Dare-Devils All

The Texan Mier Expedition, 1842–1844

By
JOSEPH MILTON NANCE

Edited by Archie P. McDonald
with support by
The Summerlee Foundation

EAKIN PRESS ★ Austin, Texas

Library of Congress Cataloging-in-Publication Data

Nance, Joseph Milton.
    Dare-Devils all : the Texan Mier Expedition, 1842–1844 / by Joseph Milton Nance ; edited by
Archie P. McDonald with support by the Summerlee Foundation.
        p.   cm.
    Includes bibliographical references (p.   ).
    ISBN 1-57168-214-7
    1. Texan Mier Expedition (1842–1844)   I. McDonald, Archie P.   II. Title.
    F390.N34   1998
    976.4'04--dc21   97-32637
                                                                                CIP

TO

ELEANOR GLENN (HANOVER) NANCE—

FAITHFUL WIFE, COMPANION,

DEVOTED MOTHER, AND

FINE ARTIST.

The Men of Mier

Three hundred Texans, dare-devils all, were they,
    With little discipline, and no gold braid
Each man demanding justice for his pay,
    Each memory aflame with Béxar's last raid,
No waving flag, no drum or bugle corps;
    No orders from the Chief who sent them there;
Each man had one strong heart, his gun, no more;
    And each man shot his way into Mier.
Naked, half-starved, in cold captivity,
    These were the men who laughed at cow-pen slime,
Whose gay hearts mocked the show of victory;
    Who faced death calmly, glorious in their grime.
These were the men who, cursing the soft-voiced lie,
    Taught the whole world how Texans fight—and die!

— Lynn Eliot

Contents

Editor's Note

In the spring of 1996, Ed Eakin called to ask if I would take on an editing project. He had a manuscript that needed to be in print because of its value to Texas history and also because it was the final writing of Joseph Milton Nance. But, said Eakin, "It is a little too long."

Dr. Nance still lived then, but Eakin and Jerry Nance, Dr. and Mrs. Nance's son, assured me that for reasons of health he would be unable to undertake the work. So, with the financial assistance of David Jackson and John Crain via the Summerlee Foundation, Ed and I began the project for the reasons he had stated: because of the story of these "dare-devils" and because of Milton Nance.

I knew Milton Nance for approximately thirty-five years. I first heard of him when my colleague in graduate studies at the then Rice Institute, Haskell Monroe, left for College Station to work for Dr. Nance and to make something of himself and of Texas A&M. Another glimpse came when my friend Harold Grant, also a fellow graduate student but this time at LSU, left for a year to teach for Dr. Nance at A&M. I'm sure I first met Dr. Nance at a meeting of the East Texas Historical Association, which he and Mrs. Nance attended regularly, and I visited with him many times over the years at ETHA gatherings or those of the Texas State Historical Association. Dr. Nance, in a military fashion, always called me by my last name. My memory of him is that he was serious-minded; he was a bit dour sometimes, but friendly enough, and always reserved. Eleanor Nance never seemed to stop smiling in outgoing good humor. I can identify with this contrast; many who know my wife, Judy, may think that I have just described us.

Joseph Milton Nance was born in Kyle, Texas, on September 18, 1915, one of eight children born to Jeremiah Milton and Mary Louise Hutchison Nance. He worked on the family farm and ranch, and was graduated valedictorian of the Class of 1931 from Kyle High School. He attended the University of Texas, earned Phi Beta Kappa honors, and was graduated from the university with a degree in history in 1935. In 1936 he earned a master's degree and began work on a doctorate. He left Austin to work at the San Jacinto Museum, completed requirements for the

Ph.D., and began teaching at Texas A&M College in 1941. During World War II he served as an officer on the staff of Adm. Chester Nimitz.

Dr. Nance returned to Texas A&M in 1946. He succeeded Ralph W. Steen as chairman of the Department of History in 1958, held that post until 1973, and continued teaching until 1979, retiring as Professor Emeritus of History. He was a member of the Texas Institute of Letters and a Fellow of the Texas State Historical Association. And he was a scholar as long as life permitted.

State Archivist Harriet Smither showed Dr. Nance the diary of Israel Canfield, one of the "dare-devils" of the Mier Expedition, in 1937. By his testimony, thereafter his major professional ambition was to write a complete history of the expedition, and he regarded his award-winning *After San Jacinto* (1963) and *Attack and Counter-Attack* (1964) as preliminary steps in actualizing that goal. His title for the conclusion of this trilogy was taken from a poem by Lynn Eliot titled "The Men of Mier," which began, "Three-hundred Texans, dare-devils all. . . ."

Dr. Nance's manuscript filled a box that measured two feet. Because pagination started over three times, and varied sometimes within and between text and notes, I can only estimate its length is between 3,000 and 4,000 pages, plus a list of suggested illustrations that exceeded 400. Anyone familiar with Dr. Nance's thorough scholarship will not find these figures surprising. The manuscript was divided into forty chapters, multiple indices—including approximately 500 pages of biographical sketches and a complete list of participants—and a 141-page bibliography. It was, and is, a monument.

Ed Eakin initially planned a three-volume work, but modern publishing realities dictated reduction. Since Dr. Nance could not perform that function himself, the duty passed to me. Dr. Nance died on January 17, 1997, with the editorial work on his monument about half done.

I do wish to emphasize that this was and remains the scholarship and writing of Joseph Milton Nance. His concepts are maintained throughout. My work eliminated lengthy quotations, some of them extending to twenty or more pages, but I hope their substance remains in summaries. I preserved Dr. Nance's method of presenting information in notes to sources, sometimes in differing ways, to retain the flavor of his scholarship; but I also reduced the number of notes by at least fifty percent. The 500-plus-page appendix of biographical sketches was excised entirely, partially because of its length and partially to preserve it for a separate publication when Jerry Nance and Ed Eakin are ready for it. Like the biographical works of L.W. Kemp, this portion of Dr. Nance's work can and should stand alone from the narrative of the expedition itself.

Dr. Nance's table of participants, which provides identification, Texas city of residence, state or country of origin, and a brief synopsis of activity or fate connected to the expedition, and his bibliography, are preserved. These two useful tools are presented just as he composed them, with the exception of some reduction in the bibliography to eliminate duplication. Dr. Nance's first-person references in the text have been retained. Given his sixty years of study on this and related topics, he had become an incarnate primary source. If he said "I could not find . . . ," likely it is not findable.

It was necessary to combine several chapters. Some exceeded 100 pages, but others were about twenty pages. Where combination was imposed, multi-spaced intervals occur in the text. When this was done, however, Dr. Nance's conclusions and transitions were left intact.

Also eliminated are descriptions of Mexico's cities, plant and animal life, and lengthy quotations from diaries and correspondence when redundant or when they did not bear directly and immediately on some experience of the Texans involved. It will be my recommendation that the full text as prepared by Dr. Nance be deposited in some convenient archive or library so researchers can have access.

I expect there are errors. I accepted on faith his translation of Spanish language terms, especially as corrected by Malcolm McLean, who read the manuscript for him, and bow to their superior knowledge. Equally, I accepted on faith Dr. Nance's facts and conclusions. This is, always, his book; I hope my reductions have not interfered with what he intended to say.

Despite the emphasis on what I have removed, much remains. Here is the narrative that Joseph Milton Nance elected as his legacy to Texas lay and professional historians. Those historians who value this episode of Texas history will find here an exciting, sad, sometimes humorous, and always meaningful story of these "dare-devils all."

ARCHIE P. McDONALD

Preface

My lifelong ambition has been to present a complete history of the Mier Expedition of 1841. My interest commenced in 1937, when State Archivist Harriet Smither showed me the diary of Israel Canfield's experiences on that expedition. As I progressed in my research it became apparent that the story could not be told without reviewing events in Texas-Mexican frontier relations between 1836 and the collapse of the Somervell Campaign of 1842 to the Rio Grande. It was for this reason, in part, that *After San Jacinto: The Texas-Mexican Frontier, 1836-1841* (1963) and *Attack and Counter-Attack: The Texas-Mexican Frontier, 1841* (1964) were written.

Folklorist J. Frank Dobie once commented: "According to historical values, the Mier Expedition was negligible, according to human values, it was dramatic, daring, admirable—and mad—beyond almost any other episode recorded in North American life." The reader will discover that the expedition was of more historical significance than Dobie thought.

The expedition did not begin under the name of "The Mier Expedition," but as retaliation because of Mexican raids on the Texas frontier. Since the first point of attack was at Mier, it has become known as "The Texan Mier Expedition."

The Nueces frontier had been one of lawlessness and danger. Although the filibustering, robbing class did not dominate frontier life, it was a constant source of danger to law-abiding citizens. The number of plunderers seems to have declined by 1842, but the remnants played an important role in the Mier Expedition.

Until the time of their capture, most of the men involved had done little to commend themselves. Had it not been for the cruelty to which they were subjected, the Mier Expedition would have been dismissed as a filibustering expedition. Many of the men were adventurers; yet within their ranks were respected citizens. There were men of education, culture, and refinement; men who had held important positions in public affairs; men of music and art; men from Ireland, Scotland, England, and the German states; men who fought at San Jacinto or with Mexican and Indian frontier marauders; and men who had crossed the plains with the Santa Fe Expedition and survived. On the whole, they were excellent material for soldiers but required strict discipline to curb independent spirits. The men had continued on a campaign contrary to orders and without the authority or flag of their government for revenge, plunder, and self-glorification; in the end they placed the civilian population of a Mexican town under contribution for badly needed provisions. It is a mystery how 309 undisciplined citizen-soldiers kept together and fought against great odds until their powder was nearly exhausted. One may question their judgment in disobeying Arthur Somervell's orders, but not their courage.

No other campaign of the Texas Republic has had more written about it or more misinformation propagated than the Mier Expedition, partly because so many participants found the need to justify their conduct, especially the charge of disobeying orders. Not all those who left accounts of their experiences blamed President Sam Houston and other Texans for showing little concern for their suffering in Mexican prisons. One of the survivors lamented that the Mier Expedition was "a subject less understood than any other portion of Texas history," and that "the Mier prisoner is not today appreciated by the people of Texas as he was by his compeers, who knew all the facts."

Accounts by participants of the Battle of Mier and of the imprisonment of the men vary in length, detail, and accuracy. Some were written from notes and journals, some merely pirated the accounts of others. Some stem from reports that a member told of events not witnessed by the recorder. Many of the men wrote letters containing information on the battle and their experiences as prisoners. The bibliography lists all known diaries, journals, memoirs, reminiscences, and letters written by men of the expedition. Many newspaper editors published interviews or letters of Mier prisoners and returnees without identifying the individual. A number of public records, as well as some private ones, were lost in fires that swept the old Treasury Office in 1845, the Adjutant General's Office in 1855, and the state capitol in 1881. Even so, much of the record has been preserved elsewhere, making a definitive history of the expedition possible.

The story of the expedition has been a favorite of both laymen and historians for 150 years. It is embedded in the political and military history of Texas. I have attempted to produce an exhaustive study of the expedition and its personnel and have examined all available materials in an effort to arrive at the truth. It has been a delightful if not an easy task.

The research and writing of the story of the Mier Expedition has taken so many years that it is possible to mention only the names of a limited number of individuals who have given me assistance and encouragement. Such a work would have been impossible without their aid. Some of these have long passed from life but are remembered for their interest and concern for this work: Harriet Smither, former state archivist; Winnie Allen, former archivist, The University of Texas at Austin Library; Llerena B. Friend, retired librarian of the Eugene C. Barker Texas History Center, The University of Texas at Austin Library; Nettie Lee Benson, former director of the Latin American Collection of The University of Texas at Austin; E. R. Dabney, former director of the Newspaper Collection, The

University of Texas at Austin; Dr. Amelia Williams, distinguished compiler and coeditor of the writings of Sam Houston; Dorman H. Winfrey, retired director of the Texas State Library and Archives; Malcolm D. McLean, former assistant director, San Jacinto Monument Museum and Archives, and his wife, Margaret, publisher of the Robertson Colony Papers of The University of Texas at Arlington; Jane A. Kennamore, archivist of the Rosenberg Library, Galveston; Dorothy Knepper, former director of the San Jacinto Museum of History, Deer Park, Texas; Kathryn McDowell and Susan Crutchfield, former librarians, and Eugenia P. Krause and Bernice Strong, assistant librarians, Daughters of the Republic of Texas Library, The Alamo, San Antonio, Texas; Mrs. Carl Jaggers, Rusk County Historical Association, Henderson, Texas; Jack Jackson, artist and writer, Austin, Texas; David B. Gracy, former director, Texas State Archives; Dr. Jack A. Dabbs, retired head, Modern Language Department, Texas A&M University; Amelia Lara Tamburino, director of *Museo Nacional de Historia*, Castillo de Chapultepec, Mexico City; Joe B. Blanton, Albany, Texas; Bill Page, library assistant, Micro-Text Collection, Sterling C. Evans Library, Texas A&M University; Michael R. Green, reference archivist, Texas State Archives; Denise Jones, library assistant, Dallas Historical Society; Lucille Boykin, genealogy librarian, History and Social Science Division, Dallas Public Library; Marilyn McAdams Sibley, Houston Baptist College, Houston, Texas; Walter P. Fretag, LaGrange, Texas; Frances Reasonover of Kemp, Texas, for information on Andrew Barry Hanna; Virginia L. Ott, director of Fort Bend County Museum, Richmond, Texas; Lynn Bilotta, Texas Memorial Museum, The University of Texas at Austin; Harbert Davenport, attorney and South Texas historian, Brownsville, Texas; and by no means least, my wife Eleanor Hanover Nance, for her excellent cartography.

JOSEPH MILTON NANCE
College Station, Texas

CHAPTER 1

Formation of the Expedition

Under pressure from the citizens of southern Texas for retaliation for recent attacks by Mexican military units on frontier settlements, climaxed by the seizure of San Antonio in September 1842 by Gen. Adrián Woll, President Sam Houston gave broad discretionary power to Brig. Gen. Alexander Somervell, commander of the First Brigade of the Texas militia, to launch an attack on the frontier settlements of Mexico in October 1842. In November 1842, Somervell left San Antonio with an army of 750 men. He captured Laredo, but when some of his volunteers plundered the town, some of the drafted militiamen returned home. Somervell, with a reduced force, marched down the Texas side of the Rio Grande to opposite Guerrero, crossed the river, and levied a requisition on the town on December 16. The following day he sent a small force to hurry the requisition of supplies, but with little effect.

On December 18 Somervell recrossed the Rio Grande to the Texas side. Finding his troops before Guerrero[1] "more disorderly than ever and that it was impossible to enforce obedience,"[2] he concluded that "to remain any longer in the enemy's country in that situation was dangerous to the extreme," reported George L. Hammeken, his interpreter and secretary. To delay Mexican forces as long as possible, Somervell ordered the fleet of boats[3] by which he had crossed the river sunk. Some to whom the order had been given merely moved the boats a few miles below and left

1. Walter F. McCaleb, *The Mier Expedition*, p. 33.
2. Guy M. Bryan to Rutherford B. Hayes, Peach Point near Brazoria, Texas, Jan. 21, 1843, in E. W. Winkler, ed., "The Bryan-Hayes Correspondence," *SWHQ* 25 (Oct. 1921), pp. 103-7. See also Joseph Milton Nance, *Attack and Counterattack: The Texas-Mexican Frontier, 1842*, pp. 540-59.
3. George B. Erath reported that there were "half a dozen nicely painted flatboats, each one capable of carrying from eight to ten horses." See Lucy A. Erath, ed., "Memoirs of Major George Bernard Erath," *SWHQ* 27 (July 1923), pp. 42.

the general under the impression that his order had been carried out.[4] The seeds of another schism and division of the army had germinated.

On December 18, Somervell's camp was located near the Carrizo Indian village opposite the mouth of the Río Salado, a stream that emptied into the Río Bravo six miles southeast of Guerrero, twelve leagues below Dolores, and a hundred miles by water above Mier.[5] On December 19, Somervell, commander of the South Western Army of Operations, composed of militia, volunteers, and "all troops raised,"[6] ordered the men to commence the return march at ten o'clock to the settled area of Texas[7] by way of the junction of the Frío and Nueces rivers, and thence to Gonzales, where the men were to be disbanded.[8]

Although many had expected the order, its announcement disheartened a majority of them. "There was intense disgust felt by the whole force and at one time it looked as though there would be a general revolt, but better councils prevailed."[9] The men, Joseph McCutchan said, "became perfectly wild." They had long wanted to engage the Mexican army and some had hoped to plunder Mexican towns for personal gain and in retaliation for the loss of property and lives at San Antonio, Victoria, Harrisburg, and Goliad by the Mexican invading army of 1836 and later raiding expeditions. Some preferred a "grave in the desolate wilds of a western prairie" to returning home without meeting the foe.[10] Others questioned Somervell's motives and presumed he had "gained sufficient

---

4. Thomas J. Green, *Journal of the Texian Expedition Against Mier*, p. 66. Hereinafter cited as Green, *Mier Expedition*.

5. John Russell Bartlett, *Personal Narrative of Explorations and Incidents in Texas, New Mexico, California, Sonora, and Chihuahua, Connected with the United States and Mexican Boundary Commission During the Years 1850, '51, '52, and '53*, 2, p. 409.

6. Thomas W. Bell, *A Narrative of the Capture and Subsequent Sufferings of the Mier Prisoners in Mexico, Captured in the Cause of Texas, Dec. 26th, 1842 (and Liberated Sept. 16th, 1844)*, p. 13.

7. Adolphus Sterne of Nacogdoches recorded in his diary on October 11, 1842, after the Woll raid: "there is now a full determination to carry on the war into the Enemies Country—if the government will only sanction such a measure it is the only safety for Texas—for as I predicted, it was only an *annoying force* and not a *regular invading army* and so it will be every Six months till Texas crosses the Rio Grande." Harriet Smither, ed., "Diary of Adolphus Sterne," *SWHQ* 34 (Jan. 1931), pp. 260-61.

8. "Order No. 64. Head Quarters, Camp opposite the mouth of the Salado, East Bank of the Rio Grande [Dec. 19, 1842]," in A. Somervell to G. W. Hill, Secretary of War and Marine, Washington, Feb. 1, 1843, *Morning Star* (Houston), Feb. 18, 1843; John Hemphill to Anson Jones, Washington, Jan. 23, 1843, Army Papers (Texas), Tx-A; also copy in State Department (Texas), Department of State Letterbook, Home Letters, vol. 2 (1842-1846), pp. 69-71; M. C. Hamilton to Anson Jones, Department of War and Marine, Washington, Dec. 24, 1844 (being "Special Report of the Secretary of War and Marine"), in Texas Congress, *Journals of the Ninth Congress of the Republic of Texas*, app., p. 75; see also Nance, *Attack and Counterattack*, p. 557. For a full account of the Somervell Expedition to the Rio Grande, see Nance, *Attack and Counterattack*, pp. 409-578.

9. Adele B. Looscan, ed., "Journal of Lewis Birdsall Harris," *SWHQ* 25 (Jan. 1922), p. 190.

10. Joseph Milton Nance, ed., *Mier Expedition Diary: A Texan Prisoner's Account. By Joseph D. McCutchan*, pp. 209-10. Hereinafter cited as Nance, ed., *McCutchan's Narrative*.

honor and glory, by taking two defenseless towns [Laredo and Guerrero]," and was now "determined to return home with a *whole body,* and a *Hat full of glory,* while it was yet time. He thought," declared McCutchan, "'Now is the time, before it is everlastingly too late.' He could see if we stayed there much longer, we would *have* to *fight*—and that would have been far from congenial within his nice sense of feeling!"[11] "He got awfully scared," said Harvey Adams.[12]

"At this time [morning of December 19] we received a peremptory order," recorded Lewis Birdsall Harris of Capt. Gardiner Smith's company, "from Gen. Houston to return and not advance any further into Mexico."[13] At the time alleged by Harris, President Houston was not aware that the Texan army had crossed the Rio Grande. Homer S. Thrall has stated: "It has been conjectured that President Houston never intended an aggressive movement against Mexico, and that Somervell acted under secret orders, in disbanding his men. If the General had intended to make the expedition a failure, he could not have done it more effectually than he did."[14] No such recall order has been found, and there is no doubt discretion lay with the commander of the expedition. Houston's order to Somervell stated, "If the enemy evacuate and falls back, the troops [rushing to San Antonio to expel Woll] are authorized and required to pursue them to any point in the Republic, or in Mexico, and chastize the marauders for their audacity." The order then calls out the militia and volunteers of a number of counties and gives general directions to their march to the frontier, saying, "The troops will assemble at the most convenient point in their respective counties, and proceed to the organization and election of company officers. More detailed instructions are considered unnecessary, as it is presumed that every soldier will do his duty; and that the troops will call to their command an officer (captain of company) whose wisdom, discretion and valor may be relied upon."[15]

"When the order to return was issued," reminisced Erath, "a new outcry came forth; men declared that they had not had satisfaction, that they could at least remain a week longer, gone down to Mier and enforce a contribution, or at least collect a thousand horses to take back with cattle and sheep. To this I had no objection; that kind of property belonged to rich men not living there, and I had looked for nothing less than to get at least one good Spanish horse in compensation for this and former services not paid for."[16]

---

11. *Ibid.,* pp. 111-12.

12. Harvey Alexander Adams, "[Journal of an] Expedition Against the Southwest," Dec. 18, 1842, typed MS, TxU-A.

13. Looscan, ed., "Journal of Lewis Birdsall Harris," *SWHQ* 25 (Jan. 1922), p. 190.

14. Homer S. Thrall, *A Pictorial History of Texas From the Earliest Visits of European Adventurers to A.D. 1883,* p. 338.

15. By Order of Sam Houston, President. M. C. Hamilton, Acting Secretary of Marine, Houston, September 16, 1842, in Amelia Williams and Eugene C. Barker, eds., *The Writings of Sam Houston* 7, pp. 6-7. The order was printed in San Augustine, *The Red-Lander,* Oct. 6, 1842.

16. Erath, ed., "Memoirs of Major George Bernard Erath," *SWHQ* 27 (July 1923), p. 43.

Having failed to launch an effective expedition against Mexico in the summer of 1842, and still plagued by the demands of the settlers along the frontier for protection, President Houston issued an "Address to the People of Texas"[17] on July 26, proposing a plan of operation against the northern Mexican frontier. It was this policy that the militant members of the Somervell Expedition had in mind, even if the policy of government had changed and conditions outlined in Houston's plan of late July had not been met. Even so, they were insubordinate to the orders of the command.

On July 26 Houston had outlined an aggressive policy against Mexico, and in August authorized Charles A. Warfield to raise a volunteer force to attack the Santa Fé trade between New Mexico and the United States as it crossed through Texas. Houston had announced in his "Address" on July 26 and in orders to regimental commanders:

That the Executive has always had in contemplation to retaliate upon Mexico, for the late outrages upon the persons and property of Texian citizens. To accomplish this, he must rely upon voluntary service alone: For its effectuation, he proposed to receive upwards of a thousand men, to be mounted, equipped and prepared at their own expense for the proposed campaign.

The government will promise nothing but authority to march and such supplies of ammunition as may be needful for the campaign. They must look to the valley of the Rio Grande for remuneration. The government will claim no portion of the spoils—they will be divided among the victors. The flag of Texas will accompany the expedition. . . .

The Executive has great reliance upon the zeal of his countrymen, and their willingness to pursue such a course of policy as will give protection to our South Western frontier for the future—and he is satisfied, if this expedition can be carried into effect, that the country has much to hope from its results. . . .

When emergencies arise in the prosecution of the campaign, detached as the army will be in its situation, the commanding officer will have to exercise a sage discretion in relation to the subject matter which may be presented; always keeping in view the safety and success of his command, the preservation of his flag and the honor of his country. The troops, by obedience to his orders, and imitating his example will establish the highest claims to the admiration and gratitude of their fellow citizens and the government of the Republic.

I have the honor to be, very respectfully,

Your obedient servant,

[Sam Houston]

---

17. "Address to the People of Texas Proposing a Plan of Operation Against Mexico," Executive Department, City of Houston, July 26, 1842, [signed by] Sam Houston, in Executive Record of the Second Term of General Houston's Administration of the Government of Texas, MS, Tx-A. See also Circular Letter Concerning the Campaign Against Mexico, Executive Department, City of Houston, July 26, 1842, in Williams and Barker, eds., *Writings of Sam Houston* 4, pp. 129-31.

Houston's plans in July and August 1842 for an expedition against Mexico never bore fruit. Then came the Woll raid in September, and the revival of popular cry for retaliation against Mexico, culminating in Houston's orders to Somervell and the latter's march to the Rio Grande:

> You will proceed to the most eligible point on the Southwest frontier of Texas, and concentrate with the forces now under your command, all troops who may submit to your orders, and if you can advance with a prospect of success into the enemy's territory, you will do so forthwith. . . .
>
> You will receive no troops into your command but such as will march across the Rio Grande under your orders if required by you to do so. If you cross the Rio Grande you must suffer no surprise, but be always on the alert. Let your arms be inspected night and morning, and your scouts always on the lookout.
>
> You will be controlled by the rules of the most civilized warfare, and you will find the advantage of exercising great humanity towards the common people. In battle let the enemy feel the fierceness of just resentment and retribution.[18]

Later, in his veto of a bill for the relief of William G. Cooke for services in the Somervell Expedition, Houston believed that paying individuals such as Cooke and James C. Neill was improper; he repeated, "the government never promised those who should participate in the late campaign to the Rio Grande, anything more than the authority to march," and "such ammunition and arms as could be furnished. . . ." He emphasized that any spoils acquired from the enemy must be "according to laws of civilized warfare."[19]

After the Somervell Expedition had returned and the Mier fiasco had taken place, Secretary of State Anson Jones (on February 16, 1843) informed Isaac Van Zant, Texas' *chargé d'affaires* to the United States, that the policy of Texas toward Mexico was "defensive" and that "the late Campaign under Gen. Somervell was not projected or recommended by the President," but was "merely sanctioned to satisfy popular clamor, and as the volunteers under him wished to cross the Rio Grande and were determined to do so right or wrong," it had been decided "to clothe the expedition with legal authority that in case it was unfortunate, and our citizens should fall into the power of Mexico they could not be regarded or treated by the authorities of that Government otherwise than lawful belligerents acting under sanction of their own Government."[20]

---

18. Sam Houston to Brig. Gen. A. Somervell, Executive Department, Washington, October 3, 1842, in *SWHQ* 23 (Oct. 1919), pp. 112-13; copy in Domestic Correspondence (Texas), MS; Texas Congress, *Journals of the House of Representatives of the Seventh Congress*, app., pp. 3-4. These orders were similar to those issued to Somervell on Mar. 10, 1842; see also *Telegraph and Texas Register*, Oct. 12, 1842.

19. *Journals of the House of Representatives of the Congress of the Republic of Texas, Eighth Congress*, 1st Sess., pp. 375-77.

20. Anson Jones to Isaac Van Zandt, Washington, D.C., [dated] Department of State, Washington, [Texas], Feb. 16, 1843, in George P. Garrison, ed., *Diplomatic Correspondence of the Republic of Texas* 2, p. 127.

From Galveston, Charles Elliot, the British *chargé d'affaires* in Texas, reported to the British Foreign Office on December 16, 1842, that he had just received word from Houston, Texas, "that a small party of our Texian levies have advanced to the Rio Grande, and I have no doubt they will do no manner of good there. The President has done what He could to prevent this folly, but it needs other checks there than that, and I think it is safe to prophecy that they will find them."[21] Although there seemed to be unanimity in reports from the western frontier that Somervell actually had begun his advance on the Mexican frontier, Elliot concluded that "eventually" it might prove to be "entirely false," as "there is not much truth running about our natural roads in Texas."[22]

General Somervell felt the responsibility for the safety of his men. He reported to the secretary of war that "having been eleven days on the river, and knowing the various positions and bodies of the enemy's troops, I was satisfied that they were concentrating in such numbers as to render a longer stay an act of imprudence."[23] He had hoped to have 1,000 men when he commenced his march from the Medina, but he had only about 750, and at Laredo on December 8 he paraded 683 men, of whom forty were on the sick list; after the return of 187 Montgomery and Washington county drafted militia, his force was down to 496, and of these 189 returned with him from Guerrero, leaving 309, who were not yet ready to go home.[24]

Somervell failed to solve the important problem of discipline, and the expedition was in great need of good horses, food, clothing, and munitions,[25] but the order to return, declared Somervell, "was from no apprehension of the scarcity of the stores of subsistence" but out of regard to the safety of his men due to the concentration of the Mexican forces along that section of the Rio Grande frontier. Little energy had been shown by the commanding officer in a campaign which was instituted as a political move to appease western demands for an invasion of Mexico.

After eleven days on the river many of the men decided that there was no possibility of accomplishing their original objective. "There was little harmony among the many filibustering men in the command, who were

---

21. Charles Elliot to H. U. Addington, Galveston, Dec. 16, 1842 (postscript), in Ephraim D. Adams, ed., *British Correspondence Concerning the Republic of Texas*, pp. 142-45.

22. *Ibid.*

23. Report of Brig. Gen. A. Somervell to the Hon. G. W. Hill, Sec. of War and Marine, Washington, Feb. 1, 1843, in Texas Congress, *Journals of the Ninth Congress of the Republic of Texas*, app., pp. 7-75.

24. See Nance, *Attack and Counterattack*, pp. 565-66.

25. On publishing Somervell's report on his recent campaign, the editor of the *Telegraph* commented:

> When he states explicitly, the horses were so materially injured by their exertions to pass through this continuous deep and tenacious morass, that they were ever afterwards unable throughout the campaign, to make those quick marches essential to the accomplishment of the objects of the campaign. (*Telegraph and Texas Register*, Feb. 22, 1843.)

continually stirring up strife, which caused almost a mutiny in camp at times. . . . Every officer [was] seeking military fame and trammeling each other to the Generalship."[26] When the general order to return home came, a few of the "more hot headed . . . determined to separate from the command and cross the river, and as they expressed it, rake down the settlements on the Mexican side and bring in as many cattle and horses as they could manage."[27]

Many of the more reliable men had drifted homeward—some from the Medina, others from the bogs of the Atascosa, more after the plunder of Laredo—leaving a rabble of adventurers and self-willed men. Some highly respectable and intelligent men did remain with the force, but they were in the minority by the morning of December 19.

Moses Austin Bryan, first lieutenant in John S. McNeill's Brazoria company and brother of Guy M. Bryan, and George L. Hammeken reported on their return home that 300 men "mutinied and remained" on the Rio Grande.[28]

"On the morning of the 7th, previous to our taking possession of Laredo," reported Memucan Hunt,[29] "Act'g Adjutant General [John] Hemphill read an order from Gen. Somervell, which assured the troops of the property taken from the enemy, there would be an equal distribution. I regret to state, however, that Gen. Somervell forfeited this privilege as far as related to the horses and mules . . . brought into camp. In some instances Captains of companies would allow their men to detach themselves in small numbers and acquire for their purposes any number of horses and mules they could find. Other officers denied their men this privilege saying that all property thus acquired, should be procured by regular details of men, and equally divided between officers and men."

Then, said Hunt, when the retreat from Guerrero was about to begin, "Gen. Somervell failed altogether to conform to his pledge."[30] His friends were aware of his intentions and the impending order to return to Gonzales, so they collected "mules, horses, mares, and colts, which they profited by."[31] "The Captains," said Hunt, "who had been most particular in requiring and enforcing discipline and subordination from their men in not allowing parties to leave camp, acquired no horses and mules to supply those of their companies whose horses were unfit for service. . . ;

---

26. Adams, "[Journal of an] Expedition Against the Southwest," Dec. 18, 1842, typed MS, TxU-A.

27. Looscan, ed., "Journals of Lewis Birdsall Harris," *SWHQ* 25 (Jan. 1922), p. 190.

28. Guy M. Bryan to Rutherford B. Hayes, Peach Point near Brazoria, Texas, Jan. 21, 1843, in E. W. Winkler, ed., "The Bryan-Hayes Correspondence," *SWHQ* 25 (Oct. 1921), pp. 103-7.

29. Hunt came to Texas with Thomas Jefferson Green. They landed at Galveston on May 25, 1836. R. L. Jones and P. H. Jones, "Memucan Hunt," *Texana* 4 (Sum. 1966), pp. 104-28.

30. Memucan Hunt to Francis Moore, Jr., editor of the Telegraph, Houston, [dated] Béxar, January 8, 1843, in *Telegraph and Texas Register*, Jan. 18, 1843.

31. Green, *Mier Expedition*, p. 66.

consequently, on the morning of the 19th, when Gen. Somervell issued an order of march, Captains Fisher, Cameron, Eastland, Rion, and Pearson refused obedience."[32]

Responding to a request for information on the orders issued to the commander of the South Western Army, John Hemphill, acting adjutant general of the Texas Militia and a staff officer on the Somervell Expedition, informed Anson Jones, secretary of state, "that predatory warfare was not among the objects contemplated in the late expedition to the Rio Grande, and that in fact the same was neither waged or permitted by the commanding officer of the said expedition."[33]

Captain Fisher told Hunt, a member of his company, that he would take his men down the river far enough to procure horses for those who were on foot or whose horses were no longer able to carry them, and to obtain a sufficient supply of provisions to take them home. Fisher said he hoped to reach Washington County as soon as those who marched home under Somervell. Hunt claims that "this was the intent of all the officers who had separated themselves from the main command."[34]

Hunt says that he called for a meeting of the officers to see if a reconciliation could be effected, but no agreement could be reached. Hunt then requested Somervell to change the direction of march and proceed down the river for a day or two and return by a more southerly route to enable those without horses to obtain mounts. Somervell refused to change his order. Hunt then told Fisher that if he could get an order from Somervell to permit his company to go down the river, he would go; "or if, under the law authorizing volunteers to elect their own officers as high as Brigade General, an election would be called," he would vote to supersede Somervell and follow the command of any person chosen to replace him. Somervell refused to permit an election, and Hunt dared not ignore the order to return home.

Somervell's orders precluded any authorization that would entail unnecessary risks. Erath, a member of the camp guard, was elected to the House of Representatives of the Eighth Congress from Milam County in 1843. In a conversation with President Houston he learned of the scope of Somervell's orders. "In substance," Erath said,

> they were to proceed with extreme caution to the Rio Grande, to cross it only when there was no possibility of an obstruction to recrossing, and to venture no general or partial action unless victory was certain in advance. The intention was to make a demonstration—to show the world we could occupy the country we claimed and beyond it, and to maintain our occupation longer than the Mexicans could occupy our own soil. To this was

---

32. Memucan Hunt to Francis Moore, Jr., editor of the *Telegraph,* Houston, [dated] Béxar, January 8, 1843, in *Telegraph and Texas Register,* Jan. 18, 1843.

33. John Hemphill, Act[g] Adjt. Genl. of the Texas Militia, to the Honble Anson Jones, Secy of State, Washington, Texas, Jany 23d, 1843, original MS, Tx-A.

34. Memucan Hunt to Francis Moore, Jr., Béxar, January 8, 1843, in *Telegraph and Texas Register,* Jan. 18, 1843.

added a comment in substance, that should the fate of war be against us in defeat and loss, with the Army under the government's control, the consequences would be self-apparent; and if we were successful, still the future must be uncertain, especially if a quantity of property were thrown on our hands. The people of Texas had just been pacified and quieted sufficiently to go to work and rise by industry and economy, leaving the Mexicans to Providence; but with military success—the greater, the worse for us—the people would abandon the plow, turn to adventure and guerrillas and the final [outcome] would be, if not in the end defeat, at least a loss in character and honor with no real profit. As I view the past in mature age, my conviction is that it was a sensible and statesmanlike view of the situation. At the time, however, I went with the mass of my companions in condemning Houston.[35]

Failing to obtain concessions from Somervell, Hunt and Capt. Edward Smith of Harrison County withdrew from Fisher's company and joined Capt. Bartlett Sims of Bastrop, the only two to withdraw from that company.[36]

Three weeks after his arrival home, Somervell made a detailed report to the secretary of war and marine on his campaign to the Rio Grande. He did not censure Fisher and his men for remaining on the Rio Grande and proceeding to Mier after the balance of the army had countermarched. By the time Somervell made his report on February 1, 1843, the Battle of Mier had been fought and the folly of Fisher and his men had become known throughout Texas.

On reading Somervell's report, editor John N. O. Smith of the *Houstonian* defended Fisher's conduct, suggesting that Somervell had seceded from the army and left the command to Fisher. He declared:

If we have been correctly informed, when the order to take up the line of march, for the junction of the "Río Frío and Nueces," was issued, at least one-half of the troops under the command of Col. Fisher were without shoes and without horses, and but few had comfortable clothing. Under these circumstances, an attempt to return to Texas would have been attended with the loss of a great many lives. Col. Fisher therefore deemed it advisable to proceed down the river, for the purpose of procuring horses and provisions for his men. This course Gen. Somervell, if not directly, indirectly sanctioned. . . . When the order was issued it was not intended to extend to Col. Fisher's company, for Gen. Somervell knew that they were not in a condition to return, and that if they attempted it many lives would be sacrificed. Upon the withdrawal of Gen. Somervell from the army the command devolved upon Col. Fisher, who continued to act under the orders of the government.[37]

---

35. Erath, ed., "Memoirs of Major George Bernard Erath," *SWHQ* 27 (July 1923), pp. 39-40.

36. Memucan Hunt to Francis Moore, Jr., editor of the *Telegraph*, Houston, [dated] Béxar, January 8, 1843, in *Telegraph and Texas Register*, Jan. 18, 1843. For information on Hunt, see Robert L. Jones and Pauline H. Jones, "Memucan Hunt: His Private Life," *Texana* 4 (Sum. 1966), pp. 104-28; *ibid.*, (Fall 1966), pp. 213-32.

37. *Houstonian*, quoted in *Daily Picayune*, Feb. 26, 1843.

The decision of whether to return home or to repudiate Somervell's authority and continue down the river was a difficult one for more than one volunteer. John Fenn of Fort Bend County asked Lt. John M. Shipman, "John, which way shall we go?" "We are good soldiers," was the ready reply, "and must obey orders," but when the time for decision came and his captain and a majority of the company went into Mexico, Shipman went too.

John Fenn also turned his horse to follow, but Robert Herndon took hold of the bridle and said, "Come, John, you are young, go back with me," and he yielded.[38] Two others, William Sullivan and a man named Woodson came back with Fenn, but Daniel C. Sullivan went with Fisher. A lad of fourteen years, he had gone on the Somervell Expedition as a substitute for Shapley P. Ross.[39]

The men of Samuel Bogart's spy company voted by a majority of two to return home, while twelve men were out trying to find better horses. When the vote was protested because of the absent men, Bogart refused to delay or reconsider and twenty of Bogart's men joined Colonel Fisher's expedition.[40] Like many who gave extra powder or lead or other supplies to those going down the river, Lewis Birdsall Harris,[41] an orderly sergeant in Capt. James P. Lowrey's company, who had a boil on his leg and determined to return home, reported, "I divided all my ammunition with two boys 16 or 17 years old," Robert H. Beale and John C. C. Hill.[42]

On separating from Somervell, Fisher told Hunt that he had no intention of crossing the Rio Grande. Hunt declared when he learned later from Dr. Robert Watson and William Hensley of the camp guard, who reached San Antonio on January 6, that he was surprised that Fisher had crossed the Rio Grande. "Indeed," he said, "my solicitude was so great for the troops which he was elected to command, that I took the liberty from our warm friendship and intimacy, to urge him not to sanction or allow it if he could possibly avoid" doing so.[43]

The thought of an expedition against Mexico had long been in the minds of settlers on the western frontier of Texas as well as in parts of East Texas. Patrick Usher wrote to his sister in North Carolina on August 11, 1842, that "An expedition numbering about three hundred men, is now being raised to march against the Mexicans on the Rio Grande, and my name is already down as being one of the number. We propose to march about the first of September."[44]

---

38. A. J. Sowell, *History of Fort Bend County, Containing Biographical Sketches of Many Noted Characters*, p. 104.

39. Stephen B. Oates, ed., *Rip Ford's Texas* by John Salmon Ford, pp. 439-40.

40. Adams, "[Journal of an] Expedition Against the Southwest," Dec. 19, 1842, typed MS, TxU-A.

41. Looscan, ed., "Journal of Lewis Birdsall Harris," *SWHQ* 25 (Jan. 1922), p. 189.

42. *Ibid.*

43. *Ibid.*

44. Patrick Usher to Eliza A. Berry, Wilmington, N.C., [dated] Texana, August 11, 1842, copy in TxU-A; original in possession of Henry B. McKoy, Greenville, S.C.

One hundred and six citizens of Nacogdoches County in a public meeting in January 1842, on learning of the capture of the Santa Fé Expedition, drafted resolutions to Senator James Shaw, representing the district of Robertson and Milam, who introduced them on January 20 in Congress, where they were read and referred to the Committee on Military Affairs. The memorialists recommended that the naval force of the Republic and privateers be commissioned to scour the Gulf of Mexico and attack every Mexican town on the coast and a land force be organized to ravage the Mexican frontier along the Rio Grande. They urged that vengeance be pursued until Mexico should sue for peace.[45]

Many were disappointed at Somervell's about-face from his determination on the eve of the Texan seizure of Laredo. On December 6 at his camp on the Nueces he had announced the opening of "the first campaign for offensive operations against Mexico," and told his men that upon them had "fallen the honor of first carrying the war into the enemy's country. . . . Let us pursue him to his retreat, and in his strong-holds punish his audacity. . . . We are determined to chastize the enemy wherever he may be found."[46]

An alleged affidavit of George Lord[47] some forty years later claimed that on December 5, before the capture of Laredo, he overheard General Somervell remark that he had received a dispatch from President Houston to break up the expedition at all costs, and that Colonel Cook, being apprised of the instructions, replied, "Gen. we cannot break up this expedition, the men will mutinize, they are determined to cross the Rio Grande and fight the enemy, but my advice is fling every impediment in its way and let it break itself up." The dispatch referred to by Lord is not extant, but this is not conclusive proof that it was not written because many of the public records of the Republic were destroyed in the burning of the Office of the Adjutant General in 1855, and of the state capitol in November 1881. Nor can it be claimed that Houston meant to say he specifically ordered the expedition back. He would not need to, for Somervell enjoyed wide discretionary authority in this respect.

"Bigfoot" Wallace claimed that while the army was near Guerrero, "Some said that our commander, General Somerville, had received orders from the President of Texas to abandon the expedition, but whether this was so or not I never knew. . . . At any rate, he left us the next morning, and took back home with him a considerable number of men. I had good

---

45. Harriet Smither, ed., *Journals of the Sixth Congress of the Republic of Texas* 1, pp. 259-60, p. 259 n. 86; Memorials and Petitions (Texas), Tx-A.

46. A. Somervell, General Order No. 56, Head Quarters, Camp Nueces, Decr. 6, 1842, in "A Record Book of the General & Special Orders and Letters of the South Western Army, November 1842 - [January 1843]," A, MS, Manuscript Division, New York Public Library.

47. Affidavit of Geo[rge] Lord, dated Feb. 16, 1881, in Traylor, "George Lord," *Frontier Times* 15 (Sept. 1938), pp. 533-35; the original affidavit is in the Texas State Archives, but the signature thereon is not that of George Lord.

reason afterward to regret that I had not continued my retreat with this crowd, for verily 'discretion is the better part of valor.'"[48]

Even before Somervell began his march from the west bank of the Medina for Laredo, Israel Worsham wrote to his father from the head-quarters camp of the army at Camp León that a petition had been drawn up by some of the men asking the general to show his orders, for "they all believed that 'old Sam' is opposed to the expedition."[49] The "petition," reported Worsham,

> seems not to have [been] answered satisfactorily to men who were dis-posed to return home, whether they did it honorably or by desertion though he [Somervell] in my opinion answered it in a mild and prope[r] and satisfactory manner. A few however determined to break [desert] in Col. Bennett's absence. About 30 led by Jno. McRay mounted and broke through the g[u]ard bidding defiance to all authority, after which many others thought themselves excusable to follow the example set before them, whom I think are in some degree excusable. In fact I cannot blame any man that has returned. At all events I cannot approve their course. I am fair [far] from censuring them. The whole Regiment fell into such confusion that they were scattere[d] every where without any leader. We determined to return on yesterday but Col. Bennett, Maj. Smithers, Col. Gillispie [Gillespie] and three Capts. with as many privates as would stay concluded to step forward and still represent Montgomery [County] the whole amounting to about 60 in number. This evening pride prompted us to rally and continue withe them. I am sorry that we have no more than 60 me[n]. . . who have the fortitude to engage [in] a winter campaign. For further particulars apply to George Christian or to Peter Johnson who will bear this letter. They are justifiable in returning. Credit nothing you hear from persons returning for they make false statements before they leave San-Antonio and the nearer they get the worse they make them. There are about six hundred men at Madena and two pieces of artillery, twelve yoke of oxen were pressed to carry them today. Tomorrow we will join them. And the next day we are ordered to march to the Riogrande there will be no longer delay. I wish I could be at home [to] help you but my feelings will not permit me to leave 60 of my best friends to represent the whole county. If we return in safety I do not think I will return until about the middle of Jan[uar]y. Nothing more at present. Reason teaches me that the enterprise is a hazzerdus one but under existing circum-stances I cannot refuse to engage in it. I have the chill and fever every change of the weather but nothing serious the rest are well. My animal is getting thin and I am very fearful I shall loose her but I cant help it.

The editor of the *Telegraph and Texas Register*[50] reported that an

---

48. Letter in the *Galveston Times*, reproduced in the *New Orleans Tropic* and quoted in the *Daily National Intelligencer* (Washington, D.C.), Jan. 2, 1843.

49. Israel Worsham to J[eremiah] Worsham, Montgomery, [Montgomery County], Texas, [dated] Head Quarters, Camp León, S. Western Army, Nov. 22, 1842, in Chabot, ed., "Texas Letters," Yanaguana Society *Publications* 5, pp. 159-60.

50. Dec. 7, 1842.

express rider from Washington, the temporary capital of the Republic of Texas, passed through LaGrange about December 2 with orders from President Houston to General Somervell. The purpose of these orders was not known, but it was reported in LaGrange that they would delay the march of the army.

In a speech delivered in the U.S. Senate on August 1, 1854, Houston admitted that General Somervell returned from the Rio Grande "in conformity with his orders and marched his troops back again to Texas."[51]

On November 5, Houston sent a personal letter to Charles Elliot, the British *chargé d'affaires* to Texas, requesting that he obtain permission from the British Foreign Office to act as the agent of Texas in securing peace with Mexico.[52] But letters from the War Department dated two weeks later gave no indication that the expedition was to be recalled.[53] Houston's letter of November 23, written at Washington-on-the-Brazos, if it reached Somervell on the Rio Grande while the army lay before either Laredo or Guerrero, conveyed no order to return home. If anything, it urged him forward. "Unless you are marshalled to cross the Rio Grande, and with that knowledge and determination, the design as well as the wishes of the government will not be carried out."[54]

George B. Erath reported later that when objection was made by members of the expedition to returning home, "the General said nothing, and the agitation continued that night." The next morning when the men talked of going down the river, "the General made no remonstrance, and by nine o'clock the portion of the forces in favor of returning home commenced to leave,"[55] in the rain that had been falling during the past day and night. The separation took place at the Texan campsite at Carrizo. After the withdrawal of Fisher and the others who did not want to return home immediately, the rest of the Texas Army began their march for Gonzales at one o'clock on the afternoon of December 19.

As in late March 1842, the problem of military command in Texas had not changed. On March 21 General Somervell reported the lack of organization of the forces at San Antonio under his orders for a descent

51. U.S. Congress, *Congressional Globe,* 1853-55, app., pp. 1214-18; see also Williams and Barker, eds., *Writings of Sam Houston* 6, p. 79.

52. Houston to Charles Elliot, Washington, Nov. 5, 1842 (private), in Williams and Barker, eds., *Writings of Sam Houston* 3, pp. 191-92;

53. M. C. Hamilton to Alexander Somervell, Washington, Nov. 19, 1842, in Williams and Barker, eds., *Writings of Sam Houston* 3, pp. 197-99; Houston to Gen. A. Somervell, Washington, Nov. 23, 1842, in *ibid.,* 3, pp. 201-2; M. C. Hamilton to Col. William G. Cooke, Dept. of War & Marine, Washington, Nov. 22, 1842, in Army Papers (Texas), TxA; M. C. Hamilton to Brig. Gen. A. Somervell, Department of War and Marine, Nov. 21, 1842, in "Report of the Secretary of War & Marine, to Sam Houston," Dec. 14, 1842, in *Texas Congress, Journal of the House of Representatives of the Seventh Congress,* app., pp. 9-10.

54. Sam Houston to Gen. A. Somervell, Washington, Nov. 23, 1842, in Williams and Barker, eds., *Writings of Sam Houston* 3, pp. 201-3; also, in Executive Record of the Second Term of General Houston's Administration of the Government of Texas, MS, Tx-A.

55. Erath, ed., "Memoirs of Major George Bernard Erath," in *SWHQ* 27 (July 1923), p. 43.

on the Rio Grande, and that they had "elected other officers, than those provided by law."[56] The situation had not changed in December 1842. Only Somervell had discretionary orders to invade Mexico; no election could confer that power on any other commander.

In the afternoon after Somervell had moved out, those who continued the expedition moved down the river approximately four miles to a more convenient campsite where the ground was drier, the grass more plentiful, and corn was available, for, narrated Erath, they camped in "another cornfield."[57] The army was composed of volunteers "burning with anxiety to meet the enemy and exchange at least a few shots. Having joined the army merely for the sake of their country," said Thomas W. Bell, "they desired to achieve something that would at least erase the stigma cast upon her by the recent inroads of the Mexicans, and avenge in some manner the cruelties practiced upon her citizens—also to capture citizens of Mexico, to give in exchange for those taken by Gen. Woll at San Antonio. These were the main objects of the expedition and not to rob and plunder as is supposed by some as the Mexicans had done."[58]

Without supplies necessary for marching nearly 300 miles home in the inclement season of the year, and, said Bell, by no means "satisfied with what had thus far been effected (which was nothing more than striking a panic into this part of the territory), and having entered the army and marched here with the expectation of meeting the enemy in battle, and having thus far been disappointed, it was thought not at all improper to remain a while longer and at some favorable opportunity give the tawny sons of Montezuma undeniable proofs of what they might expect to receive at the hands of Texans wielding the fatal rifle and urged by resentment of their wrongs to use them with unerring skillfullness."[59]

Israel Canfield reported "that the for[ce] under the Command of Col. Wm. S. Fisher were left on the east bank of the Rio Grande (near Guerrero) with the verbal consent of Genl. Sommerville . . . to return to the nearest settlements by the lower route Viz San Patricio, Goliad, & Victoria. Owing to the inclemency of the weather (December) and the great scarcity of provisions existing at the time, this course was deemed advisable by both parties Viz those who returned with Genl. Sommerville as also those engaged in the expedition against Mier under the command of Col. Wm. S. Fisher."[60]

---

56. Sam Houston to Brigadier General Alexander Somervell, Executive Department, City of Houston, Mar. 25, 1842 (private), in Williams and Barker, eds., *Writings of Sam Houston* 4, pp. 85-86.

57. Erath, ed., "Memoirs of Major George Bernard Erath," *SWHQ* 27 (July 1923), p. 44.

58. Bell, *Narrative*, p. 14.

59. *Ibid.*, p. 17.

60. Opening statement in Israel Canfield, "Narrative of the Texan Expedition under the command of Col. Wm. S. Fisher, from their entry into Mier, December 23d 1842 untill the narrator's liberation March 7th 1844," book 1, MS, Tx-A. Hereinafter cited as Canfield diary, plus date of entry.

Thomas W. Bell says that Fisher obtained permission from General Somervell to remain on the Rio Grande for a few days.[61] More than forty years later, William A. A. ("Bigfoot") Wallace made an affidavit, "That about the 15th or 18th of December 1842 i was on duty tending post on the east bank of the Rio Grande opposite Guerrero under the command of Gen Somerville at that time there was a council held at which there was present Green Cameron Fisher and others i was on post; and i heard Gen. Somerville say to Fisher i give you permission to go down the river and fight the enemy where ever you find them on the next morning Fisher moved down the river after Fisher moved down we had an Election and Fisher was elected . . . Colonel Commanding."[62]

Orlando C. Phelps, on the same day as Wallace, also swore "that about the 18th December, 1842, after Gen Somerville recrossed the Rio Grande river opposite Guerrero on the east bank of the river I asked him and he gave me and others permission to go down the river with Colonel Fishers command and fight the enemy wherever found and I did go down with him and fought the battle of Mier and was captured."[63]

Mrs. Mary A. C. Wilson, widow of William F. Wilson, a Mier prisoner, years later contended, "I have heard Colonel Wm. S. Fisher, Captain Sam H. Walker, Major Ben McCulloch, and many others, argue the subject [authorization of the expedition] frequently in the presence of General Houston, when in the United States Senate, and *I never for one shadow of an expression heard him say that he did not authorize the action of these men,* for my husband was one of them, and my sensibilities brightened, and my heart quickened in pulsation as each word fell from the lips of General Houston. He was always most genial and pleasant when the subject was introduced, and entirely non-committal."[64]

The decision to continue the expedition was a momentous one for the rebellious troops. By breaking off from the legally constituted command they cast themselves in the role of a private band bent on plunder and, if taken prisoners, were liable to be treated as outlaws. Under international law neither the Texas government nor any other had the authority to interpose in their behalf other than to urge humane treatment.

Judging from the treatment accorded prisoners of the Santa Fé Expedition, the absence of a flag or authority from a government had little to do with the treatment shown the Mier men in Mexico. Their objective was to capture small towns along the Rio Grande between Guerrero

---

61. Bell, *Narrative*, p. 17.

62. Affidavit of W. A. A. Wallace, [dated] County of Travis, 23rd day of April A.D. 1883, and witnessed by James D. Sheeks (seal), penciled MS in shaky handwriting, in William A. A. ("Bigfoot") Wallace Papers, Daughters of the Republic Library, The Alamo, San Antonio, Texas.

63. Affidavit of O. C. Phelps, Sworn to and subscribed before me this the 27d day of April A.D. 1883. W. von Rosenberg, Justice of peace and ex-officio & Notary public of Travis Co. Texas, MS, in *ibid.*

64. M[ary] A. C. Wilson, *Reminiscences of Persons, Events, Records, and Documents of Texian Times,* p. 5.

and Matamoros. They denied that their motive was plunder; Fisher contended in 1846 that it was not the Mier men who raided and plundered Laredo in December 1842,[65] and that their decimation at Hacienda Salado was not caused by the sack of Laredo, as President Houston alleged.[66] Those who remained on the frontier, recalled a prisoner who was not a member of the Mier Expedition but who was incarcerated with them for nineteen months, wished "to retaliate upon the Mexicans" and hoped "to secure a great deal of plunder."[67] Thomas Jefferson Green, who had much to say about the Mexicans ignoring the "laws of civilized warfare," condoned the pillage of the civilian population of Laredo, although all other diarists of the Mier Expedition condemned it. Some of the Mier men wanted revenge and retaliation; many sought adventure; and the leaders were nearly all political opponents of Sam Houston.

At their new campsite they unanimously elected Capt. William S. Fisher,[68] a strong opponent of President Houston, to command them and accorded him the rank of "Colonel."[69] "Col. Fisher is a commander, in my estimation," declared Memucan Hunt, "not second to any man in the nation."[70] Born in Virginia, the son of James and Margaret (Nimmo) Fisher, he emigrated to Texas in 1834 and settled in the Municipality of Gonzales in Green C. DeWitt's Colony.[71] Fisher was "a man of finished education and remarkable intelligence and one of the tallest men in the country," commented Charles DeMorse, editor of the *Northern Standard*. "As a conversationalist he was captivating, ever governed by a keen sense of propriety and respect for others—hence a man commanding esteem wherever he appeared." DeMorse reported, "We first met him in August '36, taking a company of men to the Army of Texas under Gen. Rusk, then at the Colette. In all situations that we ever saw him, he displayed the same frank energy of character which was one of his distinguishing traits. He always inspired and retained the warm appreciation and respect of his friends."[72]

Fisher's first experience as a soldier in Texas was in a fight with the Indians on the San Marcos River in the spring of 1835.[73] Later in the sum-

---

65. William S. Fisher to the *Galveston News*, reprinted in *Northern Standard* (Clarksville, Tex.), Jan. 21, 1846.

66. *Ibid.*

67. "Reminiscences of Milvern Harrell, the Only Living Survivor of the Dawson Massacre," *Dallas Morning News*, June 16, 1907.

68. John Henry Brown, *Indian Wars and Pioneers of Texas*, pp. 140-41.

69. Thomas Jefferson Green occasionally referred to Fisher as "General Fisher." See Thomas J. Green to Dear Friends, Castle of Perote, Mexico, April 15, 1843, in *Frontier Times* 13 (Mar. 1936), p. 312. Some newspaper editors also referred to Fisher as "General Fisher."

70. Memucan Hunt to Francis Moore, Jr., editor of the *Telegraph*, Houston, [dated] Béxar, January 8, 1843, in *Telegraph and Texas Register*, Jan. 18, 1843.

71. *Texas State Gazette* (Austin), June 12, 1852; D. W. C. Baker, comp., *Texas Scrap-Book*, p. 279, says Fisher came to Texas in 1833.

72. *Northern Standard*, Nov. 28, 1846.

73. William J. [S.] Fisher, Pres. Com. Safety to Com. of Safety for Mina, [dated] Gonzales, July 4, 1835; Wm. S. Fisher, Chrm. of Com. to Col. S. F. Austin, Chairman of Committee of Austin, [dated] Gonzales, Oct° 23, 1835, in Jenkins, ed., *Papers of the Texas Revolution*, 1, pp. 188-89; 2, p. 204.

mer he was elected to represent the Municipality of Gonzales in the General Consultation at San Felipe in November 1835.[74] In October 1835 he served as a volunteer in the first resistance to the Mexicans at Gonzales, and, as chairman of the Gonzales Committee of Safety, reported the defeat of Lt. Francisco Castañeda in the Battle of Gonzales.[75]

On November 7, 1835, Fisher was appointed by the president of the consultation, Branch T. Archer, to a committee to frame a Declaration of Causes for Taking Up Arms and "the Objects for which we fight."[76] He signed the "Declaration of the People of Texas in General Convention Assembled" at San Felipe de Austin, November 7, 1835.[77]

Fisher joined the army on March 10, 1836, and raised a company of men who were incorporated into Houston's command as Company I, First Regiment of Texas Volunteers, on March 26 at Beason's on the Colorado.[78]

He was the first Texan to enter the Mexican camp in the Battle of San Jacinto on April 21.[79] After San Jacinto, he continued in the army until June 10, 1836, then enrolled for another three months from June 27 until September 27.[80]

Fisher was elected a member of the House of Representatives of the First Congress of the Republic of Texas from Matagorda County, and served as chairman of the Committee on Naval Affairs.[81] During the recess of the First Congress, Fisher was appointed acting secretary of war by President Houston on December 21, 1836, succeeding Thomas J. Rusk, and on the meeting of the second session of that congress, Houston submitted his name to the Senate on May 10, 1837, for confirmation.[82] On

---

74. *Telegraph and Texas Register,* Nov. 7, 1835.

75. *Ibid.,* Apr. 4, 1837.

76. Journal of the Consultation Held at San Felipe de Austin, October 16, 1835, 9, p. 252.

77. "Texas Collection," *SWHQ* 65 (Apr. 1962), pp. 577-80. A copy of the original broadside, printed by Baker & Bordens, San Felipe de Austin, is in the archives of the University of Texas.

78. A. Somervell, Secretary of War, under date of Velasco, June 30, 1836, certified that William S. Fisher was entitled to three months' pay as captain of Company I, First Regiment of Texas Volunteers, from March 16 to June 16, 1836. William S. Fisher, Audited Military Claims (Texas), MS, Tx-A.

79. For his services in the revolutionary army, William S. Fisher received bounty warrant 2295 for 640 A. of land from the secretary of war on February 7, 1838, for service from March 8 to September 13, 1836. The 640 A. selected in Leon County were patented to Francis F. Wells, assignee, on September 16, 1852, after the death of Fisher. Thomas L. Miller, comp., *Bounty and Donation Land Grants of Texas 1835-1888,* p. 264. On July 6, 1838, Fisher received a donation certificate, number 422, for 640 A. for being in the Battle of San Jacinto. *Ibid.,* p. 767.

80. William S. Fisher, Audited Military Claims (Texas), MS, Tx-A.

81. [Elizabeth LeNoir Jennett], *Biographical Directory of the Texan Conventions and Congresses,* pp. 23, 84; *Telegraph and Texas Register,* Nov. 2, 1836.

82. Sam Houston to the Senate, City of Houston, 10th May 1837, in E. W. Winkler, ed., *Secret Journals of the Senate, Republic of Texas, 1836-1845,* p. 42; Williams and Barker, eds., *Writings of Sam Houston* 2, p. 91. "Upon receiving word of Stephen F. Austin's death, the Secretary of War, William S. Fisher, issued an order that has become historic, beginning with the words, 'The Father of Texas is no more. The first pioneer of the wilderness has departed'." James A. Creighton, *A Narrative History of Brazoria County,* p. 152.

May 22 the nomination of Fisher was laid on the table until Wednesday, May 24, and on that date the Senate postponed action on it until the second Monday (the 13th) in November 1837 for action by the Second Congress.[83]

There is no record of Fisher's confirmation, but he continued to serve as acting secretary of war until July 15, 1837, when he resigned because of ill health.[84] Soon after his appointment as acting secretary of war, Gen. Felix Huston, absent from his command of the army near Goliad-Victoria, was at the capital talking wildly of marching on the seat of government to "'chastize the President' and 'kick Congress out of doors and give laws to Texas.'" President Houston sent Fisher to the army with sealed orders directing him to furlough the troops by companies, with the exception of 600 men.[85]

Fisher became upset by the appearance of a report by "J. W." in the New Orleans *Commercial Bulletin* on March 15, 1838, of a meeting between President Houston and himself in Houston on Friday, February 23, "and even pretending to state my intentions," reported Fisher, "in asking that interview." The correspondent ("J. W.") of the *Commercial Bulletin* reported a "disgraceful" incident on February 25 had occurred when the president of the Republic of Texas was "stopped in the streets or rather was accosted" by Colonel Fisher, former secretary of war, accompanied by his companions Samuel Rhoads Fisher, former secretary of the navy who had been removed from office by Houston, and D. F. Weymouth, former commissary general of subsistence. "Both in an angry manner" walked up to the president and arranged themselves around the president, "with the President in the center."[86]

Fisher, "a known enemy of the President," was angry because of uncomplimentary remarks that the president had made about him. He began to speak to the president, "who you know is remarkable for his politeness," reported "J. W." The president "received the gentlemen in his politest manner. Fisher then asked him to repeat or retract certain expressions made relative to him, to Col. D. T. Weightmouth [D. F. Weymouth]."[87] The president "refused to notice it,"[88] and Fisher then re-

---

83. Winkler, ed., *Secret Journals of the Senate, Republic of Texas*, pp. 54, 56; Williams and Barker, eds., *Writings of Sam Houston* 2, p. 67 n. 2; [Jennett], *Biographical Directory of the Texan Conventions and Congresses*, p. 9.

84. Order of William S. Fisher to James W. Scott, Houston, December 26, 1837, to settle for the amount of pay due him as secretary of war from December 22, 1836 - July 15, 1837. William S. Fisher, Audited Military Claims (Texas), MS, Tx-A. Charles Mason, Chief Clerk, War Department, on August 1, 1837, certified that Col. W. S. Fisher tendered his resignation by letter of July 15, 1837, to the president, which was referred to the War Department by the president.

85. Herbert Gambrell, *Mirabeau Buonaparte Lamar*, pp. 192-93.

86. New Orleans *Commercial Bulletin*, Mar. 15, 1838; *Mississippian* (Jackson), May 25, 1838.

87. The name is correctly "D. F. Weymouth" (Winkler, ed., *Secret Journals of the Senate, Republic of Texas*, pp. 44, 50).

88. New Orleans *Commercial Bulletin*, Mar. 15, 1838.

quested whether Houston "held himself responsible for his expressions and actions." "The President replied, that for his official acts he was personally responsible to the People—his constituents; but for his personal acts he was personally responsible." Fisher asked if he would receive a note from him challenging him to a duel, but Houston refused to dignify the challenge with a reply.[89]

"In an hour or two" after the meeting between Houston and Fisher, "a challenge [to a duel] was handed to the President from Col. W. S. Fisher. The President immediately referred it to his servant-boy Tom, who carelessly put it in his pocket," while Houston informed the second, "that he was getting ready to start to Nacogdoches,[90] & that he would think of the affair—at all events, said he, I shall give it the attention such a thing merits. Thus ended the disgraceful affair to all parties concerned," commented "J. W.," "with the exception of General Houston, who has with his usual tact, made the gentlemen get the worst of the affair."[91]

Seeing the report of his confrontation with Houston in the New Orleans newspaper, Fisher replied through the columns of the *Brazoria People* on June 29 and sought to learn the identity of his accuser, who, he said, had signed himself "J. W." "I now wish to intimate to J. W. in the gentlest manner possible, that if he is the supple, fawning, sycophantic, lying parasite, whom I suppose him to be, he may with safety come out under his proper signature, as I can answer him for myself and the gentlemen connected with me, that we would indefinitely prefer dealing with his dark skinned friend Tom, considering him as immensely his superior, both in intelligence, gentlemanly bearing, and moral worth. Whoever J. W. may be, however, shall very soon be ascertained beyond a doubt. . . ."[92]

In July 1838, Fisher, Edward M. Glenn, and Cornelius W. Peterson announced in Houston that they intended "to practice law in the several courts comprising the western jurisdiction, and that Colonel Fisher would be found in Gonzales, Glenn in Texana, and Peterson in Victoria.[93]

Soon after Mirabeau B. Lamar became president, he nominated Fisher to the rank of lieutenant colonel and Edward Burleson of Bastrop to be colonel of the First Regiment of Infantry. Their nominations were confirmed the day they were made, January 23, 1839, from which date Fisher drew pay until he was dropped from the army on August 18, 1840,[94] having joined the Mexican Federalists of northern Mexico. For a while Fisher acted as the chief recruiting officer of the regular army formed dur-

---

89. *Mississippian* (Jackson), May 25, 1838.

90. President Houston departed the City of Houston for Nacogdoches on Saturday, Feb. 24, 1838.

91. William S. Fisher to the editor of the *Brazoria People*, Texana, June 29, 1838, in *Telegraph and Texas Register*, July 28, 1838.

92. *Telegraph and Texas Register*, July 28, 1838.

93. Winkler, ed., *Secret Journals of the Senate, Republic of Texas*, pp. 128-29; William S. Fisher, Audited Military Claims (Texas), MS, Tx-A.

94. Brown, *Indian Wars and Pioneers of Texas*, p. 70.

ing the Lamar Administration under the law of December 21, 1838. He participated in the campaign to drive the Cherokee and other Indians out of East Texas in July 1839; and near the close of 1839 he served under Colonel Burleson in an expedition against a party of Indians under Chiefs John Bowles—son of Chief Bowles killed in the Cherokee campaign of the previous summer—and "The Egg," and took part in the fight with these Indians on Christmas Day, 1839, on the Colorado River, about three miles below the mouth of the San Saba.[95]

In March 1840 Fisher was sent to San Antonio in command of Companies A, C, and I of the First Regiment of Infantry of the regular army to provide security during the peace negotiations with the Comanches at the Council House. While in San Antonio he was injured in a fall from the walls of the San José Mission.[96] In the summer of 1840, Fisher cast his lot with the Mexican Federalist rebel Gen. Antonio Canales' third expedition.[97] Fisher organized a command of 200 men, and with military equipment belonging to the Republic of Texas joined with Canales' forces on August 19.

Fisher served in the Federalist effort to establish the Republic of the Río Grande in northern Mexico, and, by experience, was probably as well acquainted with the regions of the Rio Grande as any Texan. Certainly he had commanded larger bodies of troops than any of the other 308 men who broke off from Somervell's command.

After the collapse of Canales' Republic of the Río Grande, Fisher was restless and ripe for the ambitious plans of Felix Huston, Thomas Jefferson Green, and Albert Sidney Johnston for offensive action against Mexico. On January 28, 1841, Fisher wrote to General Huston,[98] who had proposed an expedition against Chihuahua to start about April 1, 1841, from northeastern Texas, which would greatly embarrass any Mexican army contemplating an invasion of Texas. Fisher informed Huston that he was "busily occupied in earning a base subsistence" and in consoling himself "with the hope that a big war would soon break out with 'England' and furnish a broad field for enterprize and employment for the myriads of ardent and discontented spirits, who are in the same threadbare condition" as he.

In 1841 Fisher was one of the endorsers of the second edition (1841) of Robert M. Coleman's *Houston Displayed; or, Who Won the Battle of San Jacinto? By a Farmer in the Army.*[99] The new edition was printed secretly at the office of the *Telegraph* in Houston. It is a partisan attack upon Hous-

---

95. *Telegraph and Texas Register,* Apr. 22, 1840.

96. For an account of Fisher's activities in the Republic of the Rio Grande, see Nance, *After San Jacinto: The Texas-Mexican Frontier, 1836-1841,* pp. 329-75.

97. Felix Huston to Branch T. Archer, Dec. 23, 1840, in Army Papers (Texas), MS, Tx-A.

98. William S. Fisher to Gen. Felix Huston, New Orleans, Jan. 28, 1841, in *Program* of the Forty-Fourth Annual Meeting of the Texas State Historical Association, Austin, Apr. 26-27, 1940.

99. Streeter, *Bibliography of Texas,* pt. 1, 2, pp. 253-54.

ton's character and conduct in the San Jacinto campaign, first published in 1837.

Fisher's motives in defying the command of his superior officer and to organize a guerrilla band were premeditated. In a letter to Huston, written from New Orleans soon after his return from the collapse of the Republic of the Río Grande and less than two years before the Mier Expedition, Fisher revealed his thoughts concerning another expedition into Mexico. To the "loud-mouthed Mississippian" (Huston), Fisher admitted he could not "sober down into the country schoolmaster, or the patient drudge; and as every other means of subsistence is closed to me in this happy and prosperous community; my thoughts have latterly reverted towards 'Mexico'—and her peculiar position, and after deep and mature reflection, unbiased by the opinion of others, I have come to this conclusion that this unfortunate and misgoverned Country, presents the fairest field, to a military aspirant, that has . . . offered itself within a Century."[100] He predicted that Mexico would raise funds for an army to invade Texas during the spring of 1841, but would be defeated soon after crossing the border. Mexico's defeat, he declared, would be by Americans, ostensibly warring under the flag of Texas, "but actually under the command and influence of the leading individuals who command the different Corps." Fisher believed that once the Rio Grande was crossed, Mexico, especially the northern portion, would be conquered.

As for himself, Fisher had plans, and believed that the moment had arrived for carrying them into effect. From his boarding house in New Orleans, he wrote in 1841: "The part which I have laid out for myself is humble. I have determined to go immediately to 'Texas'—and among my old associates, and the disbanded soldiery, to raise a force of from 5 to 600 men; with which force, I will take up a position which will enable me to command the Valley of the Rio Grande; to subsist upon the enemy; and to strike a blow; whenever, the opportunity presents itself. I will receive no Commission or authority from the Government of 'Texas'—and will be governed alone, by a fixed principle of revenge towards 'Mexico,' in availing myself of any opportunity which presents itself; or rewarding those who serve under me . . . with the 'riches of the land, and the fatness Thereof' and in conclusion, will have a potential voice in the disposition of the Conquered Country."[101]

Thomas Jefferson Green, Felix Huston, Thomas J. Rusk, Albert Sidney Johnston, David G. Burnet, Edward Burleson, and others advocated an aggressive military policy toward Mexico; and in several of the Texan newspapers in October 1842 articles had appeared, reported the *Civilian* and *Galveston Gazette*,[102] "recommending to those of our citizens about to under-

---

100. William S. Fisher to Gen. Felix Huston, New Orleans, Jan. 28, 1841, in *Program of the Forty-Fourth Annual Meeting of the Texas State Historical Association*, Austin, Apr. 26-27, 1940.

101. *Ibid.*

102. Oct. 22, 1842.

take an expedition to the Rio Grande [under Somervell] to disclaim all connection with, and submit to no control from the Government."

A few days after the Battle of Mier, James D. Cocke wrote a letter from prison in Matamoros, endorsed by John R. Baker and Israel Canfield, both of Cameron's company, and all the Texan captains participating in that affair, giving an account of the battle and justifying their conduct in breaking off from the Somervell Expedition. Cocke declared that their crossing of the river was

> mainly prompted by disgust and mortification at the fact that the frontier of our country had been three times invaded, and our inhabitants are repeatedly desolated, and yet no blow of vengeance or retaliation had been struck by Texas. We crossed the river to stir up the whirlwind of war about the dwellings of the enemy, [even] if their houses should tumble on our devoted heads. If we are charged with acting in disobedience of the orders and wishes of the commander-in-chief, in not returning to Texas with him, I answer, that we were more afraid of being branded on our return as recreants, than we were of the worst possible results to be apprehended from disobedience; and, moreover, we were not supplied with a sufficiency of provisions to take us home from Guerrero, and this fact operated upon many of the men who were willing, had the case been otherwise, to have returned. It was stamped at the time as unofficer-like conduct of Gen. S[omervell] to presume to march the command home without adequate supplies and horses, many of the men being on foot and others with weak horses.[103]

This was not the whole story. In reporting the occurrence at Mier, Guy M. Bryan informed Rutherford B. Hayes, a close friend and former classmate at Kenyon College, that "16 of the Brazoria company [Shelby McNeill's], were taken prisoner; with the exception of three they were all transient persons. All of those who had an interest in the country returned with Somervell. Brother [Moses Austin Bryan, first lieutenant of the Brazoria Company] says that three-fourths of those who went on were expressly for plunder, that they were men who had no interest in the country, who had nothing and wished to make something by the expedition.[104] In consequence, they would obey no one, not even after they had selected Fisher, one of their own choice. Some of them were boys and others never before had tried Mexican clemency."[105] Bryan, however, admit-

---

103. James D. Cocke to ———, Matamoros, Jan. 12, 1843, quoted from the *New Orleans Bulletin* in the *Morning Star*, Mar. 4 and 7, 1843, and in *Telegraph and Texas Register*, Mar. 8, 1843.

104. Fourteen of the 309 Mier men owned land varying in quantities from eighty to 48,708 acres; thirteen had from 200 to 54,512 acres under surveys based on grants made, but without a final title confirmed by the General Land Office; one owned land and had other land under survey; and eight had town lots only, while six others had both land and town lots. This information is derived from tax rolls of various counties. See *The 1840 Census of the Republic of Texas*, edited by Gifford White (1966).

105. Guy M. Bryan to Rutherford B. Hayes, Peach Point near Brazoria, Texas, Jan. 21, 1843, in Winkler, ed., "The Bryan-Hayes Correspondence," *SWHQ* 25 (Oct. 1921), pp. 103-7.

ted that the expedition to the Rio Grande would be of some "advantage to the country for the war hereafter will be carried on there." Philip Young, in his *History of Mexico,* published in 1847, says that Fisher's men were "actuated by a spirit of adventure." The Mier men, he declared, "had no other object in view than to gratify a vague feeling of reckless courage, which courted dangerous enterprises for their own sake, rather than the hope of gain or even the glory of having achieved them."[106] It was a motley, reckless group, including individuals such as Andrew Janeway Yates. "Yates," wrote James Morgan in September 1841, "now edits a paper, the *Intelligencer* at Galveston. He is so poor he can hardly keep soul and body together. He took charge of this paper to write Gen. Houston down in that quarter—And was very bitter in his publications against him—publishing Slanderous reports and &c."[107]

David G. Burnet said, "It is well known that by far the major part of Colonel Fisher's command were the political opponents of the wily demagogue [Houston], and that some of them were the objects of his special personal enmity; and those who know General Houston as well as you and I," he told Thomas Jefferson Green, "know that he never forgave an enemy or sustained a professed friendship beyond his own interest or convenience. His utter destitution of moral principle, and, signally, his habitual and entire disregard of the truth, render it no breach of charity to suspect him, on slighter evidence than is furnished in this instance, of an extreme of baseness."[108]

On the Somervell Expedition there were eleven newspapermen and printers, all of whom but one refused to return with Somervell. There was also Edward E. Este, whose wife, Elizabeth Jane Smith, had died a few weeks prior to September 1842. In a moment of despair, Este joined William Ryon's Company for the Somervell campaign. There were Alexander Armstrong and William Morris, half-brothers and orphans, who in November 1835 were, respectively, fifteen and eleven years of age. They lived on the plantation of Dr. Pleasant W. Rose, father of Mrs. Dilue (Rose) Harris, who had come to Texas and settled at Stafford's Point. They were "talking war all the time," reported Mrs. Dilue Harris. They left Somervell's army to join Fisher's expedition because it offered the possibility of a fight.[109]

And there was Chief Justice Patrick Usher of Jackson County, who had become disgusted with politics and sought something more worthwhile. Raiding parties of Texans and Mexicans had virtually depopulated the Goliad-Victoria-San Patricio area. Late in February 1842 he wrote to

---

106. *Ibid.,* pp. 290-91.
107. J[ames] Morgan to Genl. Swartout, N.Y., [dated] New Washington, Galveston Bay, Texas, 15th Sept. 1841, MS in James Morgan Papers, Rosenberg Library, Galveston.
108. David G. Burnet to Gen. Thomas J. Green, Oakland, January 4, 1845, in Green, *Mier Expedition,* pp. 480-82.
109. "The Reminiscences of Mrs. Dilue Harris, Part II," *QTSHA* 4 (Jan. 1901), p. 157.

his sister in North Carolina that he did not know when he "would disentangle" himself "from so unprofitable and unthankful an occupation. I am truly sorry that I ever engaged in political life, as it has embarrassed me in my circumstances."[110] The Vásquez and Woll invasions had provided excitement, and the Somervell campaign to the Rio Grande had made him feel that he was doing something useful. But the order to return home had been frustrating and he was determined to go forward.

Erath said that those who broke off from Somervell and went down the river wished to acquire property—"supplies, clothing, and portable property of any kind" to take home. "There were many in the party," he declared, "who positively believed that no Mexican force could be got together strong enough to defeat us, or even damage us much. A bitterness against the Mexicans," he continued, "was expressed that I never heard equalled before or since. Young men just grown up and newcomers were equally swayed in the matter. I would have been rather glad to go back with Somervell, but had not the courage to express myself."[111]

In the words of John C. Duval, "Bigfoot" Wallace reported, "A motley, mixed-up crowd we were, you may be certain—broken-down politicians from the 'old States,' that somehow had got on the wrong side of the fence, and been left out in the cold; renegades and refugees from justice, that had 'left their country for their country's good,' and adventurers of all sorts, ready for anything or any enterprise that afforded a reasonable prospect of excitement and plunder. Dare-devils they were all, and afraid of nothing under the sun (except a due-bill or a bailiff)."[112]

On December 20, at their campsite below Carrizo, those who had decided to remain on the river organized. Fisher, who commanded forty-two men largely from Fort Bend County[113] in the Somervell Expedition, was elected to command those remaining upon the river, and was accorded the title of "Colonel." He began at once "with energy, decision, and alacrity" to organize the men under his command. On his election to overall command, his company selected its second lieutenant, Claudius Buster, as its captain. Staff officers included Thomas Jefferson Green, aide; Thomas W. Murray, adjutant; Fenton M. Gibson, second quartermaster; Dr. William M. Shepherd, surgeon; Dr. John J. Sinnickson, assistant surgeon; and William J. McMath, who is listed among the staff as an assistant surgeon, but who actually was not a doctor.

The men were divided into six companies with substantially the same personnel and organization they had in the Somervell Expedition, except

---

110. Patrick Usher to [Mrs. Eliza Anne Berry, Wilmington, N.C., dated] Texana, Feb. 24, 1842, in Friend, ed., "Sidelights and Supplements on the Perote Prisoners," *SWHQ* 68 (Jan. 1965), p. 368.

111. Erath, ed., "Memoirs of Major George Bernard Erath," *SWHQ* 27 (July 1923), p. 44.

112. Duval, *Big-Foot Wallace*, p. 167.

113. Erath, ed., "Memoirs of Major George Bernard Erath," *SWHQ* 27 (July 1923), p. 4.

some of the men of these companies returned home with Somervell and others from companies returning home stayed and affiliated with the companies that went down the river. Only two members of Fisher's company—Memucan Hunt and Edward W. Smith of Harrison County—returned home. The six companies were commanded, respectively, by Captains Ewen Cameron (Company A, sixty-six men, largely from the Goliad-Refugio-Victoria-San Patricio area); William M. Eastland (Company B, sixty men, who came mostly from the vicinity of LaGrange); John G. W. Pierson (Company C, twenty-seven men, drawn largely from Milam County and the surrounding area and were referred to as the Milam County company); Claudius Buster (Company D, forty-two men, mainly from the Bastrop area); William Ryon (Company E, sixty-one men, principally from the Fort Bend and Harris County areas); and Charles K. Reese (Company F, forty-two men, composed largely of those belonging to Capt. Shelby McNeill's company who did not wish to return home). The expedition totaled 307 men rank and file.

Thomas Jefferson Green, a bitter enemy of President Houston and of General Somervell and who served as an aide to Colonel Fisher, was placed in command of about forty men to take charge of the six large boats[114] which had been found near the mouth of the Salado and had escaped destruction, contrary to the orders of General Somervell.[115] Even though the river was at a low stage, it was not fordable below Laredo. These vessels resembled a ferryboat. They had copper bottoms and each could easily transport twelve to fifteen men, including baggage.[116] They were not, however, as large as one would presume from Green's statement that they had a carrying capacity of 125 men.[117] Other boats, smaller in size, described as "canoes" or "dugouts," carried even a fewer number of persons. "We had to sit in the bottom of the canoe," reported one of the Texans before Guerrero, "each with his rifle across his knees and were not allowed to touch the gunwales" for fear of upsetting "the frail craft."[118] The smaller craft were of little use, "being very clumsy and hard to manage owing . . . [to their] irregular shape and the swiftness of the current."[119] "Two of the large boats," with several of the smaller ones, "were burned for want of men to occupy them," reported Green.[120] Thus, in the end, the

---

114. Joseph D. McCutchan says four lighters were placed in Green's charge, but apparently McCutchan had reference only to those vessels that were actually used. Nance, ed., *McCutchan's Narrative*, pp. 34-35.

115. Nance, ed., *McCutchan's Narrative*, p. 35.

116. Adams, "[Journal of an] Expedition Against the Southwest in 1842 and 1843," Dec. 14, 1842, typed MS, TxU-A.

117. Green, *Mier Expedition*, p. 70.

118. Adams, "[Journal of an] Expedition Against the Southwest in 1842 and 1843," Dec. 14, 1842, typed MS, TxU-A; see also Looscan, ed., "Journal of Lewis Birdsall Harris," *SWHQ* 25 (Jan. 1922), pp. 189-90.

119. Adams, "[Journal of an] Expedition Against the Southwest in 1842 and 1843," Dec. 14, 1842, typed MS, TxU-A.

120. Green, *Mier Expedition*, p. 7.

flotilla came to consist of four large copper-bottomed boats, carrying twelve to fifteen men each, and four dugouts, used as tenders, carrying luggage and equipment. It was planned that the vessels be floated downstream with the land force, which would ride or walk leading the horses along the east bank. At night the two units would camp together.

A small scouting party, not affiliated with the expedition, was led by Lt. Benjamin McCulloch, a twenty-eight-year-old, self-educated Tennessean who had been the lieutenant in Maj. John C. Hays' ranger scouts in the Somervell Expedition, and who now performed scouting duty for those bent on going down the Rio Grande.

Although most of Hays' spy company returned with Somervell, Hays himself did not reach San Antonio with Somervell, although most of his men did.[121]

Ben McCulloch was to follow down the west bank of the Rio Grande with a small force consisting of his brother Henry E. McCulloch, Thomas Green, C. C. Cady, Ephraim W. McLean, James H. Gillespie, probably Dr. Edmund J. Felder, and one other serving as a spy company. The boats under Green were available to ferry McCulloch's spies across to the Texan side of the river if a strong enemy force were encountered. The "Texan fleet" was instructed to destroy all boats found on the river to prevent a sudden crossing and a surprise attack. If we are to judge by a description left by one of the men, "Commodore" Green was not highly respected by some of the men in the expedition. He was pictured as a man "possessed with that degree of vanity, that prompted him, rather to rashness than cool, determined valour. He might be termed, by some, a man of talent; which he did to some degree possess; but they were of an order, that I would believe quite ordinary. Vain, bombastic, fond of praise, and with all, ambitious of military glory, he could well be called daring, even fearless; but he was unfit to command an army, though he had . . . held the rank of general."[122]

---

121. Nance, *Attack and Counterattack*, p. 566 n. 3.
122. Nance, ed., *McCutchan's Narrative*, pp. 34-35.

CHAPTER 2

The March to and Capture of Mier

O N THE MORNING OF December 20 the band of "dare-devils" set forth on their hazardous course in high spirits, "as ever a bridegroom went to his wedding . . . and with equal impatience; all were anxious to try their rifles on the foe of Texas. They were much pleased with the spirit of their commander."[1] Their destination was Mier, some seventy miles away. The leaders were nearly all opponents of Houston; and "perhaps," wrote George B. Erath, "he had no personal or political friends left among us."[2] They met the detachment of approximately forty men under General Green that had secured the boats which Somervell had ordered destroyed before commencing his march homeward; instead, they had been hidden.

"Commodore" Green appointed Maj. George W. Bonnell, a member of the Santa Fé Expedition and a former commissioner of Indian affairs in Houston's first administration, to serve as first lieutenant of the miniature navy. Dr. Richard F. Brenham was named surgeon, and a "commandant" was assigned to each of the vessels. A red bandana with a crudely cut five-pointed star that Green had unfurled at Guerrero was hoisted as a flag.[3]

With sailing master Samuel C. Lyon guiding the "flag ship," the flotilla of about forty men[4] floated down the river capturing and burning all

1. Nance, ed., *McCutchan's Narrative*, p. 36.

2. Erath, ed., "Memoirs of George Bernard Erath," in *SWHQ* 27 (July 1923), pp. 43-44.

3. "John Rufus Alexander's Story of the Mier Expedition as Told to John Warren Hunter," in Wade, comp., *Notes and Fragments of the Mier Expedition* 2, p. 22.

4. Nance, ed., *McCutchan's Narrative*, pp. 34-35. Samuel H. Walker reported the number was about sixty men in four boats and an equal number of canoes; see Marilyn McAdams Sibley, ed., *Samuel H. Walker's Account of the Mier Expedition*, p. 34. Hereinafter cited: Sibley, ed., *Samuel H. Walker's Account*.

canoes and small boats of every description found anchored or secreted on the Mexican side of the river.[5]

The Rio Grande was not fordable between Laredo and Mier, except near Guerrero, where there was "a continued series of shoals, rocks and rapids."[6] Winding through a beautiful valley, the river had left "high bluffs generally on one side or the other," and the side opposite was fertile bottomland, especially along the small valleys running back to the tablelands, where, in season, corn, wheat, cotton, potatoes, beans, and other products were grown. Above Mier the soil appeared to be better than in the vicinity of the town. Most of the desirable agricultural land was found on the west bank, while the eastern high bank bluffs were covered with a dense growth of chaparral, matted with vines and shrubbery of sage, peyote, catclaw, nopal (prickly pear), pitahaya, creosote and retama bushes, mesquite, huisache, amargoso, maguey, sotol, peyotl (peyote), grasses, and the ocatillo, all bearing thorns or burrs in some shape or other. "The man who possessed leagues of this disgusting 'territory,'" reported William A. McClintock, who traveled through the area in 1846, "would be like he who hath self righteousness—the more he had, the worse would be his condition."[7] It was December, so the grass was brown and scarce. Deer, javelinas, wolves, and rabbits darted from their path, and occasionally a covey of quail sprang into the air. Sometimes in the distance could be seen the dust clouds of wild horses (mustangs) or a small herd of wild cattle.

While riding through the chaparral George B. Erath stuck a long prickly pear thorn in a knee which lamed him for several days. Often the men rode single file through growths of prickly pear, some crossing their legs on the saddle to protect them from the thorns.

As the "navy" floated down the Río Bravo, the land force followed along the east bank of one of the most crooked rivers in North America through a dense, thorny chaparral and across deep gullies. Their march led over hills and across valleys, through thickets and prairies, and occasionally over a high hill where visions of beauty and grandeur burst upon them. Along the west bank followed the eight rangers who served as a spy company under McCulloch. Each night the land and "navy" forces camped together. The land forces turned their horses into the unfenced Mexican and Indian cornfields. Like their horses, the men lived off the land as they proceeded, appropriating the cattle, sheep, goats, beans, corn, red peppers, and other food they found in the huts abandoned by Mexicans in their hurry to escape the approach of the Texans.[8]

Occasionally the scouts collected a few horses. At the end of the first

---

5. Erath, ed., "Memoirs of George Bernard Erath," in *SWHQ* 27 (July 1923), pp. 49-50; Reid, *The Scouting Expeditions of McCulloch's Texas Rangers*, p. 25; Sibley, ed., *Samuel H. Walker's Account of the Mier Expedition*, p. 34.

6. Bartlett, *Personal Narrative of Explorations and Incidents* 2, p. 509.

7. William A. McClintock, "Journal of a Trip Through Texas and Northern Mexico in 1846-1847," *SWHQ* 34 (Jan. 1931), p. 238.

8. Bell, *Narrative*, p. 18.

day's march, the Texans encamped at *rancho* Guardado de Abajo, near the river. Shortly after mid-afternoon Captain Baker's advance party of forty to fifty men came upon seven Karankawa Indians[9] who, a short time previously, had raided Live Oak Point on the Texas coast and had robbed a merchant in Lamar.[10] The Karankawa tribe, once numerous, now numbered only about forty warriors. Since it was believed that their recent threatening and hostile attitude toward the Texas settlers in the vicinity of Aransas Bay had been instigated by Mexican emissaries, the Texans were wary of them. Karankawas were unusually large and tall, some being six feet or more in height. The men wore only a breech cloth fastened around the waist, and were hideously painted.

The Indians tried to convince the Texans of their friendship and their desire to return to Texas. The Texans, however, were not convinced, and as a precaution disarmed them of all implements of war. The seven captured warriors were tied up and placed under guard in a boat for the night.[11]

The next day, December 21, after freeing the Karankawa warriors and restoring their bows and arrows, the adventurers proceeded twenty miles down the river and camped in a cornfield on the Rio Grande at a point one mile west of modern Roma[12] near present U.S. Highway 83 in Starr County. As the men, some with long beards and mustaches, dressed in every variety of garment, squatted in small groups around the evening campfires with their tin cups, iron spoons, and knives, partaking of coffee, roasted corn, and mutton, few were lacking in ready wit and rough, crude jokes. At least for the moment all hardship was forgotten as they regaled each other.

The following day, December 22, a march of about fifteen miles brought the expedition within seven miles of Mier, the largest town on the Rio Grande between Laredo and Matamoros. Mier had been founded on March 6, 1752, on the east bank of the Alcantro.[13] The Alcantro flowed eastward into the Rio Grande. In a bend nearly four miles from its junction with the Rio Grande rested the town of Mier. José Florencio Chapa petitioned José de Escandón in 1751 for permission to bring nineteen families (ranchers) from Cerralvo to establish a colony a few leagues to the

---

9. Erath, ed., "Memoirs of George Bernard Erath," *SWHQ* 27 (July 1923), p. 44.

10. *Telegraph and Texas Register*, Sept. 21, 1842, and Jan. 4, 1843.

11. Memucan Hunt to Francis Moore, Jr., Editor of the *Telegraph*, Houston, [dated] Béxar, Jan. 8, 1843, in *Telegraph and Texas Register*, Jan. 18, 1843, and in *Morning Star*, Jan. 17, 1843; Green, *Mier Expedition*, p. 73; Erath, ed., "Memoirs of George Bernard Erath," in *SWHQ* 27 (July 1923), p. 44.

12. Roma was founded in 1760 by colonists from Mier and Camargo. Schoen comp., *Monuments Erected by the State of Texas to Commemorate the Centenary of Texas Independence*, p. 154.

13. Vito Alessio Robels, *Coahuila y Texas, 1821-1848*, p. 216; *Telegraph and Texas Register*, Jan. 11, 1843; Herbert E. Bolton, *Texas in the Middle Eighteenth Century*, p. 297. The river is more appropriately called "El Cantaro," but is commonly shown on maps as "Alcantro"; Florence Johnson Scott, *Royal Grants North of the Rio Grande*, p. 8.

west of Camargo to be known as Mier. In founding Mier, the Spaniards secured control of the *Paso de El Cántaro* on the Rio Grande, "which had long been known to the residents of Cerralvo who had ranches in the same vicinity. . . . The original eighteen families were stockmen since their land was not suitable for [farming]. They had long engaged in the salt trade"[14] with the Indians, with whom they exchanged livestock and hides for salt. Many of the houses of Mier were of stone and mud (adobe). The construction of the church of Mier was completed in 1798 and was considered one of the finest buildings on the frontier. In true mission-style architecture, it was built of native stones. Its heavy timbers were hauled over ox trails from Monterrey. "The altar fixtures and ornaments were in the early days all made of silver and gold, fashioned by artisans who worked the ore brought from the Cerralvo mines, sixty miles away." Even today the "church is well preserved but its beauty has been somewhat marred by the addition of a clock tower built of brick."[15]

Above Mier the banks of the Rio Grande were more abrupt and rocky than below the town, and the bottom of the river was rocky in contrast to the muddy and sandy bed elsewhere. The town was built around a single plaza and had become a center for trade and household textile manufacturers. Almost every home contained a loom or spinning wheel for making woolen yarn and cloth. It did not appear that the land surrounding the town could be irrigated.[16]

Having arrived near their objective, the Texan force was, with the exception of a small party of eight that included Samuel H. Walker—the expedition's choicest scouts under Lt. Ben McCulloch—concentrated in camp above a big bend in the river on the east bank of the Rio Grande. The scouting party had been dispatched to reconnoiter the town to become acquainted with the terrain and to estimate the size of the enemy force in the area. Failing to find enemy troops, Lieutenant McCulloch entered the city and conferred with the *alcalde* and several resident Americans. He learned that Colonel Canales' cavalry had evacuated, but a large Mexican force under Gen. Pedro de Ampudia was expected within the hour.[17] Canales, the "Chaparral Fox," apparently was hovering in the vicinity, awaiting reinforcements.

The scouting party returned to the Texan camp with the information.

---

14. *Ibid.*

15. Scott, *Historical Heritage of the Lower Rio Grande*, p. 115.

16. John Russell Bartlett, *Personal Narrative of Explorations and Incidents in Texas, New Mexico, California, Sonora, and Chihuahua, Connected with the United States and Mexican Boundary Commission During the Years 1850, '51, '52, and '53*, 2, pp. 507-8. Hereinafter cited as Bartlett, *Personal Narrative of Explorations.*

17. Ralph A. Wooster has written that Fisher "already knew that General Pedro Ampudia was somewhere in the vicinity with an army nearly ten times as large" as his. Ralph A. Wooster, "Texas Military Operations Against Mexico, 1842-1843," in *SWHQ* 67 (Apr. 1964), p. 475. Had Fisher known that Ampudia's force was as large as this he would never have attempted to re-enter Mier three days later.

That night unusual care was taken in posting sentries, and the next morning, December 23, a council of war determined that the army should enter Mier and levy a requisition for supplies. Ben McCulloch and several others declared that it was evident that Mexican troops were massing and he was opposed to crossing the river. He pointed out that there was little prospect of success without better discipline among the men. Crossing the river and taking the town would delay the expedition several days, which could be hazardous.[18] McCulloch, a brave and able officer, knew when it was time to fight and when it was time to withdraw in the face of a hopeless situation. Some in McCulloch's spy company, seeing the determination of a majority to go into Mier, let it be known they would have no part in the attack and planned to leave immediately for the Texas settlements. Those who went home included McCulloch, his brother Henry E. McCulloch, Ephraim W. McLean, Thomas Green, Capt. James H. Gillespie, C. C. Cady, probably Dr. Edmund J. Felder, and possibly one other. Only Samuel H. Walker determined to stay with the expedition.[19]

About midmorning the men quietly withdrew from the expedition and headed for home. "The final outcome was exactly as they, with their not inconsiderable military experience, had foreseen," reported Erath. "Doubtless there were others among us whose experience should have been of equal service to them."[20] John R. Baker, a lieutenant in Captain Cameron's company and sheriff of Refugio County, succeeded to the command of the spy company.

Fisher ordered a camp guard of forty to fifty men to be left on the east bank of the river to guard the horses, baggage, and other equipment[21] while the main body, with ten horses for spying, crossed the river in flatboats. The spy company swam across with their horses. "Bigfoot" Wallace reported that one "became entangled with the rope he had attached to his saddle, and his horse got mixed up with it and both went down."[22] On the west bank, Fisher informed the men they were now in the enemy's territory and embarked on "an honourable service, and not one of pillage, and that their country would look to them for a soldier-like discharge of that service. . . ."[23]

---

18. Marvin Hunter, "General Benjamin McCulloch," in *Frontier Times* 5 (June 3, 1928), pp. 353-54; Jack W. Gunn, "Ben McCulloch: A Big Captain," in *SWHQ* 58 (July 1954), pp. 1-21.

19. *Southern Intelligencer* (Austin), Sept. 16, 1857; Erath, ed., "Memoirs of George Bernard Erath," in *SWHQ* 27 (July 1923), pp. 49-50; Reid, *The Scouting Expeditions of McCulloch's Texas Rangers*, p. 25; Sibley, ed., *Samuel H. Walker's Account*, p. 34.

20. Erath, ed., "Memoirs of George Bernard Erath," in *SWHQ* 27 (July 1923), p. 50.

21. McCutchan says the camp guard was about fifty in number, and Erath makes the same statement. See Nance, ed., *McCutchan's Narrative*, p. 36; Erath, ed., "Memoirs of George Bernard Erath," *SWHQ* 27 (July 1923), p. 44. Canfield and Glasscock gave the number as forty, Canfield diary, Dec. 23, 1842; Glasscock diary, Dec. 24, 1842.

22. Walter F. McCaleb, *The Mier Expedition*, pp. 42-43. No other participant reported such an incident. McCaleb says that "Bigfoot" Wallace's account as told by others varies from that dictated to him by "Bigfoot." *Ibid.*, p. 10.

23. Green, *Mier Expedition*, pp. 74-75; Memucan Hunt to Francis Moore, Jr., editor of the *Telegraph*, Houston, [dated] Béxar, Jan. 8, 1943, *Morning Star*, Jan. 17, 1843.

After Fisher concluded his speech, the march on foot to Mier, approximately seven miles distant, was begun with the mounted spy company out in front under the command of its new leader, Capt. John R. Baker.[24] Baker's party scoured the countryside, but failed to discover an armed enemy.[25] Colonel Fisher and his men crossed the lower ford of the Alcantro, "a beautiful stream which danced merrily along, and rippled over its rocky bed, pure, cool, and as limpid as a mountain rivulet."[26] The Texans took up a position in the plaza and posted a guard. Plundering was strictly prohibited. A large portion of the population had fled, but the *alcalde*, Juan Francisco Perez, and several other men of the town welcomed the Texans and treated them in a friendly manner—so much so that the Texans learned a sad lesson: "And beware of the Mexicans, [wrote Wallace], when they press you to hot coffee and 'tortillas.' Put fresh caps on your revolver, and see that your 'shooting-irons' are all in order, for you will probably need them before long. . . . He will feed you on his best, 'señor' you, and *'muchas gracias'* you, and bow to you like a French dancing-master, and wind it all up by slipping a knife under your left shoulder-blade! And that is one reason I hate them so."[27]

Colonel Fisher, accompanied by Green, was invited into the *cabildo* (city hall). Fisher informed the Mexican officials that the inhabitants need not fear the Texans but that he wished certain supplies furnished for the use of his army. The *alcalde* was handed the following document, which Fisher had instructed Green to draft:

> The Alcalde of Mier will forthwith furnish and deliver at headquarters upon the Rio Grande the following requisition for the use of the army, to wit: All the government stores of every kind, including cannon, small fire-arms, powder, lead, munitions of war of every kind, tobacco, and &c., also, 5 days' rations for 1200 men, to wit: 40 sacks of flour of 6 arrobas each, 1200 lbs. sugar, 600 lbs. coffee, 200 pairs of strong coarse shoes, 100 pairs of do pantaloons, and 100 blankets.[28]

The amounts requested were in excess of the needs of the Texans and were intended to mislead the Mexicans about the size of the Texan force.

---

24. A. Wislizenus, *Memoir of a Tour to Northern Mexico, Connected with Doniphan's Expedition, in 1846 and 1847*, p. 79 (*U.S. Senate, Misc. Doc.* 26, 30th Cong., 1 Sess.) reports the distance from the Rio Grande to Mier as five miles, but most of the accounts given by men of the Mier Expedition say that it was seven. William H. Emory, *Report on the United States and Mexican Boundary Survey*, 1, p. 66, says Mier was four miles from the Rio Grande.

25. Nance, ed., *McCutchan's Narrative*, p. 38; Israel Canfield diary, Dec. 23, 1842 (original MS., Tx-A).

26. Reid, *The Scouting Expeditions of McCulloch's Texas Rangers*, p. 73.

27. Duval, *Big-Foot Wallace*, pp. 170-71.

28. Green, *Mier Expedition*, pp. 75-76. Basing his report on accounts given by Dr. R. Watson and William Hensely, Memucan Hunt says the requistion called for "25 sacks flour, 1250 lbs. coffee, 1250 lbs. sugar, and about 150 blankets, and 100 pair of shoes." Memucan Hunt to Francis Moore, Jr., editor of the *Telegraph*, Houston, [dated] Béxar, Jan. 8, 1843, in *Telegraph and Texas Register*, Jan. 18, 1843, and in *Morning Star*, Jan. 17, 1843.

The Texans considered the amounts to represent seven days' supply and sufficient to enable them to march on Matamoros.[29]

The *alcalde* agreed to the requisition, and remarked that since he had to do the same for the Mexican army, he saw no reason why he should do less for the Texans.[30] He even showed a strong disposition to furnish more than what had been demanded, if he could only get rid of the Texan "devils." As was customary when a requisition was levied, officials apportioned it among the inhabitants. So the *alcalde* requested time to collect the desired supplies from the citizens, but was told it must be done at once. He issued orders to commence collecting the articles. To some of the Texans it was evident that the *alcalde* intended to prolong the collection and delivery of the supplies as much as possible. Meanwhile, the Texans visited all parts of the town, "being invited into private houses, where they were treated with coffee," and other items of food, "and to the praise of our Soldiers," reported Thomas Washington Cox, "no acts of waste or depredations were committed."[31] "Everything we took from the inhabitants," declared Wallace, "was duly paid for according to our own estimate of its value, and of course the prices were quite reasonable."[32] The Texans remained in possession of the plaza until five o'clock in the afternoon, when the Mexicans had fulfilled most of the requisition. Rufus Alexander remembered that "The response was prompt and energetic; the contributions were piled in heaps and heaps on the plaza until Fisher soon found he had more than he expected."[33] Then there arose the problem of transporting the supplies to the Texan camp on the other side of the river. The Texans had no desire to carry the supplies, and the inhabitants claimed that their teams had been driven into the chaparral.

Colonel Fisher, having been in the town four hours,[34] decided to return to the camp east of the Rio Grande for the night after extracting a promise that the supplies would be delivered the next morning, Saturday, December 24, in wagons or carts at the river crossing below the Texan camp. The point decided upon for the delivery of the supplies was at Los Calavasas, opposite Mier and nearer to the town than to the Texan camp. At this point the river was about two and one-half miles from the town.

The Texan officers considered it advisable to spend the night on the Texan side of the river since Canales had a sizable cavalry force in the area. To ensure that the town fathers acted in good faith, Fisher ordered

---

29. See Thomas Washington Cox in *Texian and Brazos Farmer*, quoted in Adams, "[Journal of an] Expedition Against the Southwest," Part II, Dec. 19, 1842.

30. Green, *Mier Expedition*, p. 75; Canfield's diary, Dec. 23, 1842.

31. Thomas Washington Cox in *Texian and Brazos Farmer*, quoted in Adams, "[Journal of an] Expedition Against the Southwest," Part II, Dec. 19, 1842. Israel Canfield (diary, Dec. 23, 1842) recorded that during the Texian occupation of the town "the property of the Citizens was respected in the strictest sense of the word."

32. Duval, *Big-Foot Wallace*, p. 172.

33. "John Rufus Alexander's Story of the Mier Expedition as told by John Warren Hunter," in Wade, comp., *Notes and Fragments of the Mier Expedition* 2, p. 23.

34. Bell, *Narrative*, p. 19.

Green to take the *alcalde* in tow as a hostage to guarantee the fulfilling of the promise.[35] The *alcalde* was bound and placed under guard. As soon as the supplies were delivered, it was Colonel Fisher's intent, reported Thomas W. Bell, to march "immediately homewards, judging very reasonably that with his small force it would be useless and even hazardous to remain longer on the borders of the enemy's country, and thereby give them time to bring a force of far superior numbers to bear upon his inconsiderable numbers."[36]

Toward late afternoon of December 23, the Texan army evacuated Mier. The behavior of the men had been excellent, but as soon as they were out of town they became careless. Near sundown the advance reached the river when suddenly a shot felled one of the "smallest boys in the army."[37] Each man brought his rifle to the ready while word passed back that Jesse Yocum, a lad of only seventeen years, had been shot accidentally when the branch of a tree struck the hammer of a gun carried by John Christopher Columbus Hill, who was walking immediately behind Yocum.[38] The ball passed through the small of the youth's back, killing him instantly. The boy's body was carried across to the Texan camp, "which was upon the second bottom above the landing" on the east side of the river.[39] The next morning, Yocum received a soldier's burial with "a farewell volley over his grave."[40] His comrades marked the grave of the first casualty of the Mier Expedition with a pile of rocks.

The army was late in crossing the river on the evening of December 23, and some of the men failed to reach the new campsite until long after dark. Colonel Fisher, Joseph D. McCutchan, and two or three others arrived at the river after dark, but found no boat for transport across. They became alarmed that they would not be missed for some time unless they hailed for a boat, but, if they did so, Canales' force might find them. The small band took refuge in a thicket near the river while one of their number slipped away some distance to shout for the boat. Immediately one was dispatched to their relief. "I know not what may have been the feelings of the others," reported McCutchan, "but I was greatly relieved in mind, when I found myself, beyond gunshot from the enemy's shore, and rapidly approaching the encampment of the Texian army."[41]

The expedition passed the night encamped about four miles east of

---

35. Green, *Mier Expedition*, p. 76; Canfield's diary, Dec. 23, 1842.

36. Bell, *Narrative*, p. 19.

37. Green, *Mier Expedition*, p. 77.

38. Nance, ed., *McCutchan's Narrative*, pp. 38-39; Sibley, ed., *Samuel H. Walker's Account*, p. 35; Green, *Mier Expedition*, p. 77; Canfield diary, Dec. 23, 1842; *Galveston Daily News*, Aug. 4, 1901; Elmer L. Callihan, "Little John Hill, the Boy Hero of Mier," in *Daily Herald* (Dallas), Mar. 25, 1880.

39. Green, *Mier Expedition*, p. 77.

40. Nance, ed., *McCutchan's Narrative*, p. 39.

41. *Ibid.*

Mier.[42] As the men squatted around several campfires eating their supper and discussing the events of the day, they occasionally glanced at the *alcalde*. The *alcalde* was anxious to have his "protector" take him before the Texan general, since he had assumed that the Texans who had entered Mier were only the advance guard of a much larger force. Needless to say, "Commodore Verde," as Green was called by his prisoner, had no intention of revealing the small size of the Texan army; he told Perez that he must wait until the requisition had been delivered. After supper Green and a fellow Texan lay down to sleep with the *alcalde* between them.

December 24 dawned cloudy and cold. After breakfast, the army under Colonel Fisher and the boats under "Commodore" Green proceeded to the point of rendezvous six miles below their encampment two and one-half miles from Mier.[43] The Texan scouts, operating under Captain Baker from the opposite bank of the river, discovered several trails made by enemy cavalry on the west side of the river that passed in the direction of the abandoned Texan camp.[44] It was learned later that these trails had been made by Ampudia's force, and that Ampudia was, in part, responsible for the nondelivery of the promised supplies.

Before the scouts reported their discovery to Fisher, Alexander Mathews and Allen S. Holderman crossed the river to search for horses. They came upon a small detachment of Mexican cavalry which gave pursuit. Mathews fled toward the river and called for the boats which were passing, and they put in to take him on board. Mathews excitedly explained that six or eight Mexicans had attacked with "such suddenness and skill" that Holderman had been captured and that he had barely escaped. One of the Texans working the boats that morning recorded: "I . . . well remember the fear stricken features of Mathews, as, standing upon the bank he called to us, 'For God Sake! . . . bring over a boat and take . . . [me] on board.'"[45]

After the Texan "navy" proceeded about four miles down the river, the Texan spies, still operating on the west bank, halted the boats to inform Green that a party of 200 to 300 Mexicans was stationed a mile or so down the river prepared to fire artillery on the boats.[46] The boats were anchored on the Texan side of the river to await the arrival Fisher.

The Texas land force arrived about sunset and the two groups proceeded another mile or two down the Rio Grande, but found that the Mexican commander had withdrawn his force. The Texan scouts reported that the supplies had not yet arrived. The Texans decided to camp for

---

42. Erath, ed., "Memoirs of George Bernard Erath," *SWHQ* 27 (July 1923), p. 45; Stapp, *Prisoners of Perote*, p. 31; Green, *Mier Expedition*, pp. 77-78.

43. Guy M. Bryan to Rutherford B. Hayes, Peace Point, Texas, Jan. 21, 1843, in Winkler, ed., "The Bryan-Hayes Correspondence," *SWHQ* 25 (Oct. 1921), pp. 103-7.

44. Canfield's diary, Dec. 24, 1842; Stapp, *Prisoners of Perote*, p. 32.

45. Nance, ed., *McCutchan's Narrative*, p. 40.

46. Memucan Hunt to Francis Moore, Jr., editor of the *Telegraph*, Houston, [dated] Béxar, Jan. 8, 1843, in *Morning Star*, Jan. 17, 1843.

the night in the "handsome place" in which they found themselves, called by the Mexicans *Casas Blancas.*[47]

As the men hovered about the campfires threats were cast in the direction of the *alcalde,* who grew more anxious by the hour. There was talk among the hungry Texans of sacking and burning the town for failure to abide by its promise. The *alcalde* tried to assure the Texans that some unforeseen development must have prevented the delivery. He repeatedly assured them that *en la mañana* the supplies would be delivered to the rendezvous point opposite the mouth of the Alcantro, approximately two miles below.

Near dusk Gideon K. ("Legs") Lewis,[48] a member of Baker's spy company, was captured within 200 yards of Baker's camp on the west side of the river. "Bigfoot" Wallace, and probably several others, had advanced to the edge of Mier, when they discovered a large body of Mexican cavalry coming out of town, and fled in the direction of Baker's camp. As they neared the camp, they saw "Legs" Lewis on picket guard, and Wallace "yelled out to him, 'you had better run, the Mexicans will get you sure.'"[49] Not giving heed, Lewis kept his post and was captured by Agatón Quiñones, the celebrated Rio Grande freebooter.[50]

As night descended, the *alcalde* "grew still more restiff." Again he slept between "Commodore Verde" and another guard in the same manner as the previous night. The *alcalde*'s dreams were anything but pleasant, if judged by his "nervous excitability and sleeping exclamations of halters and bullets."[51] He may well have surmised that the real reason for the nondelivery of the supplies had been due to the arrival of Mexican troops.

47. Nance, ed., *McCutchan's Narrative*, p. 40.

48. Canfield diary, Dec. 24, 1842.

49. Sowell, *History of Fort Bend County*, p. 187.

50. For his part in the Mier campaign, Agatón Quiñones was later made captain of the 3rd Squadron of Camargo, José María Tornel, *Ministro de guerra y marina, a Pedro de Ampudia, México, Enero 27, de 1843*, in *El Cosmopolita*, Feb. 1, 1843.

51. Green, *Mier Expedition*, p. 78.

CHAPTER 3

Mexican Preparations to Defend the Frontier

DEFENSE OF THE NORTHERN frontier of Mexico against Indians had been a matter of concern to Mexican officials since early September.[1] A sizable portion of the troops for the defense of the frontier had marched under Gen. Adrián Woll to San Antonio and did not return to Presidio del Río Grande until October 1. The Indians had been emboldened, though it is doubtful that they needed much encouragement.[2] The governor of the Department of Nuevo León issued orders on August 15 to the *alcaldes* and justices of the peace to have assembled at Monterrey by September 15 money, horses, and one-third of the men of their forces; the second third on November 15; and the remaining third on January 15, ready for service. Nearly 200 militiamen were ordered assembled at Lampazos on September 29 for service against the Indians.[3]

On September 22, 800 troops sailed from Tampico for Matamoros. Hostile Indians were not the only worry of the Mexican frontier authorities; there was also a potential threat from Texas. News in Matamoros on September 18 reported the Texans rallying to resist the invasion of Mexicans. Capt. Henry W. Allen was reported to be at Galveston, where the Texans had received large quantities of provisions from the United States for the defense of the western frontier of Texas, whose citizens were reported armed and ready. Unknown to the Mexicans, Allen's troops had dispersed.[4] Col. Anastasio Parrodi left Matamoros on September 2 for the

1. *El Cosmopolita* (Mexico City), Dec. 17, 1842; *Jesús Cárdenas en Matamoros a Juez de Paz del Estero, dando ordenes sobre la conducta de una marcha a Refugio, Prefectura del N. de Tamaulipas, Matamoros, Diciembre 10 de 1842*, in Matamoros Archives, 43, pp. 131-32.
2. *El Provisional* (Matamoros), Oct. 7, 1842.
3. Circular: *Nuevo León, secretaría del gobierno del departamento*, [signed] Monterrey, *15 de Agosto de 1842.*—Santiago Vidaurri, quoted from *El Semanario* (Monterrey), in *El Cosmopolita*, Sept. 3, 1842.
4. *El Provisional* (Matamoros), Oct. 7, 1842.

37

Texas frontier, traveling as far as the Nueces River before he returned to Matamoros on October 16. His return left no Mexican troops north of the Rio Grande.[5] "Texas is in great misery, and in spite of what the [New Orleans] *Bee* of [September] 1 says has not even one regular soldier," declared the editor of *El Provisional*[6] of Matamoros. While immigrants were flocking to Texas in an "extraordinary manner," they were finding "the greatest consternation and misery."[7]

Receiving reports of Indian incursions on the frontier, Governor Francisco Mejía of Nuevo León left Monterrey on September 29 to inspect and reinforce the line of frontier defense. He found the reports he had received to be exaggerated and that there had not been an invasion, but the inhabitants of the frontier were alarmed and accused the authorities of failing to protect them. Some 500 Comanches and a party of Cherokees had penetrated the frontier of Coahuila and ravaged *pueblos* and *ranchos* near Monclova and Saltillo,[8] and it was feared that the presidial companies from La Bahía, San Fernando, and Presidio del Río Grande had not been detached from the Army of the North and sent to cover the important points along that frontier as ordered. There was strong evidence that the Indians were supported by "adventurers from Texas not only because of the good clothes they wore but because they were armed with repeating rifles," "pistols in the belt," and a pair of shell guns, the latter for throwing shells or explosive projectiles.[9]

Finding that the Indians had made their *entradas* by the passes of the Río Salado, Mejía had, by December 1, established a first line of 200 men along the right bank of the Río Salado, and a second line of 400 men prepared to move in any direction. Finally, the governor ordered a unit of 100 men from the Eleventh Squadron to maintain a constant scout of the endangered area. With these and the frontier auxiliaries, a force of 1,450 could be mustered to defend the frontier against the Indians and the "usurpers of our territory."[10]

On November 12 a party of Comanches attacked a Mexican mule-train on Mesa Grande, ten leagues north of the Rio Grande, killing two muleteers, wounding a third, and carrying off seventy mules.[11] The retreating Indians were pursued by fifty citizens and soldiers of the First Squadron from Camargo under the command of D. Matias Ramírez. He followed them as far as Agua Nueva, where he left Lt. D. Félix Gutiérrez

---

5. I. D. Marks to Daniel Webster, Secretary of State, Washington, D. C., [dated] Consulate of the U. States, Matamoros, October 17, 1842, in Despatches from the United States Consuls in Matamoros (Jan. 1, 1840-Dec. 29, 1848), National Archives (microfilm).

6. Oct. 7, 1842.

7. *El Provisional* (Matamoros), Oct. 14, 1842.

8. *El Cosmopolita*, Dec. 7, 1842.

9. *Ibid.*, Dec. 14, 1842.

10. *Ibid.*, Dec. 17, 1842.

11. *Antonio Canales a Gobernador del Departamento de Tamaulipas, Comandancia de las Villas del Norte, Camargo, Noviembre 21 de 1842,* quoted from the *Gaceta de Tampico* in *El Cosmopolita*, Dec. 31, 1842.

to continue the pursuit. After six days, Gutiérrez overtook the Indians in the Zancajo Aredeno. He defeated them, recovered the mules, and relieved the Indians of buffalo hides and other items. "Also, he recovered and brought [back] the scalp of one of the dead [muleteers] who was [in his grave] without it, killing the Indian who wore it."[12] On the basis of information obtained from Indian captives, Governor Mejía believed the raids were being instigated by the Texans.[13]

By November 14 Brig. Gen. Isidro Reyes, commander-in-chief of the Army of the North headquartered in Sabinas, had received information of the assembling in Béxar of 3,000 Texan volunteers to attack the Mexican frontier and "invad[e] the Mexican territory beyond that which they had so vilely usurped." This information was passed to the various defense units on the northern frontier.[14] At Saltillo, Gen. Francisco Mejía issued a broadside calling on the inhabitants of the department to enlist under General Reyes for the defense of the country.[15]

Reyes informed the secretary of war on November 17[16] that he was preparing to move the Second Division under Brig. Gen. Adrián Woll at San Fernando de Agua Verde and the Reserve Brigade under Gen. Rafael Vásquez at Sabinas to Presidio del Río Grande. From Vera Cruz on December 19 it was reported that the 3,000 Texan troops were marching toward the Rio Grande,[17] but that the invincible Reyes, Ampudia, and Woll, with violence such as that with which "the thunderbolt breaks through the black cloud to fall upon earth, will hurl the scandalous emigration from the North from the territory the Mexicans esteem as their own and float the national banner on the Sabine."[18]

The slow advance of Somervell's forces from the Medina enabled the Mexicans to deploy their forces along the Rio Grande below Presidio,[19] which troubled Somervell at Guerrero.

At Matamoros, Bvt. Gen. Pedro de Ampudia, who commanded the First Division of the Army Corps of the North, prepared for the defense of the city and surrounding area,[20] even making a feint across the Rio

---

12. *Ibid.*

13. *El Cosmopolita*, Dec. 14, 1842.

14. *Ibid.*, Dec. 3, 1842; see also *Pedro de Ampudia a ministro de Guerra y Marina D. José María Tornel, Mier, Diciembre 29 de 1842*, in *El Cosmopolita*, Jan. 25, 1843.

15. *Francisco Mejía, General de brigada, gobernador y comandante general del Departamento de Coahuila a sus habitantes*, [Saltillo, Dec. 8, 1842], copy in *Archivo General del Estado*, San Luis Potosí, Mexico; cited in Streeter, comp., *Bibliography of Texas*, Part 2, p. 229, vol. 3, item 976.

16. *El Cosmopolita*, Dec. 3, 1842; see also *Pedro de Ampudia a ministro de Guerra y Marina D. José María Tornel, Mier, Diciembre 29 de 1842*, in *El Cosmopolita*, Jan. 25, 1843.

17. *New York Union*, quoted in *Daily National Intelligencer* (Washington, D.C.), Jan. 12, 1843.

18. J. M. Carrillo in *El Provisional* (Matamoros), Oct. 7, 1842.

19. *Telegraph and Texas Register*, Jan. 25, 1843.

20. *Pedro de Ampudia a Ministro de Guerra y Marina D. José María Tornel, Cuerpo de ejército del Norte, División primeró, Mier, Diciembre 29 de 1842*, in *El Látigo de Texas* (Matamoros), Jan. 23, 1843 (vol. 1 no. 3), and *El Cosmopolita*, Jan. 25, 1843; *El Nacional* (Jalapa), Dec. 15, 1842; *El Siglo Diez y Nueve* (Mexico City), Mar. 31, 1843.

Grande as far as the Arroyo Colorado. Reyes advanced from San Fernando to Presidio del Rio Grande with the Second Division to meet a possible Texan advance in that direction. He arrived at Presidio del Río Grande on November 7.[21] With the Second Division and the Reserve Brigade under Woll, he had approximately 1,500 men. He urged the secretary of war to send reinforcements to counter the Texans he expected to strike at Laredo, Presidio del Río Grande, or along the Las Moras road, since he would not be able to protect these points with his present force. The commandant of Squadron D, Antonio Pérez, was ordered to Béxar to investigate the object of the Texan rendezvous at that place.

Reyes ordered Ampudia to send 300 infantrymen to Laredo to escort 20,000 *pesos* for the payment of Ampudia's troops. Ampudia sent only 100 select *zapadores* under Capt. Mamascio Martínez up the river toward Laredo, and his own son and Capt. Miguel Aznar by stage to Laredo to hurry the money. Aznar was instructed to hold in readiness at Guerrero fifty well-mounted men from the Regiment of Auxiliaries from the Villas del Norte, so upon his return from Laredo to Guerrero the money might be brought quickly to Matamoros.[22]

Pérez reported to Reyes' headquarters at Presidio del Río Grande that 1,000 Anglo-Texans volunteers had commenced their march from Béxar on November 25 for the Mexican frontier with one six-pound artillery piece, and had crossed the Medina.[23] With the Second Division and the Reserve Brigade under his command, Reyes marched immediately to Las Adjuntas, approximately thirty-seven miles north of Presidio del Río Grande, to a better position. As he left Presidio del Río Grande, other spies arrived, confirmed Pérez's report, and added that "the French flag had been trampled under foot at Béxar by the chief of the enemy force, Tamavil [Somervell] taking from the home of the Consul lead, flour, and other things. Just punishment to those who have recognized the independence of those pirates,"[24] commented Reyes. On December 3 he reached Paso del Aguila (Eagle Pass), encamped, and sent two cavalry units out to scout.

On December 5 Reyes dispatched a letter to the secretary of war saying that "the Supremc Government need not doubt that if the Knight errants of Texas should dare invade the frontier" that they would be "ex-

---

21. Miguel A. Sánchez Lamego, *The Second Mexican-Texas War*, p. 44.

22. *Pedro de Ampudia a Ministro de Guerra y Marina D. José María Tornel, Cuerpo de ejército del Norte, División primeró, Mier, Diciembre 29 de 1842*, in *El Látigo de Texas* (Matamoros), Jan. 23, 1843 (vol. 1, no. 3); also in *El Cosmopolita*, Jan. 25, 1843; see also *Pedro de Ampudia a Ministro de Guerra y Marina, Mier, Diciembre 26 de 1842*, in *El Cosmopolita*, Jan. 6, 1843; *Republican Banner* (Nashville), Feb. 8, 1843; *Niles' National Register* 63, p. 269, Feb. 11, 1843.

23. *Isidro Reyes al Sr. Ministro de la Guerra, [Presidio del] Río Grande, Diciembre 1 de 1842*, reprinted from *Diario del Gobierno* in *El Cosmopolita*, Dec. 14, 1842.

24. *Ibid*.

emplarily punished" by the troops under his command.[25] From his position at Paso del Aguila he could operate on either San Fernando or Presidio del Río Grande, depending on the direction the enemy might take, "either by one of the two detachments on the other side of the Rio Grande and on the Nueces, or by . . . [the] outposts which . . . [he had] placed before . . . [his] camp at the fords known on the Río Grande." He expressed appreciation that the substitute president had ordered money sent to him to pay his troops, which would enable them to "acquire the necessaries of life in this place, where everything is so dear on account of the distance from which it is brought, and the danger on their transit from the savage Indians."[26]

Early in December General Reyes apprised Ampudia that a force of some 3,000 Texans was advancing against the northern frontier and that he was moving to meet them. Ampudia was advised not to maneuver troops of his brigade farther than a radius of ten leagues from Matamoros, for that city must be held at any cost.

From Laredo, Aznar wrote that the money had not yet arrived and that he had learned that General Reyes was moving in the direction of the Nueces on information that the Texans had crossed the Río Frío. Colonel Canales, who commanded the Auxiliary Regiment of the Villas del Norte, informed Ampudia in dispatches dated December 7 and 8 on the Rio Grande, and sent by special courier who reached Matamoros on the December 14,[27] that Laredo had fallen to the Texan adventurers and he had returned to Guerrero without munitions and sufficient force to check their advance.

With the fall of Laredo, Reyes abandoned his camp at Paso del Aguila and returned to Presidio del Río Grande on December 10. Reyes ordered Canales to do everything possible to harass the Texans if they crossed the Rio Grande.[28] At Monterrey, on December 16 Governor José María de Ortega issued a broadside announcing the fall of the Villa de Laredo to the usurpers from Texas "who have dared to offer a new outrage to the nation."[29]

---

25. Isidro Reyes to His Excellency the Secretary of War and Marine, Headquarters of the Army of the North, Passo del Aguila, December 5, 1842, translated from the *Diario del Gobierno* in *Telegraph and Texas Register*, Feb. 1, 1843.

26. *Ibid.*

27. I. D. Marks to Daniel Webster, Secretary of State, Consulate U.S.A., Matamoros, 18th December, 1842, in Despatches from United States Consuls in Matamoros (Jan. 1, 1840-Dec. 29, 1848), National Archives (microfilm).

28. I. D. Marks to Daniel Webster, Secretary of State, Consulate of the U.S.A., Matamoros, 18th December 1842, no. 2, in Despatches from United States Consuls in Matamoros (Jan. 1, 1840-Dec. 29, 1848), National Archives (microfilm). The fall of Laredo to seven hundred Texans, "with three pieces of artillery," was reported in the *Vera Cruz Siglo* on December 19, 1842. Quoted in *Daily National Intelligencer* (Washington, D.C.), Jan. 23, 1843; and in *Niles' National Register* 58, p. 338 (Jan. 28, 1843).

29. *José María de Ortega, Gobernador y Comandante General del Departamento de Nuevo León, a los habitantes del mismo. Monterrey, Diciembre 16 de 1842.* Broadside. Copy in Yale University Library, New Haven, Connecticut; cited in Streeter, comp., *Bibliography of Texas*, 2nd ed., p. 309, item 984.2.

Ampudia found it difficult to comprehend the fall of Laredo to Texans, knowing that to the left of the river were over 500 cavalrymen who could have been used against the invaders. Believing that a portion of the Texans had marched toward San Fernando, Ampudia sent 400 infantrymen commanded by Col. Rómulo Díaz de la Vega to unite with Canales, whom he supposed was reconnoitering the enemy.[30] He dispatched a courier to Captain Aznar, who was returning from Laredo, ordering him to unite his fifty *defensores* and 100 *sappers* under Captain Martínez with Canales at Guerrero.[31] Before Aznar received the order he had reached Camargo.

Preparations for the march of Colonel de la Vega's troops from Matamoros were made in spite of rain, muddy streets, and a lack of "resources." Ampudia borrowed 1,500 *pesos* from leading citizens of the city, pledging the tobacco tax, "to exhibit something to the troops." A special courier from General Woll, who was with Reyes near Presidio del Río Grande, reached Matamoros on December 14 with further word of the fall of Laredo to a Texan force and a new report of the Texans taking the northern route along the river toward Matamoros.[32] The next afternoon, December 16, Colonel de la Vega moved up the river in a rainstorm toward Guerrero. That same day Canales sent word to Ampudia that the Texans had appeared before Guerrero and would occupy it the next day. "This news," reaching him early on December 20, "confirmed my predictions," Ampudia reported later, "and therefore, without considering my poor health, I arranged without loss of time the defenses of Matamoros" under Col. Anastasio Parrodi.[33] He left half of the Second Brigade there and made preparations to go to the relief of the northern river towns with the other half of the brigade.[34]

Disregarding Reyes' earlier order for him not to leave the vicinity of Matamoros, Ampudia hastened north in the face of rain and snow on December 17 along the west bank of the Rio Grande toward Mier. He realized its strategic importance before the Texans did. As he hurried north along the river road, he pressed into service the *rancheros* from the *ranchos* and river towns of Reynosa Viejo, Reynosa, and Camargo.

At Reynosa, Ampudia found the *Auxiliaries* who had not gone with Canales, organized under Prefect Jesús Cárdenas of the Northern District of the Department of Tamaulipas. Adding them to his command, he pushed on toward Camargo, sending word ahead for the local com-

30. *Pedro de Ampudia a Escmo Sr. Ministro de Guerra y marina D. José María Tornel, Cuerpo de ejército del Norte, Mier, Diciembre 29 de 1842*, in *El Cosmopolita*, Jan. 25, 1843.

31. Sánchez Lamego, *The Second Mexican-Texas War, 1841-1843*, p. 44.

32. *New Orleans Bee*, Jan. 26, 1843.

33. Sánchez Lamego, *The Second Mexican-Texas War*, p. 43.

34. *Pedro de Ampudia a Ministro de Guerra y Marina José María Tornel, Mier, Diciembre 29 de 1842*, in *El Cosmopolita*, Jan. 25, 1843; idem., *Mier, Diciembre 26 de 1842*, in *ibid.*, Jan. 6, 1843; *Republican Banner* (Nashville), Feb. 8, 1843; *Niles' National Register* 68, p. 369, Feb. 11, 1843.

mander, Lt. Col. José María Cárdenas, to join him with his *Auxiliaries* when properly organized. He left behind at both Reynosa and Camargo small parties of organized citizens to report the movements of the enemy should they appear. Some 100 miles upriver from Matamoros, he overtook Colonel de la Vega at Camargo[35] and met the troops under Martínez and Aznar, which he incorporated into his command. Aznar carried a letter from General Reyes ordering the authorities in Monterrey to credit Ampudia with the 20,000 *pesos* needed to pay his troops. Although the men were disheartened at Aznar's failure to obtain the money at Laredo or at Reyes' headquarters, they moved on toward Mier in spite of their fatigued condition because Ampudia considered it imperative that he should arrive there before the Texans.

Ampudia encountered a delay at Camargo and the San Juan River. He commenced crossing the Río San Juan at four o'clock in the afternoon on December 22 and did not finish until two the next morning. In the meantime, Reyes reached Guerrero, and learned from Canales that the Texan force had divided, with a portion of them going on down the river and the other turning toward Texas. This might be a feint for they could still cross the river at some point higher up. Concluding that the latter was the stratagem of the Texan commander, Reyes turned back and headed up the river.

At Buey Creek, four leagues from Mier, Ampudia met Canales with his 100 *zapadores* and 137 *ranchero* cavalry.[36] As it was reported that the Texans had occupied Mier that day (December 23), Ampudia allowed his men only long enough to eat before the march was resumed, with the expectation of reaching Mier that night. Small reconnaissance parties were sent out in all directions; one was to go as far as Mier to check on the movement of the Texans. It reported that the Texans had evacuated the town and fallen back to their camp at Chapeño on the left bank of the Río Bravo, carrying with them as hostage the *alcalde,* Don Francisco Pérez, to guarantee delivery of the contribution they had demanded.

With this information, Ampudia entered the town that night without the sound of drum or cornet to reveal his nearness to the invaders. The Mexican infantry and a small group of cavalry was stationed around the town; the rest of the cavalry was posted a half league to the west on a hillock.[37]

When the Texans did not move against the town, and learning from spies that they had gone up the left bank of the Río Bravo toward Guerrero, Ampudia went out during the morning with some 300 men to

35. *Pedro de Ampudia a Exmo. Sr. Ministro de Guerra y marina, D. José María Tornel, Mier, 29 Diciembre de 1842*, in *El Látigo de Texas* (Matamoros), Jan. 23, 1843.

36. Sánchez Lamego, *The Second Mexican-Texas War*, p. 47.

37. *Pedro de Ampudia a Ministro de Guerra y Marina José María Tornel, Mier, Diciembre 29 de 1842*, in *El Cosmopolita*, Jan. 25, 1843; idem., *Mier, Diciembre 26 de 1842*, in *ibid.*, Jan. 6, 1843.

look at the enemy camp. While following the road that led from Mier to Guerrero along the right bank of the Río Bravo, he learned that the Texans had moved downstream to the point where town officials were expected to deliver the supplies. He turned to the right, hoping to intercept them at the confluence of the Bravo and the Alcantro. He hoped to issue to "the Texan Colonel and his ragamuffin followers . . . a few thousand blue pills hurled by fire and [brimstone] from a convenient distance across the Rio Grande . . . to cure them," reported Bell, "of a disease which he supposed they must be extremely afflicted; viz, that of marching three hundred miles to kill and rob the Mexicans."[38] At the junction of the two rivers, Ampudia picked a high point to wait in ambush with artillery. As night fell he was advised by his spies that the Texans had halted at Casas Blancas, nearly two miles northeast of the junction of the rivers, where they had gone into camp.[39]

Ampudia countermarched to Mier to feed both men and animals, protect the town against a night attack, and avail himself of better and drier sleeping accommodations. He left behind forty cavalrymen under Capt. Luciano García as observers. That evening or early the next morning (December 25), Ampudia was joined by 105 *Auxiliaries* in two squadrons from the Department of Nuevo León.[40] It was during the morning of December 24 that Mexican "guerrillas" apprehended Allen Holderman and near dusk when Gideon K. Lewis was captured by a Mexican reconnaissance party. Holderman "had in his possession," reported Chalk, "a correct journal of all our movements and force from the time we left San Antonio until he was taken, which led to our attack at Mier and final discomfiture."[41] When taken before Ampudia they admitted that their comrades intended to take the three remaining towns (Mier, Camargo, and Reynosa), "until arriving at the summer pastures of Matamoros."[42]

Until the capture of Holderman, it appears that the Mexicans were unsure of the size, character, and organization of the Texan force. The Texans learned later that the Mexicans had believed there were three divisions: one going north to attack General Reyes at San Fernando; a second going downriver to Matamoros; and a third party operating between them to create a diversion. Holderman's journal cleared up the mystery of "three armies," correct the situation concerning in the split of Somervell's

38. Bell, *Narrative*, pp. 19-20.

39. *Pedro de Ampudia a Ministro de Guerra y Marina D. José María Tornel, Cuerpo ejército del Norte, División primeró, Mier, Diciembre 29 de 1842,* in *El Cosmopolita,* Jan. 25, 1843.

40. *Rafael del Bosque a Gobernador y Comandante general D. José María de Ortega, Mier, Diciembre 26 de 1842,* in *El Cosmopolita,* Jan. 7, 1843; *José María de Ortega a [José María Tornel], Gobierno superior del departamento de Nuevo León, Monterrey, Diciembre 28 de 1842 (Núm. 85),* in *Diario del Gobierno,* Jan. 11, 1843; see also *El Semañario* (Monterrey), Dec. 29, 1843, quoted in *Diario del Gobierno,* Jan. 13, 1843.

41. A. Gardenier to Messrs. Cruger & Moore, LaGrange, January 12, 1843, in *Telegraph and Texas Register,* Jan. 25, 1843; *Morning Star,* Jan. 9, 1843.

42. *Pedro de Ampudia a Ministro de Guerra y Marina, D. José María Tornel, Cuerpo de ejército del Norte, División primeró, Mier, Diciembre 29 de 1842,* in *El Cosmopolita,* Jan. 25, 1843.

forces below Laredo, and the confusion caused by the Texan party crossing to the west bank of the river.

On the morning of December 25 the Texans marched to the delivery
point for the supplies. At ten o'clock they camped at the site about two
miles below their camp of the past evening.[43] No supplies had arrived. A
strong demand developed to cross the river and collect the requisition
with force. Captain Baker's Spy Company captured a one-armed Mexican
ranchero a short distance from the Texans' camp.[44] Although the man appeared to be harmless, George Lord thought it best to take him before
Fisher for questioning. The prisoner stated that the supplies had been
started on their way to the Texan camp but General Ampudia and Colonel
Canales had arrived and stopped them.[45] The prisoner also informed
Fisher that Ampudia had taken up a position in Mier with 350 men and
two pieces of artillery.

Lord and the Texan spies disagreed with the *ranchero* as to the size of
the Mexican force in the vicinity, believing it to be considerably larger.[46]
Lord estimated that the Mexican cavalry numbered "at least six hundred,
but . . . from the breadth of the trail, he would say *not less than one thousand.*"[47] Actually, Ampudia's force totaled over 2,000 men.[48] The rank and
file included many of Indian blood, and many were recruited from the
criminal classes or by a crude system of press-gangs. There were a few volunteers.

Fisher summoned his officers in a council of war.[49] After a few minutes of deliberation, Fisher assembled the army and declared, "Well boys,
as the enemy have made the necessary preparations to give us *powder* and
lead, instead of *sugar* and *coffee,* we will attend the summons and draw our
rations."[50] "This would seem a poor substitute in the eyes of hungry men,"
recorded McCutchan, "but one, nevertheless, which the Texian army was
glad to anticipate."[51] "The officers," recalled Erath years later, "had little
to say in the excitement that followed. The men were the grand movers,

---

43. Nance, ed., *McCutchan's Narrative*, p. 41.

44. Stapp, *Prisoners of Perote*, p. 32; Green, *Mier Expedition*, p. 79; Nance, ed.,
McCutchan's Narrative, p. 41.

45. Canfield diary, Dec. 25, 1842; Green, *Mier Expedition*, p. 79; Bell, *Narrative*, p. 20.

46. Canfield reported that the Texan spies thought "the force of Ampudia could not
be less than 500 to 800." Canfield diary, Dec. 25, 1842.

47. Nance, ed., *McCutchan's Narrative*, p. 41; *Telegraph and Texas Register*, Feb. 15,
1843.

48. Bancroft, *History of Texas and the North Mexican States* 2, p. 364, n. 32.

49. Ralph A. Wooster, "Texas Military Operations Against Mexico, 1842-1843," in
SWHQ 47 (Apr. 1964), p. 475.

50. Quoted in Nance, ed., *McCutchan's Narrative*, p. 42; see also, "A Texian" to ——,
[Matamoros], January 25, 1843, in *Morning Star*, Feb. 9, 1843.

51. Nance, ed., *McCutchan's Narrative*, p. 42.

and prepared at once and without any caution to cross the river and go back to town."[52]

"Bigfoot" Wallace told Walter F. McCaleb, "every time I think about it, I can hardly keep from crying. We were such a bunch of headstrong, foolish men. Many of us were hardly more than boys. We had no common sense. If we had, we would have known that 300 men were no match for 1,500 armed soldiers, supported by cannon. Yet most of us thought we could lick anything. We were a fighting bunch and could beat three times our number. Some of us remembered what we had done at Salado."[53]

To the hungry Texans there seemed to be no alternative; besides, many had been anxious for a fight. Their position on the river left them two choices—fight or retreat, and in the latter case, to go hungry. The requisition "was absolutely necessary to us now," wrote Stapp, "our provisions were entirely exhausted."[54]

The decision having been made, Fisher detailed a camp guard of thirty-nine men commanded by Oliver Buckman.[55] The guard, which was left at a point the Mexicans called *"Casas Blancas,"*[56] would protect the camp, boats, horses, and baggage. Many wanted to accompany the main body into Mier, but realized the necessity of a camp guard to keep the river crossing open. "Bigfoot" Wallace, chosen for camp guard duty, preferred a more active assignment and exchanged with his messmate, who desired to stay. Wallace later commented, "it wasn't a great while before I rued the trade I had made with him, and would gladly have swaped back again and given considerable 'boot.' "[57]

Having stuck a prickly pear thorn in his knee which had been aggravated by walking to Mier two days before, Erath requested permission to ride in the advance. Fisher said that there were already too many on horseback and that they would all have to dismount before reaching Mier; he advised Erath to remain in camp with the guard.[58]

As Fisher prepared to cross the river, Major Bonnell, Dr. Watson, and John L. Hackstaff were detailed by Green to take a boat and go down the river to destroy all boats that they discovered to prevent Mexican troops from crossing the Río Bravo in their wake.[59] When the three reached the point where the supplies were to have been delivered, they occupied themselves in cooking "a fat sheep with a stick run through it, the ends of which rested upon the sides of a large canoe, with the fire in the bottom."[60]

52. Erath, ed., "Memoirs of Major George Bernard Erath," *SWHQ* 27 (July 1923) p. 45.

53. Wallace quoted by McCaleb in *The Mier Expedition*, pp. 43-44.

54. Stapp, *Prisoners of Perote*, p. 32.

55. Erath, ed., "Memoirs of George Bernard Erath," *SWHQ* 27 (July 1923), p. 46.

56. *Pedro de Ampudia a Ministro de Guerra y Marina, Mier, Diciembre 26 de 1842*, in *Diario del Gobierno*, Jan. 6, 1843.

57. Duval, *Big-Foot Wallace*, pp. 172-73.

58. Erath, ed., "Memoirs of George Bernard Erath," *SWHQ* 27 (July 1923), p. 45.

59. Memucan Hunt to Francis Moore, Jr., editor of the *Telegraph*, Houston, [dated] Béxar, January 8, 1843, in *Telegraph and Texas Register*, Jan. 18, 1843.

60. Green, *Mier Expedition*, pp. 114-15.

"We expected to have warm work with Ampudia," said Green, "and ordered these gentlemen to float the canoe down opposite the battle-ground, hitch it to a bush, come up, take a hand, and then we could relish our dinner the better. As we . . . arrived in sight of the Mexican army, they retreated to the city at right angles from the river, leaving my friends and my dinner behind, they having no alternative then but to join the camp-guard."[61]

Captain Baker was sent forward with ten or twelve mounted men, including Samuel H. Walker, George Lord, Patrick Lusk, and John McMullen, to reconnoiter,[62] while the main force of the Texan army began crossing the river in boats at two in the afternoon, and by four o'clock the small army of 259 men was on the West Bank.[63]

While the Texans had anxiously awaited the delivery of the supplies on December 25, General Ampudia, near midafternoon, again headed for the confluence of the rivers. Before he reached his destination two other Texans, Patrick H. Lusk and Samuel H. Walker, had been captured. Baker's company had not proceeded far when it discovered several of the enemy's spies. Samuel H. Walker, Patrick H. Lusk, John McMullen and one other of Baker's men immediately gave pursuit. As the Mexican spies fell back, the pursuers found themselves within gunshot of about fifty Mexican cavalrymen under Dón Luciano García. Walker raised his gun, then decided to reserve his fire "until the last resort,"[64] since only his three companions were in sight. The four fled but the girt of Lusk's saddle broke and he was forced to dismount to repair it. While remounting, he was surrounded and taken. Walker claimed that he and the two others would have made a safe retreat had not their messmate, John McMullen, who was ahead of them, "taken the wrong trail which led us into a labour [Spanish *labor* (field)] surrounded by a high bulrush fence from which it was impossible to escape with our horses."[65] Walker's two companions effected their escape by climbing over the brush fence. Walker might have escaped, "had I not been too anxious to give them a shot. When I raised my gun they were in thirty feet of me. I then discovered I had lost both caps of my gun and before I could recap it a half dozen of them had seized me. They tied my arms. One of them took me behind him and hurried me off to town."[66]

The captured Texans, said Ampudia, reported their comrades had

---

61. *Ibid.*

62. Samuel H. Walker says that all of the Texan horses, except "about 15" for the spy company, were left in the Texan camp. He seems to imply that Baker's spy company numbered "about 15" men. Sibley, ed., *Samuel H. Walker's Account*, p. 36.

63. Erath, ed., "Memoirs of Major George Bernard Erath," in *SWHQ* 27 (July 1923), pp. 45-46, says 258 crossed.

64. Bell, *Narrative*, p. 21.

65. A field. A Spanish or Mexican *"labor"* was a grant of 177.1 acres of land for farming.

66. Sibley, ed., *Samuel H. Walker's Account*, p. 35.

crossed the Rio Grande to capture the town. Again Ampudia ordered a countermarch, happy, he said, at the thought of having attained his objective of having the enemy attack him in his base of operations.[67] He ordered Dón Luciano García to remain behind, and, as the Texans advanced, to fire at them by echelons, "alluring" them to his line. Later he said that he purposely let the enemy occupy all the houses adjacent to the Río Alcantro in the lower part of town while he prepared strong defenses at the entrances to the plaza.

The Texans were in high spirits, eager to advance against the enemy. As they formed for their advance, the sun was sinking below the horizon. They had not gone far before "the report of firearms came booming on the breeze. Many were the conjectures, of the probable cause of these reports, and what their result," for they lasted only momentarily.[68] Colonel Fisher was giving instructions when the "clatter of horse's hoofs on the smooth hard ground caught his ear, and suspended his harangue."[69] A moment later a courier from Captain Baker galloped up and informed Fisher that three of the spies had been "decoyed from the main body of the Spy Company by two Mexican spies" and that two of them, Patrick H. Lusk and Samuel H. Walker, had been captured.[70] Baker sent word that he would seek to hold his position until relief could arrive. Turning to his men, Fisher ordered a march for the relief of the spy company, shouting, "Column! Forward! March!" Like "magic, and with rapid strides, . . . the little band moved off towards the foe."[71] Within a mile of the town the Texans encountered enemy scouts and pickets who discharged their *escopetas* at "long taw" and fell back, losing themselves in the night; but as one Mexican historian said, "nimbly feigned retreat, drawing his enemies behind him toward Mier, in compliance with the orders he had received, but continuing to harass his pursuers all through his retreat."[72] As the Texans continued to move forward, the enemy's outposts were driven in without loss in killed and wounded on either side. As night closed in, the band of Texan invaders halted at seven o'clock on the high bluff overlooking Mier on the east side of the Alcantro. Only the Río Alcantro separated them from the town.[73] The immediate problem for the Texans was to find a place for protection against the elements and enemy gunfire.

---

67. *Pedro de Ampudia a Sr. Ministro de Guerra y Marina, José María Tornel, Cuerpo ejército del Norte, Primero División, Mier, Diciembre 29 de 1842*, in *El Látigo de Texas*, Jan. 25, 1843; also in *El Cosmopolita*, Jan. 25, 1843.

68. J. N. M. Thomson to William D. Thomson, Matamoros, Jan. 13, 1843, copy in Tx-A, original MS owned by Mrs. L. H. Jones, Austin, Texas.

69. Nance, ed., *McCutchan's Narrative*, p. 42.

70. Sowell, *Early Settlers and Indian Fighters of Southwest Texas*, p. 61; see also Sibley, ed., *Samuel H. Walker's Account*, pp. 35-36.

71. Nance, ed., *McCutchan's Narrative*, p. 43.

72. *Pedro de Ampudia a Ministro de Guerra y Marina D. José Mariá Tornel, Cuerpo del ejército del Norte, Primero División, Mier, Diciembre 29 de 1842*, in *El Látigo de Texas*, Jan. 23, 1843.

73. Nance, ed., *McCutchan's Narrative*, p. 43; Letter of "A Texian," [Matamoros], Jan. 25, 1843, in *Morning Star*, Feb. 9, 1843.

Ampudia fortified the town and deployed his troops. He sought unsuccessfully to extract information from the several Texans who had been captured. Walker was questioned at length through an interpreter concerning the Texan forces on the frontier, particularly Fisher's command. He was warned that he must "tell the truth" or he would be shot.[74] Walker replied that threats would make no difference in his answers, that he was a prisoner and that Ampudia could dispose of him as he thought proper. The interpreter asked if Walker considered himself a spy. Walker reported, "I told him I was a scout, but he insisted otherwise while I stated that a spie was one who tried to obtain important information by palming himself on the enemy as a friend. Nothing more was said on the subject."[75] To the numerous questions asked about Fisher's movements and intentions and the forces of Generals Rusk, Burleson, and Somervell, Walker gave evasive answers, "except as regarded the disposition of our men to fight to which," he said, "I told him (Ampudia) they had been waiting for some time to get a fight and were not willing to go home without it—that they were resolved on death or victory."[76]

The interrogation ended, Walker joined Lusk, who had apparently already been questioned. The two Texans were taken "to a small prison adjoining the *alcalde*'s office" where they found Lewis and Holderman, who had been captured the day before. The four were locked up, but before they could finish relating their individual experiences, heard musketfire answered by a volley of riflefire. Bullets whistled about their cell door, and the sentinels hastily departed their posts, "ran into the house but soon returned, and tied us so tight," said Walker, "with our arms behind us that we were in much pain, not forgetting to rifle our pockets for the small change."[77] The guard left to take up a position on the opposite side of the plaza.

The battle for Mier had been joined.

---

74. Sibley, ed., *Samuel H. Walker's Account*, p. 36.
75. *Ibid.*
76. *Ibid.*
77. *Ibid.*

CHAPTER 4

The Battle of Mier Begins

THE LUGAR OF MIER, named in honor of Don José Servando Teresa de Mier, a delegate to the Spanish Cortes, by José de Escandón on March 6, 1753,[1] was on a limestone hill in a bend of the east bank of the Alcantro, nearly four miles from its junction with the Río Bravo. On the left bank of the Alcantro at a distance of one and a quarter to a mile and a half east of the town was a low hill that forced the river to curve before flowing east into the Río Bravo. The town was located "in a pocket of hills near the best ford on the lower Rio Grande," which was used to carry salt from the salines north of Reynosa. Formerly a part of the Spanish *provincias internas,* Mier had been included in the Department of Tamaulipas. Its location today is thirteen miles west of Roma, formerly *Rancho Gracía,* near the site of Mission Nuestra Señora de la Inmaculada Concepción de Mier, founded in 1751.[2] The houses and public buildings of Mier were of mud, adobe, and river sandstone, with walls two or three feet thick, which had weathered to a rich brown. The town was built around a plaza on whose west side, fronting east, was a church, Our Lady of the Immaculate Concepción, built in 1794,[3] and now, in 1842, the military headquarters of General Ampudia. The church was approximately 200 feet deep and sixty feet across the front with massive hand-carved doors. It was "surrounded by a very thick and high wall."[4] Capt. William S. Henry visited Mier on September 3, 1846, and thus described the interior of the church: "There

---

1. Herbert E. Bolton, *Texas in the Middle Eighteenth Century,* pp. 58 and 297.

2. Directly across the river from Roma today is Ciudad Miguel Alemán, formerly Pedro de Roma. See also Ed Syers, "Ciudad Mier Still Almost Like Attackers Saw It," *San Antonio Express-News,* Aug. 10, 1963.

3. The date 1794 is carved over the entrance to the church. See Virgil N. Lott and Virginia M. Fenwick, *People and Plots on the Río Grande,* p. 80. Scott, *Historical Heritage of the Lower Río Grande Valley,* p. 115, says the church was completed in 1798.

4. Henry, *Campaign Sketches of the War with Mexico,* p. 167.

is a main aisle, at the foot of which is the grand altar. Upon either side, near the door and grand altar, are four alcoves twenty feet deep by twelve broad, in which are altars, making five altars in the church. The decorations were very creditable, although not rich; the walls were hung with paintings, some of which were fine specimens of the art. It boasts of an organ, and a belfry with a chime of bells."[5]

Opposite stood the town hall and courthouse buildings. The best built and more substantial houses were located around the plaza. The streets were narrow but clean. In the suburbs were the more humble cottages built of sun-dried adobe bricks with thatched roofs. On the southeast side of town was a second plaza with a church fronting upon it. Mier had two advantages over other Rio Grande towns.[6] A ford across the Rio Grande, called *El Cantaro*, could be crossed more easily than at any other point between Laredo and Camargo, and the limestone beds in the vicinity afforded the best building materials along the Rio Grande. Ranching was the principal occupation in the area. Two fords crossed the Alcantro at Mier. The main ford, adjacent to the northwestern corner of the town, was of chief interest to the Texans because it was nearest their line of march. It had a smooth, pebbly bottom, and the ground sloped gently toward it on both sides. The upper ford was at the opposite side, but at a greater distance from the town. In between the two fords the bed of the stream contained many large, jagged rocks, and a number of deep holes.

Although dusk obscured visibility, the 261 Texans,[7] from their position on the bluff between the two fords, could see the stream and the town. Darkness was soon upon them, and it had again begun to drizzle, but they realized that a crossing must be made that night for in the daylight they might be cut off and surrounded. So the Texans prepared to assault the town on Christmas night, seize a few of the houses, and work their way through the walls of the houses to gain control of the plaza.

The troops were ordered to protect their arms from dampness while the terrain was explored for a place to descend the bluff and cross the Alcantro. Capt. Charles K. Reese of the Brazoria Company and Joseph Berry were "dispatched from the left wing to fire into a picket-guard some two hundred yards to their left, for the purpose of extracting [the Mexicans'] fire and exploring the situation of their different pickets."[8]

While Reese and Berry attracted the enemy's attention, Green felt his way down the steep bluff. Drawing near the ford, he heard "the rattling of the cavalry gear when the horses would shake themselves." Although his eyes could not pierce darkness, he concluded that the crossing was strongly guarded. Feeling his way back to where the main body of Texans had

---

5. *Ibid.*, pp. 167-68; see also Sánchez Lamego, *The Second Mexican-Texas War*, p. 49.
6. Scott, *Historical Heritage of the Lower Río Grande Valley*, pp. 4 and 40.
7. Green, *Mier Expedition*, pp. 437-43, lists the residence and nativity of the men who fought at Mier.
8. Green, *Mier Expedition*, p. 82.

halted, he obtained permission from Fisher to have Baker's spy company and a few of the boatmen, about twenty-five men, go to the lower crossing and open fire on the cavalry while he tried to cross the stream between the two fords.[9] Baker's men were guided to a point directly opposite the cavalry at the lower crossing. There on the east bank of the bend of the Alcantro the Texans crouched behind a three-foot embankment and awaited Green's signal. Slipping down to the water's edge, Green fired nine shots, the prearranged signal, in rapid succession into the supposed position of the enemy cavalry guarding the crossing. The Texans higher up on the bank immediately opened fire. The enemy replied to the Texans' fire with their *escopetas*,[10] but "no damage was done by these vollies save to make a novice wince a little when a whistling ball passed too near his head."[11] While this fire, now being directed at the flashes of the Mexican muskets, was continued, Green worked rapidly along the river's edge in search of an intermediate crossing that would not be guarded by the enemy. He located a place which could be descended with difficulty and marked it by tying a handkerchief to a bush and returned to lead the army down.[12]

Reese and Joseph Berry had fired into the picket on the left of the Texan position, then retreated. Young Berry fell from a thirty-foot precipice and fractured his thigh bone. The crossing of the river was delayed while the injured lad was hoisted up with ropes. A guard was left for his protection until the Texans could enter the town.[13]

Green led the way to where he had placed the handkerchief, and in single file the Texans slid down the clay bluff, grasping at bushes, "it being too perpendicular to walk down."[14] They moved upriver for several hundred yards. The *alcalde* was near the front of the line in the custody of Sailing Master Lyon, who had instructions to see that he made no mistake about where to cross the stream. The *alcalde* was asked frequently if the river could be forded at this or that point, but always his answer was *"poco mas arriba,"* as he was anxious to put as much distance as possible between himself and the firing below. The Mexican cavalrymen, who randomly returned the Texans' fire at the main crossing, wounded David Allen and Harbert H. Oats. On reaching a place where the water roared over the rocks, Green endeavored to cross alone. Wading through the rapids, he found the main channel only waist-deep and fifty feet wide.[15] Returning to the east bank, Green, Fisher, and Brenham headed the vanguard of six-

9. *Ibid.*, pp. 82-83.

10. An *escopeta* was a smoothbore cavalry gun.

11. Bell, *Narrative*, p. 21.

12. Green, *Mier Expedition*, p. 83.

13. Nance, ed., *McCutchan's Narrative*, pp. 48-50, and n. 28, pp. 48-49.

14. Smith, "Mier which Texans Hoped to Capture, Defies the March of Time," in *San Antonio Express*, Feb. 25, 1934.

15. Green, *Mier Expedition*, pp. 84-85; Stapp, *Prisoners of Perote*, p. 33; Bell, *Narrative*, p. 22.

teen Texans who led the men across.[16] As the party advanced with guns raised above their heads, some barked their shins and knees against the rocks, but the noise of their crossing was drowned by the roar of the rapids. When they gained the opposite bank, the right wing under Green's command ran into an enemy picket whose attention had been diverted by the firing below. To their *"Quién vivas?"* Green replied, "Let them have it boys!" The Texans poured a murderous fire into the enemy picket; those Mexicans who did not fall fled in great disorder, "bearing down their officers, who vainly vociferated and resisted their tumultuous flight into the town."[17] Col. Simón Ramírez ordered the cavalry to charge. As it bore down on the company, it was met with a withering fire, which killed and wounded so many that the cavalry vanished for the night.

The *alcalde* "bounded with the strides of a chamois up the hill" and disappeared.[18] Again a prisoner had escaped who could furnish information to the enemy about the size of the Texan force. While the Texans forded the stream, the Mexican infantry kept up a heavy fire of grapeshot, canister, and musket, which, because of the distance, proved harmless, except for the slight wounding of one man. After crossing the stream, the Texan line headed for the plaza. It was now about eight o'clock and dark.[19] As the column of Texans advanced up the bank, its marksmen drove the enemy into the town.

Fifty yards beyond the annihilated picket, the Texans reached the nearest street intersection just as a mounted Mexican officer crossed the intersection at full gallop. "As he passed the head of the line," wrote Green, "some dozen shots were fired at him, with what effect we do not know. His horse floundered, and passed out of our immediate path."[20]

The Texan line turned to the right and as it advanced, the enemy kept up an ineffectual fire. A halt was ordered while Green went forward once more to examine the position of the enemy. While awaiting Green's reconnaissance, several Texans responded to the Mexicans firing from the housetops and thus exposed the position of their own left wing. The Washington County Company under Captain Buster was the most exposed. Captain Buster "coolly ordered his men to kneel, and well it was that he gave this order; for, although the night was dark, the Mexican balls were so well directed, that they fell like hail against a wall immediately in the rear of Buster's Company, which was not over five feet tall."[21] For a few minutes the Texans received the enemy's fire without returning it, hoping

---

16. Richard F. Brenham to ———, Matamoros, Jan. 14, 1843, quoted from *New Orleans Tropic* in *Northern Standard*, June 8, 1843.

17. Stapp, *Prisoners of Perote*, p. 33.

18. *Ibid.*

19. A Prisoner's Account written at Matamoros, Jan. 13, 1843, in *Daily National Intelligencer* (Washington, D.C.), Mar. 6, 1843; see also William S. Fisher to ———, Perote, May 20, 1843, in *Northern Standard*, Sept. 21, 1843.

20. Green, *Mier Expedition*, p. 86.

21. Nance, ed., *McCutchan's Narrative*, pp. 44-45.

Fisher would either lead them on or order them to return the fire; when he failed to act, Buster ordered his men to "rise and fire." In executing this order, John E. Jones of Houston was killed.[22] The bullet that killed Jones passed so near to "Bigfoot" Wallace that he felt the wind.

The enemy firing ceased, and from Ampudia's report one would gather that everything was working out as he had planned it. In the exuberance of victory, he informed the minister of war and marine that he had ordered Captain García of his scouts "to start firing on the enemies alternately" as they advanced on Mier, "drawing them closer to my line, and by seven o'clock at night, the flashes of firing revealed to . . . [him] the direction of the enemy's advance." "Intentionally," he continued, "I left unoccupied and at his disposal a few of the houses [in the lower end of the town] close to the said Alamo [Alcantro] River, while I deployed my Infantry on the higher elevations, setting up my two cannon at the entrance to the town square, toward the side where the affray began."[23]

The rain continued as the Texans awaited Green's return, making it not only unpleasant but also decreased the efficiency of their powder, some of which already had become wet crossing the Alcantro. It was necessary to seek protection from the cold rain to dry out clothing and refix rifles.

During the lull, Green, still on reconnaissance, noticed that the cross street led into the plaza, and at the opening of the street into the plaza was stationed one of the enemy's two cannon. Retracing his steps, he asked and secured Fisher's permission to lead the right wing to the intersection to command the street where the artillery had been placed.

Following the example set at San Antonio in 1835, the right wing was ordered to seize a row of stone houses on the north side of the Plaza de Armas.[24] Cautiously approaching the intersection, the Texans fired a volley at the artillerymen and "passed the corner in quick time to make room for their 'grape and canister.'"[25] Sure enough, "the first Cannon shot boomed through the air" as the Texans darted across the street, followed by repeated peal after peal of cannon.[26]

The Texans had no cannon to reply, so they commenced firing on artillerymen down the street to their left. They were determined to seize houses across the street and closer to the plaza. The Texans darted across the street between cannon shots at the rate of twice per minute. The Texan fire was accurate and destructive, but the grapeshot from the

---

22. "John Rufus Alexander's story of the Mier Expedition as Told to John Warren Hunter," in Wade, comp., *Notes and Fragments of the Mier Expedition*, p. 25; Duval, *Big-Foot Wallace*, p. 174.

23. *Pedro de Ampudia a Ministro de Guerra y Marina D. José María Tornel, Cuerpo de Ejército del Norte, División primero, Mier, Diciembre 29 de 1842*, in *El Latigo de Texas* (Matamoros), Jan. 23, 1843 (vol. 1, no. 3).

24. William S. Fisher to ———, Perote, 20th May, 1843, in *Northern Standard*, Sept. 21, 1843.

25. Green, *Mier Expedition*, pp. 86-87.

26. Nance, ed., *McCutchan's Narrative*, p. 45.

Mexican artillery played upon a vacant street. The Mexicans had placed their two cannon at the northeast and southeast corners of the plaza to protect government buildings and supplies. The Texans broke down the corner doors to the first house, and then, with the use of a crowbar found in it, breached the walls into the house facing toward the plaza.[27] One of the houses entered belonged to Don Domingo Moricio, an Italian tavern keeper. Moricio's house was located about 100 yards from the north side of the plaza, and from it the Texans did much of their fighting. The house and the sheet-iron door of the oven in the yard was "riddled with bullet holes"—in fact, "five holes made by canister shot."[28]

After gaining possession of the fourth house, the Texans discovered that the next lot, toward the plaza, was vacant,[29] there was no cover leading to the plaza beyond, and that it was too late to change their position. They decided to breach the upper part of the end wall of the building so the artillery could be covered by their rifle fire. When the Texans commenced hammering away at the wall from the inside, the artillery was directed against that point on the outside. The wall was thick and strong, and "the twelve-pound shots driving against it in rapid succession tended greatly to facilitate our work," reported Green.[30] As soon as the opening in the wall had been made, rifles poured a withering fire on the artillerymen.

To make amends for entering a range of houses through which they could not tunnel to the square because of a vacant lot between the houses, Major Murray, second in command of the Texan troops,[31] with approximately 100 men, was ordered, just before daylight, to seize a house on the opposite side of the street. They accomplished this by running across the street between the firing of the cannon.[32] Thus protected from the fire of the Mexicans "a part of the men quietly laid themselves down to sleep."[33] The musket and cannon balls fell harmless at the foot of the stone walls, arresting "their mad career or flew above spending their angry fury on the darkened air and fell lifeless to the earth." Others "engaged in conversation" relative to "their domestic affairs at home with as much composure as if in the house of a friend or in a peaceful land,"[34] "while about forty amused themselves by picking their chance to fire upon the enemy's

27. Reid, *The Scouting Expeditions of McCulloch's Texas Rangers*, pp. 101-2. "Bigfoot" Wallace has reported that the men used pocket knives, Bowie knives, and their bare hands to breach the walls of the houses. Quoted in McCaleb, *The Mier Expedition*, pp. 44.

28. Reid, *The Scouting Expeditions of McCulloch's Texas Rangers*, p. 102. Henry, *Campaign Sketches of the War with Mexico*, p. 169.

29. Israel Canfield, "Narrative of the Texan expedition under the command of Col. Wm. S. Fisher, from the entry into Mier, December 23d, 1842, until the narrators liberation, March 7th, 1844," Dec. 25, 1842, MS, Tx-A.

30. Green, *Mier Expedition*, p. 88.

31. Canfield diary, Apr. 20, 1843.

32. Nance, ed., *McCutchan's Narrative*, pp. 44-46; John R. Alexander, "Account of the Mier Expedition," written at Round Mountain, Texas, July 13, 1897, typed MS, Tx-A.

33. Nance, ed., *McCutchan's Narrative*, p. 45.

34. Bell, *Narrative*, p. 23.

artillery, which was planted within one hundred yards of the position of the Texan army."[35] Conserving their ammunition, the Texans awaited the coming of dawn and the real test. So far they had been fortunate—only one man had been killed and two wounded.[36]

In a room of one of the houses "Bigfoot" Wallace and several others found *chile con carne,* tortillas, several bottles of *pulque* (or *aguardiente*), and a box of fine *puros* (Spanish cigars). At first the Texans were suspicious, thinking they were poisoned, "but hunger at length," said Wallace, "got the better of our suspicions, for we had not eaten a bite all day, and we pitched into them, regardless of consequences, and made a jolly night of it."[37] Some of our "boys," reminisced Wallace, "didn't know any better than to get drunk with bullets falling all around them. They began to sing, to shout, and to holler; they forgot that they were fighting for their lives—and some of the boys got so drunk that they fell down on the floor and were worse than useless."[38]

A baby was discovered in one of the houses; as the Texans entered the room "The little devil squalled like a panther," said Wallace. Seizing the baby, Wallace advanced to the wall of the yard surrounding the house, climbed up on a stack of wood, and dropped the baby over, at the same time shouting *"muchacho."* Soon a woman's voice was heard on the opposite side of the rock wall; the crying ceased, and it was presumed that the child was found by its mother.[39]

The Mexicans kept up artillery and musket fire to distract the Texans from the erection of barricades. Scaling ladders were attached to the walls of the houses to permit ready ascent of reinforcements "for the morrow's busy work of death."[40] The houses the Texans occupied "were large stone buildings, containing several rooms each, and one story high, with tall grated windows, and fronted each other at the terminus of a principal avenue, leading to the great square" which was entirely in the hands of the Mexicans. The square enclosed an area of about an acre, reported Stapp, and "was formed by parallel rows of stone buildings" intersected at each corner by streets running at right angles, that gave the Mexicans an advantage. "At the northeastern and northwestern debouchures, two six-pound cannon [actually four-pounders] were stationed, whilst the houses around, and the square itself, were filled with Mexican troops, and a strong reserve stationed beyond the western wall. But for the darkness when we entered, and the overwhelming numbers of the foe, we might have possessed ourselves of houses on the square, where we could have

35. Nance, ed., *McCutchan's Narrative,* p. 45.

36. Green, *Mier Expedition,* pp. 88-89. Canfield (Diary, Dec. 25, 1842) says two Texans were killed while crossing the Alcantro into town.

37. Duval, *Big-foot Wallace,* p. 175.

38. Quoted in McCaleb, *The Mier Expedition,* p. 47.

39. Sowell, *Early Settlers and Indian Fighters of Southwest Texas,* p. 62; see also idem, *History of Fort Bend County,* p. 188. Sowell says Wallace told him the story.

40. Stapp, *Prisoners of Perote,* p. 33.

driven the enemy from the town." Stapp added, "The population had abandoned the place early in the day, carrying off with them all that was valuable, and taken refuge in the woods some distance from the scene of conflict."[41]

As the rain ceased and the moon rose, the Texans could see "numerous squads of cavalry careening around the village," obviously intent on cutting off escape, retreat, or aid reaching the Texans."[42] Throughout the night Ampudia maintained 100 infantrymen armed with bayonets and drawn up in a column ready to be sent to repel any breakthrough of the Texans into the plaza. Mexican troops also swarmed over the flat housetops. Others were stationed at the corners of streets leading into the plaza and in houses along the southern edge of town.

On the Texan left, Col. D. Ramón Valera with the Third Regiment guarded against a flank attack or retreat by the Texans. A charge was made on the Texan left by the First Squadron of Camargo but was repelled. On the right flank of the Texans was stationed a company of Auxiliary Cavalry under Col. D. Cristoval Ramírez. The remainder of the Second Squadron of Nuevo León under José María Villarreal covered the Texan rear; and eventually 100 of these were ordered to tie their horses and advance on foot to attack the Texans in the rear. The Third Squadron of Reynosa, under José María Cárdeñas, covered the flat roofs of the houses.[43] While the Texans conserved their ammunition, the Mexicans, whose supply of powder and lead was much greater, were not so conservative. Their artillery and musket fire throughout the night was incessant but ineffective. "The hoarse roar of musketry" and "awful thunder of artillery" were answered intermittently by a "ringing report" of the Texans to let the enemy know the Texans were still there. "This night," wrote McCutchan, "was by far the most exciting Christmas scene that ever I had witnessed! Never shall I witness another such! and there were more powder bursts, and more oppressive shower of iron and lead than I desire to encounter again to as little purpose."[44]

As dawn tinged the gray horizon, the sharp notes of reveille rang out from the Mexican headquarters in the church. The Mexican soldiers aroused from their slumbers, and the Texans were alerted and on their feet. Daylight gave the Texans a better picture of buildings, streets, and layout of the town. They recognized the *alcalde*'s office near the center of the east side of the plaza, now used as a military station. On the west side was the church, now serving as the headquarters of the Mexican command. Adjacent to it was the García mansion. While they had known during the night that the enemy occupied the flat rooftops of the houses, they

41. *Ibid.*, pp. 33-34.

42. *Ibid.*

43. *Pedro de Ampudia a Ministro de Guerra, José María Tornel, Mier, Diciembre 29 de 1842,* in *El Cosmopolita,* Jan. 25, 1843.

44. Nance, ed., *McCutchan's Narrative*, p. 45.

now discovered the housetops and streets heavily lined with Mexican soldiers and learned the odds that opposed them. Their position was precarious, but they prepared to offer a desperate resistance.

The battle was renewed with energy. Artillery balls struck the houses with a terrible crash and riddled doors, breached walls, and tore holes in yard walls. "A grape-shot bent one of the window bars to one of the houses in which the Texans had taken refuge, and glanced into the room hitting a Texan lad in the act of discharging his rifle."[45] The roar of rifles, musketry, and artillery was music to those who had long spoiled for a fight. The cannonading of the Texans was not effective, since the buildings in which they had taken refuge did not face the cannon and the balls and grapeshot struck them at an angle and ricocheted, "doing no further damage than to scale the surface, and glance off down the street."[46] From portholes, window gratings, and a rooftop, the Texans poured a withering crossfire on the cannon nearest them in the plaza. Three times the Mexicans manned their artillery piece and each time it was silenced. Fifty soldiers were piled around it, and "the remainder deserted it and dared not approach it again."[47]

The abandonment of the cannon prompted requests to Fisher for permission to charge the cannon and to spike them, but always the reply was, "Spare your ammunition."[48] The battle raged on. "The way the Mexicans fell," reported Chalk, "was a caution."[49] It was phenomenal how the Texans handled firearms. They fired with extreme deliberation and seldom missed their mark. "The way our riflemen picked them off," reported one of the participants, "was a sin to Davy Crockett. Such was the deadly aim of our rifles that we cleared the cannon four times, and not a Mexican could show his head without getting a rifle ball to feel his different lumps —the examination was generally very hasty, and the patient was surely to lose his life."[50] Frontier fighting had taught them teamwork: one man loaded while another fired. When Fisher perceived that the enemy was "discouraged and showed a disposition to evacuate the town,"[51] he thought the time had arrived to seize the artillery and to turn it on the enemy. He ordered the doors of the houses thrown open for a charge, but was surprised "when an officer who possessed considerable reputation, and as much or more influence than myself with the troops, positively refused to

---

45. Henry, *Campaign Sketches of the War with Mexico*, pp. 168-69.

46. Nance, ed., *McCutchan's Narrative*, p. 208; Stapp, *Prisoners of Perote*, p. 34.

47. Bell, *Narrative*, p. 23.

48. Nance, ed., *McCutchan's Narrative*, p. 208; Stapp, *Prisoners of Perote*, p. 34.

49. New Orleans *Daily Picayune* quoted in the *Republic Banner*, Feb. 3, 1843; see also A. Gardinier to Messrs. Cruger & Moore, LaGrange, Jan. 12, 1843, in *Morning Star*, Jan. 19, 1843.

50. Letter from "A Texian," [Matamoros], January 25, 1843, in *Telegraph and Texas Register*, Feb. 15, 1843.

51. William S. Fisher to ———, Perote, 20th May, 1843, in *Northern Standard*, Sept. 21, 1843; also in *Telegraph and Texas Register*, Aug. 2, 1843.

obey the order, exclaiming that my rashness would destroy his men. . . .
The charge was therefore necessarily abandoned, and the enemy perceiv-
ing that we showed no disposition to improve our advantage, profited by
our inactivity to recover their artillery [by lassoing it from behind a house],
and remove[d] it to a position from which their fire annoyed us extremely."[52] The recovered artillery piece, served now by the *zapadores,* was
mounted in the consistorial houses, where a large hole was knocked in the
wall through which the muzzle of the cannon was thrust. The cannon was
now personally aimed by General Ampudia, who had served as commandant general of artillery in the Army of the North from 1835 to 1841 and
as an engineer in the siege of the Alamo in 1836.[53] The cannon raked the
corral where Cameron's men fought and battered down the walls protecting the Texans.

While Ampudia rearranged his cannon and a portion of his forces, his
men fought from the housetops. Occasionally a shot from the concentrated fire of the Mexicans wounded or killed someone among the little band
of dare-devils. As the Texans' supply of powder and lead was meager and
likely to become embarrassing before another day, only the best marksmen were permitted to fire, and then only "with dead rest and sure aim."[54]
Among the Texans were a number of backwoodsmen from Kentucky, Tennessee, and Arkansas, representing some of the best marksmen in the
world. One of the most accurate marksmen was Col. William F. Wilson.
"Bigfoot's" gun "Sweetlips" also took its toll among the Mexicans.[55] "I
never raised a gun," wrote Richard F. Brenham from Matamoros, "without thinking of the indignities I had formerly suffered in this country, and
you [may] be assured that I wasted no powder by long shooting."[56] However, "as fast as we would shoot them down from the parapets on top of
the house," said Thomson, "they would fill up the vacancy.[57]

During the morning, the Mexicans received limited reinforcements
when 100 auxiliaries, in two squadrons, arrived from the Department of
Nuevo León.[58] To improve their position, some of the Texans punched
holes in the roofs of the houses that they occupied and themselves ascended to the roof.[59]

52. *Ibid.*

53. *Pedro de Ampudia a Ministro de Guerra, José María Tornel, Mier, Diciembre 29 de 1842,*
in *El Cosmopolita,* Jan. 25, 1843; Carreño, ed., *Jefes del Ejército Méxicano en 1847,* pp. 141-54.

54. *Morning Star,* Jan. 19, 1843; Pace, ed., "The Diary and Letters of William P.
Rogers," in *SWHQ* 33 (Apr. 1929), p. 262.

55. Letter from "A Texian," [Mier], Jan. 25, 1843, in *Morning Star,* Feb. 9, 1843, and
Northern Standard, Mar. 2, 1843; Nance, ed., *McCutchan's Narrative,* p. 46; Green, *Mier
Expedition,* 89, n. 89.

56. Richard F. Brenham to ———, Matamoros, January 14, 1843, quoted from the
New Orleans Tropic in the *Northern Standard,* June 8, 1843.

57. J. N. M. Thomson to William D. Thomson, Matamoros, Jan. 13, 1843, copy in
Tx-A.

58. *José María Ortega, Gobernador superior del departamento de Nuevo León, a [José María
Tornel], no. 85, Monterey, Diciembre 28 de 1842,* in *Diario del Gobierno,* Jan. 11, 1843.

59. John McMullen's diary quoted in Shannon, "12 Miles to Mier Thunder the 300,"
in *Dallas Morning News,* Oct. 19, 1930.

Becoming exasperated, Ampudia withdrew his infantry from the housetops after two hours of fighting. Out of range of the invaders' fire, he collected infantry to charge the Texan positions with the bayonet. He ordered skirmishers to attack from the left and right, and 100 *defensores* to fetter their horses and advance on foot on the Texan rear. Simultaneous charges were made by the Mexicans on every house occupied by the Texans.

With cool, calculating, resolute, and comparatively inexhaustible courage, the Texans awaited the onslaught:

At length the assaulting collum of infantry began its advance. Their progress was rapid, and in most beautiful and impressive order [and led by their officers]; on, on, they came, a dark frowning mass, with arms to the shoulder, and bayonets set; in short they presented a front, that it would seem hard to break. About forty or fifty Texians, the only ones disengaged, led on by Col. Fisher, stepped proudly and firmly into the street, formed in a . . . line across the street, and calmly awaited the onset of that grim band of mustached soldiers. Not an eye quailed, nor a muscle quivered, nor a hand trimbled, of that little band, as quietly abiding their time, they carefully inspected their arms! It seemed, indeed, as if every one felt that his single arm alone would decide the coming struggle, which, appearance justified them in believing would probably be hand to hand! At length, when within Eighty yards of the Texian line the Mexican musquets came to a present, as if by the movement of a single hand—a momentary halt, and their whole front was involved in flame and smoke, a long contin[u]ed roar burst forth, and the Leaden messengers of death speed on the way to the invaders of Mexican soil and redressers of the wrongs of Texas! Hark, that shout of exultation from Mexico, and wail from the Prairies of Texas, as another deadly, awful volley, is poured in by the still advancing collum, now spread into a mass of Platoons, filling the street, through which they advance as if the day were their own. A few of the band of Texians have fallen. Capt. William Ryan is down, but up again as if by magic, while his eye is still fierce, and his arm nerved for the contest! But few, perhaps two, remain on the earth, the rest stand unmoved—unawed! The Mexicans have advanced to within forty yards, the smoke has cleared away; and now—mark nerved arms and steady eyes—the rifle is aimed—and hear the sharp clear ring of those rifles as they belch forth death to numbers of the advancing soldiery! Now pause and behold the sene, that fire was too well aimed, and the effect too deadly, for the objects of it to stand another. It has done its duty well; the enemy are broken—panic struck—and now that lastly "Hurra for Texas" coming from the Texian line is heard by a retreating foe. The Mexican[s] fled to shelter, leaving numbers on the ground, to rise no more, till the last trump[et] shall thunder in their ears a summons to judgment.[60]

---

60. Nance, ed., *McCutchan's Narrative*, pp. 46-47.

In the repulse of the Mexican assault, Henry Weeks displayed an energy and spirit seldom excelled in battle. Twice shot down by the advancing column of infantry, "receiving wounds that seemingly would have disable[ed] ordinary men at each of the two shots," he was brought to earth a third time. "When friends bore him to the house, he begged them to let him remain in the street to witness the glory of the arms of Texas."[61]

"Bigfoot" Wallace pursued a party of retreating soldiers, when suddenly the Mexicans turned on him. "I was determined, however," said Wallace, "to retreat to all hazards, and turned and dashed through their line. One fellow, as I passed, made a lunge at me with his bayonet, slightly wounding me in the left arm; but I made good my escape and rejoined my comrades, who had given me up for loss."[62] Thereafter he never ventured beyond supporting distance of his comrades.

Fisher lost the ball of his right thumb in the first volley fired by the enemy. Later Fisher became nauseated and some thought his injury affected his judgment.[63]

Two other infantry assaults were made between ten and twelve o'clock,[64] but were "so gallantly repelled and with such loss to the assailants that the Mexicans soon abandoned the hazardous attempts and kept at a respectful distance."[65] Although these assaults were daring and several of the men reached to within a few yards of the Texan lines, the Mexican soldiers later revealed that they were all drunk on *pulque* furnished by their officers for the purpose of stimulating their courage.[66]

The third assault was directed primarily against Captain Cameron's position to the south of Green's right wing. Cameron's Company, composed mostly of men from Victoria, had taken up a position in the backyard of one of the houses enclosed by a low wall. He ordered his men to pile up stones for throwing if they could not reload fast enough or ammunition ran short.[67] From this position, the "Men-Slayers," as they were sometimes called, wrought havoc on their enemies. When hard-pressed by superior numbers, Cameron set aside his empty "death dealing yager,"[68] which carried twelve balls to the pound, and threw stones at the assaulting enemy column. He repelled the effort to scale the wall almost single-handedly until his men could reload their rifles.

Realizing that their ammunition was being depleted, a council of the

---

61. Nance, ed., *McCutchan's Narrative*, pp. 58-59.
62. Duval, *Big-Foot Wallace*, p. 176.
63. Green, *Mier Expedition*, p. 93, and note.
64. William S. Fisher to ———, Perote, 20th May, 1843, in *Telegraph and Texas Register*, Aug. 2, 1843.
65. Bell, *Narrative*, p. 24.
66. Duval, *Big-Foot Wallace*, p. 176.
67. Green, *Mier Expedition*, p. 286.
68. "Yager" means hunter, marksman, or gamekeeper in German but came to be applied to a specially designed rifle developed and used by hunters and trained marksmen in military units. Harold Leslie Peterson and Robert Elman, *The Great Guns*, pp. 88-89, with illustrations.

Texan officers agreed that their "present position should be maintained . . . until night and then retreat, for it was now very evident," wrote Bell, "that the enemy's number was so far superior . . . that it would be difficult . . . to extricate themselves from their perilous situation."[69] The Texans' firing now became slower but, recorded Bell, "the Texans were still in high spirits and determined to fight; making their rifles tell with a precision and coolness when they did fire."[70] The Mexican firing also seemed to taper off.

About eleven o'clock the Mexicans sent forward a white flag to request a parley, but it was shot down and the battle was renewed with vigor. For a second time since crossing the Rio Grande, discipline cracked. "Confusion took place. Many were talking, and each one had his plan of defense, and the voice of each was drowned in cabal."[71] Green leaped upon a table, demanded silence, and assigned the men to various positions, and the men obeyed the orders without arguing.

The battle raged fiercely. Mexicans fired from all points of the town— some from too far away to have any effect. "The Texian rifles answered promptly, belching forth death to the foe. . . ."[72] While the battle raged at its hottest, the attention of the Texans was directed by Pvt. William D. Cody pointing his finger toward the guard across the Alcantro and exclaiming, "Look, . . . yonder is the almightiest fight you ever did see."[73] The small guard of men which had been left to protect Joseph Berry was engaged in a fight with the Mexicans. When the guard was posted it was promised that when the main body had secured a sheltered position in the town, the guard and Berry would be moved. "[I]n the hurry, confusion and excitement of the evening, they were forgotten and thus neglected until after daylight on the morning of the 26th, when it had become to[o] late to bring them over, or even inform them of the locality of the Texian forces."[74]

From their position in an adobe hut they had viewed the fight in the town. At about nine o'clock, sixty Auxiliary Cavalry under Col. D. Cristóval Ramírez passed near the hut, and the guard could not resist the temptation to become participants in the battle. Knocking holes in the walls of the hut, they fired on the passing Mexicans, killing their commander and eight or ten others.[75] The survivors fled, but a few minutes later returned 300 strong under Captain Alderete.[76] Not to be outdone by so small a gar-

---

69. Bell, *Narrative*, p. 24.

70. *Ibid.*

71. Green, *Mier Expedition*, pp. 94, 285-86; Bell, *Narrative*, p. 24; J. N. M. Thomson to William D. Thomson, Matamoros, Jan. 13, 1843, copy in Tx-A.

72. Nance, ed., *McCutchan's Narrative*, p. 48.

73. Green, *Mier Expedition*, p. 91.

74. Nance, ed., *McCutchan's Narrative*, pp. 48-50.

75. *Ibid.*, p. 49; Green, *Mier Expedition*, p. 91; *El Latigo de Texas*, Jan. 23, 1843.

76. Reid, *The Scouting Expeditions of McCulloch's Texas Rangers*, pp. 84-85; see also Rose, *The Life and Services of Gen. Ben McCulloch*, p. 90.

rison, Alderete ordered a cannon to be brought up but was careful to keep it out of range of the Texan rifles. A cannonade commenced. The first shots passed well over their mark, but Berry's guard realized that the gunners would get the correct trajectory and their chances of survival would be hopeless. Berry tried to persuade his guards to make a break to join the main body in town.

John Bate Berry was reluctant to abandon his brother. Joseph explained: "Your presence here cannot avail me; you would give me no protection; if the[y] kill me, they would also you; and I am crippled, and they may not hurt me; but if you remain, they may kill us both. Your presence might make against me, while it can do me no good. Go, then; and if I die, live to avenge my death!" Finally, Bate Berry consented to go, after it was agreed that Dr. Sinnickson, "being naturally crippled" himself, would remain.[77] William Hobson and A. Jackson were shot down immediately outside the house; Richard Keene ducked into a small house about midway to the river, hoping to elude the oncoming cavalry, where he was captured. David H. E. Beasley was captured.[78] Thomas ("Walking") Davis and Bate Berry reached the Alcantro, turned to fire at their pursuers, and saw young James Austin cut down. Davis and Berry crossed the stream near buildings occupied by their countrymen, and were admitted to their lines around eleven o'clock.

Throughout the morning the Texans "were generally firm, . . . feeling confident that they would be able to maintain themselves against such odds."[79] By noon their losses had reached eleven killed and twenty-two wounded. Around noon the Mexican officers ordered their horses saddled, and aides held them in readiness "near the gate of the backyard, open evidently for the purpose of retreating," reported Samuel H. Walker,[80] prisoner at the enemy headquarters.

77. Nance, ed., *McCutchan's Narrative*, pp. 49-50; see also Green, *Mier Expedition*, p. 91. In the attempt to fight clear, three were taken prisoners, four were killed, and two escaped.

78. Green, *Mier Expedition*, p. 92; Nance, ed., *McCutchan's Narrative*, pp. 49-50.

79. Canfield's diary, Dec. 26, 1842.

80. Sibley, ed., *Samuel H. Walker's Account*, p. 37.

CHAPTER 5

The Texans Surrender

SHORTLY AFTER ONE O'CLOCK the battle again slackened. "Both sides seemed tired of the conflict,"[1] and Mexican bodies, reported Wallace, "lay scattered around the square like so many dead chickens."[2] Keene, Beasley, and Sinnickson, who had been captured on the other side of the Alcantro, were brought to Ampudia's headquarters.[3] What information General Ampudia may have obtained from them is not known. Combining what information he may have obtained from Mexican spies with the fact that the Texans had reduced their fire, he may have concluded that a favorable opportunity had arrived to end the battle. He reported to the minister of war and marine that, having overwhelmed the enemy on all sides,[4] that "out of respect for humanity and in proof of the magnanimity of the Mexican heart," he ordered his troops to cease firing.[5] He ordered a parley sounded, and a white flag was borne down the street toward the Texan position.[6] Some of the Texans requested permission to shoot it down, but Fisher requested the men "not to molest the flag." As the men with the flag approached, the Texans recognized their own Dr. Sinnickson as the bearer of the flag.

It is impossible to determine the purpose the white flag was intended to accomplish. Some of the Texans who were critical of Fisher on this occasion believed Ampudia meant to surrender, to penetrate the Texan lines to gain valuable information, or to gain a truce so he could reorga-

---

1. Bell, *Narrative*, p. 24.
2. Quoted in McCaleb, *The Mier Expedition*, p. 48.
3. Sibley, ed., *Samuel H. Walker's Account*, p. 37.
4. *Pedro de Ampudia a Escmo. ministro de guerra y marina D. José María Tornel, Cuerpo de ejército del Norte, Primera División, Mier, Diciembre 29, de 1842*, in *El Cosmopolita*, Jan. 25, 1843.
5. Nance, ed., *McCutchan's Narrative*, p. 50.
6. *Pedro de Ampudia a Escmo. ministro de guerra y marina D. José María Tornel, Cuerpo de ejército del Norte, Primera División, Mier, Diciembre 29, 1842*, in *El Cosmopolita*, Jan. 25, 1843.

nize his forces, receive reinforcements, or evacuate the town. Most likely General Ampudia hoped to bluff the Texans into surrendering.

As soon as Dr. Sinnickson drew near the Texan line, he was recognized by Fisher, who advanced toward him. As they met, Dr. Sinnickson said: "Gen. Ampudia occupies the town with 1,700 troops of the line and 800 'defensores'—he bids me say, if you will lay down your arms in five minutes your lives shall be spared, otherwise the whole shall be put to the sword."[7] Fisher could not hear the message because of the renewed firing by Texans. He turned and again ordered, "Cease Fire!" Once more turning to Sinnickson, Fisher inquired, "What does this flag mean?" The doctor repeated his message. "Without saying a word," Fisher "cast his eyes upon the ground as if undetermined, and endeavoring to decide upon what course he should pursue."[8]

The demand to surrender took Fisher by surprise. "A capitulation had never been made a question with us," wrote James D. Cocke, "until the parley was sounded by the enemy."[9] After a moment's reflection, Fisher replied that he would listen to no such proposition and ordered Sinnickson and his guard to return immediately to the Mexican lines as he intended to renew the action.[10] A captain rushed from the Texan lines to inquire the terms of surrender, and other men and *"some officers"* began to crowd around Fisher, Sinnickson, and the Mexican officer, "who, governed by curiosity and perhaps a worse motive, prevented their passage back to the Mexican lines," declared Fisher. Fisher "leaped the wall and advanced to the position occupied by Cameron and Ryan's Companies," where he relayed Ampudia's proposition to the officers. Many of the privates and sergeants gathered around to listen. He reported that the Mexicans claimed they had 1,500 men engaged in the battle and expected 1,000 reinforcements.[11] Hearing these number, some of the Texans became "panic stricken,"[12] "while others shed tears that so disgraceful a surrender was about to be made."[13] Later William Rupley, hearing a rumor that Cameron was the first to propose surrender, declared such a thought

---

7. Quoted by Fisher in William S. Fisher to [Editor of the *Telegraph*], Perote, May 20, 1843, in *Telegraph and Texas Register*.

8. J. J. Sinnickson to Gen. Thomas J. Green, n.d., in Green, *Mier Expedition*, appendix 4, pp. 474-76; William S. Fisher to the [Editor of the *Telegraph*], Perote, May 20, 1843, in *Telegraph and Texas Register*, Aug. 2, 1843.

9. James D. Cocke to ———, Matamoros, Jan. 12, 1843, reprinted from the *New Orleans Weekly Bulletin* in the *Telegraph and Texas Register*, Mar. 2, 1843.

10. William S. Fisher to the [Editor of the *Telegraph*], Perote, May 20, 1843, in *Telegraph and Texas Register*, Aug. 2, 1843, and in *Northern Standard*, Sept. 21, 1843.

11. A. Gardenier to Crugar & Moore, LaGrange, Jan. 12, 1843, in *Morning Star*, Jan. 14, 1843; *Telegraph and Texas Register*, Jan. 25, 1843.

12. Letter of "A Texian," dated [Mier], Jan. 25, 1843, in *Morning Star*, Feb. 9, 1843; William S. Fisher to the [Editor of the *Telegraph*], Perote, May 20, 1843, in *Northern Standard*, Sept. 21, 1843; James D. Cocke to ———, Matamoros, Jan. 12, 1843, in *Telegraph and Texas Register*, Mar. 8, 1843.

13. Canfield diary, Dec. 26, 1842.

preposterous. Cameron, he said, spurned the idea of surrender with indignation and declared that he "would fight to the last and conquer the
treacherous Mexicans or perish in the attempt."[14] It was Rupley's conclusion that if the Texans had renewed the fight, the Mexican army would
have surrendered or withdrawn within half an hour.[15]

The Texans were divided on what course to pursue. Some believed
that Ampudia was ready to abandon the town and thought that a truce
might be acceptable to him for that purpose. Others suggested a truce to
enable the Texans to reorganize and reestablish discipline. Still others
contended that this was simply a ruse to surprise the Texans while their
attention was diverted by the white flag.[16] To substantiate the latter opinion, they pointed out that while Dr. Sinnickson had approached with the
white flag, Mexican infantry had advanced. By the time Fisher reached the
wall of the courtyard to meet the flag, the Mexican infantry, "without their
guns being reversed," had arrived within a few feet of the buildings occupied by Green before being detected. Green quickly ordered the men
nearest him to shoot the foremost Mexican. As the Mexican fell, Green
fired twice "with equal good effect," and "the remainder of the column
dodged around a stone wall to their right."[17]

As Fisher leaped the wall, Sinnickson "instantly followed to await his
instructions." In the midst of the council of war several Mexican officers,
seeing the flag detained and the discussion going on, advanced to the
Texan position and penetrated the ranks of the Texans. Those who did so
included an adjutant to General Ampudia, who informed Fisher that
Ampudia demanded he "surrender his whole force in five minutes, or I
[Ampudia] will cause them all to be put to the sword."[18]

Several of these men had known Fisher from his participation in the
Federal War. Padre Rafael de Lira and others among the Mexican officers
assured the Texans they would be treated "as prisoners of war." Further,
they claimed that things were different in Mexico since Santa Anna had
retreated to his estate near Vera Cruz and Gen. Nicolás Bravo, president
of the Council, had been acting as president since October 26. There were
even hints of a new revolution fermenting in northern Mexico.

Convinced that the Mexicans were not acting in good faith, as evidenced by their reoccupation of lost positions[19] during the truce, Green
pointed his rifle at the Mexican officers. He believed they should not be
permitted to return to their lines with a knowledge of the strength of the

14. *Morning Star*, Mar. 14, 1843.

15. *Ibid.*

16. Wallace, in Duval, *Big-Foot Wallace*, p. 171.

17. Green, *Mier Expedition*, p. 97.

18. John J. Sinnickson to General Thomas J. Green, n.d., in Green, *Mier Expedition*,
appendix 4, pp. 474–76; Nance, ed., *McCutchan's Narrative*, p. 51; Canfield diary, Dec. 26,
1842.

19. Nance, ed., *McCutchan's Narrative*, pp. 51, 51 n. 34; Green, *Mier Expedition*, pp.
97–98.

Texan army. Captain Ryon leaped between Green and the Mexicans. Ryon begged Green not to shoot the Mexicans until more could be learned, and Fisher "most positively and emphatically refused to allow General Green to shoot down or interfere in any offensive manner whatever with the Mexican officers who accompanied the flag of truce."[20] While the Mexican officers made pledges to Fisher, Eastland, Ryon, and others, Green ordered Cameron "to form his company near by and be in readiness for farther [sic] orders."[21] When Cameron had assembled his men, Green requested that Fisher stand aside so Cameron's men could shoot the Mexican officers. Fisher refused, so Green asked permission to take the Mexican prisoners and "march them unharmed, at the head of our column, to the camp, upon the east side of the Rio Grande, where under any possible circumstances, . . . [the Texans] would be safe."[22] This request was likewise refused.

The discussions showed that the Texans were divided, so Fisher, by agreement with his council, sent word to Ampudia that the fight would cease "if [the Texans] were allowed to retire unmolested," and he asked for Ampudia to come for personal negotiations. Ampudia reported that his officers begged him not to enter the Texan lines, and he refused to do so. Colonel Vega, who had conveyed Fisher's request to Ampudia, returned to report that the general did not think it necessary to come,[23] and insisted they surrender, "promising them fair and honorable terms."[24]

Fisher requested an hour to consider surrender. With Ampudia's approval, Colonel Blanco, his adjutant, granted a truce of one hour, believing that the Mexican scheme had succeeded. The Mexican officers, accompanied by the priest and Dr. Sinnickson, returned to Ampudia's headquarters. During the truce, Ampudia brought his forces in sight. Mexican soldiers could be seen on housetops, at street intersections, in the plaza, and at all avenues of exit from the town. The display, reported J. N. M. Thomson, "had the desired effect upon some of the men who became intimidated at their numbers" and wanted to surrender.[25]

The Texans now began to consider seriously their situation, "surrounded as they were by an enemy ten times their number," and the dare-devils' thoughts turned from hope of victory to survival. "Their stock of ammunition [was] nearly exhausted," and if they should seek to retire from the town, it was "four miles to march . . . before they could reach the

20. William S. Fisher to the editor of the [*Galveston?*] *News*, reprinted in the *Northern Standard*, Jan. 14, 1846.

21. Green, *Mier Expedition*, p. 99.

22. *Ibid.*

23. *Pedro de Ampudia á Ministro de Guerra y Marina D. José María Tornel, Cuerpo del ejército del Norte, División primero, Mier, Diciembre 29 de 1842*, in *El Latigo de Texas* (Matamoros), Jan. 23, 1843; also in *El Cosmopolita*, Jan. 25, 1843.

24. *Daily Picayune*, Jan. 16, 1843; *Telegraph and Texas Register*, Jan. 25, 1843.

25. J. N. M. Thomson to William D. Thomson, Matamoros, Jan. 13, 1843, copy in Tx-A.

Río del Norte . . . the whole liable to be exposed to the attacks of the Mexican cavalry and probably when they reached the river no means of crossing it would be had. All these dark prospects rushed in sad array before their already dismal imaginations," reported one of their number, "to heighten the gloom of their critical situation."[26]

The men assembled in groups without regard to order or superiors and gave their opinion of what ought to be done. Some favored maintaining their position until night, then retreat; some were for an immediate retreat through the enemy's lines; and others, believing that little chance was left for retreat or defense, were for an immediate surrender.[27] The Santa Fé men in the command had been talked into a surrender before and had lived through the horrors of a Mexican imprisonment. "My informant [Chalk]," reported Gardinier, "thinks they never would have been taken, if they had not been panic struck, as they could have held their position till night and made good their retreat."[28]

Fisher was not satisfied with the terms for they did not afford protection to such persons who previously had been captured and had taken an oath not to take up arms again against Mexico on penalty of forfeiting their lives. Chalk and St. Clair reported that Fisher proposed that the men fight their way out of Mier to a thicket from which "the old devil himself could not have got them out." But the lack of discipline and the declaration of a captain that he would not cooperate prevented the execution of the plan.[29]

Fisher decided to visit Ampudia to offer to end the battle "if allowed to return [across the Rio Grande] unmolested."[30] Another claimed that he visited Ampudia to request additional time to consider the Mexican proposal. Green, Cameron, Reese, and others tried to restore order in the ranks, but some of the Texans became distraught.[31] Those who wanted to continue the fight pointed out that either the Mexicans were utilizing the truce to prepare for a more vigorous onslaught, or they were in dire straits themselves. In their opinion the truce was a ruse to get within the Texan lines to appraise the Texans' coalition. The Texans' losses, up to this time, had been eleven killed and twenty-three wounded.[32]

Disappointed by Ampudia's refusal to permit the Texans to withdraw peacefully or grant further time to consider surrender, and not overanxious to rely upon Ampudia's promise of equal treatment to the Santa Fé

26. Bell, *Narrative*, p. 25.

27. *Ibid.*, pp. 25-26.

28. A. Gardinier to Messrs. Cruger & Moore, LaGrange, January 12, 1843, in *Morning Star*, Jan. 19, 1843.

29. Guy M. Bryan to Rutherford B. Hayes, Peach Point, near Brazoria, Texas, Jan. 21, 1843, in Winkler, ed., "The Bryan-Hayes Correspondence," in *SWHQ* 25 (Oct. 1921), pp. 103-7.

30. "Report of Captain Auld on the Battle of Mier," in *Telegraph and Texas Register*, Jan. 25, 1843; also in *Morning Star*, Jan. 24, 1843.

31. Canfield diary, Dec. 26, 1842.

32. *Ibid.*; Nance, ed., *McCutchan's Narrative*, p. 52

men, Fisher returned to his own lines and used the remainder of the hour trying to restore order in his ranks. He said, "I would rather die than surrender."[33]

At the end of the hour Fisher met Ampudia halfway between the Texan position and the Plaza del Armas and informed him that he "rejected his terms and would renew the action in ten minutes."[34] Returning to his lines, Fisher met some Texans moving toward the plaza to surrender. When they ignored his command to return to duty, he ordered the companies formed so he could inform those remaining of his interview with Ampudia and of the terms of surrender he had been offered. Fisher explained that he had known Ampudia for several years and believed him to be an honorable man. He pointed to the lack of discipline and the impossibility of fighting their way out of Mier and crossing the Rio Grande without sustaining a loss of two-thirds or more of the men, but, "if you are determined to fight, I will be with you, and sell my life as dear as possible." The men were to prepare for battle in five minutes or march to the square and lay down their arms.[35] The question was "put to a vote," narrated McMullen several years later, "and as our men were badly cut up it was thought prudent to comply with Ampudia's demands."[36] Those who did not wish to submit sought out those who did trying to change their minds by picturing the uncertain fate which lay before them as Mexican prisoners. Green, who had arrived at Velasco on June 3, 1836, with 230 volunteers and had prevented the Texas government from releasing Santa Anna in accordance with an agreement that had been made, had ample reason not to fall into that individual's hands.[37]

Green asked Cameron for his opinion on surrendering. "I asked him," reported Green, "if it was possible that he was in favor of a *surrender*."[38] In the words of Green, "The bare mention of the word [surrender] choked him; he [Cameron] was too full for utterance; but, taking me by the hand, he carried me to the building where our wounded were. Here he had seven of his old company, who had followed him for three years through many dangers and hard-fought battles. . . . Cameron asked 'General what would you do?'"[39] Green answered, "Men, if by staying with you we could save your pain or heal your wounds, the sooner my will would be to remain, but you will have your own physician, and will doubtless be treated as well as [with] our going as if we were to remain and surrender for even then we would be separated."[40] Cameron replied: "I cannot nor

---

33. Bell, *Narrative*, p. 26.
34. William S. Fisher to the [Editor of the *Telegraph*], Perote, May 20, 1843, in *Northern Standard*, Sept. 21, 1843.
35. Green, *Mier Expedition*, pp. 102-3.
36. Dallas *Morning News*, Oct. 19, 1930, Feature Section, p. 6.
37. A. K. Christian, "Mirbeau Buonaparte Lamar," in *SWHQ* 23 (Jan. 1920), pp. 161-62.
38. Green, *Mier Expedition*, p. 100.
39. *Ibid.*
40. *Ibid.*, p. 101.

will not leave my wounded men."[41] The wounded constituted a serious problem. To leave them, it was believed, would be abandoning them to certain death, but it would be impossible to take them along.

As Green and Cameron left the wounded, Green asked Ryon if he was in favor of fighting their way out of Mier. Ryon said that he and most of his men would do so.[42] While Green was conversing with Ryon, Cameron returned, and "in a voice of harsh determination, which his Highland Scotch accent rendered peculiarly impressive," reported Green, declared: "By God, general, me and the whole of my company will go it!"[43]

Green has reported that the men in Reese's and Pierson's companies were opposed to surrendering and that all but twenty of the Texans were in favor of fighting their way out of town.[44] This is difficult to believe. Though Green called for 100 volunteers to fight their way out of Mier and claims that all but twenty of the Texans were in favor of doing so, there is no evidence to prove that more than a handful of diehards were willing to follow such reckless leadership.[45] Fisher found that only the companies of Reese and Pierson "were united to a man and prepared to fight to the last extremity,"[46] and these were willing to fight only under Major Murray. "The others were in indescribable confusion," wrote Fisher, "some exclaiming let us fight our way out, others let us remain in the houses till night, both parties contending in a vociferous manner, which drowned the voice of command, while another party was silently repairing to the 'Plaza' to deliver up their arms."[47] "Bigfoot" Wallace, remembering the fate of his kinsmen who had fought under James Fannin at the Coleto, did not wish to trust the Mexicans.

Realizing "that we were utterly defeated," wrote Fisher, "not by the enemy, but by ourselves," he determined to accept the proposed terms of capitulation offered by Ampudia before it was too late. Large numbers of the men already were surrendering on the verbal pledge of Ampudia to spare their lives. Fisher returned to Ampudia's headquarters, and wrote:

> Mier, December 26, 1842
> Gen. Pedro Ampudia
> Com[m]anding Mexican Army
>   Sir,—The force which through the chances of War I now surrender to you are composed of the most valient and intelligent citizens of Texas. They have contended manfully against your superior force and have yielded only when it was folly longer to contend. Your well established

---

41. Bell, *Narrative*, p. 26.
42. Green, *Mier Expedition*, p. 101.
43. *Ibid.*
44. *Ibid.*
45. Bell, *Narrative*, p. 26.
46. William S. Fisher to the [Editor of the *Telegraph*], Perote, May 20, 1843, in *Telegraph and Texas Register*, Aug. 2, 1843.
47. *Ibid.*

character as a brave and magnanimous officer is a certain guarantee to me they will be treated as brave men deserve to be.

I have the honour to be most respectfully yours,

W.S. Fisher, Com[manding] S[outh] W[estern] A[rmy][48]

"Now if any man, still asserts that any action on my part could have produced a different result in the fortunes of the day," wrote Fisher from prison, "I must either consider him as a most determined slanderer or a most superlative ass."[49]

At three o'clock in the afternoon the Texans began to lay down their arms with no other conditions than the guarantee of their lives.[50] Those opposed to surrender were full of "disappointment, sorrow, rage; and many shed tears, some swore, while others maintained a sullen determination, which showed that they were prepared for the worst," possibly another Goliad massacre. Some, like Green, "nearly frantic with rage," smashed their rifles so they could not be used by the Mexicans.[51] "Had I fortunately been placed in the same irresponsible situation as Gen. Green," wrote Fisher in the defense of his own conduct, "I also might have *blustered, vavooed, tore my hair and broke my gun;* but, alas, as the lives of two hundred and forty-one men, and the issue of the happiness or misery of their families depended upon my decision, I acted as I did; therefore, the convenient safety-valve for an overcharged spirit adopted by Gen. Green, from circumstances, denied myself."[52]

As the first of the Texans filed out to surrender, they passed the companies of Reese and Pierson, still formed, and received a shower of abuse. "Go!" said one; "I hope you may never enjoy the sight of your country and liberty again!" "Go," yelled another, "you ——— cowards! and rot in chains and slavery."[53] The first to surrender were three men who filed out "while yet in tears," to cast down their arms.[54] Every few minutes a few weary, battle-worn Texans, with faces begrimed and often streaked with

48. William S. Fisher, Gen Com. S[outh] W[estern] A[rmy] to Gen. Pedro Ampudia, Commanding Mexican Army, Mier, Dec. 26, 1842, in *El Latigo de Texas*, Jan. 23, 1843 (vol. I, no. 3), in both English and Spanish; Samuel H. Dixon, *Romance and Tragedy of Texas History* 1, p. 291; Green, *Mier Expedition*, p. 110.

49. William S. Fisher to [Editor of the *Telegraph*], Perote, May 20, 1843, in *Northern Standard*, Sept. 21, 1843.

50. *Jesús Cárdenas al Alcalde de Matamoros, Prefectura del N. de Tamaulipas, Mier, Diciembre 26 de 1842*, in Matamoros Archives, 44, p. 20 (photostat, TxU-A); *Jesús Cárdenas y Alvino Cortínas al Alcalde de la villa de Laredo, Prefectura del este de Tamaulipas, Mier, Dic[iembre] 26 de 1842*, original MS in the Spanish Archives of Laredo, and a copy is in Miscellaneous Papers, Tx-A; Brown, *History of Texas* 2, p. 244.

51. *Morning Star*, Jan. 19, 1843; *Telegraph and Texas Register*, Jan. 25, 1843; Bell, *Narrative*, p. 26; see also Duval, *Big-Foot Wallace*, p. 179.

52. William S. Fisher to the Editor of the [*Galveston?*] *News*, reprinted in *Northern Standard*, Jan. 14, 1843.

53. Quoted in Green, *Mier Expedition*, p. 103.

54. Nance, ed., *McCutchan's Narrative*, pp. 51, 56-57; Brown, *History of Texas* 2, p. 244.

tears, "accompanied by a few unarmed Mexicans,"[55] entered the plaza to stack their arms at the feet of a Mexican officer and surrender to the Mexicans to whom "good fortune belong."[56] During the surrender a Mexican infantry battalion was drawn up in the plaza, and the rest of the infantrymen held their positions.

John Day Morgan "carried his friend and neighbor, James Barber, into the [improvised] hospital, the poor fellow being wounded in the breast." Knowing that he had not long to live, Barber requested Morgan to say to his friends and family, "I die for Texas!"[57]

The twenty-three who were wounded seriously in the Battle of Mier included: David Allen, James Barber, Robert H. Beale, John Bideler, Lynn Bobo (mortally), D. H. Gattis, Lewis Hays, Jeffrey B. Hill, Francis Hughes, Edward Y. Keene, Stanley Lockerman (mortally), Malcolm McCauley (mortally), Alexander McKindel (mortally), William McLeyea (mortally), Theodore D. Maltby, Nathaniel R. Mallon, Harbert H. Oats, George B. Pilant (permanently disabled), James O. Rice, William Rupley, William Y. Scott, James H. Ury (mortally), and Henry D. Weeks (permanently disabled).

Others wounded did not require hospitalization. Among these were: Capt. William M. Ryon, who "received a slight wound on the head," which knocked him down and stunned him for a few minutes;[58] Col. William S. Fisher, who had the end of a thumb shot off; William Beard, who received a slight wound in the shoulder; William A. A. Wallace, who received a slight wound in the left arm from a bayonet; and William Kinchen Davis,[59] wounded in the left hand.

Confusion continued among the Texans. While some were surrendering, others were firing, for they had not yet become reconciled to the idea of surrendering. Forty or fifty men, looking to Cameron for leadership after Murray surrendered, held back to the last. To his men Cameron said, "Boys, it is no use for us to continue to fight; they are all gone but us."[60] Finally, Cameron, wishing to save the lives of the men, and especially the wounded, took the lead and the men filed out. "Bigfoot" Wallace stayed behind "until the last, closely watching every incident of the surrender, thinking it might be necessary to kill another Mexican if the slaughter, which he expected, should commence too soon."[61] He walked out empty-handed, having broken his gun.

55. Canfield diary, Dec. 26, 1842.

56. *Pedro de Ampudia a Ministro de Guerra y Marina D. José María Tornel, Cuerpo del Ejército del Norte, División primero, Mier, Diciembre 29, 1842*, in *El Latigo de Texas* (Matamoros), Jan. 23, 1843.

57. Jenkins, *Recollections of Early Texas*, p. 134.

58. Sowell, *History of Fort Bend County*, p. 208; William Ryon to Abner Harris, Brazoria, Texas, [dated] Castle of Perote, Mexico, June 27, 1844, copy in Houston Wade Papers, Tx-A.

59. William K. Davis, Pension Papers (Tx-A).

60. Sowell, *History of Fort Bend County*, p. 191.

61. Sowell, *Early Settlers and Indian Fighters of Southwest Texas*, pp. 64-65.

When the Texans surrendered they were searched for knives and pistols, relieved of personal possessions, and marched off in pairs into three small rooms.[62] They were guarded by soldiers with loaded muskets and fixed bayonets. They would never forget the humiliation, but "there was no use to complain," reported Wallace, "we knew we were 'in for it,' and principally through our own stupidity and folly, and we resolved to make the best of the worst situation in which we might be placed."[63] The wounded were taken to the church, now serving as a hospital, and there they had the care of their own physicians, Drs. William M. Shepherd, John J. Sinnickson, and William F. McMath. Ampudia's headquarters were moved to the nearby García mansion.

Within two hours all had surrendered but two, Caleb St. Clair and Whitfield Chalk, although some when leaving home had vowed the Mexicans would never take them prisoner.[64] Had the Texans, as a group, realized the suffering, privations, indignities, and cruel treatment they would incur for the next twenty months, it is doubtful if they would have surrendered.

After the surrender, Fisher and Green were summoned to Ampudia's headquarters at the García mansion to receive and sign the terms of surrender agreed upon earlier by Fisher and Ampudia. On the floor of the *sala grande* in the general's quarters was sprawled Ampudia's son, Capt. Miguel Anzar,[65] the twenty-four-year-old adjutant-general of the enemy forces, writhing in agony. "There," pointed his father, with tears in his eyes, "is my son, the hope of the army, the pride of the service. He has a death-shot through the kidneys, and must soon die."[66] Also in the room, seated at a table, was Canales drafting the "Articles of Capitulation." While Canales wrote, Ampudia ordered the Texans served coffee and chocolate, for which they were very grateful, having been without food since the previous morning. Canales finished drafting the terms of surrender and Ampudia signed them and had his interpreter, Aldrete, read the terms in English:

> Camp of the Army of the North
> 1st Division, December 26th 1842
> Agreeable to the conference I have with General William S. Fisher, I have decided to grant,

---

62. A picture of the alleged three rooms in which the Texans were held prisoners may be found in the *Dallas Morning News*, June 23, 1929.

63. Duval, *Big-Foot Wallace*, p. 181.

64. Jonnie Lockhart Wallis and Laurance L. Hill, *Sixty Years on the Brazos: The Life and Letters of Doctor John Washington Lockhart, 1824-1900*, p. 186. Hereinafter cited: Wallis and Hill, *Sixty Years on the Brazos*.

65. Fanny Chambers Gooch-Iglehart, *The Boy Captive of the Texan Mier Expedition*, p. 139. Hereinafter cited as Gooch-Iglehart, *Boy Captive*.

66. Green, *Mier Expedition*, pp. 105-6; see also *Discurso pronunciado por el presbitero Rafael de Lira Capellán accidental de la 1ª división del ejército Norte al concluir la tercera parte del entierro del valiente Captain Aznar en el mismo lugar de la plaza de la villa de Mier a donde fue herido por el enemigo*, in *Gaceta del Gobierno de Tamaulipas*, Mar. 18, 1843; *Diario del Gobierno*, Mar. 31, 1843.

1st. that all who will give up their arms will be treated with the consideration which is in accordance with the magnanimous Mexican nation.

2nd. That [in conforming with] the petition which the said General Fisher has made to me, all persons belonging to the Santa Fé Expedition will receive the same treatment and guarantees as the rest.

3rd. All who desire to avail themselves of these terms will enter the square and there deliver up their arms to us.

Pedro D'Ampudia[67]

Green suggested to Fisher that the Texans bring in their own interpreter, but Fisher said that although he could not speak Spanish he could read and translate it.[68] Fisher found no objections, so he and Green signed the terms of capitulation. The Mexican interpreter then read the articles of surrender to the other Texan officers and no objections were raised.

Later some of the Texans claimed that the terms which had been signed were not those originally agreed to by Fisher when he negotiated with Ampudia. If such were the case, nothing was said at the time the articles were signed. Either the Texans were ignorant of the terms, or little credence can be placed in their later statements. Fisher read the terms before he signed them. He could read and translate Spanish, for we know that he was soon engaged in translating for the governor of Perote Castle. Fisher knew what he signed, and in spite of what the Texans said later, it is unlikely that either the Mexican government or its military officers would have recognized the independence of Texas by permitting the Texans to surrender as "prisoners of war." Any admission on their part that the defeated Texans had the status of "prisoners of war" would have been an indirect acknowledgement that the Texas government had the power to designate a commander to conduct a war against Mexico. Mexico still contended that Texas was a "rebelled province" and that the Texans were in insurrection against constituted authority. Furthermore, Gen. Jesús Cárdeñas advised the *alcalde* of Laredo from Mier on December 26, 1842, that "today at three o'clock in the afternoon the Texans surrendered after seventeen hours of continuous fighting . . . the only guarantee being that their lives would be spared."[69]

The schooner *Doric,* commanded by Captain Auld, left Matamoros on January 14 for New Orleans, bringing news confirming reports of the capture of the Texans at Mier. It was reported that the Texans "capitulated on fair and honorable terms, which," declared the editor of the Nashville *Republican Banner,*[70] "it is presumed, however, will not ultimately be complied with." It was conjectured that Fisher and his comrades would be shot upon their arrival at Mexico City. But, declared the editor of the *Daily*

67. Copy in translation in *Telegraph and Texas Register*, May 3, 1843.

68. Green, *Mier Expedition*, pp. 106-7; Nance, ed., *McCutchan's Narrative*, p. 51.

69. *General Jesús Cárdenas al Alcalde de Laredo, Mier, Dec. 26, 1842*, in Laredo Archives, MS.

70. Feb. 8, 1843. See also *Niles National Register* 63, p. 369, Feb. 11, 1843.

Picayune, "we cannot for one moment entertain such a belief. Even if so disposed, which we much doubt, the Government of Mexico would never dare commit such an outrage."[71]

Some have accused the Mier men of cowardice, of acting unwisely, of being too trustful of the Mexicans, and still others have said that Fisher lacked the necessary qualities of leadership. Samuel H. Walker informed Albert Sidney Johnston: "but I will assure you that we had whiped them at Mier, and the fault of surrendering was mainly attributed to the officers particularly the commander."[72] Glasscock vented his criticism in his diary,[73] saying that "during the whole day Col. Fisher was very inactive, he appeared to be perfectly stupid. When he was asked what was best to do, [he] would give an evasive answer. He was asked frequently to let the men charge out and repulse the several charges of the enemy," and eventually a charge was made, "although the order was given by Capt. Cameron." Most bitter became their criticism when, after surrender, they learned from some of the Mexican officers "that if Col. F. had not showed a disposition to accede to the terms of capitulation, . . . the town would have been left to our disposal," reported one of the diarists of the expedition, "as their loss was too great to have continued the action, they having seen the determination of our little band to hold out to the last."[74]

Most vehement were the accusations against Fisher, but "if any officer is culpable," declared Bell, "all are equally so for allowing themselves to be so far duped as to believe that only a small body of Mexicans were there, and to lead so small a party into a town near which every demonstration of a large force of the enemy was plainly visible."[75]

A study of the motives prompting the surrender reveals that the accusations made against Fisher and other officers are not borne out by the facts. Critics among the Mier men would have criticized their commander under any circumstances, for they were men who had little regard for discipline or rules. They agreed to obey Somervell when he led them from Laredo to Guerrero. At Guerrero they changed their mind. They elected Fisher to lead them on down the river, but in the Battle of Mier they ignored his commands.

There is no doubt that Fisher was a brave and generous man and a faithful commander. He had been tested many times in the field, and his command of the Mier Expedition was not the first position of trust he had held. "He entered . . . Mier, under the impression that there were but few soldiers in the place."[76] While he may have erred in that assumption, the

---

71. *Daily Picayune,* Jan. 30, 1843.

72. S.H. Walker to Gen. A. Sidney Johns[t]on, Prison Santiago, City of Mexico, May 4, 1843, in Army Papers (Republic), Tx-A.

73. Glasscock diary, Dec. 26, 1842.

74. *Ibid.,* Dec. 26, 1842; see also Canfield diary, Dec. 26, 1842.

75. Bell, *Narrative,* p. 26.

76. Nance, ed., *McCutchan's Narrative,* p. 55; George W. Trahern diary, p. 7.

entire responsibility was not his. He had retained a company of scouts under McCulloch on the west bank of the Rio Grande to keep him informed
of changes in the situation after the Texans abandoned Mier on December
23. McCulloch, after advising against further lingering on the river, returned home, and a small spy company was formed under a less experienced individual, John R. Baker, acting as captain, which failed to keep
Fisher properly informed of the approach of a sizable Mexican force until
the enemy was at hand. Fisher falsely assumed that the enemy force was a
small one since it failed to take up a position opposite his camp and made
no attempt to cross the river. "The real force of the Mexicans was not
ascertained until the following morning, the 26th, and it was then too late
to justify a retreat, by the Texans."[77]

After the surrender, the prisoners at Ampudia's headquarters were
untied and put in with their unfortunate comrades. "From them we
learned," recorded Walker, "that the entering of the town on the part of
Green & Fisher was a very gallant affair, but after Col. Fisher became satisfied of the force he had to contend with which amounted to about 3,000
men, he became low spirited and gave his men no encouragement."[78]

The men, such as Bell and McCutchan, did not hold Fisher solely
responsible for misjudging the size of the Mexican force:

"What *could* he [Fisher] do, with a set of men who obeyed but few, if
any orders, save those which agreed with their own notions of Generalship? Fisher felt all the responsibility of his station, without the means of
prosecuting any plan of his own; and hence, what could he do, more than
to save, if possible, the lives of his men? True, an *honorable death* would
have been far—far preferable to that life preserved at such costs; but let
all the world remember, that had Fisher refused this flag, and had the
Texians been butchered—massacred—the town of Mier would have been
remembered and pointed out as the place of *Fisher's* consumate head
strong folly; he would have been remembered as the reckless adventurer
who led to slaughter a small band of noble Texians!"[79]

Disobedience of commanders and disrespect for orders seem to have
been quite common among Texan volunteers. "Under all the circumstances," reported Canfield, "owing to the disunion in our band, Col. F.
might possibly be warranted in pursuing the course he did."[80]

A further weakness in discipline is evidenced by the fact that one of
the rooms occupied by the Texans during the battle contained liquor, and
some of the officers and men drank to excess. One of the officers became
so intoxicated that he fell to the floor, and while in that condition was
wounded by a bullet.

On the other hand, it may be argued, discipline is no substitute for

---

77. *Ibid.*, p. 56; see also Duval, *Big-Foot Wallace*, p. 180.
78. Sibley, ed., *Samuel H. Walker's Account*, p. 37.
79. Nance, ed., *McCutchan's Narrative*, pp. 56-57.
80. Canfield diary, Dec. 26, 1842.

leadership, and the border wars with the Mexicans showed that trained leadership was often absent. As Vestal assessed, "Many of the leaders were brave men, resourceful and intelligent, but not many can be fairly credited with victories won by their men. Time after time, Mexican officers outwitted the Texans and the Americans [and] time after time the Texan and American volunteers outfought the Mexican levies. Their victories were victories of the rifle over lance and musket."[81]

Aside from poor discipline, other factors motivated the Texans to accept surrender. Not only were they without food, water, and hope of reinforcements, but their supply of ammunition was almost exhausted.[82] Had the battle lasted a few hours longer, more than one half of the Texans would have been without this essential element of warfare. "All accounts," from Texas, reported the *Daily National Intelligencer,*[83] "agree that a want of ammunition was the main cause of the surrender." Even if they could have held their position until night, they would have found it difficult to extricate themselves from Mier and reach their camp east of the Rio Grande because they were overwhelmingly outnumbered. Some disliked the idea of abandoning their wounded, which would have been necessary if it were decided to retreat. The Mexican cavalry and a piece of artillery were posted on the only route by which the Texans could hope to withdraw from their position. Finally, there were a few individuals among the Texans who had not fired a single shot during the battle.[84]

In view of these circumstances, Fisher considered surrender "the only means of saving the lives of even a portion of the command."[85] The Texan willingness to call off the contest was also due to statements made by the enemy that Santa Anna was no longer at the head of affairs in Mexico, that Gen. Nicolás Bravo had taken over the presidency, that Gen. Mariano Arista would soon issue his *pronunciamento* for Federalism and the Constitution of 1824, and that the Texans would then become auxiliaries in the campaign against Central troops. Fisher formerly had engaged in the cause of Federalism in northern Mexico until double-crossed by Canales and his Mexican associates. Why, then, should the Texans feel they could trust Canales or the Mexican Federalists? If any Texan did so on December 26, it was misplaced. The prisoners who later escaped from Mier reported that they believed Fisher would not have surrendered if he had not received positive assurances from the Mexican officers with whom he had served in the Federalist wars that he and his men would not be sent

81. Vestal, *Bigfoot Wallace*, p. 85.

82. *Charleston Courier*, Feb. 15, 1843; New Orleans *Daily Picayune*, Feb. 8, 1843; *Dallas Morning News*, Oct. 19, 1930, Feature Section, p. 6; Brown, *History of Texas*, 2, p. 244; A. Gardenier to Cruger & Moore, LaGrange, Jan. 12, 1843, in *Telegraph and Texas Register*, Jan. 25, 1843.

83. Feb. 6, 1843.

84. Nance, ed., *McCutchan's Narrative*, pp. 55, 57.

85. William S. Fisher to the [Editor of the *Galveston?*] *News*, reprinted in *Northern Standard*, Jan. 14, 1846.

to Mexico City, but would be kept east of the mountains and treated "as Federal troops."[86]

When news of the surrender reached Texas, many of the journals denounced "Gen. Houston for imbecility, more especially in relation to his remissness in not fostering and assisting the volunteers on the Mexican frontier. The entire blame of the late defeat of Col. Fisher," reported the *Daily Picayune*, "is thrown upon the shoulders of Gen. Somerville in one of the papers, *unless* he acted under orders from the President, and the same editor goes on to say that he thinks he *did*, thus casting the censure on the head of the Republic."[87]

Even forty years later, some of the Mier survivors sought to blame Houston for their misfortune. In 1881 George Lord made "an affidavit . . . to the effect that Gen. Sam Houston was altogether to blame for the failure of the Mier Expedition," and hoped, "although rather late, to right history in this matter."[88]

The editor of the *Galveston Daily News* presented an excellent summary of news events in 1881:

> It is no part of the object of the *News* at this time to discuss the questions of whether they were in any way to blame for their own misfortunes, or whether president Houston was liable, as many contended, to censure for [*sic*, but should probably read: "to censure them"] them. Few, except some of the sufferers themselves, or their immediate friends, will be apt to take the later view of the subject at this late date. If the soldiers were in fault, they certainly atoned in full for the offense. Very few, however, have ever regarded the expedition as "a move that panned out splendidly." It was, in fact, full of suffering and disaster both to those engaged in it and to Texas at large.[89]

---

86. *Morning Star*, Feb. 25, 1843.

87. *Daily Picayune*, quoted in *Daily National Intelligencer* (Washington, D.C.), Feb. 6, 1843.

88. The report was datelined San Antonio, Feb. 16, [1881], in *Galveston Daily News*, Feb. 17, 1881.

89. *Ibid.*

CHAPTER 6

Significance of the Battle of Mier and the Fate of the Camp Guard

THE EFFECT OF THE Texan defeat at Mier in diplomatic circles abroad was negative for Texas. Movements of the Texas Navy off the coasts of Mexico in defiance of Houston's orders, resistance to the collection of tariff duties on the Red River, and publicized meetings in the Republic against Houston and his policies—all encouraged and given wide publicity by the anti-Houston press—and the defiance and failure at Mier hurt the name and prestige of Texas abroad. U.S. Secretary of State Daniel Webster considered the action so detrimental that the United States could not mediate between Texas and Mexico as it had intended.

The position of the United States was complicated by Commodore Thomas ap Catesby Jones' unauthorized seizure of California, causing Webster to instruct Waddy Thompson, "If . . . the account of that event should prove to be authentic, you will take occasion to inform the Mexican Minister of Foreign Affairs, orally, that Commodore Jones had no warrant from this government for the proceeding and that the President exceedingly regrets its occurrence."[1] Thompson apologized, but his reports indicated that any effort to interpose good offices in behalf of Texas would be useless.[2] Isaac Van Zandt reported on March 13 that in his recent interview with Webster he had endeavored to show "that any apparant [sic] diversion from our former course was not to be attributed to the Gov't authorities but to individuals acting in violation of orders, these things I am unable to fully establish, for the want of authentic information concerning the facts as they existed." Webster replied that "it was impossible to draw the distinction at all times between those who acted by authority and those

---

1. Daniel Webster to Waddy Thompson, Department of State, January 17, 1843, in Instructions of the Department of State, Mexico (May 29, 1833-Mar. 29, 1845), National Archives (microfilm).

2. Isaac Van Zandt to Anson Jones, Legation of Texas, Washington [City], March 13, 1843, in Garrison, ed., *Diplomatic Correspondence of the Republic of Texas* 2, pp. 132-38.

who acted without it, and if such numbers acted not only without but in violation of orders it was one of the strongest grounds to prove that we were without a government or in other words the Govt had lost its force."[3]

William H. Daingerfield, Texas' newly appointed *chargé d'affaires* to the Netherlands, stopping in Washington en route to Europe, wrote home that the treaty of commerce and navigation pending between Texas and the United States had not been ratified and "this failure I am convinced, not only by what I learn here but by information obtained before my arrival is the result of our own demagogical madness and diabolical insubordination *at home*. An entire want of confidence in the stability of our institutions, the result of our own folly and wickedness forbids the possibility at present of this treaty being ratified."[4]

In an effort to offset unfavorable opinion created in the United States toward Texas, Van Zandt claimed that England was greatly interested in maintaining the integrity of Texas and that its assistance could be counted on to see that Texas was a free and independent nation inhabited by Anglo-Americans. He told Jones that he was careful not to place such statements in writing. Van Zandt also told Jones that he had received a copy of Andrew Neill's report of his captivity and a copy of the orders given to General Somervell, "which must fully (as I conceive) vindicate the course of the govt in the measures which I have taken." These he sent to Webster on March 23. He reported that he had "privately and confidentially presented" to President John Tyler "the propriety of the United States announcing to the world that the independence of Texas shall be maintained and that the war against us shall cease in toto. . . . The President listened with much attention and replied he would take the matter into serious consideration."[5]

Armed with further official information received from Texas, Van Zandt lost no time in trying "to correct the erroneous impressions, which had been made here [Washington City], in relation to the later movements of the Government of Texas, and to place it in its proper light; and to again impress upon the Government, of the United States, the propriety, of a prompt and efficient interposition upon their part, in arresting the war between Mexico and Texas; and to secure a proper treatment to those of our countrymen whom the fortunes of war had placed, as prisoners, in the power of Mexico."[6]

In an endeavor to modify the unfavorable impression created among officials in the United States by the Mier Expedition, Van Zandt attempted a lengthy defense of that action. Webster did not reply, and thus matters on this point rested for a while. Early in May 1843, Isaac Van Zandt

---

3. *Ibid.*

4. William H. Daingerfield to Anson Jones, Washington City, March 10, 1843, in Garrison, ed., *Diplomatic Correspondence of the Republic of Texas* 2, pp. 130-31.

5. Van Zandt to Jones, Legation of Texas, Washington City, April 5, in Garrison, ed., *Diplomatic Correspondence of the Republic of Texas* 2, pp. 149-52.

6. *Ibid.*

wrote privately to his counterpart, Ashbel Smith, in London, explaining how the situation in Texas had affected negotiations in Washington:

> Unfortunately for us . . . our people had rendezvoused upon the frontier for the purpose of making an inroad upon Mexico; the President finding himself unable to control the persons assembled otherwise; the manner in which this campaign was carried out is of course familiar to you; its disorganized movements and mutinous character in its prosecution and its unfortunate termination was all made known here in quick succession which together with the unlimited abuse cast upon the Govt by the newspapers and letter writers, swept every thing before them and in the shortest notice it might have been truly said that confidence had fled and nothing was left sav|c| the suspicion and mistrust which seemed to shroud all that pertained to us.[7]

As soon as the news that Fisher's party had crossed the Rio Grande in defiance of Somervell's order, the United States and Great Britain lodged strong complaints that this type of warfare was the same as that which they had protested in Mexico recently. "In consequence of the generally unfavorable character of the news circulated in Europe about Texas, based in a good degree on the defeat of Col. Fisher, and still more on the atrocious statements of the condition of our country copied from the opposition newspapers of Texas," reported Ashbel Smith from France, "I have abstained from any endeavors recently to extend our international relations with the single exception of Belgium."[8]

The U.S. *chargé d'affaires* to Texas, Joseph Eve, was instructed by his government to "seek an early interview with the secretary of state of Texas and address to him *orally* a remonstrance of the tenor referred to in instructions to General Thompson of the 7th ultimo [February,]"[9] relative to expeditions on the Texas-Mexican frontier.[10] Instead of confining himself to an "oral" protest, Eve addressed a letter to the Texas secretary of state saying that he had been instructed by his government to address "a strong, but kind and friendly remonstrance, to abstain on the part of Texas from carrying on the war (should it continue) against Mexico by means of predatory incursions whether with a view to retaliation or otherwise. But so long as the war continues, to carry it on openly, honorably, and according to the rules recognized by all civilized and Christian States in modern times. Texas owes this to herself, and to the character of the

---

7. Isaac Van Zandt to Ashbel Smith, Washington City, D.C., May 3, 1843 (Private), in Ashbel Smith Papers, TxU-A.

8. Ashbel Smith to Anson Jones, Legation of Texas, Paris, April 11, 1843, in Garrison, ed., *Diplomatic Correspondence of the Republic of Texas*, 3, pp. 1431-33.

9. Daniel Webster to Joseph Eve, Department of State, Washington, March 17, 1843, in Diplomatic Instructions of the Department of State, Texas (May 21, 1837-Aug. 7, 1845), National Archives (microfilm); see also A. P. Upshur to W. S. Murphy, Department of State, Washington, 8th November, 1843, in *ibid*.

10. Daniel Webster to Waddy Thompson, Department of State, Washington, January 31, 1843; *idem* to *idem*, February 7, 1843, in Diplomatic Instructions of the Department of State, Mexico (May 29, 1833-Mar. 29, 1845), National Archives (microfilm).

Anglo-Saxon race."[11] The United States also remonstrated against Mexico's predatory warfare carried on against Texas.

On January 31, 1843, as a result of a request from Van Zandt for the interposition of the United States to pressure the Mexican government "to abstain from carrying on the war against Texas by means of predatory incursions, in which the proclamations and promises of the Mexican commanders are flagrantly violated, non-combatants seized and detained as prisoners of war, and private property used or destroyed, this department," Webster wrote Thompson, "entirely concurs in the opinion of Mr. Van Zandt that practices such as these are not justifiable or sanctioned by the modern law of nations." Thompson was instructed to communicate with Bocanegra, the Mexican secretary of foreign relations, "in a friendly manner," and "represent to him how greatly it would contribute to the advantage as well as the honor of Mexico to abstain altogether from predatory warfare. Mexico has an undoubted right to re-subjugate Texas, if she can, so far as other States are concerned, by the common and lawful means of war. But other states are interested and especially the United States, . . . not only in the restoration of peace between them, but also in the manner in which the war shall be conducted, if it shall continue."[12]

For the present this was all that Thompson was expected to say to the Mexican government, but, added Webster, "I may add for your information, that it is in the contemplation of this government to remonstrate in a more formal manner with Mexico, at a period not far distant, unless she shall consent to make peace with Texas, or shall show the disposition and ability to prosecute the war with respectable forces."[13]

A week later, after word had reached Washington that Texans had attacked Mexican settlements along the Rio Grande, Webster instructed Waddy Thompson to inform the Mexican secretary of foreign relations that the United States, in the same way that it had remonstrated with Mexico against "predatory" warfare on Texas, intended "to take steps for the purpose of remonstrating with the Texan government upon the subject of marauding incursions into Mexico, whether with a view to retaliation or otherwise."[14]

President Houston took a definite step toward ending the predatory warfare on the frontier by issuing a proclamation on April 27, 1843, declaring martial law in the region from the Nueces and Frío rivers to the Rio Grande. John C. Hays' ranger company was ordered to arrest any person found there without authority from the government of Texas.[15]

---

11. Joseph Eve to Anson Jones, Galveston, April 13, 1843, in Garrison, ed., *Diplomatic Correspondence of the Republic of Texas* 2, p. 163.

12. Daniel Webster to Waddy Thompson, Department of State, Washington, January 31, 1843, in Diplomatic Instructions of the Department of State, Mexico (May 29, 1833-Mar. 29, 1845), National Archives (microfilm).

13. *Ibid.*

14. Daniel Webster to Waddy Thompson, Department of State, Washington, February 7, 1843, in *ibid.*

15. Proclamation of the President of the Republic of Texas, Washington, April 27, 1843, in *Writings of Sam Houston* 3, pp. 366-67.

Texans had different opinions about what had been accomplished by the attack on Mier. The editor of the *Northern Standard* praised Fisher and his men for "striking a blow useful for purposes of policy and protection, and necessary to sustain our character as fighting men. To have longer suffered the depredations of the Mexicans without retaliation would have lessened our reputation," he said, "and it would have injured our settlements."[16] From prison at Perote, Anderson Hutchinson commented: "To the brave men who justly won it, their inglorious surrender proved a sore defeat; but in all the moral and political consequences of this battle to Texas, a glorious Triumph!"[17] Homer S. Thrall, after listing the names of a number of the Texan participants in the battle, thought otherwise: "A failure in an army with such material is both humiliating and unaccountable."[18]

By his victory at Mier, Ampudia dispelled the rumor that a three-section Texas army, comprised of 3,000 troops, was operating along the Rio Grande.[19] The defeat of the Texans was hailed throughout Mexico as a great victory. It strengthened the confidence of the Mexicans in the ability of Mexican arms and removed some of the tarnish inflicted by the Texan victory at San Jacinto. It was the most significant defeat of Texans since the capture of Fannin near Coleto Creek in March 1836. Canales reported, "We see ourselves so united and such friends, when in August it was not so."[20] Later, he claimed that he had played a leading role in the defeat of the Texans at Mier.[21] On January 3 José Antonio de Castillo, commandant of Santa Aña de Tamaulipas, informed Tornel that "by special despatch several hours before this you should have enjoyed receiving the fullest satisfaction from the news that the Texas section which invaded the northern part of the Department of Tamaulipas had been completely defeated and made prisoners in Mier."[22]

The Texan invasion of northern Mexico resulted in a shakeup of the Mexican command on the frontier. Gen. Isidro Reyes, the commander-in-chief of the Army Corps of the North, reached Presidio del Río Grande on December 27, where he received word of the Mexican victory. Reyes was

---

16. *Northern Standard*, Apr. 13, 1843.

17. Hutchinson diary, Sunday, Jan. 8, 1843.

18. Thrall, *A Pictorial History of Texas*, p. 328, note.

19. Isaac Van Zandt to Anson Jones, Washington City, Jan. 11, 1843, in Garrison, ed., *Diplomatic Correspondence of the Republic of Texas* 2, pp. 103-5.

20. *Antonio Canales a Exmo. Sr. general D. José María Tornel, Mier, Diciembre 26 de 1842*, in *Diario del Gobierno*, Jan. 6, 1843.

21. *Antonio Canales, Contestación dada al General Woll por las injurias y calumnias que en el núm. 101 del Monitor constitución de 17 de abril y bajo el disfraz de Pedro Grullo hace el que subscribe.* [signed and dated at end: *Monterrey, Mayo 29 de 1845. Antonio Canales] Monterrey: Impreso por Francisco Hernández. En la imprenta del Nivel.* Cited in Streeter, *Bibliography of Texas*, 2nd ed., p. 316, Item 1006. Copy in Yale University Library, New Haven, Connecticut.

22. *José Antonio de Castillo a Exmo. Sr. Ministro de la Guerra y marina, Comandancia principal de Santa Ana de Tamaulipas, Santa Ana de Tamaulipas, Enero 3 de 1843* (no. 11), in *Diario del Gobierno*, Jan. 11, 1843.

suspended and summoned to the capital to explain why he had not pre-vented the Texans from sacking Laredo and capturing Guerrero.[23] Brig. Gen. Adrián Woll, second-in-command of the Army of the North, became commander of that army,[24] and Ampudia was named second-in-command. Reyes turned over his command to Woll on January 30, 1843.[25] An inves-tigation exonerated Reyes and his suspension was revoked; as testimony of his good reputation, Santa Anna, now back in control, appointed Reyes governor and commandant general of the Department of Puebla.[26]

After much delay, the government of Mexico announced it would pay the auxiliary troops who had participated in the Battle of Mier.[27] For his service to the nation, his "glorious, bloody and decisive victory at Mier," Ampudia received a "personal cross" of gold adorned with precious stones on which would be inscribed his name in gold letters surrounded by a sprig of laurel and another of olive, and on the face of which would be the inscription *Pericia y valor distinguido,*[28] and on the back of which the inscrip-tion would read *"Vencío en Mier, en 26 de Diciembre de 1842."*[29]

Before proceeding with the story of the Mier men, let us address the fate of the Camp Guard, left waiting on the east bank of the Rio Grande for news from the battle.

Before Green crossed the Rio Grande, he had detailed George W. Bonnell, Dr. Robert Watson, and John L. Hackstaff to reconnoiter down-stream and secure or destroy all boats they found. The detail was to join the army, which would cross the river and encamp until Baker's spies returned with information on the Mexican forces.

Bonnell and his companions returned to where they expected to find the army. Bonnell landed on the west bank, but "all was calm and quiet." On his way back to the boat, a party of horsemen guarding the lower cross-ing ran away from the river and discharged their guns. Bonnell and his comrades crossed to the east side of the river to "extinguish the fire he had made in obedience to an order of Gen. Green," reported Watson,

---

23. *Diario del Gobierno*, Mar. 22, 1843; *El Cosmopolita*, Feb. 8, 1843; *Telegraph and Texas Register*, Apr. 5, 1843.

24. *El General en gefe del cuerpo de ejército del Norte, a las tropas de la 1. división.* [Procla-mation on taking command of the division. Signed and dated at end:] Adrián Woll. *Cuartel general en Matamoros, Julio 3 de 1843.* [At end:] *Imprenta del Látigo de Texas,* [Matamoros, 1843]. Broadside. Copy in Thomas W. Streeter Collection.

25. *Adrián Woll a Exmo. Sr. Ministro de la Guerra, General en gefe del ejército del Norte, Cuartel general en Ciudad Guerrero, Enero 31 de 1843* (no. 38), in *Diario del Gobierno*, Feb. 17, 1843.

26. *José María Tornel a General D. Isidro Reyes, gobernador y comandante general del depar-tamento de Puebla, Ministrio de guerra y marina, México, Mayo 3 de 1843.*

27. *Santiago Vidaurri, Secretaría de Gobierno del Departamento de Nuevo León, a las tropas aucsiliares, Monterrey, Agosto 14 de 1843,* copy in Yale University Library.

28. Translated "Distinguished skill and valor."

29. Translated "Triumphed in Mier, December 26, 1842."

"that they might cross again undiscovered and endeavor to join the army previous to or at the time it reached its . . . destination."[30] But their boat leaked to such an extent that they considered it unsafe to attempt to recross the river.

During the night Bonnell and his companions remained on the east bank. About ten o'clock in the evening they heard the reports of the Mexican artillery and small arms, and from an adjacent bluff could see "the light produced from the explosion of the powder of each which was kept up at intervals during the night, and commenced at dawn of day with greater rapidity."[31] Early the next morning, Bonnell and his two companions went up the river about three miles to the Texan camp.

As the Battle of Mier raged, the Camp Guard at the *Casas Blancas* camp eagerly awaited information from their comrades. At daybreak on the morning of the battle the horses were watered and fed. Besides the mounts of the expedition, there were over 300 captured horses, but corn fodder and grass were plentiful. While the guard cooked breakfast, two men, one on foot and the other on horseback, came into camp. One was a Mexican named "Vásquez" who claimed he had accompanied the Texans as far as the town of Mier. He reported that the Mexicans had surrounded the town with their cavalry and had opened fire with their artillery. "Vásquez" estimated the Mexican force to be between 2,000 and 3,000 men.[32] The other man was Michael Cronican of Reese's Company, who had started into town with his company but "by some accident, or mistake, or perhaps intentionally," returned to camp.[33] He reported that he had gone near the town while the battle raged, and was convinced when the firing ceased that the Texans had won.[34]

At ten in the morning, as the rain began to slacken and the clouds became higher, Francis Hancock and George B. Erath went down the east bank about a half mile where they could see the smoke of battle and masses of Mexicans outside the town. The firing became heavy, then stopped. "A considerable smoke arose," and they supposed the Texans had won. They returned to camp, hoping to have their conclusion confirmed. After waiting until three o'clock in the afternoon and no messenger having arrived from Fisher, Erath and Hancock "went down the river to a higher bluff" nearer the town, but could see nothing, and returned once more to camp disheartened.[35]

Late in the afternoon of December 26, before the escapees arrived,

---

30. Memucan Hunt to Francis Moore, Jr., editor of the *Telegraph*, Houston, [dated] Béxar, Jan. 8, 1843, in *Morning Star*, Jan. 17, 1843.
31. *Ibid.*
32. *Ibid.*
33. Nance, ed., *McCutchan's Narrative*, pp. 201-2.
34. Report of "Mr. Chronican," in *Telegraph and Texas Register*, Jan. 18, 1843.
35. Erath, ed., "Memoirs of George Bernard Erath," in *SWHQ* 27 (July 1923), p. 46.

gloom crept over the camp. Buckman, in charge of the guard, offered to surrender his command to Erath, who refused to accept it, but as a matter of precaution, Erath advised that as soon as it was dark the men move a mile from the camp to sleep and then return in the morning. Most of the guard prepared to leave at a moment's notice.

The rain, which had commenced late in the afternoon, now ceased and, although the night was cloudy, the moon gave a little light. "Some time after dark," wrote Erath, "we distinctly heard the words 'Bring over the boat, bring over the boat!' coming from over the river. Buckman and several of us ran down to the river, but no reply came to our challenge. Some said we had imagined the call . . . Buckman . . . thought it time to leave the camp. He called for all who wanted to go with him, and mustered about twenty. . . . Probably twenty-two or twenty-three of us remained in camp. I prepared to go, and there were thirteen with me. . . . After going about a mile and a half, hardly knowing where, as we had left the river, we heard the sound of a gun some distance off. It was about midnight; we camped."[36]

Between ten and eleven o'clock that night, all the Texans in camp, except William Hensley, William S. Holton, Archibald C. Hyde, Gabriel Smith, Thomas Oldham, John L. Hackstaff, Milton Hicks, George W. Bonnell, and Dr. Robert Watson had withdrawn, leaving nine men in charge of the camp boat and thirteen Mexican prisoners.[37]

Previously in Mier, when Whitfield Chalk and Caleb St. Clair of Gonzales learned the intention was to surrender, they executed a bold plan of escape.[38] Without informing anyone they hid in a yard behind a large stand of cane. "We stood verra still for we did not know how soon we wold be foun[d] . . . never saw a darker nite with a litel mist of rain and a cool norther blowing About 8 o'clock everra thing becam stil we got out with grate caution there was a gap in the back of the wal we got over tham," but in doing so St. Clair sprained an ankle. "We was vera cautious until we crosed the creak [Alcantro] then we had to turn easte to find the rode that led to the river."[39]

Chalk traveled the rest of the night barefoot through prickly pear and thorny shrubs, but his life depended on reaching the river. Slowed by St. Clair's injury, the two men reached the Rio Grande about daylight and hallooed for the boat.

36. Erath, ed., "Memoirs of George Bernard Erath," in *SWHQ* 27 (July 1923), pp. 37, 46-48.

37. Memucan Hunt to Francis Moore, Jr., editor of the *Telegraph*, Houston, [dated] Béxar, Jan. 8, 1843, in *Morning Star*, Jan. 17, 1843; *Telegraph and Texas Register*, Jan. 18, 1843.

38. Erath says St. Clair induced Chalk to hide with him. Erath, ed., "Memoirs of George Bernard Erath," in *SWHQ* 27 (July 1923), p. 48.

39. Whitfield Chalk, "Reminiscences of Whitfield Chalk," 15. MS, Rosenberg Library, Galveston, Texas.

Supposing them couriers from the battle, the remnant of the Camp Guard dispatched a boat to bring them over. A shout of welcome arose as the men recognized their companions. "I than[ked] the blessed lord['s] name at last for my escape," said Chalk, but "there were no provisions in camp, and for several days we had nothing to eat."[40]

Saddened by the news of Chalk's and St. Clair's report of the capture of their comrades, and learning that the Mexican cavalry was crossing the river a few miles away, the remnant of the Camp Guard prepared for flight. All of the boats but one or two were now destroyed. The best horses and camp equipment was collected, but they left behind what baggage and horses they could not take to be pillaged.

When St. Clair and Chalk had eaten, Erath's party began its return march on the morning of December 27. The first day the men made good time, having "a very good open route"; but traveling by night they became lost. At daylight, December 28, they made another start and that evening reached "a watering spot known as the Palo Blanco, on a trail leading to San Patricio."[41] They were now sixty miles from Mier. Buckman's party had left camp ahead of Erath's but it, too, got lost, and in a few days they met.

After the Texans crossed the Nueces at San Patricio, they separated into small parties, "the better to find game, which was scarce except for wild horse[s]." Erath, St. Clair, Chalk, and Thomas Oldham continued together and were the first to reach the San Antonio River, at Goliad. While contemplating swimming the river, they saw side six men who had just crossed on an improvised raft. The men offered the new arrivals the raft if one of their number would swim over for it. They also invited the four to join them six miles farther on at a camp they intended to make on the trail to Lockhart's house on the Guadalupe. They had killed a wild horse and had plenty of meat for all. Erath's party crossed the San Antonio and late in the afternoon found the camp of the six Texans, who were Ben McCulloch's party returning from the Rio Grande. That night, while sitting around the campfire eating horsemeat, each man related his experiences of the last few days.[42]

The next afternoon the ten Texans reached Lockhart's house, obtained supplies, and the following day crossed the Guadalupe and separated. Erath, Chalk, and Oldham went to Victoria, arriving on January 5, two days in the wake of a report said to have been brought by a Mexican "who came directly from Mier," that the Texans had defeated the Mexicans and captured three field pieces.[43] After resting several days, Erath, Chalk, and Oldham crossed the Colorado to LaGrange to bring the first news of the defeat on the evening of January 11, where Aaron A. Gardi-

---

40. "How Whitfield Chalk Escaped from Mier," newspaper clipping in Littlejohn, comp., "Texas Scrapbook," 2, p. 68.
41. Erath, ed., "Memoirs of George Bernard Erath," in *SWHQ* 27 (July 1923), p. 49.
42. *Ibid.*
43. *Morning Star*, Jan. 19, 1843.

nier recorded Chalk's story in a letter dated January 12 to the editors of the *Telegraph and Texas Register.*[44]

The story told by Chalk seemed incredible. For "300 Texians, all well armed, and having at least fifty rounds of ammunition each, while strongly posted in stone houses, should have tamely surrendered to 1,500 or 2,000 Mexicans, when only four of their number had been killed" was hard to believe. "If they had fought until half their number had been slain," declared the editor of the *Morning Star,*[45] "and their ammunition and supplies had been exhausted, there would have been some excuse for them to surrender; but for them to have yielded under the circumstances mentioned by Chalk and Sinclair *[sic]*, exhibits a spirit of imbecility and cowardice so totally at variance with the known character of Texians, and so much in contrast with the former achievements of the gallant Fisher, Cameron, and the comrades of Jourdan [Jordan], that we still view all these statements with suspicion."[46]

The editor of the *New Orleans Bulletin* on January 20 received a letter dated January 15 from Galveston "from a man of high standing, and one whose opinions are formed on strong grounds": "Sir: Under cover I send you an extra containing the latest accounts from our little army. My private information convinces me that the worst therein stated is true, whilst the better part (killing 400 Mexicans) is untrue. There can be no doubt but that Col. Fisher's division has been captured."[47]

The terms of surrender having been signed in Mier, Ampudia told Fisher to address a note to the Camp Guard ordering them to surrender. Fisher replied that he would have to send a force to capture them, as he was a prisoner and could not advise free men to surrender. Ampudia stamped his right foot in indignation and shouted that if he had to send for them, many of the Texan guards would be killed. He issued an order to Capt. Miguel de la Peña to take 150 cavalrymen and bring in the Camp Guard.[48]

That night Ampudia wrote two letters to the minister of war and marine announcing victory over the Texans. "Notwithstanding duty, beneath the rain and the snow, I arrived by forced marches at the center of the line! I saw and I conquered! This is certain, at least the nation has filled itself with honor, while Texas remains trembling."[49]

---

44. A. Gardinier to Messrs. Cruger & Moore [of the *Telegraph*], LaGrange, January 12, 1843, in *Morning Star*, Jan. 19, 1843; *Telegraph and Texas Register*, Jan. 25, 1843.

45. Jan. 17, 1843; same copied in *Telegraph and Texas Register*, Jan. 18, 1843.

46. *Ibid.*

47. *New Orleans Bulletin*, Jan. 21, [1843], quoted in *Daily National Intelligencer* (Washington, D.C.), Feb. 1, 1843.

48. *Pedro de Ampudia a Gen. José María Tornel, Ministro de Guerra, Mier, Diciembre 26 de 1842*, in *Diario del Gobierno*, Jan. 6, 1843.

49. *Ibid.*

Early on the morning of December 27, Capt. Samuel C. Lyon was taken from the prison at Green's request and sent along with the Mexican cavalry to contact the Texas Camp Guard. As they approached the Rio Grande opposite the Texan camp, Lyon and a single guard advanced while the cavalry remained out of sight. Lyon convinced his escort that he would have to communicate to the Camp Guard in English. Reaching the river opposite the camp, Lyon halloed across. Hearing the call, Hicks and Bonnell hurried to the edge of the east bank. Lyon, not realizing that they had learned of the surrender, summarized the situation to them and urged that they flee at once. They told Lyon that Chalk and St. Clair had arrived already with the sad news. The conversation was broken off by the departure of Bonnell and his companion. When last seen by Lyon, the two were climbing up the second bank of the river, with Hicks some distance in advance.

Lyon was now sent back under a guard while Captain Peña prepared to cross the river in pursuit of the fleeing Camp Guard. When the guard reached Mier and reported to Ampudia that the Camp Guard was in flight, Ampudia "was angered to excess—foiled, as he conceived, and beaten."[50]

As Bonnell and Hicks fled on the morning of December 27 with two horses each, Dr. Robert Watson tarried. Bonnell and Hicks missed the trail their comrades had taken and got lost in the chaparral, but finally struck the Camp Guard's trail late the next day. In the meantime, more than 100 dismounted Mexican cavalry under the command of Captain Peña crossed the river in "our boats" to "our camp," reported Erath, expecting to seize the Camp Guard. Finding it had fled, Peña's men rounded up the horses and mules, camp equipment, and other items that had been left behind and returned to Mier late in the afternoon of December 27. Captain Peña explained to General Ampudia that the Camp Guard, whom he estimated at 120 strong, had fled on the best horses, leaving the "culls" behind. Ampudia accused Fisher of breaking the terms of surrender and declared that Fisher had said that he had surrendered his whole force. Fisher responded that he had only surrendered "those that could be taken by the Mexican troops," reported McCutchan.[51] Ampudia then ordered Col. José María Carrasco to take 600 cavalry and pursue the Camp Guard.

Colonel Carrasco set out in pursuit of the Texans. After a day or two he gave up the chase, but while returning discovered Hicks and Bonnell. The two unfortunate Texans were taken to their old camp on the river. Bonnell was placed in a boat under guard, and Hicks "was told to push the boat from shore and jump in."[52] Hicks gave the boat a vigorous shove, then he leaped in the opposite direction. Several shots were fired, but he escaped and walked all the way to Victoria, swimming streams and sus-

---

50. Nance, ed., *McCutchan's Narrative*, p. 62.
51. *Ibid.*
52. Erath, ed., "Memoirs of George Bernard Erath," in *SWHQ* 27 (July 1923), pp. 48-49.

taining life without even the assistance of a pocket knife. The fate of Bon-nell is unknown, but it was rumored that he was shot in exasperation over the escape of his companion, or, that in the confusion created by Hicks, he, too, tried to flee and was killed.

Disappointed that he could not add to the list of prisoners, Ampudia sought trophies of victory. He demanded that the Texan flag be brought to him, but was told that there was none. The absence of a Texan flag was in part responsible later for the Mexican government terming the Mier men adventurers and pirates, not soldiers of the Texas government. During the battle the Texans had but one flag; it "belonged to the La-Grange Company and bore the inscription 'REVENGE OR DEATH!' "[53] When surrender was certain, the bearer "cut the flag into 'mince pieces,' and disposed of the fragments in some secure way, no one knew how."[54]

Ampudia offered $100 for the pieces of the flag, but none were pro-duced. His displeasure was appeased by an old English Union Jack which Captain Peña found in a saddlebag taken from the Texan camp. When it was exhibited in Mexico City as a trophy captured by the Mexicans in bat-tle, it caused diplomatic repercussions with Great Britain. Some Texans doubted that Ampudia understood that the Union Jack was not a Texas flag.

None of the prisoners passed the threshold of their improvised cells on the evening following their capture. As they sat on the cold brick floor with their backs against the wall, thirsty, hungry, and exhausted, they vied with one another in telling of their mighty exploits in the campaign, as well as the exploits of others, and of the events that led to disaster. The discussions ended "in a vow of vengeance on the foe, if fortune should allow them to return to a land of liberty," or the consolatory remark, "We'll live to pay them for all this."[55]

In time, many dropped off to sleep. They were awakened by an inter-preter who wanted to know if they would rather have their beef raw, believing them to be savages who ate raw meat.[56] They informed him that they preferred their meat cooked. About midnight a large kettle filled with badly boiled meat was brought and served without knives, forks, plates, or cups. Small in quantity and poor in quality, the boiled beef was eaten. The meat was so tough "Bigfoot" Wallace found it expedient to give half of his ration to a messmate who possessed a strong set of teeth, as compensation for chewing the remaining portion for Wallace so he could swallow it.[57] Muddy water was also brought in and the next day a small

---

53. Nance, ed., *McCutchan's Narrative*, p. 62.
54. *Ibid.*
55. Quoted in Bell, *Narrative*, p. 28.
56. *Ibid.*, p. 29.
57. Duval, *Big-Foot Wallace*, p. 180; see also Nance, ed., *McCutchan's Narrative*, pp. 65-66.

amount of flour was given each prisoner "without any means of making bread or anything else eatable of it."[58] After finishing their late evening meal, the Texans slept soundly in spite of the hardness of their beds and the chill of the night. Just inside the door to each room a sentinel stood and numerous others were stationed outside the door.

Most of the Texans had left their coats and hats in camp when they attacked Mier expecting victory and an early return to camp. Ampudia ordered their baggage delivered to the owners, but little appeared. Peña's *ranchero* cavalry plundered what was left of the Texan camp and appropriated all wearing apparel of any value, leaving the Texans virtually destitute of clothing except for what they wore.[59]

The prisoners remained at Mier four days while the Mexicans buried their dead and Ampudia awaited the return of the cavalry unit sent in search of the Camp Guard.

The Texan field officers—Col. William S. Fisher, Gen. Thomas Jefferson Green, Adjt. Thomas W. Murray, Second Quartermaster Fenton M. Gibson, Dr. William M. Shepherd, and Dr. John J. Sinnickson—and four boys were assigned separate quarters from the main body of prisoners, placed on parole, and given the freedom of the town. The remaining prisoners were kept under a watchful guard. The Texans received only two meals a day, one around midday and the other at ten at night. The fare was meager and of poor quality, and usually consisted of boiled beef, although occasionally boiled beans without much seasoning would be substituted.[60]

On the second morning, "a little Mexican maiden—bless her little tawny hide—came trippling alone," recorded Wallace, to the small grated window of one of the rooms in which the prisoners were held, and made signs to ask if they wanted something to eat. Wallace, whose knowledge of Spanish was quite limited, signaled through the window, which was not much bigger than the mouth of a "bottle guard." The girl hurried off but returned with "a batch of the inevitable tortillas, some red peppers, and a considerable chunk of roast kid-meat," which she handed through the grating of the window.[61] In appreciation, said Wallace, "I made her a low bow, pulled my forelock, and smiled as sweetly and as amiably as I could with my powder-burnt and dirt begrimed countenance. She went off laughing at my grimaces, and turning the corner, I lost sight of my pumpkin-colored angel forever."[62] Although "the tortillas were cold and tougher than army 'flap jacks,' and the red pepper was as hot as mesquite coals," all were devoured by the hungry Texans.

On December 27, about three o'clock in the afternoon, the able-

58. Bell, *Narrative*, pp. 28-29.
59. Stapp, *Prisoners of Perote*, p. 38.
60. *Ibid.;* Nance, ed., *McCutchan's Narrative*, p. 66.
61. Duval, *Big-Foot Wallace*, p. 181.
62. *Ibid.*

bodied Texans were ordered to prepare to march. They were formed in a unit in the square and marched approximately 300 yards under heavy guard to a "gloomy looking dwelling" and into a backyard surrounded by a high stone wall. As they entered each Texan was searched for knives, which they had hitherto been allowed to retain, and other weapons.[63] Inside the yard was a double line of armed soldiers with loaded muskets and fixed bayonets. The Texans were marched in a single file between the soldiers and the wall, and the entrance to the courtyard was blocked by a forest of bayonets. "A solemn silence stole over guards and prisoners, occasionally interrupted . . . by short and husky interrogations of [the Texans as to] what the infernal muster meant."[64]

An hour of torturing uncertainty dragged by while Mexican officers pretended to be in search of a notorious robber on the Rio Grande who had been with the Texans after they crossed the river. Later it was learned that "the officers were holding a Court Martial upon the lives of their prisoners; and it was said, and received as true, that the lives of the whole were saved by barely one vote,"[65] the vote of Ampudia himself. Finally, the Texans were marched to new and better quarters in the town.[66]

As the burial of the dead neared conclusion, complaints about the number of Mexicans killed in the battle were voiced on Wednesday, December 28. The Mexican losses were considerably greater than the eleven Texans killed and twenty-three wounded. The Texans estimated that probably more than 600 Mexicans had been killed and 200 wounded.[67] Thomas W. Bell said the Mexicans estimated their losses as 900 killed and wounded.[68] It was reported in the United States that the Mexicans estimated their losses at 420 killed and 130 wounded.[69] Green said that all the Mexican officers with whom he conversed gave their losses as over 700 killed and wounded, and that upon arrival at Matamoros "the United States Consul and several American and English gentlemen, who had it in confidence from the Mexican officers, reported the Mexican losses exceeded 800 in killed and wounded."[70]

While the Mexicans reorganized their forces, buried their dead, and awaited the return of Captain Peña, the church in Mier was converted into a hospital and wounded Texans were placed there with wounded Mexicans. So great was their number that many of the less seriously wounded

---

63. Canfield diary, Dec. 27, 1842; Nance, ed., *McCutchan's Narrative*, pp. 64-65; Stapp, *Prisoners of Perote*, p. 38.

64. Stapp, *Prisoners of Perote*, p. 39.

65. Nance, ed., *McCutchan's Narrative*, pp. 64-65; Stapp, *Prisoners of Perote*, p. 39.

66. Canfield diary, Dec. 27, 1842; Nance, ed., *McCutchan's Narrative*, p. 65.

67. Nance, ed., *McCutchan's Narrative*, p. 52.

68. Bell, *Narrative*, p. 27.

69. *New Orleans Bee*, Jan. 26, 1843, quoted in *Daily National Intelligencer*, Feb. 4, 1843.

70. Green, *Mier Expedition*, pp. 108-9.

had to be billeted about the town with citizens.[71] Doctors Sinnickson, Brenham, Shepherd, and McMath administered to the needs of their wounded comrades. From all accounts the hospital had more the semblance of a *"slaughter pen or hog stye* at the time," than an institution of mercy.[72]

Dr. John J. Sinnickson was placed on parole to perform his professional duties, although some of his comrades believed that his liberty had been promised if he bore the white flag.[73] "He must have known something of the Mexican position," wrote McCutchan accusingly, "but nothing escaped his lips in relation to it when he came up with the flag of truce."[74] It must be remembered that McCutchan's criticism was recorded four months and many bitter experiences after the surrender at Mier. Green declared that "Dr. Sinnickson is a gentleman long and favorably known in Texas."[75]

Before he left Mexico, Sinnickson, apparently at Green's request, wrote his version of the "white flag" incident.[76] He stated that he had been compelled to bear the "white flag," and several days after the surrender that he had had an interview with Colonel Fisher, and that the latter in no way ever "intimated in the slightest degree, that he had given me . . . an order" to return the flag; "but, on the contrary, when the subject of my bearing the flag was introduced, he assured me that himself nor any other person had or could attach any censure to me for the course I was compelled to pursue."

By the close of December 30 the last of the Mexican dead had been buried, Peña and Carrasco had returned, and the official report of the battle had been written and sent with Col. José María Carrasco and Ens. Cayetano Ocampo to Mexico City, along with the only banner ("flag") found in the enemy's camp.[77] Ampudia took full credit for the victory. "Without obligation [orders], resources, and cavalry, in the face of rain and snow," he reported, "I left Matamoros. I arrived by forced marches at the center of the line! I saw and I conquered. This is certain: the fatherland has been honored, while Texas remains trembling."[78]

---

71. *Ibid.,* p. 116.

72. Nance, ed., *McCutchan's Narrative,* p. 64; see also Stapp, *Prisoners of Perote,* p. 38.

73. Nance, ed., *McCutchan's Narrative,* p. 53.

74. *Ibid.*

75. Green, *Mier Expedition,* p. 112.

76. "Dr. Sinnickson's Statement about the 'White Flag' at the Battle of Mier," in *ibid.,* pp. 474-76.

77. *Pedro de Ampudia a Ministro de guerra, José María Tornel, Mier, Diciembre 26 de 1842,* in *El Cosmopolita,* Jan. 25, 1843; also in *El Látigo de Texas,* Jan. 23, 1843.

78. *Pedro de Ampudia a Ministro de guerra, José María Tornel, Cuerpo de ejército del Norte, Mier, Diciembre 29 de 1842,* in *El Cosmopolita,* Jan. 25, 1843; and *El Látigo de Texas,* Jan. 23, 1843.

CHAPTER 7

The March to Matamoros

GENERAL AMPUDIA WAS READY to return to Matamoros. Early Saturday morning December 31, the Texans were formed in the plaza, with the exception of their twenty-one surviving wounded, Dr. Sinnickson, and interpreter John Brennan, who were to be left temporarily at Mier.[1] Captain Ryon felt well enough to travel and went forward with the main body of prisoners, although later, he wrote: "I wish I had stayed in the hospital at Mier; if I had of done so I would now be at home."[2] Fisher, Green, Murray and three boys—William Reese, William Harvey Sellers, and Orlando C. Phelps—were placed under the charge of Capt. Clemente Castro. Young John C. C. Hill rode along beside General Ampudia.[3]

The procession got under way with the Texans marched two abreast down the center of the road, one cannon before and another behind. Only 460 of the Mexican troops returned to Matamoros from Mier. Ampudia dared not march 217 Texan prisoners to Matamoros with so small a force without the assistance of Canales' *ranchero* cavalry, so the guard consisted of 200 cavalrymen and 600 infantrymen.[4] The cavalry, the Mexican staff, and one artillery piece preceded by drum, fife, and horns announced the advance of the victorious Mexican army. On each side of the double column of prisoners was a single file of infantry with bayonets at the ready, flanked by cavalry. At their rear followed four columns of infantry and a large body of reserve cavalry. The Texans possessed no baggage; all they had was the clothing on their backs.

The prisoners were marched at a steady pace along the river route,

---

1. Canfield diary, Dec. 31, 1842.

2. W[illia]m Ryon to Abner Harris, Brazoria, Texas [dated] Castle Perote, Mexico, June 27, 1844, in Houston Wade Papers, Tx-A. Original in possession of Willie Mae Weiner, Seguin, Texas.

3. Canfield diary, Jan. 10-13, 1843: see also Glasscock diary, Jan. 9, 1843.

4. Stapp, *Prisoners of Perote*, p. 39.

which wound along a high limestone ridge from Mier to Matamoros never far from the Rio Grande. They marched through a forest of chaparral and bare hills past forlorn *jacals* made of mud and cane, with no order or neatness about them, and occasionally past fairly prosperous *ranchos*—such as El Jacal Blanco, El Jacal Difunto Angel (Dead Angel Ranch); El Rancho Guardado (now Gareno), where there was a beautiful fresh water lake; El Rancho Risa; and Carnestolendas (now Rio Grande City) on the left-hand side of the Rio Grande. Along the route from Mier to Matamoros, the country was covered with fine grass and seemed to be more fitted for grazing.

Prodded on bayonet or ox goad[5] amid constant cries of "*Adelante! Adelante!* (Forward! Forward!)" by their guard, the Texans moved along. They were not permitted to stop for water; and, as they had no way to carry water, they suffered from thirst during the day. Dust stirred by the cavalry did not help. Although walking down grade—a drop of 250 feet —to Matamoros, the walking was injurious to men's feet accustomed to riding. Those wearing high-heeled boots found the going almost as difficult as those who had no shoes. Near noon of the first day they halted at a *rancho* for rest and water. By nightfall, foot-sore and exhausted, they reached the San Juan River opposite the town of Camargo. Beautifully situated in a sandy plain on the east bank of the picturesque San Juan River four miles from the Rio Grande, Camargo contained a population of approximately 4,000 people.[6] The bottomlands of the Rio Grande and San Juan were fertile and to some extent cultivated, but in 1842 many of the *ranchos* near Camargo were abandoned. The San Juan was not fordable opposite the town, but there was a ford about six miles upstream.

The town was built around a plaza, or square. Camargo had been founded on March 5, 1749, by Col. José de Escandón, as La Villa Santa Aña de Camargo,[7] and was at one time regarded by Spaniards as one of the best sites for agriculture on the Rio Grande. In January 1843, however, its barren limestone hills did not appeal to the tired prisoners. A bleak norther was blowing when the weary Texans were quartered at Rancho Tiququajo in a corral; its fence partially protected them from the north wind. Their supper consisted of half-boiled beef, their beds the cold ground, and the sky was their cover.[8] Although brushwood fires were started, the Texans suffered from the cold and the dampness of the night. Most were without blankets, so when the brushwood fires burned down some raked away the hot coals and laid down in the ashes to keep warm.[9] The biting wind was so cold that sleep proved almost impossible.

---

5. An ox goad was usually a sharpened piece of iron on the end of a long stick. It could be nothing more than a long sharpened stick.

6. Emory, *Report on the United States and Mexican Boundary Survey* 1, p. 62; Nance, ed., *McCutchan's Narrative*, p. 66, n. 3; Canfield diary, Dec. 31, 1842.

7. Polly Pearl Crawford, "The Beginnings of Spanish Settlement in the Lower Río Grande Valley," pp. 61-116 (M. A. thesis, The University of Texas, 1925).

8. Bell, *Narrative*, p. 31.

9. Nance, ed., *McCutchan's Narrative*, p. 66.

On New Year's morning the prisoners were crossed over the San Juan River in boats into the city amid the ringing of church bells.[10] "Here commenced the grand menagerie show" of the "wild Texians," a common occurrence throughout their zigzag march of 1,500 miles through Mexico. Rather than seeming to be Sunday and a day of rest and worship, the town was in a festive mood. All was excitement and commotion; it was a gala day. Camargo was the first town to welcome the chastizers of their country's arrogant foe. Men, women, and children ran in every direction seeking a view of the prisoners. The *rancheros*, dressed in their *sombreros*, showy scarves, and "slashed" trousers, turned out to view the "demons" from beyond the Nueces. To a disinterested foreigner it might have seemed as if a circus had arrived in town. The Texans were marched to the center of the town and then around the military plaza, "under the ringing of bells, the firing of crackers and guns, and the *'vivas'* of the populace."[11] On one side of the military plaza was "a neat little Church," built of brown limestone, and all around the plaza were fine buildings.

Colorful handkerchiefs, banners, and ribbons streamed from buildings. Children paraded around the plaza in front of the prisoners carrying long rolls of paper on which were printed mottoes such as "Long live the Mexican Republic," "Ampudia the Invincible and Canales the Brave," "Glory and gratitude to the brave Canales," "Eternal honour to the immortal Ampudia," "Long live the brave Ampudia," and similar declarations.[12] The town boasted a few low stone buildings of very thick walls and flat roofs, and many miserable *"jacals,"* a few donkeys, and numerous dogs.

On New Year's Day, the prisoners, after being paraded about the square, were furnished with a small amount of *aguardiente* (or mescal), a strong, spirituous drink made from the juice of the maguey century plant. The prisoners were distributed among three prisons within the city, and the officers and boys were lodged in the home of Don Trinidad, a hospitable and kind man. That night *fandangos* were got up in the houses on the plaza, and the citizens and soldiers enjoyed a night of revel, riot, and rejoicing. The next morning, January 2, the march to Matamoros, 127 miles from Camargo,[13] was resumed, but only fifteen miles were covered that day, owing to the sore feet of the Texans and the desire of their captors to lodge them in an enclosure for the night.[14] When they reached a *rancho* six miles upriver from Sabaritas, Ampudia ordered a halt. The prisoners were herded into a cow pen and, although incredibly tired and weary, a few of them were determined to have their fun by getting down "upon their all-fours, bow their necks, paw up the dirt, and low like bulls,

---

10. Green, *Mier Expedition*, p. 118.
11. *Ibid.;* Duval, *Big-Foot Wallace*, p. 183.
12. Canfield diary, Jan. 1, 1843; Green, *Mier Expedition*, p. 119.
13. Henry, *Campaign Sketches of the War with Mexico*, pp. 151-52.
14. Canfield diary, Jan. 2, 1843, reported fifteen miles traveled, but Green, *Mier Expedition*, p. 119, and Sibley, ed., *Samuel H. Walker's Account*, p. 38, say they marched ten miles.

to the no small astonishment of their captors."[15] A strong guard for the night was placed around the compound.

At daylight the prisoners were formed, counted, and the march resumed to Nuestra Señora de Guadalupe de Reynosa. During the day they traveled twenty-one miles through flat plains sprinkled with cactus and mesquite. About dark they reached Old Reynosa and were herded into a sheep pen, where the comedians among them bleated like sheep. Reynosa contained only 200 inhabitants, but the Texans were shown greater hospitality than at any previous point along the route to Matamoros, and "more than we had a right to expect, so said those who had been prisoners with these mongrels before," reported Canfield.[16] The fare furnished by their guard was supplemented by the benevolence of some of the inhabitants, who brought them *frijoles, chile quisado, olla podrida* (hash of stewed mutton, strongly seasoned with red peppers), *atole, miel, tortillas,* and *huevos* (eggs).

The next morning, January 4, the journey was renewed at an early hour, but as exercise warmed the aching limbs of the prisoners they moved with less pain. Nevertheless, the men suffered from hunger, thirst, and lameness. By two they reached the outskirts of Nueva Reynosa, some seventy miles from Matamoros and eighteen miles past their previous stop.[17] The prisoners and their escort halted to allow the artillery to move forward to fire in tribute of Ampudia and give the inhabitants time to make arrangements for the reception of the victorious general and his army.[18] Situated on a steep, rocky limestone point sixty to eighty feet above sea level, the town had been built about a mile from the Rio Grande. A steep road descended from the town to the river. Nueva Reynosa, or simply Reynosa, was dominated by a church tower which reminded one of an ancient castle. The town contained approximately 2,000 inhabitants who subsisted by raising black cattle, transporting lime to Matamoros in carts, and conveying merchandise into the interior. From the character of "its population and its reputation," wrote Reid in 1847, "we were disposed to consider the town of Reynosa as the most rascally place in all Mexico. The town itself is well enough, but the inhabitants are a set of the most irreclaimable scoundrels that are to be found anywhere in the valley of the Rio Grande —a race of brigands, whose avowed occcupation is rapine and murder."[19]

The plaza was laid out on the summit of the hill and was surrounded "by some twenty stone houses plastered and mostly in a rude dilapidated state," yet had the appearance of being clean.[20] The street leading from

---

15. Green, *Mier Expedition*, p. 119.
16. Canfield diary, Jan. 3, 1843.
17. *Ibid.,* see also Nance, ed., *McCutchan's Narrative*, p. 67.
18. "John Rufus Alexander's Story of the Mier Expeditions as Told to John Warren Hunter," in Wade, comp., *Notes and Fragments of the Mier Expedition*, p. 28.
19. Reid, *The Scouting Expeditions of McCulloch's Texas Rangers*, p. 53.
20. *Telegraph and Texas Register*, July 13, 1842; see also, Reid, *The Scouting Expeditions of McCulloch's Texas Rangers*, pp. 29-32; Henry, *Campaign Sketches of the War with Mexico*, p. 139.

the square to the river was lined by long, narrow stone buildings. Beyond the plaza most of the buildings were common *jacals*. The Rio Grande opposite Reynosa was approximately 100 yards wide and three to five fathoms deep.

At Reynosa "great preparations had been made for the victor's triumphal entry."[21] A dispatch bearer arrived to notify Ampudia that a royal reception for the victorious army had been arranged. In preparation for entering the town, the guards adjusted their dress, brushed their clothing, and assumed a more martial air.[22] The procession ascended the steep hill with the prisoners ordered "to march two & two."[23] About halfway up, the procession was met by a group of painted warriors of the Carrizo Indian tribe, who, wearing only breech-cloths, suddenly popped into their path and uttered shrill war whoops and fired blank charges from their guns into the prisoners' faces. The procession entered the town's principal street through an elaborate triumphal arch constructed of reeds arranged in the form of a rope and raised in the center by an upright pole. Decorating the rope was a variety of colored cloth ranging from blankets to petticoats, and including laces, calicoes, scarves, ladies' shawls, veils, handkerchiefs, colored shirts, ribbons, and muslin of almost every conceivable color, size, and shape.[24] Flags and ensigns floated from buildings. Placards and banners proclaimed "glory," "honour," and "immortality" to Ampudia and his officers as they rode through the streets at the head of the column of prisoners.

The town was entered amid the firing of artillery, the clanging of church bells, and shouts of *"Viva Ampudia!" "Viva México!" "Viva! Viva! Viva!"* The procession was met by approximately twenty small, dirty-faced boys between the ages of ten and fourteen, dressed in robes with varied colored ribbons fluttering from their heads and shoulders. Their hair was filled with withered flowers or encircled with faded wreaths, and on their heads were fastened small, four-sided obelisk glass mirrors. They were led by a man, no larger than a twelve-year-old boy, although he appeared to be sixty years of age.

Women, children, and Indians danced in the street. "The ladies cheered from the housetops, the men shouted, the Indians yelled," and all the church bells, seemingly hundreds,[25] clattering as if they would be tossed from their axles, gave "forth a doubled tongued welcome in thun-

---

21. Green, *Mier Expedition*, p. 120; see also, Samuel C. Reid, Jr., *The Scouting Expeditions of McCulloch's Texas Rangers*, p. 29; Emory, *Report on the United States and Mexican Boundary Survey* 1, p. 62.

22. Stapp, *Prisoners of Perote*, p. 40.

23. Sibley, ed., *Samuel H. Walker's Account*, p. 38.

24. Nance, ed., *McCutchan's Narrative*, p. 67; Canfield diary, Jan. 4, 1843.

25. W. S. Henry reported in 1847 that the cathedral possessed "two discordant bells"; see Henry, *Campaign Sketches of the War with Mexico*, p. 139. If there had been more bells in 1843, most of them must have been removed on account of the war with the United States.

der tones,"[26] as the Texans were paraded in dishonor about the town, hooted at by the mob, pelted by stones, clods of dirt, and stale eggs, cursed, called all sorts of hard names, and spit upon by the women, "with all the malice of she-wolves." "Oh! that town," cried McCutchan, "should be razed to the earth, and its hundred bells run into cannon, with which to batter down the pride of that self-conceited people."[27] Some of the Texans laughed at the parade; "others would occasionally give a yell as the muskets & firecrackers went off, while others . . . [could] scarcely contain themselves with indignation and rage."[28]

The prisoners were marched three times around the square to the music of *"la Cachucha"* (an Andalusian *baile*-tune) before the curiosity of the citizenry had been satisfied. They were marched to their quarters in an unfinished brick building, where they were "caged for the night"[29] and fed on the meat of "either a mule or a Jack Ass."[30] They lay down to rest on the cold stone floor only to be tormented by fleas and lice.

Seldom during their march to Matamoros were the prisoners given bread and vegetables, usually supplied only with some form of meat. It must be remembered that the Mexican army was no better provisioned and that often the principal fare among the settlers of Texas was meat. On the march, the meat ration was supplemented by a few tortillas or a handful of corn. Even these rations were supplied without system, for, in general, troops on the march lived off the country. Essential supplies were carried on mule-back, or sometimes in country carts commandeered to transport impressed supplies. There was no organized transport system. "Our fare, and the miserable bivouacs assigned us on our march from Mier," reported one of the Texans, "rather sprung from the vile condition of the Mexican commissariat, than any meditated neglect" of Ampudia or other officers.[31]

The prisoners were retained at Nueva Reynosa until January 6. During this time, Dr. William M. Shepherd, who had prevented one of the Texans from firing on Padre de Lira, Ampudia's father-confessor, when he entered the Texan lines before the surrender, was taken from the main body of prisoners and placed with the officers. The *padre* furnished Shepherd with a horse and money and indicated his gratitude for Shepherd's saving his life by drinking from his pocket flask of brandy *(vino mescal)* with the Texan officers.[32]

On January 6 the prisoners were taken from their quarters and marched to the plaza, where they stood at attention for two hours upon a

---

26. Canfield diary, Jan. 4, 1843; see also Nance, ed., *McCutchan's Narrative*, p. 67; Bell, *Narrative*, p. 32.
27. Nance, ed., *McCutchan's Narrative*, p. 67.
28. Sibley, ed., *Samuel H. Walker's Account*, pp. 38-39.
29. Canfield diary, Jan. 4, 1843.
30. Nance, ed., *McCutchan's Narrative*, p. 67; Stapp, *Prisoners of Perote*, p. 41.
31. Stapp, *Prisoners of Perote*, p. 45.
32. Green, *Mier Expedition*, p. 121.

cold stone floor,[33] while Padre Lira and "a few sleek old priests"[34] went through the ceremony of mass in Spanish. The devotional services were followed by the firing of crackers and cannon as Ampudia prepared to renew the march.[35]

Samuel McDade, who had been ill since leaving Mier, was left lying on a rawhide at Nueva Reynosa, where he soon died.[36] Early in the day they passed La Mesa, an extensive *rancho* on the Mexican side of the Rio Grande about forty-five miles above Matamoros and four miles in a southerly direction from Agua Negra. After a march of twenty-five miles the Texans were driven into a picketed enclosure used for holding cattle and "left to pick the softest heaps of manure" on which to rest their weary bodies.[37] The next morning the march was renewed but covered only eighteen miles because the Mexicans found it convenient to place their captives in a cow pen or sheep pen[38] of a *hacienda* along the route, and obtain water and forage for the horses and men; such might not be available a few miles farther. This accounts for the variations in distance covered from day to day.

The corrals used for penning livestock were constructed of pickets placed upright and close together with one end fixed in the ground. Their tops were fastened to a horizontal pole by rawhide strings, thus making a strong fence. The prisoners were herded into such corrals for the night during their march through Mexico, and a strong guard surrounded the pen. A cannon faced the only exit from the enclosure. Usually it was more pleasant on the road than being confined in the filthy corrals of the towns and *haciendas.* On the road the Texans were generally free from the vile remarks of the mob that congregated when they halted in town.

As they marched along, a few of the men discussed overthrowing their guard and making a dash for Texas. They received very little encouragement within the group because most of the men were too tired from the hardships they had suffered traveling on foot, since they were accustomed to riding. But, as the prisoners were led toward the interior of Mexico others became more interested in escape. Some thought that on reaching Matamoros, military headquarters for the northeastern area of Mexico, they would be paroled.

As the procession approached Matamoros, the good horse ranges appealed to the Texans. The rolling prairies were carpeted with rich mesquite grass over which herds of fine cattle grazed, and doubtless some made mental notes for a future cow-stealing business.[39]

---

33. Canfield and Glasscock say they were formed in front of the church. Canfield diary, Jan. 6, 1843; Glasscock diary, Jan. 6, 1843.

34. "John Rufus Alexander's Story of the Mier Expedition as Told to John Warren Hunter," in Wade, comp., *Notes and Fragments of the Mier Expedition*, p. 28.

35. Stapp, *Prisoners of Perote*, p. 42; Canfield diary, Jan. 6, 1843; Green, *Mier Expedition*, p. 121; see also, Sibley, ed., *Samuel H. Walker's Account*, p. 39.

36. Nance, ed., *McCutchan's Narrative*, p. 67; Canfield diary, Jan. 4, 1843; Sibley, ed., *Samuel H. Walker's Account*, p. 39.

37. Stapp, *Prisoners of Perote*, p. 42; see also, Glasscock diary, Jan. 6, 1843.

38. They encamped the night of January 7, 1843, in a cow pen. Glasscock diary, Jan. 7, 1843.

39. Canfield diary, Jan. 8, 1843; Stapp, *Prisoners of Perote*, p. 42.

On the evening of Sunday, January 8, after a fifteen-mile march[40] "over a low musquet country"[41] and through "a rich [oblong] flat country well adapted to the cultivation of sugar cane," in the center of which "was an extensive slash, filled with every species of plover," the prisoners arrived at the small village of Guadalupe and were quartered for the night in a cow pen at Rancho Guadalupe. Here Ampudia was met by the leading citizens of Matamoros who had ridden out to welcome the hero and see the "barbarians" from the North. Among those who came from Matamoros in a coach with a great deal of curiosity were two runaway slaves from Texas named Tom and Esau, who in 1841 had escaped from Gen. Sam Houston, for whom they had worked as barbers.[42] Tom "treated us with marked respect and attention," reported Green, and often spoke of his activities in Mexico and of his intended marriage.[43] He invited the Texans to his wedding, at which he said Ampudia was to act as "godfather." Meeting Ampudia, Tom remarked: "Well, general, I told you, before leaving Matamoros, that when you met these gentlemen, you would catch them." Esau was disliked by most of the Texans because of the insults which he hurled at them. Esau, who sulked and spoke disrespectfully of Houston, was afraid to circulate among the Texans as Tom did.

As soon as the first demonstrations of joy at Matamoros on receipt of the news of the victory at Mier had subsided, Col. Anastasio Parrodi, in charge of the military defenses of the city, instructed the *alcalde* to make provision for receiving the Texan prisoners on the way to their city.[44] A *junta* of notables was assembled in the large room of the consistory to formulate plans for a public demonstration by which the people of the area might celebrate the entrance of the victorious troops and their general. Three citizens and the first *alcalde* were designated a welcoming committee to go out with musicians to meet Ampudia. Other committees were established to decorate the streets and erect a triumphal arch at the corner of the plaza major, and prepare a "gorgeous" ball.

Since daybreak on January 9, the town had been a busy place. Excited voices mingled with the noise from the movement of coaches, horses, and a "multitude of persons of all classes, sexes, and ages." The welcoming party, with the members of the committee riding at its head in a coach, left the city to greet the advancing army, and "it had the honor of saluting with acclamations of the most profound joy, General Ampudia,

40. Green, *Mier Expedition*, p. 122. Walker says thirteen miles were covered; Sibley, ed., *Samuel H. Walker's Account*, p. 39.

41. Green, *Mier Expedition*, p. 122; Henry, *Campaign Sketches of the War with Mexico*, p. 133.

42. Sam Houston to Genl. William G. Harding, Cedar Point, Texas, July 17, 1841, in Williams and Barker, eds., *Writings of Sam Houston* 3, pp. 10-11; see also *Galveston Civilian* quoted in *Northern Standard*, May 22, 1844.

43. Green, *Mier Expedition*, pp. 122-23; Nance, ed., *McCutchan's Narrative*, pp. 67-68.

44. *Anastasio Parrodi en Matamoros al Alcalde de la ciudad, sobre prisioneros texanos que arriban, Cuerpo de Ejército de Norte, 1.ª división, 2.ᵈ Brigada, Enero 6 de 1843*, in Matamoros Archives, 44, pp. 149-50 (photostat), TxU-A; *Diario del Gobierno*, Feb. 27, 1843.

Colonels D. Rómulo Díaz de la Vega [who commanded the First Brigade of Infantry and Artillery] and D. Antonio Canales [commander of the Auxiliary Cavalry] who [rode] . . . in front of the invincible first division and valiant auxiliaries from the villages."[45] Ampudia was invited to take a seat in the committee's coach, which he readily accepted. Within a mile or so of the town the inhabitants commenced flocking out in great numbers —some on foot, others on horseback, and a number of ladies and gentlemen in costly and elaborately carved coaches drawn by five or seven well-fed mules. Some of the women cried as the poor, half-starved, half-naked, hollow-eyed, tired *Tejanos* passed by.[46]

The guards were questioned by an anxious mother, wife, or sweetheart about some loved one missing from the ranks, and "the general reply was a sudden stroke upon the forehead with the end of the forefinger and a significant shrug of the shoulders, which invariably produced a shriek of woe," followed by "curse upon curse uttered upon . . . disarmed Texians." "Many of the females reprimanded us en masse," reported Canfield, "because forsooth some of their favorites were Accidentally (or rather Bullet-dentally) left at Mier."[47] "Many of the female sex [were] abusive on account of some of their husbands or connexions being left at Mier by our Rifle Balls," recorded Glasscock,[48] "whilst the more enlightened seemed to think we had made a desperate resistance against our formidable enemies, and pitied us."

Amid the confusion, as well as apprehension for their safety, "the little disarmed band of Texians stood as men whose bosoms had never known evil, and whose hearts," declared McCutchan, "had never felt a single pulsation of fear! They seemed insensible to all things around [them]; for they felt that they had gone as far as possible towards the performance of their duty."[49] In moody silence they submitted to the taunts of the multitude whose fury was controlled only by the bayonets of their captors. Such triumphant rejoicings, it may be surmised, "added nothing sweet to the bitter reflections of the Texan prisoners, who treasured them up like brands and brooding over them in silent agony," consoled themselves with the hope that their captivity might yet have a favorable termination.

At the outskirts of the city the 216 prisoners were halted for Ampudia to receive the congratulations of many friends who had come out to meet him. As the town was entered, a splendid reception was accorded the victorious Mexican army. Amid the din of artillery salvos, the joyful sound of church bells, and the crack of innumerable skyrockets, the Texans, decked in tattered clothing but with heads high, entered Matamoros. Every part of the city resounded to the strains of martial music from the fifers, trum-

---

45. *Diario del Gobierno*, Jan. 18 and Feb. 27, 1843.
46. *Daily Picayune*, Jan. 26, 1843.
47. Canfield diary, Jan. 9, 1843.
48. Glasscock diary, Jan. 9, 1843.
49. Nance, ed., *McCutchan's Narrative*, p. 69.

peters, buglers, and drummers from each corps of the garrison, and placards announcing the heroic deeds of Ampudia and the other officers were posted at the various street corners. Music and fluttering banners welcomed the army, "whilst gay cavaliers, on spirited *mustangs,* with flowing manes and tails, caracoled" before the procession, almost checking its advance by their numbers and curiosity.[50]

The procession entered from the west and moved along the Calle de Iturbide, passing beneath triumphal arches of flowers that extended across the street at intervals along both sides of the street. At every thirty feet soldiers stood at attention. The sidewalks, terraces, windows, doorways, and even houstops were filled with spectators eager to get a look at the "terrible Texians."[51] Only the bayonets of the soldiers protected the stone-faced Texan prisoners from bodily harm. There was hurry, bustle, and confusion. *"Mira! Mira! Los Tejanos! Los Tejanos!"* exclaimed the eager populace, pointing to the prisoners as if they were animals. Pushing his way through the crowd, Ampudia went immediately to the church "to render to the God of battle," reported the Mexican newspapers, "the homage owed for having deigned to adorn his brow with a crown of unfading laurel."[52]

The Texan officers were brought to the church and placed under the charge of Capt. Clemente Castro, who then hurried them "at full gallop" to the general's quarters to prevent the populace from hurling insults. The main body of prisoners was not so fortunate; they were marched "slowly and solemnly up one street and down another, to give the brutal populace full opportunity to gaze at them, to hiss, to hurl dirty epithets upon them, and to pelt them with stones and clods of earth and stale eggs."[53]

After the ceremony of high mass and a solemn *"Te Deum,"* Ampudia appeared on a raised platform in front of the church where he was formally received by the *ayuntamiento* and the ecclesiastical authority, after which the march continued to the principal plaza. The group halted before a triumphal arch covered with inscriptions and mottoes in honor of those who had subdued "the pride of the adventurers who pretended to convert themselves into conquerors."[54] The leading dignitaries mounted the rostrum at the side of the arch.

A youth by the name of Andrés Treviño stepped forward to deliver a short speech followed by a lengthy panegyric in verse by another youth. Then three girls presented Ampudia with a crown made of palm leaf and laurel, and pronounced the dedication in verse in a "sweet and expressive voice."[55] After this, the same girls sang a patriotic hymn.

---

50. Stapp, *Prisoners of Perote*, p. 43.
51. Canfield diary, Jan. 9, 1843; Stapp, *Prisoners of Perote*, p. 43; Sibley, ed., *Samuel H. Walker's Account*, p. 39.
52. *Diario del Gobierno*, Feb. 27, 1843.
53. Duval, *Big-Foot Wallace*, p. 183; Green, *Mier Expedition*, pp. 123-24.
54. *Diario del Gobierno*, Feb. 27, 1843.
55. *Ibid.*

The singing ended, the march continued to Ampudia's residence. In the reception room Agustín Menchaca, a member of the arrangements committee, arose and congratulated the general for his readiness to punish the enemy who had occupied "the defenseless and uninhabited towns of Laredo and Guerrero." In their defeat, "the ungrateful colonials owe their lives to your clemency, and in their surrender found humane and generous treatment. The people of Matamoros salute and congratulate you for . . . the glorious victory which you have obtained over the rebels in Texas in Mier, the 26th day of December last."[56] Ampudia modestly replied, "As a General of the Republic, I could not be indifferent to the incursions of those new vandals, and for that reason I marched quickly to save the towns that are so dear to me. I value much the felicitations of the citizens of Matamoros, because they recognize the noble and elevated principles of patriotic love."[57] That evening a sumptuous dinner was given in honor of Ampudia and his officers, during which many toasts were offered, followed by a magnificent ball.[58]

After being paraded about the streets for nearly two hours, the prisoners were lodged in uncomfortable quarters near the outskirts of the town "with the common felons of the country," where they remained until January 14.[59] The first night their rations were meager, but later the military not only supplied them "most abundantly with wholesome and palatable food, but the citizens generously contributed large supplies of clothing," blankets, money, and other necessities, without which the Texans would have suffered more then they did.[60]

During the evening another officer relieved Captain Castro so he could attend the entertainment. The new officer ordered the Texan officers removed to an unfinished room in the prison for greater security. Locked in their quarters, the Texans found themselves without heat, bedding, or furniture. Displeased with this sudden reversal in treatment, Green persuaded the officer of the guard to furnish him with pen, ink, and paper. He drafted a note to Ampudia expressing astonishment at the little consideration accorded the prisoners and accusing their captors of acting in bad faith in carrying out the "gratuitous promises" which had been made to them.[61] An hour later Ampudia's aide-de-camp appeared and returned the Texan officers to their former quarters. Green attributed the prompt attention to their plight to the intercession of Gen. Romúlo de

---

56. *Ibid.*

57. *Ibid.*

58. Green, *Mier Expedition*, p. 124.

59. Maj[or] J. D. Cocke to ———, Matamoros, Jan. 12, 1843, reprinted from the *New Orleans Bulletin* in the *Morning Star*, Mar. 4 and 7, 1843; in the *Telegraph and Texas Register*, Mar. 8, 1843; and in the *Northern Standard*, Apr. 13, 1843.

60. Stapp, *Prisoners of Perote*, p. 44; Canfield diary, Jan. 10-13, 1843; Nance, ed., *McCutchan's Narrative*, pp. 69-70; Duval, *Big-Foot Wallace*, p. 186; *Morning Star*, Jan. 24, 1843.

61. Green, *Mier Expedition*, pp. 124-25.

la Vega and Capt. Clemente Castro. The next morning Ampudia apologized and informed them that the prisoners were to be sent to Mexico City. Fisher and Green were to be sent in advance as hostages to guarantee the conduct of the others and that they were expected to meet their own expenses on the road. "We replied," reported Green "that if we were denied the privilege of accompanying our men, which we most preferred, we would cheerfully go in their advance to Mexico, to endeavour to do them all possible service. We also desired a day to make preparations and write letters to the United States and Texas, which was granted. After our letters were written, they were submitted to his inspection, which he in the most gentlemanly manner declined, and endorsed a free passport upon them."[62]

Green wrote another letter on January 11, this one to the president of the United States, John Tyler, on their captivity and solicited his intercession in their behalf as the head of a neutral and friendly power.[63]

The foreign consuls and merchants in the city spoke in the highest terms of Ampudia's conduct toward the prisoners. It was reported in Nashville and in New Orleans early in February 1843 that Colonel Fisher, General Green, and "all the other Texian officers and men acknowledge that they have been humanely treated by Gen. Ampudia."[64] The officers were given the privilege of the town accompanied by a Mexican officer of the same grade. They dined and spent their evenings at Ampudia's home and were treated very kindly.[65]

Ampudia reportedly adopted the youngest of the Texan boys, John Christopher Columbus Hill, and it was said that the little fellow was running about the town "as gay as a lark." Soon after the arrival of the prisoners at Matamoros, one of the Mexican colonels, in the presence of a number of citizens, placed his hand on Hill's head and allegedly told him, "You are too small; they would run over you in battle," to which the youth replied, "As small as I am, I made twelve of your countrymen bow low to me the other day."[66]

When the main body of Texan prisoners went forward to Mexico City, three boy members of the expedition, including Hill, were left behind on parole in Matamoros.[67] Ampudia had obtained the consent of John Hill's father to retain the boy as a member of his household and to send him to the best school in Matamoros, where he was enrolled as Juan Cristóbal Gil

---

62. Green, *Mier Expedition*, p. 125.

63. See Thomas J. Green to John Tyler, President of the United States of America, Castle of Perote, Mexico, April 25, 1843, in Green, *Mier Expedition*, pp. 287-95.

64. *New Orleans Picayune* quoted in *Republican Banner* (Nashville), Feb. 8, 1843.

65. Captain Auld's Report of the Battle of Mier, in *Telegraph and Texas Register,* Jan. 25, 1843; William S. Fisher and Thomas J. Green to Gen. Pedro de Ampudia, Matamoros, Jan. 11, 1843, in *ibid.*, May 3, 1843. A photostat copy of Fisher's and Green's letter to Ampudia is in the San Jacinto Museum of History.

66. Captain Auld's Report of the Battle of Mier, in *Telegraph and Texas Register*, Jan. 25, 1843.

67. Nance, ed., *McCuthan's Narrative*, pp. 71-72.

de Ampudia and received his first lessons[68] in Spanish from a teacher named Treviño. Later, word came from Santa Anna to Ampudia to have the boy sent to him in México City.[69]

On the eve of his departure from Matamoros, Green wrote to two old friends in New Orleans, Gen. Felix Huston and Col. Bailey Peyton, indicating his deep need for funds and that he had found "a noble generous fellow" named J. P. Schatzell, who had agreed to advance him $400 on a sixty-day draft drawn upon them. "My Dear Friends I have only to say to you to pay it if you have to inconvenience [yourselves] greatly. My brother I expect will be in Orleans before its maturity and if he does he must pay it; but if <u>not</u> do meet it. Col.° Wm. Christy will surely assist you in this matter if necessary for reasons known to us."[70]

The higher classes of both the native and the foreign population of the city were humane in their treatment of the Texans. The ladies, "ever foremost in the blessed ministrations of charity," sent "various sums of money in addition to their other bounties,"[71] and donations came from the Mexican gentry and foreign merchants. Among the foreigners who called on the prisoners and rendered assistance was Green's benefactor, Joseph P. Schatzell, a wealthy German merchant who formerly had resided in Louisville, Kentucky,[72] where he and Oldham had been friends. He provided articles needed by the Texans and distributedd $5 to each Kentuckian. On that occasion there was more than the usual number of Kentucky boys among the prisoners. Schatzell also advanced several hundred dollars on drafts to several members of the party, including Green. He loaned his friend Oldham $100.[73] In all, he gave and loaned between $2,000 and $3,000. He also succeeded in getting permission from Ampudia for the Texans to write home, then ensured their transmittal.[74]

A number of the prisoners eagerly wrote letters to family or friends in Texas and the United States. Robert S. Beard wrote to his father in Texas saying that he and his brother William were "in verry good health and stand the fategue we are bound to undergo verry well. I verry little expected this when I left home."[75] He wrote that Bill, his brother, "acted a verry good part in the battle and was skelped [slapped] on the sho[u]lder by a musket ball."

---

68. "Little John Hill, the Boy Hero of Mier," in *Dallas Morning News*, Dec. 22, 1929, Feature Section, pp. 7-8.

69. Gooch-Inglehart, *The Boy Captive*, pp. 209-11.

70. Tho[ma]s J. Green to Genl. Felix Huston & Colo. Bailey Peyton, New Orleans, [dated] Matamoros, Jany. 12, 1843, MS, in Domestic Correspondence (Texas), Tx-A.

71. Stapp, *Prisoners of Perote*, p. 44.

72. Canfield diary, Jan. 10, 1843; Nance, ed., *McCutchan's Narrative*, p. 69; Alexander, "Account of the Mier Expedition."

73. "John Rufus Alexander's Story of the Mier Expedition as Told to John Warren Hunter," in Wade, comp., *Notes and Fragments of the Mier Expedition*, p. 29.

74. Sibley, ed., *Samuel H. Walker's Account*, p. 39.

75. Robert S. Beard to Wm. Beard, Fort Bend County, Texas, via New Orleans [dated] Matamoros Prison, January 13, 1843.

Richard F. Brenham, who had been a commissioner on the Santa Fé Expedition in 1841, and was now once more a prisoner in Mexico, wrote: "Melancholy as is my fate, I have of late years learned philosophy in a hard school, and can submit to the vicissitudes of life with little murmuring. Although from my previous relations with this country, my condition is more perilous and uncertain than that of my companions, I believe it affects my spirits far less seriously. We leave this place tomorrow for Mexico."[76]

Green wrote to his brother Charles that he should get President Tyler to send him to Mexico as a dispatch bearer to General Thompson.[77] From Matamoros, Patrick Usher wrote to his sister in North Carolina on January 11, telling her that as a result of the Battle of Mier he was a prisoner and explaining his predicament as a prisoner "without clothing, without money and without friends." He hoped that his friends in Wilmington would write to Waddy Thompson, the American minister to Mexico, who seemingly had much influence with President Santa Anna, to intercede for his release. He requested that his sister convey to brother William that now was the time for him to pay the money he owed Patrick from his father's estate, because Patrick was now "in a loathsome prison, in a strange land without friends and without money," and that the rations he received were "of the coarset kind, and only sufficient to sustain life."[78]

Having made his campaign, a few months later Usher again wrote his sister: It is rumored in prison this morning "that they would in a few days be sent to Mexico City in irons." Though he now wrote in haste, he stated he would write more fully from Mexico City, "if I live to reach there, which is very doubtful as my health is bad. So much that I fear I can not undergo the fatigue and exposure attendant on so long a march on foot."[79]

---

76. Richard F. Brenham to ____, Matamoros, January 14, 1843, reprinted from the New Orleans *Tropic* in *Northern Standard*, June 8, 1843.

77. C.P. Green to Willie P. Mangum, Warren County, NC, March 24, 1843, in Henry Thomas Shanks, ed., *Papers of Willie Person Mangum*, 3, pp. 439-40.

78. Patrick Usher to Mrs. Eliza Anne Berry, Wilmington, NC, [dated] Matamoros, Mexico, Jan. 11, 1843, original in possession of Henry B. McKay, Greenville, SC; copy in TxU-A.

79. Idem to [Mrs. Eliza Anne Berry, Wilmington, NC], Matamoros, Mexico, Jan. 11, 1843, original in possession of Henry B. McKay, Greenville, S.X.; copy in TxU-A.

CHAPTER 8

The Béxar Prisoners from San Antonio to Saltillo

W HEN GEN. ADRIÁN WOLL, commander of the Second Division of the Mexican Army of the North, captured San Antonio on September 11, 1842, sixty-two persons were made prisoners, ten of whom were subsequently released because of their youth, indisposition, or promises of loyalty to Mexico in the future. The remaining fifty-two captured persons, largely Texans, included a number of men of importance who were sent to Gen. Isidro Reyes' headquarters at San Fernando de Agua Verde.

When the Texans defending San Antonio learned their foes were a regular Mexican army force of superior strength, they responded to Woll's white flag with a commission composed of William E. Jones, George Van Ness, Cornelius W. Peterson, and Anderson Hutchinson that went to Woll's headquarters to investigate terms of surrender. They "agreed to surrender as prisoners of war—our lives and property (arms excepted)," reported Jones, "to be spared and secured."[1] Woll told Judge Hutchinson, and probably several others on September 13, that he would write ahead to Santa Anna to request his release.[2]

With only a few hours' notice, the prisoners were marched out of San Antonio on September 15 under a heavy guard of 150 cavalrymen and infantry commanded by Capt. Emeterio Posas.[3] By special favor some of the prisoners were permitted to ride horses. Andrew Neill, however, was not permitted to ride, for he had been one of the few prisoners who had

---

1. William E. Jones to [M. B. Lamar], Washington, 1 Feby 1844, in E. W. Winkler, ed., "The Béxar and Dawson Prisoners," *QTSHA* 13 (Apr. 1910), p. 323.

2. Anderson Hutchinson diary, Sept. 13-15, 1842, in Winkler, ed., "The Béxar and Dawson Prisoners," *QTSHA* 13 (Apr. 1910), p. 296. Hereinafter cited as Hutchinson diary, plus date of entry.

3. Maverick diary, Sept. 15, 1842. For a detailed account of the capture of San Antonio by Gen. Adrián Woll and the removal of the Texas prisoners to San Fernando, see Nance, *Attack and Counterattack*, pp. 297-334.

refused "to sign his name to one of the many documents drawn up for signature to be sent into Texas or left behind us," he said, "respecting our treatment."[4]

Arriving at a campsite at the Alazán, four miles from town, the Texans were made to lie down and told not to move unless accompanied by a guard. A portion of the escort was then sent back to Béxar. On September 16, the prisoners were started on the march shortly after sunrise. Late that afternoon after a fatiguing march of thirty-four miles, they reached the Medina at the Presidio ford and pushed up the river to Woll's crossing, where they crossed and camped on the west side of the river about three miles from the crossing. During the night the prisoners discussed the feasibility of escaping, but according to Hutchinson, several were so "desirous to avail themselves of the opportunity of being taken into Mexico" that they were unwilling to attempt it.[5] Trueheart also claims that "the prisoners were so wearied by the day's tramp that they were unwilling to attempt it."[6] Judge Hutchinson believed that if any ten had made the attempt to escape, they would have succeeded.

Leaving their overnight camp at sunrise, September 17, the prisoners marched along the Upper Presidio Road. During the day, John R. Cunningham, who suffered from a high fever, fell from his horse and was placed in a cart with Mexican wounded. No fellow Texan was permitted to remain with him. On arrival at the Río Hondo, Shields Booker and Francis McKay, both physicians, requested permission to administer aid to Cunningham, but Captain Posas refused. A brief halt was made at the Hondo to permit the troops and prisoners to rest. Capt. Luis Vidal, aide-de-camp to General Woll, found Hutchinson exhausted, made a tent for him, and "gave him of his rice and assured him of his friendship."[7] After a short rest, the guard and prisoners moved on, reaching the Río Seco about eight at night, where they camped on the east bank. The prisoners were arranged in two lines with the soldiers camped on both sides of them.

By the next morning, September 18, Cunningham had improved. He wanted to ride horseback, but friends advised against it so he rode once more in the cart. The Texans never saw him again.[8] They reached the Río Frío, crossed, and camped on its west bank. The following day they crossed the Leona and the Nueces, and that evening camped near the head of La Laguna Espantosa, in the rain, seven miles west of the Nueces. On September 20, the prisoners passed Chaparrosa Creek and camped.

The next day a heavy rain forced an early rising to keep their blan-

---

4. A. Neill to Anson Jones, Washington, Texas, Jany 29, 1843, in Winkler, ed., "The Béxar and Dawson Prisoners," *QTSHA* 13 (Apr. 1910), p. 315.

5. Hutchinson diary, Sept. 16, 1842.

6. Trueheart diary, Sept. 16, 1842.

7. Hutchinson diary, Sept. 17, 1842.

8. Maverick diary, Sept. 18, 1842.

kets dry, so they got started at an unusually early hour. After marching thirty miles, they arrived in sight of the Rio Grande. Captain Posas said they could go on to the river or stop at watering holes on nearby Cuevas Creek.[9] They chose the latter.

For the past two or three days, the Mexican soldiers had amused themselves by killing rattlesnakes, which were abundant in the area west of the Nueces. An officer offered a soldier a *real* to capture a snake by taking it by the back of its head. The soldier made the attempt. He stepped on the snake's tail and "was boldly walking up, when the snake, too quick for that, bit him through a hole in his old shoe."[10] Friends carried him to the creek where Dr. Booker lanced the wound and poured salt into it. The soldier survived.

Early on September 22, the prisoners and their escort reached Nogal Pass on the Rio Grande, described by one of their number as "a bold, rapid river 250 or 300 yards wide."[11] Woll had crossed his army into Texas there late in August. In view upriver was Kinto's *rancho*.

The march from San Antonio had been slowed by the Mexican carts loaded with wounded soldiers. It took a day for them to cross the river in two dugout canoes. While the prisoners and their guard crossed in parties of eight or ten, others awaited their turn to cross in a corral near the crossing under the shade of a large pecan tree.

By sunset nearly everything had been taken across and camp was made in a sheep pen on a hill near the river. Here the prisoners learned of the death on September 19 of their comrade, John R. Cunningham, a lawyer, who had been left desperately ill on the Leona, "and was buried after being stripped of his apparel on the west side of the Leona about a mile or a mile and a half from the creek on one side of the road made by General Woll, a short distance from the terminus of the bottom as you ascend a slight hill."[12] The next day, September 20, the prisoners bathed in the river, which proved to be a source of great pleasure although the water was quite muddy. Afterwards, they marched to Presidio del Río Grande through sheep-and-cattle country with good *labors* (farms). Presidio del Río Grande was a town of approximately 1,000 "villanous" looking inhabitants situated about six miles below the crossing of the Rio Grande.[13]

The town appeared to be in decay. Water was plentiful, but salty and unfit to drink.[14] As they entered the town every door and window was occupied by curious residents. The prisoners were quartered in an old house fronting on the plaza, and remained there until September 27, when the

9. Trueheart diary, Sept. 21, 1842.
10. Maverick diary, Sept. 21, 1842.
11. [William E. Jones to M. B. Lamar], Washington, 1 Feby 1844, in Winkler, ed., "The Béxar and Dawson Prisoners," *QTSHA* 13 (Apr., 1910), p. 320.
12. Trueheart diary, Sept. 28-Oct. 7, 1842.
13. Maverick diary, Sept. 23 and 27, 1842.
14. *Ibid.*, Sept. 23, 1842.

prisoners were marched twenty-six miles in a westward direction from the Rio Grande through a rich prairie to San Juan de Nava, located near the old Spanish mission of San Juan Bautista.

The Woll prisoners found the inhabitants of Nava kind and hospitable.[15] Along the way to Nava they learned that the Texans had captured Don Refugio de la Garza (Pedro Garza), the parish priest of Béxar and chaplain in the Río Grande Company, but had released him when Woll threatened to have the Béxar prisoners shot. At Nava the prisoners were quartered in a granary. A short while after they arrived, three or four were invited out to cook provisions for the other prisoners.

The next day they reached San Fernando de Agua Verde, or San Fernando de Rosas, a beautiful city of white "gleaming through the dark green foliage."[16] As they entered the main plaza they found General Reyes, commander of the Army of the North, gazing at them through a window of his quarters.[17] The prisoners were held in formation in front of Reyes' quarters and under the gaze of a crowd of curious men and women. Afterwards the prisoners were conducted to quarters in a single large room, which Neill, upon his arrival in Texas, described as "a small loathsome dungeon."[18] A sentinel stood inside the door, and others were stationed outside, each "bawling every ten minutes, *Centinela alerto!*" Hutchinson was taken to the home of General Cela, adjutant general to General Reyes, where he was entertained during his stay in San Fernando.[19]

At San Fernando the prisoners learned that Woll had reached Presidio del Río Grande, "accompanied by a large number of families from Béxar, bringing with them 200 carts containing their furniture, [other] moveables, cattle, horses and in fact everything is brought." Other families from Béxar were arriving at San Fernando, including Peter Ford, a former resident of Béxar.[20]

On Sunday, October 2, Reyes visited the prisoners in their quarters, where he received a protest of their incarceration and a written statement of the facts of their resistance and surrender at San Antonio drafted by William E. Jones and signed by him and Samuel A. Maverick as representatives of the prisoners. Reyes promised to forward the document to Santa Anna with his favorable recommendation. He thought they would soon be released.[21] This was duplicity. Woll had the power to release some of the prisoners taken at San Antonio and he could have released all of them if he thought they had been taken unjustifiably because they believed they were defending their homes against bandits. If Reyes believed that this might have been the case when the prisoners reached San Fernando, he

---

15. Maverick diary, Sept. 27, 1842.
16. Bayliss, *A Narrative of Major General Wool's Campaign in Mexico*, p. 14.
17. Maverick diary, Sept. 28, 1842; Trueheart diary, Sept. 23, 1842.
18. *Morning Star*, Feb. 18, 1843.
19. Hutchinson diary, Oct. 2, 1842.
20. Trueheart diary, Sept. 28, 1842.
21. Hutchinson diary, Oct. 2, 1842.

could have released them. The only excuse that can be offered for Woll and Reyes is political. What would be the popular reaction to turning loose hated "colonials and usurpers of Mexican soil"? How else could they demonstrate prowess over the Texans except by the exhibition of Texan prisoners?

Doña Marina Rodríguez y Taylor visited the prisoners twice and furnished some with food and coffee three times a day while the prisoners were in town.[22] Her coffee pot got broken in their service. Upon leaving San Fernando, five of the prisoners left behind a note testifying to the kindness of Doña Marina Taylor.[23]

From San Fernando Andrew Neill wrote Francisco Vidaurri y Villaseñor at Santa Rosa, asking him to pay at least the interest on a note Vidaurri had given Samuel G. Powell, dated November 5, 1839, because Neill was badly in need of money for himself and friends. Neill, who was probably Powell's lawyer, offered a receipt for the amount.[24] On October 4, ten of the Dawson captives arrived.[25] They were placed in a separate prison and not allowed to visit the Béxar men, but Bradley was able to pencil "a line or two to us," reported Maverick, "in which he gave some a/c of his fight—and ended his note with the statement 'God & the Future.'" The wounded Dawson men had been left in the hospital at Presidio del Río Grande, where they were confined under a guard for two months.[26] They plotted escape when sufficiently recovered to travel, but concluded they could not get across the river and gave up on the idea. Shortly thereafter a Frenchman visited the Texan prisoners and learned of their earlier plan for escaping. He assured them that crossing the river would be no problem, "as it was low at that season of the year." Encouraged, the Texans revived their plans to escape. Because of some difficulty between John Higgerson and the others, "Higgerson was not invited to participate in the attempt to escape."[27]

Noticing that their guards played cards a great deal and left their guns unloaded, the four Texan prisoners, though not recovered fully from their wounds, determined to act at the first opportunity. They also re-

---

22. Samuel A. Maverick to Mary A. Maverick, Castle of Perote, 150 miles East of the City of Mexico on the Road to (80 miles off) Vera Cruz, Jan. 27, 1843, in Green, ed., *Samuel Maverick*, pp. 223-27.

23. James W. Robinson, S. A. Maverick, Geo. C. Hatch, A. Neill, and Chauncey Johnson, to All to Whom this May Come, San Fernando, Oct. 8, 1842, in Maverick diary, p. 198.

24. A. Neill to Francisco Vidaurri y Villaseñor in Santa Rosa, [dated] San Fernando, Oct. 3, 1842, in Domestic Correspondence (Texas), MS, Tx-A.

25. Samuel A. Maverick to Mary A. Maverick, Castle of Perote, 150 miles East of the City of Mexico on the Road to Vera Cruz, Jan. 27, 1843, in Green, ed., *Samuel Maverick*, pp. 223-27.

26. R. A. Barkl[e]y to H. G. Woods, LaGrange, Fayette Co., Texas [dated] Mexico, Castle of Perote, May 8, 1843, [postmarked] Galveston, June 5, Texas, in Spellman, ed., "Letters of the 'Dawson Men' from Perote Prison, Mexico," *SWHQ* 38 (Apr. 1935), pp. 252-53.

27. Weyand and Wade, *An Early History of Fayette County*, p. 160.

alized that as soon as the authorities became aware of their ability to travel, they likely would be sent to join their comrades. So, on a moonlit but cold night in November, the prisoners ran toward the river some three or four miles away, stumbling over the rocks that littered the ground and falling several times.[28] Norman Woods was recaptured easily. The other three—John MacCredae, W. D. Patterson, and Milvern Harrell—ran upstream for some ten or twelve miles from the ford, then cut toward the river and reached it about daylight.[29]

Since Patterson was oldest, the other two followed his advice. They searched for a shoally place to cross, and selected a point where the river narrowed and "bent in towards the Texas side." A sandbar lay near the bank and on the opposite side of the river was a high bluff. The three had waded beyond the sandbar when unexpectedly Patterson, who was in the lead, stepped into deep water and commenced to swim. He called for his companions to follow. MacCredae and Patterson drowned and Harrell was recaptured when he gave up and returned to the Mexican side of the river.

In a few days, Higgerson, Harrell, and Woods were taken to San Fernando under guard, where they found George Van Ness, Thomas Hancock, and Fitzgerald. On his march from San Fernando to Mexico City, Woods was permitted "to ride a horse or burro—the latter of which," he said, "I found to be far the *superior* animal of the two, at least in my situation."[30] Between Presidio del Río Grande and San Fernando, Woods lost a handkerchief that covered his head wounds, and in the inclement weather took a severe cold which forced him to keep to his bed in San Fernando for about two months. Finally, an order reached Reyes' headquarters commuting the death sentence of the three former Santa Fé prisoners to ten years' imprisonment in the Castle of San Juan de Ulúa and ordering all Texan prisoners at San Fernando to be sent to Mexico City.[31] By the time they reached Saltillo, Woods had become delirious and would have died without the care given by his nephew, Milvern Harrell. At Saltillo the five BéxarDawson prisoners were overtaken by the Mier men headed also for Mexico City.

As for the Dawson men, upon arrival at San Fernando, Bradley was able to supply the Béxar prisoners with a list of comrades who had been

28. Norman Woods to H. G. Woods, Molino Del Rey, July 5, 1843, in Spellman, ed., "Letters of the 'Dawson Men'," *SWHQ* 38 (Apr. 1935), pp. 257-60.

29. "Reminiscences of Milvern Harrell, The Only Living Survivor of the Dawson Massacre," in *Dallas Morning News*, June 16, 1907; see also Winkler, ed., "The Béxar and Dawson Prisoners," *QTSHA* 13 (Apr. 1910), pp. 299-300; R. A. Barkley to "My Friends," Perote, Mar. 25, 1843 (fragment of a letter), in Spellman, ed., "Letters of the 'Dawson Men,'" *SWHQ* 38 (Apr. 1935), pp. 248-49.

30. Norman Woods to H. G. Woods, LaGrange, Fayette County, Texas, [dated] Prison of the Po[wder] Mills, near the City of Mex[ico], n.d. [postmarked] Galveston, Aug. 18, [1843] and probably written in June, [1843], in Spellman, ed., "Letters of the 'Dawson Men,'" *SWHQ* 38 (Apr. 1935), pp. 264-65.

31. Norman Woods to H. G. Woods, Molino del Rey, July 5, 1843, in Spellman, ed., "Letters of the 'Dawson Men'," in *SWHQ* 38 (Apr. 1932), pp. 257-60.

captured or wounded, but with only a partial list of those who had been killed in the engagement near Salado Creek.[32] On October 6, the day before the prisoners left San Fernando for Mexico City, one wrote that he had spent the previous day with General Cela, a Spaniard, who was serving as adjutant general to General Reyes, and, "taking everything into consideration, passed a very agreeable time of it. We played chess during the afternoon, dined about seven o'clock—the dinner excellent, coffee, butter, &c. So far I have found the Mexican officers gentlemen, and the soldiers generally kind and disposed to make our situation as comfortable as possible."[33] During their stay at San Fernando most of the officers who came with the prisoners from San Antonio to the Rio Grande visited them frequently.

Except for George Van Ness and Thomas Hancock, who were separated from the group on October 6 and put in the "common prison" to await their fate as Santa Fé prisoners, the San Antonio prisoners were ordered from their quarters on Friday, October 7, to begin their march to Mexico City. The ten survivors from Dawson's command, who could travel, joined them in the plaza, making a total of fifty-eight to commence the long march to the capital. From the Salado prisoners, the San Antonio prisoners obtained a more complete story of the Dawson Fight. As preparations were made to leave, Mrs. Rodríguez y Taylor purchased a horse for Judge James W. Robinson. Maverick's horse was judged too fine an animal for a Texan to ride in Mexico, so it was taken from him by Col. José María Carrasco, who gave him in exchange "a little black, tender footed horse," and to Judge Hutchinson he presented a mule for the long journey to Mexico City. Francisco Ruíz, formerly of San Antonio and a signer of the Texas Declaration of Independence, supplied Trueheart with a small amount of money.[34] When the prisoners left San Fernando, twenty-two of them were riding horses, mules, or burros.

As the names of those captured by Woll at San Antonio became known, relatives and friends tried to gain their release. The Woll prisoners had scarcely reached the Rio Grande when John Neill wrote to Charles Elliot, the British *chargé d'affaires* in Texas, pleading for assistance in getting his brother Andrew freed from imprisonment in Mexico. Neill stated that Andrew, at the time of his seizure, had intended to return to Scotland. Elliot informed Lord Aberdeen that Andrew Neill had "assumed the privileges of Texian citizenship," lending doubt to his case; however, Elliot afforded Neill "the benefit of that state of doubt" and wrote a letter to Woll via President Houston, hoping he would find a way to transmit it.[35]

---

32. Trueheart diary, Sept. 28-Oct. 7, 1842.

33. *Telegraph and Texas Register*, Nov. 23, 1842; see also Trueheart diary, Sept. 28-Oct. 7, 1842.

34. Maverick diary, Oct. 7, 1842.

35. Charles Elliot to Don Andrew [Adrián] Woll, etc. The Officer in Command of the Mexican Force in Advance, Galveston, October 18, 1842 (true copy), in *QTSHA* 15 (Apr. 1912), pp. 349-50. This is enclosed in Charles Elliot to Earl of Aberdeen, in *QTSHA* 15 (Apr. 1912), pp. 347-49.

After being at San Fernando eight days, much to the disappointment of those who believed they would be released upon their arrival at that point, an order came for the prisoners to be sent to the capital. The long journey to Mexico City was about to begin. The guard was commanded by Lt. Bernerdo Cabazas, who had treated the Texans kindly from the time they left San Antonio. The guard consisted of eighty cavalrymen who rode on each side of the prisoners.

The country from San Fernando to Monclova was "generally poor, broken, and sometimes mountainous."[36] The region was devoid of trees, except mesquite and chaparral thickets.[37] Their route lay through a fine valley to Morelos, located about three leagues to the southeast of San Fernando. From Morelos they continued to San Juan de Matas, situated on a small creek in a well-irrigated valley. San Juan was reached at three in the afternoon, after traveling twelve miles. Here Judge Hutchinson was lodged in the home of *Alcalde* Treviño.

The country was rich in sugar cane, cornfields, and pecan trees. They met several escaped slaves, including "Old Solomon," from Texas, and more refugee families from San Antonio de Béxar.[38] On October 9 they arose at daybreak; as they commenced their march a severe norther began to blow a drizzling rain. By midday the sun beamed down intensely hot. Near noon their quartermaster presented the prisoners with a bag of "*biz-cochoes*" (biscuits). The road soon became rocky and was in a hilly terrain, and toward late afternoon they reached the mountains and Rosita, twenty miles from their previous encampment.[39] Their camp was beside a rocky branch of the San Juan River. Santa Rosa was almost in sight on their right. The night at Rosita was cold and rainy, and a sleepless one for many. Two beeves were killed for supper; for fires they burned bear-grass stalks. The commander of the guard, believing that the prisoners were planning an escape, became uneasy, "so much so, as to keep him nearly the whole night watching and reconnoitering the camp."[40]

The following day, with "the sun shining out in all its brilliancy," they came out of the mountains about noon, and struck the Río Sabinas, a deep, rapid stream about the size of the Brazos River. They descended two or three miles along its east bank, where some of the men encamped after sunset near a stone ranch house in a cow pen with cow dung a foot deep, and others camped nearby, but on the outside of the corral.[41] They had traveled about thirty-five miles that day. William Trimble amused the local inhabitants "by hooting like an owl, for which he received bread and many

36. Trueheart diary, Sept. 28, 1842.

37. [William E. Jones to M. B. Lamar], Washington, 1 Feby 1844, in Winkler, ed., "The Béxar and Dawson Prisoners," *QTSHA* 13 (Apr., 1910), p. 322.

38. Hutchinson diary, Oct. 7, 1842; Trueheart diary, Oct. 7, 1842.

39. Trueheart diary, Oct. 8, 1842; Hutchinson diary, Oct. 10, 1842.

40. Maverick diary, Oct. 8, 1842.

41. Trueheart diary, Oct. 8, 1842.

other things." Here, also, the prisoners had plenty of good water and delicious milk.[42]

The next morning they spent most of the day in crossing the river in canoes. The river was between fifty and sixty yards wide. Its water was the finest ever tasted, recorded Maverick. Having crossed the river, they again moved down it on the west side about a mile and encamped. At this point some planned an escape, but changed their minds.

The following morning their route continued down the west side of the Sabinas towards Candela over a high, well-watered *mesa* (plain) with a view of the mountains of Candelia and Monclova. After ten or twelve miles the prisoners left the river on the right. At night they camped at the old Hacienda de los Alamos on the Río Salado (Alamo) after a march of thirty miles.[43] They were placed in a large room, and those who had money bought *tortillas* and kid meat. Here Hutchinson urged the prisoners to make an effort to escape before they got too far into the country.[44] Again, nothing came of the idea. The next morning the Salado was crossed and the prisoners continued southwestwardly toward the gap in the mountains at the eastern edge of the Sierra Madre Occidental. "The profile of the Candelia mountains," recorded Maverick, "is so striking, for beauty, variety and high sublimity I cannot forget it."[45] At night they camped in the mountains at Hacienda de las Encinas (Green Oaks, or Live Oaks).[46]

Earlier in the day Captain Posas had sent forward an officer to have a beef butchered by the time the escort arrived with the prisoners, but none had been butchered and the officer blamed the *alcalde,* who, upon being summoned, said, "the cattle were some distance of[f], and as yet one had not been obtained."[47] Posas flew into a rage. "The altercation increased and at length <u>Colonel Posas</u> . . . told him [the *alcalde*] that he had to call on the *alcaldes* orders for what he needed upon his giving him a fair consideration, and that unless he (P.) was supplied with a fat beef in a short time he would tie and carry him to the city of Mexico. The *alcalde* finding that he could do nothing in opposing Posas, and that he might be roughly handled in not complying, made all haste in having one brought, which was really fat. The dispute afforded us some amusement while it lasted," reported Trueheart, "as well as information."[48] The prisoners took a bath in the beautiful fountain of the *hacienda.*

On October 13 the Texans and their escort reached the pass of Las Hermanas, which had been visible to them for the past two days, and in the distance they could see the extensive Hacienda de las Hermanas (Hacienda of the Sisters). Late in the afternoon they reached the *hacienda,* a splendid

---

42. Maverick diary, Oct. 9, 1842.
43. Trueheart diary, Oct. 11, 1842.
44. *Ibid.*
45. Maverick diary, Oct. 11, 1842.
46. *Ibid.*, Oct. 12, 1842.
47. *Ibid.*
48. Trueheart diary, Oct. 12, 1842.

sheep ranch. They were conducted into a large yard surrounded by a high rock wall. The buildings were laid out in the form of two contiguous squares with a solid wall on all sides. Entrance was through a single gate into each plaza. The inner side of the wall was made up mostly of houses occupied by servants and constructed around two courtyards of 100 or more square yards each. On one side of the wall were large storerooms for grain. The Texan prisoners were lodged in one of the granaries.[49] One of the courtyards was surrounded by stables. The whole establishment was built of hard rock and constituted a strong fortification against Indians and *banditti*. During their stay at Las Hermanas, some of the prisoners were permitted to bathe in the tank and stroll about the *hacienda*.

Beyond Las Hermanas the prisoners crossed the Salado twice and passed Buena Ventura, the Vicente Pass, and the old Rancho de Zapeda before arriving at Las Adjuntas. Las Adjuntas was another *hacienda* devoted to the raising of sheep. There they met Jesús de la Garza, a Mexican officer on his way to Woll's headquarters. During the evening William Trimble "and a Mexican commenced dancing to see which could out do the other. A crowd of Americans and Mexicans assembled to see the sport. They both exerted themselves very much to the intense amusement of the spectators. The American finding that he was about to be beat[en] suddenly stop[ped] and clapping his hands, he crowed like a chicken cock, which so startled the Mexican with words and arguments that he quit dancing and retired out of the circle, the American returning his salutation. The way the Mexican out did us," commented Trueheart, "afforded great mirth to the bystanders."[50]

After an easy march of fifteen miles on October 14, the prisoners reached Monclova. As usual on entering a town, they found the streets lined with spectators. The Texans were quartered "on the public square where soldiers were accustomed to be lodged."[51] They were visited by several foreigners and Mexican gentlemen friendly to the Americans, including Victor Blanco and his son Don Miguel, son-in-law of Don Ramón Músquiz, and Ramón Eca y Músquiz. Blanco and Músquiz promised to return the next day and hoped in the meantime to prevail upon Posas to remain another day in Monclova. They promised that he would "be at no expense," as they would agree to feed the prisoners during their extended stay. They also arranged for some of the prisoners "to go that evening and visit their acquaintances."[52] Posas agreed to stay over one day so the footsore prisoners could rest. On October 16 some prisoners were permitted to dine with friends and visit the town. Hutchinson dined with Músquiz, former governor of Coahuila y Texas and Federalist leader."[53]

---

49. Maverick diary, Oct. 13, 1842; Trueheart diary, Oct. 13, 1842.
50. Trueheart diary, Oct. 14, 1842.
51. Maverick diary, Oct. 15, 1842.
52. Trueheart diary, Oct. 15, 1842.
53. Maverick diary, Oct. 15, 1842.

Not only were the prisoners "kindly received," they were "abundantly supplied by the inhabitants" with food, drink, and other necessities.[54] Baskets of cake and bread were brought to the prisoners in their quarters. Músquiz supplied Trueheart with a small quantity of coffee, sugar, and pork, and gave him a blanket and five dollars.[55] During the extra day in Monclova, those who wished to do so were permitted to wash their clothes. "As soon as they arrived at the creek, the wash women perceiveing their object, came in a body, and offered to do it for them," reported one of the prisoners. "As soon as one of the first party gets through, they returned and others come, thus proceeding until every man who wished to have his clothes washed" had done so.[56]

The prisoners remained at Monclova until three o'clock, October 17. They camped first at Hacienda Castaño, eight miles from Monclova, in a cow pen near excellent water, and the next night they camped in a cow pen near some waterholes.[57]

On October 19 they reached the tank of San Felipe, and the next day the Hacienda de Anelo, where they bathed in a warm tank attached to the *hacienda.* On October 21 they traveled through several hailstorms to the Hacienda de Mesías only fifteen miles from their destination. They were placed in a stable, practically roofless, against which they remonstrated to Captain Posas. Posas said he regretted the poor quarters selected by the quartermaster who had been sent ahead to make arrangements.[58] He had the prisoners taken to a larger room used as a granary, and none too soon, for while the Mexicans were killing a beef, "a tremendous shower of rain and hail" descended.

The next morning they passed the mouth of the Parrajo, and followed along its banks, first on one side and then on the other. They passed through the mountains, occasionally observing mountain tops above the clouds, and descended into the valley of Saltillo twenty-one miles to Capellanilla, where they were provided with both good quarters and food. On Sunday, October 23, as they prepared to resume their journey, they were requested by Posas to change their clothes, "so as to appear as clean and as comely as possible."[59] Just before entering Saltillo, they were "met by some officers, and a crowd of citizens, which . . . enlarged every step we take," recorded Trueheart. "Those that do not join in, gaze at us as we march along. An American acquaintance of one of the prisoners is recognized and hailed by him, but [the American] does not reply, appearing not

54. Trueheart diary, Oct. 16, 1842.

55. A. Neill to Anson Jones, Sec. of State, Washington, Texas, Jany 29th, 1843, in Winkler, ed., "The Béxar and Dawson Prisoners," *QTSHA* 13 (Apr. 1910), pp. 315-16.

56. Trueheart diary, Oct. 17, 1842.

57. Maverick diary, Oct. 18, 1842.

58. *Ibid.*

59. [William E. Jones to M. B. Lamar], Washington, 1 Feby 1844, in Winkler, ed., "The Béxar and Dawson Prisoners," *QTSHA* 13 (Apr. 1910), pp. 322.

to know him."[60] On arrival at the barracks, they were "kept huddled toget-her [for] several days like sheep in a little room hardly 16 feet square," Neill reported, and were guarded by soldiers little better than "rogues."[61] "The Mexicans themselves were ashamed of this treatment, and said that there were not soldiers enough in that section to guard them, and they were afraid they would make their escape if they gave them greater liberty."[62]

The prisoners remained at Saltillo two weeks awaiting the arrival of a new guard from San Luis Potosí. They were closely confined and on no oc-casion were they permitted to leave their quarters, for Woll, having learned of the liberties given to the prisoners at Monclova, had sent an order to Captain Posas not to permit such privileges again.[63] The new guard, com-manded by Benito Cortéz, described as "a gentlemanly little officer," arrived, and the prisoners were moved to three "tolerably" good rooms.[64]

At Saltillo they "met that bad treatment which was to be expected from that robber city of 30 thousand people," wrote Maverick.[65] "None of the Mexican inhabitants visited us or showed the least feeling for us," declared Hutchinson.[66] The prisoners "were badly treated by the soldiery and abused and insulted" if they dared ask for better treatment, said Neill.[67]

Through a petition they drew up at Saltillo to Governor Francisco Mejía the San Antonio prisoners sought relief for the Dawson men, who had been added to their group just before leaving San Fernando, and who had been stripped on the battlefield by the Mexican soldiers of every-thing—money, watches, clothes, and blanket. Mejía turned a deaf ear and would have sent them on, as near naked as they were, but for the kindness of Dr. J. D. Knight, Dr. James Hewetson, and a Mr. Rogers, who visited the prisoners every day during the two weeks they were in Saltillo and gave them supplies.[68] Hewetson gave Hutchinson $25 and promised to supply him with additional funds when he reached Mexico City.

From Saltillo on October 31, Maverick wrote to his cousin Waddy Thompson, the U.S. minister to Mexico, of his apprehension of being taken to some secret prison. He wanted Thompson to know where they were so that he could inquire about their treatment.

---

60. Trueheart diary, Oct. 23, 1842.

61. *Morning Star*, Feb. 18, 1843.

62. Maverick diary, Oct. 23, 1842.

63. Samuel A. Maverick to Mary A. Maverick, Castle of Perote, 150 miles East of the City of Mexico on the Road to (80 miles off) Vera Cruz, Jan. 27, 1843, in Green, ed., *Samuel Maverick*, pp. 223-27.

64. Trueheart diary, Oct. 24, 1842.

65. Samuel A. Maverick to Mary A. Maverick, Castle of Perote, 150 miles East of the City of Mexico on the Road to (80 miles off) Vera Cruz, Jan. 27, 1843, in Green, ed., *Samuel Maverick*, pp. 223-27.

66. Hutchinson diary, Oct. 23, 1842.

67. A. Neill to Anson Jones, Washington, Texas, Jan. 29th, 1843, in Winkler, ed., "The Béxar and Dawson Prisoners," *QTSHA* 13 (Apr. 1910), p. 316.

68. Trueheart diary, Oct. 23, 1842.

On November 7 the prisoners were started south once more, this time under the command of Capt. Emeterio Posas, nicknamed by the Texans "Old Seguin" because he was always "*seganos*" [sigamos] them ("go ahead," "go along," "move along").[69] Posas, who had guarded the prisoners from San Antonio to the Rio Grande, was described as "an ignorant man who had risen from the ranks after near thirty years' service."[70]

The prisoners left the city accompanied for two or three miles by Doctors Knight and Hewetson. Their immediate guard of forty troops was commanded by Benito Cortéz, who marched them by way of Buena Vista, on October 8, to Hacienda de Agua Nueva, some twelve leagues below Saltillo. They were quartered on a porch fronting the main buildings of the *hacienda,* where they spent a miserably cold night. The soldiers were more fortunate, being billeted in a church attached to the *hacienda.* At Agua Nueva one of the prisoners was struck by a soldier and several others were threatened. They had no complaint against the officers of the guard on the march from Saltillo, reported one of the prisoners, "but the [Red Cap] soldiers were of the most insolent and villanous character, using every opportunity of maltreating us."[71]

On October 9 they started at an unusually early hour. The morning was cold, and the men walked briskly to keep warm. A mile and a half from the *hacienda* they entered Encarnación Pass, and at noon they arrived at a large sheep ranch, where they halted at a tank to rest. Continuing their journey through rugged terrain, they passed along the edge of the Saline Valley, and toward late afternoon arrived at the Hacienda de la Encarnación.[72] They found the water to be very salty, but some of the prisoners were able to obtain good water by paying a Mexican to bring it to them from a well.

The next day a Texan became ill and was left behind with a soldier. Although still sick, he rejoined the main body during the night of October 10 at El Rancho de San Salvador, where he found his comrades sleeping upon "cold bloody rocks where a beef had been killed and burned."[73] From the desolate area of San Salvador the prisoners were taken to the commodious Hacienda de Salado. During the day they passed a well dug where the corners of four departments—Coahuila, Nuevo León, Zacatecas, and San Luis Potosí—came together.

At Salado the Texans were housed in neatly whitewashed rooms, with good floors, of a *meson* [inn]; as at San Salvador, the water was salty. The next day those unable to walk because of sore feet were provided with burros. At the poor ranch of Las Animas it was found that only a few prison-

69. Trueheart diary, Nov. 1, 1842; Maverick diary, Nov. 4, 1842.

70. Hutchinson diary, Sept. 15, 1842.

71. Trueheart diary, Nov. 8, 1842.

72. *Ibid.,* Nov. 9, 1842.

73. Maverick diary, Nov. 10, 1842.

ers could be accommodated in the house picked for their quarters, so most of the men spent a miserable night camped in the cold.[74]

On Sunday, November 13, at three in the afternoon, they reached the beautiful Hacienda de San Juan de Vanegas, noted for its mineral waters, hot baths, and its extraction of silver from the ores taken from the nearby mines of Real de Catorce. Some prisoners visited the extracting works, and while out sought "the bath house and enjoyed the luxury of bathing."[75] They were provided with quarters and meals a little better than usual. They waited a day at Vanegas for the arrival of an infantry guard from San Luis Potosí to replace the one from Saltillo. The exchange was joyful news to the prisoners, who disliked their current guard.

The new guard was commanded by an officer who had been taken prisoner with General Cós at San Antonio in December 1835. He discussed with Captain Posas the need of keeping the Texan prisoners locked in the calaboose for the night, "but Posas stopped him in the middle of his harangue by telling him that he was in charge of us and would not do with us as requested," reported Trueheart, "as there was no occasion for it." As they renewed their march on October 15, the new guard boasted of being able to out-walk the Texan prisoners, but soon learned to the contrary, "there being more broken down soldiers than prisoners."[76]

They next stopped at Cedral, a town of some 5,000 population, ten miles below Vanegas, where silver ore was smeltered. At Cedral the natives brought large qunatities of various kinds of fruit, which they sold cheaply to the soldiers and to the prisoners. In Mexican newspapers they read Woll's report on the Battle of Salado. A mock trial was held before Judge Hutchinson to determine who would pay for a bottle of brandy. One of the Mexican women, taking pity upon some of the prisoners who had no money, gave fifteen of them one dollar.[77]

On October 17 at Hacienda Represada a woman who attended a small store entertained the Texans with guitar music "and other diversions,"[78] and one of the Texans presented those present with a bottle of liquor. When it had been consumed Captain Posas obtained another bottle for the party.

The next morning on the road they lost their way, but after retracing their steps discovered a pass in the mountains that led to the tableland above. By midday they reached the beautiful Hacienda de la Laguna Seca, devoted exclusively to raising horses—six to seven thousand of them.[79] They were quartered in a "stable, . . . soap house and chikaronmi [chichar-

---

74. Trueheart diary, Nov. 12, 1842.
75. *Ibid.*, Nov. 13, 1842.
76. *Ibid.*, Nov. 14, 1842.
77. Maverick diary, Nov. 16, 1842.
78. Trueheart diary, Nov. 17, 1842. Maverick reported: "Two gentlemen play and sing on guitar aided by two ladies," Maverick diary, Nov. 17, 1842.
79. Truehart diary, Nov. 18, 1842.

ron, crackling] house."[80] At Laguna Seca they were given a fat beef, and took advantage of their early arrival to prepare provisions for the next day's journey. As night descended it became cold and they requested transfer to another room, which proved to be warmer.

Saturday, November 19, the prisoners started at an early hour and had a long march before reaching a suitable stopping point. The weather was cold, and those who had mounts were glad to walk, leaving others to ride their horses or burros. In the middle of the afternoon, after a rapid march in an effort to keep warm, they arrived at Benado, a town of some 6,000 population, surrounded by numerous maguey and organ trees. They were quartered in a *meson* (tavern), where they were furnished fine rooms. From Matehuala to San Luis Potosí the water was tolerable. En route to Las Bocas the next day, they rested about thirty minutes at the *hacienda* and city of Hedionda, and arrived cold and tired after dark.[81] Because of the late arrival, many prisoners went to bed without supper. The captain apologized for traveling so late and promised not to do so in the future. On October 21 they spent the night at the Hacienda de Penasco, owned by the Count of Moras. The *hacienda* had many pretty pine trees and was situated at the junction of the Tampico and Saltillo roads to Mexico City. A march of fifteen miles the next day brought them to San Luis Potosí, a city of some 40,000 population, where they remained until October 25.

San Luis Potosí was situated in a wide valley, much of which was fertile and productive of wheat, barley, oats, and Indian corn. On entering the city, the prisoners were "paraded through every public street . . . as a show, followed by an immense crowd of people chiefly of the lower class," reported William E. Jones,[82] and were viewed by "a large collection of persons of almost every size, age, and complexion, all anxious to see the Texan prisoners."[83] After halting several times in the parade around the plaza, the prisoners were quartered in a military hospital and delivered over to a new guard. They were furnished beds from an adjoining apartment and provided with food.[84] On the following day, foreign residents of the city, principally Germans, called upon them and gave their fellow countrymen among the prisoners money, clothes, and other articles. San Luis Potosí was one of "the best-built cities in Mexico, regularly laid out, and with an air of cleanliness not common in a Mexican town," reported Kendall.[85]

From street vendors the prisoners purchased fruit, *frijoles, chili quisado,* and *tamales.* Two or three of the Texans were permitted to go out into the city, but stayed only a short time.

---

80. Maverick diary, Nov. 18, 1842.
81. *Ibid.,* Nov. 20, 1842.
82. [William E. Jones to M. B. Lamar], Washington, 1 Feby 1844, in Winkler, ed., "The Béxar and Dawson Prisoners," *QTSHA* 13 (Apr. 1910), p. 323; see also Trueheart diary, Nov. 22, 1842; Hutchinson diary, Nov. 22, 1842.
83. Trueheart diary, Nov. 21, 1842.
84. *Ibid.,* Nov. 22, 1842.
85. Kendall, *Narrative of the Texan Santa Fé Expedition* 2, p. 158.

During their two days in the city, the Texans were visited by Governor José Ignacio Gutiérrez and several other Mexicans of distinction. The governor promised to send blankets, which he did, and these were distributed to the most needy of the prisoners. An elderly Frenchman presented the Texans with four or five cases of ale, which, upon being distributed, quickly disappeared.

From San Luis Potosí, under a new guard commanded by Maj. José María Quijano, the march was resumed. The new commander told his soldiers, reported Trueheart, "that if they insult or mistreat the prisoners in any way," they would be severely punished.[86]

On October 26 they continued through the Valley of San Francisco, one of the most fertile in Mexico, to the Hacienda Jaral. From Cubo they passed where the Aztecs under Montezuma were defeated in the Battle of Ganalleras with heavy losses, and proceeded to the old Indian town of Dolores. During the day, many of the prisoners and guards became fatigued and scattered for several miles along the road. Before entering Dolores, the vanguard awaited the stragglers. When all had arrived, they entered the village about a half hour before sunset, and were "lodged in splendid quarters, the *meson* being the best we had stopped at," declared Trueheart.[87]

The next morning they started at an early hour, and at noon stopped briefly in a small village where those who wished to do so visited the ancient church of Atotonilco. The church possessed many sacred paintings and relics of the Mexican Revolution.

On October 29 they proceeded to the ancient city of San Miguel el Grande (or San Miguel de Allende), founded in 1543 as a bulwark against the hostile Chichimec Indians. Its inhabitants made saddle cloths and blankets. The Texan prisoners were quartered in good rooms at a *meson*, and during the afternoon and evening several were permitted to visit about the town.[88] Before setting out, they made out lists for shoes, but none could be obtained.[89] They were, however, able to procure oranges, nopals, and dried mutton.

On November 30 they proceeded to the Hacienda de la Santa Rosa, where they were assigned poor quarters in a lime house since the calaboose was full, and were badly fed. On December 1, they passed along a paved road, "out of repair,"[90] through a rich valley, and near midday, after ten miles, arrived at Querétaro, ten miles from Santa Rosa. As they prepared to enter the city, Major Quijano requested the prisoners to march in files of four abreast, as the governor would most likely come out to view them. "To please him," recorded one of the prisoners, "as he had been

---

86. Trueheart diary, Nov. 25, 1842.
87. *Ibid.*, Nov. 28, 1842.
88. *Ibid.*, Nov. 29, 1842.
89. Maverick diary, Nov. 29, 1842.
90. *Ibid.*, Dec. 1, 1842.

uniformly kind and obliging, we determined to use great care in marching with order."[91] As they passed through the streets of the city, they spied
Captain Posas, "who as soon as he sees us," remembered Trueheart, "crys
out, *'dos a dos'* ('two and two') affording us great mirth, he joining in the
sport."

The prisoners were taken to the Convent of Santa Cruz, a portion of
which had been converted for the garrisoning of troops, where they were
"provided with good quarters, the same that were occupied by the Santa
Fé prisoners" the year before.[92] Shortly after they arrived, fruit peddlers
appeared. At Querétaro, Hutchinson met Major Quijano and called on
Doña Catalina.[93] On December 2 several of the Texans were permitted to
go out to view the city; some bought clothing.[94] During the day, they were
visited at their quarters by a number of ladies who showed great interest
in their welfare.

From San Luis Potosí to the outskirts of Mexico City, the prisoners
passed through many splendid *haciendas,* "the entire grounds of which . . .
[were] enclosed by stone walls beautifully constructed. One enclosure was
said to contain 36 square miles."[95]

Near midday the prisoners reached Hacienda de Colorado and were
quartered in a granary, near where natives were treading out wheat. It
being Saturday night, they witnessed payment of "the natives [who] came
up to receive their week's pay—and rations—pay [of] a bit a day and
rations [of] an almud and a half of an almud."[96] From the Hacienda de
Colorado they continued to San Juan del Río, where there was a circus in
town; thence to Arroyo Seco on the Vera Cruz stage route, thirty miles
from San Juan del Río, and through the mountains to the Indian village
of Tula, twenty leagues from Mexico City.

San Juan del Río was the last town of any importance before reaching
Mexico City. At San Juan del Río on December 4, through the politeness
of Col. Gregorio González, Maverick "got out of the mail a letter from
Genl. Thompson[97] which was directed to [him at] San Luis Potosí," which
they already had passed. Thompson explained that he had made a request for Maverick's "liberation as that of a relation and for Wm. E. Jones,
Esq., as a personal friend."[98] The remainder of the prisoners received lit-

---

91. Trueheart diary, Dec. 1, 1842.

92. *Ibid.*

93. Hutchinson diary, Dec. 1, 1842.

94. Trueheart diary, Dec. 2, 1842.

95. [William E. Jones to M. B. Lamar], Washington, 1 Feby 1844, in Winkler, ed., "The
Béxar and Dawson Prisoners," *QTSHA* 13 (Apr. 1910), p. 323.

96. Hutchinson diary, Dec. 3, 1842. A "bit" was 12 1/2 cents; an "almud" was a measure of grain amounting to 8/10ths of a liter, or approximately .84536 of a U.S. liquid
quart.

97. Waddy Thompson to Samuel A. Maverick, Saint Luis Potosí [dated] Mexico, Nov.
19, 1842, in Green, ed., *Samuel Maverick,* pp. 207-8.

98. Samuel A. Maverick to Mary A. Maverick, Castle of Perote, 150 miles East of the
City of Mexico on the Road to (80 miles off) Vera Cruz, Jan. 27, 1843, in Green, ed.,
Samuel Maverick, pp. 223-27; see also Trueheart diary, Dec. 4, 1842.

tle consolation from Thompson's statement that he "could not ask for any more of your companions but will [do so] at a fitting time on that matter." There seemed little grounds for hope since Gen. Nicolás Bravo, the acting president, was "the open and avowed enemy of the Anglo-Americans," and had, "on more than one occasion, expressed his hostility to those adventurers whom he believes" were "constantly endeavoring to conquer the country. The recent inroad of our army [under Somervell], and its disgraceful retreat," declared editor Moore of the *Telegraph*,[99] "will serve still further to excite his hatred, and, perhaps to induce him to exercise his power to inflict a summary punishment upon these helpless captives."

From San Juan del Río they proceeded thirty miles to Arroyo Seco on December 5.[100] At Arroyo Seco the prisoners were put up for the night in miserable quarters and received poor fare. The stage between Vera Cruz, Zacatecas, and Mexico City was operated by Americans.[101]

The following day they reached Tula, passing the high gap in the mountains of Chapulalpa, considered to be the highest point between the Rio Grande and the City of Mexico. Their route took them through a series of red hills thick with oak and pine trees. Several villages and a tank of water were at the foot of the mountains. "White tunas, Indians and pulque [were] everywhere."[102] As they approached the city, they passed "a splendid mill" operated by water power.

During their stay in Tula, several of the Texans were permitted to roam about the town. Maverick enjoyed the good fortune of dining with Don Eduardo Rodríguez, Col. Gregorio González, Colonel Durán, the local priest, and several other notables. Having the opportunity to send letters to Mexico City, the prisoners sent off a memorial prepared by Judge Hutchinson and Andrew Neill from Tula to Acting President Nicolás Bravo requesting their release and asking that they "might be allowed to enter Mexico [City] to set forth to the nation the nature and cause of their capture and [be] not sent to a distant prison, in a cold and uncharitable climate," and that they "might have communication with . . . friends through the foreigners of the city."[103] The memorial was conveyed to the capital by Col. Gregorio Gonzáles and delivered to Señor del Llano. Their petition seems to have gone either "unheeded or neglected."[104]

After five days at Tula awaiting the arrival of a new guard, the prisoners were informed that their point of destination had been changed.

99. Jan. 18, 1843,

100. Maverick diary, Dec. 5, 1842.

101. Trueheart diary, Dec. 5, 1842.

102. Maverick diary, Dec. 6, 1842.

103. A. Neill to Anson Jones, Washington, Texas, Jany 24th, 1843, in Winkler, ed., "The Béxar and Dawson Prisoners," *QTSHA* 13 (Apr. 1910), p. 316; Trueheart Diary, Dec. 14, 1842.

104. A. Neill to Anson Jones, Washington, Texas, Jan. 29, 1843, in Winkler, ed., "The Béxar and Dawson Prisoners," *QTSHA* 13 (Apr. 1910), p. 316; see also Hutchinson diary, Dec. 10, 1842.

They would not go to Mexico City, but "to that most desolated and dilapidated [place], the Castle of Perote."[105] The change of destination became
"a matter of repeated and lengthy conversation." Their journey was renewed on December 11. At four in the afternoon, after going thirty miles,
they reached Huehuetoca and were lodged in comfortable quarters at a
meson. Captain Madrid ordered each prisoner to be given the government's daily allowance of two-bits *(dos reales),* out of which those who
desired could hire burros, or, in lieu of the allowance, he would furnish
them everything necessary for their march. During the evening eight or
ten of the Texans were permitted to go out into the town without the usual
guard to view the celebration "of the eve of the Santa Guadalupe," the
patron saint of Mexico.[106]

On December 12 the prisoners passed through a valley to Cuantitlán,
eight leagues from the City of Mexico, where they were lodged in a *meson*
and provided good rooms. The lieutenant was sent to Mexico City for the
necessary money to pay the prisoners their daily allowance. In the meantime, the prisoners were visited by Captain Posas, who was on his way to
Mexico City. From Cuantitlán they had their "first view of the snow mountains."[107]

On December 13 the Texans left the main road to Mexico City and
turned into the Puebla Road toward San Cristóbal de Ecatepec, which lay
between lakes Cristóbal and Tezcoco, some twelve miles northeast of Mexico City. Near midday they reached San Cristóbal with its celebrated lake
and great bridge. They were within sight of the volcanic peaks of Popo-
catépete and San Martín, covered with snow. The view was splendid in
spite of the cold weather. "Maguey farms and pulque [were] everywhere."[108]

They spent the night at San Cristóbal in the schoolhouse. A few of the
prisoners were "permitted to sleep in one of the rooms attached to the
church." The prisoners were permitted to go out into the community in
parties of eight or ten. "Our commander grants us many privileges and
permits us to act as we wish," reported Trueheart.[109]

The next day they crossed a large bridge and headed across the
Valley of Mexico, parallel to the stone dam on the other side of the valley.
In the distance they could see the City of Mexico. In the evening of December 14, while the prisoners were at San Juan de Tehuacán, they were
permitted, as on the previous night at San Cristóbal, to roam about the
town in parties of ten or twelve, "sometimes with one soldier as a guard

105. Trueheart diary, Dec. 6, 1842; see also A. Neill to Anson Jones, Washington,
Texas, Jan. 29, 1843, in Winkler, ed., "The Béxar and Dawson Prisoners," *QTSHA* 13 (Apr.
1910), p. 316; Hutchinson diary, Dec. 10, 1842.
106. Trueheart diary, Dec. 11, 1842.
107. Hutchinson diary, Dec. 12, 1842.
108. Maverick diary, Dec. 13, 1842.
109. Trueheart diary, Dec. 13, 1842.

and sometimes none" to purchase provisions.[110] Early in the evening, Colonel Neill, bidding his captain "farwell," took advantage of an opportunity to take "French leave" from his party and the next morning was in Mexico City. Having money enough for three or four days, he stopped at a hotel for several days to recuperate. He "shaved off a large pair of whiskers and otherwise disguised himself." His escape was not discovered by the guard at Tehuacán until early the next morning, causing a delay of several hours in the march of the other prisoners.[111]

When Neill's absence was discovered, Captain Madrid sent an express to Mexico City to apprise the authorities and placed restrictions on the other Texas prisoners, but told them "that he was sorry that he was obliged to abridge our liberties," recorded Trueheart; "he does not get angry and abuse us, but preserves his temper and appears to be obliging and accommodating as ever. We are all much pleased with the manner with which he deported himself."[112]

On his second evening in Mexico City, Neill ventured out of the hotel to search for a particular street. The next evening he again searched for a house on that street, entered, and was embraced by his friend, who concealed him for two weeks. He then took the stage for Vera Cruz under an assumed name and even stopped for a night in the town of Perote, where he learned of his own escape, saw some of his companions in chains, and learned that they had been set to work on January 2.[113] In Vera Cruz, he was concealed on board a vessel until another was ready to take him to Havana. His safety was made known to his comrades at Perote Castle on March 2 by Lt. H. A. Hartstene, dispatch bearer from Commodore Jones of the Pacific Squadron.[114] From Havana, Neill went by way of Key West and Pensacola to New Orleans,[115] and through New Orleans newspapers brought to Perote Castle on February 13 the prisoners learned of the safe arrival of their comrade.[116]

Neill reached Houston aboard the *Dayton* on Sunday evening, January 22, 1843, and reported "that the treatment of the Texian captives gradually became more and more severe and cruel as they retired from their own borders."[117] He was confident that an army of 1,000 Texans could conquer all of northern Mexico to the mountains in a few weeks, "and we would scarcely meet with serious opposition." Neill believed that

---

110. Trueheart diary, Dec. 14, 1842; Maverick diary, Dec. 14, 1842; A. Neill to Anson Jones, Washington, Texas, Jan. 29, 1843, in Winkler, ed., "The Béxar and Dawson Prisoners," *QTSHA* 13 (Apr. 1910), pp. 316-17.

111. Andrew Neill's report of his escape is given in the *Daily Picayune*, Jan. 13, 1843, and in the *New Orleans Bulletin*.

112. Trueheart diary, Dec. 14, 1842.

113. A. Neill to Anson Jones, Washington, Texas, Jan. 29, in Winkler, ed., "The Béxar and Dawson Prisoners," *QTSHA* 13 (Apr. 1910), p. 317.

114. Trueheart diary, Mar. 2, 1843.

115. *Daily Picayune*, Jan. 13, 1843, reports Neill's arrival in New Orleans.

116. Hutchinson diary, Feb. 13, 1843.

117. *Morning Star*, Feb. 18, 1843.

"we can never expect to release our citizens in bondage, unless we invade those provinces and compel the Mexican government to yield to our demands," reported the editor of the *Morning Star*.[118] Neill reported that fifty-five Texans were imprisoned at Perote Castle, but he listed the names of only forty-two of the San Antonio prisoners, omitting the names of Capt. Chauncey Johnson, H. A. Alsbury, and George C. Hatch. Thomas Hancock, Archibald Fitzgerald, and George Van Ness, who were still at San Fernando as former Santa Fé prisoners, under penalty to be shot; and Simon Glenn and Samuel Norvell had been left ill at San Luis Potosí and Querétaro. Neill thus accounted for all of the San Antonio prisoners marched from Béxar. He made no mention of the Dawson captives.

From San Juan de Tehuacán, the route of the San Antonio-Dawson prisoners continued through the villages of Chalpulalpán, San Martín, Puebla de los Angeles, Acajete, Cuapeseda, and Tepiohualela to Perote Castle, which they reached in the afternoon of Thursday, December 22, 1842, in the face of a "fierce norther."[119]

Their long journey had come to an end. About three in the afternoon of December 22, the day that Fisher's men first entered Mier, the Béxar-Dawson prisoners reached Perote Castle, where they were formed in the courtyard of the fortress in the presence of the governor and placed in his custody. They were marched to two large rooms and locked up for an hour or two. The "common herd" Texans were lodged in Cell No. 10, and a small group of "well-off" or "Aristocrats," primarily military and civil officers, except Samuel A. Maverick, who preferred to be with the less pretentious members, was placed in Cell No. 9. It was customary for the Mexican officers to keep the leaders separate in prison from the rank and file. The cells adjoined in the east wing of the castle.

After an hour or so, the cell doors were unlocked and the men were permitted to go out to buy provisions at the small store in the castle maintained by Don Francisco, "a superannuated lieutenant. The old man was a dried-up octogenarian, who had served under Napoleon in Italy. He occasionally looked after our men at work, and was not a bad man," reported Green.[120]

---

118. Jan. 24, 1843.
119. Trueheart, Maverick, and Hutchinson diaries.
120. Green, *Mier Expedition*, p. 276.

CHAPTER 9

The Béxar Prisoners Protest
Their Treatment and The
Santa Anna-Robinson Proposals

WHEN THE FIRST CONTINGENT of Texan prisoners arrived at Perote Castle, the Mexican officers there included Gen. José M. Duran, governor, commandant of the fort, and commander of the Fourth Infantry Regiment, who owned an estate near Jalapa;[1] Capt. Isidro Pombo, the mayor de Plaza and second-in-command and called by the Texans *"limpin' Jesus,"* because he had a wooden leg;[2] Captains Bonilla, José Piñeda, Angel de Campo, Petronilo Zicontencalt, José María Díaz de Guzmán— "Old Guts" to the Texans—and Lieutenants García, Unkatanka, and "Old" Dejalor Ventura; and Ensigns Mara and Castro.

For the first four or five days the prisoners were allowed to roam about the castle, and on Christmas Day each was given two small cakes of soap and a drink of eggnog.[3] Trueheart and seven or eight others were permitted to go into the town where they passed the day quietly.[4]

On December 28, after dinner, the prisoners were ordered into formation and told they were to be chained two and two by the legs and that each should select his companion.[5] They were marched in pairs to the blacksmith shop for ironing. Wilson I. Riddle and William E. Jones were chained together, and John Riddle and John Twohig were partners in chains.[6] Hutchinson was chained to French Strother Gray, but two days later their chains were severed.[7] The Texas carpenters, whom the officers intended to work at their trade, were not chained. Those who acted as

---

1. Trueheart diary, May 10, 1843. From April 29 to May 10, 1843, General Duran was absent from the castle at his *hacienda*, and Col. Rafael Hernández was in charge of the fortress.

2. Green, *Mier Expedition*, pp. 267-68.

3. [William E. Jones to M. B. Lamar], Washington, 1 Feby. 1844, in Winkler, ed., "The Béxar and Dawson Prisoners," *QTSHA* 13, p. 323.

4. Trueheart diary, Dec. 26, 1842.

5. Hutchinson diary, Dec. 28, 1842.

6. Barnes, "Houses with Histories," in *San Antonio Express,* Feb. 9, 1908.

7. Hutchinson diary, Dec. 30, 1842.

interpreters, and a few others, such as Trueheart, who "messed and slept with the interpreter," were chained alone.[8] The prisoners were usually chained with a crude iron band attached to the right ankle of one man and another to the left ankle of his partner, with the two bands connected by a chain eight feet long and weighing twenty pounds.[9] While the men were chained they were searched and deprived of all ropes and nails.

Being chained to another was an uncomfortable experience, and "unpleasant in the day time, but much more so in the night (chains being rather cold bedfellows)."[10] Many ingenious ways of removing the chains developed. The Mexicans never succeeded in fashioning chains and rivets that could not be broken, cut, manipulated, or removed; and dire threats of punishment, blows, or solitary confinement were ineffective deterrents to the Texan prisoners, whose spirit of independence and contempt of the Mexicans could not be squelched. The Texans bitterly resented having to wear irons, or "jewels" as they termed them, not only because of the inconvenience and humiliation, but also because they were the distinguishing marks of a criminal; they regarded themselves as soldiers who had the misfortune to become "prisoners of war."

Although Santa Anna was once a prisoner in Texas and had been chained, he had not been forced to work. But the proud spirit of a Castillian soldier and the head of a nation had been humbled and there was no reason, in his mind, why the Texans should not feel the pinch of chains and be forced to perform manual labor for having defied the laws of Mexico.

Within a week many of the chains were secretly and even openly shed by the prisoners. Sometimes, when a man could no longer bear the weight of the heavy chain on his inflamed ankle, he would boldly cut the chain loose at night and leave it on the floor of his cell or fearlessly cast it into the street or courtyard. Many contemptuously freed themselves completely from their chains when not in the presence of a guard. They learned that the blacksmith could be bribed to give them a large ring so that they could slip it off, or to use lead rivets instead of iron ones which could be removed, reinserted, and reheaded. When blackened with charcoal, the lead rivet gave the appearance of being an iron one. A lead rivet could be acquired for one *medio*.[11] After many hassles with unchained Texans, "Old Guts" finally told the governor "that it would require as many blacksmiths to keep us ironed as there were Texans in the castle."

Whenever the men heard the key in the lock of their cell door, they jumped to their chains and adjusted them about their ankles; as soon as the officer left the room, the chains were dropped again.[12] It was the de-

---

8. Trueheart diary, Dec. 26, 1842.

9. Green, *Mier Expedition*, p. 244.

10. Edward Manton to Uncle Edward ———, Peroty (Mexico), Jan. 1, 1843, in Weyand and Wade, *An Early History of Fayette County*, pp. 22-24.

11. A *medio* was one-half of a *real* or six and one-fourth cents in United States money.

12. Nance, ed., *McCutchan's Narrative*, p. 123.

light of "Old Guts," or more appropriately Captain Guzmán, and a few of the officers to enter the cells suddenly and unexpectedly, hoping to catch the Texans performing some illegal act. The unjeweled Texans would jump to their irons and clamp them on with "a magic celerity which entirely bewildered the senses of the officers, and then as suddenly put on a demure inoffensive countenance."[13] If an individual got caught, the offender usually was punished by beatings or sword cuts and cudgel blows across the head by an enraged officer, and then double-ironed and thrown into the dungeon by a standing order of the governor.

On April 4, 1843, the day after Maverick and his two companions had left for Vera Cruz, the chains of the San Antonio prisoners and of Fisher's party, when they arrived later, were carefully examined. Finding some of them badly in need of repair, the guard ordered the prisoners to the blacksmith shop. "This did but little good," reported one of the prisoners a few days later, for "before the last was fast the first was loos[e]."[14]

The New Year brought no joy to Texans confined in Mexican prisons. Sunday, January 1, 1843, at Perote Castle was a "sad day—cold—and clear," for the Béxar-Dawson prisoners.[15] The men desperately needed clothes, blankets, shoes, coats, and hats.[16] Edward Manton found himself in need of clothing and wrote on January 1 to his uncle in Rhode Island. He reported that everything he possessed had been taken from him at the battlefield near Salado Creek where he had surrendered as a member of Dawson's command. "There were some of us," he wrote, "who were thinly clad that suffered from the cold, myself for one not having anything but one pair of thin pantaloons, shirt, hat, and shoes, which are now so far gone that it is with difficulty that I can keep them together. . . . My clothes are so rotten and threadbare that they will hardly undergo the operation of getting off and on. . . . On the road I had an old roundabout and a small thin blanket given to me without which I don't know what I should have done, suffereing from the cold more than I ever did before. This [Perote] is said to be one of the coldest places in Mexico."[17] Then he said, "We are as lousy as we can be, make a regular business every day to pull off our shirts and kill them. While I write my companion [Nathaniel W. Faison] whom I am chained to is sitting by me lousing himself." He ended by requesting his uncle send $150 which he needed to buy necessities and get out of the country if they should be liberated.

---

13. Green, *Mier Expedition*, p. 246.

14. [Richard A. Barkley] to Woodses, Harrell[s], Robinsons, Willson Kenady, Broosher and Others, Castle of Perote and Strange [land], April 10, 1843, in Spellman, ed., "Letters of the 'Dawson Men,'" *SWHQ* 38 (Apr. 1935), pp. 249-51; Bell, *Narrative*, p. 80.

15. Extract of a letter from Edward Manton to [Uncle] Edward ———, Peroty (Mexico), Jan. 1, 1843, in D. C. Jenckes to A. A. Gardenier, Lime Rock, R.I., Feby 19th 1843, in Edward Manton Papers, TxU-A.

16. Weyand and Wade, *An Early History of Fayette County*, p. 24.

17. Extract of a letter of Edward Manton to [Uncle] Edward ———, Peroty (Mexico), Jan. 1, 1843, in D. C. Jenckes to A. A. Gardenier, Lime Rock, R.I., Feby 19, 1843, in Edward Manton Papers, TxU-A.

The San Antonio-Dawson prisoners and the Mier officers who joined them seem to have enjoyed better treatment than those assigned to work at Tacubaya. On January 1, 1843, Edward Manton informed his uncle in Rhode Island, we "eat all we can get and would be glad to get more. Our breakfast consists of a piece of bread about the size of one of your biscuits, at dinner 2 pieces, a saucer of boiled potatoes, and the broth with onions and red pepper in it and another saucer of rice, at night a saucer of beans and then comes on lock-up hour until morning. We then have liberty of the yard during the day which enables those who have money to live quite well, there being a store inside where bread and many other things can be bought, fruit is very cheap, 12 oranges for 6 cents."

"We are allowed to go where we please inside the outer wall during the day," reported Chauncey Johnson on June 8, 1843. "Every room and the pavements are swept early each morning by Mexican prisoners. Coffee is furnished us twice a day, with plenty of good bread. Beans, rice, potatoes and beef are also given us; but beef of a good quality is not to be had in this part of the country," he wrote.[18]

Those who remained at the Santiago hospital and prison in Mexico City when the men at Tacubaya were moved to Perote Castle were believed to be better off than those at Perote Prison or those held at the castle of San Juan de Ulúa. The degree of treatment varied, and was dependent on the Mexican officers and soldiers responsible for their security and welfare. In July 1843, Trueheart was of the opinion that the prisoners of Mexico City were treated better than those at Perote Castle, since many were reported exempt from chains and not closely guarded, for there had been four escapes.

Despite the pledge of Woll in San Antonio that they would be treated well, shortly after their arrival at Perote Castle the Texan prisoners were informed by Capt. José María Díaz de Guzmán, "who could be Exceedingly civil at times,"[19] that they must prepare to go to work in a few days to offset the nation's expenses for their care. Lt. Henry J. Hartstene[20] of the United States Navy, on his way to the United States bearing dispatches from Commodore Thomas ap Catesby Jones of the Pacific Squadron and Waddy Thompson, visited the Texan prisoners at Perote on December 30 and afterwards sent them $50 from Vera Cruz.[21] When he arrived at Charleston, South Carolina, he reported the prisoners to be in good health and spirits, but "badly clad & chained two and two together" and

---

18. Chauncey Johnson to the Editors of the *Picayune*, Castle of Perote, June 8, 1843, in *Daily Picayune*, July 13, 1843.

19. Green, *Mier Expedition*, p. 244.

20. Lt. Hartstene sailed from Monterey, California, on November 22 aboard the *USS Yorktown*; landed on the coast of Mexico at San Blas on December 7, and traveled wearing the uniform of the United States Navy and was well-treated. *Daily Picayune*, Jan. 13, 1843.

21. Trueheart diary, Dec. 31, 1842.

that they had been scheduled to be put to work on the streets the following Monday morning, January 2,[22] after his visit at Perote Castle.

On January 5 Maverick was placed in solitary confinement for several days because he told Guzmán "that we were not of right in the condition of slaves: that the slavish labor exacted from us at the point of the bayonet, was in violation of the laws and usages of nations, and [was] directly opposed to the express terms of our surrender, and moreover, that, if it was determined, in our case to violate all law and compacts, all justice and mercy, all public faith and private honor, even then it still remained and was a physical impossibility and high treason against God and Nature to require and exact from us labor without sufficient food."[23]

It was not until January 6, 1843, however, that some of the men were ordered out to work.[24] When they were first informed that they were to be put to work, "there was scarcely one who would believe it."[25] The Béxar-Dawson prisoners contended that they had surrendered on conditions "that our lives should [be spared] and property (arms [excepted]) should be respected and that we should be kindly and human[e]ly treated; not as prisoners of war but as gentlemen."[26] They "did not relish" the idea of working and there was some talk of refusing to do so, but since there was no "unanimity of opinion and concert of action" among the prisoners, the idea was abandoned.[27]

On January 7, Judge Hutchinson was accorded a "Gentlemen's" assignment in charge of ten Texans assigned to carry out manure in a dump cart and to bring in sand, stone, lime, and other items. At the end of the day, Hutchinson "treated" the detail on their return,[28] but he does not say to what he treated them, presumably to a little *aguardiente* (brandy). On January 11 Hutchinson recorded that "six of us [are] compelled to work as oxen in a tumbel, carrying out dung and bringing in sand and rocks."[29] "We are treated precisely as the most degraded felons in the prison," complained Wilson Riddle to the British minister, "fed in the same way, chained in the same manner—and driven to work side by side with convict murderers and thieves!"[30] But, "the abstemousness that

22. D. C. Jenckes to A. A. Garinier, Lime Rock, R.I., Feby. 19, 1843, in Edward Manton Papers, TxU-A.

23. S. A. Maverick to José María Bocanegra, Secretary of State and Foreign Affairs, &c., Perote (fort and prison), 21st January 1843, in "Extension of Remarks of Hon. Maury Maverick of Texas in the House of Representatives, Monday, March 28, 1938" (an undelivered letter), *Congressional Record*, 75th Cong., 3rd Sess., Appendix, Vol. 83, Pt. 10 (Mar. 28, 1938-June 1, 1938), pp. 1199-1202.

24. Samuel Maverick to Mrs. Mary A. Maverick, Pendleton, So. Carolina, Feb. 15, 1843, in Green, ed., *Samuel Maverick*, pp. 229-32.

25. Trueheart diary, Dec. 26, 1842.

26. *Ibid.*, Sept. 11, 1842.

27. *Ibid.*, Jan. 4, 1843.

28. Hutchinson diary, Jan. 7, 1843.

29. *Ibid.*, Jan. 11, 1843.

30. Wilson I. Riddle to R. Pakenham, Castle of Perote, 24 Jany. 1842 [1843], in *Texana* 5 (Winter 1967), pp. 380-83.

we have forced upon us," declared Maverick, "with the exercise attendant on our labor, has had the happy effect of making me heartier than I have been since we were first acquainted," he wrote on March 15 to his wife: "I expect to be liberated before many days, say a week or two—these are *'poco tiempo'* people."[31]

Reports were afloat on January 27, 1843, that when the 240 prisoners taken at Mier reached Mexico City, they would be "detained to work upon a new road cutting from this city [Mexico] to Acapulco on the Pacific," and that the Texan "prisoners now at Perote" would "also be employed on this national road."[32] A new flagstaff was erected with the assistance of the Texan prisoners. The erection of the new pole has become a part of the folklore associated with the Mier Expedition and the Mexican War. It has been erroneously stated that when erecting the new staff, Samuel H. Walker spit on a ten-cent piece, some say a picayune, and slapped it on the bottom of the pole as it was lowered into the hole. Turning to the Mexican supervisors, he reportedly said in broken Spanish that he "will yet see the American banner wave over this castle."[33] To this the Mexicans gave a hearty laugh. During the war between the United States and Mexico, so goes the story, when General Gaona was ordered by Gen. Valentín Canalizo to abandon Perote Castle on April 22, 1847, Walker was stationed by Gen. Winfield Scott at the fortress with two companies of Rangers to keep the road open between Perote and Jalapa. According to legend, Walker retrieved his coin from the base of the flagstaff by having Mexican prisoners pull up the pole. Word spread along the road from Perote to Mexico City for guerrillas and robbers to take warning "for the renowned Capt. Samuel H. Walker takes no prisoners."[34] In truth, Walker was never imprisoned at Perote Castle. No eyewitness recorder of the events of 1842-44 has mentioned any Texan placing a coin at the base of a flagpole.

News of the capture of Monterey, California, by Commodore Thomas ap Catesby Jones on October 20, 1842, and of Somervell's attack upon the Rio Grande frontier "tended to render the Mexicans more exasperated against the prisoners and induced them to treat the poor fellows with extreme rigor."[35] One of the prisoners wrote to his brothers in Texas, presumably late in January or early in February 1843, that "the treatment of the captives . . . is intolerably severe," and he advised them, reported the *Telegraph* and *Texas Register,* that "if they should ever be engaged in another combat with Mexicans, never to surrender; for death is preferable to

31. Samuel A. Maverick to Mary A. Maverick, Castle of Perote, March 15, 1843, in Green, ed., *Samuel Maverick,* pp. 234-38.

32. Report from the City of Mexico, Jan. 27, 1843, from the *Western Advocate* (Austin) reprinted in the *Morning Star,* May 2, 1843, and *Telegraph and Texas Register,* May 3, 1843.

33. J. Jacob Soswandel, *Notes on the Mexican War, 1846-47-48,* pp. 171-72, 176-78, 182; story repeated in Webb, *The Texas Rangers,* p. 116.

34. Soswandel, *Notes on the Mexican War,* pp. 171-72.

35. *Daily Picayune,* Jan. 13, 1843, *Niles' National Register,* Jan. 28, 1843.

the insults and cruelties which are inflicted by the Mexicans upon their captives." Yet, commented the editor, "this gentleman, when at Béxar, and during the parley, was among the foremost to advocate a surrender, he felt so confident that the pledges of Gen. Woll would be fulfilled, and he considered it not only unnecessary to continue the fight, but criminal, because many might be killed on both sides, without effecting any beneficial object to either. But, he now bitterly laments his error, and wishes they had fought on."[36]

As soon as Waddy Thompson, United States minister plenipotentiary and envoy extraordinary, learned of the capture of his relative and others at San Antonio, he attempted to see José María de Bocanegra, but the minister of foreign relations was out of his office on November 19, 1842, so Thompson left a message requesting the release of his relative, Samuel A. Maverick, and William E. Jones, of Georgia, a close personal friend, as a "Personal favor."[37]

While Thompson had sympathy for the Texans, he could do little officially. His position was always a difficult one. On the one hand, there were the claims of humanity and a desire to assure the prisoners of the treatment to which they were entitled under international law. On the other hand he had the responsibility of "discharging the duties of the Representative of a Neutral Nation, and . . . of not seeming to espouse the cause of Texas."[38] He had received no instructions from his government on the matter of the current Texan prisoners in Mexican hands, but the expected attitude of the United States might be gauged from the position it had taken in respect to the Santa Fé prisoners the year before. The Texan representative in Washington had requested the good offices of the United States in getting the Santa Fé prisoners released. Secretary of State Daniel Webster had sent instructions to Powhatan Ellis, U.S. minister in Mexico, to procure the release of the citizens of the United States and to say to the Mexican government that undue punishment of the Texans in their custody would be more apt to defeat the object of that punishment than if the offenders were to have a fair trial, and that harsh treatment of them would excite and foment in the United States a bitterness of feeling prejudicial to Mexico. Thompson was instructed by Webster on February 26, 1842, to remonstrate "against any cruel and improper treatment of the Texan prisoners." Thompson visited General Tornel, minister of war and marine, to discuss the Santa Fé prisoners and communicate "the just and humane views of our Government." Tornel said he would look into the complaints made in letters sent by the prisoners at Perote Castle and

36. *Telegraph and Texas Register*, Feb. 22, 1843.

37. Waddy Thompson to Samuel A. Maverick, [at] San Luis Potosí, [dated] Mexico, Nov. 19, 1842, in Green, ed., *Samuel Maverick*, pp. 207-08.

38. Waddy Thompson to Daniel Webster, Legation of the U. S. of A., Mexico, 20th June 1842, in Despatches from U. S. Ministers to Mexico (Mar. 12, 1842-Mar. 25, 1844), National Archives (microfilm).

Puebla to Thompson complaining of ill-treatment, "but that Mr. Webster was mistaken in supposing that . . . [the] prisoners were entitled to rights of prisoners of War." Thompson told the Mexican minister of war that he was wrong in his conclusion, because Texas was a nation recognized by several governments and Mexico had not in six years made a serious effort to reconquer it.

In matters relating to Texas and Texan prisoners, Thompson found that whoever was at the head of the Mexican government held power "so insecurely that the Foreign Relations, even, of the Country" were "conducted mainly with a view to domestick politicks. I have not changed the opinion I heretofore expressed to you," he told Webster, "& before the liberation of the Texan [Santa Fé] prisoners that this movement of apparent menace fierceness was intended to satisfy the Mexicans with that act." Their strong language in the press against the United States was intended mainly for home consumption, and "forbearance to them is the course . . . [best] prescribed by a just regard for our own National character." When he sought to show the concern of his government for the Béxar-Dawson-Mier prisoners and to seek an amelioration of their condition, he found that the attitude of the Mexican government had not changed.

After contacting the foreign ministry, Thompson informed Maverick that he believed that he could not ask for the release of more of the prisoners at that time, but that he would do so at a more fitting date.[39] Thompson promised to send United States and Texas newspapers to Maverick whenever he received them and urged Maverick to draw on him for money he needed. "I have been badly treated by Texas as well as by those [Santa Fé prisoners] who have been released," he wrote, "but that in no way diminishes the interest I feel in your behalf. I have written to your father, & inclose him your letter." In conclusion, he wrote: "I have no doubt you will all be soon released so bear up."

Three weeks later Thompson wrote Maverick that on December 10 he had called on Bocanegra and renewed his request for the release of Maverick and Jones as a personal favor to him, and that Bocanegra had promised to use his influence with the president. "I do not doubt that it will be done. I can not say exactly when; I think before long."[40] He also requested Bocanegra, in the event Maverick could not be released, to have him sent to Mexico City. When after a week there had been no answer, he again wrote to Maverick: "I can not calculate on this government about anything. But when St. Anna comes [to the capital], and he is expected, I think I shall be able to procure your release. I shall go home in March and if you are not released before [then], he cannot refuse to release you to me

39. Waddy Thompson to Samuel A. Maverick, [at] San Luis Potosí, [dated] Mexico, Nov. 19, 1842, in Green, ed., *Samuel Maverick*, pp. 207-08.

40. Waddy Thompson to Samuel A. Maverick, [at] Perote, [dated] Mexico, Dec. 12, 1842, in Green, ed., *Samuel Maverick*, p. 208.

as a favor."[41] Thus, by December 30 Maverick had received three letters from his cousin, the U.S. minister, detailing his efforts to free him.[42]

Maverick assured his cousin that he felt "a weight of gratitude suited to the immense sympathy and service you have so kindly extended to me in my abject situation. When I speak of my situation as deplorable," he continued, "I do not allude to the chains, labor & starvation of this Hell, but I speak in reference to my wife & children and then my adopted and suffering country." He thanked Thompson for the offer of money, but was happy to report that "there is one Texian who does not stand in need of such assistance. But if I should run out, I will make free to let you know it."[43]

Early in January 1843, Thompson made an effort through Louis S. Hargous, the U.S. vice-consul at Vera Cruz and brother-in-law of Ignacio Trigueres, the minister of finance,[44] to reach Santa Anna at his *hacienda* to request, in Thompson's name and as a personal favor, to release Maverick and Jones and Judge Hutchinson, "a gentleman of 60 years old, and who probably never fired a gun in his life."[45] Hargous replied on January 19 that Santa Anna told Trigueres to show the United States minister the friendly disposition that he held for him and to assure him "that he would give the order for the liberation of the three prisoners, . . . but that for political reasons he could not do so immediately, but it would be very shortly." The "political reasons" centered around reports of the recent seizure of California by U.S. forces, the invasion of Mexico's northern frontier by Somervell, and the Battle of Mier, which had rendered the Mexicans "more exasperated than ever against the prisoners" and had "induced them to treat the poor fellows with extreme rigor." The *Daily Picayune* reported, "The utmost severity the Mexicans can exercise toward these men, according to the usages of all civilized nations, is to treat them as prisoners of war; and we even doubt if they can be long held even as prisoners. . . . We doubt not that foreign governments will look into this matter, and we cannot but believe that Santa Anna will be informed that other than humane treatment will not be tolerated towards these men."[46]

As time passed, Maverick became more impatient. On January 21 he wrote a lengthy, disorganized, and impolitic letter to Bocanegra, but had

41. Waddy Thompson to Samuel A. Maverick, Mexico, Dec. 20, 1842, in Green, ed., *Samuel Maverick*, p. 210.

42. S. A. Maverick to Mary A. Maverick, Perote, Dec. 30, 1842, in Green, ed., *Samuel Maverick*, p. 210.

43. S. A. Maverick to Gen. Waddy Thompson, Castle of Perote, Dec. 5 [Jan. 5], '43, facsimile of first page of letter (with extracts) in *San Antonio Express*, Sept. 15, 1912.

44. Ben E. Green to A. P. Upshur, Legation of the U.S. of A., Mexico, Nov. 25, 1843, in Despatches from the United States Ministers to Mexico (Mar. 12, 1842-Mar. 25, 1844), National Archives (microfilm).

45. Waddy Thompson to Provisional President of the Mexican Republic, Mexico, March 12, 1843 (copy); Thompson to Daniel Webster, Legation of the United States of America, Mar. 14, 1843, in Despatches from the United States Ministers to Mexico (Mar. 12, 1842-Mar. 25, 1844), National Archives (microfilm).

46. *Daily Picayune*, Jan. 13, 1843.

the good sense to send it through Thompson for transmittal. He described the circumstances under which he and others had fallen captives to Woll on September 11 of the preceding year and told of the hideous conditions under which they now suffered as prisoners. Thompson believed the letter would do more harm than good for its author and his companions, so he refused to present it to Bocanegra.

On Sunday, January 8, news of the Mexican victory at Mier reached Perote Castle. The report was read to the soldiers by the governor and was celebrated by the ringing of bells, the firing of cannon, and expressions of great joy.[47] At first, reported Trueheart, "We could not believe . . . that the Mexicans had taken so many prisoners, but were compelled to credit it when we saw a list of their names in the *Diario de Gobierno,* at which we were much concerned. . . . Many portions of General Ampudia's report was disbelieved by us."[48] "Poor fellows," wrote Maverick to his wife, "it is a dreadful thing to be made prisoners to the coward[ly] Mexican[s]—and much worse for them, invaders of Mexico!"[49] And of the battle, Judge Hutchinson commented: "To the brave men who justly won it, their inglorious surrender proved a sore defeat; but in all the moral and political consequences of this battle to Texas, [it was] a glorious triumph!"[50]

They sent petitions to "all the members of the [Mexican] government, including one to Bocanegra, Minister of Foreign Relations; and finally," on January 10 to "Santa Anna at his Hacienda near Vera Cruz." The memorial to Santa Anna drawn by William E. Jones and Judge Hutchinson detailed the circumstances under which they had been made prisoners, told of their treatment and forced labor as "prisoners of war," and requested their liberation.

Santa Anna sent back word that he had received their memorial and petition and that he would have a translation made "very so[o]n and then return an answer," reported Maverick; but weeks passed before the reply was received in a letter dated February 1 to the governor of the castle. On February 5 Captain Pombo read it to the Texan prisoners. Santa Anna stated that he had received their memorial and also letters from Booker, Davis, and Robinson, but that, not being the president, he could not act; Robinson's letter, however, concerning matters of grave national concern, would be forwarded to the authorities at the capital.[51]

From Perote Prison on January 9, 1843, the day after the news of the Mexican victory at Mier reached Perote, James W. Robinson, provisional

47. Hutchinson diary, Jan. 8, 1843.

48. Trueheart diary, Jan. 8, 1843.

49. Samuel A. Maverick to Mary A. Maverick, Castle of Perote, 150 miles east of the City of Mexico on the road to (80 miles off) to Vera Cruz, 27 January 1843, in Green, ed., *Samuel Maverick,* pp. 223-27; Green, *Mier Expedition,* p. 110.

50. Hutchinson diary, Jan. 10, 1843.

51. Trueheart diary, p. 177.

lieutenant governor of Texas during the days of the Consultation, wrote to Santa Anna suggesting a rapprochement between Mexico and Texas. He stated that he had "resided many years in Texas as a colonist" and falsely followed with the statement that he had "never been wanting in obedience to the laws of the government of Mexico, whose goodness enabled me to enjoy fortune and prosperity."[52] He explained that Mariano Arista's proclamation of January 9, 1842, to the inhabitants of the "Department of Texas" had offered protection to all persons and their property, at the time of Vásquez's entry into Texas, who would not take up arms against Mexico. Further, General Woll, on his entry into San Antonio in September 1842, had announced that only persons found in arms against Mexico would be taken prisoner. Robinson explained that, although he had rallied with others for the defense of San Antonio in September, it was only because he thought a robber band was attempting to plunder the place. He declared: "I . . . did not make use of my arms, and laid them down as soon as I knew they were troops of your excellency—an error which had made me appear a rebel."

Referring to a weakness in Arista's proclamation, Robinson said if a proposition similar to one recently offered Yucatán had been offered to Texas, it might have been accepted. For peace to be brought about, there must be an armistice. Robinson suggested that Mexico appoint commissioners "and unite one or two of the gentlemen who are with me, who, I before said, are of my opinion; and permit me to recommend that the steps which are to be taken in the matter should be taken immediately, for the purpose of counteracting whatever measure the Congress of Texas might take, which ought to meet the first Monday in this month."

Santa Anna transmitted Robinson's letter to the minister of war and marine, José Mariá de Tornel, with the request that he submit it to Gen. Nicolás Bravo, the "Substitute President," with the suggestion that he interview Robinson. "Robinson perhaps will operate solely with a desire to obtain his liberty," said Santa Anna, "but if it should not be so, and he should act in good faith, nothing can be lost on hearing him, and some favourable result may be obtained." If the "Substitute President" thought it proper, Santa Anna would be willing to hear Robinson's ideas, but "I will not make concessions which can affect the interests and sacred rights of the nation," he said.

After conferring with Bravo, Tornel informed Santa Anna that the "Substitute President" requested that he hear Robinson and do what he thought proper, relying on his good judgment. "The government," said Tornel, "abstains from giving directions of any kind, resting as it should,

---

52. J. W. Robinson to Gen. Antonio López de Santa Anna, Castle of Perote, January 9, 1843, in Green, *Mier Expedition*, pp. 464-66. This letter was not published in Texas until October 4, 1843, when the editor of the *Telegraph* printed it.

in the just opinion that your excellency should direct the matter according to your own judgment."[53]

On receipt of Tornel's letter, Santa Anna directed Robinson be sent to Manga de Clavo for a conference, "in which he perfectly convinced me," reported Santa Anna, "that he was not wanting in influence or means to produce the conviction in Texas of the importance of the colonists of again embracing the protection of our laws."[54] Robinson left Perote Prison under armed escort for Santa Anna's *hacienda* on February 13. The Texan break at Salado had occurred two days earlier, but was not known at Perote or Manga de Clavo at this time, though Santa Anna may have received intelligence from Monterrey "that 2,000 Texians were crossing the Rio Grande at Laredo." From Mexico City word arrived that Gen. T. J. Rusk was preparing to invade the eastern provinces of Mexico, which may have caused him to try to forestall hostile movements from Texas while he suppressed the rebellion in Yucatán. It was the opinion of the editor of the Houston *Morning Star* that Santa Anna welcomed the opportunity to negotiate a peaceful adjustment with Texas, even if it were only temporary. Surely he was aware of the strong Texan drive for absolute independence and smart enough to know that there could be no lasting reconciliation between the two countries on any other basis.[55]

After some discussion, a series of propositions calling for an armistice were signed on February 18, 1843, by Santa Anna, and Robinson was given his liberty and urged to return to Texas immediately with the proposals. In the meantime, Santa Anna gave assurances to Tornel, Bravo, and Bocanegra that he had shown "care and prudence . . . to avoid a single expression which can in any manner compromise the rights of the nation, so dear to all Mexicans, so sacred to me in my natural sentiments, because it has made me its keeper." In conclusion, he said: "As the whole subject is submitted to negotiations, in which the government should act with due caution," nothing is hazarded by planting "the seeds of reconciliation among the people of a department whose dispositions have been entirely alienated."

When notified of the agreement, Bravo gave his approval,[56] but the administration's newspaper, the *Diario del Gobierno*,[57] was quick to point out that the proposals in no way restricted the government; indeed, Robinson scarcely had left Mexico when Santa Anna issued a decree on March 18 declaring that the war "against the rebels and adventurers of Texas"

---

53. Gen. José María de Tornel to Antonio López de Santa Anna, Mexico, Feb. 11, 1843, in Green, *Mier Expedition*, p. 466.

54. Antonio López de Santa Anna to José María de Tornel, Manga de Clavo, February 18, 1843, in Green, *Mier Expedition*, pp. 466-67.

55. *Morning Star*, Apr. 1, 1843.

56. Extract of letter from José María de Tornel to Santa Anna, Mexico, February 23, 1843, in Green, *Mier Expedition*, p. 469.

57. May 21, 1843.

was a national one to preserve the integrity of the nation's territory and that the war against the traitors of Yucatán was also a national war.[58]

Nevertheless, while the administration prepared a division to penetrate to the heart of Texas to force submission to the laws of Mexico, it sought to bring that "rebelled" province again under its sovereignty by peaceful means. The sole thought of the government, declared the editor, was for the good of the nation and the procurement of the public interest.

The U.S. minister in Mexico, Waddy Thompson, gave a candid evaluation of the situation and of the Robinson proposals. Having heard much in recent weeks of a possible rapprochement between Mexico and its "rebelled" province and of "a reannexation of Texas to Mexico" and of "negotiations about being entered into to that end," he said, "I knew that Mexico only desired to save, in some degree, the point of honor, and that almost any terms would be conceded; such as that Texas should have her laws, religion, &c.; that no Mexican troops should be quartered in Texas, the Texians to make their own revenue laws, appoint their own revenue and other officers, pay only a nominal amount to Mexico; in one word, and in the language of a distinguished member of the Mexican Cabinet, in conversing with me on the subject, 'actual independence, with a mere nominal recognition of the sovereignty of Mexico.'"[59]

Robinson left Vera Cruz on March 2, on the U.S. brig-of-war *Dolphin* for New Orleans. En route, the *Dolphin* stopped at Tampico, where one of the passengers received news that an official dispatch had reached there saying that 110 of the escaped Texan prisoners had been recaptured and that it was thought that the remainder had no chance to make good their escape.[60] The *Dolphin* reached the Belize on March 22, and Robinson arrived at Galveston aboard the *New York* on March 27 but took his time in contacting the Texas government.[61] However, in a letter to the editor of the *Galveston Times* and to the editors of the *Galveston Civilian,* dated March 27, the day of his arrival, he detailed the propositions agreed to by Santa Anna, and "as a matter of good faith, perhaps, to Santa Anna," reported Francis R. Lubbock,[62] and urged they be accepted.[63]

As to the points referred to by Robinson, the editor of the *Telegraph* stated on April 5 that Santa Anna had expressed to Robinson a willingness "That Texas shall elect all her own officers, civil and military; That the right to property in the soil, acquired by citizens under the present Gov-

---

58. Decree of Santa Anna, March 18, 1843 [Mexico, 1843]. No copy. See Manuel Dublan and José M. Lozano, comp., *Legislación Méxicana ó Colección de las Disposiciónes Legislativas expedias Desde la Independencia de la Republica. Ordenada por . . . Manuel Dublan y José Lozano. Edicion Oficial.* Tomo I [-V], Mexico, 1876, IV, no. 2539, p. 406.

59. Thompson, *Recollections of Mexico,* pp. 95-96.

60. *Daily Picayune,* Mar. 24, 1843; see also, *Morning Star,* Apr. 1, 1843.

61. *Telegraph and Texas Register,* Apr. 5, 1843.

62. C. W. Raines, ed., *Six Decades in Texas or Memoirs of Francis Richard Lubbock,* pp. 153-54.

63. James W. Robinson to the Editor of the *Civilian,* Galveston, Mar. 27, 1843, in *Galveston Civilian,* Mar. 27, 1843; reprinted in *Morning Star,* Apr. 1, 1843.

ernment, shall be secured, as also the right of property in their slaves; That no laws affecting religion shall be enacted; These and many other points, including the subject of revenue, trade, &c., are reserved to be discussed and settled by agents appointed for the purpose, should Texas consent to entertain the subject."[64]

The *Galveston Civilian* spoke very favorably of the propositions, and demanded a serious and respectful consideration of them. But the editor of the *Galveston Times* declared: "Whatever impression a superficial consideration of these propositions may excite—however pleased we may at the moment be with the flattering deductions of Judge Robinson founded upon them, we have no hesitation in expressing our decided conviction that upon calm and mature reflection they will be, by reflecting Texians, consigned to the contempt which alone they merit."[65]

Robinson proceeded to Houston on the *Dayton,* arriving there on Friday, March 31.[66] When the proposals that he had brought from Mexico became known in Galveston and elsewhere, Robinson encountered personal indignities and threats to his life. A letter received at Perote Castle in mid-July from a correspondent in Houston told of "the gloomy position of Texans at this time, divided with civil dissensions and discord; and of the utmost contempt with which Judge Robinson is treated in Texas, and of the wish of the populace to mob him."[67]

There were those who believed that the propositions should be considered. In Houston on April 4, Gen. Moseley Baker addressed a group of citizens assembled at the courthouse "in favor of considering said propositions. After this a general anxiety prevailed to hear the subject more fully discussed"; on the next day, the District Court being in session, there was no opportunity to discuss in a meeting the Robinson proposals, but General Portis and C. N. Bassett expressed themselves as strongly opposed to the "propositions or any other that did not directly 'acknowledge the Independence of Texas.'"[68]

A general meeting of the citizens called for Friday, April 7, produced a similar conclusion. The Texas prisoners in Mexico were of but one sentiment, wrote Green, "that we would rather rot in these walls [of Perote Prison], ere Texas by any act, directly or indirectly, should acknowledge the supremacy of Mexico, or do anything on our account which would compromise her dignity and honour."[69]

Being aware of some of Robinson's plans, but not sure of the details, Maverick wrote to his wife in mid-March that Robinson was up to some-

---

64. *Telegraph and Texas Register,* Apr. 5, 1843.
65. Quoted in *Niles National Register* 64 (Apr. 15, 1843), p. 97.
66. *Telegraph and Texas Register,* Apr. 5, 1843. The terms agreed upon by Santa Anna and Robinson, Manga de Clavo, Feb. 18, 1843, are in Green, *Mier Expedition,* pp. 467-69.
67. Trueheart diary, July 29, 1843.
68. *Telegraph and Texas Register,* Apr. 26, 1843.
69. Thomas J. Green to Gen. Waddy Thompson, Perote Castle, April 5, 1843, in Green, ed., *Samuel Maverick,* pp. 257-58.

thing that spelled "no good for Texas." He requested her to inform Col. John W. Dancy on the Colorado River opposite LaGrange, where some of the refugee families from San Antonio, including Mrs. Maverick, were living, that Robinson's "business was secret & I know bad. A petition is reported in Mexico asking to go back [under Mexican rule]. If this is possible it behooves us to look out, and oppose them at once."[70] Another San Antonio prisoner wrote on March 9: "Many of our prisoners think we shall be released directly. I hope we shall soon, if no recent interference has been made by some of us, and I do hope that nothing but honorable propositions will be made, or I hope they will not be entertained by the Texian government."[71]

From Santiago Prison, Samuel H. Walker pleaded with Albert Sidney Johnston in Texas to reject the Robinson proposals. "We all here unanimously scorn the idea of such a thing [being brought back under Mexico] and would rather run the risk of dieing with old age in prison than Texas should listen to any such a proposition."[72] The editor of the New Orleans *Daily Picayune* of May 5, 1843, was not sure what Houston would do about the propositions brought by Robinson, but he was sure that the people of Texas would "submit to no other conditions than those of independence and freedom from Mexican connexion."

Richard A. Barkley, who was captured in the Dawson Fight, was perplexed by the release of Robinson. He wrote: "In my last letter I told you of a Mr. Roberson [Robinson] that had been set at liberty & sent to Texas & for what purpose I could not tell."[73] At the stage stop in Perote, where he had gone for the mail on April 30, Reese met with Peyton A. Southall, who bore dispatches to Thompson in Mexico City. Southall showed him a copy of Santa Anna's propositions to Texas made through Judge Robinson.[74] Until then, the prisoners at Perote Castle had no definite information on what had been proposed to Texas. Three days later, May 3, the prisoners received a New Orleans newspaper containing the propositions arising out of Robinson's letter and conference with Santa Anna, and they were much upset. A letter was sent to Messrs. Cruger and Moore, publishers of the Houston *Telegraph and Texas Register,* protesting Robinson's conduct.[75] It declared that Robinson's motive was simply to gain his per-

---

70. Samuel A. Maverick to Mary A. Maverick, Castle of Perote, March 15, 1843, in Green, ed., *Samuel Maverick*, pp. 234-38.

71. A San Antonio Prisoner to Col. James P. Lowery, Castle of Perote, March 9, 1843, in *Telegraph and Texas Register*, June 7, 1843.

72. S. H. Walker to Gen. A. Sidney Johns[t]on, Galveston, Texas, [addressed from] Prison Santiago, City of Mexico, May 4, 1843, in Army Papers (Texas), Tx-A.

73. [Richard A. Barkley] to H. G. Woods, William Harrell, Wood Prairie, Fayette County, Texas, [dated] Perote, Mar. 22, 1843, in Spellman, ed., "Letters of the 'Dawson Men' from Perote Prison," in *SWHQ* 38 (Apr. 1935), p. 247.

74. Trueheart diary, Apr. 30, 1843.

75. [Thomas J. Green?] to Messrs. Cruger & Moore of the *Telegraph and Texas Register*, In Prison, Mexico, May 4, 1843, in *Telegraph and Texas Register*, June 14, 1843. The tone and language used sound as if it were written by Thomas Jefferson Green.

sonal freedom, but, on second thought, its author wrote another lengthy letter to Cruger and Moore, condemning Robinson's conduct and the propositions carried to Texas by him for fear that they might be believed by the gullible in Texas.

The writer stated that it was his belief that only the people of the nation could make a decision on the propositions presented by Robinson, and since his current situation denied him the right to express himself at the ballot box, he took this opportunity to speak out against the proposals for himself and "for my unfortunate companions, with perhaps a few dastardly exceptions."[76]

A few days later, through the courtesy of some of the Mier men returning home, Barkley was able to send a letter to Henry Gonzalvo Woods at LaGrange: "I see in a late *Picayune* [March 24, 1843] the *Proposition of Santa Anna* through Roberson the worst man Texas ever had within her borders—say to him for me that his blood shall atone for his conduct towards us. His conduct is the sole cause of our lengthy confinement there in this hell I might call it."[77]

Because of the defeats in Yucatán and restlessness at home, Santa Anna was thought by some of the Texan prisoners to "have been induced as a matter of self-preservation to give in to something like a cessation of arms with Texas, in order to get through with Yucatán, and seat himself firmly in the Presidential chair." It was believed to be the intention of Santa Anna never to recognize the independence of Texas unless forced to do so. "The *milk and water* policy pursued by the United States, England and France, by their peaceable half-way interference, have only operated to the prejudice of Texas, by inducing this republic [Mexico] to think we are in a much weaker and disaffected situation than we truly are, (and as it may be) so I am told by intelligent Mexican officers," wrote a San Antonio prisoner. "*War, unceasing war* . . . carried into their country, and in their mode of warfare, is the only thing which will ever give peace, respected peace to our country"; even more important than offensive war there must be a "total expulsion of the Mexicans entirely from our border," for their disloyalty in giving information to the Mexican enemy.[78]

Mexican newspapers supporting the cause of Federalism, as contrasted to the Centralism and dictatorship of Santa Anna, attacked the proposed terms of pacification with Texas. "The Federalist urge—and not without force," commented the editor of the *Daily National Intelligencer* in Washington, "that the terms offered are too liberal, useless, indeed, [if] the federal system is to be adopted throughout Mexico; for these condi-

---

76. Letter from a Texan Prisoner in Mexico to Messrs. Cruger & Moore, In Prison, Mexico, May 4, 1843, in *Telegraph and Texas Register*, June 14, 1843.

77. R. A. Barkl[e]y to H. G. Woods, LaGrange, Fayette Co., Texas, [dated] Mexico, Castle of Perote, May 8, 1843, in Spellman, ed., "Letters of the 'Dawson Men,'" *SWHQ* 38 (Apr. 1935), p. 252.

78. San Antonio Prisoner to Col. James P. Lowery, Castle of Perote, March 9, 1843, in *Telegraph and Texas Register*, June 7, 1843.

tions would really confer on Texas the local independence, the government by her own local laws, and the exclusion of all Mexican troops from her territory, which none of the existing departments possess."[79]

The administration papers sought to justify the liberal terms, declaring that they were not absolute offers, but were only intended as a basis for discussion between Mexico and Texas; and that Santa Anna in his private, not official, character had only consented "that it should be ascertained whether or not a peace between the two states could be made to spring from these proposals." In the meantime, unaware of Robinson's activities, Waddy Thompson learned that the Mexican authorities were anxious to come to some arrangement to end hostilities with Texas. In conversations with Bocanegra, he gained the impression that Mexico was anxious to make concession to Texas but that there must be a reunion, if only in name. Thompson suggested to Maverick that he would say that he was in favor of such a reunion if Santa Anna would release him as an emissary to Texas to further the cause of rapprochement. Maverick hastily replied: "You say that you think Santa Anna will release me if I say that I am in favor of reannexation on any terms that would be advantageous to Texas & I therefore cannot say so, for I regard a lie as a crime, & one which I cannot commit even to secure my release; I must therefore continue to wear my chains, galling as they are."[80]

Houston and Anson Jones, his secretary of state, did not look on the proposals as being submitted by the Mexican government to the government of Texas. When Elliot, the British diplomat, visited Houston at Washington-on-the-Brazos relative to some claims of English subjects, in the course of the conversation, knowing that Robinson was in town, he referred to the Robinson affair. President Houston showed him "the original . . . paper General Santa Anna had delivered to Mr. Robinson . . . I did not detect that that Gentleman had more to communicate to General Houston than had already been made known to him through the medium of his Newspaper."[81] Houston declared that although the propositions "came to him in a strange and informal manner indeed, still He would [state] his belief that it evinced a peacefulness of Spirit on the part of the Mexican Government and [he was] disposed on his own side to proceed to all proper lengths for the Establishment of an honorable, and desirable pacification." Elliot told Richard Pakenham that he hoped it would not be incompatible with his position "to state to General Santa Anna that he [Houston] was ready to send Commissioners to Mexico in furtherance of that object." Houston made it clear, however, "that an Armistice would be indispensably necessary before any proposals of a peaceful Nature could be entertained."

---

79. *Daily National Intelligencer* (Washington, D.C.), June 30, 1843.

80. Note copied from Waddy Thompson's book, penned to the end of Maverick's diary.

81. Charles Elliot to Richard Pakenham, April 14, 1843 (Private) in Adams, ed., *British Correspondence Concerning the Republic of Texas*, pp. 172-78.

"No proposition of any character," Jones informed Isaac Van Zandt in Washington, "have been submitted by Mexico to this Government nor was Mr. Robinson charged with any communication to it."[82] Houston and Jones took the view that "Mr. Robinson was authorized by that functionary [Santa Anna] on behalf of the Mexican Government" to make propositions "to the *people* of Texas" and had been given "instructions in relation to the same." On May 8, Jones sent to Van Zandt a translation of the proposals brought by Robinson.

As late as May 22, the government of Texas had taken no action, either directly or indirectly, on the overtures from Mexico, "which, since the execution of the Texian prisoners, are more than ever regarded," reported the French *chargé d'affaires* in Texas, "as a snare and a trap."[83]

---

82. Anson Jones to Isaac Van Zandt, Dept. of State, Galveston, May 8, 1843, in Isaac Van Zandt Letters, 1839-1843, TxU-A.

83. Vte. J. de Cramayel to François Guizot, Galveston, May 22, 1843, in Barker, trans. and ed., *The French Legation in Texas* 2, pp. 436-37.

CHAPTER 10

The Release and Return of the First of the Béxar and Mier Prisoners

LATE IN JANUARY 1843, Samuel G. Norvell, who had been left sick at Querétaro, was released upon his arrival at Mexico City through the intercession of Col. José María Carrasco.[1] From there he accompanied Payton A. Southall, a U.S. Navy purser and dispatch bearer, on his way to Washington. Southall, at Thompson's request, visited the Texan prisoners at the castle on February 2. He conveyed news that "we are all to be liberated in a month," reported Maverick.[2] He told Maverick that Thompson had written to Santa Anna for his release as Thompson's cousin.[3] The visitors said they had been requested by Thompson to advise the prisoners against any attempt to escape or "to run off" for it could only jeopardize his chances of getting them released and that the risk to them would be great.[4] "It was rumored that . . . Hutchinson, James W. Robinson, W[illia]m F. Jones, [H. Alexander] Alsbury, and Maverick would be almost immediately released, and the current report at Mexico was that all [the San Antonio prisoners] were to be shortly liberated with the exception of those taken at the Salado belonging to Capt. Dawson's unfortunate company."[5]

The prisoners sent letters to the United States through Southall and Norvell. Hutchinson wrote to Foote, but upon the advice of William E. Jones did not send the letter he had written to George W. Terrell, attorney general of Texas, presumably to resign his position as district judge,

---

1. *Telegraph and Texas Register*, Mar. 8, 1843; *Northern Standard*, Mar. 16, 1843.

2. Samuel A. Maverick to Mrs. Mary A. Maverick, Perote, Feb. 2, 1843, in Green, ed., *Samuel Maverick*, p. 228.

3. *Ibid.*

4. Trueheart diary, Mar. 2-18, 1843, but includes information under date of Mar. 2, dating back to Jan. 25, 1843, while Trueheart was in the hospital. The month of February 1843 is missing from the diary.

5. *Daily Picayune*, Feb. 16, 1843, quoted in *Northern Standard,* Mar. 16, 1843.

"on account of a special interposition in my favor at Mexico," he said, which could result in an early release.[6] Southall and Norvell proceeded to Vera Cruz and took passage on the U.S. revenue cutter *Woodbury,* for New Orleans, where they arrived on February 15.[7] Arriving with them were William Eppes and his wife, "and one of the Santa Fé prisoners, who up to this time had remained in Mexico.[8] From New Orleans Norvell went to Galveston and then to Houston, reaching there on Friday morning, March 5.

Norvell reported that the Texan prisoners in Mexico "had entertained hopes that a sufficient number of Mexicans would be captured to exchange for them; but since they have learned that the [Texas] government is opposed to an offensive war, they have abandoned this hope in despair."[9]

It required some time for Santa Anna to implement his promise to Thompson to free Maverick and William E. Jones. Santa Anna had been at his *hacienda* "ever since we were prisoners," reported Maverick, from where he kept in close touch with affairs in the capital but let others bear "the heat."[10] The political situation in Mexico was volatile and unstable. With the fall of Bustamante early in 1841, a council of generals met at Tacubaya and framed the *Bases Provisionales de Tacubaya,* issued on September 28, 1841. Under the *Bases Provisionales,* deputies to represent the various departments were to be named by Santa Anna who then would name a provisional president who would summon a Congress to meet within eight months to frame a new constitution for Mexico.[11] Santa Anna was named provisional (often called substitute) president on October 7, 1841. Santa Anna was described as tall and graceful, with a "small oval face stamped by thought and energy, with . . . closely set eyes, brilliantly reflecting an impulsive nature and a talented mind."[12] "Oily duplicity, treachery, avarice, and sensuality," were evident in every feature and were clearly stamped upon his face.[13] "A sparkling of gray in his hair added dignity, and the dark, bilious complexion, with its striking expression of anxious melancholy hovering around the mouth when in repose, generally brightened during conversation into sympathizing affability and winning smiles. When giving command the voice assumed a well balanced, dictatorial tone, which was effectively imposing, and when roused his face changed into repelling fierceness."[14]

The Congress was summoned by Santa Anna to meet on June 10,

---

6. Hutchinson diary, Feb. 2, 1843.

7. *Daily Picayune,* Feb. 16, 1843.

8. *Northern Standard,* Mar. 16, 1843.

9. *Telegraph and Texas Register,* Mar. 8, 1843.

10. Samuel A. Maverick to Mrs. Mary A. Maverick, Castle of Perote, March 15, 1843, in *Samuel Maverick,* pp. 233-34.

11. Bancroft, *History of Mexico* 5, pp. 233-37.

12. Crawford, ed., *The Eagle,* p. 269, based on Bancroft, *History of Mexico* 5, pp. 236-37.

13. George Frederick Ruxton, *Adventures in Mexico, from Vera Cruz to Chihuahua in the Days of the Mexican War,* p. 45.

14. Crawford, ed., *The Eagle,* p. 269, based on Bancroft, *History of Mexico* 5, pp. 236-37.

1842. Not liking the way matters were going in the Chamber of Deputies in revising the Constitution, Santa Anna planned to retire to his estate near Vera Cruz to watch and direct operations, "leaving the brunt of the contest to be borne by a proxy [Nicolás Bravo], with perhaps the humiliation of defeat, while in the case of success he could step forward to reap the fruit."[15] On September 27, 1842, before he left the city, Santa Anna's left leg, which had been amputated at Pozitos, near Vera Cruz, and buried at Manga de Clavo, was disinterred and reburied in a monument especially built for that purpose.[16]

It was not long before new revolutionary disturbances broke out, and throughout almost all of the departments the cry *"Abajo el Congreso"* ("Down with the Congress!") sounded. Were one to judge alone from the tone of the different accounts appearing in the Mexican journals, "he would be led to believe that this voice . . . preceded from, and [had] been echoed by the people, and only the people."[17] The deputies, who neared the conclusion of their discussions on the Constitution, found they "could obtain no assurances of protection from the government, [and] finding the hall of congress closed against them, they recognized the futility of resistance, and dissolved on their own accord on the 19th" of December 1842.

It was clear to those who understood the situation that "the people had nothing to do with pulling down the late Congress; but that, on the contrary, it . . . [had] been entirely a military crusade, headed by Santa Anna himself . . . [from] Manga de Clavo, . . . [where] undoubtedly proceeded all the machinations," declared the editor of the *Picayune,* "which upset the recent Federal Congress," and from there, too, "emanated the call for a new assembly to be elected by his own partisans. To prove this we have but to state, that before a cry against the old Congress was heard, a list of members of the new assembly was actually in the hands of Gen. Bravo, at Mexico [City], sent by Santa Anna himself."[18]

Following the dissolution of the old Congress, Provisional President Bravo announced that since the public interest demanded the formation of the Constitution, the government would appoint a council to draft one, assisted, of course, by the ministry. The dissolved constitutional convention was replaced on January 6, 1843, by a body of eight hand-picked Centralists as an Assembly of Notables. They commenced work on a new con-

---

15. Bancroft, *History of Mexico* 5, p. 253.

16. Santa Anna claimed that he had forced the French to flee Vera Cruz and that they had set up an eight-pound cannon to protect their rearguard. When charging the cannon he was seriously wounded by cannon fire which mangled the bones in his left leg and broke one of the fingers of his right hand, leading to amputation of the lower part of his leg. Crawford, ed., *The Eagle*, pp. 64-65.

17. *Daily Picayune,* Jan. 13, 1843.

18. *Ibid.*; see also Waddy Thompson to Daniel Webster, Secretary of State, Washington City, [dated] Legation of the United States of America, Mexico, December 28, 1842, in Despatches from United States Ministers to Mexico (Mar. 12, 1842-Mar. 25, 1844), National Archives (microfilm).

stitution to be completed in six months. Soon official Mexican journals arriving in New Orleans from Vera Cruz stated that "reports had been received from almost every department of the nation, and that they were unanimous in the opinion that the Federal form of Government was not suitable for the Mexican people, and declaring their adhesion to the new consolidated system of Santa Anna."[19]

Santa Anna's delay in acting on Thompson's request was caused by distraction over this political unrest and maneuverings among members of his cabinet. Reports from individuals in Mexico represented "a strong feeling and even a conspiracy as existing against the Dictator in the capital."[20] From Jalapa it was reported that troops stationed there, "and which were destined to act against Yucatán, had been ordered by Santa Anna to march forthwith to the city of Mexico." Santa Anna was expected to return to Mexico City on March 1, and Thompson thought the matter of Maverick's release would be taken up at that time.[21] Thompson now concluded to seek also the release of Judge Hutchinson "on account of his age."[22] He also worked for Hutchinson's release because of the American Secretary of State Daniel Webster's request: "It would be gratifying to the friends of that gentleman, many of whom are persons of distinction in this country, if his liberation could be obtained. You will accordingly endeavor unofficially to effect that object or at least to alleviate the rigors of the Judge's captivity."[23] Thompson instructed Maverick to "tell him [Hutchinson] confidentially that if he needs any moderate sum of money in the meantime" that he would send it to him through Maverick. He also told Maverick that he had sent Maverick $25 through Colonel Gonzáles and hoped that he had received it, for he was afraid that he might be in need of it and had too much of "a delicacy in asking for it."

Thompson obtained and forwarded to Secretary of State Webster, on February 16, 1843, a copy of the terms under which the Texans had surrendered at Mier.[24] He reported that he had "this day received information that five of them who had belonged to the Santa Fé expedition had been ordered to be shot which I have not a doubt has been done," and that the remaining Mier prisoners, when they arrived in Mexico City, would be sent to work on a road south of the city. "I desire to know," he wrote Webster, "whether your instructions to me of the 5th of April [1842] last,

19. *Daily National Intelligencer,* Jan. 23, 1843.

20. *Daily Picayune*, March 24, 1843.

21. Samuel A. Maverick to Mrs. Mary A. Maverick, Castle of Perote, March 15, 1843, in Green, ed., *Samuel Maverick*, pp. 233-34.

22. Waddy Thompson to Samuel A. Maverick, Mexico, Feb. 16, 1843, in Green, ed., *Samuel Maverick.*

23. Daniel Webster to Waddy Thompson, Department of State, Washington, 15th February, 1843, in Instructions of the Department of State, Mexico (May 29, 1833-Mar. 29, 1843), National Archives (microfilm).

24. Waddy Thompson to Daniel Webster, Legation of the United States, Mexico, Feb. 16, 1843, in Despatches from the United States Ministers in Mexico, Mar. 12, 1842-Mar. 25, 1844, National Archives (microfilm).

in which the interference on the part of our Government is threatened to prevent cruel treatment to prisoners of war and to enforce the observance of the terms of Capitulation are to be regarded as applying to these new batches of prisoners."

Santa Anna came out of seclusion and it was predicted that upon his arrival in Mexico City he would make changes in the cabinet—especially in the ministers of treasury and of war and marine—and that, because of the difficulties on the home front, he probably would send "a commissioner to Texas with propositions for peace and a recognition of the independence of the republic."[25]

News of the overthrow of the guard at Salado reached him on February 27 as he was leaving Manga de Clavo. On February 28 amid the ringing of bells and the boom of cannon, Santa Anna entered Perote Castle for an overnight stop. During his stay at the castle, the Texan prisoners were "kept locked up."[26]

Texas Independence Day, March 2, was celebrated by the Béxar prisoners in Perote Castle with an egg-nog frolic in their rooms, during the course of which they made so much noise that the sentinel at the door threatened to fire upon them if they did not quiet down. "We told him," reported Trueheart, "to shoot and be da————."[27]

The prisoners hoped they would be released when Santa Anna reached the capital, "if no recent interference has been made by some of us," wrote one of the prisoners.[28] During the day the prisoners were visited by Lt. H. A. Hartstene, dispatch bearer for Commodore Thomas ap Catesby Jones of the Pacific Squadron, and Peyton A. Southall, dispatch bearer from the United States of Waddy Thompson. Hartstene reported that Neill had reached New Orleans safely, and he promised to send the prisoners money upon his arrival at Vera Cruz—he did send $50. Southall promised to stop again at the castle upon his way back to the United States.

On March 5, Santa Anna made a splendid entry into the City of Mexico, then seething with revolutionary sentiment. After resuming the duties of provisional president, his attention was directed toward settling the political unrest among the members of his cabinet, which he did by putting all members of the cabinet, except Tornel, in prison for a few days. "This brought them all to the feet of S[anta Anna]," reported Maverick, "and he is now probably as firmly & absolutely settled on the people or more so, than he ever was in his life."[29] Santa Anna also intervened in the controversy between the *Ayuntamiento* of the city and the governor and commandant general of the district, and settled it by dismissing the latter and de-

25. *Daily Picayune*, Mar. 26, 1843.

26. Trueheart diary, Mar. 1, 1843.

27. *Ibid.*, Mar. 2, 1843.

28. "A San Antonio Prisoner" to James P. Lowery, Castle of Perote, March 9, 1843, in *Telegraph and Texas Register*, June 7, 1843.

29. Samuel A. Maverick to Mrs. Mary A. Maverick, Castle of Perote, March 15, 1843, in Green ed., *Samuel Maverick*, pp. 234–38.

claring null and void "all the measures he had taken against the *'Ayuntamiento.'*"[30] Santa Anna then named Gen. Mariano Paredes y Arrillaga governor and commandant general, but he had scarcely been in office three hours when he was arrested by order of Santa Anna because it had been learned that he was involved in the conspiracy against the provisional president. "I conclude," reported Maverick in reference to Santa Anna, "that the greater and to him more interesting events of his first days in the Capitol has prevented his attending to what he promised the Am[eri]c[a]n Minister in my behalf."[31]

A few days after George S. Curson's departure from Perote to Mexico City, the Texan prisoners learned through the American consul in Vera Cruz of the arrival of the revenue cutter *Woodbury* at that port and that a United States dispatch bearer on the way to Mexico City would reach the castle on March 9. "We hope for something *late* and encouraging," wrote one of the prisoners to Captain Lowery in Texas.[32]

Thomas L. Crittenden, brother of George B. Crittenden, from Frankfort, Kentucky, on February 8, 1843, forwarded to his father, Senator John J. Crittenden, a letter received from Texas telling of his brother's capture. He requested Thomas Francis Marshall, a member of the U.S. House of Representatives, to use his influence with the administration to secure the release of his brother.[33] On March 9 Thompson sent Santa Anna letters from Secretary of State Webster, written privately, and from Senator John J. Crittenden soliciting the release of Crittenden's son.[34] Also, in behalf of Crittenden, General Almonte, Mexico's minister to the United States, wrote to Santa Anna.

Thompson explained to Santa Anna that while Senator Crittenden was absent in Washington, his son had gone to Texas, "where he was induced to join what his father very properly" describes as "that miserable expedition." "I beg that you will regard this communication as entirely unofficial, for in my official character I have no right to interfere," but "Mr. Crittenden is one of the dearest friends I have upon earth, and is the very best man I ever knew, and one universally beloved, and you will see how strongly he condemns the conduct of his son. That you may have a just idea of the interest which is felt for Mr. Crittenden, I will mention that a Government ship has been sent to Vera Cruz for no other purpose than to instruct me to make this appeal to you."

---

30. *Daily Picayune* reprinted in *Northern Standard,* May 18, 1843.

31. Samuel A. Maverick to Mrs. Mary A. Maverick, Castle of Perote, March 15, 1843, in Green, ed., *Samuel Maverick,* pp. 234-38.

32. "A San Antonio Prisoner" to Col. James P. Lowery, Castle of Perote, March 9, 1843, in *Telegraph and Texas Register,* June 7, 1843.

33. Thomas L. Crittenden to Hon. T. F. Marshall, Frankfort, February 8, 1843, in Lyon G. Tyler, *The Letters and Times of the Tylers* 2, p. 265.

34. Waddy Thompson to Gen. Antonio López de Santa Anna, Provisional President of the Mexican Republic, Mexico, March 9, 1843 (copy), in Waddy Thompson to Daniel Webster, March 14, 1843, Despatches from United States Ministers in Mexico, Mar. 12, 1842-Mar. 25, 1844, National Archives (microfilm).

It was not enough to appeal only to the provisional president in regard to Crittenden. Thompson "took many other steps to obtain his release, including an effort to enlist the assistance of Richard Pakenham, the British minister, who, "enjoys," reported Thompson, "a very great and deserved influence here." The help of others would not have been asked if it were simply "a matter of right" he had been demanding; in that case he "would not have asked or received the aid of any one, but it was not— but a matter of favor, the case was different."

Having learned of the poor prison fare and the loathsome tasks forced upon the Texan prisoners, Thompson wanted to know from Webster what stand the United States intended to take in respect to the treatment of the prisoners in Mexico. "The prisoners taken at San Antonio," he reported, "are confined in the Castle of Perote, and until the last two or three weeks have not a mouthful to eat, except a small supply of beans and bread. Since then they have had small quantities of beef offal given to them, and are daily hitched to carts like mules or oxen, and made to labor in cleaning out the Castle, and other loathsome and degrading employment. If it is intended by our Government to take ground in this business it cannot be done too soon, nor too high ground assumed."[35]

At the end of February, Andrew Jackson, at the solicitation of Francis P. Blair in Washington City, wrote a strong letter to Santa Anna in behalf of Crittenden. Jackson sent the letter to James W. Breedlove in New Orleans to be sent through the Mexican consul to Mexico. He explained that he thought Santa Anna had "too much wisdom" not to treat the Texan prisoners "as prisoners of War, as any other course would arouse the whole civilized world against such barbarity" as "destroying them as rebels."[36] Jackson's letter reached Santa Anna after he already had agreed to release Crittenden.

In the meantime, George S. Curson, dispatch bearer from the U.S. State Department, arrived at Vera Cruz on February 28, 1843, on the United States sloop of war *Falmouth,* and on his way to Mexico City stopped at Perote Castle on March 4 and informed Hutchinson that Senator Robert J. Walker of Mississippi and Jacob Thompson, representative from Mississippi, had applied to Daniel Webster for the aid in obtaining his release.[37] This was encouraging news.

Curson brought issues of the *Telegraph and Texas Register* for February 1 and 8, and recent Alabama papers. On March 6 he reached Mexico City with dispatches from Webster regarding California and Texas, and on the evening of February 15, visited the vanguard of the Mier prisoners at Tacubaya. The day after his arrival at the capital, Thompson called on

35. Waddy Thompson to Daniel Webster, Legation of the United States of America, Mexico, March 14, 1843, no. 15, in Despatches from United States Ministers to Mexico, Mar. 12, 1842-Mar. 25, 1844, National Archives (microfilm).

36. Andrew Jackson to James W. Breedlove, Hermitage, February 27, 1843, in Bassett, ed., *Correspondence of Andrew Jackson* 6, pp. 212-13.

37. Hutchinson diary, Mar. 11, 1843.

Bocanegra and, in obedience to Webster's instructions, "in the most friendly and respectful terms" alluded to the character of the war now going on between Mexico and Texas and told Bocanegra "that whilst our government was determined to strictest neutrality in that war, that it felt that it was its duty to remonstrate in the most respectful manner with both governments against the predatory forays—really not war which were now made by both Mexico and Texas—and to urge upon both the abandonment of such a system. The only consequence of which were individual suffering and calamity." Bocanegra replied vehemently "that Mexico did not regard Texas as an independent power but as a rebellious province and that prisoners taken were not entitled to any of the privileges of prisoners of war, but that they were rebels and would be so treated, and that no suggestions on the subject from other Governments would be received or listened to."[38] To this Thompson replied, "if Mexico regarded these men as rebels, that she ought not to enter into capitulations with them, and then violate them."[39] After his audience with Bocanegra, Thompson told Webster that he was "very well satisfied that nothing can be effected on this subject, by any thing short of a decided stand by our Government."

A week after Santa Anna arrived in Mexico City, and no action having been taken on his request for the release of Maverick, Hutchinson, and Jones, Thompson again addressed the president on March 12 on the matter, reminding him of his promise and stating that he now had "an opportunity of sending these men to the United States by a Government ship together with any others whom you may choose to liberate." Thompson added: "The Secretary of State of the United States has also directed me to request in my own individual character that Mr. Truhart [Trueheart] and Mr. Peterson now confined in Perote, may be also set at liberty if Your Excellency should think it compatible with the interest of Mexico to do so."

Thompson wrote Maverick that he expected the order to come through any day for his release and for that of Hutchinson, and that he had no doubt but that all of the San Antonio prisoners would be released shortly. "Indeed Santa Anna told me so." On February 16, according to Maverick, Thompson wrote again, saying "he had just obtained Santa Anna's promise for the release of all of us prisoners in a very short time."[40]

One of the major difficulties encountered in his efforts to obtain the release of all of the San Antonio prisoners was the violation by some of

38. Waddy Thompson to Daniel Webster, Legation of the United States of America, March 14, 1843, in Despatches from United States Ministers in Mexico, Mar. 12, 1842-Mar. 25, 1844, National Archives (microfilm); William R. Manning, ed., *Diplomatic Correspondence of the United States* 8 (Mexico), pp. 542-43 (extract).

39. Waddy Thompson to the Provisional President of the Mexican Republic, Mexico, March 12, 1843 (copy), in Despatches from United States Ministers in Mexico, March 12, 1842-March 25, 1844, National Archives (microfilm).

40. Waddy Thompson to Samuel A. Maverick, Mexico, March 14, 1843, in Green, ed., *Samuel Maverick*, p. 234. Samuel A. Maverick to Mary A. Maverick, Perote, March 22, 1843, in Green, ed., *Samuel Maverick*, pp. 239-42.

them of their parole as Santa Fé prisoners.[41] In view of these violations, Thompson informed Webster that he could not "see any just ground of complaint against Mexico for refusing to release any more prisoners."[42]

Finally, on March 15, the day the vanguard of the Mier prisoners reached Tacubaya, Santa Anna informed Thompson that the three men he had specifically requested to be released would be freed, including Crittenden, as soon as the latter reached the capital.[43]

When Santa Anna informed Thompson of his determination to release them, he ordered Tornel to have the chains removed from Hutchinson, Jones, and Maverick, and to have them sent to Mexico City to be placed at the disposal of the American minister. "On taking these measures which is only for [because of] the private intervention of yourself and some other respectable persons in the United States," he told Thompson, "I lose no occasion to exercise acts of generosity peculiar to the Mexican character." He then said: "I hope you will be sensible of my friendly disposition towards the American Nation. . . . I have to expect from you, that you will interpose your influence that the citizens of the United States may not stain their name by making common cause with the Texan Rebels who have been treated with hospitality by the Mexican Republic, and have paid it with ingratitude, and have practised a robbery which has filled the world with astonishment."[44]

The next day, March 16, Thompson acknowledged the receipt of Santa Anna's letter and indulged in a little flattery: "I have this moment received your kind letter of yesterday and feel deeply sensible of this additional act of generosity on your part. . . . I feel no less so from the reflection that it will reflect additional honor upon the character of Your Excellency." Thompson went on to say that he had learned that Crittenden was not with the party that rose on the guard, but, being sick, had been permitted by Ampudia to remain at Matamoros when the prisoners were marched to Mexico City, and was apparently still there.[45]

On Saturday, March 18, Maverick received a letter from Thompson

---

41. Waddy Thompson to Samuel A. Maverick, Mexico, Jan. 26, 1843, in Green, ed., *Samuel Maverick*, pp. 222-23.

42. Waddy Thompson to Daniel Webster, Secretary of State, Legation of the U. States, Mexico, May 16, 1843, in Despatches from United States Ministers in Mexico, Mar. 12, 1842-Mar. 25, 1844, National Archives (microfilm).

43. A. L. S[an]ta Anna to Waddy Thompson, Envoy Extraordinary and Minister Plenipotentiary of the United States, National Palace, 15th March 1843 (translation), in Waddy Thompson to Daniel Webster, Mexico, March 14, 1843, Despatches from United States Ministers in Mexico, Mar. 12, 1842-Mar. 25, 1844, National Archives (microfilm).

44. A. L. S[an]ta Anna to Waddy Thompson, Envoy Extraordinary and Minister Plenipotentiary of the United States, National Palace of México, 15th March 1843 (translation), in Waddy Thompson to Daniel Webster, March 14, 1843, in Despatches from United States Ministers in Mexico, Mar. 12, 1842-Mar. 25, 1844, National Archives (microfilm).

45. Waddy Thompson to The Most Excellent Provisional President of the Mexican Republic D. Antonio López de Santa Anna, Mexico, March 16, 1843 (copy), in Waddy Thompson to Daniel Webster, March 14, 1843, in Despatches from United States Ministers in Mexico, Mar. 12, 1842-Mar. 25, 1844, National Archives (microfilm).

"communicating the order of the Govt. of Mexico for the release of your-self, Jones & Hutchinson," but stating that they would have to go to Mexico City to see the president. The next day the commandant of the castle sent for the three men. Upon arrival at the governor's quarters, the order for their release was read to them. It confirmed that they were to be sent to Mexico City "by the first opportunity under a safe guard." "We of-fered to go in 5 minutes," reported Maverick, "but had to wait their plea-sure."[46] The governor ordered the chains of the three men cut off.

On March 20, the Riddle brothers and Captain O'Phelan of the San Antonio prisoners received notice from Richard Pakenham, British minis-ter in Mexico, that he had obtained their release.[47] As soon as the guard changed the next morning, their chains were removed. Since they were practically without funds, Maverick advanced money to assist them on the journey home.

On March 22 Maverick and his companions found three horses in the courtyard "awaiting with saddles on—as they say, for us to go to the Capi-tol which is 150 miles distant," wrote Maverick. "Am quite grieved to think we are obliged to go to Mexico [City]."[48] They took leave of their comrades and left the castle under armed escort for the capital, carrying with them letters of their companions for mailing. "We were permitted to ride to Mexico City," said Jones, "by paying the hire of horses; we paid also our own expenses although we were still prisoners."[49] Their comrades at the castle anxiously awaited their return. "We expect to be liberated on their return, which will be some 11 days," wrote Richard Barkley.[50]

The first night on the road they were lodged at Tepiohualela. The night of March 23 was spent at Hacienda Floreta, where they were robbed of some of their clothing.[51] Although no letter or diary shows it, it is pos-sible that Colonel Fisher and his party on their way to Perote Castle also spent the same night at Floreta in near proximity of the three Béxar pris-

---

46. Samuel A. Maverick to Mary A. Maverick, Perote, March 22, 1843, in Green, ed., *Samuel Maverick*, pp. 239-42; Hutchinson diary, Mar. 18, 1843; Hutchinson diary, Mar. 19, 1843.

47. Trueheart diary, Mar. 20, 1843. The correspondence of the British minister with Gen. Tornel, minister of war and marine, relative to the release of British subjects held in the Castle of Perote, may be found in Legajo 5, 1843. See Herbert E. Bolton, *Guide to Ma-terials for the History of the United States in the Principal Archives of Mexico*, p. 289. See also —— —— to the Editors of the *Bulletin* (New Orleans), Monterey, 26th March, 1843, in *Telegraph and Texas Register*, May 3, 1843.

48. Samuel A. Maverick to Mrs. Mary A. Maverick, Perote, March 22, 1843, in Green, ed., *Samuel Maverick*, pp. 239-42.

49. [William E. Jones to M. B. Lamar], Washington, 1 Feby. 1844, in Winkler, ed., "The Béxar and Dawson Prisoners," in *QTSHA* 13 (Apr. 1910), p. 323; see also Trueheart diary, Mar. 22, 1843.

50. [Richard A. Barkley] to H. G. Woods, William Harrell, Woods Prairie, Fayette County, Texas, [dated] Perote, Mar[ch] 22, 1843, in Spellman, ed., "Letters of the 'Dawson Men,'" in *SWHQ* 38 (April 1935), p. 247.

51. Hutchinson diary, Mar. 23, 1843.

oners.[52] The three Texans reached Mexico City on March 27 and were "paraded for a quarter of an hour ragged and dirty in front of the Palace —and then escorted into it and finally sent to prison," after a short audience with President Santa Anna. According to Maverick, who claimed that he was from South Carolina, he was told by the president that he had been released, as had William E. Jones of Georgia and Judge Anderson Hutchinson of Mississippi,[53] and George B. Crittenden of Kentucky, out of respect for him (Maverick) and for General Thompson.[54]

Soon after the three Texans arrived at the prison they were visited by John Black, the U.S. consul, and were released to him. Black took them to General Thompson's quarters. Maverick, Jones, and Hutchinson were handed passports on March 30, turned over to General Thompson, and told that they were free to go. The three, now fully at liberty, obtained lodging for three days during which they endeavored "to see everything to be seen in that remarkable place, in that short time,"[55] including a visit to the cathedral. As Hutchinson, Jones, and Maverick left Mexico City, it was being reported that Captain Elliot had written a letter to Santa Anna from Texas which stated that "at the express request of President Houston, that the latter hopes that Santa Anna will treat the Mier prisoners with all clemency, *but that they crossed the Rio Grande contrary to his (Houston's) orders!*"[56]

The three left Mexico City by stagecoach on April 3 for Vera Cruz, a four-day journey of 280 miles. The evening before their departure, Judge Hutchinson drew a draft on Dobbins & Co. of New Orleans for money to pay his expenses home, and the men visited with various friends in the city. They stopped at Perote to visit their comrades and the Mier men in the nearby castle. They arrived at the castle at lockup time and gave hopes of early liberation soon to those yet in irons. On behalf of Thompson, they conveyed a message to Trueheart and to two others that he had received letters from the United States in their behalf, but that Santa Anna was ill. As soon as he recovered, Thompson promised to press their claims for liberation.

On their arrival at Vera Cruz on April 5, Maverick, Jones, and Hutchinson took breakfast "at a large hotel" where they met F. M. Dimond, the American consul, and were invited to the home of Louis S. Hargous, a prominent American merchant and the vice-consul. They expected to find

---

52. Diaries of both groups fix their position on the Mexico City-Vera Cruz road at or adjacent to that point on the road on the same night.

53. All three had been residents of Texas for many years and had held various public offices in Texas.

54. Samuel Maverick to Mary A. Maverick, Pendleton [dated] April 16, 1832, in Green, ed., *Samuel Maverick*, p. 243.

55. [William E. Jones to M. B. Lamar], Washington, 1 Feby 1844, in Winkler, ed., "The Béxar and Dawson Prisoners," *QTSHA* 13 (Apr. 1910), pp. 323-24.

56. Report of Samuel A. Maverick upon his arrival at New Orleans, in New Orleans *Daily Picayune*, Apr. 22, 1843; copied in *Republican Banner* (Nashville), May 3, 1843.

the *Woodbury* waiting to take them home, as Thompson had written on March 16 that he had ordered it to standby, but this vessel was awaiting the payment of the indemnity and there was no other available transportation. While at Hargous' they were visited by John Bryan of Georgia, the purser of the United States sloop-of-war *Vincennes.* Waddy Thompson had requested that the three Texans be accorded passage on the *Vincennes,* then about to leave for Pensacola with dispatches for the U.S. State Department. Bryan came to complete the arrangements for their passage. Capt. Franklin Buchanan of the *Vincennes,* who hailed from Philadelphia, was under instruction to stop en route at Tampico to pick up George B. Crittenden, who had been released by Santa Anna, and where he was believed to have arrived on his way to Mexico City.

The *Vincennes,* a 22-gun vessel mounting 24-pounders, was delayed three days in sailing owing to a stiff norther. By Sunday, April 9, the wind from the north had subsided sufficiently to permit vessels to clear the harbor, and Hutchinson, Maverick, and Jones were conducted on board. Hutchinson was taken to the captain's cabin to lodge with him, while his two companions were taken to the wardroom to lodge with the lieutenants. The *Vincennes* got under way from the island of Sacrificios at two in the afternoon for Pensacola.

On April 12 the *Vincennes* found itself nineteen miles north of Tampico, and turned back.[57] That evening it tacked and cast anchor off the bar before Tampico, and Lieutenant Lewis from Philadelphia and Purser Bryan were sent ashore in a boat to bring off young Crittenden. They returned the next morning without him, for he had been sent on toward Mexico City three days previous to the arrival of the *Vincennes.*[58] Lewis came back with information that the British consul had received a report of the decimation at Hacienda Salado.[59] The *Vincennes* got under way for Pensacola, arrived off the Belize on the evening of April 17, and reached Pensacola at sunset on Tuesday, April 18.[60] From Pensacola the three Texans proceeded by stagecoach to Mobile, which they reached on April 20. Jones and Maverick left for New Orleans, arriving there on the morning of April 21. They reported Santa Anna as being extremely unwell when they left Mexico City.[61]

Hutchinson stopped off at Mobile, where he borrowed $20 from William P. Aubrey of Matagorda, enabling him to continue on April 23 on the steamer *Fashion* for New Orleans.[62] He arrived there the next morning, where he expressed "his warmest gratitude to Gen. Thompson, to

---

57. Green, ed., *Samuel Maverick,* p. 191.
58. *Daily Picayune,* Apr. 27, 1843.
59. *Telegraph and Texas Register,* May 3, 1843.
60. Hutchinson diary, Apr. 9-18, 1843; A. Hutchinson to W. D. Miller, Jackson, Mississippi, June 10, 1843, in W. D. Miller Papers, Tx-A; *Diario del Gobierno,* June 8, 1843; *Daily Missouri Republican,* May 1, 1843.
61. *Daily Picayune,* Apr. 22, 1843; see also *New Orleans Bee,* Apr. 22, 1843.
62. Hutchinson diary, Apr. 19-23, 1843.

President [John] Tyler, to Mr. [Daniel] Webster [Secretary of State], to the Senators and Members of Congress of Mississippi and Alabama, and also to Gen. H. S. Foote of the latter State, for their unsolicited interposition for his liberation. He also spoke in warmest of terms of Gen. Cela and Capt. Vidal of the Mexican army for their many attentions, and of the kindness shown him by Doña Catalina Canal de Semamigo of Querétaro."[63]

From New Orleans on April 28, Hutchinson, with his "health even improved by the many hardships of his imprisonment,"[64] took the steamer *Buckeye* to Vicksburg, where he arrived on May 1 and was met by Gen. Henry S. Foote. Foote took him to his home in Raymond, Mississippi—the place where Hutchinson had lived before going to Texas, and where he now met his daughter Ellen. On May 23, he met his wife, Mariana, in Montgomery, Alabama.

Hutchinson gave up the idea of returning to Texas and entered into a law partnership with Foote & Russell, effective June 19, 1843, in Jackson, Mississippi.[65] From Jackson, he sent a letter to Texas resigning the judgeship of the Fourth Judicial District, effective June 5, 1843.

In New Orleans Maverick reported the spirit and health of the Texans at Perote Prison to be good but said that many of the men were quite destitute and would often suffer for the ordinary necessities of life if it were not for a few generous foreigners who lived near the castle.[66] On April 22 Jones and Maverick left New Orleans aboard the *New York* for Galveston, arriving there three days later.[67] On April 28, Maverick crossed on horseback to Virginia Point on the mainland. He reached Houston on the evening of April 30,[68] where he again reported the prisoners at Perote to be "in good health and spirits." He said: "If the friends or relatives of the prisoners could remit twenty or thirty dollars to each prisoner, it would render their condition comparatively comfortable. The money could be sent to any respectable merchant in New Orleans, and a draft for the amount could readily be sold for a premium in Mexico."

On May 4, Maverick reached his family on the Colorado at Colonel Dancy's, near LaGrange.[69] His granddaughter, Rena Maverick Green, has said: "Mr. Maverick's only sorrow was that he had left so many friends and comrades in prison, and he felt almost ashamed when he met any of their families and friends, who all, of course came to see him—to tell him of his own good luck and of the continued ill luck of the other captives." He was

---

63. *Daily Picayune*, Apr. 29, 1843.
64. *Ibid.*
65. Hutchinson diary, April 27-June 14, 1843.
66. *Telegraph and Texas Register*, May 3, 1843; *Daily Picayune*, Apr. 22, 1843.
67. *Telegraph and Texas Register*, May 3, 1843, reported that Maverick arrived at Galveston on April 24, 1843.
68. *Telegraph and Texas Register*, May 3, 1843.
69. Green, ed., *Samuel Maverick*, p. 172.

elected to the Eighth Congress, House of Representatives, Congress of Texas, while in prison in Mexico.[70] He returned home in time to serve.

From Galveston, Jones went to San Augustine, where, in an address, he expounded at length "upon the cruel and barbarous conduct of the Mexican government." He stated that peace between Texas and Mexico could only be attained through the force of arms.[71] Proceeding to Nacogdoches, he delivered another address on Texas-Mexican relations, and stated "his views upon our Mexican policy generally," reported the editor of the *Northern Standard*, "and the practicability of an invasion of Western Mexico in particular."[72]

Billy Reese, the oldest of the four boys taken prisoner, who had "the downy evidences upon his upper lip, resembling a young frost, bespoke the confidence of sixteen,"[73] was released, at General Ampudia's request, shortly after his arrival on March 25, 1843, at Tacubaya. Reese had "just recovered from a dangerous illness in Mexico," and was expected to visit Perote Castle on the evening of April 11 on his way to the coast by stage to visit his brother, Captain Reese, and friends. He did not arrive until Friday, April 14, and brought no cheering news relative to the release of the prisoners. He "confirmed the melancholy intelligence of the decimation . . . at Salado,"[74] casting a still darker gloom over the disheartened prisoners, who shed tears in memory of their murdered companions.

On arrival at New Orleans early in June, Billy Reese was interviewed by the editor of the *New Orleans Tropic* on June 3, and reported that five Texans and twenty-three Mexicans had fallen in the struggle at Hacienda Salado. He confirmed the report from an American citizen in Mexico City who had reached New Orleans giving the melancholy fate of those drawing black beans at Salado.[75] Crittenden, on reaching Mexico City from Tampico with nine other Mier prisoners, gained his freedom and made his way to the coast for passage to the United States. He carried a letter from Thompson to the Texan prisoners at Perote Castle, where he stopped on April 23.[76] He was unable to give any account of the overthrow of the guard at Salado, but confirmed the report that seventeen had been shot by order of Santa Anna. He reported "the prospects of the Béxar men as bad, and that of the Mier men worse,"[77] but Thompson's letter conveyed

---

70. Eighth Congress, Dec. 4, 1843-Feb. 5, 1844. Maverick had been elected to the Seventh Congress (Called Session, Nov. 14, 1842-Dec. 4, 1842; Regular Session, Dec. 5, 1842-Jan. 16, 1843), but being one of the Woll prisoners, was unable to serve. His seat was declared vacant, and Hugh McLeod served from Béxar County, *Biographical Directory of the Texan Conventions and Congresses*, pp. 35-38.

71. *Telegraph and Texas Register*, May 24, 1843.

72. *Northern Standard*, May 18, 1843.

73. Green, *Mier Expedition*, p. 193. The Trueheart diary, Apr. 14, 1843, says Reese was released "on account of his youth."

74. Green, *Mier Expedition*, p. 283; see also Trueheart diary, Apr. 14, 1843.

75. *New Orleans Tropic*, June 4, 1843, quoted in *Northern Standard*, June 8, 1843.

76. Trueheart diary, Apr. 24 [23], 1843.

77. *Ibid.*

a ray of hope that the Béxar men probably would be released about June 13. From Perote Castle, Crittenden, carrying messages and many letters to be mailed in New Orleans, "to wives, sweethearts, and countrymen,"[78] proceeded to Vera Cruz, where he met Southall, the dispatch bearer who had arrived on the *Falmouth,* which remained in port awaiting the first payment of the Mexican indemnity.

At Vera Cruz, Crittenden took passage to Havana, and from that port on the steamer *Alabama* to New Orleans, arriving on May 7, along with David Morgan and George C. Hatch, who had escaped from the town of Perote. They had gone there on April 7 to bring back bread and a trunk of clothes. Morgan was "a noble fellow," who "spoke the Spanish language well."[79] At New Orleans, Hatch and Morgan reported that the Texan prisoners "were often fed tainted beef and stale, musty bread."

---

78. Green, *Mier Expedition*, p. 186.

79. Crittenden gave a verbal account of his imprisonment to the editor of the *New Orleans Bee,* May 8, 1843, upon his arrival in New Orleans, and was quoted in the *Republican Banner* (Nashville, Tenn.), May 19, 1843, and in the *Daily National Intelligencer,* May 16, 1843.

CHAPTER 11

Hard Times at Perote Castle — Hopes for Early Liberation Fade

RICHARD A. BARKLEY, WHO was as cantankerous and obnoxious to the Mexicans as any of the prisoners, wrote on April 10, 1843: "I would say that we are to see [hard times]. When we shall get out of this snap, God only [knows]. My only hope is an exchange of prisoners. . . . Things growes daily more gloomey . . . they treat us worse every [day]."[1]

On April 15, about ten days after Jones, Maverick, and Hutchinson left Perote Castle for Vera Cruz, Barkley wrote to Maverick:

> Things has changed verry mutch since you left this place or I might add this hell for it has become a perfect hell in every particular. Immediately after you left here the Mexicans Or devils I might add became more enraged they examoned our Chanes and finding them you know how they ordered us to the Shop they fastoned our Chanes as fast to our ankles as they could. the next day they agane examoned our chanes and finding them in the like condition they agane revited them after this the Govoner issued an order that the first man that was caught with his chanes off should be punished. . . .
>
> I will give you my case on yestedy my chane was off. Old Guts sliped in he carried me to limpy and he simply ordered me to the Calaboos this I took in good umer this he disliked he ordered me out again and had a pare of Spancels riveted to my ankels this I took in the Like maner this made him still mader—On this morning he said to Trewhart [Trueheart] I dont wish to punish anny man Iff he will promis to keep on his chanes and obey my orders and not make funn of him any more he would let me loose—I said to him I make you no promes I am a prisoner doo your damnedest—[2]

---

1. [Richard A. Barkley] to the Woodses, Harrell, Robinsons, Wilson Kenady, Brooksher, [and Others,] Castle of Perote and a strange [land], aprile 10 1843, in Spellman, ed., "Letters of the 'Dawson Men' from Perote Prison," *SWHQ* 38 (Apr. 1935), pp. 249-51; typed transcript of original in Woods Papers and Letters, TxU-A.

2. R. A. Barkley to Samuel A. Maverick, Castle of Perote, Saturday, April 15, 1843, in Green, ed., *Samuel Maverick*, pp. 245-47.

The harsh treatment Barkley received—often the result of his own stubbornness and recalcitrance—ended in his successful escape on July 2, 1843, with a number of others. Barkley reported that when the first Texans reached Perote Prison and were assigned to work that they worked every other day and were allowed to be their own judge as to the size of loads they would carry. But by May 1843, they were forced to work nearly every day and were made to pack as much as they could. "To add to our mizery," he said, "a large body of cavelry has binn stationed" here; and "we have their filth to carry out every morning."[3]

Toward the end of April, a letter was sent to President John Tyler of the United States by Thomas Jefferson Green. He sent the original to his mother and "expressed a wish that a copy might be sent to each of the [U.S.] senators [William A. Graham and Willie P. Mangum] from N.C."[4] In his communication, Green recalled that he had written the president a hurried note from Matamoros with Ampudia's permission. Now he wished to give a more detailed history of their march on Mier and capture. He sought Tyler's intervention in behalf of the Texans imprisoned in Mexico. "Our desire," he said, "is that we should be liberated because it is just that we should be; and then that the war should be conducted upon principles of civilized warfare, because we are too brave to retaliate by such dastardly perfidy and cowardice. Let this be done, and we are willing, anxious and able to carry on the war."

Two months after his outspoken opposition to Bocanegra in regard to the predatory warfare being waged on the Texas-Mexican frontier, Waddy Thompson informed Webster on May 16: "I have strong hopes that all the Texans will be released on the 15th of the next month [June]," but expressed little hope for the further release of individuals, since his recent private request for the liberation of Dr. Sinnickson had been rejected. "And after the violation of their parol[e] by so many of the Santa Fé prisoners [1841-1842] I can not see any just ground of complaint against Mexico for refusing to release any more prisoners."[5] Thompson's assumption concerning the release of all the prisoners proved false.

On May 19 Southall arrived at Perote on mail day and visited the prisoners. He informed them that it was generally believed that all would be released on June 13, Santa Anna's saint's day.[6] Chauncey Johnson thought they would all be released on June 13, 1843.[7]

---

3. R. A. Barkl[e]y to H. G. Woods, Mexico Castle of Perote, May 8, 1843, typed transcript of original in Woods papers and Letters, TxU-A.

4. Thomas J. Green to His Excellency John Tyler, President of the United States of America, Castle of Perote, Mexico, April 25, 1843, in Green, *Mier Expedition*, pp. 287-95; also in "The Texan Expedition Against Mier, 1842; Petition of Gen. Thos. J. Green," *Publications* of the Southern Historical Association 3, no. 2 (Apr. 1899), pp. 115-21.

5. Waddy Thompson to Daniel Webster, Secretary of State, Legation of the U. States, Mexico, May 16, 1843, in Despatches from United States Ministers to Mexico, Mar. 12, 1842—Mar. 25, 1844, National Archives (microfilm).

6. Trueheart diary, May 19, 1843.

7. Chauncey Johnson to the Editors of the *Picayune*, Castle of Perote, June 8, 1843, in *Daily Picayune*, July 13, 1843.

Word came more directly and with a higher degree of authenticity from Thompson and others that the Texans were to be released on June 13. "Our information appeared to be so authentic," declared Green, "we did not doubt it, and consequently knocked off from our work upon the breach in the wall."[8] Two letters were received at Perote Castle on May 8, 1843, from Thompson saying he had no doubt they would be freed on June 13, if not before.[9] In New Orleans it was reported from a alleged "reliable" Mexican source that "The Perote prisoners will, I think, all be released on the 13th June. So say those who know. They comprise all the San Antonio prisoners with Gen'ls Fisher and Green and sixteen others taken at Mier."[10] However, it was also learned through a letter from Mexico City that the Mier men there had been chained and put to work, "and that their treatment and fare was miserable in the extreme."[11]

Thompson wrote to Texas in May saying that when the Texan prisoners were released they would not have the means to defray their expenses to Vera Cruz and "many of them will be liable to starve or perish miserably unless means are furnished to enable them to return with all possible speed to Galveston."[12] While Louis Hargous and Thompson were willing to aid any returning prisoners, they did not have the means to defray the expenses of so large a group, and it was suggested by the editor of the *Telegraph* that the president of Texas use the reputed $3,000 left in the "contingent fund," for "we know of no method by which it could be disposed of more advanteously than by relieving the wants of those gallant men."[13]

Thompson sent word to the prisoners to prepare to go home, and Green, knowing that yellow fever was raging in Vera Cruz, wrote to the prisoners in Mexico City: "We are informed from various unofficial sources, besides through the letters of the United States minister in Mexico, that we are to be liberated on the 13th instant. . . . Should we be liberated on that day, I have advised our companions here to stop at Xalapa . . . until I can go to Vera Cruz and perfect an arrangement for their sailing, as it would be very dangerous for them to remain in that place. . . . I also advise you to come to that place, where you will join your comrades, and where I hope to meet you with the arrangements for sailing."[14] We find Green assuming the position of directing the men of the Mier Expedition and becoming more officious, a condition that pursued him throughout his career in Texas.

On June 2 there was a full dress review of the troops in the courtyard

---

8. Green, *Mier Expedition*, p. 302.

9. Trueheart diary, May 8, 1843.

10. *New Orleans Bee,* May 8, 1843, quoted in *Northern Standard*, July 13, 1843.

11. Trueheart diary, May 14, 1843.

12. Editor of the *Telegraph and Texas Register,* July 5, 1843, reporting content of Thompson's letter.

13. *Telegraph and Texas Register*, July 5, 1843.

14. Thomas J. Green to Captains Ryan, Pierson, Baker, and other Texan prisoners at War at Mexico, Castle of Perote, June 5, 1843, in Green, *Mier Expedition*, pp. 302-3.

of the castle, and the next day, when a new flag was raised in the courtyard, the prisoners were told again that they would be released on June 13.[15]

In anticipation of the completion of a new constitution for Mexico, President Ad Interim Valentín Canalizo summoned the national Congress in extraordinary session on June 18, 1844, "to receive the oath of the Constitutional President of the Republic, in order that he may enter on the discharge of his functions," and to grant power to the government to increase the size of the army and permit it to procure the "pecuniary resources and everything necessary to recover Texas and preserve the integrity of the national territory."[16]

By June 12 the Assembly of Notables had framed a new constitution, known as the *Bases Orgánicas,* calling for a central or consolidated representative government. It was signed by Santa Anna, and the next day in an elaborate ceremony he proclaimed it in effect.[17]

June 13 arrived, but no order came for the release of the Texan prisoners. Surely, said some of the Mexican officers, it will come tomorrow. Buoyant spirits of hope began to sink into gloom and disappointment, if but for a little while. Dr. William Shepherd wrote from Perote: "We have again resumed our accustomed feelings of indifference and despair, at least for the present. When we shall be liberated can be answered alone by the President of Mexico."[18]

In a few days word came from the capital that Santa Anna, learning that Houston had commissioned two parties to prey on the trade between the border of the United States and Santa Fé, New Mexico, had changed his mind about liberating the Texan prisoners. With this "*petit larceny* of waylaying the road, and robbing a few harmless traders of handkerchiefs and calicoes," declared Green, "all hopes of speedy liberation vanished, and we again set to work upon the breach in the wall."[19] A correspondent of the *Daily Picayune* wrote from Mexico on July 15 that he "was very much disappointed in the Texans not being released on the 13th of June. It was resolved on and would have been done, but for the arrival of your newspaper a few days before, containing a statement of a new invasion of Santa Fé."[20]

Colonel Hernández furnished the Texan prisoners with United States and Mexican newspapers reporting the invasion of New Mexico by "Americans again approaching Santa Fé," who "had surprised a Mexican spy

15. Trueheart diary, June 2-3, 1843.

16. Valentín Canalizo, President *ad interim* of the Republic of Mexico, to All the Inhabitants, Given at the National Palace of Mexico, 13th May, 1844, translation in *Telegraph and Texas Register*, July 17, 1844.

17. *Diario del Gobierno*, June 13, 1843; see also *Telegraph and Texas Register,* July 12, 1843.

18. Wm. M. Shepherd to the Editors of the *Picayune*, Castle of Perote, Mexico, July 4, 1843, in *Daily Picayune*, Aug. 1, 1843.

19. Green, *Mier Expedition*, pp. 304-5.

20. Correspondent of the *Picayune* to the Editors of the *Daily Picayune*, Mexico, July 15, 1843, in *Daily Picayune*, Aug. 8, 1843.

party of 100 on the Masseste River near Santa Fé," killing "the greater portion of them, capturing the balance, with the exception of one," who made his escape and reached Colonel Armijo with news of the attack. A few days later, the rumor was that the Americans were "committing great atrocities in New Mexico."[21] Any benevolent attitude that the Mexican authorities may have exhibited toward the Texan prisoners stiffened as news of the Texan advance on Santa Fé reached Mexico City.

Among the prisoners there was a faint hope that the recently appointed Texan commissioners might succeed in obtaining their freedom, even if they should fail to bring about a reconciliation between the two governments. "Many of us," recorded Trueheart, "awaiting with all the fortitude we are possessed with, would that something may happen to free us from this painful situation, and may the authors of it meet with punishment, they so necessarily merit. The manner of my capture, and my unjust detainment in this place and peculiar situation prey on my mind so that at times I feel unable to bear it, and become reckless of the future."

The men were disappointed that June 13 had passed and they had not been freed. Santa Anna did issue a proclamation on June 13 granting liberty to persons confined for political offenses, although its terms were not extended to the Texans; but, declared the editor of the Houston *Telegraph*, "It is scarcely probable that they will be imprisoned much longer, as Santa Anna can have no excuse for detaining them since he has received official notice that our government has assented to the armistice he proposed."[22] The latest word from Thompson on June 17 was that there was no chance that they would be granted their freedom soon, so Barkley, on June 18, wrote to Gonzalvo Woods in Texas, "I shall resor[t] to the project that I last spoke of in a leter of the 8 May," which he said he had sent by Orlando Phelps. He would now go through with his plans to escape. He stated that he had "binn able to guet hold of a few dollars," which would come in handy. "Iff I am not mistaken," he said, "this is the last leter I shall writ at least I hope so none of the boys of our Prairie will go with me it being a haserdous undertaking it is my advice to them to stay." He then proceeded to give full instructions about the payment of his debts and the collection of money owed to him and his father.[23]

The prisoners in Perote were visited by James F. B. Marshall, who reported them heavily chained and "compelled to perform the most servile offices, and are otherwise treated with great severity." The editor of the *New Orleans Bulletin* reported, "They have sent a letter to the President of the United States, soliciting the interposition of our Government in their

---

21. Trueheart diary, July 17, 22, and 27, 1843.
22. *Telegraph and Texas Register*, Aug. 2, 1843.
23. A. Barclay [Barkely], to H. G. Woods, LaGrange, Fayette Co., Texas [dated] Castle of Perote, June the 18, 1843, in Spellman, ed., "Letters of the 'Dawson Men' from Perote Prison," *SWHQ* 38 (Apr. 1935), pp. 254-56.

behalf. . . . [We] cannot but hope that the universal sense of the country will unite with the prayer of these poor prisoners, and our Government make at once a peremptory demand for their release and indemnification."[24]

Many became impatient to go home. As soon as the vanguard of the Mier prisoners reached the Castle of Perote, the minds of several turned to escape, having lost hope for an early liberation. When their chains were inspected on April 7, 1843, some were badly in need of repair; in such cases they were ordered to the blacksmith shop, where their chains were reriveted fast to their legs. "This did but little good," reported one of the men, for "before the last was fast the first was loos[e]." This enraged the guard, "but hell . . . [was] yet to pay the same evening." At one o'clock eight Texans were sent into Perote under heavy guard to bring back bread, as was the custom, and a trunk of clothing sent from Mexico City to Colonel Fisher and his men.[25] Later in the afternoon the main party returned, leaving George C. Hatch and Maj. David Morgan, who spoke Spanish[26] fluently, with several of the guard.

When lockup time came, they had not returned to the castle. The officer of the day became alarmed and checked the cells to determine if they had returned; they had not, and it was reported by those who had returned that the others had been seen in town playing billiards. As the night advanced their comrades did a lot of conjecturing. Morning came, and there was still no information about the two Texans. During the morning, the chains of all the Texan prisoners were checked carefully and those needing repairs were mended. None of the Texans were permitted to leave the castle and their guard was doubled. "We are told," recorded Trueheart, "by the officer that it [the escape] would operate to the prejudice of us all."[27]

Mexican criminals were dispatched for the bread and the governor ordered the two escapees shot if taken.[28] All of the Texan prisoners were ordered out to work, and the overseers and guards were instructed by the officers "to make us bring [good] loads and not to let us stop one moment," wrote Barkley.[29]

It was soon realized that Morgan and Hatch, both taken at San Antonio by Woll the previous September, had outwitted the guard and had effected their escape with the aid of friends in Mexico. Making their way to Vera Cruz, they obtained passage on an American vessel bound for New

---

24. *New Orleans Bulletin*, quoted in *Northern Standard*, June 15, 1843.
25. Trueheart diary, April 7, 1843.
26. Nance, *Attack and Counterattack*, pp. 323, 323-24, n. 85, pp. 600-3.
27. Trueheart diary, Apr. 7-8, 1843.
28. R. A. Barkley to Samuel A. Maverick, Castle of Perote, April 15, 1843, in Green, ed., *Samuel Maverick*, pp. 245-47.
29. [R. A. Barkley] to Woodses—Harrell—Robinsons—Willson Kenady—Brooksher and Others, April 10, 1843, Castle of Perote and a Strange [land], in Spellman, ed., "The Letters of the 'Dawson Men,'" *SWHQ* 38 (Apr. 1935), pp. 249-50.

Orleans, where they arrived on May 7, 1843.[30] They traveled first to Galveston, then to Houston, and arrived there on May 12, in fine health.[31]

The prisoners at Perote Castle were somewhat relieved on May 23 concerning the Robinson proposals, when one of them received a letter from Morgan telling of his safe arrival at New Orleans on May 7 and informing them that the Robinson proposals were a "no go" in Texas, all of which was pleasing news to the Texans at the castle.[32]

The escape of Morgan and Hatch encouraged others to make the attempt. Reese and Green planned to scale the castle walls, the height of which could be estimated by counting the number of layers of squared stones from the bottom of the moat. Their ignorance of the country made it necessary to have a map of that section of Mexico, so Green wrote to a friend in Mexico City to procure one for him. The friend replied that on a certain day he would pass by stagecoach from Mexico City to Vera Cruz and for Green to meet him at the stage-office in Perote, where the Vera Cruz and Mexico City stages met and the passengers spent the night at the local *posada*. Since it was customary for the governor to permit a few Texans under strong guard to meet the stage to receive mail intended for the Texans,[33] it was easy for Green to obtain permission to go after the mail on the appointed day. When Green reached the stage office his friend was waiting. Neither spoke or gave any indication of recognizing the other. The problem was how to transfer the map without being detected. The Mexican officer stood not more than three feet away, and on each side of the door the soldiers stood in single file.

After a few minutes, Green's friend, who spoke Spanish well, approached the officer and, pointing to the prisoner, asked:

"Is not that a Texian prisoner?"

"Yes," replied the officer.

Walking around Green, and eyeing him from head to foot as something of a novelty, the friend once more turned to the officer to remark: "Well, such is the fortune of war; will you join me in something to drink?"[34]

The officer accepted the invitation and after the first drink had been finished, the friend asked if he might not give one to the poor Texan. The courtesy was permitted, and thereafter the officer was plied with drink after drink until he became quite good-natured and loquacious. After a while, the friend stepped into an adjoining room and "returned in a few minutes with a razor, hairbrush, and comb, so folded in a rumpled paper" that their ends plainly showed. He requested permission from the officer to give the items to the Texan, who appeared to be badly in need of them.

30. *New Orleans Bee*, May 7, 1843, quoted in *Daily National Intelligencer* (Washington, D.C.), May 16, 1843; Trueheart diary, May 23, 1843.

31. *Telegraph and Texas Register*, May 17, 1843.

32. Trueheart diary, May 23, 1843. The printed Trueheart diary gives the date as May 1, but the date seems to be May 7. See *New Orleans Bee*, May 7, 1843.

33. Stapp, *Prisoners of Perote*, p. 114.

34. Green, *Mier Expedition*, p. 299.

The officer gave his consent, little dreaming that the rumpled wrapper was a map of the area between Mexico City and Vera Cruz.

On his return to the castle, Green had Ludovic Colquhoun make copies of the map for the use of those who were planning to escape. Taking as few as possible of the other Texans into their confidence, Reese and Green collected the items necessary for their planned escape over the walls of the fort. Rope could be purchased in town. From time to time, Mexican soldiers and civilians were bribed or encouraged to purchase short pieces of rope so as not to attract attention, and to smuggle it into the castle. The pieces were woven into a unit. They gradually accumulated small quantities of bread and hoarded coins to purchase bacon and chocolate. A stormy, cold night was considered ideal for crawling past sentinels to the gate that blocked steps that led to the top of the gate. To get over the gate, one man would stand on the shoulders of the other to reach the top; while his partner held one end of the rope, the other would descend to the opposite side of the gate. He would hold the rope for the other to ascend to the top of the gate and let himself down on the shoulders of the one already over. They would then ascend by the stairs to the top of the castle, crawl past the sentinels at the top, tie the rope to the wheel of a cannon, and descend to the moat below.[35]

Having worked out the details of their plan, Green and Reese were awaiting a favorable night when they became aware of tunneling operations in the middle cell, which contained thirty-six of their comrades. In his narrative of the escape plans, Green leaves us with the impression that he and Reese were prevailed on by the others to await the outcome of the tunneling efforts, which, if successful, would give an opportunity for a greater number to escape.

The men in the middle cell had been working for several weeks, in accordance with a suggestion made by [David] Joe Davis, one of Captain Hays' rangers,[36] digging a tunnel through the eight-foot wall, and the men were elated with the prospect of success. Efforts to enlarge the window at the rear of the room were frustrated by "the hard character of the stones, and the secure fastenings immediately around the hole." Another hole was commenced a short distance to the left of the window and cut through the barrier wall. To avoid discovery, "a careless rap upon the door or post by . . . [a] *look-out* man was sufficient for the operator in the hole to *lie low*." The men worked alternately in the tunnel, "as only one at a time could operate, and he was secreted by the shutter enclosing the loophole, and blankets carefully hung about it. The labour was extremely tiresome, as the hole had to be made horizontally through the wall, and consequently required the operator to lay upon his abdomen, and rest upon his elbows, which position after a few hours' work, became very painful."[37] The men

35. Green, *Mier Expedition*, p. 301.
36. Sowell, *Early Settlers and Indian Fighters of Southwest Texas*, p. 81.
37. Green, *Mier Expedition*, p. 306.

used narrow carpenter's chisels smuggled in the folds of their blankets from the shops. With these tools small holes were gouged into the masonry and chips of stone and mortar pried loose. Often, after "a hard day's labor, not more than a hatful could be disengaged." The fragments of stone and mortar were buried under loose stone or brick in the cell floor, and when the quantity of it raised the pavement too high, it was smuggled out in the clothing and blankets of the men and dumped in the common privy, the moat, or allowed to sift out on the courtyard. As the hole developed, one of the greatest problems was to keep it from growing too small. By the time the outer wall was reached, the hole had a funnel shape with the outer opening only about ten by fourteen inches. It would be difficult for anyone to squeeze through, and impossible for more than one, even in their "lean" condition. On July 1 the tunnel was complete except for a thin shell on the outer end which could easily be knocked out when the men were ready to leave.

For weeks those who were counting on escaping through the tunnel had been making "knapsacks" cut from old saddlebags or grass sacks and filling them with bread, fat bacon, coffee, sugar, and chocolate which they saved from their daily rations or purchased. Green, having more money than the others, procured sugar, coffee, and bacon for several men to compensate for his lack of work in the hole. A minimum of two weeks' food supply was regarded as sufficient to enable them to get through the mountains to a settled area.

On Sunday, July 2, the officer of the guard was one known for his laxity in counting and inspecting at lockup time. During the day, the conspirators passed the word for all who intended to make the attempt to go to be in readiness by night. Johann G. Andreas Voss, a Béxar prisoner and the *cuartelero* of the center room for the day to keep the room clean, tied up his head and jaw about an hour before lockup time, so he would be absolved from responsibility in the escape plans. Late in the afternoon, several of the Texans suddenly changed their minds. It was a risky business, and failure would mean death. Green also realized the risks were great, especially to him personally; he believed that Santa Anna would relish an opportunity to have him shot if recaptured. In his book, Green says that he had grown tired of living "the life of an insulted slave." But his life as a prisoner was far superior to that of the majority of his comrades.

Others were reluctant to make the attempt at a time when liberty seemed close at hand; furthermore, Edward Manton declared, there was "a hint that a man that was no Woods Man would be a drawback and I had rather be here than be a burden to any man." He added, "It was also thought by some men that were best acquainted with the people and Country to be impracticable and foolish, and I believe their calculation was about rite, as one half were retaken, . . . and I think . . . most of the others would have be[e]n for the exertions of one man, among them who had a plenty of money and friends, and knew how to manage matters."[38] Sixteen of the men determined to make the effort, no matter what the risk.

Green has left an account of the leave-taking of friends at half past five, shortly before the usual lockup time. Many, he reported, said, "God grant that you may reach home in safety, for then we know we will be fearlessly and truly represented." One wonders how much Fisher's blood pressure rose when he saw this statement in print two years later. At the time of departure, in Green's words, Fisher told him: "As you have determined upon the hazard, though the chances are greatly against you, God grant that you may reach home in safety."[39]

Those planning to escape included: Samuel Stone, Isaac Allen, Augustus Elley, Thomas Hancock, Truman B. Beck, David J. Davis, John Young, David S. Kornegay, Richard A. Barkley, John Forester, John Dalrymple, John Twohig, Duncan C. Ogden, Charles K. Reese, Daniel Drake Henrie, and Green. All their personal items that could not be taken were distributed among those who remained. Green left his diary and other papers in the hands of Ludovic Colquhoun, who buried them and thus kept them from falling into the hands of the guard who later carefully searched those who remained.[40] Green left a note on his table addressed to President Santa Anna. In it he says, he "exculpated the officers of the castle from either knowledge of our going, or neglect of duty in closely guarding us."

It was difficult to persuade the five men in the center room who were not planning to leave to exchange places with those from the other two rooms who desired to go as it entailed great risk to the five who remained. If we believe Green's account, Fisher tried to discourage the undertaking; others have reported that Fisher refused to leave, saying he had "brought the command into the 'Scrape,' and that he thought it his duty to stay untill all could go." In a letter he wrote: "I could have availed myself of the same mode of liberation with Green, but preferred to wait and witness the result of the captivity of my companions." Fisher's attitude is further illustrated by his rebuttal of the Mexican effort "to attach blame to those who escaped upon what principles &c I cannot understand, as it is certain that where no confidence existed none could be violated." Since the prisoners had not been paroled on their word of honor, Fisher saw no reason why they should not leave if the opportunity afforded. While he may have discussed the possible effect such an escape would have on those who remained, Fisher did not consider his personal safety in the matter; more than once he had told the men to use their own judgment in the matter of escaping. The Mexicans, he thought, "might save themselves a vast deal

---

38. Edward Manton to Hezekiah Smith, LaGrange, Fayette County, Texas, [dated] Castle of Perote, Sept. 22, 1843, in Edward Manton Papers (photostats), TxU-A.

39. Green, *Mier Expedition*, p. 313.

40. When John Bradley was released several weeks later by Santa Anna the papers were forwarded through him to Green. Green, *Mier Expedition*, p. 312.

of trouble and disagreeable feeling by at once admitting our claim to consideration as gentlemen, and placing confidence in our pledge of honor, which they would find a better security against escape than chains, prison walls and double guards."[41]

At six o'clock the bugles in the plaza sounded, and the turnkey began to lock the cell doors. It was a moment of excitement when the officer of the guard entered the cells to count the men because the discovery of a single man out of place would delay the escape. A cold rain was falling and darkness came earlier than usual that evening. Because of the inclement weather, the officer did not order the men to line up in front of the prison doors for the count. The men were counted in their rooms, the rear of which were fairly dark. The men in the cell on the right were counted first while the men in the center cell, with the tunnel, anxiously awaited the outcome. The grating of a heavy door and the jingle of keys told them that all was well. Then the turnkey, the counting sergeant, and the officer of the guard, followed by a squad of soldiers with fixed bayonets, entered the center room. *"Formarse! Formarse!"* ("Form yourselves! Form yourselves!") ordered the officer. The count began. With the exception of Green and Ogden, who lay on the floor with blankets closely drawn around them, the prospective escapees, with slouched hats and blankets well up about their faces, lurked at the rear of the long, narrow, dimly lighted room. The count revealed two men missing, but "Tecolote" Trimble, pointing to the two on the floor, sang out: *"Aquí son dos que muy malo."* ("Here are two who are very sick.") *"Bueno"* ("Good"), shouted the officer, and the guard passed out of the cell, pulling the door behind him with a heavy crash. Soon the slamming of the door to the left-hand cell told the Texans that so far all was well and that their plans could proceed on schedule.

Still there was danger of being detected by the sentinel at the door, should he stand on the sill and look through the grating. Some of the men now sought to make him good-natured and to divert his attention by passing through the grating of the door small quantities of *vino mescal* in an eggshell. Soon another group of four or five Texans spread a blanket on the floor near the door. They placed two candles on it and began a game of monte. The sentinel became interested in the progress of the game and as a means of furthering that interest he was provided with a handful of *clacos* so that he could participate in the betting, which he soon passed back through the grate of the door, indicating at the same time the card upon which the bet was to be placed.

A short distance away from the game of monte, eight or ten of the prisoners, chained *dos-a-dos*, engaged in "a 'bull-dance,' being the only one" they "could perform in" their " 'jewelry'; the twenty pound festoons which coupled the partners not being well adapted to the 'chases' and 'bal-

___

    41. William S. Fisher to the Editor of the *New Orleans Bulletin*, Castle of Perote, Aug. 4, 1843, in *Northern Standard*, Dec. 16, 1843.

ance.'" They danced to the clank of their chains and to "Tecolote's" (Trimble's) call or sing-song. "Tecolote" concluded each dance with the hoot of an owl, or the "flap of his wings," and the crow of a rooster in the early morn of "the gamest cock that ever graced a pit."[42] When one set of dancers tired, another took its place to cover the noise of the men knocking out the end of the tunnel and worming their way through to freedom.

By seven o'clock, the outer end of the tunnel had been removed, and as the hole proved only large enough for the smallest men to pass through, two hours of feverish work were required to scale away pieces of stone and mortar to permit the larger men to pass. Then a rope was made fast to permit the men to descend thirty feet to the bottom of the moat. The first to go through the tunnel was John Twohig, a small man, who went feet foremost, drawing his knapsack after him. If he had become stuck in the tunnel, no one would have gotten out. Because of his size and energy, he had done more than anyone else in performing work in the tunnel. "It was less difficult for him than some others," said Green, "to get through the perforation in the wall." Inch by inch he squeezed out, "and descended hand over hand to the bottom of the moat." The depth of the tunnel and the smallness of the hole made it exceedingly slow, but by half past twelve all sixteen had landed safely on the other side of the wall. Ike Allen lost his grip on the rope and fell into the midst of his friends below. The ankle-deep sand prevented injury.

The smallest men went through first, leaving the larger ones to the last for fear of someone getting stuck in the hole and preventing others from escaping. Though Green's normal weight of 160 pounds was down to 120, he found "much difficulty" in going through the tunnel. "The gradual funnel-shape of the breach made it like driving a pin into an auger-hole, for the deeper . . . [one] went the closer the fit." The next-to-the-last man to go through was Samuel Stone, a large man, who lodged fast in the funnel-shaped tunnel. He could move neither forward nor backward. Finally, his friends on the inside of the cell reached into the hole, tied ropes to his hand and drew him back. This operation was very painful, but he was still determined to go. "I have a wife and children at home," he said, "and I would rather die than stay here longer: I will go through, or leave no skin upon my bones." Accordingly, he undressed and again entered the hole feet first, pulling his clothes after him along with his knapsack. His vigorous efforts caused the perspiration to flow freely, which had the same effect as if he had been greased. After much effort, Stone went through, "leaving both skin and flesh behind. Probably a larger man than Stone was John Young, who had well-developed shoulders, which reminded one of a wrestler or boxer; he stood six feet two inches in height. He was the last to go through the tunnel, dragging thirty pounds of bacon after him.

---

42. Green, *Mier Expedition*, pp. 316-17.

While the Texans quietly whispered instructions from one to the other and adjusted their knapsacks and blankets, the Mexican sentinels on both the right and left bastions monotonously cried *"centinela alerto."* With their packs adjusted, the tense little band slinked across the moat between the two bastions, favored by the darkness. The moon had gone down at eight o'clock, and through the inky blackness of the deep dry moat the Texans slowly crossed to the outer wall in Indian file, then groped along the wall until they came to a flight of narrow steps eighteen inches wide, up which they crawled upon all fours.

Thirty minutes past midnight, the Texans were 200 yards beyond the fortifications. Here they halted to await the return of Reese, Ogden, and Twohig, who, accompanied by Allen, had gone forward to contact a confidential guide with whom they had made arrangements through a friend. The guide was to meet them some distance from Perote with three horses between the hours of ten and one at a point one mile east of the castle. He was to kindle a fire to signal his location and to arrange for a relay of horses to carry the Texans to Vera Cruz before the alarm of their escape could reach there. The guide, it was later learned, had waited at the designated spot, but had not kindled a signal fire for fear of attracting the attention of some shepherds in the neighborhood. Allen hoped to contact a second guide who would conduct the others on foot through the mountains toward Vera Cruz. The failure to light the signal-fire caused the Texans, who were unfamiliar with the terrain, to search for their friend in vain. Ogden and Allen returned to the main group while Reese and Twohig continued the search for the guide. "They are without a Pilot," wrote Norman Woods from Molino del Rey on July 20 when he learned of the escape. "God noes whether they will make good their retreat."[43]

The Texans fell back on their original plan to escape in pairs. They divided into six groups: Thomas Hancock, Duncan C. Ogden, and John Forester, headed in a northeasterly direction.[44] Isaac Allen, with Samuel Stone and Augustus Elley, kept the north star on his left and headed more to the north than did Hancock for the Rio Grande. John Young, with Truman B. Beck and David J. Davis, started for Tampico, taking a route that lay between those of the Hancock and Allen parties. Richard A. Barkley and David S. Kornegay struck a course still farther to the east of Hancock and succeeded in reaching Vera Cruz. Green and Daniel Drake Henrie took the stagecoach road toward Vera Cruz and had only gone a few miles when they were overtaken by Reese, Twohig, and John Dalrymple, whose partner had refused to come at the last moment and headed alone for the main road to the City of Mexico. On arrival at the capital, he represented himself as a Canadian to the British minister and obtained a passport,

43. Postscript to Norman Woods, letter to H. G. Woods, LaGrange, Fayette County, Texas, Moleino del Rey, July 20, 1843, in Spellman, ed., "Letters of the 'Dawson Men' from Perote Prison," *SWHQ* 38 (Apr. 1935), pp. 260-62.

44. Green, *Mier Expedition*, p. 327.

which enabled him to travel to Tampico with little or no hindrance.[45] At Vera Cruz, Twohig "hired himself on board a Mexican war Steamer bound to the United States, which landed him at Charleston, S.C., without the officers or crew being aware of his having escaped from one of their . . . prisons."[46] Forester's group reached Texas eventually. The night following their separation, John Young fell over a precipice in the mountains and crippled himself so badly that he was easily recaptured the next day and returned to the castle, then was sent to the hospital in Perote. His companions, Beck and Davis, were soon retaken by the pursuing cavalry. Hancock, on venturing into a *rancho* to buy supplies, was recaptured; and Ogden, who had become separated from his companions, was caught entering Jalapa on July 9, the night that Green and his companions left the place.

Those recaptured were closely chained.[47] Green, Reese, and Henrie reached Jalapa safely[48] on the evening of July 8, and were hidden in the home of a Mexican friend, who obtained a guide, "the most noted robber and murderer in Mexico," to conduct them to Vera Cruz. The guide was assisted by two others. After many harrowing experiences, including the crossing of Santa Anna's estate, the three reached Vera Cruz on the fifth night—July 13, and eventually made their way to New Orleans.[49]

At New Orleans, Green, Henrie, and Reese stayed in the St. Charles Hotel at the rate of one dollar each day paid in advance, until passage could be arranged to Texas.[50] In New Orleans, Reese and Dr. Sinnickson exhibited consideration for their friends left in Mexico by publishing letters thanking a number of officials for the favors the prisoners received, including Col. Manuel Barragán, Col. Juan Ortiz, and Capt. Felix Llera of the Mexican army; Gen. José María Bocanegra for the release of his brother, William E. Reese; Gen. José M. Duran "for his leniency towards myself whilst a prisoner at Perote, and beg leave to assure him that my escape was affected without the knowledge of any officer or soldier at the castle"; and to Gen. Waddy Thompson, the United States minister to Mexico, to whom "I shall ever feel the greatest gratitude for the interest manifested by him towards those who could have no claim to his good offices, more than common humanity would prompt."[51]

Sinnickson expressed through the columns of the *Daily Picayune* of

45. *Daily Picayune*, Sept. 12, 1843.

46. Bell, *Narrative*, p. 92.

47. Those recaptured were John Young, Truman B. Beck, David J. Davis, Thomas Hancock, Duncan C. Ogden, reported the *Daily National Intelligencer* (Washington, D.C.), Aug. 16, 1843.

48. Green, *Mier Expedition*, pp. 327-60, 364-69.

49. For additional details, not reported here, of the journey of these three dare-devils to Vera Cruz and thence by way of New Orleans to Texas, see Green, *Mier Expedition*, pp. 364-69.

50. Green, *Mier Expedition*, pp. 368-69.

51. Charles K. Reese to the Editors of the *Picayune*, New Orleans, Aug. 10, 1843, in *Daily Picayune*, Aug. 10, 1843.

August 10, 1843, his thanks to those to whom he was "greatly indebted for his release from confinement as a prisoner of war"; namely, the "many eminent members of the U.S. Congress . . . for the interest they manifested in his behalf, in addressing the American Minister near the City of Mexico"; to Waddy Thompson; to John Black, the United States consul in Mexico City, "for the many services rendered him, both prior to and after his release"; and he said he might be accused of ingratitude if he did not "acknowledge his indebtedness to the President of the Republic of Mexico, for granting the application of the American Minister for his liberty, so soon as the political affairs of the country would admit"; and he would not pass unnoticed General Tornel, the minister of war, "for the promptness with which he issued an order for his discharge, within about four hours after Gen. Thompson's application had been made."[52] Dr. Sinnickson did not return to Texas.

The day after Green and his companions arrived in New Orleans, William M. Beal generously supplied the men with funds for food, and two days later, August 10, Green, Reese, Henrie, Forester, and Kornegay left New Orleans aboard Captain Furgarson's ship for Texas. Six days later they reached Quintana, near the mouth of the Brazos River.[53] Soon after his return, Green announced from Velasco in the columns of the *Columbia Planter* that he was a candidate to represent Brazoria County in the House of Representatives of the next Congress.[54]

Returning to the men in the castle, after the last man had gone through the hole, William Bugg stuffed a dirty blanket in the opening and awaited the coming of daybreak and the order to form. There was much apprehension concerning the safety of the escapees as well as the fate of those who stayed behind, although it was known that those who had not participated in the break at Salado had not been held accountable for the action of their colleagues. Those remaining planned to reveal nothing, and as far as possible to throw as many stumbling-blocks in the way of the Mexican command to delay the search for those who had fled. At the usual hour of nine o'clock the next morning, Captain Guzmán and the new guard appeared and ordered the prisoners to turn out and form in front of the prison doors to be counted and turned over to the day guard. The prisoners emerged from their cells, some holding back and delaying for various reasons. "Old Guts" stormed at their slowness and finally rushed furiously into the center cell to drive the missing men out. None were there. He asked in an uncertain voice for the whereabouts of the missing men. Some suggested that they had gone to the privy; others hinted that they were at the *tienda;* and still others inferred that they had gone early

---

52. John J. Sinnickson to the Editors of the *Picayune*, New Orleans, Aug. 10, 1843, in *Daily Picayune*, Aug. 10, 1843.

53. Green, *Mier Expedition*, p. 369.

54. *Telegraph and Texas Register* and *National Vindicator* (Washington), quoted in *Northern Standard*, Sept. 14, 1843.

to the carpenter shop. All of these places were quickly searched by units of the guard without success. Guzmán "swelled and raved." "Where are they?" he demanded of the interpreter. After all, the castle was regarded as impregnable and one of the strongest fortifications in Mexico.

Seeing that they could no longer stall, Van Ness whispered to Trueheart, asking if he should now make known the escape. Receiving an affirmative answer, he announced that sixteen of the men were missing. "It is almost impossible," reported a witness, "to describe the mingled emotion of surprise, mortification and fear detected on his [Guzmán's] face, the vaines in his neck swelling and appearing as though he was laboring under some dreadful malady."[55]

For a moment "Old Guts" "seemed to have lost in a measure, his power of speech." Soon in a quivering voice he blurted in a thundering rage: "Where did they go, and how did they get out?" "*Quien sabe?*" ("Who knows?") replied Van Ness, with a shrug of his shoulders. "Then commenced the greatest possible row: The whole castle was alarmed—officers and soldiers turned out—the Govenor came forth with deathlike horror upon his countenance—officers and guards flew all over the castle; examined every nook and corner—the top walls—went around the great moat, but still did not discover the breach, the hole having been so carefully stopped with the blanket." The dark tyrants of Mexico were between a lather and a sweat. "The last place . . . they thought of looking was in the prison cells, and after much useless search, one of the officers pulled back the small shutter in the center room which covered the loophole, and found to his inexpressible horror . . . [the] breach obliquing to the left."[56] "Here is where the d——— rascals got out," he cried.[57]

Trueheart suggested that Guzmán might find out who was missing by calling the roll of prisoners. The cooks and carpenters were sent for and, in the presence of the officers who had assembled in front of the cells, the list of names was called. For a moment, some of the officers seemed puzzled as to how some of those in rooms 9 and 11 had gotten into room 10. Finally, one of the officers observed that was easy enough; they had simply changed places prior to being locked in the cells for the night.

The governor, his lady, and many of the officers came to view the hole, and when news of the escape spread into the town of Perote, a good many persons came out to the castle the next day, July 4, to see the place where the Texan devils had dug out. In the more than seventy years since the building of the castle, no one had escaped through or over the walls. This was, indeed, an extraordinary achievement and worthy to be seen.

Green's letter to Santa Anna was handed to the governor, as he examined the hole, and he quickly read and dispatched it at once since "It

---

55. Trueheart diary, July 3, 1843.
56. Green, *Mier Expedition*, pp. 361-62. Green got his information later from those who were on the scene.
57. Trueheart diary, July 3, 1843.

exonerated the governor and officers from any neglect."[58] Nevertheless, upon receipt of the news of the escape, Santa Anna ordered the governor, Isidro Pombo ("Limpy"), and Guzmán ("Guts") arrested. Major Coxo was placed under arrest by the governor and temporarily relieved of his supervision of the prisoners' quarters, and for a brief spell, Major Bonilla, officer of the plaza, a more humane and kind officer, took over the supervision of the prisoners. When Major Coxo was exonerated and restored to his former position, the Texans felt his wrath, torments, and vexations. When Guzmán was relieved of his office, "a very good man" replaced him, "all though he is not to be trifled with," reported Manton, "but makes us wear our chains night and day."[59]

By ten o'clock, the cavalry was mounted and sent in pursuit of the fleeing Texans but they lost the trail at the point where the sixteen had separated. The cavalry divided into several small units, each going in a different direction; others hurried to close the mountain passes. Citizens were called on to render assistance in reapprehending *los tejanos.* The Texans who remained behind were confined to their cells. On July 4 the windows of rooms 9, 10, and 11 were "well stopped," greatly restricting the circulation of air.[60] The four prisoners in the hospital were brought back to the castle and in the evening all chains were examined carefully and any found loose were riveted tight; those who had been exempted from or freed of their chains were now reironed.

For that night and the next two days all of the Texian prisoners were placed in room number 11 under double guard day and night. The four Texan officers and former civil officials who occupied the "Star Room" were "obliged to admit a few of the Common Stock and the two house[s] agree a little better than they used to."[61] For several days after the escape, those left behind were kept securely locked in their cells, for every soldier who could be spared had gone in search of the fleeing Texans. For a few days, no small degree of excitement prevailed among the prisoners themselves, "feeling naturally a warm solicitation for our companions in so daring and hazardous an undertaking," reported Dr. William Shepherd, "as well as our own condition not knowing the effect which might be produced upon the officers in charge relative to ourselves."[62]

On July 6 the fourteen prisoners who had occupied cell number 9 were permitted to return to it and two additional members were added. The prisoners now occupied two rooms instead of three as formerly. The

58. Green, *Mier Expedition*, p. 363.
59. Edward Manton to Hezekiah Smith, LaGrange, Fayette Cty., Texas, [dated] Perote, Aug. 15, 1843, in Edward Manton Papers (photostat), TxU-A.
60. Trueheart diary, July 4, 1843.
61. Edward Manton to Hezekiah Smith, LaGrange, Fayette Cty., Texas [dated] Aug. 15, 1843, in Edward Manton Papers (photostat), TxU-A. The officers and top court officials were referred to as "Stars."
62. Wm M. Shepherd to the Editor of the *Picayune*, Castle of Perote, Mexico July 4, 1843, in *Daily Picayune*, Aug. 1, 1843.

floors in the rooms were ripped out and the hole in the door was enlarged to permit the sentinels more visibility to see if there was any digging going on or if the prisoners took off their chains.[63] No threats to punish or actual punishment, however, kept the Texans from taking off their chains. "As soon as our doors are locked," recorded Trueheart, "we as usual take off our chains."[64]

To impede the planning of future escapes, guards shuffled the prisoners—exchanging rooms, changing companions to whom shackled, and changing job assignments and the personnel within work crews. On July 8 all rope and nails found among the prisoners were seized, and their quarters were examined minutely. Chains were reexamined constantly. On July 9 the *mayor de la Plaza* was "very much indisposed," being "confined to his bed with his lame leg, originating no doubt, from his being up over night," reported Trueheart, "endeavoring to catch some of us separated from our companions." Just before lockup time on July 12, all chains were examined. "The person who examined them," recorded Trueheart, "reported favorable notwithstanding the bad condition of a good many— one being tied with a string.

Two of the escapees, Beck and Davis, were captured by a squad of cavalry. In the excitement over their return, a letter arrived from Vera Cruz containing a copy of Houston's proclamation of a cessation of hostilities.[65] A few days later, the prisoners learned that the suspension of hostilities had been acknowledged in the Mexican newspapers.

On July 10 Ogden and Hancock were brought in, rechained, and placed in the calaboose. A few days later three more of the fugitives— Allen, Elley, and Stone—who had been apprehended near Papantla were returned, bringing to eight the number recaptured. Two days later a declaration was taken from them, after which they were returned to room 9. On July 17 declarations were taken on the remaining fugitives, and they, too, were returned to cell number 9, bringing the number in the cell to twenty-three.[66]

As an added precaution and with the hope of locating some of the fugitives still at large, the guard examined the mail received by the prisoners. When letters written by the fugitives on the eve of their embarkation to their friends at the castle arrived on July 17, the guard intercepted, read, and retained two or three of them, creating apprehension among the prisoners for fear that the letters might incriminate someone who had favored or aided in their escape. Their suspense was soon relieved when they learned through their new interpreter that no one had been compro-

---

63. Edward Manton to Hezekiah Smith, LaGrange, Fayette Cty., Texas, [dated] Perote, August 15, 1843 (photostat) in Edward Manton Papers, TxU-A.

64. Trueheart diary, July 12, 1843.

65. Proclamation of an Armistice with Mexico issued at Washington, June 15, 1843, in Proclamations of the Presidents, Republic to Texas, Tx-A; *Morning Star,* June 20, 1843; *Telegraph and Texas Register,* June 21, 1843.

66. Trueheart diary, July 16, 1843.

mised, but word was sent to Vera Cruz and Jalapa, from whence the letters had come, to have the fugitives arrested and returned. The authorities there failed to locate them.

News of the Snively Expedition against the Santa Fé trade, gained from Mexican newspapers, created great excitement among the prisoners, and later reports were that the Americans were "committing great atrocities in New Mexico." This caused gloom among the prisoners concerning the possibility of an early release. On the heels of this news, word was received from General Thompson that no "prisoners will be released until the negotiations between Texas [and Mexico] are completed."[67]

The cells were entered at unexpected intervals, day and night, by guards in search of evidence of tunneling operations. In spite of all these added precautions, the Mier men soon began digging another tunnel to connect with the outside.

Charles Elliot, the British *chargé d'affaires* in Texas, then in Galveston, notified Sam Houston in Washington on the Brazos that he had received from H. B. M. *chargé d'affaires* in Mexico, Percy Doyle, a dispatch informing him that Doyle had requested Santa Anna to release all the Texan prisoners still held in Mexico. Santa Anna reportedly replied that there were still Mexican prisoners held in Texas, some of whom had been captured at San Jacinto, although he admitted that they were fewer in number than the Texan prisoners held in Mexico. Santa Anna requested Doyle to inform the government of Texas that he would "at once consent to the release of all the Prisoners, whatever may be the difference in numbers, upon the Mexicans still kept prisoners in Texas, being sent to the Head Quarters of General Woll."[68]

Houston, knowing there were no Mexican prisoners from San Jacinto being held in Texas,[69] moved immediately to issue a proclamation freeing all Mexican prisoners captured by the Texan forces since the commencement of hostilities. He instructed that they report to Colonel Hays at San Antonio by October 10, 1843, and be given an escort to Woll's headquarters. All military and civil officers in Texas were "enjoined and required to aid and assist in effecting the objects and provisions" of the proclamation.[70]

A similar proclamation had been issued on April 25, 1837, by Houston freeing all Mexican prisoners in Texas with permission to return home. Many, however, preferred to remain in Texas.[71] "It is somewhat

67. Trueheart diary, July 27, 1843.

68. Charles Elliot to Anson Jones, Washington-on-the-Brazos, [dated] Galveston, August 28, 1843, in Garrison, ed., *Diplomatic Correspondence of the Republic of Texas*, pp. 253-54.

69. The captive Mexicans were released throughout the Republic of Texas on April 17, 1838, by order of President Houston. *Telegraph and Texas Register*, Mar. 17, 1838.

70. By the President of the Republic [of] Texas, a Proclamation, Washington, September 4, 1843, [signed by] Sam Houston, in Proclamations of the Presidents, Republic of Texas, Tx-A; also in Executive Record Book, No. 48, p. 79, Tx-A; *Telegraph and Texas Register*, Sept. 20, 1843; *The Red-Lander*, Oct. 7, 1843; *Northern Standard*, Oct. 14, 1843; *Writings of Sam Houston* 3, pp. 427-28.

71. Brown, *History of Texas* 2, p. 124.

strange," commented the editor of *The Planter,* "that the Santa Fé prisoners should have been released, without a reclamation for Mexican prisoners, and that now the Mexican Government, should pretend to believe that there are prisoners in Texas, still held in confinement."[72]

Captain Elliot was informed of the issuance of the proclamation, and was requested to pass on to the British *chargé d'affaires* in Mexico and through him to Santa Anna the information that Houston was "not aware that there is a single Mexican prisoner in Texas, except those who have voluntarily chosen to remain in this country, since orders were issued in 1837 and subsequently for their release and restoration to entire liberty, still that no doubt might remain on this subject and perfectly willing to accede to the arrangement proposed by Santa Anna he has deemed it proper to issue a proclamation," and enclosed a copy for his information.[73]

"An early opportunity will be embraced," said Anson Jones, "to apprize Gen. Woll of the steps taken by his Govt. in relation to this matter and to arrange the details of the exchange of prisoners, and a vessel will be sent to Vera Cruz for the purpose of removing our prisoners from Mexico so soon as the same may seem adviseable."

The prospect of the release of the Texan prisoners in Mexico gave "hopes of a better understanding between the two Governments, as well as healed the wounded sympathies of the prisoners' friends," reported a correspondent from Galveston on September 6.[74]

When John Bradley returned from imprisonment in Mexico, he reported that there was a belief among the lower classes in that country that many Mexicans were held captive in Texas and compelled to work on plantations.[75]

---

72. *Planter,* Sept. 23, 1843.

73. Anson Jones to Capt. Charles Elliot, Department of State, Washington, Sept[r]. 4, 1843, in Garrison, ed., *Diplomatic Correspondence of the Republic of Texas* 3, pp. 1125-26.

74. *London Times,* Oct. 19, 1843, p. 7, col. 1.

75. *Telegraph and Texas Register,* Dec. 6, 1843.

CHAPTER 12

Early Efforts to Effect the Release of the Prisoners and Reaction in Texas

No SOONER WAS WORD received in Texas and the United States of the capture of the Texans at Béxar and Mier than their friends and relatives began to work for their release. Few had sufficient influence with the Mexican authorities, and diplomacy worked slowly. The prisoners often became critical even of the governments which sought their release. Those who could or did claim citizenship of some country other than Texas were more fortunate in obtaining an early release. A few secured their release as a result of requests by foreign friends of Santa Anna, or because of other special considerations.

Friends and relatives made plans to send money to enable the prisoners to obtain necessities.[1] Joseph C. Morgan received $50 from Messrs. Montgomery Nechod & Co., through the U.S. legation in Mexico.[2] John A. King, uncle by marriage to Thomas W. Bell, wrote Bell's father in Tennessee about his son's imprisonment in Mexico and of his efforts to send the boy money through safe channels for badly needed clothes. "There is no money in this country [Texas] that can be commanded, or we would even sacrifice some of his effects that we have control of and send him some money."[3] It was hoped that the father might be able to do better.

After reading the report of the Mier Expedition's disaster in the Washington *Daily National Intelligencer*, Charles Plummer Green, of Ridgeway, North Carolina, became concerned for the safety of his brother, Gen. Thomas J. Green. He sought the assistance of U.S. Senator Willie P. Man-

---

1. D. C. Jenckes to A. A. Gardenier, Lime Rock, R.I., Feb. 14, 1843, in Edward Manton Papers, TxU-A (photostat).
2. Waddy Thopson to Samuel A. Maverick, Mexico City, Feb. 16, 1843, in Green, ed., *Samuel Maverick*, pp. 233-34.
3. John A. King to W[illia]m A. Bell, Rutersville, February 10, 1843, in Friend, ed., "Thomas W. Bell Letters," *SWHQ* 58 (Apr. 1960), pp. 590-93.

gum and Senator William A. Graham in protecting his brother from "the cruel fate which I fear [he] will have to suffer if he has not already—he I know does not enjoy any of Santa Anna['s] good will as he was partly responsible in causing him to desembark from aboard of a vessel at the mouth of the Broad [Brazos] River in June 1836 just in the act of leaving for Mexico with Col Almonte the present [Mexican] Minister at Washington." Almonte, having been educated in the United States, was expected to understand the situation and presumably would know the fate of the prisoners. It was suggested that they enlist the aid of Gov. Thomas W. Gilmer in getting President John Tyler's aid, and that they write to Thompson in Mexico "under cover of a letter from the President or one of the Departments and I am sure he will use his particular talents in the matter." Charles P. Green indicated that he was seriously considering going to Mexico to see what he could do in behalf of his brother.[4]

Mangum wrote Charles Green, saying that the latest reports left no doubt that his brother was among the captured. "We shall do, & at once, all that we can. Through Webster we shall transmit earnest requests to Gen. Thompson to exert his best offices—yet, by the last papers from N. Orleans, it is reported that Thompson is on his return to the United States. It however, wants confirmation. I know not how Gen. Almonte can be approached with success on the subject. We hope, through Webster, who will doubtless use his best efforts. Mr. Graham & myself were to have seen Webster last night [February 23]—We cannot probably, before to-morrow night. Dispatches will be forwarded as early as possible."[5]

Green thanked Mangum and Graham on March 1 for their interest and declared: "Should Santa Anna carry out his tyranny by the Masacree of my brother I hope that I possess enough of the spirit of revenge to give my feeble aid in overthrowing his majestry. I much prefer the situation of Genl Green to that of Genl Sommerville who *retreated*. I knew him when in Texas & always doubted *his capacity* to stand a *crisis*."[6]

Green's father, Judge Nathan Green of Winchester, Tennessee, first appealed to Senator John C. Calhoun for help in securing information about the Texans being held prisoners in Mexico. On February 23, Calhoun passed Green's letter to Secretary of State Daniel Webster, and Calhoun was immediately apprised that "no authentic information has yet reached the Department in regard to the Texan prisoners taken at Mier." He would "forthwith instruct General Thompson to transmit the information which you request."[7] On the same day eleven members of the U.S.

---

4. Charles P[lummer] Green to Willie P. Mangum and William A. Graham, Near Ridgeway, N.C., Feb. 14, 1843, in Shanks, ed., *The Papers of Willie Person Mangum* 3, pp. 431-32.

5. Willie P. Mangum to Charles P. Green, Washington City, 24th Feby. 1843, in Shanks, ed., *The Papers of Willie Person Mangum* 3, pp. 433-34.

6. C. P. Green to Willie P. Mangum and Will A. Graham, Warren County, N.C., March 1, 1843, in Shanks, ed., *The Papers of Willie Person Mangum* 3, pp. 434-35.

7. Dan[l] Webster to J. C. Calhoun, Senate, [dated], Department of State, Washington, February 24, 1843, in Domestic Letters, Department of State, vol. 33, Dec. 1, 1842-Jan. 24, 1844, National Archives (microfilm).

House of Representatives appealed to the Department of State to use its influence to obtain Green's release. "In reply," said Webster, "I have the honor to acquaint you that the information contained in your letter and received at the department from other quarters has interested me much in the fate of Col. Green. The Executive cannot officially demand his release, but I have written a private letter to General Thompson, the Minister of the United States at Mexico, requesting him to use his best endeavors in a private way towards effecting the liberation of the Colonel, or a mitigation of the rigors of his captivity." On February 10 Judge Green appealed directly to the Department of State for its assistance in respect to his son. On the same day, he wrote to the Texan *chargé d'affaires* in Washington, Isaac Van Zandt, that he had learned "from the New Orleans papers that information has been received at that city of the capture of 212 Texians by the Mexican army under Genl. Ampudia at the town of Mier. My son Thomas is stated to be one of the captives." He requested Van Zandt's aid in getting him released, paroled, or in securing better treatment for him as a prisoner.[8]

Others who showed an interest in getting Green released were John Knox of Boydton, Virginia, and William O. Goode, a member of the Virginia House of Delegates. Knox wrote to Acting Secretary of State H. S. Legaré on May 20, 1843, and enclosed a letter from Goode. He also sent a letter addressed to General Almonte, the Mexican minister in Washington, and requested that it be forwarded to him.[9]

Charles P. Green's concern for the safety of his brother increased. On May 4 he again communicated with Van Zandt, seeking "information relative to the Mier prisoners" and confirmation of the rumor that England, France, and the United States had joined to protest Mexico's continuance of the war against Texas, and the effect it might have.[10] He wished to know if General Thompson had "any idea of leaving Mexico"; if it were possible that Houston had written to Santa Anna, as rumored, "that Fisher and my brother invaded Mexico without orders"; did he "think it probable that the prisoners . . . [would] eventually be liberated"; whether "there [was] any prospect of the war [between Mexico and Texas] soon terminating and if not will there be an invasion from Texas"; and whether a visit to his brother in Mexico would be useful in gaining his liberation. The family had received several letters from his brother, the latest being dated April 13 from Perote. For the past two months, Thomas had been expecting his brother in Mexico, but Charles Green's health for the past four months had been such that he could not make the trip.

---

8. Nathan Green to Isaac Van Zandt, Washington City, [dated], Winchester, Tenn., 10 February 1843, in Van Zandt Papers, TxU-A.

9. H. S. Legaré to John Knox, Boydton, Mecklenburg Co., Virginia, [dated] Department of State, Washington, May 26, 1843, in Domestic Letters, Department of State (Dec. 1, 1842-Jan. 24, 1844), National Archives (microfilm).

10. C. P. Green to Isaac Van Zandt, Ridgeway, N.C., May 24, 1843, in Isaac Van Zandt Letters, 1839-1843, TxU-A.

Thomas Jefferson Green thought it important that his brother go to Mexico as a dispatch bearer from the U.S. government to Waddy Thompson so he would be clothed with "diplomatic immunity" and have his expenses paid. "I *know* the President [Tyler]" wrote Charles, "& think that he could be prevailed upon to act in this matter. Independent of my ardent attachment to my brother I am willing to do all in the power of an humble individual," he declared, "to save the lives of the noble fellows, now in bondage under a tyrant."

Numerous letters were written from the United States in behalf of individual prisoners. Some were by relatives and friends, or by important persons in state and national government in response to the solicitation of relatives and friends. Austin Kilbourn of Hartford, Connecticut, appealed to the U.S. Department of State in behalf of J. N. Torrey;[11] Congressman Joseph L. Tillinghast of Providence, Rhode Island, made a plea in behalf of Edward Manton;[12] Governor Wilson Shannon of Ohio appealed to Secretary of State A. P. Upshur on August 21, 1843, and enclosed two letters to Thompson in Mexico seeking the release of Thomas S. Smith;[13] William C. Rives, senator from Albemarle County, Virginia, made an appeal to the Department of State on March 3, 1843, and enclosed a letter to be forwarded to Waddy Thompson in Mexico urging assistance in obtaining the release of Joseph A. Crews of that state;[14] and on May 2, 1843, Senator Robert J. Walker and William M. Green of Jackson, Mississippi, jointly appealed to the State Department for help in getting the release of Patrick H. Lusk.[15]

Reuben Chapman of Somerville, Alabama, on March 3, 1843, and W. H. Solomon of New York, on May 19 appealed to the State Department to request the release of John Bradley.[16] Governor Campbell of Virginia appealed to Senator Rives in behalf of Bradley. The attitude of the United States Government in all cases was expressed by Upshur to Senator Rives in respect to Bradley: it would be improper for the United States "officially to demand the release of Mr. Bradley," or to "officially ask for that as a matter either of favor or right," but, as "the only eligible" course, the Department wrote "a private letter to General Thompson requesting

---

11. Danl. Webster to Austin Kilbourn, Hartford, Connecticut, [dated] Department of State, Washington, May 6, 1843, in Domestic Letters, Department of State, Dec. 1, 1842-Jan. 24, 1844, National Archives (microfilm).

12. Danl. Webster to J. L. Tillinghast, House of Representative, [dated], Department of State, Washington, March 1, 1843.

13. W. S. Derrick to Wilson Shannon, Governor of the State of Ohio, [dated] Department of State, Washington, Aug. 26, 1843.

14. Danl. Webster to W. C. Rives, Department of State, Washington, March 6, 1843.

15. H. S. Legaré to R. J. Walker and William M. Green, Department of State, Washington, 15th May, 1843.

16. Danl. Webster to Reuben Chapman, Department of State, Washington, March 8, 1843; H. S. Legaré to W. H. Solomon, Department of State, Washington 23rd May 1843.

him to use his personal good offices for the purpose of obtaining Mr. Bradley's release," or to mitigate his condition as a prisoner.[17]

Finally, at the solicitation of David Campbell, former governor of Virginia, Gen. Andrew Jackson wrote to Waddy Thompson urging him to request Santa Anna to release John Bradley, uncle of Mrs. Samuel Ann (Adams) Maverick, wife of Samuel A. Maverick, who already had been released. Jackson enclosed to Thompson the letters he had received in behalf of Bradley.[18]

Although "backed by many of the most distinguished names in the United States," including Secretary of State Abel P. Upshur and Henry Clay, Thompson, in spite of his repeated efforts, had been unable to get Bradley freed; "but your letter to me," he informed Jackson, "which I communicated to President Santa Anna" on September 13, "immediately produced the desired effect, as you will see from his letter [of September 21], a translation of which I send you."[19] Santa Anna wrote, in part: "the mediation of the Hon. General Jackson for me is highly respectable, as much so for his being one of the most distinguished men of the United States as for the special favors which he bestowed on me in 1836, when I returned from my captivity in Texas. This interposition has induced me to grant the order for the liberty of Bradley."

When informed on September 22, 1843, the day after the arrival of the main body of Mier prisoners, of the order for his release, Bradley was much surprised. "His transports of happiness, at being liberated," reported Stapp, "diffused a sympathy of joy throughout the whole prison. Squalid, penniless, and without a friend outside from whom he could hope to receive relief, he scarce stayed to bid us adieu, so impatient was he to answer the summons of home and freedom."[20]

Thompson hoped that Colquhoun would be released in a few days, and he added, "I have strong hopes that Prest Santa Anna will release them all to me, when I go home. I am on the best of terms with him, & he is in the habit of conversing with me in the *most* confidential manner."[21]

Bradley arrived in the LaGrange area, where his family was staying, on November 21, 1843, and two days later was visited at his home by Jane Woods, Mrs. Trimble, Amanda Pendleton, whose husband had been killed in the Dawson Fight, and Gonzalvo Woods, all anxious for news about the prisoners in Mexico. "You cant tell the satisfaction tha[t] he gave us to

---

17. A. P. Upshur to W. C. Rives, Bentwoglo [?], Albemarle County, Va., [dated] Department of State, Wash., July 28, 1843.

18. Andrew Jackson to Waddy Thompson, Hermitage, July 12, 1843, in Bassett, ed., *Correspondence of Andrew Jackson* 6, p. 224.

19. Waddy Thompson to Gen. A. Jackson, Mexico, Sept. 24, 1843, in *Niles' National Register* 65, pp. 338-39 (Jan. 27, 1844); also in *Telegraph and Texas Register*, Mar. 6, 1844.

20. Stapp, *Prisoners of Perote*, p. 113; *Telegraph and Texas Register,* Nov. 8, 1843.

21. Waddy Thompson to A. P. Upshur, Legation of the U.S. of America, Mexico, Oct. 29, 1843, in Despatches from United States Ministers to Mexico, Mar. 12, 1842-Mar. 25, 1844, National Archives (microfilm).

hear From you all," wrote Gonzalvo to his brother Norman at Perote, "and to [hear] that you were all well & in good spirits & it has releved your wifes mind very much to [know] that you were at Perota with Milvern & Joe & the rest of the boys from th[is] County."[22]

With the arrival of the first contingent of Mier prisoners under Colonel Fisher at Perote Castle on March 25, 1843, the Béxar-Dawson prisoners received their report of the Battle of Mier. The new arrivals found themselves in chains and ordered to work. The idea of performing menial labor did not set well with Fisher and his fellow officers, who politely refused to do it, alleging that they had surrendered as prisoners-of-war and expected to be treated as such. Fisher and Green, who were chained together, wrote to Tornel, minister of war and marine, protesting the order to work because they had surrendered "with all the honours of prisoners of war."[23] The letter contained two gross misstatements of facts. The Mier men had not surrendered as prisoners-of-war, nor were they the "humble representatives" of their country, even though most of them claimed Texas citizenship.

Referring to Fisher's and Green's letter to Tornel, the editor of the New Orleans *Daily Picayune* commented: "We believe, according to strict usages, that Santa Anna has a right to confine these men in irons if he thinks there is any danger of their escaping." Unaware of the terms of their surrender, the *Picayune* continued, "he cannot be justified in compelling them to work like criminals and in actual association with them. It is in violation of the express terms of the capitulation," and contrary to international law.[24]

A week later, a second letter was sent protesting being forced to work. This time the letter was addressed to the governor of the castle and signed by Fisher, Green, Captain Reese, and Lt. Charles A. Clark. "We had," they said, "been ordered out by your officers to perform unnatural and degrading labor. In the name of our country and the whole civilized world, we as officers, solemnly protest against the imposition of this degradation. We furthermore respectfully protest, that even were we willing tamely to submit to such a disgrace, that our country has claims upon us which we never can abuse. We herewith enclose [to] your Excellency, a copy of our articles of capitulation."[25] In a letter to Thompson, Green declared that it was for

---

22. H. G. Woods to Norman Woods, Castle of Perote, [dated] November 24, 1843 (To the car[e] of Mr. F. M. Dimond, U.S. Concal, Vera Cruz), in Spellman, ed., "Letters of the 'Dawson Men' from Perote Prison," *SWHQ* 38 (Apr. 1935), pp. 267-69.

23. William S. Fisher and Thomas J. Green to General [José María] Tornel, Minister of War and Marine, Castle of Perote, March 31, 1843, in *Daily Picayune*, Apr. 23, 1843; *Telegraph and Texas Register*, May 3, 1843; also in Green, *Mier Expedition*, pp. 250-52.

24. Apr. 23, 1843.

25. William S. Fisher, Thomas J. Green, Charles K. Reese, and Charles A. Clark to Governor-General of the Castle of Perote, April 5, 1843, in *Telegraph and Texas Register*, May 3, 1843; also in Green, *Mier Expedition*, p. 253, but here the date of the letter is given as April 6, 1843.

Santa Anna to do him justice or to "exercise cruelty over my body at his sovereign will. I ask nothing for myself which the laws of civilized warfare does not guarantee to me, and must believe that upon second thought His Excellency will concede this much, not only for myself but brave companions in arms, who, through the fortune of war, have been made prisoners with me."[26]

After receiving the letter from the Texan officers, General Durán, governor of the castle, sent for Fisher and Green to convince them to work, since he had his orders and would have to carry them out. He did agree to communicate once more with his superiors in the government on the subject. Meanwhile, the Texan officers did not work, although the remainder of the men, except those excused for illness, performed the tasks assigned to them.

Those who were carpenters were assigned tasks in the carpenter shop of the fort. For their work they were to receive twenty-five cents per day,[27] but the pay was received irregularly and sometimes not at all. The hours of work for skilled craftsmen were from six in the morning to six in the evening.[28] At first, each person wore a single chain while working inside the shop or within the castle. Occasionally, they might be chained two and two and put to work outside the castle under a heavy guard.[29]

After the main body of Mier men reached the fortress, the authorities made a special appeal to all the skilled workers among the Texans, such as wheelwrights, blacksmiths, carpenters, masons, painters, and others to work at their trade for the Mexican government. The governor promised to pay them well, that those who performed such work would be exempt from regular chores assigned to prisoners, and would gain freedom from wearing chains while at work inside the castle.[30]

The promises were appealing, and there were soon six or seven volunteers among the Texans. The money allowance would be useful in obtaining additional food, and the work was less degrading than that which they might otherwise have to perform. Only a limited number of workers could be accommodated in the *maestranza*,[31] and there was strong competition among the prisoners for the opportunity to work in the carpenter's shop. On November 6, Trueheart recorded: "Today I am admitted in the carpenter shop, which I at last effected after a great deal of trouble. . . . We have in the *mastrasa* 22 workmen and two in the hospital. Our pay is two bits."

---

26. Thos. J. Green to Gen. Waddy Thompson, United States Minister to Mexico, Castle of Perote, April 5, 1843, in *Telegraph and Texas Register,* May 10, 1843. This same letter is printed in Green, *Mier Expedition,* pp. 254-55, with slightly different wording.

27. Glasscock diary, Oct. 15, 1843; Trueheart diary, Nov. 6, 1843.

28. Edward Manton to Hezekiah Smith, LaGrange, Fayette Cty., Texas [dated] Perote, August 15, 1843, in Edward Manton Papers (photostat), TxU-A.

29. Nance, ed., *McCutchan's Narrative,* p. 138.

30. Trueheart diary, Nov. 6, 1843.

31. *Ibid.,* Dec. 2, 1843. *"Maestranza"* technically means "storeroom," but Trueheart probably meant "shop," "work shop," or "carpenter shop."

On October 17, 1843, the Mexican officers drafted an agreement for the Texan carpenters to sign, stating that if they would agree to work for eight years they would be paid thirty dollars a month. The Texans refused to sign any such peonage contract,[32] but continued to work under the earlier understanding. On October 24 one of the Texan carpenters was struck by the Mexican overseer, but no diarist or letter writer has said for what reason. The next day, another carpenter was struck by the overseer. Less than a month after the arrival of the main body of Mier men, one of the guards discovered a knife in possession of one of the carpenters outside the carpenter shop. The guard threatened punishment if he should ever catch him again outside of the shop with such an instrument.[33]

On Saturday, December 2, 1843, three of the carpenters, including Trueheart, were told that they could continue to work in the *maestranza* but would receive only twenty-five cents per week instead of the twelve "bits" per day they had been promised and received during the past several weeks. The carpenters unanimously agreed that they would no longer work in the carpenter shop unless the order was changed. On July 7 they received $1.00 each for the first time in three months. The authorities "promised to pay them regular[ly] if they would work well."[34]

On July 7 the masons were also paid a meager $1.00 for the first time in three months, although they, too, had been promised that they would be paid well if they worked regularly and faithfully. The masons resolved that if they were not to be paid well, they would not work well. They were thrown into the calaboose with a threat that they would be chained in the morning if they did not mend their ways. The masons were let out but not chained.

Three weeks later, the governor had another problem with the carpenters, now reduced to about twelve in number. They refused to work for $4 a month when they had been receiving $7.50. So they were chained two and two and put to packing sand.

After a few weeks, rumors again suggested an impending release. When Houston proclaimed an armistice with Mexico on June 15, 1843, they hoped that it would lead to their release. On Monday, July 24, the prisoners learned through letters and newspapers received that the British man-of-war *Scylla* had reached Vera Cruz from Galveston with important dispatches for the Mexican government and was still lying at anchorage there; also, it was reported that the Texan warship *Wharton* would soon arrive with two commissioners—Samuel May Williams and George W. Hockley—to negotiate with Mexico, and that they would demand the release of the Texan prisoners as a preliminary step to negotiation. "They may succeed in obtaining our liberty, a matter of para-

---

32. Glasscock diary, Oct. 16-17, 1843.
33. Trueheart diary, Oct. 15, 1843.
34. Glasscock diary, July 8, 1844.

mount importance to us," recorded Trueheart, "but to bring about a reconciliation between the two governments I hardly think probable." A letter written by "one of our members," and published in the New Orleans *Picayune* "creates a considerable *disopinion* among us; *'Veremos como saldra la cosa'* (we shall see what comes of it)," declared Trueheart.[35]

The prisoners had little hope that the Texan commissioners would be able to effect their release. "The news of Texans' commissioners coming to this country, does not create much sensation among us," recorded Trueheart. "Many of us, awaiting with all the fortitude we are possessed with, would that something would happen to free us from this painful situation, and may the authors of it meet with punishment, they so necessarily merit. The manner of my capture, and my unjust detainment in this place and peculiar situation prey upon my mind so, that at times I feel unable to bear it, and become reckless of the future. May its duration be short."[36]

Early in August 1843, Fisher again wrote to a friend saying that it had been some time since he had heard from him, but attributed the neglect to rumors that the prisoners would be released. He said, "I again charge you to put no faith in such idle rumors, as I can assure you that our liberation depends upon the cessation of this war, of which the 'Supreme Being' can alone assign the termination, as I am satisfied, that the most calculating and discriminating of human beings can as yet affix no end to it."[37]

On August 4 only three of Fisher's command were with him at Perote. The remaining forty-seven were citizens of Béxar and from the battlefield of Salado, "stolen from their homes" by Woll, whom Fisher described as "that gallant 'French gentleman,' as he styles himself, but whom from his ingratitude to myself, who twice saved his life at the immense risk of my own, I now consider is a gentleman of no description whatever. I applied to him to use his influence with the Government to procure my release on my parole of honor, this he never even deigned to answer, though I am satisfied he received it."[38]

Edward Manton, a Dawson prisoner, wrote to Hezekiah Smith, "I have often thought of you, and the good advice you have given me, and had I of taken it and stayed until the next day I should not of been here; but so it [is] a man know not how to value good health or a friend, until he is deprived of them for a time. . . . [They still] have me by the leg." Since he had been separated, after seven months, from Faison, now em-

35. Trueheart diary, July 24, 1843.

36. *Ibid.*, July 27, 1843.

37. Wm. S. Fisher to the Editor of the *New Orleans Bulletin*, Castle of Perote, Aug. 4, 1843, in *New Orleans Bulletin*, Sept. 20, 1843; also in *Telegraph and Texas Register*, Oct. 11, 1843; and *Northern Standard*, Dec. 16, 1843.

38. W[illiam] S. Fisher to the Editor of the *New Orleans Bulletin*, Castle of Perote, Aug. 4, 1843, in *New Orleans Bulletin*, Scpt. 20, 1843; also in *Telegraph and Texas Register*, Oct. 11, 1843, and the *Northern Standard*, Dec. 16, 1843.

ployed in the carpenter shop, Milvern Harrell had become his partner in
chains. He "makes a first rate pard." He and Faison "never had a cross
word" during the time they were chained together, "the only two I think
that can say it," and he saw no reason why he and Milvern Harrell could
not get along equally as well. "Our chain is about the size we use to plow
with," he wrote, "and is about eight feet long. . . . I can form no idea when
I shall get home but am in hopes of getting home [in] time a nough to
make a crop next year."[39]

On August 23, 1843, the prisoners learned of an order for the release
of Charles A. Clark. His friends had vainly sought his release, until his
mother remembered that he had been born in Halifax and had been
brought to the United States when only a few days old. "This fact," declared Green, "when made know to the English minister, procured his immediate release."[40]

A communication from General Thompson on August 28 brought
news that no more prisoners would be released until the negotiations between Texas and Mexico had been completed.[41] Nevertheless, new rumors
of an impending general release inspired hope. On September 10, Trueheart, substituting for the regular mailman who was ill, went to Perote to
get the mail. At the mail stop he met a New Yorker, an Englishman, and
a Spaniard, from whom he learned that, most likely, the prisoners would
be released on September 16.[42] A letter from one of the prisoners in Mexico City stated that they had hopes of being released on that day.

An order came from the governor on September 10 to chain all of the
prisoners, causing much bustle and confusion in trying to get "all accomodated to their liking." Trueheart was permitted to remain chained
singly, but on the next day, he was "again united by a damnable chain" to
a companion.[43]

September 11 brought sad memories of the anniversary of the capture of San Antonio by Woll and of their capture. At dawn the prisoners
were aroused from their slumbers by the firing of the batteries in celebration, not of their capture as they first thought, but of the Mexican victory
over the Spaniards in 1829 near Tampico. The firing of the cannon was
repeated at midday and at dusk.

On September 14 the governor received word that the prisoners from
Tacubaya would be leaving Mexico City and he should be prepared to
receive them within the next few days. On September 16 a salute was fired
at daybreak, noon, and nightfall in honor of Mexican Independence Day.
The celebration included a military parade at the castle and in the evening

---

39. Edward Manton to Hezekiah Smith, LaGrange, Fayette Cty., Texas, [dated]
Perote, August 15, 1843 (photostat), in Edward Manton Papers, TxU-A.
40. Green, *Mier Expedition*, pp. 220-21.
41. Chabot, ed., *The Perote Prisoners*, pp. 226-27.
42. Trueheart diary, Sept. 10, 1843.
43. *Ibid.*, Sept. 12, 1843.

a dance in Perote. The prisoners were kept locked in their cells until one o'clock, because so many of their guard were involved in the parade. In the afternoon they were permitted to send several of their number into town for the mail, but the mail contained no order for their release. They were "not much disappointed," for they had been repeatedly "gulled and deceived" so often about being liberated since that they had become "miserably resigned" to their fate.

On September 17 it was reported that their Mexican interpreter had been ordered to join his regiment in Vera Cruz, as there was no further need for him at the castle, "as the Texans are to be released at Jalapa. "It is said," reported Trueheart, "that we are to leave on Thursday [September 21], after being joined by our companions from Mexico, who were expected to arrive on the 20th." It was rumored that Santa Anna would visit the castle on his way to his *hacienda* and that they would "be released in his presence"; but the next day the president's expected arrival had been changed to October 7, causing one of the prisoners to lament that he "should prefer having something definite; but such a thing from a Mexican is not to be expected," he commented. In the evening of September 18, the prisoners were informed by the captain of the guard that chains were being prepared in Vera Cruz for their companions soon to arrive from the capital. Late that night the new governor, Gen. José María Jarero, reached the castle to replace Governor Durán for two months, who was much disliked by everyone— "officers, soldiers and Texans."[44] The rumor was that the new governor was a good man, and certainly he "cannot be worser" than Durán. In the evening of September 20 the prisoners were marched out to see the new governor. "We are much pleased," reported one of the Texans, "with his manner and deportment thus far."

The Texans in rooms 9 and 11 were informed that they would have to move the next day to the rooms occupied by Fisher and his party. The upper storage areas of the rooms were then removed "and the under [area] stopped up, the walls whitewashed and the floor recleaned." Room "no. 10. . .[was] prepared in the some manner" and was to be occupied by those in number 7. "We are not permitted to build our stores in the back part of the rooms as on the former ones, but [are] requested [to do so], in the front part."

Then on September 23, the word was that Santa Anna would be at the castle in a week. Three days later, the date of his arrival was announced as October 5. On November 9 they learned of Houston's proclamation freeing all Mexican prisoners in Texas taken during the Revolution and believed by the Mexicans to be still held in Texas. In exchange, Santa Anna would release the Texans confined in Mexico. News of an impending mutual release of prisoners bolstered the spirit of the prisoners, who believed that their liberation was not far away; although Patrick H. Lusk, in

---

44. *Ibid.*, Sept. 18, 1843.

a letter to his brother-in-law, wrote from Perote Castle: "I have learned from a letter from the American Minister to Col. Fisher, that the Commissioners could do us (the prisoners) no good whatever, that Mexico would not recognize the independence of Texas, nor would she accede to any propositions that our country proposed, except a reannexation and submission to slavery."[45]

The return of the mounted militiamen under Colonels Joseph L. Bennett and Jesse L. McCrocklin, who had gone west with Somervell, caused those who had loved ones still at the front to worry about the outcome of the expedition weakened by the return of one-third of the men. Although it was said that the drafted militiamen had been "regularly discharged by Gen. Somervell, because they were unwilling to cross the Rio Grande, it is a fact worthy of notice," declared Dr. Francis Moore, editor of the *Telegraph*, "that nearly every drafted soldier forsook the army, either just before it set out for Laredo, or when it arrived at that place."[46]

"The political condition in Texas is squally at this time as usual," wrote William W. Holman, a former member of Congress from San Augustine. "The people [of the] West," he continued, "are the most dissatisfied people in all North America. Summerville has gone to take the City of Mexico. He has a very formidable force consisting of 400 men. The world is anxiously awaiting the result. It is thought," he added sarcastically, "a change in the monatorial concerns of the world will be wrought when he leaves the City. Now I will tell you," he informed Van Zandt, "there is no danger of Genl. Somerville being killed clost to the City."[47]

"Our country," wrote James Morgan, "is in a rather deplorable situation at present for want of money and [there is] very little sympathy felt for our situation abroad."[48] The chance to seek "greener fields" in Mexico to exploit was more than a restless youth or a person who had little to hope for in Texas could resist. As Morgan explained to Samuel Swartwout: "There is no credit handy & but little confidence between man & man in promise to pay! This will account to you for so many leaving Somervell to go & fight on their own hook across the *Rio Grande*. Their object was plunder. They had nothing at home, nor in fact no homes & many of them went forward as an alternative, having no fear of Houston."[49]

In January 1843 it was reported throughout Texas that Somervell had

45. Quoted in *Northern Standard*, Feb. 17, 1844.

46. *Telegraph and Texas Register*, Jan. 18, 1843.

47. W. W. Holman to Isaac Van Zandt, San Augustine, Jan. 20, 1843, in Isaac Van Zandt Letters, 1839-1843, TxU-A [Jennett], *Biographical Directory of the Texan Conventions and Congresses*, p. 105.

48. J. Morgan to Saml. Swartwout, New Washington, Galveston Bay, Texas, Nov. 22, 1842, in James Morgan Papers. MS, Rosenberg Library, Galveston.

49. James Morgan to Samuel Swartwout, Feb. 20, 1843, in James Morgan Papers, Rosenberg Library, Galveston.

returned from the Rio Grande with approximately one-third of the men who had marched upon Guerrero, and that the remainder of his force, some 300, had defied his order to return and had marched down the river under the command of Col. William S. Fisher, "but were enjoined not to recross—they did, however," reported the correspondent of the *Northern Standard* on January 17, 1843, from Washington-on-the-Brazos.[50] On February 4, Thomas F. Smith reached Clarksville from Washington with a copy of the *Brazos Farmer* of January 21, in which its editor declared, "The Campaign of General Somervell has ended more disastrously than we could possibly have anticipated from its commencement. . . . This appears to have arisen more from the unhappy spirit of insubordination, which seems to be peculiar to Texas volunteers, than from any want of skill or energy on the part of the General."[51] The editor quoted from "the Journal of a Gentleman, upon whose veracity, we can implicitly rely," giving details of Somervell's march upon Laredo, its capture and plunder, the descent on Guerrero and its capture, the order to return to the Texas settlements, the split in the army, Fisher's march upon Mier, the Battle of Mier, and the surrender of the Texans.

"It is really surprising," wrote the editor of the Houston *Morning Star*, "to notice the remarkably healthy and robust appearance of the soldiers who have recently returned from the army."[52] Two weeks later, the editor of the *Star*, on publishing Somervell's report, absolved him from responsibility for the failure of his campaign because of factors beyond his control. "His remarkable humane and charitable disposition is manifested in every sentence [of his Report]. He is indeed one of the kindest and most forebearing of men; and he seems so unwilling to cast censure upon others, that it would be almost cruel to censure him. It appears, from this report that the bog between the La Parita and the Presidio road, was the main cause, of the ill-success of this campaign."

One of the earliest reports of the Battle of Mier to reach Texas was brought to the settlements above Victoria by a Mexican, who reached there on January 3, from Mier. The report was that the Texans had defeated the Mexicans and captured three fieldpieces.[53] In Houston it was reported on January 7 by "a gentleman who recently arrived from the Colorado, that a courier arrived at LaGrange a few days since from the army" with news that the Texan troops had "marched to Camargo, capturing one or two villages on the route, but when they reached Camargo, they encountered a detachment of the Mexican army, consisting of about 600 men, with four fieldpieces. They immediately gave battle, and after a short

---

50. *Northern Standard*, Feb. 4, 1843.

51. *Brazos Farmer* (Washington), Jan. 21, 1843, quoted in *Northern Standard*, Feb. 4, 1843.

52. *Morning Star*, Feb. 1, 1843.

53. *Telegraph and Texas Register*, Jan 18, 1843; *Morning Star*, Jan. 14, 1843.

but severe engagement, completely defeated the Mexicans" and captured the four fieldpieces.[54]

"A silly rumor has been circulating on the Brazos for the last five or six days," declared the editor of the *Morning Star*, "that the army has been defeated, two-thirds killed, and the rest taken prisoners except one—a lying rogue probably who originated the rumor."[55]

"Hopes and expectations were further stimulated when G. W. Whitesides, on furlough from Capt. E. S. C. Robertson's Company D of Somervell's Army, arrived in Houston on January 13, from Washington, and stated that just before he left town, a messenger had arrived from the West and confirmed the account of the battle fought near Comargo. . . . Mr. Whitesides says the Mexican army consisted of over sixteen hundred men, commanded by Gen. Woll. The Texians, after a severe engagement, defeated it, killed four hundred Mexicans, and captured several hundred prisoners, Gen. Woll escaped. Three fieldpieces and a large number of horses were captured. A large drove of the horses captured by the army have arrived at Béxar. . . . Thirty Texians were disabled in this battle, and thirty were killed."[56]

From Galveston on January 15, the British *chargé d'affaires* wrote his government and enclosed a clipping from the Houston *Morning Star* on January 14. "It is much to be wished, that these confusedly reported accounts may be exaggerated, but there is certainly reason to apprehend that some sinister event has occurred"; the "sinister event" to which he had reference was the capture of the Mier Expedition.[57]

Sobering news soon came from the Rio Grande. St. Clair and Chalk arrived at Victoria fresh from the Battle at Mier and gave details of the Texan surrender. On January 13 William Needham, quartermaster in the First Regiment, Second Brigade, of Somervell's army reached Houston from Béxar. He reported the return of Somervell to San Antonio with 200 of his men while another 300 had broken off from the command, elected Col. William S. Fisher commander, and had gone down to Mier, and had captured the town, but "a shower of rain came up just after they had captured it, so that they could not use their rifles to advantage, and the Mexican army arrived, and after a desperate engagement retook the town and captured about two hundred or two hundred and fifty of our troops."[58]

It was from St. Clair and Chalk that Needham derived his information. "This story seems quite too incredible for belief," commented the

---

54. *Daily National Intelligencer*, Jan. 24, 1843; see also *Morning Star* quoted in *Telegraph and Texas Register*, Jan. 11, 1843.

55. *Morning Star*, Jan. 14, 1843.

56. The account was said to have been published in the *Daily Texian* (Austin).

57. Charles Elliot to Earl of Aberdeen, Galveston, Jan. 15, 1843, no. 2, in Adams, ed., *British Diplomatic Correspondence Concerning the Republic of Texas*, p. 150. The clipping from the Houston *Morning Star* was dated Jan. 14, 1843.

58. *Morning Star*, Jan. 14, 1843; see also *New Orleans Bee*, Jan. 19, 1843; *Daily Picayune*, Jan. 19, 1843.

editor of the Houston *Morning Star*. But St. Clair gave details of their own escape, reported that the Mexican army was commanded by General Ampudia and Canales, and that the whole Mexican force amounted to 1,500 to 2,000 men. The *Picayune*'s correspondent in Galveston urged caution in accepting the Needham story: "The whole story about the battle of Mier and its results, [he said] needs confirmation. There is perhaps some truth in it. I think it not unlikely that a battle was fought at the time and place mentioned, but so many as 400 Mexicans were killed, with so small a loss as four on the part of the Texans, is not to be credited; nor is it much more probable that so large a portion of the Texans were captured as the amount represents."[59]

That confirmation was soon to come, with its disheartening effects on individuals and upon Texas as a nation. News confirming the capture of the Texans at Mier in detail arrived in Galveston on January 24 by passengers on the *New York,* which had met the schooner *Doric* at sea. The *Doric* had left Matamoros on January 14, bearing letters and reports from the Mier captives.

On January 25, Captain Auld on the *Doric* reached New Orleans from Matamoros, and confirmed the disaster that had overtaken the Mier men. His report, containing a copy of the articles of surrender furnished by Fisher, was substantiated by Cocke's letter.[60] The editor of the *Morning Star* thought it almost incredible "that nearly 300 Texians, all well armed, and having at least fifty rounds of ammunition each, while strongly posted in stone houses, should have tamely surrendered to 1,500 or 2,000 Mexicans, when only four of their number had been killed. If they had fought until half of their number were slain, and their ammunition and provisions had been exhausted, there would have been some excuse for them to surrender; but for them to have yielded under the circumstances mentioned by Chalk and Sinclair, exhibits a picture of imbecility and cowardice so totally at various with the known character of Texians, and so much in contrast with the former achievements of the gallant Fisher, Cameron, and the comrades of Jourdan, that we still view these statements with suspicions."[61]

News of the fate of Fisher and his men reached Texas almost simultaneously with the return of the South Western Army of Operations. The defeat of Mier was reported in an extra of the *Civilian and Galveston City Gazette*.[62]

Captain Elliot reported to the British Foreign Office on January 28

---

59. Quoted in *Daily Picayune*, Jan. 19, 1843.

60. *New Orleans Bee*, Thur. Jan. 26, 1843; *Daily Picayune*, Jan. 26, 1843; "Report of Captain Auld on the Battle of Mier," from the *Galveston Civilian* in *Telegraph and Texas Register*, Jan. 25, 1843.

61. *Morning Star*, Jan. 17, 1843.

62. No copy of this extra has been located, but the account is republished from it in the *Civilian and Galveston City Gazette*, Jan. 18, 1843.

"that authentic information has reached this place from Matamoras via New Orleans, confirming the surrender of that portion of the Texian force, under Colonel Fisher, which had separated from the direction of the Officer appointed by the Government, and continued the movement beyond the Rio Grande: a movement to which the disregard of the authority of the Officer, acting under the orders of the Government has given a character that may be attended with very unhappy consequences to these prisoners."[63]

News of the disaster at Mier cast a heavy gloom over Texas, especially in the west, from where so many of the Mier men had come. From Washington-on-the-Brazos, C. M. C. Smith wrote to his sister in East Texas that "on tomorrow night," February 9, there was to be a "special prayer meeting for our countrymen who are now in prison in Mexico. Oh what thrilling interest. Fayette is almost broken up it has be[en] deprived of 1/3 of her men since Spring."[64]

The opponents of the Houston Administration attributed "the capture of the men under Col. Fisher to the Executive," but "he is about as much to blame for the circumstance," declared the editor of the *Civilian and Galveston Gazette*, "as for most of the other evils laid to his charge— bad crops, bad roads, and weather included. If, contrary, to the order of Gen. Somervell and of the Executive, Col. Fisher with less than three hundred men, chose to remain in Mexico two weeks, and until all the regular forces at Matamoros and within a hundred and fifty miles of the scene of his operations could be concentrated and brought against him—the fault is [alleged to be] that of the Executive."[65]

It was a sad day in Texas. The reaction was mixed and varied. Some took the attitude, "I told you so"; some demanded that the administration take action to free the prisoners; some wanted to march to the Rio Grande and punish Mexico for having been so ready to defend its own frontier against a band of invading Texans; others were stunned by the news and knew not what to do; and still others—probably many others—were completely indifferent and believed that a small, rash, impetuous group of adventurers, without the sanction of the government, had launched an attack upon the enemy and had gotten themselves into a tight fix. Texas was in deplorable straits. The economic outlook was bad; trade was stagnant; the nation's currency was practically worthless; and foreign powers were becoming more skeptical of the ability of Texas to sustain itself as a nation, or even to maintain a responsible government. "We have noticed, with regret," reported the editor of the *Telegraph and Texas Register*,[66] "that an

---

63. Charles Elliot to the Earl of Aberdeen, Galveston, Jan. 28, 1843, in Adams ed., *British Correspondence Concerning Texas*, pp. 154-56.

64. C. M. C. Smith to Mrs. Missouri M. Fowler, San Augustine, Texas [dated] Was[hington] City, Gay Hill, Feb. 8, 1843, in L. Fowler Papers, TxU-A.

65. *Civilian and Galveston Gazette*, Jan. 28, 1843.

66. Mar. 22, 1843.

unusual degree of despondency pervades all classes of citizens throughout the country." James Webb wrote to his friend former President Mirabeau B. Lamar, that "Poor Austin has sadly changed since you saw it, as indeed, has all the Western part of the Country. We have now but a small population, no business, and are living under great privations," but still hold on to the Archives.[67] For several weeks there was great concern in Texas about another Mexican invasion. Many felt that Mexico, encouraged by the victory at Mier, would send an army to reconquer Texas. [68]

---

67. James Webb to M. B. Lamar, Austin, May 4, 1843, in Gulick *et al*, eds., *Lamar Papers* 4, pt. 1, pp. 19-20.

68. *Telegraph and Texas Register*, Dec. 21, 1842; also *Daily Picayune*, Dec. 31, 1842.

CHAPTER 13

Mier Prisoners are Marched to the Interior—Texan Wounded Escape from Hospital at Mier

T HE TEXANS HELD AT Matamoros awaited the arrival of instructions from Mexico City as to their disposition. In preparing for a possible transfer of the prisoners to the interior of the country, General Ampudia informed the "notorious" Antonio Canales[1] that he would be placed in command of the prisoners in the event they were ordered to the interior. The "mean, traitorous, and dastardly" Canales, soon to be promoted to the rank of brigadier-general of the Active Militia for his part in defending the frontier,[2] insisted on having the men placed in irons and stated that he would not guard them with less than 1,000 men. The Mexican officers held a consultation upon the issue of ironing the Texans,[3] and soon rumors reached the Texan officers that plans were being made to shackle the prisoners and to march them to the City of Mexico. Fisher and Green protested to Ampudia not only against ironing of the men but also in regard to sending them into the interior, claiming that at the time of their surrender some of the men had been under the impression that they would be retained upon the frontier until released.[4] Ampudia assured them that, while Canales wanted to have the men ironed since he was to guard the prisoners en route to Monterrey, that he had overruled Canales. But to appease Canales, Ampudia ordered the Texan staff officers to be sent ahead of the main body of prisoners "as a precautionary measure to prevent us from attempting an escape," recorded Walker, "being told that if any attempt was made they would be held responsible."[5]

---

1. For a description of Antonio Canales and his personality, see Nance, ed., *McCutchan's Narrative*, pp. 36-37; Nance, *After San Jacinto*, pp. 188, 198, 213-14, 227, 234, 247-48, 368.

2. *José María Tornel, Ministro de guerra y marina, a Pedro de Ampudia, México, Enero de 1843*, in *El Cosmopolita*, Feb. 1, 1843.

3. Sibley, ed., *Samuel H. Walker's Account*, pp. 39-40.

4. Green, *Mier Expedition*, p. 127.

5. Sibley, ed., *Samuel H. Walker's Account*, p. 40.

Soon the order from President Santa Anna arrived. From Mexico City Waddy Thompson informed Daniel Webster, the United States secretary of state, that the prisoners were "to be sent to the South of this City to work on the road which the Government is opening. They have," he said, "been treated with great cruelty as have also those taken in San Antonio." Thompson wanted to know if the State Department's instructions of April 5, 1842, in regard to the Santa Fé prisoners, "in which the interference on the part of our Government is threatened to prevent cruel treatment to prisoners of war and to enforce the observance of the terms of Capitulation are to be regarded as applying to those new batches of prisoners."[6]

On January 11 Fisher and Green again wrote to Ampudia, acknowledging "the officer-like conduct and gentlemanly deportment of General Ampudia and his officers during the battle and since the time of the capitulation,"[7] and thanking him for the kind treatment the men had received. The American consul reported "that when the prisoners were about setting out Gen. Ampudia applied personally to each of the [Texan] officers and obtained certificates of his good treatment towards them and their unfortunate companions. At the same time the blacksmith of this city was by his orders making the chains to fetter them."[8]

The Texans were disheartened by news that they were to be taken into the interior. Those who had been Santa Fé prisoners remembered well the hardships that a march to Mexico City entailed. They knew that even if they survived the journey, an uncertain fate awaited them at its termination. With the concurrence of Fisher, Green said, on the day previous to the departure of the Texan officers for Mexico City, he addressed a note of encouragement to the main body of prisoners accompanied by a small amount of money sent by Adjutant-General Murray for the assistance of those who might become sick upon the road. "Let us nerve our souls," wrote Green, "in that impregnable armour which lightens the weary limb, and which the steel of our enemy cannot penetrate. That immortal spirit will make us superior to our condition, and triumph over our misfortunes. . . . Indulge, therefore, all reasonable hope in the magnanimity of our enemy, and in that justice which is the all-prevailing providence of God. . . . Now, dear friends and neighbors, let us part, but with that hope which stimulates man to look beyond the present, and which, with God's pleasuse *[sic]*, will one day unite us again in our homes."[9]

---

6. Waddy Thompson to Daniel Webster, Secretary of State, Washington City, [dated] Legation of the United States of America, Mexico, Feb. 16, 1843, in Despatches from the United States Ministers in Mexico, Mar. 12, 1842-Mar. 25, 1844, National Archives (microfilm).

7. Reported the editor of the *Civilian and Galveston Gazette* quoted in *Telegraph and Texas Register*, Jan. 25, 1843; see William S. Fisher and Thomas J. Green to Pedro De Ampudia, Matamoros, January 11, 1843, in *Telegraph and Texas Register,* May 3, 1843.

8. I. D. Marks to Daniel Webster, Secretary of State, Consulate of the U.S.A. Matamoros, 31st Jan.[y]. 1843, No 5, in Despatches from United States Consuls in Matamoros, Jan. 1, 1840-Dec. 29, 1848, National Archives (microfilm).

9. Green, *Mier Expedition*, pp. 127-29.

The small group of officers was to take the lead under the command of Lt. Col. Manuel Savariego of the regular cavalry, who commanded approximately forty men. The Texan officers were to pay their "own individual expenses on the road."[10] A report from Matamoros by the schooner *Zerviah,* which reached New Orleans on March 22, said "the Texan officers when they left that place, were well supplied with money—raised for them by contribution in the town."[11] Prior to commencing the march from Matamoros, Green obtained permission from Ampudia to take along his "servant," Samuel C. Lyon, the old sailing-master, and an interpreter, Daniel Drake Henrie, a former midshipmen in the United States Navy, who had learned Spanish while stationed in the Pacific.[12] Lyon, who had been Green's next door neighbor in Texas for six years, was not Green's servant, but Green thought that he might receive better treatment if he rode along with the officers than if he had to walk with the privates. It was pointed out to the Mexican general that the Texans commonly granted similar privileges to Mexican officers when prisoners of the Texans. The advance group, serving as security for the good behavior of the main body, was furnished with a horse for each man and the march began. The advance party consisted of Fisher, Green, Major Murray, Captain Lyon, Henrie, and Dr. Shepherd. As he had learned that some of the prisoners contemplated overpowering the guard and escaping, Ampudia insisted that Fisher and Green visit the main body of prisoners and inform them that such an attempt would bring retribution upon their officers in the advance party. Fisher informed Captain Cameron, the leader of those contemplating making a break, "to use his own judgment in the matter" and Green admonished them "to let no opportunity slip in overpowering their guards and getting home, and to do so regardless of any consequence" to himself.[13]

Savariego commenced his march with the Texan officers on January 12, three days in advance of the main body of prisoners. Ten days were required for the officer-prisoners to cover the 275 miles from Matamoros to Monterrey. From Matamoros the road wound in a northwest direction through a level valley laced with ponds and lakes. It then ascended to the central plain and continued to Zacate, on the San Juan River, 200 miles from Matamoros. Three more days through the valley of the San Juan with frequent crossing of the river brought them to Cadereyta on the Topo Grande. Colonel Savariego proved to be a kind, intelligent, humane, and generous officer, with whom the Texans found no fault, except at Cadereyta.[14] Cadereyta, a town of some 10,000 inhabitants, was located on

---

10. Thos. J. Green to Genl. Felix Huston & Colo. Bailey Peyton, New Orleans, [dated] Matamoros, Jan. 12, 1843, MS, in Domestic Correspondence (Texas), Tx-A.

11. *Daily Picayune,* Mar. 23, 1843.

12. Green, *Mier Expedition,* p. 278.

13. *Ibid.,* p. 129.

14. William S. Fisher and Thomas J. Green to Col. Severiego, of the Mexican Army, Monterrey, Jan. 23, 1843, *Telegraph and Texas Register,* May 10, 1843. The San Jacinto Museum of History, San Jacinto, Texas, has a copy of the original letter.

a bluff about twenty-five miles from Monterrey. Its inhabitants had made great preparations to welcome Savariego and his prisoners, whom they wanted paraded for the amusement of the populace. This Colonel Savariego refused to do, and the *alcalde* refused to furnish bedding for the prisoners or to permit its hire. Monterrey was reached on January 22. Here they remained six days in the home of José María Bermúdez, the *mayor de la Plaza,* who permitted his daughters to sing and play the guitar and piano for the Texans.[15] On the third day Green and Fisher were taken before Governor and Commandant Gen. José de Ortega of Nuevo León. He received them kindly and expressed a desire to have them furnished every comfort possible. While in Monterrey the Texans' table was supplied from the best French restaurant in the city.

On January 14 the main body of prisoners, with approximately half of the men without shoes and blankets, left Matamoros under the guard of the Auxiliaries of Nuevo León "in consequences of the apprehensions entertained by the Mexicans," reported Brenham, "that we will make an effort at our liberation."[16] The guard, consisting of new recruits, was another reason for Mexican apprehensions. It was composed of 100 cavalry, 400 infantry of the Seventh Regiment of Infantry, and one fieldpiece—all under the command of Colonel Canales. In view of the numerous escort, recorded Walker, "We did not have strong hopes of whipping our guard and making our escape home."[17] Learning that they were to be moved farther into the interior, six of the Texans "determined on playing sick."[18] Just before leaving, their "illness" was reported to the commandant. The Mexican surgeon-general, Votager, was sent to investigate, and he reported that six prisoners were unfit for the rigors of the journey. These were Lt. George B. Crittenden, Ezekiel Smith, Patrick Usher, James Charles Wilson, Joseph D. McCutchan, and John Day Morgan, who was masquerading under the name of John Day because he had been one of the Santa Fé prisoners. These men were ordered to the hospital Malta, which was large and well built.

The main body of prisoners commenced their march for Mexico City by way of Monterrey and Saltillo. The signal for their departure also brought out a large part of the population of the city. Both sides of the streets were thronged with a crowd eager to obtain one last view of *los Tejanos diablos.* The raw recruits under Canales were more brutal and insolent than the members of their previous guard. The prisoners' new masters were noted for their many petty tyrannies, and Canales, who feared

---

15. William S. Fisher and Thomas J. Green to Col. [José María] Bermúdez of the Mexican Army, Monterey, Jan. 26, 1843. The San Jacinto Museum of History, San Jacinto, Texas, has a copy of the original letter.

16. Richard F. Brenham to ———, Matamoros, January 14, 1843, reprinted from the New Orleans *Tropic* in the *Northern Standard*, June 8, 1843.

17. Sibley, ed., *Samuel H. Walker's Account,* p. 40.

18. Canfield diary, Jan. 13, 1843.

the Texans, never ventured nearer than 100 yards of their lines during the march.[19] As the procession passed through each village along its route, the customary crowd of men, women, and children assembled to pay homage to the conquering Mexican soldiery and view with awe the Texans, often shouting "death to the robbers," and "down with the heretics." One "little scamp," reported Wallace, "in the excitement of the moment, ventured within reach of my foot, which . . . is a No. 12, and I gave him a kick which would have done credit to a vicious mule. . . . He went off howling like a full-grown cayote, but, fortunately for me, none of the guard noticed this little by-play, as otherwise, I should certainly have been punished for it with a thrust from a bayonet, or cut from a broadsword."[20] The "Federalist Texans" had no doubt left behind a great deal of ill-will in northern Mexico and the recent slaughter of the frontier militiamen or *defensores* at Mier had not increased their popularity.

The march from Matamoros led through a valley dotted with ponds and lakes. Soon they commenced the ascent of the central plateau known as La Mesa Central de Anáhuac. That night the Texans, having traveled twelve miles, were lodged in a cow pen, with dung a foot thick, at a ranch near a water hole, where there was nothing to eat "except a few scraggy goats, and naked, sore-eyed dogs."[21] Not even *tortillas* were available; so a few of the Texans "pressed one of the little naked dogs into service for supper," but found it to be exceedingly tough. They reported that when cooked, it "'smelt worse than a wet dog,'" and was certainly a poor substitute for roast beef or pork. Other messes were more fortunate and obtained goats. During the day Wallace "met with a serious misfortune" in the loss of his "'fine tooth comb,'" [his] only 'ark of safety' against the swarms of vermin with which they were infested." Wallace reported, "I have since lost articles of a thousand times more intrinsic value than that little brown comb, but never anything the want of which I felt so sensibly . . . [as] a 'ridding comb.'"[22]

At times the prisoners and their guards suffered from lack of food during the march. Some "spoiled sea-bread" had been supplied by the Mexican *comissariat* at Matamoros for the march, "which being after various trials positively rejected by the men, was substituted by meager rations of the cheapest flour to be obtained. And two meals a day of this, with refuse beef, to be cooked as we could best prepare it, without utensils or a sufficiency of firewood, was the provisions for our support, whilst undergoing marches that would have worn down well-fed men," recorded

19. Stapp, *Prisoners of Perote*, pp. 45-46; *El Semanario Político del Gobierno de Nuevo León* (Monterey), Dec. 29, 1842, quoted in *Diario del Gobierno*, Jan. 13, 1843; T. W. Cox's account in the *Texian and Brazos Farmer*, quoted in Adams, "[Journal of an] Expedition against the Southwest," Part 2, pp. 74-77; *Northern Standard*, Mar. 2, 1843.

20. Duval, *Big-Foot Wallace*, p. 191.

21. Canfield diary, Jan 14, 1843.

22. Duval, *Big-Foot Wallace*, p. 189.

Stapp.[23] When the prisoners protested the scantiness of the fare furnished them, one of their guard "went out and collected from the barn-yard a quantity of old bones and other filthy offal," and on returning, threw them on the ground before the Texans, bidding them to eat, "as that was good enough for such abominable heretics" as they.[24]

At best, the daily allowance of food barely saved the prisoners from starvation. No doubt a part of the Mexican policy was to weaken the prisoners by keeping them on a subsistence ration to facilitate guarding and handling them more easily. The Mexican commissary received, or more often, was supposed to receive, an allowance of twenty-five cents per diem from the government for rations for each prisoner, "of which amount not five cents a man was expended" upon the prisoners. "This money was properly and legally payable by . . . [the commissary] to the prisoners in specie; but the commutation was insisted upon by the officer" of the commissary.[25] When possible, Texans who had money purchased food from the ranches and the peddlers along the route. "Our coming seemed to have been heralded far in advance, and every old *palado [pelado]* that could scrape together a few eggs, tortillas, goat milk or goat milk cheese, got out on the road to wait our coming," remembered John Rufus Alexander, "and those who had money could buy, while the moneyless man had to resort to stealing. And if the man without money got to the peddler first the latter soon found his stock entirely exhausted; [for] he was soon surrounded by the friendliest people in the world, who oggled him clean away from his basket of goods, and when he carried his complaint to the officers they treated it as a huge joke—on the pelado."[26]

Occasionally, long marches of twelve to fifteen hours were made without water and at night they usually camped in cow pens or sheep pens exposed to the elements.

On January 15 they advanced twenty miles through a "tolerably good country."[27] On January 18 they camped at a "Stone Rancho."[28] Unknown to the prisoners, the minister of war canceled Ampudia's commitment in the terms of surrender exempting the Santa Fé men among the Texan prisoners from the death penalty if apprehended in arms against Mexico, and had sent an order to Ampudia "to shoot those of the prisoners who had accompanied the Santa Fé expedition." The order reached Matamoros on January 28, two weeks after the main body of the prisoners had

---

23. Stapp, *Prisoners of Perote,* p. 47.

24. Duval, *Big-Foot Wallace,* p. 193.

25. Stapp, *Prisoners of Perote,* p. 47; William S. Fisher and Thomas J. Green to the Commander-in-Chief of the Department of San Luis Potosí, Prison, San Luis Potosí, Feb. 22, 1843, *Telegraph and Texas Register,* May 10, 1843.

26. John Rufus Alexander, "Story of the Mier Expedition as Told to John Warren Hunter," in Wade, comp., *Notes and Fragments of the Mier Expedition* 1, p. 30.

27. Sibley, ed., *Samuel H. Walker's Account,* p. 40.

28. Canfield diary, Jan. 18, 1843.

left there, "which order," reported Consul Marks on January 31, "will no doubt be executed."[29]

Before the Texans had proceeded far into the interior some renewed talk of escape. As long as they were upon the frontier there was hope of an early release; but when word came for them to be sent to Mexico City, more serious thought was given to planning an escape. Brenham wrote to New Orleans, "We contemplate making the effort for our escape, before we leave here many days—it will be against fearful odds, but I have no doubt of our success, if the matter is conducted properly, The peculiarity of my own situation and choice also, will place me," he wrote, "in the front rank in an unarmed charge upon Mexican bayonets. Although I feel confident in the success of the enterprise, if conducted properly, yet still I have occasionally a presentiment that my career is shortly to be closed." If his colleagues would not revolt against the guard, Brenham declared he would resort to some other means of releasing himself "from this painful thraldom," and, "Be it as it may, I am determined not again to appear in Mexico as a prisoner."[30]

The captains of the six companies were delegated the task of laying the plans for a break. At Rancho Lacoma some of the men had intended to charge the guard, but decided to wait until the following night when they would be encamped upon the Matamoros side of the San Juan.[31] At this point, declared Glasscock, "we came very near charging the guard."[32] Zacate Pass, from Camargo, was reached early in the evening of January 21. The Mexican cavalry was distributed equally on the left and rear of the pen containing the prisoners. Their infantry occupied the right and front, and extended from the corral gate to the six-pounder, 150 yards away, that pointed toward the Texan quarters. Artillerymen lolled nearby, and fires were placed near the cannon and burning matches were in the hands of several artillerymen standing near the cannon ready for instant use. Everything having been previously arranged, it was determined to charge the guard under the leadership of Ewen Cameron, the oldest and most experienced captain among the prisoners, at the time their evening meal was brought in.[33]

The Texans were divided into four companies and each company was assigned a specific task, and a special group of twenty-five daring men chosen and led by Dr. Richard F. Brenham was assigned to charge the cannon. The enemy was to be assailed simultaneously on all sides. The bars across the gateway were up and two men stood in readiness to draw

29. I. D. Marks to Daniel Webster, Secretary of State, Consulate of the U.S. A., Matamoros, 31st Jany. 1843, No. 5, in Despatches from United States Consuls in Matamoros. Jan. 1, 1840-Dec. 29, 1848, National Archives (microfilm).

30. Richard F. Brenham to ———, Matamoros, Jan. 14, 1843, reprinted from the New Orleans *Tropic* in the *Northern Standard*, June 8, 1843.

31. Canfield diary, Jan. 20-21, 1843; see also Stapp, *Prisoners of Perote*, p. 47.

32. Glasscock diary, Jan. 20, 1843.

33. Stapp, *Prisoners of Perote*, p. 48.

them out at the proper signal to enable the men to exit from the compound as quickly as possible.[34] The prearranged signal was the word "draw," the expression the men used when their rations were brought in by the guard.

About four o'clock, the time for the delivery of the prisoners' supper, four burros, loaded with fuel and accompanied by their drivers, approached the corral. The Texans anxiously awaited the signal. "Outside of the enclosure could be seen the glittering muskets, stacked in tempting piles; whilst the unconscious guard were lolling at their ease, smoking, gossiping, or sleeping, as their various humours or inclinations invited. Every eye in our desperate batallion," reported Stapp, "seemed riveted with the potency of fascination upon the towering and athletic Cameron; whose own were bent . . . upon the approaching troop of servitors, . . . already entering the coural. *'Draw your rations first,'* was the ambiguous signal that saluted our ears, delivered in the common place tone of daily custom, and unattended by a single demonstration or look, explanatory, beyond the simple counsel it implied. The men looked bewildered—hesitated—gazed out over the pickets as apprehending a discovery of the plot, and some certain precautions for its defeat; they looked at Cameron again, who was busily engaged with his supper."[35] A moment of hesitancy, and Captain Baker coolly and quietly whispered "wait until we get into the mountains."[36] "In a moment . . . they were all," like Cameron, "similarly absorbed in the base employments of baking, roasting and gorging."[37] It was soon known that the change in plans resulted from Charles K. Reese's refusal to take the position assigned to him by Cameron.[38] Also some believed that the guard had been informed of the plan because fires had been placed beside the cannon, immediately upon making camp, and extra sentinels with firebrands continually in hand had been stationed about the compound for illumination.[39] Stapp tells us that "a portion of Cameron's Company, . . . had appealed successfully, on the spur of the moment, for the postponement of the enterprise," but we are not told why, except that a few days later Cameron was "acquitted of all blame or dishonor for balking the attempt."[40] No further serious consideration was given to attempting an escape before Monterrey was reached on February 1.

The next day they reached the village of Mantaca, at twelve miles' distance, and camped once more in a corral.[41] The next day they crossed a creek early in the morning and proceeded twenty-four miles and camped in a cow pen. On the following morning, Wednesday, January 25, a march

34. Sibley, ed., *Samuel H. Walker's Account*, p. 41.
35. Stapp, *Prisoners of Perote*, pp. 47-49.
36. Sibley, ed., *Samuel H. Walker's Account*, p. 41.
37. Stapp, *Prisoners of Perote*, pp. 47-49.
38. Canfield diary, Jan. 21, 1843; Glasscock diary, Jan 21, 1843.
39. Canfield diary, Jan. 21, 1843.
40. Stapp, *Prisoners of Perote*, pp. 47-49.
41. Canfield diary, Jan. 23 and 24, 1843.

of five miles brought them to Capisaro on the Capisaro River, a branch of the San Juan. Crossing the Capisaro, they proceeded up along its bank. The road inclined upwards toward the Sierra Madres, which they soon entered. The scene, said Canfield, "would present a beautiful appearance to a person *riding*" but not so to walking prisoners.[42] Eighteen miles beyond Capisaro they camped in a corral. On January 26 they reached Cadereyta Jiménez, or simply Cadereyta, and, after crossing a small stream at the edge of the town, were marched, as usual, under triumphal arches. Cadereyta was perched upon a knoll overlooking the San Juan, at the edge of the Sierra Gorda.

Great preparations had been made for according a gala reception to the conquering heroes. The citizens had been disappointed by the refusal to parade the Texan officers a few days earlier. The guard, with its prisoners, was escorted into the town by a band. Triumphal arches were formed in all of the streets through which they passed, and the houses were decorated *"a la Comanche."* Salvos of cannon fire resounded through the city and countryside. As the procession turned the corner of a street leading into the public square the firing of rockets and the ringing of bells commenced, and the Texans passed in review before the principal men of the town and its inhabitants.

At Cadereyta "more pretty gals made their appearance, than in any other town" through which the Texans had yet passed. They were "all of the Indian order, with fine eyes and devilish-looking."[43]

The prisoners were surprised to find quarters in the backyard of the soldiers' barracks. These were the most filthy, unsanitary, and uncomfortable of any in which they had been placed in their march from Mier to Cadereyta. Soon it began to rain and became very cold. Some of the citizens of the town overheard the complaints of the Texans and persuaded Canales to move the prisoners to more comfortable quarters on January 27,[44] where they were plentifully supplied with *frijoles*, hot *tortillas*, fowls, and various kinds of fruit. They were visited several times by a Dr. Bullock, "a young and very popular American physician," who displayed sympathy and supplied some of the men with "tolerable" tobacco, which could only be had in the "black-market" at fantastic prices.[45] January 27 a heavy rain made the roads almost impassable and delayed the march to Mexico City, but it was resumed on the next day.

Late in the afternoon the prisoners and their escort camped at a large *rancho*. There were several irrigated sugar cane farms in the neighborhood. On Sunday, January 29, after marching six miles, the procession reached the mission of Guadalupe, a small thriving settlement nine miles

---

42. *Ibid.*, Jan 25, 1843.

43. *Ibid.*, Jan. 26, 1843; [Folsom], *México in 1842*, p. 90.

44. Canfield diary, Jan. 26, 1843.

45. Stapp, *Prisoners of Perote*, p. 51; see also Bell, *Narrative*, p. 34; Canfield diary, Jan. 27, 1843; Sibley, ed., *Samuel H. Walker's Account*, p. 42.

from Monterrey, "the holy city of the frontier,"[46] nestling in a niche of the vast sierra. Monterrey lay 130 miles below the Rio Grande. Before night-fall the Texans and their guard reached the city. The Texans were con-ducted into the city without that "vulgar triumph" which had character-ized their entrance into other Mexican towns. Large crowds came out to meet and to view the prisoners. The Texans remained in Monterrey until the afternoon of February 2, and were treated kindly and shown more courtesy and respect than at any other point along the way. The inhabi-tants generally professed great friendship for them, referring to them as *pobrecitos* (poor fellows)! There was no parade in Monterrey for the amuse-ment of the populace. In passing along the city streets toward the prison, Canfield spied "A beautiful young lady (white) but liberty had left us," he wrote, "as *we* soon did the fair one." It is doubtful that Canfield actually saw the face of the lady, but judging from "the brilliancy and sweet expres-sion of her dark, melting eye, peeping like a star through the folds of her reboso," might have concluded that she was beautiful.

The Texans' quarters, although completely devoid of furniture, were cleaner and more comfortable than any they had occupied since leaving home. The bare stone walls of their abode were "scribbled over with pieces of charcoal by some former occupants of these luxurious abodes."[47] Their rations were the best that could be secured and included well-cooked meats, eggs, *frijoles*, and many kinds of fresh fruits. The prisoners were supplied with sandals and clothing, and six and one-fourth cents per diem with which to take care of any other necessary items.

It must have grated to praise Canales for his conduct of the prisoners to Monterrey and it must have been politic on their part to have done so. Before leaving Monterrey, Gibson and six captains wrote to Canales, "we have awaited the convenient opportunity . . . to thank you for the kind treatment that you have shown us on the road from Matamoros to this place. . . . Permit us to express our most pure gratitude and our most vehement desires for your individual happiness and that of your brother officers."

The Texan prisoners left at Mier as the main body marched toward Matamoros were accorded reasonable care, considering the inefficiency of the Mexican medical corps and lack of cooperation from their own doc-tor.[48] The Texans had no desire to remain in Mexico longer than absolute-ly necessary, and since they were not on parole they had no hesitation to try to escape. To elude a vigilant guard would take careful planning, so

---

46. Henry, *Campaign Sketches of the War with Mexico*, p. 273, says Guadalupe was four miles from Monterrey.

47. Canfield diary, Jan. 29, 1843.

48. T. [F.] M. Gibson, Quarter Master General, William Ryon, Captain, Esven [Ewen] Cameron, J. G. W. Pierson, William M. Eastlam [Eastman], Charles K. Reise [Reese]. Clau-dius Buster to Sr. General Canales, *Comandant de la escolta de prisoneros*, originally published in *Semanario* (Monterey), Feb. 2, 1843; reprinted in *El Látigo de Texas*, and copied from it in *Diario del Gobierno*, Feb. 24, 1843.

several of the men pretended to be more seriously wounded than was the case, and those whose recovery progressed satisfactorily tried to give the impression that their condition was serious, hoping that the guard would relax its vigilance.

Henry L. Kinney, on a business trip from Corpus Christi to the Rio Grande, visited the Texans at the hospital in Mier and left $500 with James O. Rice for the purchase of food, clothing, and other necessities required by the wounded. Rice and seven others, who had recovered sufficiently to travel, used the money to bribe a guard to supply them with ammunition, three guns, and provisions for their escape to Texas. With everything in readiness for the escape, the eight Texans   James O. Rice, Robert H. Beale, George B. Pilant, Henry D. Weeks, William Rupley, Nathaniel R. Mallon, John Bideler, and Lewis Hays—were escorted to a point outside the town. The men were halted and instructed by the guard to pursue a northeast course after crossing the Rio Grande, while he, after raising the alarm, would cross the river some fifteen miles above at the Palo Blanco road leading to San Patricio, with a small party of cavalry in pursuit.[49]

After crossing the Rio Grande the Texans became confused as to the direction they should pursue, and spent the night wandering in the chaparral. When daylight came, they found themselves near the Palo Blanco road, along which their pursuers were expected to come. Once more they took to the chaparral, but again found themselves at the Palo Blanco road, leading in the direction of Casa Blanca on the lower Nueces a few miles above old Fort Lipantitlán and less than forty-five miles from Corpus Christi. Across the river from the old fort was San Patricio.

The Texans were now sorely puzzled, having failed to pursue a continuous forward course through the brush and every moment expecting to hear the pursuing cavalry. As they stood at the edge of the road, pondering what course to take, and believing that it necessary to cross the road where tell-tale tracks would be left, William Rupley, an Irishman, exclaimed, "'By the Howly Saint Patrick can't we jest walk across the road backwards, and make the divils think we are going the other way?'"[50] The men backed across the road into the chaparral on the other side. After going a short distance, they turned north, paralleled the road for a mile or more, then re-entered the old trail (road). Limping and hobbling along they made the weary journey from the Rio Grande to Victoria, subsisting on the measly rations they had laid up in store for the journey, supplemented by a couple of mule-rabbits and two Mexican buzzards they were able to kill on the way.

The eight escapees arrived safely at Victoria.[51] They reported that

---

49. *Morning Star*, Feb. 28, 1843.
50. *Telegraph and Texas Register*, Mar. 15, 1843.
51. *New Orleans Bee*, Mar. 7, 1843; see also *Daily National Intelligencer* (Washington, DC), Mar. 16, 1843.

thirty others had escaped "about the close of the battle, . . . but as they have not come in," declared the editor of the New Orleans *Daily Picayune*, "it is thought that they have been captured by the bands of Mexican robbers who are continually roving along the frontier."[52] Actually, the only other escapees from Mier or its vicinity were members of the Camp Guard, and it is these that the recent arrivals at Victoria must have had in mind.

Robert Harper Beale arrived in Richmond around mid-March from the Rio Grande. The overland journey on foot had not been easy for him. Shot through the lung in the battle, his wound gave him considerable trouble and necessitated frequent stops for rest. He stumbled into Richmond "more like a ghost than a man"—more dead than alive. Thompson McMahan, a merchant in the community, recognized him and "embraced him with so much fervor that it caused his wound to break and he came near to bleeding to death."[53] Beale reported that Kuykendall and several others had died of their wounds at Mier.[54]

The Texans who remained at Mier were guarded more carefully and there were no more escapes. In the meantime, after the surrender, four of the wounded Texans died at Mier, and as soon as those remaining had recovered sufficiently from their wounds to travel, they were started, nine weeks after the main body of Texan prisoners had marched from Matamoros, on the long route to Mexico City by way of Matamoros and Tampico. These were: David Allen, Lynn Bobo, James Barber, Jeffrey B. Hill, Frank [Francis] Hughes, Edward Y. Keene, Malcolm McCauley, Theodore D. Maltby, Harbert H. Oats, William Y. Scott, and Dr. John J. Sinnickson. Of these the following died in Matamoros: Lynn Bobo (prior to March 4, 1843); James Barber (March 14, 1843); and Malcolm McCauley (July 14, 1843).

In Matamoros their journey was temporarily halted with receipt of the news of the escape of the main body of prisoners at Hacienda Salado. For some time they were held in close confinement in Matamoros, and after a while were ordered, along with the three boys who had been left on parole in the city since early January by Ampudia, to Mexico City. Their movement into the interior was further hastened by the talk in Texas of organizing an expedition under Gen. Thomas J. Rusk to effect a release of the Texan prisoners in Mexico.

When the boys and those who had been wounded in battle were sufficiently recovered to travel, they were marched south toward Tampico for Mexico City. Four of the Texan wounded, regarded as not yet sufficiently recovered for the trip, were retained in Matamoros, along with several who were still ill. Frank Hughes and William Y. Scott were still in Matamoros when the last of the Mier prisoners were released on September 16,

---

52. *Daily Picayune*, Feb. 26, 1843.
53. *Ibid.*
54. Wharton, *History of Fort Bend County*, p. 116.

1844. They were given their freedom under the same order that released the other Mier men.

In Matamoros, John Day Morgan and nine others who had charge of their sick and wounded colleagues were allowed the privilege of the town until word arrived of the overthrow of the guard at Hacienda Salado. "They were suddenly arrested and placed in a cell about ten feet square, with no light or anything of comfort or satisfaction." They set about with "an old pocket-knife" to remove a few bricks so as to effect their escape, when "late one evening the door [to their cell] was suddenly thrown open and the ten prisoners were rushed into the street to find themselves suddenly and completely surrounded."[55] With a company of infantry on each side, cavalry on the outside, artillery before and behind, they were marched to Victoria. A march of eleven leagues the first day left them tired and low spirited that night, with no possible chance for escape. Suspense and despair filled their minds as they wound their way to Tampico. They believed that death awaited them at Mexico City.

In Tampico they were treated kindly and were allowed some liberty, but there was no possible chance to escape. Upon arrival at Mexico City, Morgan was much relieved to find himself "unrecognized as one of the old Santa Fé band." A few days later, the new arrivals were sent to work on the road at Tacubaya. There "he was recognized and much disturbed in mind by one Mexican, who was disagreeably inquisitive and showed himself by no means satisfied when Morgan evaded his questions, assuring him he was mistaken."

The Mier men who had been left at Matamoros to recover from their wounds or illnesses "were treated with more kindness than had previously fallen to our lot," recorded McCutchan.[56] A Frenchman, who had formerly lived in San Antonio, Texas, was superintendent and chief physician at the hospital. As for H. L. Kinney, he returned to Matamoros from Mier, and visited McCutchan and his companions early in February. He told them "that he would make arrangements for us to escape," recorded McCutchan, "but before he could effect his *Noble* and *Generous* purpose, *he was taken,* and *thrown* into prison . . . accused of having assisted eight of our Men off from Mier."[57] He was held prisoner for several months, then paroled, but confined to the limits of the city.[58] On June 13, 1843, he escaped and made his way overland to his *rancho* on Corpus Christi Bay. From there he took the schooner *Santa Anna* to Galveston, and from there went to Houston, where he arrived on Friday, June 22, and confirmed "the opinion, so often expressed by intelligent travelers from that section [of southwestern Texas], that an army of 800 Texians could capture the whole country east of the mountains without the firing of a gun." Kinney

---

55. Jenkins, *Recollections of Early Texas*, pp. 134-35.
56. Nance, ed., *McCutchan's Narrative*, p. 73.
57. *Ibid.*, p. 74.
58. *Ibid.*, pp. 73-74.

reported the Mexican troops on the frontier "ill-clothed, ill-fed and generally dissatisfied. They have often been heard while intoxicated to declare," he said, "that they wished the Texians would come and take them prisoners for they would be better treated."

"It is a singular fact," surmised the editor of the Houston *Telegraph,* "that while our army under Gen. Somervill was at Laredo, the *rancheros* in several of the Mexican towns held meetings and agreed to send delegates to inform Gen. Somervill that they would submit to the Texian Government. If Somervill had advanced with his army directly towards Matamoros, he would have been joined by a large body of the citizens and would have probably been able to conquer the whole country."[59]

---

59. *Niles' National Register* LXIV, p. 309 (July 15, 1843).

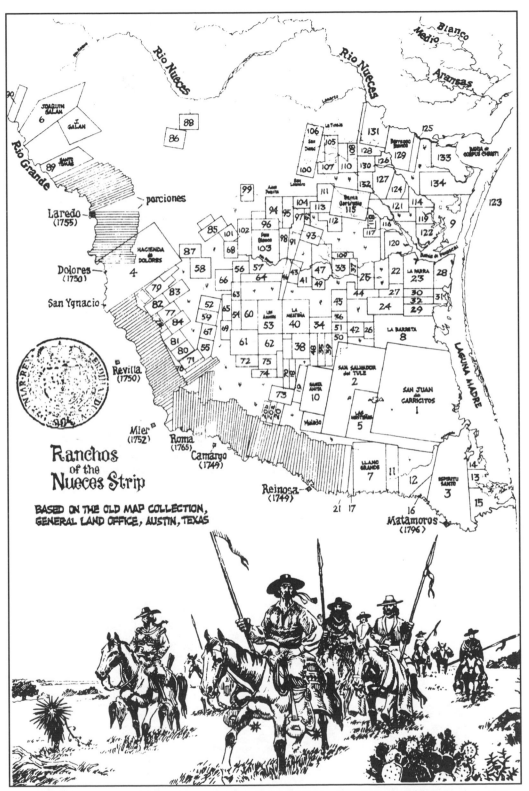

Blanco

Medio

Aransas

Rio Nueces

Rio Nueces

Rio Grande

porciones

Laredo
(1755)

HACIENDA de
DOLORES

Dolores
(1750)

San Ygnacio

Revilla
(1750)

Mier
(1752)

Roma
(1765)

Camargo
(1749)

Reinosa
(1749)

Matamoros
(1796)

Ranchos
of the
Nueces Strip

BASED ON THE OLD MAP COLLECTION,
GENERAL LAND OFFICE, AUSTIN, TEXAS

BAHIA de
CORPUS CHRISTI

LAGUNA MADRE

SAN JUAN
de
CARRICITOS
1

SAN SALVADOR
del TULE
2

LA BARRETA
8

LA PARRA
23

LLANO
GRANDE
7

ESPIRITU
SANTO
3

"As Many Horses as Circumstances Permit," by permission of Jackson, Los Mesteños, *445.*

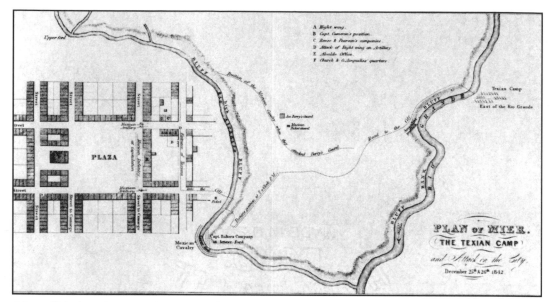

Map of Texian Camp, Mier. From The Journal of the Texian Expedition Against Mier, *by Thomas Jefferson Green.*

The Plaza in Mier. The building on the extreme left was used as Ampudia's headquarters. From Gooch-Iglehart, The Boy Captive of the Texas Mier Expedition, *120.*

Mier Expedition descending the Rio Grande. From Green, . . . Texian Expedition Against Mier, *70.*

Matamoros. From Mayer, Mexico, Aztec, Spanish and Republican *(1853), 1:337.*

Arroyo Secate, two miles below Laredo. From Nance, Attack and Counter-Attack, *339.*

Queretaro. From Mayer, Mexico, Aztec, Spanish and Republican *(1853), 2:307.*

Sierra Madre Pass. From Mayer, Mexico, Aztec, Spanish and Republican *(1853), 1:354.*

Monterrey from the Bishop's Palace. From Mayer, Mexico, Aztec, Spanish and Republican *(1853), 1:344.*

San Luis Potosí Cathedral.
From author's collection.

Mexican Lancer, ca. 1839. From
Cisneros, "Riders of the Border,"
Southwestern Studies, *monograph*
number 30, p. 35.

City of San Luis Potosí.
From Mayer, Mexico, Aztec,
Spanish and Republican *(1853),*
2:325.

Camp at Querétaro, Qro. From author's collection.

Jalapa. From author's collection.

William A. A. "Bigfoot" Wallace. From Nance, Attack and Counter-Attack, *338f.*

Memucan Hunt. From Nance, Attack and Counter-Attack, *338f.*

Adrián Woll. From Nance, Attack and Counter-Attack, *338f.*

Pedro de Ampudia. From Manuel Glugliazza, Documentos y datos para la historia de Tabasco.

"Arrieros and Mules." From author's collection.

John C. C. Hill. From Fanny Chambers Gooch-Iglehart, 303.

Orlando C. Phelps. From Gooch-Iglehart, The Boy Captive of the Mier Expedition, *29.*

Israel Canfield. Courtesy Texas State Archives.

Samuel H. Walker, from a deguerreotype by J. McGuire, New Orleans. Courtesy The University of Texas.

Governor P. Hansborough Bell, 1849. From Daniell, Personnel of the Texas State Government, *34.*

Henry Journeay. Courtesy Texas State Archives.

Henry L. Kinney. From Nance, Attack and Counter-Attack, *338f.*

Richard Brown. From Rusk County Historical Survey Committee program for historical marker dedication, 1971.

The dashing and gallant Capt. Jack Hays. From author's collection.

B. Z. Boone of San Bernard, grandson of Daniel Boone. From Wharton, History of Fort Bend County, 118.

Anson Jones, Republic of Texas President, 1844. From Daniell, Personell of the Texas State Government, 28.

Samuel A. Maverick. From Nance, Attack and Counter-Attack, *338f.*

Charles Elliot, R.N. From Blake, Charles Elliot, R.N., *frontispiece.*

Colonel William Ryon. From Wharton, History of Fort Bend County, *112.*

General Thomas J. Rusk. From Wooten, A Comprehensive History of Texas, *2:20.*

General José Maria Tornel. From Manuel Rivera Cambas, Los gobernantes de México, *UT Library.*

José María Bocanegra. From Nance, Attack and Counter-Attack, *338f.*

Archbishop Posada. From Gooch-Iglehart, The Boy Captive of the Mier Expedition, *212.*

General Mariano Paredes y Arrillaga. From Crawford (ed.), The Eagle, 136.

Nicolas Bravo. From Crawford (ed.), The Eagle, *182.*

Juan N. Almonte. Courtesy The University of Texas Library.

Mariano Arista. From Crawford (ed.), The Eagle, *174.*

Vice-President Gomez Farias. From Gooch-Iglehart, The Boy Captive of the Mier Expedition, *230.*

Valentin Canalizo. From Crawford (ed.), The Eagle, *178.*

Antonio López de Santa Anna, President of the Republic of Mexico and Senior General of Division D.

Dolores Tosta de Santa Anna, wife of the dictator. From a painting by Mexican artist Juan Cordreo, which shows the ostentatious luxury common to the court of Santa Anna. From author's collection.

The entrance to Perote Prison, showing effigies in stone of two colonial soldiers who were executed for sleeping while on guard. From McGrath and Hawkins, "Perote Fort . . .," SWHQ, *48:342.*

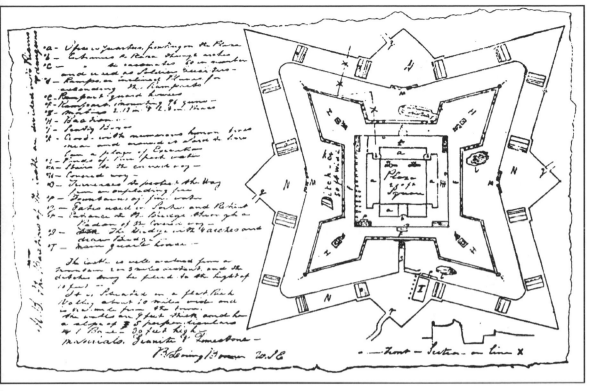

Above: *Pen and ink ground plan of the Castle of Perote, accompanying letter of April 29, 1846, by B. Lorring Boomer, U.S. Engineer.*

Below: *Ground plan of the Castle of Perote drawn by Charles McLaughlin, one of the Mier prisoners.*

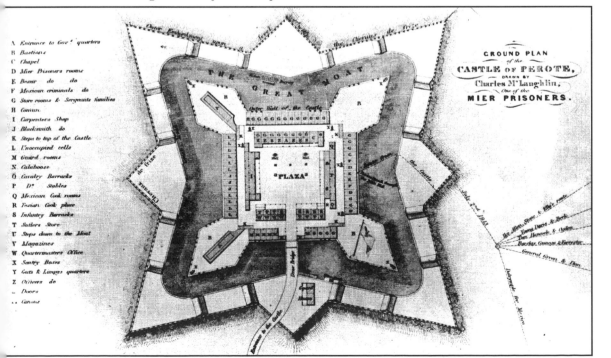

View of Jalapa and the Castle of Perote. From author's collection.

Guts and Ike Allen at the Calaboose. From Green, ...Texian Expedition Against Mier, 324.

Texians killing their horses in the mountains for sustenance. From Green, ...Texian Expedition Against Mier, 160.

CHAPTER 14

The Mier Men Overpower their Guard and Escape

ON JANUARY 28, TWO DAYS before the arrival of the main body of prisoners at Monterrey, the Texan officers were placed under a troop of cavalry commanded by Capt. Rafael Ugartechea and started for Saltillo. Reaching Saltillo on January 30 they were quartered in a filthy cavalry barracks. After a strong protest they were moved to an infantry *cuartel*. In their new quarters they found three of Captain Dawson's men who had been wounded and taken prisoners,[1] and three who had been captured at San Antonio on September 11 by General Woll and had been detained as Santa Fé prisoners at San Fernando to be shot.[2] On the recommendation of Woll, their death sentences were commuted to ten years' imprisonment. The Texan officers were detained in Saltillo eight days until the arrival of the other prisoners.

The Texan officers with their guard left Saltillo for San Luis Potosí on February 6. At Hacienda Salado they were quartered in a room opening upon a small courtyard in which was stationed the escort-guard. Adjoining on the south was a larger courtyard or corral, separated from the smaller one by a fifteen-foot wall, into which the main body of the Texan prisoners was placed. They resumed their march toward Mexico City at two o'clock on February 2. Their guard had been changed and greatly reduced. Lt. Col. Manuel R. Barragán, an accomplished and humane officer, replaced Canales. Their new guard consisted of 100 cavalrymen and 100 infantry. They were primarily raw recruits impressed from the prisons of Monterrey and poor soldiers both in discipline and military bearing. The character of the guard was severely criticized by several of the Mexi-

---

1. Norman B. Woods, Milvern Harrell, and John Higgerson. Green, *Mier Expedition*, p. 141.

2. Archibald Fitzgerald, George Van Ness, and Thomas Hancock. Gulick *et al.*, eds., *The Papers of Mirabeau Buonaparte Lamar* 6, p. 117; *Telegraph and Texas Register*, Jan. 25, 1843.

can officers. Gen. Severo Ruíz later asserted that he had warned Lt. Col. José María Bermúdez and Barragán against marching from Monterrey to San Luis Potosí with only 200 guards for 209 Texan prisoners.[3] Lt. Col. Antonio Tenorio declared later at the court martial of Colonel Barragán that he informed General Ortega, the commandant general of Nuevo León, that he feared the Texans would make a break because the Mexican escort was composed of raw recruits but that Ortega had assured him that they were picked men.[4]

The Texans were elated at the change in their guard. Not only were they rid of Canales, but they became more hopeful of effecting a successful escape. Their course from Monterrey led west past a cemetery and then along a road that diverged toward the river, passing between the Bishop's Palace and the river. To their left across the river stood a ridge of foothills known as the Loma Federación, which rose sharply from the river. From Monterrey to La Encantada the going was uphill, rising from a level of 1,600 feet above sea level to 6,100 feet.

After traveling approximately twelve miles, Colonel Barragán ordered the men to encamp at the *rancho* Santa Catarina. The prisoners were quartered in a stone church. The next morning the journey was resumed, and after going some fifteen miles, they crossed a small bridge. The road now descended a little, and "enclosed much of the way by lines of trees and maguey plants, pursued the same general direction until it reached the Hacienda de Rinconada, a mile or so farther on." Rinconada was a beautifully located *rancho* of several thousand acres situated in a cove near a high mountain pass. Colonel Barragán permitted frequent rest stops in the heat of the day on the long marches between Monterrey and Saltillo.[5] In the evening the prisoners reached the Rancho Rinconada.

At Rinconada the Texans were incarcerated in an old compound consisting of "three connected courts or pens, separated by mud walls some six feet high, opening into each other by gateways, closed by poles or bars. The first was occupied by the infantry, the second by . . . [the Texans], and the third, to the rear of . . . [them], by the cavalry."[6]

The situation seemed to offer an opportunity to escape. It was determined that just before daybreak the Texans would charge their guard and seize their arms. As the hour approached, the Texans were quietly awakened by their leaders. It had been expected that the cavalrymen would still be asleep and could be overcome before they could reach guns stacked against the wall of their compound. About the time for making the assault, the prisoners heard drums and found that the position of the guard had

---

3. Deposition of Severo Ruíz, Matamoros, Feb., 22, 1843. The San Jacinto Museum of History has a copy of the original document.

4. Deposition of Lt. Col. Antonio Tenorio, Matamoros, Feb. 22, 1843. The San Jacinto Museum of History has a copy of the original document.

5. Bell, *Narrative*, pp. 34-35.

6. Stapp, *Prisoners of Perote*, p. 55; see also Duval, *Big-Foot Wallace*, p. 195.

been changed. Again, the prisoners concluded that their captors were aware of their plans.

Opinions about who informed the guard varied. Some believed that Capt. Charles K. Reese and others who hoped to make individual escapes and were opposed to a general uprising had informed Colonel Barragán.[7] Others suspected a black man named Swaney, who had followed the Mexican troops from Matamoros and had circulated freely among the Texans, gaining the confidence of some "from his professed devotion and attention to their interest," and may have overheard them discussing plans for escape.[8] Others who had opposed the plan as being too desperate may have turned "informer." There is no evidence to prove that the Mexicans were informed. Since there had been some discussion at Monterrey of the possibility of the Texans attempting to revolt against the guard, Colonel Barragán may simply have been taking added precautions.

Leaving Rinconada on Saturday, February 4, the procession wound up a steep ravine. The way led mostly over hilly and broken country. Along the route from Monterrey Barragán permitted the Texans to stop frequently to rest during their march in a hot climate at an altitude higher than that to which they were accustomed.[9] Each day took the prisoners farther into the enemy's country, and they realized that the possiblity of a successful escape lessened.

On the night of February 4 they were driven into an enclosure at Rancho Gonzáles and herded for the night, having come twenty-seven miles that day. On February 5, about noon, they reached Saltillo, on the San Juan, "in a pretty little valley surrounded by rocky, dreary looking mountains without vegetation."[10]

Their entry into the city was through lanes of adobe walls until they came to the principal street which led them up a hill to the town proper. Their guard was reinforced, thus giving more credence to the belief among the men that their plans to escape had been divulged.[11]

The Texans were marched directly to prison without being paraded. They found bread plentiful and cheap in Saltillo, and those who had money could buy provisions reasonably. The women brought cooked food of various kinds to sell to the soldiers and to the prisoners, and "a liberal Frenchman" made a gift of tobacco to the prisoners.[12]

Since Fisher's party was quartered in different barracks, several of the men, in company with Barragán, were permitted to visit with their officers. On the following day the main body of Texans was joined by five of the

7. Canfield diary, Feb. 3, 1843; Stapp, *Prisoners of Perote*, p. 55; Sibley, ed., *Samuel H. Walker's Account*, p. 42; Glasscock diary, Feb. 3, 1843.

8. Stapp, *Prisoners of Perote*, p. 55.

9. Bell, *Narrative*, pp. 34-35.

10. Sibley, ed., *Samuel H. Walker's Account*, p. 42.

11. Duval, *Big-Foot Wallace*, p. 196; Stapp, *Prisoners of Perote*, p. 56.

12. Sibley, ed., *Samuel H. Walker's Account*, p. 43.

persons who had been captured by Woll during his campaign in Texas and who had been quartered temporarily with Fisher's group. These included Norman Woods, Milvern Harrell, and John Higgerson of the Dawson captives, and Archibald Fitzgerald and Thomas Hancock, who had been captured at San Antonio.[13] George Van Ness was added to the Texan officer party as an interpreter.

With the escort supplemented by a company of infantrymen known as "Red Caps," clearly indicating apprehension of the authorities for the security of their prisoners, the march southward in the direction of San Luis Potosí was resumed at an early hour on February 7, the day after the Texan officers had left under Captain Ugartechea. Orders from the Central Government required all of the Texans to be brought to Mexico City. "The sick were, therefore, mounted upon donkeys or thrown into carts and thus dragged through the burning sun for whole days consuming with fever and raging thirst."[14] A stiff breeze drove the powdery dust which the columns raised in marching. Water was available only from lakes formed by damming ravines or from wells of brackish water found at habitations, usually a day's journey apart. After going twenty-four miles, constantly ascending by way of gorges and narrow valleys through a rugged, barren, mountainous country, they camped at the Hacienda de Agua Nueva, where a large spring of water gushed from the foot of the mountain and collected in a large natural basin.[15] At Agua Nueva plans once more were concocted for charging the guard but, owing to the soreness of their feet and the weariness and vigilance of their guard, the Texans again postponed their plans. The night of February 8 they encamped at the Hacienda de Encarnación on the edge of the Saline Valley about sixty miles from Saltillo. The guard seems to have been *"fagged,"* but many of the Texans, having become acclimated and conditioned to walking, "at the end of the day's march would dance a jig for a piece of *peloncia* (piloncillo)."[16]

From Saltillo they had passed through a land of cactus and Spanish daggers, some attaining a height of twenty feet, with branches that made them look like trees. Much of the country through which they passed between Saltillo and the Hacienda del Salado had no water, except that "supplied from deep wells of brackish water."[17] The next day, February 9, they arrived at San Salvador, about three leagues beyond La Ventura. On February 10, they drew near *el rancho Salado* (Salt Farm) a small establishment located in a desert plain some 110 miles southeast of Saltillo on the main road to Mexico City. The conversation "this day . . . on the road was

13. Canfield diary, Feb. 6, 1843.

14. Bell, *Narrative*, p. 36.

15. "Bigfoot" Wallace called the place "Big Springs." W. A. A. Wallace to Miss Nora C. Franklin, Bigfoot, Oct. 13, '88. in TxU-A; it is also printed in *Frontier Times* 8 (June 1931), pp. 418-19.

16. Canfield diary, Feb. 8, 1843.

17. Green, *Mier Expedition*, p. 144; Bell, *Narrative*, p. 36.

regarding the propriety of charging the guard, the first opportunity that offered," reported Glasscock, "as we had now reached the mountainous part of the country, which we intended to take advantage of, in case we were pursued by a large force."[18] During the day, said Canfield, "several of us came to the Conclusion We had gone far enough, if not too far, into the country, and were determined . . . [no longer] to be driven this way through the country, if it could be avoided."[19] Here the main body of prisoners again overtook their officers. "The men appeared now to be more desperate and determined at all hazards to strike a blow which might once more gain their liberty." Until the last two days Barragán's treatment had not been very harsh, but his conduct toward the prisoners was beginning to cause concern. Within the last two days, reported Walker, "he had given the soldiers liberty to whip us and several of our men had already experienced their cruelty."[20]

After refreshing themselves from a well of brackish water, the Texans were ushered to their quarters, a horse corral amid a large block of adobe houses surrounding a central square. The houses were connected by a thick stone wall ten feet high. The prisoners were conducted through a wide gate into an open courtyard in which the infantrymen of the guard were to be quartered. They crossed the courtyard to the opposite side through a narrow gate in a lower wall closed by poles or bars and into the horse corral which was to be their quarters. The corral was surrounded on three sides by thick stone walls ten feet high. On the fourth side and connected with this corral was a quadrangular stone court surrounded by the main buildings of the ranch, with walls of equal height and thickness. The wall between the corral and the courtyard was only about four or five feet high, or as one account says, "about as high as a man's shoulders."[21]

The infantry of the guard, now about 150 men, occupied the main stone courtyard; the cavalry was stationed outside and surrounded the other three sides of the corral containing the prisoners.[22] A chain of sentinels was placed on the lower wall between the corral and the courtyard and on one of the other walls. The "Red Caps" occupied the houses which formed the wall on the west end of the courtyard. Texans who charged the guard would have to pass through two gates blocked by wooden rails. The inner gate was only wide enough to permit the passage of one man at a time, and on each side of this narrow exit stood a sentinel. At a distance of ten feet behind these two sentinels stood two more, and another pair guarded the outer gate. In the courtyard between the first and second doors was a much stronger guard. By night it became evident that Barra-

18. Glasscock diary, Feb. 10, 1843.

19. Canfield diary, Feb. 10, 1843; see also Stapp, *Prisoners of Perote*, p. 56.

20. Sibley, ed., *Samuel H. Walker's Account*, pp. 43-44.

21. Capt. Claudius Buster to John H. Jenkins, Sr., [n.p., n.d.], in *Frontier Times* 16 (June, 1939), pp. 35-40.

22. Stapp, *Prisoners of Perote*, p. 57; *Telegraph and Texas Register*, Nov. 29, 1843.

gán was suspicious. "The sentries were doubled, their guns examined, discharged and reloaded; and every precaution taken to insure against surprise that vigilance and prudence could suggest," reported Stapp.[23]

On entering the corral, many of the prisoners stretched out on the ground, overpowered by the heat of the day and the fatigue of the march. The leaders circulated among them, polling opinions and laying plans. Dr. Richard F. Brenham, Dr. William F. McMath, Judge Fenton M. Gibson, Samuel H. Walker, Maj. James D. Cocke, John Lyons, Col. William F. Wilson, and others urged that the proposal to escape be no longer postponed. The sun dipped below the crest of the sierras and the air became chilly from a cold wind that swept down from the mountains. John Rufus Alexander remembered that as night closed in he made a little fire from the small quantity of wood that had been given the prisoners, and sat beside it. He was joined by Brenham and Willis Copeland, who in low tones spoke of overthrowing the guard. Alexander says he told them that he did not believe a successful break could be made because they were so deep into the country, but if the men determined to overthrow the guard he would join in the attempt. Captain O'Phelan of the San Antonio prisoners, after his release and return to Texas, reported that Archibald Fitzgerald was among those opposed to the break, but from a spirit of chivalry he went along with the majority and took a leading part in it.[24] O'Phelan seems to have been the only one who thought Fitzgerald was opposed to the break, and there is no supporting evidence to prove the correctness of his statement. Brenham declared that his own life was already in jeopardy, having been on the Santa Fé Expedition of the year before, and most likely he would be executed upon arrival at Mexico City, despite the promises made by Ampudia.

After a brief discussion, a poll was taken among the men. It revealed that approximately one-third of the 214 prisoners were willing to charge the guard, the others believing it extremely imprudent and unsafe to do so at so great a distance from the frontier settlements of Texas. More favorable opportunities, both for attack and retreat, had been passed up. The minority, however, continued to urge and to entreat until all opposition was silenced.

Several of the Texans, including Captain Ryon, Brenham, Edwards, Maxwell, and Capt. Archibald ("Madcap") Fitzgerald, accompanied by Barragán, visited Fisher and party whose passage to Mexico City had been delayed a day owing to the illness of Lt. Col. D. Rafael Ugartechea and who were at the time quartered in a room opening upon a small courtyard.[25] The courtyard adjoined the larger one in which the main body of

23. Stapp, *Prisoners of Perote*, p. 56; Bell, *Narrative*, pp. 37-38.

24. *Telegraph and Texas Register*, May 10, 1843.

25. William S. Fisher and Thomas J. Green to Commander-in-Chief of the Department of San Luis Potosí, Prison, San Luis Potosí, Feb. 26, 1843, in *Telegraph and Texas Register*, May 10, 1843.

prisoners was quartered, and the two were accessible to one another only by the outer gate. Green claimed he urged that the attack be made, and that Colonel Fisher was opposed to the proposed charge upon the guard, thinking it "injudicious" and that "the whole of our men would be killed." Fisher sent word to Captain Cameron, however, "to use his own good sense in the matter."[26]

From our knowledge of the character, bravery, and gentlemanly conduct of Colonel Fisher, we may rest assured that he sought to place no impediment in the way of the proposed attack, even though Green would have us believe that the origin of the idea, the plans for the escape, and the success of the attack all came from him. "I was in favour of it, as I had uniformly been, and my plan of attack was freely communicated to Captain Ryon and Fitzgerald, and Dr. Brennam [Brenham]. They informed me that their plan was to charge at midnight. I opposed this hour, [declared Green], as being unpropitious for securing the horses of the cavalry, as they would most probably be out grazing, and recommended sunrise, at which time the horses would be herded."[27] After the main body of prisoners had broken free, Captain Fitzgerald was to lead a party around the building and assist in freeing the officers. If the latter, however, should leave before the attack, Fitzgerald promised to pursue them and rescue the officers on the road.

The Texans hoped to overthrow the armed guard, which outnumbered them but slightly, before the Mexicans could recover from the suddenness of their attack. The plans were discussed in low tones late into the night while Mexican sentinels dozed at their posts or drowsily uttered an occasional *"centinela alerto!"* and the Mexican officers slept. Brenham, who had done so much to keep alive the spirit of revolt, would have been their leader, said Thomas W. Cox, "but for the fear that his impetuous daring and ardent feelings would urge him into measures beyond prudence."[28] Instead, Captain Cameron was reaffirmed as the leader. It was understood that he would give the signal for the attack when Colonel Barragán came into the compound to order the men to draw their rations and to get ready to resume the march. The men were instructed not to kill unnecessarily, as the sick, the wounded, and a few unwilling souls would have to be left behind and their lives would be endangered if the Mexicans were shot down ruthlessly.

The prisoners acted as nonchalantly as possible. Some of the 214 men danced, sang, and cut capers until late at night, while others discreetly watched every movement of the guard. When a petty officer of the guard

---

26. Green, *Mier Expedition*, p. 146; Claudius Buster to John H. Jenkins, Sr., [n.p., n.d.], quoted in *Frontier Times* 16 (June 1939), p. 359; Sibley, ed., *Samuel H. Walker's Account*, p. 43.

27. Green, *Mier Expedition*, p. 146.

28. Thomas W. Cox in the *Texian and Brazos Farmer*, quoted in Adams, "[Journal of an] Expedition against the Southwest," Dec. 19, 1842.

was sent in to inquire what was the occasion for so much general good humor, Cameron informed him "that it was in view of the near approach of St. Valentine's, our Saint's day," which they "always celebrated with great rejoicing and hilarity, since it never failed to bring good luck."[29]

The decision made, the men lay down to rest, resolved that the morning's sun would shine upon free men or set on their graves. A few still maintained a lookout and the "watchers" were rotated so that each could get as much sleep as possible. Without arms or knives—not even a penknife—they were about to embark upon a daring undertaking.

With a glimmer of light in the east on February 11, the prisoners stirred and rekindled their fires. The positions of the guard were the same as the evening before; the sentinels were still in double formation and were "closely observing what was going on among their prisoners,"[30] but some of the Texans, no doubt a little edgy, thought their guard unusually alert and that they had lost the advantage of surprise.

As the dawn gave way to the new day, Colonel Barragán, as was his usual custom, entered the compound and ordered the prisoners to arise, draw their rations, and make ready to resume the march as soon as they had eaten.[31] He "discovered our excitement," reported Walker, and sensing that something was wrong retired immediately before the word could be given, and the prisoners lost the important advantage of taking the commander a prisoner. The Texan leadership hesitated for a moment, but there was a strong undercurrent to go ahead as if this were the last chance; the word was passed that they would go forward with the plan. Their breakfast of boiled rice was brought in and the prisoners milled around in apparent listlessness near the huge kettles and gulped their morning repast. The "men looked into each other with inquiring eyes and read decision in every countenance and grim determination in every eye."[32]

As the guards began to prepare their own breakfast, the Texans steeled themselves for the coming attack. They noticed that many of the infantrymen in the adjoining corral had stacked their guns with fixed bayonets in the courtyard against the wall about ten paces from the gate while cooking their meal.[33] Some stowed their blankets while others loitered near the outer gate talking with the cavalrymen. The Texans continued to devour their rice, with an occasional glance cast from beneath "the slouched brims of their hats and caps" in the direction of the gate and toward their leader. On the lower wall separating the corral from the courtyard, "four sleepy-looking sentinels" stood at ease, resting upon their

29. "John Rufus Alexander's Story of the Mier Expedition as Told to John Warren Hunter," in Wade, comp., *Notes and Fragments of the Mier Expedition* 1, p. 32.

30. Bell, *Narrative*, p. 37.

31. Sibley, ed., *Samuel H. Walker's Account*, p. 44.

32. "John Rufus Alexander's Story of the Mier Expedition as Told to John Warren Hunter," in Wade, comp., *Notes and Fragments of the Mier Expedition* 1, p. 34.

33. Duval, *Big-Foot Wallace*, p. 197; Claudius Buster to John H. Jenkins, Sr., [n.p., n.d.], extract in Houston Wade Papers, Tx-A.

escopetas; beyond the low wall just outside the gate the two sentinels leaned on their muskets, watching the noisy Texans consume their breakfast.

As Cameron, the chief conspirator, "with an air of vulgar relish, . . . continued to munch his gourd of rice, . . . he advanced with a careless and loitering step nearer and nearer the doorway of the coural *[sic]*," until he stood foremost, and within a few steps of the sentries at the gate.[34] Suddenly, about seven in the morning, as the sun began to peep over the mountains, he faced about and for an instant, "an unbroken silence reigned over that daring band; every eye is turned to the noble Cameron, who stan[d]s like a statue, his head erect, his eye fixed upon vacancy, his nerves steady; no one moves, none seemed excited, but anxiety has a place upon the features of all, save Cameron. The moment arrives; his piercing eye lights up, and throwing his timeworn hat far above his head—the preconcerted signal—he utters the word[s]: ["Come it Boys"]: the door is reached; placing the hand upon the breast of each sentinel at the narrow door way the Lionlike Cameron hurls them far away in opposite directions, as the w[h]irlwind scatters chaff, and with a bound he rushes through the remaining door. The Texians pour out after their leader."[35]

Samuel H. Walker was probably the second man through the narrow gate leading into the adjoining courtyard. He was followed closely by Brenham, Major Cocke, Lyons, and others. Cameron seized the musket of the sentinel at the left of the gate and Walker that of the one on the right.[36] Like men possessed, the Texans dashed upon the startled enemy.

Simultaneous with Cameron's rush for the gate, a volley of sun-dried bricks and stones hurled by *los diablos Tejanos* toppled several of the sentinels from the walls.[37] A piercing yell which "might have been heard for miles" frightened the raw recruits of the guard as their charges poured through the gate and over the low wall to dash for the muskets stacked against the south wall where they grappled for the guns held by the sentries.[38] At the same time, the Mexican soldiers rushed for the same guns, causing a fierce hand-to-hand struggle for about five minutes. Alexander reported that when he got "to the stack of guns," he grabbed a short musket, "but imagine our chagrin when we found that the guns were not loaded."

---

34. [A Mier Prisoner] to the Editor of the *New York American*, Prison of the Powder Mill, near the City of Mexico, June 3, 1843, quoted from the *New York American* in *Niles' National Register* 65, pp. 3-4, Sept. 2, 1843.

35. Nance, ed., *McCutchan's Narrative*, p. 84; see also Canfield diary, Feb. 11, 1843; Glasscock diary, Feb. 11, 1843; W. A. A. Wallace to Miss Nora C. Franklin, Big Foot, Sept. 24, 1888, in "Letters of Big Foot Wallace," *Frontier Times* 8 (June 1931), pp. 417-18; Wilson, *Reminiscences of Persons, Events, Records and Documents of Texian Times*, p. 6; Stapp, *Prisoners of Perote*, p. 58.

36. Sibley, ed., *Samuel H. Walker's Account*, p. 44.

37. *Telegraph and Texas Register*, Nov. 29, 1843.

38. "John Rufus Alexander's Story of the Mier Expedition as Told to John Warren Hunter," in Wade, comp., *Notes and Fragments of the Mier Expedition*, p. 36; see also McCaleb, *The Mier Expedition*, p. 66.

Using a "sling shot," as he described it, made from the sleeve of an infantryman's coat that had been thrown derisively at his feet at Saltillo by one of the guards, and which he had concealed under his clothes, Bate Berry inserted "a stone weighing about two pounds" and "brained two of the 'Red Cap' guards" and "knocked" a third "into insensibility."[39] Scarcely ten guns were fired before the courtyard was empty of Mexicans, except for the sentries who had been disarmed.[40]

In the struggle for the guns the Texans had the advantage in strength and weight, and soon were in possession of the weapons.

Those Texans who remained behind, thinking they could avoid the affray, felt the brunt of the Mexican gunfire directed into the enclosure from which their comrades were escaping. John Harvey was wounded although he took no part in the action.[41]

About fifty cavalrymen under Colonel Barragán escaped into the plain while a small group took refuge in some of the adjacent buildings, from which they fired their pistols and *escopetas* at the Texans in the corral and courtyard. Outside the courtyard Barragán tried to rally a company of infantrymen and his mounted cavalry to make a stand.[42] As the Texans charged through the outer gate of the courtyard Brenham and Patrick Lyons, leading the sortie, were killed. Lyons was shot down in the gateway by the Mexicans sheltered in the buildings on the left. Brenham was killed in the brief fight at the outer gate. Brenham met his death more or less accidentally while rushing a Mexican soldier who fell to the ground, "and his gun fell toward the Doctor, who rushed upon it inadvertently and the bayonet passed directly through his body."[43] On arrival in Texas, O'Phelan reported Brenham had killed three of the enemy with a bayonet before he fell.[44] When the fight was over, Brenham's comrades gathered around his body, and "shed tears of regret at the loss of one who had shared their hardships, accomplished their release, and fell in the moment of success, and whose brilliant qualities had made forcible impressions upon them."[45]

As the Texans cleared the outside gate the cavalry fell back and the "Red Cap" infantrymen retreated around the main wall of the building to the south and through the gate into the courtyard, which had only a short

---

39. John Warren Hunter, "The Vengeance of Bate Berry," *Frontier Times* 30 (Oct.-Dec., 1953), p. 465; see also, "John Rufus Alexander's Story of the Mier Expedition as Told to John Warren Hunter," in Wade, comp., *Notes and Fragments of the Mier Expedition*, p. 35.

40. Stapp, *Prisoners of Perote*, p. 58.

41. Sibley, ed., *Samuel H. Walker's Account*, p. 45.

42. Stapp, *Prisoners of Perote*, p. 59; Green, *Mier Expedition*, p. 158.

43. Sibley, ed., *Samuel H. Walker's Account*. p. 45; Stapp, *Prisoners of Perote*, p. 59; "John Rufus Alexander's Story of the Mier Expedition as Told to John Warren Hunter," in Wade, comp., *Notes and Fragments of the Mier Expedition*, p. 66; Sowell, *Early Settlers and Indian Fighters of Southwest Texas*, p. 67; *Northern Standard*, Apr. 20, 1843.

44. *Northern Standard*, Apr. 20, 1843.

45. *Telegraph and Texas Register*, Apr. 12, May 3 and 10, 1843.

time before been occupied by Fisher and his party. A number of the Texans under the leadership of Captain Fitzgerald, believing that their officers were yet in their quarters, sought to force that gate to free them. Fitzgerald fell wounded in the shoulder and died two days later while being transported in a cart.[46]

In the charge at the outer gate, "Bigfoot" Wallace rushed upon a Mexican, who had just fired his gun, with the intent of disarming him. "The fellow had a bayonet on his musket, however, and made a vicious thrust at the big Texan, who seized the bayonet, and a hard struggle commenced for the mastery. The bayonet came off in the hands of Wallace, and another unarmed prisoner came up behind and seized the gun by the breach and obtained possession of it. The Mexican fell to his knees, held up his hands, and in Spanish called for mercy, which was granted him." Lieutenant Barragán, whose father commanded the escort, showed great bravery during the fight. Six Texans confronted him with fixed bayonets and demanded his surrender. Backing against a wall, he brandished his sword, parried their thrusts, and refused to surrender except to an officer. "His saber made such rapid movements that it was hardly visible. About this time Big Foot Wallace came up and some one told him to get a loaded gun and shoot the fellow. Wallace said no; that a brave man like him should be spared. The brave young Mexican now called for Captain Cameron. He came at once, and the sword was then turned over to him. With a proud look the Mexican stepped back and folded his arms."[47]

While in the act of grabbing at the musket of a Mexican soldier standing upon the wall above him, youthful George W. Trahern was shot through the top of his right hand and his clothes were set on fire by the discharge.[48]

An order was "now given to cease firing."[49] Wallace reported that "there was an awful rattling of bayonets for about two minutes." Cameron had cautioned his men not to kill any of the Mexicans if they could avoid doing so.[50] Little firing took place in this momentary engagement, but what did occur was at close range and generally effective. Many loaded muskets were snatched from the hands of the sentinels and guards before they could even discharge them. There followed a few sporadic shots as the Mexicans tried to restrain pursuing Texans or as Texan frontiersmen sought to subdue their opponents. Men, women, children, and dogs raced madly in all directions in fear of *"los diablos Tejanos."* The hand-to-hand encounter was brief but deadly and it lasted only about five minutes, ac-

---

46. *Daily Picayune*, Apr. 28, 1843.

47. Sowell, *Early Settlers and Indian Fighters of Southwest Texas*, p. 68.

48. Trahern diary, p. 8. George W. Trahern Pension Papers, Tx-A. MS.

49. Sibley, ed., *Samuel H. Walker's Account*, p. 45.

50. Wilson, *Reminiscences of Persons, Events, Records and Documents of Texian Times*, pp. 5-8; Capt. S. H. Walker to Gen. A. Sidney Johns[t]on, Prison Santiago, City of Mexico, May 4, 1843, in Army Papers (Republic), Tx-A.

cording to William F. Wilson, or fifteen minutes, according to Capt. Samuel H. Walker.[51]

In what many of the Texans termed the "Battle of the Rescue," the Mexicans had five killed and five wounded.[52] All other members of the escort were captured except those who escaped into the plain. The smallness of the Mexican losses may be attributed to the desire of the Texans to shed no more blood than was necessary for the preservation of their own lives, and "those [Mexicans] who threw aside their arms were not molested, and the officers were treated with the utmost respect and their sword returned to them." The Texan losses were three killed and eight wounded,[53] two of whom subsequently died of their wounds. Those killed in the action were Lorenzo Rice, Patrick Lyons, and Richard F. Brenham. Capt. John R. Baker, Capt. Archibald Fitzgerald, Thomas Hancock, John A. Sansberry, John Harvey, John Higgerson, Leonidas Sanders, and George W. Trahern were wounded.[54] Baker, Sansberry, Fitzgerald, and Higgerson were seriously wounded. Higgerson died that same day of his wounds, but Trahern's wound was not serious enough to prevent him from attempting to escape with the others. Harvey, though he took no part in the fight, and Hancock were only slightly wounded.[55] Hancock decided not to go with the escapees, and in Fitzgerald and Hancock, both of whom a few weeks past had come over the route from San Fernando, the Mier men lost the two they needed to guide them through the country over which they intended to pass.[56]

The Texan officers—Fisher, Green, and five others,[57] with their new commander, Capt. J. German Romano, who replaced Lt. Col. Rafael Ugartechea, had started on their way eight or ten minutes before sunup, or about fifteen minutes before the attack on the guard began, so as to keep the officers separated from the men, a policy which had been followed since leaving Matamoros. The Mexican guard of twenty-five dragoons, Capt. J. German Romano, and their seven prisoners had progressed only three-fourths of a mile before the noise of gunfire reached them. Green and his companions, anticipating the break, heard the fire of the first gun, but it was not until several shots had been fired before

---

51. Wilson, *Reminiscences of Persons, Events, Records and Documents of Texian Times*, pp. 5-8; see also Capt. S. H. Walker to Gen. A. Sidney Johns[t]on, Prison Santiago, City of Mexico, May 4, 1843, in Army Papers (Republic).

52. "Narrative of 'Mier' and 'Perote' By one of the Expedition," in *Telegraph and Texas Register*, Nov. 28, 1843.

53. *Francisco Mejía a Exmo, Sr. comandante general de San Luis Potosí, Departamento de Coahuila, Saltillo, Febrero 12 de 1843*, in *Diario del Gobierno*, Feb. 24, 1843.

54. *Telegraph and Texas Register*, May 10, 1843; Duval, *Big-Foot Wallace*, p. 198; Thomas J. Green to Dear Friends, Castle of Perote, Mexico, Apr. 15, 1843, in *Telegraph and Texas Register*, May 17, 1843.

55. Sibley, ed., *Samuel H. Walker's Account*, p. 45.

56. *Ibid.*

57. *J. Germán Romano a Exmo. Sr. comandante general de San Luis Potosí, Matehuala, Febrero 11 de 1843*, in *Diario del Gobierno*, Feb. 24, 1843; Green, *Mier Expedition*, p. 147.

Captain Romano recognized the gunfire.[58] He halted the prisoners, and ordered Lt. D. Antonio Arredondo to go back with fifteen men to learn what the shooting was about.

While Arredondo was dashing back to Salado, Captain Romano urged the small band of prisoners and the guard on at a full gallop at the point of the lance to avoid any attempt by the escaping prisoners to lay hands upon their officers. As they hurried along, the guards rode on each side with fixed cavalry lances. After going about a hundred yards, the prisoners were halted and ordered to dismount. Soon the firing in the distance ceased, and the repeated Texan shouts of victory—of "Hurrah for Texas!" and "to Hell with Mexico!"—could be heard. The Texan officers could see men, women, children, infantry, and cavalry scampering to the four winds, leaving clouds of dust behind.

A sergeant major from the auxiliaries arrived with verbal orders from Barragán to Romano to shoot his prisoners and to come at once to his assistance.[59] The sergeant major reported that the Texans had taken possession of the arms and buildings, and that Barragán's situation was desperate. Comprehending his orders, Captain Romano cast a glance in the direction of the prisoners, and nervously, but without hesitation, ordered his men to reprime their *escopetas* and make ready to receive further orders.

Fisher met the situation with coolness by appealing to the captain's sense of honor and self-respect. Fisher asked him if he were not bound to obey Governor Ortega's order to take them to Mexico City, rather than some subsequent order issued by Colonel Barragán; and, he continued, we thought "'we were in the hands of a gentlemen and a soldier, not a murderer,'"[60] Captain Romano's "eyes were instantly lowered to the pommel of his saddle, and his countenance underwent hesitation, change, and satisfaction in as many seconds, when he raised himself in his stirrups, and, proudly clapping his hand upon his bosom, ordered the interpreter to say to the gentleman 'that they are in the hands of a *gentleman* and a *soldier,* and I will carry out Governor Ortega's orders.'"[61] The Texans were ordered to mount and started at a fast gallop toward Mexico City with the lancers on each side.

Diverging from the route assigned to him, Romano bypassed Vanegas and the Hacienda Guadalupe del Carnicero, and directed his course to

---

58. *J. Germán Romano al Sr. comandante general de San Luis Potosí, Matehuala, Febrero 11 de 1843,* in *Diario del Gobierno,* Feb. 24, 1843; Thos. J. Green to My Dear Friends, Castle of Perote, Mexico, Apr. 15, 1843, in *Morning Star,* May 12, 1843; *Telegraph and Texas Register,* May 17, 1843.

59. Quoted in Green, *Mier Expedition,* p. 149; Thomas J. Green to Dear Friends, Castle of Perote, Mexico, Apr. 15, 1843, in *Telegraph and Texas Register,* May 17, 1843.

60. Green, *Mier Expedition,* p. 149; William S. Fisher and Thomas J. Green to Capt. Germán Romano, of the Mexican Army, San Luis Potosí, Feb. 20, 1843, in *Telegraph and Texas Register,* May 10, 1843. Photostat of original in San Jacinto Museum of History.

61. *Germán Romano al Sr. comandante general de San Luis Potosí, Matehuala, Febrero 11 de 1843,* in *Diario del Gobierno,* Feb. 24, 1843.

Cedral. Stopping only at the large Rancho de la Punta for water and to dispatch messengers to Vanegas and Catorce, the group arrived at Cedral at about four in the afternoon. News of the revolt upon the guard at Salado had preceded them; and in order to protect the Texans from the populace, Romano ordered them to dismount and immediately enter a room before which he placed his cavalry. During the hour that the prisoners remained at Cedral, they were supplied with crackers, cheese, and a bottle of *vino muscal,* while the Mexican escort recruited fresh horses and Romano prepared to proceed to Matehuala.

Romano decided that it was his duty to return to Hacienda Salado to assist Colonel Barragán and turned his charges over to the *alcalde.* No regular troops were available, so the *alcalde* prevailed upon Matias Martin y Aguirre, an old and sickly retired colonel, to collect a party of *rurales* to guard the seven Texan prisoners.[62] Soon after Romano left, Aguirre decided to organize a small force to rush to Salado, too,[63] and the prisoners were turned over to citizen Juan Mata to guard while Aguirre made plans to unite with other *rurales* in the district to go to the assistance of Barragán.

With a new guard of thirty of the most "perfect savages we ever met before or since," reported Green,[64] the Texans renewed their journey. It was now night, but a fair moon revealed the countenances of their guard and caused the prisoners to suspect that their guard intended to assassinate them before reaching Matehuala. No doubt with some idea of effecting their escape, Lyon pretended to have difficulty in keeping in line; and, when several of the guards cocked their guns under pretense of shooting him, Henrie, the interpreter, informed the guards that the old sailor was unaccustomed to riding horseback. His conduct was forgiven. Henrie, however, pieced together some of the general's conversation and informed Green that the prisoners were to be shot, and that it was his intention to die as gloriously as possible. So saying, he reached over and took from the horn of Green's saddle his flask of *muscal,* from which he drank so heavily that he became drunk and in that condition occasionally rode up against the guard. As they rode along a guard was on the point of spearing Henrie with his lance, when Green, seeing what was about to happen, grabbed the bridle of Henrie's horse and drew him to his side, thus protecting the "supposed" drunk Texan from serious injury, if not death.

Captain Romano unexpectedly rode up with the "old guard." He said that he had learned of the murderous intent of the rogues after the prisoners had left Cedral, changed his mind about returning to Salado, and had dashed after the prisoners to reach them before they had been mur-

62. *Matias M. y Aguirre a Sr. gobernador y comandante general del departamento [San Luis Potosí], Matehuala, Febrero 12 de 1843,* in *Diario del Gobierno,* Feb. 24, 1843.
    63. Green, *Mier Expedition,* p. 151.
    64. *Ibid.,* pp. 151-53.

dered.[65] At nine o'clock, after nearly seventy miles of travel that day, Matehuala was reached. Despite the hour a large segment of the population had turned out to view *los diablos Téjanos*. The prisoners were hurried through the crowd to quarters in a tavern and turned over to the local authorities.

On the morning after the arrival of the prisoners at Matehuala, Col. D. Matías de Aguirre visited them. Aguirre exhibited a spirit of kindness. He ordered the prisoners removed to better quarters and placed them under the care of citizen Juan Mata to guard until his return or until ordered to San Luis Potosí by the governor. Juan Mata was "a humane gentleman" and an accomplished scholar. A lawyer, D. Manuel Fernández Palos, supplied the Texan officers with food from his own table during their three days at Matehuala. They were visited by several persons of distinction in the community, including the local priest, who generously sent them "several rich viands from his table."[66] One of the visitors was the Baron de Kawinsky, a member of the scientific corps of the Russian Emperor, who had been exploring the northern states of Mexico. Upon parting, he left with them "some of his excellent tea, which we highly enjoyed," said Green, "during our trip to Mexico."[67]

With Romano's troops as their escort, the prisoners left Matehuala on February 16 for San Luis Potosí, 140 miles away. The Texan officers spent the night of February 17 at the *hacienda* of the Count of Zivyes, who showed the Texans fine hospitality, inviting them that night and the next morning to his mansion for supper and breakfast served under "a dozen covers." He showed them around "his extensive buildings, and all the appurtenances belonging to the establishment, particularly his farming utensils, which we found," reported Green, "to be exceedingly crude, at least one hundred years behind Texas in this respect."[68]

Leaving the *hacienda* the next morning, the officers reached San Luis Potosí on February 20, where they remained until March 1—the day their recaptured comrades reentered Saltillo. The prisoners were halted in the street before the governor's quarters, where they remained in the hot sun for twenty minutes without permission to dismount while the captain sought to learn the disposition to be made of the prisoners. Being greatly fatigued from the excessive heat and dust of the road, the Texans purchased a flask of *muscal* from a street vendor as they waited, and a corporal relieved them of their purchase. The privilege of buying *vino muscal* had never before been denied them. Shortly after this incident they were

---

65. *J. German Romano a Sr. comandante general de San Luis Potosí, Matehuala, Febrero 11 de 1843, and [Matias M. y Aguirre] a Sr. Comandante de los priseoneros, Matehuala, Febrero 12, 1843,* in *Diario del Gobierno*, Feb. 24, 1843; Thos. J. Green to My Dear Friends, Castle of Perote, Mexico, Apr. 15, 1843, in *Morning Star*, May 12, 1843.

66. Green, *Mier Expedition*, pp. 151-52.

67. *Ibid.*

68. *Ibid.*, p. 154.

ordered locked up in miserable quarters and a strong guard was placed over them.

Fisher dispatched a letter to the commander-in-chief of the Department of San Luis Potosí, saying that he had seen it stated "in your newspaper" that the Texans had surrendered at discretion, but that such, as he could plainly see from the enclosed copy of the surrender terms, was not true; Fisher did admit that the Texans did not have their interpreter present at the reading of the terms at Mier.[69] Fisher was by no means totally ignorant of the Spanish language, but he tried to make a case for being treated as "prisoners of war." He said Ampudia voluntarily promised that if the Texans surrendered "they would be treated *with all the honours* and considerations of prisoners of war."

While the governor refused to reply in writing to the prisoners' protest regarding their treatment "as prisoners of war," he inquired verbally through his secretary to know what it was they desired so their conditions could be improved. On February 22 the two officers put into writing a list of grievances. They objected to being treated as common state criminals, and complained of a breach of parole of a general officer and of being housed in bare walls, with no furniture of any kind, neither bed nor chair, and with no privacy for acts of nature; they had been denied the purchase of *vino muscal;* their guard had been quadrupled and sentinels with bayonets paced their room during the whole night "uttering every few minutes the most unearthly exclamations as if the luxury of the brick pavement was too good a bed for us. These with the magnanimous allowance of fifty cents per day for our support is the situation in which we are at present."[70]

Again the governor's secretary contacted the Texan officers and said that orders had been issued which should ameliorate their situation, but implied that the rigorous treatment and the curtailment of customary privileges had been due to the break at Salado. Fisher and Green again wrote to the governor, thanking him for the use of a table, chairs, and other items of convenience, and "for the amelioration of the rigors of guard discipline." They stated: "But when your Secretary makes you assume the position, that our privileges have been curtailed on account of the Texian prisoners, having escaped from their guards on the 11th Inst. at Salado we are bound to object to such position." They claimed that they were in no way responsible for the break, and that Ampudia, contrary to their own wishes, had separated the Texan command from the men, and thus "removed any influence we might have exercised over the men, and consequently freed us from any responsibility for their conduct whether

69. William S. Fisher to the Commander-in-Chief of the department of San Luis Potosí, San Luis Potosí, Feb. 19, 1843, photostat of original in San Jacinto Museum of History; reprinted in *Telegraph and Texas Register,* May 10, 1843.

70. William S. Fisher and Thomas J. Green to Commander-in-Chief of the Department of San Luis Potosí, Prison, San Luis Potosí, Feb. 22, 1843, photostat of original in San Jacinto Museum of History; printed in *Telegraph and Texas Register,* May 10, 1843; Green, *Mier Expedition,* pp. 180-83.

for good or for bad." However, Ampudia had personally been very considerate of the Texan officers, permitting them to share his house, purse, wardrobe, and his table. Thereafter, the governor reduced their guard, permitted them greater freedom, and provided various items of furniture.

The Texan and Mexican wounded in the "break," and those who had not absconded, were started later in the morning of February 11 under Capt. Emeterio Posas, with a small cavalry unit, on the road south toward San Luis Potosí. On February 21 Captain Posas, the wounded, and remnants of the Texans left at Salado were overtaken by Lt. Col. Juan de Dios Ortiz, who assumed command of the unit. On February 26, Ortiz and sixteen Texans, including William Reese, reached San Luis Potosí, and the Texan officers for the first time received an account of the successful overthrow of the guard. Ortiz had advanced to the Hacienda Salado with the force under his command, where he united with a small number of infantrymen from Catorce. In vain he had pursued the "traitorous" Texans for thirty leagues. They were all mounted and well armed, he reported. By last accounts on February 12, they had passed beyond Encarnación and were now probably beyond Saltillo, Ortiz reported to the commandant-general of the Department of San Luis Potosí from Salado.[71]

Nineteen of the Texans, excluding the wounded and sick, were started for Mexico City on March 1 from San Luis Potosí under Colonel Teris of the 4th Regiment of infantry. Milvern Harrell was forced to go forward, leaving his Uncle Norman behind. Simon Glenn, who had been left ill at San Luis Potosí, was sent forward with Fisher's party. Before leaving Fisher and Green addressed a letter of appreciation to Captain Romano for the kind treatment shown to them and to their party while in his charge,[72] and another to Capt. José María Reyes of the Mexican army, expressing warm thanks for his kind and humane treatment of them while in prison.[73]

Their route carried them through the Hacienda de Plata; Hacienda Jaral (Xaral), where they were quartered in the *meson;* San Juan del Río; Arroyo Seco; Cuautitlán; and the western suburbs of Mexico City to Tacubaya, which they reached on March 15.[74]

At three in the morning, "the bugle sounded the march," and at daylight they commenced their descent into the beautiful Valley of Mexico. On reaching the western suburbs of the City of Mexico, they halted for a short interval in front of a church, and were allowed to purchase some

71. *Juan Ortiz, Comandancia general del Departamento de San Luis Potosí, a Señor comandante general del Departamento de San Luis Potosí, Hacienda del Salado, Febrero 12 de 1843,* in *Diario del Gobierno,* Feb. 24, 1843.

72. William S. Fisher and Thomas J. Green to Capt. Germán Romano, of the Mexican Army, San Luis Potosí, Feb. 20, 1843, photostat of original in the San Jacinto Museum of History; printed in *Telegraph and Texas Register,* May 10, 1843.

73. William S. Fisher to Capt. José María Reyes of the Mexican Army, San Luis Potosí, Feb. 28, 1843, photostat of original is in San Jacinto Museum of History; printed in *Telegraph and Texas Register,* May 10, 1843.

74. Green, *Mier Expedition,* pp. 188, 210.

fruit and bread for breakfast.[75] Resuming their march, they passed through the western edge of Mexico City and "fell into a road that led to Tacubaya, which place they reached about noon." It was falsely rumored that Fisher's party of Mier men had been sentenced to work on the road between Mexico City and Acapulco and that those at Perote Castle who had fought at Salado Creek would be brought back to work with them. The Texans were quartered at the Archbishop's Palace on the brick pavement of its open patio, where they enjoyed the cool fresh water from the fountain supplied by the Chapultepec aqueduct. That afternoon an order came for the release of Billy Reese, who had pretty well recovered from his illness.[76]

In the evening the Texans were visited by Captain West and Mr. G. S. Curson, bearer of dispatches from the U.S. government. They reported "that an order had gone forth several days [before] from Santa Anna to shoot all our companions behind" us, reported Green. Fisher sent his original copy of the articles of surrender to General Thompson, "for safe keeping," with the request that he send a copy to General Tornel, the minister of war and marine.[77]

From the Americans they learned also, for the first time, that President Houston had written to Capt. Charles Elliot, the British *chargé d'affaires* to Texas, that the Mier men had gone "without orders" and thereby had "placed themselves out of the protection of the rules of war," and that the government of Texas, according to Houston, was not responsible for their acts.[78] Elliot, on behalf of Houston, had appealed to Richard Pakenham, the British minister to Mexico, to request Santa Anna to treat the Mier men kindly although they had crossed the Rio Grande without orders.[79] Green, the penman of the Mier men, wrote to friends in Texas, hoping to confirm or to disprove the information he had received. In 1845, Green succeeded in getting the substance of Houston's letter to Elliot in regard to the Mier Expedition, but not a copy of the letter. He falsely alleged that Houston officially called the Mier men "robbers," and "in effect pronounced them *brigands* and *marauders*," and he referred to the president as a "slanderer," "murderer," and "traducer of the dead."[80]

When the editors of the *Daily Picayune* heard the rumor concerning the Houston-Elliot-Pakenham correspondence, they were quick to comment: "For the sake of humanity we trust this rumor may not prove true. It would be virtually signing the death warrant of these brave men, in case Santa Anna wanted an excuse for shooting them."[81] The editor of the

---

75. *Daily Picayune*, Feb. 16, 1843.
76. Green, *Mier Expedition*, p. 215.
77. *Ibid.*, p. 222.
78. Sam Houston to Captain Charles Elliot, Washington, Jan. 24, 1843, in *Writings of Sam Houston* 3, pp. 299-302.
79. Reported by Samuel A. Maverick on his arrival in *Telegraph and Texas Register*, May 3, 1843.
80. Green, *Mier Expedition*, pp. 451-53.
81. Reported in *Daily Picayune*, May 5, 1843.

Civilian and Galveston Gazette, however, challenged the rumor that Houston had written to Santa Anna (through Elliot and Pakenham) that the Mier men had invaded Mexico contrary to his orders.[82]

During the first night at Tacubaya, the Texans suffered much from the cold and found little comfort from their blankets, quartered as they were upon the pavement of the courtyard, though "there were hundreds of unoccupied rooms" in the Archbishop's Palace, "which had been used as a convent" and in which the regiment was quartered in some of the rooms." Although they suffered in body, "the anguish of mind" was far greater.[83] During the evening William Reese, who had been released a few hours earlier to the U.S. minister, visited General Thompson in Mexico City and received confirmation of the order to shoot those who had revolted against the guard. Reese informed Thompson that his brother Charles was engaged to be married; besides, he said, he knew that Charles would be much more useful to their father and mother than he would, " 'and I should like, sir,' " he continued, " 'to take his place as a prisoner, and let him go home.' " "In this," recorded Thompson, "he was not acting a part; he spoke under deep excitement and with a glistening eye, and I do not know that his was the only moist eye in the room."[84]

The next day, March 16, Curson, Capt. W. W. West, and other friends again visited the prisoners and brought the news that the U.S. and British ministers had prevailed upon Santa Anna to cancel the order to shoot the prisoners. During the evening, Green asked a friend to see the two ministers, and request that they visit the prisoners the next day.[85]

The prisoners were permitted to visit the second floor of the palace, and from there ascended to the azotea of the building, where they had a splendid view of Tacubaya, Mexico City, Chapultepec Castle, the snow-capped volcanoes of Popocatépetl and Ixtaccíhuatl, and the whole valley below, "and a more charming landscape," according to Green, did not exist.[86]

General Thompson did not come out to see them, but sent word that "he thought he could be of more service by not evincing too great anxiety in our behalf," reported Green, "and that everything in his power should be done for us."[87] Pakenham came to the prison and conferred with Green and others. Green requested that he intercede with the Mexican government for them, and especially in behalf of the English subjects among them such as Cameron, Samuel C. Lyon, and others. Pakenham assured them that "he would do everything in his power for these men," but said that he " 'feared much difficulty would interpose in this service; that these

---

82. June 3, 1843.
83. *Daily Picayune*, Feb. 27, 1843.
84. *Telegraph and Texas Register*, July 5, 1843.
85. Green, *Mier Expedition*, p. 222.
86. *Ibid.*, p. 218.
87. *Ibid.*, p. 219.

men, though they were British subjects, had made their own election in taking up arms against Mexico, and consequently had subjected themselves to all the penalties of the laws of war.'"[88]

Pakenham asked how they had been treated, and Green pointed to the dirty blankets upon the pavement used as their beds. "He looked indignant, and replied that 'by the laws of war, as officers, we were entitled to our parole, and *doubtless* it would be extended to us,'" reported Green; but Pakenham added that those "'same laws also required, as a matter of security, that the soldier prisoners should be kept securely.'"[89]

These answers were not heartening, and when coupled with news that arrived of a new order, this time for the decimation of the prisoners who had escaped at Salado and been recaptured, their apprehensions skyrocketed. As the days, weeks, and months passed, the Anglo-Texans, who had defied the orders of their commanding general before Guerrero, had gradually come to realize that there was a considerable difference between international law and "the consideration which is in accordance with the magnanimous Mexican nation." No longer were they a law unto themselves, but were now dependent on the skillful manipulations of international relations and power politics.

News also reached them through friends, later confirmed by an officer of the guard, that the Texans were to be moved into the city the next day. They looked forward to this move as one placing them in closer contact with friends who were interested in their welfare. Instead, on the next day, after youthful Billy Reese of Brazoria had been taken from their ranks under orders from Santa Anna to be released, they were marched toward Tacubaya. They carried their dirty blankets and sheepskins without being furnished horses, mules, or burros. As they commenced their march, they were accompanied by a file of mounted lancers on each side.

Passing through the southern suburbs of the city the prisoners were driven in the direction of Perote to lessen the pressure from representatives of foreign governments, foreign citizens, and others in the capital on their behalf.

Early on the morning of March 19, as they were preparing to get under way, the officer-in-charge stopped "an unladen drove of pack-mules" going in their direction and gave the Texan prisoners the opportunity of riding that day at fifty cents each.[90] During the day they crossed the mountains "and descended into a deep cove" to Río Frío, eighteen leagues from Mexico City. A Frenchman and lady, who kept the stagehouse, furnished them supper at a low price and divided "all her husband's old clothes" among the more destitute Texans.[91]

Having procured for the Texans "the most miserable burros we have

88. *Ibid.*, p. 220.
89. *Ibid.*, pp. 226-29.
90. *Ibid.*, pp. 227-28.
91. *Ibid.*, p. 229.

ever seen," recorded Green, the Mexican guard commenced the march on the 20th and in eight leagues reached San Martín. At San Martín, "a considerable village in a broad, cultivated, and well-watered plain," on March 21, and again at Puebla, the guard was changed. At San Martín the prisoners were turned over "to two lieutenants; the oldest long, lean, and lank —a dyspeptic-looking man who appeared always hungry—a fine specimen of ill-nature and low breeding; the other quite a youth, but evidently the son of a gentleman; he was well bred, and exceedingly civil."[92]

Sometimes the prisoners rode; at other times they walked, and often found it necessary to leave a part of their accumulated luggage behind. After eight leagues, they were "quartered in a horribly filthy room in a cavalry barracks," and when they requested their tall lieutenant "to have the filth removed from our room," reported one of the prisoners, adding "that we would pay the soldiers for so doing," the lieutenant refused. Lieutenant Velarde, overhearing the commotion, ordered the room to be cleaned, and in reasonably good English "apologized in a handsome manner for the want of civility of some of their officers, and said 'they had never travelled out of Mexico, and knew little of the customs of other countries.'"[93]

On March 22, when Daniel Drake Henrie was too ill to walk, he was thrown on a mule. "With great difficulty he made out to hold on to the mane of the animal for two miles, and in the act of falling was caught and laid upon the ground." When it was explained to the officer in charge that it would be impossible to carry him in his condition, the officer replied, "'Let him die then.'" The word die "had no pleasant sound . . . to Dan, who was not so far gone but that he knew its meaning, and after giving him water," he was lifted upon the mule and the march was resumed with one of his comrades walking on each side to hold him on.[94]

The prisoners reached Acajete on the night of March 22, hungry and tired, after nine leagues on the road. The prisoners were sent to "a *meson* to purchase supper, which was contracted for at twenty-five cents each for sixteen. After much delay, it was brought . . . [to the] prison, about enough for three hungry men," and from the whispered conversation between the red-eyed officer and the person bringing the food, "it was clear that he divided the four dollars with the sutler."[95]

In the prison at Acajete, as well as in other prisons along the route, the Mier men were amused by the caricatures left on the walls by the Santa Fé prisoners who had preceded them. Most of these drawings featured Santa Anna. In one, he was shown "crouched in a Texas prairie, hiding from the sons of Freedom"; in another, he was shown "upon his knees, yielding up his sword with a most penitential phiz"; and in a third, he was

---

92. *Ibid.*
93. *Ibid.*, pp. 230-31.
94. *Ibid.*, p. 231.
95. *Ibid.*, p. 233.

depicted "stalking forth upon his wooden leg, under a chapeau extremely ludicrous from its immense size with a huge sword, dictating laws to his enslaved countrymen."

On March 24 the prisoners marched ten leagues to Tepiohualela. They sent the Mexican orderly of the guard to purchase their supper, but "the fellow had hardly turned his back before the sentinel at the door . . . told . . . [the Texans] that that fellow was a noted rogue; that he would cheat us of the best half of our money; that it was a great pity the Mexican officers allowed us gentleman prisoners," reported Green, "to be so swindled; that in a few minutes his [the sentinel's] tour of the guard service would be over, when it would give him pleasure to wait upon us; and that he would see we had the full benefit of our purchase. This fellow also told us that he had been in the United States, and knew the difference between a gentleman and a *pillo* [peón or day laborer]." During the conversation the sentinel appeared to be such an honest man that Green handed him "two-bits" (twenty-five cents) for his honesty, believing him to be the first honest soldier he had encountered in his long tramp through Mexico. Green's companions, "rejoicing in the opportunity of having an 'honest man' to buy their food, gave him their extra bits and this was the last," declared Green, "we ever saw of the money or the fellow."[96]

Colonel Fisher and his thirteen Mier Expedition companions, Thomas Hancock, Simon Glenn, and George Van Ness of the San Antonio prisoners, and Milvern Harrell of the Dawson men, reached the Castle of Perote at three on the afternoon of March 25.[97] They wound their way through the entrance "and across the drawbridge over the great moat, thence through an archway into the great plaza, fronting the governor's quarters, amid the bugle's blast and the roll of drums, the din of arms and the clank of chains."[98] In the castle they found the forty-four San Antonio prisoners in rags and in chains.

The rest of the afternoon was spent discussing the Battle of Mier and the experiences of both groups since leaving San Antonio by different routes. Barkley complained, "I cant guet a chance to ask . . . [Harrell] two questions at a time," owning to everyone trying to get information from the new arrivals.[99]

The first Mier men to reach the Castle of Perote were placed in a room adjacent to Béxar prisoners, who were "occupying two. . . long, narrow, dark archways, adjoining each other, in the eastern rampart of the castle." The Texan prisoners occupied rooms Number 9, 10, and 11.[100] Life was no bed of roses for Fisher's party and the Woll prisoners at Perote

---

96. *Ibid.*, pp. 233-34.
97. *Ibid.*, p. 235.
98. Trueheart diary, Apr. 13 [14th], 1843.
99. R. A. Barkl[e]y to "Dear fr[i]ends," Perote, Mar. 25, 1843, in Spellman, ed., "Letters of the 'Dawson Men' from Perote Prison," *SWHQ* 38 (Jan. 1935), p. 249.
100. Trueheart diary, July 2, 1843.

Castle. Although the two groups were confined in separate cells, many of their problems were the same. On March 26 the new arrivals witnessed the Béxar-Dawson men being taken out to gather up the filth of the castle in wheelbarrows and after that pack in sand and stones to make repairs on the fortifications. The sand came from a wash about a mile away, while the stones were brought from the mountains a mile and a half away. The Woll prisoners were chained in pairs by the leg with about four feet of chain between them and guarded on each side by a file of soldiers with fixed bayonets. On the fourth day after the arrival of Fisher and his party at the castle, the Mier men were chained by order of the commandant of the fortress, Gen. José María Durán. A large quantity of chains was brought out and laid in a heap upon the floor of the blacksmith shop, "with a corresponding quantity of cumbrous ready-made clevises to fit around the ankles."[101] The chaining was carried out under the supervision of Capt. Díaz Guzmán. Some were chained singly but most of the men were chained *dos a dos* by the right ankle of one of the left ankle of the other. To get the process started, Guzmán invited Fisher and Green to choose their chains, but, reports Green, "there was no choice between them, the lightest weighing about twenty pound; and even if there had been any difference, neither of us was in a temper to make the choice."[102] Each man was permitted to choose his companion in chains. Fisher and Green were chained together.[103] "All of the Texan prisoners," reported Waddy Thompson, "concur in stating, that they were very well treated until after the attack on the guard." But the increasing harsh treatment cannot be solely blamed upon the Mexican troops' reaction to the revolt against the guard. As long as the prisoners were north of Saltillo, they were among Mexicans who had had more contacts with the Texans, both through trade during the Federalist wars, when more than one Texan had fought side by side with them against the Centralists. After his arrival in Texas, Fisher gave his opinion why the Texans had been kindly treated while in the north. After breaking off from Somervell, "we proceeded to Mier and held possession of the town for eight hours, during the whole of which time the men remained under arms, and the houses of no citizen was entered except upon the invitation of the owner, nor were the rights or property of the citizens interferred with in any case."[104]

After their arrival at Perote Castle, Fisher and Green made copies of the articles of capitulation and of all letters they had written to Mexican

---

101. Green, *Mier Expedition,* p. 244.

102. *Ibid.*

103. Waddy Thompson to Daniel Webster, Legation of the United States of America, Mexico, Apr. 11, 1843, in Despatches from United States Ministers in Mexico, Mar. 12, 1842-Mar. 25, 1844, National Archives (microfilm); copy in Justin H. Smith Papers, 2 TxU-A; see also Manning, ed., *Diplomatic Correspondence of the United States* 8 (Mexico), pp. 543-44.

104. William S. Fisher to the Editor of the *Galveston News*, reproduced in the *Northern Standard*, Jan. 21, 1846.

officials since their surrender. On March 31, having experienced the indignity of wearing chains for two days, Fisher and Green sent a vigorous protest to Secretary of War and Marine Gen. José María Tornel, criticizing the violations of the terms under which they had surrendered.[105]

On April 6 Captain Guzmán told Fisher, Green, and his companions that he had received orders to put the Texans to work. Green says that Colonel Fisher, Captain Reese, and Lieutenant Clarke, the only Mier officers present, "pledged themselves to me that they would be shot down sooner than submit to the order,"[106] and Guzmán was so informed.

Governor Durán asked for Fisher and Green to be brought to his quarters. He informed them that he had received orders from his government to put all of the prisoners to work, argued that they were not entitled to protection from work under the terms of their capitulation, and that he had his duty to perform. The two Texans told him that working was not in accord to the pledge of magnanimous treatment and that they were determined not to deviate from their duty to their country. The governor finally stated that he would once more communicate with his government on the subject.[107] As the days passed, the Texan officers were told repeatedly that they must work, but they absolutely refused to do so, and the prison authorities declined to compel them to do so, although all other Texan prisoners were forced to work.

We now leave the officers of the Mier Expedition to learn what happened to their comrades who overpowered the guard at Hacienda Salado.

---

105. W[illia]m S. Fisher [and] Thomas J. Green to Gen. Tornel, Minister of War and Marine, Castle of Perote, Mar. 31, 1843, in *Daily Picayune*, Apr. 23, 1843; see also Green, *Mier Expedition*, pp. 250-52; *Telegraph and Texas Register*, May 3, 1843.

106. Green, *Mier Expedition*, p. 253.

107. *Ibid.*, pp. 253-54.

CHAPTER 15

The Mier Men Head for Home

ONLY ONE-FOURTH OF THE prisoners had taken part in the "Battle of the Rescue,"[1] as some termed it, but it was not long before they were joined by most of the others. Several of the Texans who were sick had been quartered in a house separate from the main body. Among these was Benjamin Z. Boone. John R. Baker came into the room bleeding profusely from a bayonet wound. Lying down beside Boone, he told him of the successful break. Although weak, Boone determined to go with his companions. Bidding farewell to Baker, who was too badly hurt to travel, Boone left the house and joined the main body of Texans.[2] Captain Reese and eleven others refused to have anything to do with the charge.[3] These were: Capt. Charles K. Reese, Daniel Davis, Richard Keene, George W. Bush, A. B. Hanna, Charles A. Clark, Simon Glenn, Leonidas Sanders, D. F. Barney, Milvern Harrell, D. R. Hallowell, and William Reese.

Thomas Jefferson Green reported that eighteen men refused to "go it" at Salado, but included in this number five who were wounded in the fight, including John R. Baker, Archibald Fitzgerald (mortally), John Higgerson (mortally), Thomas Hancock, John Sansberry, and Norman Woods, the latter still suffering greatly from wounds received in the Dawson Fight. It is doubtful that the wounded and sick could be said to have refused to "go it." Milvern Harrell, making the number eighteen, stayed behind to take care of Norman Woods.[4]

William Reese did fight in the "Battle of the Rescue" but upon persuasion of his brother stayed behind. Others, such as Orlando C. Phelps,

---

1. Captain Claudius Buster to John H. Jenkins, Sr. [n.p.,n.d.], in *Frontier Times* 16 (June 1939), p. 395.
2. Sowell, *History of Fort Bend County*, pp. 196, 341.
3. Stapp, *Prisoners of Perote*, p. 59.
4. Thomas J. Green to "Dear Friends," Castle of Perote, Mexico, April 15, 1843, in *Telegraph and Texas Register*, May 17, 1843.

Freeman Douglass, and John Harvey, took no part in the charge but went with the homeward bound. Canfield said: ". . . this young Phelps took no part in the charge upon the guard, but secured a Horse rode without intermission as long as he could ride & even refused to carry a gun, a Freeman Douglas was of the same stamp."[5]

Having dispersed their guard, the Texans quickly set about burying their dead, and collecting horses, mules, arms, ammunition, and provisions.[6] By nine in the morning they had collected about 100 horses and mules, 150 to 160 of the best carbines, muskets, and *escopetas,* most of the latter from the 180 stands of arms captured, and remainder destroyed beyond usage;[7] several dozen swords, lances, knives, and pistols; 4,000 rounds of ammunition in two boxes,[8] which they packed on three mules; and $1,400 of public money in silver, "which was taken," they said "for the purpose of satisfying the citizens for such articles as we received from them on our way home."[9] Before leaving, the Texans burned all tents and camp equipment. Each claimed the horse he saddled, and Captain Buster carried the money on a burro.[10]

Wallace appropriated Captain Arroyo's dun pacing mule.[11] The Mexican horses were small but well trained. The prisoners found the Mexican saddles not quite as comfortable as American ones, owing to the fact that the wooden stirrups hung directly under the rider, so that he was compelled to sit almost as erect on horseback as though he were standing.

While the Texans prepared to leave, Colonel Barragán managed to round up a small group of "stampeded" soldiers. As the main body of escapees formed under their leader,[12] Cameron, for the long journey homeward, Captain Reese and his followers joined a small party of Mexican cavalry hovering about a quarter mile distant from the camp commanded by Captain Posas. Reese had opposed the break, but when the action started he took part in it rigorously. He had decided to go with Cameron, and would have gone, provided his younger brother, William—a mere lad— would remain; but William refused to stay, so Reese changed his mind and they both stayed behind.[13] Also left behind were six wounded, two of whom died later.

---

5. Canfield diary, Feb. 11 and Mar. 1, 1843.

6. "John Rufus Alexander's Story of the Mier Expedition as Told to John Warren Hunter," in Wade, comp., *Notes and Fragments of the Mier Expedition* 1, p. 37.

7. A. A. Wallace to Nora C. Franklin, San Antonio, Texas [dated] Big Foot [Frío County, Texas], Sept. 24, 1888 [Postmarked] Big Foot, Oct. 3 Tex, photostat of original MS., TxU-A; see also Duval, *Big-Foot Wallace,* p. 199.

8. This was "more ammunition than we left home with," reported one of the prisoners, *Telegraph and Texas Register,* Aug. 23, 1843.

9. Canfield diary, Feb. 11, 1843; Duval, *Big-Foot Wallace,* p. 199; Stapp, *Prisoners of Perote,* p. 59.

10. Captain Claudius Buster to John H. Jenkins, Sr., [n.p., n.d.], in *Frontier Times* 16 (June 1939), pp. 395-400.

11. Sowell, *Early Settlers and Indian Fighters of Southwest Texas,* p. 69.

12. Canfield diary, Feb. 11, 1843.

13. Green, *Mier Expedition,* p. 178; Sibley, ed., *Samuel H. Walker's Account,* pp. 45-47.

At nine o'clock the Texans were formed. Their Mexican prisoners, being largely the "Red Caps" who had taken refuge during the assault in the buildings and small corral to the left of the main gate, were released under promises that they would not harm the wounded Texans left behind.[14] The race towards the Rio Grande and home began. Half a mile north of Hacienda Salado they encountered Colonel Barragán with a small cavalry unit drawn up across the road. Barragán, accompanied by his interpreter, advanced toward the Texans. The Texan interpreter, Alfred S. Thurmond, went forward to meet him. Barragán asked to speak with their leader, and Cameron, followed by several of his men, advanced to meet him. Barragán asked Cameron and his followers to surrender, promising that they would be treated kindly and would not be punished for anything they had done, *"but every thing goes as before, and kind treatment be our award."*[15] He pointed out the impossibility of their reaching the Rio Grande in safety. Doubtless he was thinking of the wrath that might descend on his head from his superiors. The Texans refused to submit and accept the amnesty which he promised for their recent acts. He was told that the Texans had accomplished that which they so ardently desired—their liberty—and that they could not now comply with his wish. Cameron also told Barragán that they had released their prisoners with an understanding that the Texan wounded would be treated kindly. In order to placate the colonel as much as possible, Cameron ordered his horse, sword, and other personal effects returned as a token of appreciation for the kind and humane treatment shown the prisoners while under his command and also in the hope that he would afford similar treatment to the wounded Texans left behind.[16]

The Texans pushed forward, taking the road toward Agua Nueva. Barragán's cavalry did not attempt to stop them but hung on its rear during the day and night, keeping the fleeing Texans constantly in view, but at a distance of about 600 yards.[17] They continued to pursue and track the fleeing prisoners, sending up smoke signals by day and lighting fires by night.[18] Couriers were dispatched in all directions to inform state and local officials of the escape of *los Tejanos,* and orders were quickly released for intercepting the homeward-bound "prisoners."

Although great distance lay between them and home, and the Mexican guns they carried were inferior to the rifles they had used at Mier, the

14. "John Rufus Alexander's Story as Told to John Warren Hunter," in Wade, comp., *Notes and Fragments of the Mier Expedition* 1, p. 37.

15. "Narrative of 'Mier' and 'Perote' By One of the Expedition," *Telegraph and Texas Register,* Nov. 29, 1843.

16. Bancroft, *History of Texas and the North Mexican States* 2, p. 366; Duval, *Big-Foot Wallace,* pp. 198-99; Stapp, *Prisoners of Perote,* p. 59; Green, *Mier Expedition,* p. 158; Canfield diary, Feb. 11, 1843.

17. [A Mier Prisoner] to the Editor of the *New York American,* Prison of the Powder Mill, near the City of Mexico, June 3, 1843, quoted from the *New York American* in *Niles' National Register* 65, pp. 3-4, Sept. 2, 1843.

18. Stapp, *Prisoners of Perote,* p. 59.

Texans were free, light-hearted, enthusiastic, and in a more jovial mood than at any time since their surrender at Mier. As they hurried north, they sang hymns of home and country "and scared with their jovial echoes the startled wild-bird from its perch."[19] From the time they left Salado, smoke signals could be seen rising and soon Mexican troops guarded watering places, including those just east of the Rio Grande, hoping to intercept the escapees.[20] Couriers alerted the personnel of the *ranchos* along the escape route and soon the Mier men found *rancheros* in arms with no hesitancy in firing on any Texan approaching them for food or water.

The Texans continued their retreat without intermission until they halted at midnight at Rancho Encarnación[21] to feed their horses, paying for corn from their "Military Chest."[22] As soon as the men and animals had eaten and rested, the trek was resumed.

On the road they "went at a trot the whole time, those on foot keeping up with the horsemen at the gait until exhausted, when they would take their turn in riding."[23] The sick and infirm rode at all times. A few of the stronger mules carried double. "When the moon came out to set her watch in the sky, and star by star climbed up to its burning throne we halted," reported Stapp, "on the mountain to scan the jewelled host, and search amongst its radiant galaxies for that lone and newborn gem, that mirrored the stainless flag of Texas."[24] Two hours before daylight the weary band lay down in line of march and ten minutes later its members were asleep.

At sunrise, Sunday, February 12, the march was renewed. The Texans left the main road to Saltillo on their right to avoid going too near that place, and cut north for five miles up a deep gorge filled with palmettos and plants loaded with spines until they reached the road which ran west of Saltillo from Monclova to Zacatecas.[25] They turned left about three in the afternoon toward a ranch to secure water from a tank near the house. As they approached the buildings of the *rancho*, which constituted a strong fort, a group of armed Mexicans hoisted a red flag, shook their lances in hostility, and fired from the housetops and windows in the direction of the Texans, wounding a horse and breaking one man's stirrup. Rather than waste time and ammunition by engaging the Mexicans in fight, the Texans filed off to the right as bullets whizzed about their heads. "It was our intention from the start to commit no depredation upon the property of the inhabitants; and to demand nothing from them, without exchanging an equivalence in money," reported one of them.[26] Taking a northerly

19. Stapp, *Prisoners of Perote*, p. 60.

20. *Telegraph and Texas Register*, Apr. 26, 1843.

21. Stapp, *Prisoners of Perote*, p. 60.

22. *Ibid.*; Green, *Mier Expedition*, p. 158.

23. Duval, *Big-Foot Wallace*, p. 200; *Telegraph and Texas Register*, Apr. 26, 1843; Stapp, *Prisoners of Perote*, p. 60; Bell, *Narrative*, p. 40.

24. Stapp, *Prisoners of Perote*, p. 60.

25. Canfield diary, Feb. 12, 1843.

26. "Narrative of 'Mier' and 'Perote' By One of the Expedition," in *Morning Star*, Nov. 25, 1843.

course toward a gap in the mountains, they continued on their way without firing a shot.[27]

At sunset they reached the crest of the mountains by a narrow footpath and descended into an uninhabited valley, where they located a pool of muddy water sufficient to quench their thirst. This was their first water in twenty hours. "It was truly a godsend," reported one of the men, "and just about as much as would give us a drink around."[28] They filled their gourds, and dogged by a party of Mexicans, resumed their march guided by the stars. Six miles farther on they located provisions and water at a *rancho.* They found the men at the ranch in arms, but the Texan interpreter, Thurmond, informed them that the Texans had no intention of injuring or molesting them; the Texans appeased their appetites, then continued in a westward direction without a road. During the night, brothers William Sargeant and Carter Sargeant, who had taken no part in the charge on the guard, took two of the best horses and provisions and deserted. They returned to the *rancho,* where they "professed great friendship for the Mexicans stating that they had been forced to fight" by their officers at Salado.[29] Also during the night Captain Buster lost his jenny, which he had loaned "to a big near-sighted Dutchman [Henry Miller],"[30] which, in descending the mountain, fell and "rolled from under him." In the dark of the night, he could not find her. The Texans halted at three in the morning for a rest and to plan their course, then moved on. Near daylight a Mexican joined them, saying that he had been sent by a certain American [English] gentleman who lived near Saltillo to guide them.[31] The Texans kept him under close surveillance but decided to use him as long as his directions seemed practical. He agreed to conduct them to the Monclova road, from which they could see the Paso Lampazos, some sixty miles from the Rio Grande. At daylight, February 13, when the journey was renewed, John ("Jack") Sweezy was left asleep and was "picked up" by the Mexicans trailing the fleeing prisoners. Canfield thought that it was "rather an odd place . . . to take a nap, '1,000 miles from home & no mule to ride.'"[32]

Continuing a westerly course, the Texans struck the Monclova road. Following along it for a few miles with their guide, they again found water. Dr. John Cameron, an Englishman, former resident of Texas, and a relative of Ewen Cameron, rode up with two companions. Cameron went for-

27. Canfield diary, Feb. 12, 1843.

28. Sibley, ed., *Samuel H. Walker's Account*, p. 48.

29. Glasscock diary, Feb. 12, 1843; Canfield diary, Feb. 12, 1843, reports they "deserted"; but Stapp, *Prisoners of Perote*, p. 61, records they "wandered off and were lost." Bell, *Narrative*, p. 40, says they claimed they "got lost from the main body in the dark" and "were unable to find it again, and in two days were recaptured by the enemy and taken to Saltillo."

30. Captain Claudius Buster to John H. Jenkins, Sr., [n.p., [n.d.], in Wade, comp., *Notes and Fragments of the Mier Expedition* 1, p. 71.

31. Sibley, ed., *Samuel H. Walker's Account*, p. 48.

32. Canfield diary, Feb. 12, 1843.

ward to meet him and learned that the doctor had sent the guide the evening before to assist them, and he told them that they could take him as their guide. Dr. Cameron invited the Texans to visit his ranch, saying that he would be happy to supply them with provisions. Although nearly destitute of supplies, the offer was declined; the Texans needed to get to the Rio Grande as soon as possible. The doctor urged the Texans to keep to the road. Colonel Barragán, he said, had sent couriers to all points within 200 miles, but there were no troops along the road to intercept them. He believed that by keeping to the road and making long marches they could escape.[33] He urged that they escape as speedily as possible, for he expected no mercy to be "shown by the Mexican Government to any who might be recaptured."[34] Only too soon they would recall with anguish these recommendations. The doctor gave them directions and said that at the first *rancho* they would reach they would find the inhabitants hostile; with the second *rancho* along their route "he was not so well acquainted"; but the third they would find to be "very friendly, and . . . [they] could stop there to refresh themselves."[35] Finally, he again warned that if they persisted in their course into the mountains they would inevitably perish for want of food and water. Wishing them success in their try for freedom, Dr. Cameron, accompanied by his two companions, disappeared into the chaparral, leaving the guide he had sent.[36]

The Texans resumed the journey following their guide. They passed two *ranchos*. As they approached the first—Rancho San Antonio—they found the gates barred, the doors fastened, and "a red flag hung out to indicate the hostility of the proprietor." The *rancheros* refused to do business and insisted they pass on, "which request they fortified by a flourish of rusty firelocks, and multiplied disguises of the same head at the windows, to suggest the presence of a formidable force within doors." Not wishing to be delayed or reveal their weakness, the Texans moved on, hoping to find supplies elsewhere. "Our resolution being fixed," recorded Stapp, "to practice no violence or rapine on the people, unless in the greatest extremity or self-defence."[37]

On approaching Rancho San Felipe, John Brennan, an interpreter, was sent forward with the Mexican guide to see if corn could be obtained. Coming within hailing distance of the fortified compound, "the Mexican was induced to dismount and enter the house." The inhabitants not only refused to sell any corn, for fear of offending their government, but also

33. Canfield diary, Feb. 13, 1843; Duval, *Big-Foot Wallace*, p. 201; Stapp, *Prisoners of Perote*, p. 61; Bell, *Narrative*, p. 41; *Telegraph and Texas Register*, Nov. 29, 1843.

34. Bell, *Narrative*, p. 41.

35. "Narrative of 'Mier' and 'Perote' By One of the Expedition," *Telegraph and Texas Register*, Nov. 29, 1843.

36. Canfield diary, Feb. 13, 1843; Stapp, *Prisoners of Perote*, pp. 62, 69; Glasscock diary, Feb. 13, 1843.

37. Stapp, *Prisoners of Perote*, p. 62.

retained the guide, and commanded "the Texian . . . to return to his companions if he did not wish a ball put through him."[38]

Why this hostility by the personnel of the *ranchos*? Had news of the escape of the Texans preceded their approach? Was it possible that couriers had gotten out ahead of the Texans? "The reason why every place we arrived at seemed to be aware of our approach," reported Stapp, "and prepared to resist any effort we should made [make] to molest them, even when we were far in advance of any verbal or written communication, was that it is the custom in that country, whenever the Indian or other hostile force appear there, to alarm the whole country by making a dense smoke upon the highest mountain in the day and a fire by night, then they receive the intelligence, even when the enemy is at a great distance, and warned to be upon the alert; many of their smokes and fires did we see and were unable at first to account for them."[39]

Going a short distance, about a league, the Texans found water, so they unsaddled their horses to graze and the men laid down to rest. A woman from the *rancho* came out to inquire if any of Jordan's men were in the party, and being told that there were, she said, "if they would vouch for the good behavior of the rest that we could be accomodated at the ranch with what we wanted."[40] Considering this a ruse, the Texans continued onward but were overtaken by the proprietor of the *rancho*, who expressed some regret that his men had mistaken the intentions of the Texans. He offered to show them a good place to graze and rest their horses.[41] A short distance farther brought them to water and grass at the foot of the mountains. While they halted for their horses to graze, the men began to speculate on the Englishman's visit. Some believed that he was a spy in the service of the enemy sent to decoy them into an ambush. This idea was encouraged by Captain Eastland, who advocated leaving the road for the mountains to the west, as he believed the Pass would be guarded by troops. Captain Ryon remonstrated with Eastland for wanting to deviate from the course they had determined before they had escaped. He pointed out that so far all that the Englishman had stated had turned out to be true. A spirited dispute ensued between Pierson and Eastland on the one hand, and Cameron and Ryon on the other, about turning off the road.[42] Eastland threatened that if his suggestion was not adopted that he and his men would pursue his own course. The march was resumed. The majority "influenced by officers and men," said Walker, "who attached much of prudence as being the better part of valour and opposed the

38. "Narrative of 'Mier' and 'Perote' By One of the Expedition," *Telegraph and Texas Register*, Nov. 29, 1843.

39. *Ibid.*

40. Sibley, ed., *Samuel H. Walker's Account*, p. 49.

41. *Ibid.*

42. Trahern's account, p. 8; Captain Claudius Buster to John H. Jenkins, Sr., [n.p., n.d.] in *Frontier Times* 16 (June 1939), pp. 395-400.

break at the Salado and [had] done little towards fighting out after it was begun," wished to turn west through the mountains.[43] There was increased grumbling, and "just at dark,"[44] "certain signs and surroundings led us to conclude," remembered Alexander more than fifty years later, "that he [the Englishman] was a treacherous rascal, a villainous spy in the pay of Santa Anna, and that his object was to lead us into a snare."[45] The head of the column, without previous agreement among the men and officers, suddenly turned off the Monclova road toward the dreary-looking Sierra de la Paila in the distance.[46] Others fell in line, and finally Cameron, with those who followed him, being in a decided minority, reluctantly fell in with the main unit and the road was abandoned.[47] This proved to be a fatal decision; from this point they could date their extreme suffering and eventual recapture. "To separate from them," recorded Stapp of Cameron's party, "was to insure the certain destruction of all . . . and, adopting the only alternative left us, to share their fortunes, we struck abruptly into the thicket, and encamped."[48]

The conduct of the Texans on the march was injudicious and revealed a lack of discipline and the frontiersman's obsessed idea of individual freedom where each man wanted to be his own officer and obey only when it was to his inclination or convenience. So, "instead of travelling a road that led along the frontier of the Mexican settlements," wrote one of the participants,[49] "and generally through the vallies where a sufficiency both of water and provisions could easily have been obtained, and [where there was] little or no danger to . . . [be] apprehended from any considerable force in this region of the count[r]y," all of which made for a strong probability of getting safely to Texas, the Texans entered a region which, for men mounted or afoot and with little or no knowledge of its waterholes, was practically a death sentence. Had they stuck to the open valley instead of leaving the road, they could have covered the distance to Paso de Benado in eighteen hours.

Going three leagues in the direction of the mountains, they were fired on several times during the early part of the night by several Mexicans, who they learned later were shepherds. They continued on their course for another third of a league and "encamped in a safe and secure situation,"[50] about eight o'clock, without water. A guard ensured the safety of

43. Sibley, ed., *Samuel H. Walker's Account*, p. 49.

44. Bell, *Narrative*, p. 41.

45. "John Rufus Alexander's Story of the Mier Expedition as Told to John Warren Hunter," in Wade, comp., *Notes and Fragments of the Mier Expedition* 1, p. 41.

46. Capt. S. H. Walker to A. Sidney Johns[t]on, Prison Santiago, City of Mexico, May 4, 1843, in Army Papers (Republic), Tx-A; Trahern diary, p. 9.

47. Capt. S. H. Walker to A. Sidney Johns[t]on, Prison Santiago, City of Mexico, May 4, 1843, in Army Papers (Republic), Tx-A.

48. Stapp, *Prisoners of Perote*, p. 62.

49. Bell, *Narrative*, pp. 41-42.

50. "Narrative of 'Mier' and 'Perote' By One of the Expedition," *Telegraph and Texas Register*, Nov. 29, 1843; Canfield diary, Feb. 13, 1843.

their horses. Here they remained until daybreak, Tuesday, February 14, when they resumed their journey, leaving the ravine in which they had traveled the night before.

All day they toiled through a barren region. Mountains and vegetation became harsher as they penetrated deeper into the Sierra de la Paila. Progress was slow through the mountains because of the steep terrain covered with thorny bushes which showed little respect for flesh or clothing. Their legs and feet became lacerated from the thorns. No one among them had any knowledge of the country. Sometimes they had to shove their horses and mules over little bluffs three or four feet high and often had to circuit higher precipices to find a way down or up. The country was so rough that their horses now became of little use to them. The sun beat down on the whitish soil, and the glare was blinding. Not even a solitary blade of grass could be seen. They encountered a shepherd who warned them that they would find no water in the direction they were going. Heedless of the warning the Texans pursued their course deeper into the mountains rather than attempting to return to the Monclova road.[51]

The Texans pushed on during the early hours of the night and found themselves completely surrounded once more by mountains, deep canyons, and still without water. They backtracked to a deep canyon that they had crossed that morning and turned down it with the expectation of reaching the valley that they had left the night before. The farther they went, the higher the perpendicular walls of granite grew and the more broken and difficult became the surface. Near midnight they arrived at a fifteen-foot precipice, which blocked their advance, and they decided to halt until morning. Leaving their horses and mules at the top of the precipice, they descended into a ravine in search of water, but found none.[52]

The desolate country disheartened the men, but to turn back would mean capture by a vigilant foe. Wrapping their blankets about weary bodies for protection against the night winds, they encamped on the rocks and huddled around campfires, silent and unsocial. Feeling safe from the enemy, no guard was posted.

During the night, a party sent to reconnoiter reported an "abundance" of water two or three miles distant in an excavated rock.[53] Since they had had no water for twenty-four hours, many of the men rushed in the direction of the water hole, stumbling along through the darkness over gulches and ravines, barking shins and sometimes crawling on all fours, until they arrived at the "wonderful fountain," a few barrels of water in a hole in the rocks.[54] Quenching their thirst, they lay down and slept soundly until morning. They then returned to camp to fetch the animals but the horses

---

51. Sibley, ed., *Samuel H. Walker's Account*, p. 49.

52. "Narrative of 'Mier' and 'Perote' By One of the Expedition," *Telegraph and Texas Register*, Nov. 29, 1843.

53. Duval, *Big-Foot Wallace*, p. 202; Stapp, *Prisoners of Perote*, p. 64.

54. Bell, *Narrative*, p. 44; Stapp, *Prisoners of Perote*, p. 64.

could not descend the steep precipice. Realizing that their horses and mules were useless, they stationed sentinels on the highest peaks and remained near the water hole for the remainder of the day to kill their animals and to "jerk" the meat of a few of the fattest, on which even a "decent Mexican buzzard would have disdained to whet his bill."[55]

The sentinels took up their watch while their comrades transported water in gourds back to the men getting ready to prepare the meat. "I made two trips," reported Alexander, "carrying back as many gourds as I could to the men preparing the meat."[56] Building numerous fires in the canyon, the men cut the throats of their animals with butcher knives to save their ammunition and avoid attracting the Mexicans by the firing of guns. Slaughtering their mounts was a difficult task for Texans who lived and depended so much on horses in their everyday life. Some of the men did not have the heart to play the role of executioner and left the task to their comrades. "Bigfoot" Wallace said that his horse looked "so knowingly and pleading out of his sunken hollow eyes, that my heart failed me entirely, and my comrade, who was not so 'squeamish,' had to play the role of executioner."[57] The best-conditioned animals were skinned, and some of the meat was roasted for a hearty meal. A considerable quantity of the meat was cut into narrow strips, hung on ramrods or gun barrels, and "jerked" over fires made of weeds, the only fuel available in the barren mountains. Bridles, bits, and saddles were stripped of silver ornaments. By cutting their saddle bags into two pieces, they were able to convert them into haversacks. The saddle skirts and the hides of the animals were cut to make sandals for those who were in need of shoes.

For lack of transportation, the money taken from the guard at Salado was divided by Captain Buster, each man receiving about seven dollars.[58] Not being able to make exact change, two shares were left, and these were retained by Buster.

By midafternoon all preparations for continuing their advance had been completed. Strengthened after their rest and repast, the men, knowing the value of time, were anxious to move on. Filling as many gourds as possible from the limited supply of water, and taking about ten to fifteen pounds—a ten-day supply—of meat each, the little band resumed its march at three o'clock, February 15, on foot, "with heavy packs and heavy hearts."[59] It was understood "that all who broke down were to be left."[60]

---

55. Duval, *Big-Foot Wallace*, p. 203.

56. Alexander, "Narrative of the Mier Expedition," MS, TxU-A.

57. Duval, *Big-Foot Wallace*, p. 203.

58. Canfield diary, Feb. 15, 1843; Alexander, "Narrative of the Mier Expedition," MS, TxU-A; Claudius Buster to John H. Jenkins, Sr., [n.p., n.d.], in *Frontier Times* 16 (June 1939), pp. 395-400; Bell, *Narrative*, p. 44.

59. Claudius Buster to John H. Jenkins, Sr., [n.p., n.d.], in Wade, comp., *Notes and Fragments of the Mier Expedition* 1, p. 75.

60. F. Wilson to Wm. Wilson, Lexington, Va., [dated] Castle of Perote, August 12, 1844, in *Galveston Daily News*, March 17, 1874, p. 2, col. 3.

For the next four days they traveled in a northwesterly direction. At the top of the mountain they could see behind them "the dismal valley from which [they] had just emerged, over the surface of which, scattered here and there as they had fallen, lay the dead carcasses of our animals, looking like specks in the distance."[61] Before them no vegetation, no trickle of water relieved the impression of infinite desolation.

The country through which the Texans now trudged became drier as they wound their way through gullies, ravines, and one mountain peak after another. At each peak the men hoped that the next would be the last impediment a level plain. "The way appeared interminable, and no scenery varied the tireless monotony."[62] Added to this, "a burning sun poured down its scorching rays from a cloudless sky" to intensify their thirst and cause a rapid consumption of their water supply. Some of the men would scarcely taste water, but reserved their supply for the feeble and those who were sick to enable them to keep up with the main party.

About four o'clock, Zed Iceland, E. E. Este, and John Fitzgerald gave out. Unable to travel farther, they were supplied with meat, ammunition, and water and left to be picked up by the Mexicans. Their comrades moved on.[63]

At ten that night the band camped at the bottom of a canyon, where they found plenty of firewood and the steep mountains afforded protection from the wind. "All took a most comfortable night's sleep" beside small brushwood campfires.[64] It was the first entire night's rest that they had enjoyed since their escape.

The next morning, February 16, they left behind William Miller and Robert M. Pilley, who decided to wait for the trailing Mexican force to pick them up.[65] There was no choice for their comrades but to move on if they hoped to escape. The course was still north over several mountains, but since many of the men were weak, frequent stops became necessary when the sun arose. Near noon, the Texans struck a "beautiful . . . well timbered" valley, where four more threw down their packs, and dropped by the wayside, too exhausted to proceed farther.[66] Some of their friends determined to remain with them until they recuperated sufficiently to go forward. In all, during the day, eleven men were left behind. All reached Mexican settlements and were recaptured except Thomas W. Cox and John L. D. Blackburn, who eventually got through to Texas.

On Friday, February 17, the Texans started as soon as there was enough light to travel to cover as much territory as possible before the

61. Duval, *Big-Foot Wallace*, p. 205.

62. *Ibid.*, p. 207.

63. Stapp, *Prisoners of Perote*, p. 64.

64. Bell, *Narrative*, p. 45.

65. Stapp, *Prisoners of Perote*, p. 64; Sibley, ed., *Samuel H. Walker's Account*, p. 51.

66. William F. McMath, Thomas W. Cox, William Davis, and John D. Blackburn. *Telegraph and Texas Register*, Apr. 19, 1843.

heat of the day. Refreshed, the men began their march with renewed alacrity and hope. Their scouts reported a few gallons of water three miles off, but notwithstanding the extreme suffering for lack of it, the Texans decided to push on without delay, ignoring the temptation.[67] Toops, who was among those discovering the water, drank all he wanted and carried a gourdful to Captain Buster. Buster took one mouthful and divided the remainder among his men as far as it would go.[68]

While passing down a precipitous slope only one accident occurred, and that was by "a Mr. Campfield" [Canfield], reported one of the men, "who fell and stuck his bayonet in the side which some in the crowd were in hopes would kill him, though it turned out to be slight."[69] The men stopped at the foot of the mountain for Canfield to rest.

After a short while, Mark Rogers played out at eight miles, and Allen Holderman and Levi Williams remained behind with him.[70] The men began to straggle. Their limbs, their powers of locomotion and comprehension, even their resolution, seemed palsied. At a short distance they discovered clumps of palmetto whose juice-filled stalks some of the men chewed to moisten swollen tongues and parched lips. There was disagreement as to whether it really did any good. "Short and few were the words interchanged,"[71] Stapp reported.

Some threw away their jerked horseflesh as it was too dry for their husky throats. Others cast away their musket, cartridges, machete, and other objects of weight to lighten their load. Even the silver coins carried by many of the men were thrown away "as a child would sail a flat stone."[72] Some threw away their blankets and even the rags of clothing that protected their bodies, "so that many were in a complete state of nudity, which rendered their sufferings greater, as the days were very hot, and they were exposed to a burning sun, their skin blistered and became very painful; whilst the nights were very cold and having nothing whatever to shelter and protect them, they had to endure the opposite extreme."[73] Little attention was paid now to those who fell along the way. As they progressed, the valley became narrower, "until it sunk into a ravine, penetrating between two lofty mountains."[74]

They stopped to rest and Holderman, Williams, and Rogers came up.

---

67. Stapp, *Prisoners of Perote*, p. 65.

68. Claudius Buster to John H. Jenkins, [n.p., n.d.], in Wade, comp., *Notes and Fragments of the Mier Expedition*, p. 76.

69. *Telegraph and Texas Register*, Aug. 23, 1843. The "hope" for death seems not to have been made out of malice but so he would avoid a slow death in the mountains.

70. Sibley, ed., *Samuel H. Walker's Account*, p. 51.

71. Stapp, *Prisoners of Perote*, p. 65.

72. Woodland, "The Story of the Massacre of Mier Prisoners," *Houston Daily Post*, Aug. 16, 1891, p. 8, col. 1.

73. "Narrative of 'Mier' and 'Perote' By One of the Expedition," *Telegraph and Texas Register*, Nov. 29, 1843.

74. Stapp, *Prisoners of Perote*, p. 65.

Hoping the trail would lead to a stream or pool of water, they pursued the trail through a valley for fourteen miles.

In the late afternoon of February 17, the course lay a little to the east, while westward and behind them the long, rigid rampart of the Sierra de los Alamitos broke into a fiery smile in the late afternoon sun. Arriving near dark, at some thickets of pines in a valley, they found no water. "Water? Water? Water? was the only conversation."[75] To relieve their burning throats, more men chewed the bitter palmetto wood for the juice it contained or drank the juice of the *maguey* (century) plant. The juice of the latter, at first, "was very pleasant but eventually produced such burning and inflamation of the mouth as to cause the skin to peel off wherever it touched, and the lips to blister and finally to become very bad sores."[76]

As the main body advanced, a few mounted Mexicans could be seen in one of the valleys they crossed, and considerable discussion developed among the Texans. Some contended that the objects in the distance were mustangs either coming from or going to water and if followed they might lead the men to water.[77] Nevertheless it was deemed advisable not to take a chance of getting involved with a Mexican patrol, so the Texans shifted their course more toward the north. About three-fourths of them insisted that the valley be explored for water. About dark they came across the trail of the horses. The band divided into small parties ranging in size from two to ten men, except the largest group, consisting of some eighty-five men, that remained under Cameron and continued "right across the valley."[78] Many men became bewildered and lost their way, and did not see each other again until after their recapture. A few were never heard from again.

James A. Glasscock and William H. Van Horn took a westward course and traveled the remainder of the day without finding water.[79] The next day Van Horn and Glasscock took a more northerly course in the direction of a mountain in the distance and again camped without water. When daylight came, they continued their march toward the pass, but by mid-morning the weather became so hot that they stopped to rest in the shade of a bush. Discovering a column of smoke up ahead, at about five in the evening, they concluded it was a signal from some of their party. They headed in the direction of the smoke until darkness forced a halt. When the moon came up, they renewed their journey and continued for two days along the trail until they came to where the prairie had been burnt, but still found no water. However, they again saw smoke ahead and pushed in that direction, hoping some comrade had found water.

75. Stapp, *Prisoners of Perote*, p. 65.

76. "Narrative of 'Mier' and 'Perote' By One of the Expedition," in *Telegraph and Texas Register*, Nov. 29, 1843.

77. "Narrative of 'Mier' and 'Perote' By One of the Expedition," in *Telegraph and Texas Register*, Aug. 23, 1843.

78. "Narrative of 'Mier' and 'Perote' By One of the Expedition," in *Telegraph and Texas Register*, Nov. 29, 1843.

79. Glasscock diary, Feb. 17, 1843.

About one o'clock they stopped to rest. While they rested, John Thomas Dillon overtook them. He was so weak he could scarcely travel; Van Horn was in a similar condition. Glasscock, being the strongest of the three, tried unsuccessfully to get juice from a maguey plant by pounding some of its leaves. As soon as Van Horn and Dillon felt able to travel, the three continued in the direction of the smoke and near nine at night came upon a recent campsite, but found neither water nor men. They lay down to rest until morning, when they again started early and followed the trail to the foot of a mountain. Van Horn and Dillon gave out and stopped to rest under an overhanging rock. Loading a pistol and taking a gourd to bring back water if he found any, Glasscock left his companions to await his return. He searched until dark, and lay down to rest briefly, but fell asleep. He arose the next morning and started along the trail until he arrived at some bulrushes, and supposing there might be water nearby, was on the point of turning off the road in search of it, when he was surrounded by four Mexicans, who inquired if he had any companions. Knowing that his two companions would perish for lack of water, Glasscock told the Mexicans where they could be found. The Mexicans relieved Glasscock of his money and pistols. They then left him with one of their number while the others went in search of Dillon and Van Horn. The Mexican took Glasscock to a nearby *rancho,* where for the first time in six days he got some water.[80] In about two hours, his two companions were brought in.

The three captured Texans were taken to the village of Cuatro Ciénegas, northwest of Monclova, near the headwaters of the Río Salado de los Nadadores. About dark they were started on the road toward where the Mexican army was camped. Arriving near midnight, they found twelve or thirteen of their companions in camp. They remained here for a day, and on February 23 the Mexicans herded their recaptured prisoners in the direction of the Benado Pass.

James H. Calvert, who wandered off from Cameron's party in search of water, was recaptured on the Rio Grande and taken to San Fernando, and from there to Monterrey and Saltillo. He was retained at Saltillo for five months. Claudius Buster presumed that James Calvert had died in the mountains, since by March 1844 he had not heard from him. When Willis Copeland, who had escaped near Tacubaya on July 29, was retaken near the Rio Grande and brought to Saltillo, the two were then conveyed to the City of Mexico. From Mexico City, Calvert, Copeland, and Alexander Mathews were sent to Perote Castle. Two days before their arrival there, Calvert was stabbed by a Mexican at Puebla. Mathews was left sick at Puebla, but Calvert and Copeland were sent on to Perote, arriving in April 1844. Upon his arrival at Perote Castle, Calvert was sent to the hospital in

---

80. *Ibid.*, Feb. 21, 1843.

town, where he remained until he recovered from his wound and was returned to the fort.[81]

In the meantime, the little band that had remained with Cameron continued their search for water. When night came, the men availed themselves of the first smooth ground to lie down upon. No sentinels were posted. "Many slept, but more babbled through the long chilly night of forgotten springs and streams, whose mocking mirage, flaring fancies conjured up in dreams."[82] Night brought relief from the sun, but the Texans did not sleep much because of thirst.

The next morning, February 18, Cameron's party left a sleepless camp. Their course was changed to "West of North." They climbed to the top of a high mountain. Pausing occasionally to recover their breath and strength, they gained the summit and beheld a joyful sight before them: a partially wood-covered valley lay ahead. Their spirits were raised by the prospect of finding water in the extensive valley below.[83] As they rested, "all eyes were busy in searching out the most promising localities" for signs of water. In accord with previous arrangements, Cameron made a smoke signal to guide those who were lost. "After waiting for a sufficient length of time" for stragglers to come in, "and none coming," they prepared to move on.[84] Cameron requested all those who felt strong enough to search for water to go to the right and left of the course in the direction of the pass toward which they were now headed while he went forward with the main group in search of water along their intended course. The pass was visible in the distance and appeared to be only a short distance off—a short distance of forty-five miles. It was agreed that if a party found water, it would send up a smoke signal.

The men hastened down the mountainside, but the distance was far greater than they had supposed. By the time the valley was reached, the day was well advanced,[85] and Cameron's party halted to rest during the heat of the day. The stronger men, including Canfield, Walker, Stapp, and others, broke off from Cameron's party, and fanned out in squads to search every gully, ravine, and grove in the valley for water.[86]

In the search for water the men often wandered off into the dense chaparral too far from the direction in which the main party was headed, got separated, and, becoming lost, fell in with the enemy the next day and

81. James N. Calvert to [D. H.] Vanvecten, Bremond, Robertson County, Texas, Dec. 14, 1876, photostat of original in Daughters of the Republic of Texas Library, The Alamo, San Antonio, Texas.

82. Stapp, *Prisoners of Perote*, p. 65.

83. Duval, *Big-Foot Wallace*, p. 210; Stapp, *Prisoners of Perote*, p. 66; Alexander, "Account of the Mier Expedition," MS, TxU-A.

84. "Narrative of 'Mier' and 'Perote' By One of the Expedition," in *Telegraph and Texas Register*, Nov. 29, 1843; see also Letter of a Mier Prisoner from Mexico City, in *Telegraph and Texas Register*, Aug. 23, 1843.

85. Stapp, *Prisoners of Perote*, p. 66, says it was "full noon" before the rest of the men reached the bottom.

86. Bell, *Narrative*, pp. 45-46.

were recaptured.[87] Others now gave up, dropping by the way either from fatigue or despondency, spreading their blankets on the thorn bushes to protect themselves from the rays of the sun.[88] "In the extremity of our suffering," wrote Stapp, "the enemy was entirely forgotten or if thought of at all, longed for as friends who would bring us relief, rather that as enemies from whom we had any thing to dread or endure. Had the valley that enclosed us been filled with furious [ferocious] wild beasts, they would scarce have obstructed the hunt we were then making for water."[89]

There were no signals from the water hunters. John Rufus Alexander pursued a course more to the east and to the right of Cameron, hoping to find a spring in that direction.[90] Alexander headed toward a small round mountain in the valley which Cameron had said he would leave just to the left. Upon reaching the mountain, Alexander climbed it to view the surrounding country for signs of water. Seeing none, he threw his blanket over a bush and lay down in its shade to rest. After some time, he heard a rustling noise in the bush and saw Jack (John R.) Johnson coming toward him. While they rested and waited for the heat of the day to pass, Fenton M. Gibson came up. They continued to wait, and as the afternoon advanced and Cameron did not come up, they "thought he had turned to the northeast . . . [where] there seemed to be a gap or pass in the mountain. A little to the left of the gap there were two high peaks and the mountains between them and us seemed to be low," remembered Alexander; "so Jack & I decided to go across this way fearing the gap might be guarded."[91]

Despairing of making contact with Cameron, Alexander, Johnson, and Gibson renewed their northward course, traveling as late that night as they could, their famished condition rendering their progress "slow and extremely painful."[92] When morning came, it was foggy and their vision was limited, but the damp atmosphere gave some relief to their feverish bodies. Soon after renewing their journey they entered a small valley, where suddenly they came on four of their comrades—Peter A. Ackerman, Francis Arthur, James Nealy, and John Cash—all of Cameron's Company, to whom they explained their plans. The seven agreed to travel together in the direction of the distant mountain pass. Near noon they tried to get water from the pith of a dagger tree and, while attempting to do so, Gibson "wandered away and was lost—delirious of thirst and hardship."[93]

87. Duval, *Big-Foot Wallace*, pp. 210-11.

88. Stapp, *Prisoners of Perote*, p. 66.

89. *Ibid.*

90. Canfield diary, Feb. 18, 1843; see also Alexander, "Account of the Mier Expedition," MS, TxU-A.

91. Alexander, "Account of the Mier Expedition," written at Round Mountain, Texas, July 13, 1897, typed copy of original MS, TxU-A; photostat copy, Tx-A.

92. "John Rufus Alexander's Story as Told to John Warren Hunter," in Wade, comp., *Notes and Fragments of the Mier Expedition*, 1, p. 44.

93. *Ibid.*, p. 45.

The remaining six men reached the foot of the mountains near evening. That night they sought to scale the mountains and it was not until an hour or two before daybreak that they reached the top. It was dark and the mountain was steep, so they decided to sleep until daylight. They arose at daybreak and continued their journey down the mountain. Near the foot of it, they turned in an eastward direction and, after going a short distance, "saw water glistening up on the side of the mountain" to their right—a silver sheen of waterfall," said Alexander. They "were soon upon the banks of a nice little stream of clear, cold water. It was fully four days and nights since we had had any water. We stayed there . . . drinking water, . . . eating our horse meat, and resting."[94]

The next morning they started early and followed the stream in an easterly direction. After traveling some distance they saw a man on foot cross the valley in front of them. After he disappeared, the Texans struck the road the man had been on that led in the direction of the pass. They lay off the road to hide, not wishing to enter the pass in the daylight. When night descended, they entered the pass, where they found water and filled their gourds. While doing so, they heard someone pass on horseback, going north. When he had gotten out of hearing, they followed the road and after about a mile emerged from the pass into the valley. As they continued along the road, James Nealy, who was behind as a rearguard, reported that they were being followed. They turned off the road to the right and lay down under some shrubbery. When the individual arrived near the point where they had left the road, he paused and called in a low voice: "Boys where are you?" They answered and were happy, indeed, to know that it was one of their own men, William Oldham, and, recorded Alexander, "I never saw a man more happy to find company than he."[95]

Oldham told them that he had stayed with Cameron for two days after the main body had discovered a distant mountain toward the northeast; that Cameron had halted during the heat of the day, but that several small parties had continued in the direction of the pass without pausing to rest. Oldham reported that he was with Captain Pierson and ten others and that he and Thomas A. Thompson were some distance behind the others when a squad of Mexican cavalry passed between Pierson and Oldham and Thompson. The cavalry surrounded Pierson and the nine men with him, but failed to see Oldham and Thompson. After the cavalry left, Oldham and Thompson continued their search for water and came near the pass in the mountains. Not far away, near the pass, was a Mexican camp. Thompson, maddened by thirst, declared that he could not go on without water and would give himself up. He handed his gun and ammu-

94. Alexander, "Account of the Mier Expedition" MS, TxU-A.
95. Quoted in Alexander, "Account of the Mier Expedition," MS., TxU-A.96. "John Rufus Alexander's Story of the Mier Expedition as Told to John Warren Hunter," Wade, comp., *Notes and Fragments of the Mier Expedition* 1, pp. 48-49.

nition to Oldham; they shook hands, and Thompson went off in the direction of the Mexican camp. Oldham, however, lay low, hiding in a gully within sight of the Mexican camp until dark. That night Oldham climbed the mountain around the Mexican encampment and descended to the other side of the gap where he found water—the first he had had in five days.[96]

After appeasing his thirst, Oldham continued along the road to the north, taking with him his tin cup filled with water. He traveled until tired, then lay down to sleep. When he awoke he found a little bird sitting on his "breast almost splitting his little throat with his morning song." His spirits were buoyed and he felt that the happy little creature was a good omen. Continuing northward, he met with Alexander and his companions.

Alexander, Oldham, and their companions now lay by until nightfall and then traveled all night and the ensuing day. Finally they came to the bed of a small creek, but there was no water. "After resting a while," reported Alexander, "Johnson and Cash proposed going up the creek aways, which they pointed out, and there to wait until we overtook them. When we reached the place they were no where to be seen, and after resting awhile we called to them, but no one answered. We kept on our journey from here, there being only five of us left. We soon found ourselves between two hollows ["'draws' or 'valleys'"]. Ackerman said he would follow down the one on the right while we moved down the one on the left, and that we would meet at the confluence of the two, which did not seem very far away. To this we agreed. Upon arriving there we waited but he did not come. We rested awhile and called him, but getting no reply, we again took up our journey, there now being only four of us."[97]

About nine o'clock in the morning they came to a dry bed of sand, where they found fresh signs of cattle. Thinking that water must be near, they began a search for it. Arthur and Oldham gave out and stopped to rest. Soon Alexander also stopped to rest, while Jim Nealy continued on. He was to shout if he found water. In about half an hour Alexander heard Nealy call; going in his direction, he met Nealy returning for him. Alexander told Nealy, since he had had water, to go for Oldham and Arthur, while he went on to the water hole. Nealy said that there was an old bull at the water hole and told Alexander to kill him when he got there. "I found little water," said Alexander, "but dug a hole and obtained sufficient. The bull was still there, and after the men had their water and rested, Jim Neeley [Nealy] and I started after him. We shot him three times and managed to get him down, but having only one dull knife amongst us, we had rather a hard time skinning him. We stayed there two days and nights, drying the meat and mending our shoes, with the hide. Maj. Oldham also mended his gun stock which he broke over the Bull's head."[98]

96. Alexander, "Account of the Mier Expedition," MS, TxU-A.
97. *Ibid.*
98. *Morning Star*, Apr. 15 and 20, 1843; *Telegraph and Texas Register*, Apr. 20, 1843.

They continued northward, but Nealy and Arthur soon dropped behind, and Alexander and Oldham stopped to look for them. Failing to see them, they continued on their way. Thus the party of seven had now been reduced to two—Alexander and Major Oldham—who pledged to each other that they would not separate until they reached home. That night they slept in a rocky hollow, and the next morning continued their journey up the hollow toward the north. That night they slept at the head of the hollow, and the next morning began to climb the mountain nearby. On reaching its summit, they could see cattle in a valley to the northeast. For some distance, the north side of the mountain was rough and steep, but as they neared the base it became smoother and finally only a gentle slope to the bottom.

Although they traveled all day in the direction of the cattle, they were unable to reach them and decided to stop for the night. Resuming their journey, they reached the stream where they had seen the cattle the day before. They heard cattle approaching for water, and stationing himself along the trail leading to the stream, Alexander waited for them. He killed a two-year-old steer while it was drinking from the stream. They camped and barbecued some of the meat.

During the next few days, they continued toward the northeast without water. Finally, they reached a dry creek bed, and following it, came to a bluff on the west side, where they discovered a small cave. Alexander dug a hole in the sand and found water that attracted bees in considerable number, and Alexander followed the bees to their hive. He and Oldham robbed the beehive to obtain honey. In the process, Oldham was stung repeatedly about the face. That evening he consumed a considerable quantity of honey. Because of overindulgence, plus the numerous bee stings, he became quite ill that evening. Before they left the next day, Oldham tied one end of one of his goatskin leggings and filled it with honey.

Traveling all day, they came upon a road and soon thereafter a young Mexican overtook them on horseback. When asked where he lived, he explained that his house was about one league from the road. They learned from the Mexican, a shepherd, that 100 Texans had been recaptured in the mountains.[99] They inquired of the shepherd about various places and distances, and told him that they were going to Candela, although they really had no intention of doing so. As soon as they were out of his sight, they turned toward the river. The next morning they proceeded down the right bank of the river for about two miles toward the east and waded across the river with difficulty. Alexander, being taller than Oldham, found the water waist deep and swift. He made two crossings carrying their luggage over, and then went back to assist Oldham.

Leaving the river, they traveled two days without water. Late on the second day, a norther descended on them, causing them to lay up all the

---

99. *Telegraph and Texas Register*, Apr. 26, 1843.

next day without water. During the night the wind lay, and there was a white frost in the morning. They renewed their journey, but in the afternoon Alexander became sick and had to stop. Oldham built up a good fire near him, but he steadily grew worse; finally, Alexander told Oldham that if he were not better by morning, Oldham should proceed without him. Oldham reminded him of their agreement and said he would stay with him for two days. When morning came, Alexander felt a little better, and they started once more about noon. Reaching the top of a ridge, they saw two deer, and Oldham, taking Alexander's gun, crawled to within eighty yards and fired. Both deer bounded away, but Oldham claimed that he had hit one of them. They tracked the deer and found that one had been hit and killed. They dressed it and went in the direction of the timber and soon arrived on the bank of a large river.

While Alexander went to the river—the Rio Grande, as it proved to be—for water, Oldham commenced to cook the meat, but "we gave it very little time to cook before we began to eat it, as it had been several days since we had had anything to eat or drink. We had no salt . . . during the whole trip, so our cooking tasted pretty flat."

They moved their camp the next morning to the bank of the river, convinced that they had reached the Rio Grande. While filling their gourds with water, they said to each other: "That is grand old Texas!" across the river. After preparing their venison, they traveled down the west bank of the river for two days, seeking a way to cross it. They found an old stock pen made of poles. From the poles the two men constructed a raft. With poles they shoved off from the bank and landed about a mile down river on the opposite bank and about ten miles above Laredo.[100]

The next morning they had gone scarcely 200 yards "before we came to a road," remembered Alexander, "which we recognized as the San Antonio road, from where we saw a Mexican not more than 300 or 400 yards north of us standing near his horse as if waiting for someone." They hid in a gulch; after a short while the Mexican mounted his horse and "came within 20 steps of us to water his horse. He then came down and reclined on the grass his horse grazing around. We decided that we would arrest him and take him and his horse and let him go a few miles farther on." Just as they were about to carry out their plan, they "saw 20 or 25 Mexicans coming. We then jumped back into the high grass where we hid again. They passed traveling towards Laredo. We were quite sure that the man who had seen us the morning before raised this company to come in search of us."[101]

After the Mexicans had passed, the two Texans took the road for San Antonio. On the second evening they reached the Nueces River.

The following morning they resumed their journey, and late in the

---

100. *Ibid.*

101. "John Rufus Alexander's Story of the Mier Expedition as Told to John Marvin Hunter," in Wade, comp., *Notes and Fragments of the Mier Expedition* 1, pp. 63-64.

afternoon reached the Medina, where they spent the night with a Mexican from whom they learned of the decimation of the Mier prisoners and that the date was April 4. On April 5 they reached San Antonio. As they entered the plaza, "Men, women, and children gazed at us," reported Alexander, "with wonder until it became quickly known that we were Mier prisoners who had escaped from Salado, and when this news was carried through the city we became the object of a solicitude and compassion which we felt that we did not altogether merit. The attentions we received were so generous and spontaneous that to an extent they became embarrassing. Homes were thrown open to us, the town was ours, every want was anticipated and [we were] supplied clothing, saddles, bridles, and horses to carry us home. For three days we enjoyed the splendid hospitalities of the great-souled people of San Antonio, . . . during which time a great many—fathers, mothers, wives and sisters—flocked to us to learn the fate of sons, brothers, husbands, or relatives."[102] After three days at San Antonio, Alexander and Oldham proceeded to LaGrange,[103] where they were received with hospitality and eagerly questioned.

The schooner *Emblem* reached New Orleans on March 1 from Matamoros. The captain reported that, while lying off the bar before Matamoros on February 22, news arrived that the prisoners "had risen upon their guard at Saltillo [Salado]" and had effected their escape. A report of the escape of the Mier prisoners, taken from the *Daily Picayune* of March 2, 1843, was published in the *Daily National Intelligencer* on March 13, 1843.

The *Neptune* reached Galveston from New Orleans on March 12 with news of the successful escape of the Texans at Salado. When Edward Hall, in New Orleans, heard of the overthrow of the guard at Salado, he wrote to Ashbel Smith: "This affair of Mier eclipses (for bravery and intrepidity) all of the Texas fights and if the prisoners have escaped will have an important bearing in our future hopes & prospects."[104] "A report was brought by the arrival from Matamoros," said the editor of the *New Orleans Bulletin*, "that the prisoners who were captured at Mier, and were being marched to the capital, had overpowered their guard and escaped by way of Saltillo, to Texas. We had the pleasure on Saturday [March 11] of conversing with Mr. Thomas Nelson, who was one of those prisoners."[105] Nelson was reported to have come by way of Gonzales, Washington-on-the-Brazos, Nacogdoches, and from thence to New Orleans, where he told his story to the editor of the *Bulletin*.

The *Houston Morning Star* reported on March 28 that news had arrived that the Mier men had escaped. The mail rider from Columbia

---

102. *Morning Star*, Apr. 20, 1843; *Telegraph and Texas Register*, Apr. 26, 1843.

103. *Telegraph and Texas Register*, Mar. 15, 1843.

104. Edward Hall to Ashbel Smith, New Orleans, March 17, 1843, MS, in Ashbel Smith Papers, TxU-A.

105. *New Orleans Bulletin* of March 13, 1843, quoted in *Northern Standard*, Apr. 13, 1843.

brought news to Richmond "on Tuesday last [April 4], that one of the prisoners escaped at Mier had arrived at Victoria, and given notice that the main body of the prisoners had reached the Rio Grande."[106] This news, declared the editor, is considered "too good to be true; but a gentleman arrived yesterday [Friday, April 7] from Washington confirms the report."[107] On Monday, April 10, a man arriving in Houston reported that before he left Washington a messenger had arrived from Béxar with news that the Mier men under Cameron, after defeating a large Mexican force near Camargo, "and having supplied themselves with all the articles they required, . . . [were] now leisurely marching home."

The *Galveston Times* on April 11 reported that a letter had been received there from Matagorda, reporting that the Mier men had "'reached the Rio Grande, and felt perfectly secure—so much so that they are determined to levy contributions on the frontier towns of Mexico, and compensate themselves for their sufferings and losses before they return to Texas. And it is said that they have sent expresses to Victoria and Gonzales calling for reinforcements to enable them to overrun the northern provinces of Mexico.' We hope," declared the editors, "they will be aided, and again take Mier and proceed to Matamoros."[108] Dr. Francis Moore, editor of the *Morning Star,* commented: "The above report is also unworthy of credit."[109]

The editors of the *Daily Picayune*[110] were reluctant to accept the news brought to New Orleans on April 18 from Houston and Galveston concerning the report that a large body of the Mier men had made a successful retreat across the Rio Grande. The successful escape of a few, but not a great many, they were willing to accept.

On April 11 a second report reached Houston. It stated "that they had all reached the Guadalupe, and that some of them had arrived in Montgomery County." In still another, "and entirely different account," it was reported that all but 11, who had made the attack upon the guard escaped; these were killed."

On the heels of this report, copies of the New Orleans *Daily Picayune* of April 5 reached Texas conveying news of the recapture of the prisoners and of the order for their decimation. All the rumors of the successful escape of the main body of prisoners were dispelled by their non-arrival in Texas and by the receipt of reliable information of their recapture and decimation. The *Marshall Review* of April 8, quoting the *Caddo Gazette,* announced the recapture of the Texan prisoners.[111] On April 29, the *Morning*

---

106. *Morning Star,* Apr. 8, 1843.
107. *Ibid.*
108. *Ibid.,* Apr. 15, 1843.
109. *Ibid.*
110. Apr. 19, 1843; see also *Daily National Intelligencer,* Mar. 23, 1843; *New Orleans Bulletin,* Mar. 12, 1843.
111. *Marshall Review,* Apr. 8, 1843.

Star reproduced from the *New Orleans Bulletin* of April 22, a letter from "P.D." written from Monterrey on March 24 reporting the recapture of 131 Texans who had escaped from *Hacienda Salado* and the order to shoot them.

The recapture of the escaped Texans was confirmed a few days later by Mexican traders from the Rio Grande arriving at Béxar. The traders were reported to have said that the escaped Texans "were surrounded about three miles from Camargo, *in the mountains!* and after a severe fight that lasted four days, surrendered. In this fight they say *seven or eight hundred Mexicans were killed*," and that only four Texans had lost their lives, but that eight had died later "from drinking too large a quantity of cold water." "We think," said the editor of the *Telegraph and Texas Register*, "there must be some error in this statement. There are no mountains near Camargo, and the Texans were marching in a contrary direction towards Presidio de Río Grande when Messrs. Cox and Blackman [Blackburn] left them."[112]

Other stragglers from the escaping prisoners in time arrived on the western frontier of Texas. Among these were Thomas W. Cox, a Baptist lay preacher and lieutenant in Eastland's Company, and his future brother-in-law, John D. L. Blackburn, who reported that they left the main body of prisoners on February 16 in search of water, and never rejoined Cameron's party. Blackburn's bare, lacerated feet greatly impaired his walking. Cox, a large man, carried Blackburn at intervals on his back. They reached Cox's home at LaGrange, eighteen days after escaping from Salado.[113] Upon Cox's arrival at LaGrange on April 2, people flocked around to hear his tale. "He was a man of much native eloquence," wrote Julia Lee Sinks, who heard Cox speak, "and the graphic description he gave of his adventures made a strong impression upon his hearers."[114]

Also making their way through to Texas were George Anderson and William T. Morehead. On Monday, April 24, news reached Houston from Washington that John J. Jacobs[115] of Independence had brought to Washington a report of two more Mier prisoners having reached Béxar. These were probably Anderson and Morehead. *McCutchan's Narrative* and other accounts report both Anderson and Morehead being left in the mountains, but make no reference to supposing them to be dead. William T. Morehead must have gotten home, for he lived to become a Confederate veteran. He was from Nacogdoches County, and later received pay of $605 for his services in the Mier Expedition.[116]

---

112. *Morning Star*, May 3, 1843.

113. *Northern Standard*, Apr. 20, 1843; see also *Morning Star*, Apr. 15, 1843.

114. Mrs. Julia Sinks, "Early Courts of Fayette County," in *QTSHA* 7 (July 1903), p. 84.

115. Worth S. Ray, *Austin County Pioneers, Including History of Bastrop, Fayette, Grimes, Montgomery, and Washington Counties, Texas*, pp. 55, 132. Hereafter cited: Ray, *Austin County Pioneers*.

116. See W. T. Morehead Confederate Veteran Pension Application No. 25035 Approved, in Confederate Veteran Pension Papers, Tx-A.

Houston Wade says John R. Alexander, William Oldham, John D. L. Blackburn, Thomas Washington Cox, "the Fighting Parson," and George Anderson reached Texas after the break at Salado.[117] In May 1843, it was incorrectly reported that ten other escapees had arrived at Béxar, including Allen S. Holderman of Bastrop,[118] but we know that Holderman died at San Luis Potosí sometime early in April 1843, after the main body of recaptured prisoners left that place.

---

117. "John Rufus Alexander's Story as Told to John Warren Hunter," in Wade, comp., *Notes and Fragments of the Mier Expedition* 1, p. 18; see also Weyand and Wade, *Early History of Fayette County*, pp. 171-72.

118. *Telegraph and Texas Register*, May 10, 1843.

CHAPTER 16

Recaptured and Returned to Hacienda Salado

IN THE EARLY EVENING of February 18, some of Cameron's men discovered a large smoke to their right, thought to have been made by water hunters. Cameron's unit proceeded in that direction, stopping every fifteen or twenty minutes to rest. As the moon began to rise, Cameron's men saw a fire and assumed that it was the fire from which the smoke seen near dusk had come. A party of ten men, including Samuel H. Walker, drew close enough to the fire to recognize that they had approached a Mexican cavalry camp.[1] Walker's party bypassed the camp to seek water and discovered that several parties of Mexican troops had preceded them by several leagues.

When Walker and his companions came upon another Mexican camp, they left it on their right and continued "in the trail that the horsemen had made leading to a large gap or pass in the mountain."[2] At daybreak, as they neared the top of the pass, they were challenged by a sentinel. The Texans scattered while Walker and John McMullen continued forward, bearing off a little to the right in the direction of the pass. In a short time, as they neared the pass, they saw that it was guarded.

They concluded that there was no choice but to surrender, for they could no longer survive without water. Throwing away the one musket they had, they strolled into the Mexican camp, "and were met by some of the *rancheros* who told us," reported Walker, "to give them our money and they would take care of us, that if we did not the regulars would take it from us."[3] Walker said he had none, but he had taken the precaution before entering the camp to conceal what money he had in the waistband of his pantaloons. Walker found several Texans already in custody, and a few

---

1. Sibley, ed., *Samuel H. Walker's Account*, p. 52.
2. *Ibid.*
3. *Ibid.*

261

minutes after he and McMullen surrendered another party of Texans was brought in, making about fifty Texans who had been recaptured at this point. By twos and threes they came in all during the day.

In the meantime, Cameron's party approached the fire they had seen, believing it to be the camp of a party of water hunters. They discovered, when hailed by a sentry within 100 yards of the fire, that they had been directing their course toward a Mexican cavalry camp—the camp which Walker and his party had bypassed earlier in the evening.

It was now about ten o'clock on the night of February 18. Cameron formed his small party, now reduced to forty-four men, as if preparing an attack, although scarcely a dozen muskets remained among the ragged band of Texans. Seeing that the Mexicans were not anxious to attack, Cameron opened a parley. The Mexicans promised that if the Texans surrendered they would "be treated as prisoners of war and conducted immediately to water," according to the Texan reports.[4] But it seems that the Mexicans made no guarantees and that the Texans in surrender placed themselves at the disposition of the Supreme Government of the Republic. With their ranks reduced to less than one-fourth of their number when they left Salado and their suffering almost intolerable, it was decided to accept the Mexican terms, especially with its promise of water. After being deprived of their arms, money, blankets, and much of their clothing, and placed under heavy guard, Cameron's "Cowboys," raving and begging for a drink, learned that with few exceptions "the rascals had been without water two days themselves" while searching for the escaped Texans.[5]

The prisoners were compelled to lie down in rows near the smoldering camp fires until daylight. The Mexicans dispatched men for water to meet them the next day as they moved the prisoners toward their main camp. The nearest water hole was twelve miles away, at Paso de Benado, guarded principally by militiamen while the cavalry scoured the countryside for the Texans.

The escaped prisoners had traveled approximately 150 miles, about half of it covered the first day and night after their escape. By leaving the road and taking to the mountains, their pace had been slowed greatly and in the next five days they had covered a distance of only about sixty miles. Had they kept to the road rather than circling through the mountains, they might have escaped, for Mejía's small unit could not have blocked their passage along the Monclova road.

No sooner had the Texans escaped at Salado than couriers began to spread the news, and word of the escape reached Mexico City on February 27. "The tenacity and audaciousness of those adventurers begins to appear, as well as their stupidity," declared the editor of the *Diario del Gobierno*, "in believing that they would be able to escape from the interior

---

4. Canfield diary, Feb. 18, 1843; Capt. S. H. Walker to A. Sidney Johns[t]on, Santiago Prison, City of Mexico, May 4, 1843, in Army Papers (Republic), Tx-A.

5. Canfield diary, Feb. 18, 1843; Stapp, *Prisoners of Perote*, pp. 66-67.

of the Republic." The government "cannot permit itself to be impudently laughed at nor allow those charged with their custody to be vilely outraged." Whether it be "near or far off, they will be apprehended," but if not, the villages through which they may pass, "eager for their own particular security, will give them the punishment merited by their haughty arrogance."[6] They have, said another editor, "committed the most scandalous transgression of scoffing at the confidence of their guards, disarming them, and even assassinating some."[7]

On February 16 Col. Calixto Bravo, commander of the garrison at Laredo, handed the *alcalde* a communication advising him of the escape of the Texan prisoners, and requesting that he let him know "how many men you wish to furnish . . . to march the day after tomorrow to occupy the two crossings on the Nueces, . . . in case some of the fugitives seek the road by which they may enter Texas at this point."[8]

Immediately after the break, Barragán dispatched couriers to the governors of Nuevo León, Coahuila, and San Luis Potosí, and to the military commander of the district of Monclova, informing them of the affair at the Salado. When apprised of the Texan assault upon the guard, the governor and commandant general of the Department of San Luis Potosí, José Ignacio Gutiérrez, prepared to send reinforcements to Barragán. Col. Juan de Dios Ortiz, who was in command of eighty-four mounted dragoons at the Hacienda de Guadalupe del Carnicero, was ordered to Salado, and the *rurales* and *auxiliaries* of Matehuala and Catorce, in the Prefecture of Venado, were ordered to supplement Ortiz's force en route. Ortiz already had been apprised by the administrator of the Hacienda de San Juan de Vanegas and by Captain Romano of the revolt against the guard and had begun to advance to Barragán's assistance when the orders and reinforcements from San Luis Potosí arrived at 5:00 o'clock on the afternoon of the break. Ortiz was ordered to handle the "ungrateful and perverse strangers" who might be retaken and brought to San Luis Potosí. If he needed additional troops he was to make a request to Gutiérrez by special messenger.

At Salado, Ortiz found that the Texans had fled along the road by which they had come from Saltillo and were already beyond Encarnación. Capt. Emeterio Posas and several infantrymen had remained with the fifteen prisoners who did not wish to follow their comrades, then had gone on in the direction of Saltillo carrying six badly wounded "strangers" and four dead in two carts.[9]

---

6. *Diario del Gobierno*, Feb. 24, 1843.

7. *Gaceta Del Gobierno de Tamaulipas* (Victoria), Mar. 11, 1843.

8. Col. Calixto Bravo, Military Commander at Laredo, to the Alcalde of Laredo, [dated] Laredo, Feb. 16, 1843, and enclosing a copy of a letter from the Commander-in-Chief of Nuevo-León, dated Feb. 12, 1843, advising Col. Bravo of the escape of the Texans at Salado. Laredo Archives, Laredo, Texas.

9. *Juan Ortiz al Sr. Comandante general del departamento de San Luis Potosí, D. J. Ignacio Gutiérrez, Hacienda del Salado, Febrero 12 de 1843*, in *Diario del Gobierno*, Feb. 24, 1843.

Ortiz ordered Capt. Emeterio Posas to return the Texans under his escort to Salado. Posas returned to Salado the night of February 12, and the next day the Texans, still under his command, were started on the road toward San Luis Potosí with "Captains Fitzgerald and Baker, and privates Sansberry and Hancock . . . in a cart,"[10] with the others who had not joined the escape. Ortiz joined them and took command of the guard, reaching San Luis Potosí on February 26, where he overtook the party of Fisher and Green.[11] The next day, Fitzgerald's condition worsened and Posas ordered him pulled from the cart. He died beside the road and was buried by his comrades.

Small parties of *rurales* from Venegas, the Hacienda de Carnicero, Matehála, Catorce, and Refugio hurried toward Salado to assist Col. D. Juan de Dios Ortiz in suppressing the revolt.[12] Upon receiving Barragán's report of the escape on February 12, Gen. Francisco Mejía, governor and commandant general and inspector of the Department of Coahuila, made arrangements for the pursuit and "prompt punishment" of the Texan "adventurers."[13] Auxiliaries (*defensores*) were called up for the defense of Saltillo. Presidial troops and *rancheros (auxiliaries)* were ordered to cover the points of Zapatero, the avenues leading to the Hacienda de Sardinas, and all others leading to the frontier. On February 12, Col. J. Juan Sánchez left Saltillo with eighty infantrymen and a four-pound artillery piece to establish himself at Venadito and watch the road. General Mejía, accompanied by thirty infantrymen, left Saltillo at four o'clock on February 12 and directed his course toward Venadito to take command in person of the military operations from that point.

Mejía's courier reached Monterrey with a report of the escape to Gen. José María de Ortega, governor and commandant general of the Department of Nuevo León. Rising from "the bed where he lay ill of health,"[14] Ortega ordered the 7th, 8th, 9th, 10th, and 11th squadrons of *auxiliaries*, amounting to 490 men, to rendezvous at Hicamole. He turned the defense of Monterrey over to Lt. Col. José María Bermúdez, and on February 13, two days after the escape, left the city with seventy infantrymen, 300 cavalrymen, and one six-pounder to cover the most likely point by which the escaped prisoners might seek to leave Mexico. By forced marches Governor Ortega arrived at the Hacienda del Venadito, north-

10. Green, *Mier Expedition*, p. 177.

11. List of Prisoners captured by Colonel Juan Ortiz, April 8, 1843, MS Document in Exp./481.3/1937, *Archivo Histórico Militar Méxicano*, Mexico City.

12. *José Ignacio Gutiérrez a Exmo Sr. Ministro de estado y del despacho de guerra y marina, San Luis Potosí, Febrero 15 de 1843*, in *Diario del Gobierno*, Feb. 24, 1843.

13. *Lt. Col. D. Manuel R. Barragán al Gobernador y comandante general é inspector de Coahuila y Tejas, Hacienda del Salado, Febrero 11 de 1843*, in *Diario del Gobierno*, Feb. 24, 1843.

14. *José María Bermúdez a Exmo, Sr. Gen. D. Josa [sic] María Ortega, Febrero 24 de 1843*, in *El Semanario Político de Nuevo León*, Feb. 23, [1843], reproduced in *Diario del Gobierno*, Mar. 10, 1843.

northwest of Saltillo, on February 18, where he found Governor Mejía encamped with a small force. Recognizing that he was outside the jurisdiction of his department, Ortega offered to cooperate with the governor of Coahuila y Tejas.

They had information that the Texans were in the rough, mountainous region called *de la Paila*. Coordinating their operations, they began a simultaneous movement against the fleeing Texans, with General Mejía leading the vanguard. The Texans, according to the latest reports, were trying to exit the *de la Paila* by way of the Cañón de San Marcos in the direction of the Villa de Cuatro Ciénegas. Ortega, with artillery, the infantrymen of Nuevo León and of Coahuila y Tejas, and the remaining cavalry, headed in the direction of La Boca de los Tres Ríos on the Monclova road, which was to serve as his base of operations. En route, in line with previous orders, he was joined by eighty *auxiliaries* from Cadereyta. He assured the minister of war that "not one of the fiendish adventurers will escape."[15]

Mejía entered the Cañón de San Marcos on February 19. That night a party of the fugitives led by Cameron, who were making their way by the Pass of San Marcos toward Cuatro Ciénegas, as we have seen, stumbled upon his camp and surrendered without a fight.[16] The Mexican militiamen were armed with hangers, machetes, carbines, and lances, and were "uniformed in leather jerkins and open pants, with low-crowned wool-hats, ornamented with white bands."[17] The Texans, whose pride had suffered tremendously during the past week, presented a pitiful scene. Some were without hats, some without shoes or with only one shoe, some half-naked, while the clothes of many hung in shreds about their bodies. One poor fellow, hatless and with but one shoe, had "one leg of his pantaloons torn entirely off, and nothing left of his coat except the collar and sleeves, and a few strips of the lining still dangling behind his back."[18]

Early the next morning, February 19, the prisoners, with the exception of Cameron, were untied,[19] and started in the direction of the water hole at the Paso Benado, some twelve miles away, where the main body of the Mexican troops, principally cavalry, was encamped.[20] With his hands tied with rawhide strings, Cameron was marched about 200 yards in advance of the other prisoners.

They were met by cavalrymen bringing water in gourds and beef paunches well mixed with grass. At intervals of ten or fifteen minutes, they stopped and the guards measured out the delicious "nectar" and gave

15. *José María de Ortega a Exmo, Sr. ministro de la guerra [y marina], Campo en la Boca de los tres Ríos, Febrerio 21 de 1843—a las doce de la mañana*, in *El Semanario Político de Nuevo León*, Feb. 23, 1843, and in *Diario del Gobierno*, Feb. 28, 1843.

16. Stapp, *Prisoners of Perote*, p. 87.

17. *Ibid.*, pp. 69-70.

18. Duval, *Big-Foot Wallace*, pp. 213-14.

19. *Ibid.*, p. 212.

20. Stapp, *Prisoners of Perote*, p. 67.

each man a small drink, but some, using money that they had concealed, bribed a guard to give them an additional "swig" from the gourd. As they moved along, some lay down or fell during the march, determined not to go any farther. But the Mexicans would dismount, tie a rope around the man's waist, lay him across the saddle of his horse, and lead the horse, thus allowing the man relief for a short distance.[21] The Mier men in their march through Mexico seem not to have been treated as brutally as the unfortunate Santa Fé prisoners of a year and a half before. There were many reports of Mexicans having compassion for the thirsty recaptured Texans. "Some of the Mexicans themselves, as they viewed these scenes of suffering could not restrain the tear of sympathy," admitted Bell, "and a few of the more humane did all they could to allay the pangs of the sufferers, but by far the greater part would have rejoiced to have seen them shot."[22]

At five o'clock, Sunday afternoon, February 19, Cameron and his party reached the Mexican camp at the artificial water hole at Benado Pass, where Walker and others of the recaptured Texans were held.[23] Woodland reported that when they arrived "they were lashed together with rawhide thongs and then made secure to the trees, and only a very little water was allowed them at a time lest they should kill themselves."[24] Noticing a cavalryman who had a water gourd taken from him at Mier, Wallace sprang at him, saying in Spanish: "'that is my gourd; give it up!'" The soldier, seeing the determination of the "mad" Texan, exclaimed *"Pobrecito"* ("Poor fellow"), and handed him the gourd containing nearly a gallon of water. Wallace commenced gurgling down its contents. Tom Davis hobbled over and said, "Give me some, Big Foot,'" but Wallace would not let go of the gourd. A struggle for it ensued, but Davis was unable to pull it away from Wallace. "A Mexican officer now took notice of what was going on in regard to the gourd, . . . and said in Spanish, 'Hell, take the water away from that fellow; he will kill himself.'" Three or four soldiers tried to seize the gourd, but were unable to do so until Wallace had exhausted its contents. Wallace was so much taller than the Mexicans that he could hold the gourd out of their reach and drink, and "kept whirling around while doing so, and stretched his neck and held his head as high as he could."[25]

The men were searched again and deprived of all articles of value that had not already been taken, including money, blankets, and even some of their remaining clothing, after which they were tied in couples by

21. W. A. A. Wallace to Nora C. Franklin, Big Foot, Sept. 24, 1888, in "Letters of Big Foot Wallace," *Frontier Times* 7 (June 1931), pp. 417-18.

22. Bell, *Narrative*, p. 46.

23. Sibley, ed., *Samuel H. Walker's Account*, p. 53.

24. Woodland, "The Story of the Massacre of the Mier Prisoners," *Houston Daily Post*, Aug. 16, 1891, p. 8, col. 1.

25. This incident was narrated to A. J. Sowell by Wallace, Sowell, *Early Settlers and Indian Fighters of Southwest Texas*, pp. 70-71.

the wrist with strings of rawhide and were carefully guarded through the day. At night they were compelled to lie down in rows.

The officers were removed to a separate camp from that of the men, for fear they might incite another rebellion. Captain Cameron, who the Mexicans supposed had been the main instigator of the revolt, was kept separate from any other Texan and closely guarded. His hands were tied securely behind his back. For three days the recaptured prisoners remained under strong guard at the water hole while Mexican scouting parties scoured the surrounding territory in search of additional escapees. The first evening that Cameron's party reached Benado Pass, thirty-four Texans were brought in. Soon Mejía had 106 recaptured Texans, and Ortega had recaptured fifty-six. Ortega assured the minister of war that "not one of the fiendish adventurers will escape, because all will become prisoners or be killed."[26] Other parties covering Mejía's rear guard caught fourteen others. At Saltillo on March 4, Mejía reported that at that date twelve others were either dead or hidden in places where no one until now has had news of them." News reached Vera Cruz about mid-March that 111 of the Texans had been recaptured, and that "the Mexicans were close up with the remainder."[27] One Texan died at Cuatro Ciénegas and two died in the Cañón de San Marcos. Some were found wandering about in a dazed condition; others "were restored to consciousness by stinted draughts of water, and led or carried to camp."[28]

During their first day in camp at the water hole, the Texans continued to receive small quantities of water at intervals of ten to fifteen minutes, but it did little to allay their thirst. They were also retied more firmly. On the second day, the prisoners were furnished corn and small quantities of beef. They were given little wood with which to cook the meat. Gradually they began to swallow small amounts of food, and their strength returned rapidly.[29]

On Wednesday, February 22, additional Mier men were brought into camp. By noon, 131 Texans had been brought into Ortega's camp at Boca de los Tres Ríos, and General Mejía continued in pursuit of the remaining escapees while Ortega kept out patrols to cover all points where the fleeing Texans might be expected to come out of the mountains, "so that none of the insolent adventurers may escape, for they all must be taken prisoners or be extinguished."[30]

Early on the morning of February 23 the prisoners were marched in

---

26. *José María de Ortega a Exmo Sr. Ministro de la Guerra, Gobierno superior del departamento de Nuevo León,* [dated] *Campo en la Boca de los tres Ríos, Febrero 21 de 1843, a las doce de la mañana,* in *Diario del Gobierno,* Feb. 28, 1843.

27. *Daily National Intelligencer,* Apr. 3, 1843.

28. Stapp, *Prisoners of Perote,* p. 66.

29. Canfield diary, Feb. 21, p. 183.

30. *José María de Ortega a Exmo Sr. ministro de guerra [y marina] Campo en la Boca de los tres Ríos, Febrero 21 de 1843, a las doce de la mañana,* in *Diario del Gobierno,* Feb. 28, 1843.

the direction of Saltillo, with the Texan officers some 200 yards in advance.[31] The hands of each man were tied behind his back with rawhide thongs, which made walking even more difficult. Late in the afternoon, after a march of eighteen miles, they arrived at a water hole and camped.

On February 24 the Texans were marched twelve miles to Rancho Benado, where they found John Taney, Allen Holderman, and Dr. William F. McMath. Years later, John H. Jenkins reported that Taney, whom he knew well, was a notorious whistler and had hidden in a thicket near the water hole where he was discovered by a Mexican peering into the undergrowth. The Mexican recognized him and called out, "Ah Mr. Whistler, how do you do? Come out, Mr. Whistler!"[32] Perry Randolph and William Mitchell died at Rancho Benado on February 25 from having imbibed water too freely.[33] The new arrivals found the Mexican infantry encamped at the ranch. They remained there through February 25, during which interval they were joined by twenty-five more of their recaptured comrades, including Glasscock, Dillon, Van Horn, Clopton, and some twelve or fifteen others who had been brought in just before daybreak.[34]

The march from Rancho Benado to Saltillo commenced on Sunday, February 26. By then the ranks of the recaptured had increased to 140. The marches were short. Each night they camped at a *rancho* or a waterhole in a horse pen or cow pen. At nearly every ranch where they stopped one or more Texans were added to their ranks. On February 26 other prisoners were brought in, increasing the ranks to 160. Those who had untied the rawhide string severely binding their arms during the night were struck blows several times or whipped.[35] On the night of February 26 they encamped in a horse pen, and on February 27 they spent the night at Rancho San Antonio, where they were supplied with beef, corn, and firewood for cooking.[36] As they marched the sixty miles from the Paso de Benado to Rancho San Antonio, they were "fully able to appreciate the fatal blunder . . . [they] had committed in turning off from the Monclova road at this ranch, and entering the mountains."[37] They realized that their circuit through the mountains, which had carried them to within fifteen miles of the pass, had taken nine days and the Mexican force had reached the pass only the day before it began to recapture the men. Had they not left the road, they would have reached Benado Pass in eighteen hours, and along the way could have found forage for their mounts, provisions and water for themselves, and gained additional horses as they approached the frontier of Texas.

---

31. Canfield diary, Feb. 23, 1843.
32. Quoted in Jenkins, ed., *Recollections of Early Texas*, p. 112.
33. Canfield diary, Feb. 25, 1843. Some reports say that Perry Randolph died in the mountains. See Nance, ed., *McCutchan's Narrative*, p. 195; Green, *Mier Expedition*, p. 444.
34. Glasscock diary, Feb. 25, 1843.
35. Sibley, ed., *Samuel H. Walker's Account*, p. 53.
36. Canfield diary, Feb. 27, 1843; Stapp, *Prisoners of Perote*, p. 67.
37. Stapp, *Prisoners of Perote*, p. 69.

The guard was apprehensive, and at Rancho San Antonio the rawhide "cuff-links were exchanged for heavy jewels" of iron, commonly used in handcuffing criminals to be moved from one place to another, since the rawhide strings were not considered sufficient by the Mexicans. The men were handcuffed two and two,[38] closely guarded, and not permitted to stand in camp for fear that they might again charge the guard. The Texans joked about the new "jewelry" decorating their wrists, "receiving their irons with smiles and promises to remunerate the Mexicans for their kindness the first opportunity."[39] As their strength returned, the prisoners could be found in the evening singing popular tunes and telling stories, "which attracted the attention of the officers and ladies about the ranch who were as much amused as astonished at the unusual fortitude of our men under such circumstances," narrated Walker.[40] In their new manacles they marched several hundred miles in pain.

The next day they marched twenty miles. They camped on open ground in a little valley ten miles from Saltillo, and during the night suffered considerably from the cold. The next morning they reached the outskirts of Saltillo and were halted at one-fourth mile from the city for four hours to await the arrival of Mejía and to give the citizens time to prepare for their reception.[41] It was learned later that the governor had been delayed "on account of an order to shoot all of us," declared Glasscock, "and that he was consulting the officers whether to put it into execution or not."[42]

Ortega, having made his official report to the minister of war and marine from his camp at Las Bocas de Los Tres Ríos on February 21,[43] and informed Col. José María Bermúdez, whom he had left in charge of the garrison at Monterrey, of his success in reapprehension of the Texans, prepared to return to Monterrey. Three days after Ortega dispatched his official report to the minister of war and marine, Bermúdez informed him that he had received his report and had ordered it printed in *El Semanario político de Nuevo León* and a special supplementary edition run.[44]

Ortega and his troops entered Monterrey amid rejoicing by a large assemblage of people lining the streets. At the cathedral a *Te Deum* was recited and mass held. Ortega issued a proclamation announcing the suc-

---

38. Canfield diary, Feb. 27, 1843.

39. Sibley, ed., *Samuel H. Walker's Account*, p. 55.

40. *Ibid.*

41. Glasscock diary, Mar. 1, 1843.

42. *Ibid.*

43. *José María de Ortega, Gobierno del departamento de Nuevo León, a D. José María Tornel, Boca de los tres Ríos, Febrero 21 de 1843*, copy in *El Semanario Político de Nuevo León*, Feb. 23, 1843.

44. *[Monterrey] Imprenta del Gobierno a cargo de Froylán de Mier.* [1843]; Broadside, in Yale University Library, New Haven, Connecticut; see Streeter, comp., *Bibliography of Texas*, 2nd ed., p. 132, item 997.1, run off; *José María Bermúdez a Exmo Sr. Gen. D. Josa [sic] María Ortega, Monterey, Febrero 24 de 1843*, in supplement to *El Semanario de Nuevo León*, Feb. 23, 1843, quoted in *Diario del Gobierno*, Mar. 1, 1843.

cessful recapture of the Texans and commending the troops of the Department for a job well done. "The nation is avenged" by you and the meritorious troops under Gen. Francisco Mejía, who have attained "unfading glory in forcing the treacherous and ungrateful fugitives" to surrender "at discretion. . . . Your valor, unblemished patriotism, subordination, activity, and clemency toward the enemy who surrendered to you" mark the fulfillment of "a brilliant march."[45]

While preparations were made in Saltillo for "the grand entry," a committee representing the *ayuntamiento,* the *alcalde,* the parish priest, and other important persons from the capital and adjoining *haciendas* and *ranchos* came out to receive the soldiers who had recaptured the Texan fugitives.[46] For the first time since they had slaughtered their horses and mules, the Texans were permitted to wash their faces. Soon everything was in readiness for the triumphal entry into Saltillo. Thousands of persons were on hand to witness a second triumph of "the bravery and prowess of the Mexican soldier, and to discover the profound hate which had fastened itself in the hearts of all our countrymen against this wicked rabble" from Texas.[47]

The expected execution of the prisoners at Saltillo[48] was a factor in drawing the crowds to witness the triumphal entry of the governor. Governor Mejía had received an order from the authorities at Mexico City for the execution of all the recaptured prisoners and popular sentiment was strongly in favor of the punishment. "In the future," declared the *Boletín de San Luis Potosí,* "it will be necessary to treat them, not as prisoners of war, but as criminals disposed always to commit new crimes, in as much as they do not recognize rights other than those of violence, nor duties other than those which are imposed upon them by force. Is it not this which they wish? Has not their very conduct shown that they are not worthy of full consideration and courtesy?" Their overthrow of the guard was in no manner to be regarded as disgraceful to the Mexican soldier, but served "only to give a second triumph to the nation, to realize more the bravery and the prowess of the Mexican soldier, and to discover the profound hate which has fastened itself in the heart of all good countrymen against this wicked rabble."[49]

The *Diario del Gobierno* declared that for their haughty insolence, the

---

45. *José María de Ortega, gobernador y comandante general de departamento de Nuevo-León, a la tropa permanente, batallón y escuadrones auxiliares del mismo, que concurrieron a la reaprehensión de los colonos téjano que se fugaron del Salado, Monterrey, 13 de Marzo, 1843,* in *El Semanario Político* de_Nueva León de 16 de Marzo, 1843, reproduced in *Diario del Gobierno,* Mar. 13, 1843; Broadside, in Yale University Library, New Haven, Connecticut.

46. *Francisco Mejía, general de brigada, gobernador y comandante general é inspector de Coahuila y Téjas, a los Coahuilenses, Saltillo, Marzo 4 de 1843,* in *El Voto de Coahuila,* Mar. 4, 1843, quoted in *Diario del Gobierno,* Mar. 21, 1843.

47. *Boletín de San Luis Potosí,* Feb. 25, 1843, quoted in *Diario del Gobierno,* Feb. 28, 1843.

48. Bell, *Narrative,* p. 48.

49. *Boletín de San Luis Potosí,* Feb. 25, 1843, quoted in *Diario del Gobierno,* Feb. 28, 1843.

Texans "well deserved punishment." If the benevolent generosity and character of the Mexicans, through their most worthy president, Santa Anna, freed the Santa Fé prisoners, they cannot permit their generosity to be made fun of with impunity or the national honor outraged by prisoners under the custody of troops.[50]

At four o'clock the procession, led by Governors Mejía and Ortega and preceded by a band of music, got under way for entry of the city. The prisoners were marched through the streets of Saltillo amid the ringing of bells, the firing of crackers and skyrockets, music from "the magnificent orchestra of the city,"[51] and "much exalting by the citizens owing to our recapture," declared Canfield.[52] They were finally brought to a halt in the public square to hear Governor Mejía's speech, after which they were placed in "good quarters"[53]—their former quarters—but without anything to eat until the next morning when they were supplied with beef and bread, "rather better than common."[54]

The Texans celebrated their country's Independence Day, March 2, in prison, feasting on the fare furnished by their captors, although they were closely confined.[55] The Texan officers were kept in separate quarters, and "never allowed to speak or correspond in any manner whatsoever with the privates." "Captain Cameron and myself," wrote William F. Wilson from Perote in 1844, "were kept apart from the balance and shut in a most loathsome dungeon, without one ray of light."[56] A sentinel was stationed at every door of the buildings occupied by the Texans, and even the housetops were guarded.

While the disposition of the prisoners was under consideration, the Texans remained in quarters for three weeks, March 1 to March 21, at Saltillo. They seldom were allowed to pass the door except for a few hours in the day when they were sometimes "allowed the liberty of a small yard. After nine o'clock in the evening they were compelled to lie down and not allowed to rise again until day light."[57]

Shortly after their arrival at Saltillo, the prisoners learned that on the morning of March 1 Mejía had received an order for their execution. When news of the recapture of the prisoners reached Mexico City by express, Gen. Nicolás Bravo, president *ad interim*, sent an order to General Mejía, who had charge of the recaptured prisoners, directing "that they should at once be shot."[58] Not only had they attacked the Mexican army,

50. *Diario Del Gobierno*, Feb. 28, 1843.

51. *El Voto de Coahuila*, quoted in *Diario del Gobierno*, Mar. 21, 1843.

52. Canfield diary, Mar. 1, 1843.

53. Walker says the quarters furnished them were "very lousy" (Sibley, ed., *Samuel H. Walker's Account*, p. 55).

54. Glasscock diary, Mar, 2, 1843.

55. Bell, *Narrative*, P. 49.

56. Quoted in Wilson, *Reminiscences of Persons, Events, Record and Documents of Texian Times*, p. 7.

57. Bell, *Narrative*, p. 49.

58. Thompson, *Recollections of Mexico*, pp. 73-75; *Daily Picayune*, Apr. 4, 5, 1843.

but it was falsely reported in Mexico City that the Texans had murdered a Mexican officer.

As soon as the U.S. minister in Mexico, Waddy Thompson, learned of the order, he called on José María de Bocanegra, the minister of foreign relations, and expressed "the hope that all the privileges of prisoners of war would be extended to the Texans, and that no act of undue severity would be committed against them."[59] In reporting the interview, Thompson recorded, "He [Bocanegra] was very much excited, and it was the only instance, in all my intercourse with him, that his conduct was not dignified and courteous; for he is a very polished and amiable gentleman. He said to me: they are not American citizens, and you have, therefore, no right to interpose in their behalf. I replied: They are human beings and prisoners of war, and it is the right and the duty of all nations to see that Mexico does not violate the principles and the usages of civilized war—more particularly it is the duty of the United States to maintain those laws of usages on this Continent. He replied with much warmth, that Mexico would listen to no suggestion upon the subject, from any quarter. I rose from my seat, and said: Then, Sir, shoot them as soon as you choose, but let me tell you, that if you do you will at once involve in this war a much more powerful enemy than Texas—and took my leave."[60]

Thompson sought the assistance of the British and French ministers in Mexico in his efforts to save the lives of the Texans. In the meantime, Santa Anna returned to Mexico City on March 5 to resume direction of affairs. Finding that a new order directing that the recaptured Texans "should at once be decimated and shot as an atonement," was on the verge of being sent, he dispatched an order "to shoot all the Texans" to "remove the difficulties as to the selection of the victims."[61] However, under pressure from the principal foreign ministers at Mexico, Santa Anna revoked his order. In its place, the order to decimate them was sent.[62]

"Though the issuance of such an order seems very doubtful, there existed a belief among some of the surviving prisoners that such an order had been issued, but that it had come too late," reported John Bradley.[63] That such an order was issued appears to be improbable. Instead, it seems that an order of just the opposite intent was issued—that Santa Anna returned to his original objective—to execute all who had escaped and who had been recaptured. When he learned that the decimation had already taken place, he followed with an order for "the massacre" of all of the reapprehended Mier men, but the British and U.S. ministers "both

---

59. Thompson, *Recollections*, p. 74.

60. *Ibid.*

61. *Daily Picayune*, Apr. 5, 1843; see *New Orleans Bee* quoted in *Daily National Intelligencer*, Apr. 13, 1843.

62. *Daily Picayune*, Apr. 5, 1843.

63. Report of John Bradley in interview on November 10, 1843, with the editor of the *Telegraph*, *Telegraph and Texas Register*, Nov. 15, 1843.

waited on him and threatened to demand their passports and leave the country if it were executed," inducing him to countermand it.[64]

"It was a cold-bloodied and atrocious murder, of as gallant men as any country can boast of," declared Thompson. "The decimation of the prisoners of Mier," he said, "I regard as an act of much greater atrocity" than the needless slaughter at the Alamo and the shooting of Fannin's command, "prisoners of war under a formal capitulation. Those prisoners were not on parole, and had a perfect right to escape if they could; . . . .[65]

When Mejía received Bravo's order to shoot the prisoners who had been recaptured, he regarded it as cruel and unjustified. Mejía's feelings of humanity led him to refuse to obey the order, and for his imprudence and disobedience he was ordered arrested and removed from office by Santa Anna.[66] Canfield remarked upon Mejía's refusal to execute the prisoners: "*recollect this ye Texians*, there are not many officers under Santa Anna who would dare to disobey an order; yet Maher [Mejía] was only complying with the terms of our capitulation."[67]

Anyone who has studied the ruthlessness of Santa Anna and other high Mexican officials toward a defeated enemy knows how little encouragement was needed, if any, to order execution of prisoners. Santa Anna's bloodthirstiness, as a young officer under Gen. Joaquín de Arredondo in the suppression of the Texas Republicans in 1813; the extensive executions that followed his suppression of the rebellion in Zacatecas in 1835; the decision to take no prisoners among the combatants in the Battle of the Alamo on March 6, 1836; and the order for the execution of all prisoners taken with arms in hand in the Goliad campaign of March of that same year are clear evidence that he needed no encouragement beyond the fact that the Texans had overpowered their guard in an effort to escape, and in doing so had killed and wounded several Mexican soldiers. In his eyes, all Texans, including the Mier men, were in rebellion against the authority of Mexico, and Mexico in March 1843, recognized no legal government in Texas.

Houston did all he could with an often unruly citizenry and navy, a bankrupt treasury, and a nonexistent army to alleviate the sufferings of the Texan prisoners in Mexico. His was a difficult situation; but, according to John S. Ford, Houston "exerted every influence and resource he possessed to procure the release of the Texan prisoners."[68]

When Houston learned that a substantial portion of Somervell's army had refused to return home, followed shortly by news of the catastrophe at Mier, he sought the assistance of friendly nations and influential individuals to bring pressure on the Mexican authorities to gain the release of

---

64. Thompson, *Recollections of Mexico*, p. 74.
65. *Ibid.*, p. 73.
66. Sánchez Lamego, *The Second Mexican-Texas War*, p. 52.
67. Canfield diary, Mar. 1, 1843.
68. Ford, *Memoirs*, 2, pp. 254-75.

the prisoners, or at least, to treat them humanely. On January 24, 1843, Houston wrote to Capt. Charles Elliot, the British *chargé d'affaires* to Texas:

> The "Campaign of the people," is ended; and I think "the eyes of the blind are opened," but they will not see. In relation to this subject, I am constrained to solicit the kindness of you, should it not be out of the line of your official action that you would address her Majesty's Minister at Mexico and, bad as matters are, make this *representation.*
>
> It is true the men went without orders; and so far as that was concerned, the Government of Texas was not responsible; and the men thereby placed themselves out of the protection of the rules of war. This is granted. But the Mexican officers, by proposing terms of capitulation to the men, relieved them from the responsibility which they had incurred; and the moment that the men surrendered in accordance with the proposals of capitulation, they became prisoners of war, and were entitled to all the immunities as such, Upon this view of the subject, I base my hopes of their salvation, if it should be speedily presented through the agency of her Majesty's Minister to the Mexican Government.
>
> Should it be proper to do so, I feel assured that your kind offices will not be wanting in an early application upon this subject. This view of the subject seems to be the only feasible one which has presented itself to my mind.[69]

Houston admitted that he had encouraged retaliation by Somervell, who had marched *under authority*. Houston was powerless to use military force to free the Mier men.

In a note attached to his letter of February 5, 1843, to the Earl of Aberdeen, Elliot reported that Houston had requested that he ask the British minister in Mexico, Pakenham, "do what He can to avert dangerous consequences from them [the Mier prisoners]. The General [Houston] grants that the disorderly action of their separation from the Officer acting under the orders of this Government is of highly serious consequence to them, but presses upon the fact that there was a Capitulation, and that the Mexican Government is bound to respect it."[70]

Elliot copied from Houston's letter and transmitted it to Pakenham.[71] Upon receipt of Elliot's letter, Pakenham either showed it or transmitted a copy of it to Waddy Thompson and requested his assistance in an effort to save the lives of the Mier prisoners.

As the two foreign diplomats interceded in behalf of the Texan filibusters, there developed a "leak" of information and a garbled interpre-

---

69. Sam Houston to Captain Charles Elliot, Washington, 24th January, 1843, in *Writings of Sam Houston* 3, pp. 299-302.

70. Note attached to Charles Elliot to the Earl of Aberdeen, Galveston, Feb. 5, 1843 (Secret), in Adams, ed., *British Correspondence Concerning the Republic of Texas*, pp. 162-64.

71. Charles Elliot to Aberdeen, Galveston, June 8, 1843 (Secret), in Adams, ed., "Correspondence from the British Archives Concerning Texas, 1837-1846, in *QTSHA* 16 (Jan. 1913), pp. 318-27.

tation of what Houston had written. Thompson either revealed the substance of the extract from Houston's letter to Elliot to one or more of the Mier prisoners or by his replies to or avoidance of their questions revealed the Texas government's attitude toward their disobedience of Somervell's orders. It was only after the decimation had taken place that this information spread throughout Mexico, to the United Sates, to other countries, to Texas, even to the Texan prisoners themselves, and back to Mexico, and Houston stood accused of having repudiated the Texans who had been captured at Mier.

Several months after receiving Houston's communication regarding the Mier prisoners, Elliot informed the Earl of Aberdeen on June 8, 1843, that he had written to Pakenham at Houston's request urging him to intercede with the Mexican authorities for the protection of the Mier prisoners and that he had included in his letter "an extract from General Houston's letter upon the subject, . . . though he did not deny that the movement beyond the Rio Grande had been made upon their own responsibility."[72]

If one believes the French diplomatic representative in Texas, the leak may not have been unintentional. He reported that he had learned from President Houston that the latter had requested Isaac Van Zandt to lodge "a formal complaint concerning the hostile conduct of Mr. Waddy Thompson in Mexico in regard to General Houston himself." He said Thompson was "a bitter enemy of General Houston," and had "not hesitated to strike up a friendship with the leaders among the Texian prisoners (General Green and Colonel Fischer [*sic*]), to communicate to them all the correspondence to which their capture had given rise, and to take part in their incessant low intrigues to hold the President responsible for the cruel treatment they had received from Santa Anna."[73]

While Hutchinson, Maverick, and Jones were in Mexico City, they learned of a report that Elliot had transmitted to Richard Pakenham a request from Houston to see that the Texans taken prisoners at Mier were treated with humanity though "they had acted contrary to his (Houston's) orders in crossing the Rio Grande!"[74]

"If this news be correct," declared the editor of the *New Orleans Bee*, "it is the most brutal act of the age, and entitles Samuel Houston to the appellation par excellence of 'monster.' It is equivalent to volunteering the information to the Mexican Government, that his unfortunate countrymen in chains were a banditti and unfit objects of humane and christian treatment."[75]

---

72. Charles Elliot to the Earl of Aberdeen, K. T., Galveston. June 8, 1843 (Secret), in Adams, ed., *British Correspondence Concerning Texas*, pp. 205-07.

73. Vte J. de Cramayel to Francisco Guizot, Galveston, Nov. 13, 1843, in Barker, trans. and ed., *The French Legation in Texas* 2, pp. 482-86.

74. *New Orleans Bee*, Apr. 22 and May 8, 1843; see also *Daily Missouri Republican* (St. Louis), May 1, 1843.

75. *New Orleans Bee*, Apr. 22 and May 8, 1843.

If Houston's letter to Elliot, as alleged by his enemies, was responsible for the decimation of the Mier men who had marched into Mexican territory without orders, why was it a decimation and not an execution of *all* of the Mier men rather than limited to the escapees who had been recaptured? Under the circumstances, one can only conclude that the decimation was punishment imposed only on those who had escaped and had been recaptured and imprisoned at Saltillo by the time the order arrived. Those subsequently recaptured or who had not arrived at Saltillo before the prisoners were marched from there were not subjected to the decimation.

The most persistent and vocal of the Mier men who criticized Houston was Thomas Jefferson Green. He has left an interesting record of his experiences on the expedition, "in the writing of which," declared Eugene C. Barker and Amelia Williams, "he was probably assisted by Branch T. Archer and David G. Burnet, two of Houston's bitterest enemies."[76] After his escape from Perote Castle on July 2, 1843, and return to Texas, Green let no opportunity pass to embarrass Houston on the subject. With the publication of the Houston Papers and a more careful search of the official documents of the Republic and of the private letters of Houston and others, it is "now possible to form a more objective, and a truer estimate of Houston's actions in this matter of relief to the Mier prisoners." And it has come to be the consensus of opinion among unprejudiced, thoughtful students that whether Houston's efforts to save the Mier prisoners, relieve their sufferings and gain their freedom "were the wisest that could have been devised, it was certainly a sincerely honest effort to do something, officially and unofficially for the benefit of those who had so foolishly marched off to Mexico, to use his influence through diplomatic channels, since he was helpless because of lack of financial means, to send out military support. Most men under similar circumstances would have been paralyzed into utter inactivity."[77]

Thompson either revealed the substance of the extract from Houston's letter to Elliot to one or more of the Mier prisoners or, by his answers to or avoidance of their questions revealed to them the Texan government's attitude toward their disobedience of Somervell's orders. "I am sure that it will be a source of great surprise and concern to Mr. Pakenham," said Elliot, "and entirely contrary to the [his?] wishes that any other use has been made of it."[78]

For some time the prisoners had been displeased with Houston's Mexican policy. Since their fiasco at Mier, they had labored under a sense

---

76. *Writings of Sam Houston*, 3, p. 303, n. 2.

77. *Ibid.*

78. Charles Elliot to the Earl of Aberdeen, Galveston, June 8, 1843 (Secret), in Adams, ed., "Correspondence from the British Archives Concerning Texas, 1837-1846," *QTSHA* 15 (Jan. 1913), pp. 318-21; see also Adams, ed., *British Correspondence Concerning Texas*, pp. 205-07.

of guilt for the open violation of their country's policies. They tried to make Houston their scapegoat by claiming he did not care for their well-being. "If the prisoners who have been released by Santa Anna have reported truly the conduct of Genl. Thompson in Mexico," wrote Houston to Elliot on May 13, 1843, "he could have had but one object in view, and that was, by the return of those gentlemen to create a strong prejudice against the representative of Her Britannic Majesty in Texas, as well as the Executive, who was understood to be on terms of personal friendship with him and entertaining at the same time for his character and capacity the highest respect."[79]

Since Texas was at war with Mexico, Houston's avenue of communication with that power had to be through the assistance of other powers. He was handicapped in meeting the accusations of his critics by the necessity of keeping his actions secret if they were to be effective with Mexico, whose officials were concerned about their own image when negotiating about or with their "rebelled province."

Several months after receiving Houston's communication regarding the Mier prisoners, Elliot informed the Earl of Aberdeen on June 8, 1843, that he had written to Pakenham at Houston's request urging him to intercede with the Mexican authorities for the protection of the Mier prisoners and that he had included in his letter "an extract from General Houston's letter upon the Subject, . . . though He did not deny that the movement beyond the Rio Grande had been made upon their own responsibility."[80]

As for Houston, he had determined not to worry about the matter, and refused to comment on his reputed letter to Elliot. "Being satisfied as I am," he told Elliot, "and being assured from your intelligence, and feelings, that you would pursue no course, but one induced by the highest principles of honor and generosity, I am very much at ease."[81]

For months, Houston said nothing publicly on his Elliot letter. The editor of the *Morning Star* on June 3, 1843, commenting upon the injustice with which the Texan prisoners in Mexico were being treated, said that Houston's silence about his alleged letter to Elliot probably encouraged the Mexican despot to aggravate the cruelties and increase the sufferings of the captives. The president, he said, should have stated publicly that he considered the Mier prisoners entitled to all the rights and privileges of prisoners of war. Overlooked was the fact that the San Antonio-Dawson prisoners had neither received better treatment nor had they been considered prisoners of war; the only reason none of them had been decimated was that they had not escaped and been recaptured.

---

79. Sam Houston to Charles Elliot, Washington, May 13, 1843 (Private), *Writings of Sam Houston* 3, pp. 385-90.

80. Charles Elliot to the Earl of Aberdeen, K. T., Galveston, June 8, 1843 (Secret), in Adams, ed., *British Correspondence Concerning the Republic of Texas*, pp. 206-07.

81. Sam Houston to Charles Elliot, Washington, May 13, 1843 (Private), in *Writings of Sam Houston* 3, pp. 385-90.

Finally, at the Presbyterian Church in Huntsville on November 8, 1843, Houston defended himself against the accusations of his enemies.[82]

> Assailed as I have been, and my motives misrepresented not by the patriotic and honest multitude, but by the malignant and mischievous, their stabs inflict no wounds upon me, but are too efficient to blast their country and traduce its character abroad. . . . I am a traitor to my country: "*bribed* by Santa Anna's gold." I am denounced as a villain, a drunkard, a blackguard and a wretch. . . . My political opponents would at one time have been willing to torture their victim, if they had him in their power. And for what? For saying to Santa Anna, as was alleged, in regard to the prisoners lately taken: these men have gone to Mexico without my orders; without the authority of government. The accusation is absurd. Would mercy to them have injured me? I asked for no mercy for them. No matter under what circumstances they went, their capitulation had brought them within the pale of prisoners of war. I demanded it as a right, that they should be treated as such. So did the government of England and France, and the United States. . . .
>
> Fellow Citizens—I cannot think that very fair. I think the course pursued was better calculated at the head of the government, than truth towards the world, or to benefit our friends in captivity."[83]

Houston declared that he had heard that it had been said on "high authority 'I had received a bribe; I was to sell my country to England; I was to be Governor-General of Texas.' And all this for five thousand pounds sterling! What! sell my country for British Gold?"[84] He referred to the excitement of 1842 and to those who wished to be heroes in Mexico. "We have seen horses, with our heroes astride of them, whipping on their sore side to battle. When they reached the enemy's border, what did they do? They were taken prisoners, and then, the President must be the 'rascal and traitor.'"[85]

In the prison camp in Mexico, occasionally stragglers would be brought in. Among these were William and Carter Sargeant, who had deserted Cameron's group and visited a Mexican *rancho* professing friendship to Mexico and saying that they had "been forced to fight" the Mexicans at Salado.[86] The Sargeant brothers had been in town several days in prison before the arrival of the main body of Mier men. On March 3 they were transferred to the cells of their comrades and placed in irons. On the same day Robert G. Waters and James N. Torrey were brought in and put

---

82. *The Weekly Citizen* (Austin), Dec. 9, 1843. Extensive extracts of this address appeared in the *Galveston City Gazette*, Nov. 25, 1843; see also *Writings of Sam Houston* 3, pp. 442-55.

83. *Writings of Sam Houston* 3, pp. 447-48.

84. *Ibid.*, p. 453.

85. *Ibid.*, pp. 459-74; *Journals of the House of Representatives of the Republic of Texas*, 8th Cong., 1st Sess., pp. 13-28.

86. Canfield diary, Mar. 1, 1843.

in irons.[87] On March 5, ten more Texans, including John Sweizy, were added to the ranks of the recaptured. Peter A. Ackerman had fled to within sixty miles of the Rio Grande when he was retaken and brought in on March 7.[88] On March 18, Joseph Watkins and E. D. Wright were added to the group. They had been picked up by the Mexicans near Monclova, where they had "laid down to die for want of water,"[89] and had been carried to Cuatro Ciénegas, "where they were very kindly treated after first being robbed of everything they had." From Watkins and Wright their comrades learned of the death of A. J. Lewis, who had died for want of water.[90]

On March 18 the Mexicans gave up the search for missing Texans, assuming that those unaccounted for had either died in the mountains or had made good their escape. Of the 191 who fled from Salado under Captain Cameron, 177 were recaptured and collected at Saltillo, from where they were soon to be marched south once more. Seven were believed to have perished in the mountains and five made good their escape to Texas, and others were eventually reapprehended and later joined the main body of prisoners.

On March 6 the prisoners received a gift of tobacco from a local citizen, and on Sunday, March 12, they were visited by several Americans who were watched closely and were not permitted to talk to the prisoners except through an interpreter.[91] The reason for the visit seems to have been to observe the condition of the prison. Stapp, probably more correctly, gives a different version of the visit of the Americans. He reported that several American wagoners from Zacatecas visited the prison on the 12th. They "informed us, with less sensibility than they would probably have displayed in recounting the loss of a horse, that an order had arrived directing every tenth man of us to be shot. The brutes seemed to consider it a special privilege to be first to communicate the tidings, thinking, no doubt, it would prove a decided mitigation of the blow to have it come from Anglo-Saxon lips, and ciphering out the exact amount of the propitiatory sacrifice, they indulged in a few strictures upon our folly in being recaptured, and went away. Of course we put no faith in their assertions, as it was uncorroborated by the guard, who were ever too delighted in harassing us to omit such an opportunity, had it been true."[92]

Five of the sick prisoners accepted baptism by a Catholic priest, apparently with the thought of getting "something better to eat."[93] Little

---

87. Sibley, ed., *Samuel H. Walker's Account*, p. 55.

88. Walker says he was brought in on March 8.

89. Sibley, ed., *Samuel H. Walker's Account*, p. 57.

90. *Ibid.*; Nance, *Attack and Counterattack*, p. 635.

91. Glasscock diary, Mar. 4-21, 1843.

92. Stapp, *Prisoners of Perote*, p. 70. Canfield described the visitors as American merchants who were on a trading expedition to Chihuahua, "who came to take a look at us" (Canfield diary, Mar. 4-21, 1843).

93. Canfield diary, Mar. 4-21, 1843; Bell, *Narrative*, p. 49; Sibley, ed., *Samuel H. Walker's Account*, p. 56.

amelioration of their condition resulted; although they received considerable attention from the local citizens, they earned no special favors from their guards.[94]

On March 9 the prisoners petitioned the governor for additional rations, and "in addition to the one meal a day . . . [they, thereafter,] got coffee in the evening." As the Mexicans at Saltillo were not very hospitable, some of the Texans devised an ingenious scheme to get more and better food. A "Blank Book" was obtained, and they let it be known among their guard that a history of the "Campaign" was to be written by one of their number as soon as they gained their freedom, and that "all those Mexicans whose names were placed in the Book, were to be spoken of in the highest terms." The idea "took." There was "much anxiety on the part of a number of gullible Mexicans to get their names in "the Book," and thereafter they unstintingly furnished the prisoners with better and increased quantities of food and drink, adding significantly to their comfort.[95]

On the whole, the captives were treated with consideration by the citizens of Saltillo during their confinement there, and by even some of the officers belonging to the army. A few of the citizens, especially "one Mexican man and a couple of pious women," attended to the Texan sick and were credited with saving the lives of several by the kindness and attentiveness shown to the unfortunate whose own physician was not permitted to attend them.[96]

The Mexican authorities conducted an investigation of the escape of the Texans at Salado. On February 21, 1843, General Ampudia, commandant-general of the Department of Tamaulipas, ordered Capt. Manuel Montero to conduct a summary investigation relative to the escape of the Mier men.[97] Second Lt. Ignacio Huerta of the 7th Infantry Regiment was named secretary to the investigation and was sworn on February 22.[98] The investigation began and was completed on February 23. It was the opinion of Captain Montero, as examining judge, that Commandant Gen. José María Ortega was to blame for having sent off the prisoners with an insufficient escort and that Lieutenant Colonel Barragán, who commanded the squadron, was to blame for not maintaining proper discipline among his troops.[99]

Capt. Octaviano Huerta, commandant of the First Battalion, 12th

94. Sibley, ed., *Samuel H. Walker's Account*, p. 56; Stapp, *Prisoners of Perote*, p. 70.

95. Canfield diary, Mar. 4-21, 1843.

96. Bell, *Narrative*, p. 49.

97. *Pedro de Ampudia a Captain Manuel Montero, Matamoros, Febrero 21 de 1843*, photostat of original in San Jacinto Museum of History.

98. *Pedro de Ampudia a D. Ignacio Huerta, Matamoros, Febrero 21 de 1843*, appointing him secretary to the hearing concerning the escape of the Mier prisoners, photostat of letter signed in San Jacinto Museum of History.

99. *Man¹ Montero al Comandante General del departmento [de Tamaulipas], Matamoros, Febrero 23 de 1843*. Photostat in San Jacinto Museum of History of autograph letter signed.

Regiment of Permanent Infantry, testified to the disorder which he observed among the escort troops from the time they left Monterrey until the prisoners escaped. He emphasized the indifference shown by Lieutenant Colonel Barragán toward the situation.[100] He observed that the infantry troops, on leaving the Plaza de Monterrey, did not open their ranks in order to place the prisoners in the center, that Barragán allowed the prisoners great freedom, and that he saw seventy of the cavalrymen from the *defensores* of the Villa de Morelos returning home and Barragán had noted in the presence of the prisoners that return, which he should not have done. Furthermore he had witnessed at the Paso de los Muertos only half of the force guarding the prisoners. The remainder of the rear guard, tired of carrying their muskets, had stowed them on the baggage train on which some of the prisoners had mounted. He observed that the majority of the infantry who guarded the prisoners were seated on the ground with their arms at their side while the others were conversing with the prisoners and Lieutenant Colonel Barragán. Huerta's testimony was reinforced by depositions given by Lt. Col. Gil Guillén and Capt. Manuel Ciriaco de Ayala.[101]

At Saltillo, Alfred S. Thurmond, William Moore, and John Brennan, who served as interpreters, were taken before a Mexican board of inquiry on March 19-20, and "examined under oath with the most rigid strictness, touching all the circumstances connected with . . . [the] charge upon the guard"[102] and the conduct of Colonel Barragán. The evidence collected by the board of inquiry was intended to be used in a court-martial of Colonel Barragán and others. He was to be tried not only on "a charge of carelessness, but actual connivance in our escape," reported Stapp.[103] According to Canfield, the purpose of the inquiry was "to ascertain who took the lead in the charge" on the guard.[104] On the question of "carelessness," Stapp did not comment; but on the charge of "connivance" in the escape of the Texans, he declared that "there was not only no foundation whatever in fact, but not the remotest ground for suspicion." If Barragán's troops had been true to him, few of the Texans would have survived the conflict. Double the number of the Mexican guard at Salado "would not have deterred our attempt, nor repelled our attack, had they reflected the cowardice of those whom we did disperse."[105]

Barragán was tried before a court-martial on charges of "carelessness" and "connivance" in the escape of the Texans at Salado, found guilty, and

---

100. Deposition of Octaviano Huerta, dated Matamoros, Feb. 22, 1843. Photostat in San Jacinto Museum of History of document signed.

101. Deposition of Lt. Col. Gil Guillen dated Matamoros, Feb. 23, 1843; and Deposition of Capt. Manuel Ciriaco de Ayala dated Matamoros, Feb. 22, 1843. Photostats in San Jacinto Museum of History of documents signed.

102. Stapp, *Prisoners of Perote*, p. 70.

103. *Ibid.*, pp. 70-71.

104. Canfield diary, Mar. 4-21, 1843.

105. Stapp, *Prisoners of Perote*, p. 71.

106. *Ibid.*, pp. 70-71.

demoted.[106] He was certainly not guilty of the latter charge. By removing Barragán from the service, "Santa Anna and the vile agents of his work," commented Stapp, got rid of a man of honor and humanity who stood as a "reproach upon their own cruelty and pusillanimity."

On March 21 the First Regiment of Cavalry under Col. Dios de Ortiz, an esteemed and generous officer, arrived from San Luis Potosí. On the following morning, amid the shedding of tears on the part of sympathetic Mexican friends over the fate that they well knew awaited some of the Texans at Salado, the march toward Mexico City, 800 miles away, resumed. Their guard consisted of thirty infantrymen wearing "Red Caps" from their previous guard at Salado. To these were added at Saltillo two full companies of cavalry of 160 men under Colonel Ortiz. The "Red Caps" were commanded by Col. Domingo Huerta. Their guard was much smaller than when they had come over the same route previously; however, the Texans were now in irons and many were induced to believe the false representations of the Mexican officers that they would all soon be liberated and sent home. By such delusions the guard sought to allay the fears of the Texans and stave off another attempt at escape, even though the Texans were now shackled two and two.

The greater portion of the prisoners were in poor condition. Almost all of the men were without blankets and many without sufficient clothing. A good many lacked shoes or sandals, and blood trickled from their feet "as they crippled over the stones that gashed them at every step."[107] Their iron handcuffs caused most excruciating pain.

During the day, the weather was extremely hot, but the nights were fairly cool. "This suffering under the manifold evils of heat and cold alternately with hunger, thirst and fatigue, as well as being closely fettered and enduring . . . stripes inflicted by their cruel and relentless guard, it is no matter of astonishment," declared Bell, "that some should wish, as they did, that the enemy would shoot them and thus put a final termination to their lives."[108]

---

107. *Ibid.*, pp. 70-71.
108. Bell, *Narrative*, p. 50.

CHAPTER 17

The Death Lottery

As THEY MARCHED SOUTH, the prisoners camped again at such previous sites as Rancho Agua Nueva, twenty miles below Saltillo; the next day the march began early in the morning and after marching thirty-six miles they reached Rancho Encarnación and were quartered in a large church. On March 24 they reached Rancho San Salvador, distant thirty-three miles, where their handcuffs were inspected and the men, including the sick, who until then were unironed, were ironed in pairs—*dos-a-dos,*[1] causing the prisoners "to suspect that something was wrong yet we hoped otherwise," declared Walker; and on the fourth day after leaving Saltillo, Rancho Salado, twenty miles from Rancho San Salvador, in the bleak mountains about 113 miles below Saltillo, was reached at one on the afternoon of Friday, March 25, after a tiring march.[2]

The prisoners observed several Mexicans digging a ditch, and Henry Whaling remarked to "Bigfoot" Wallace, standing near him, "That ditch is for us."[3] Before being penned the Texans were permitted to wash and to drink all the water they wanted from a tank supplied from water wells while a group of women rejoiced at the recapture of the "Texian Devils." "This dismal farm-house, so late the scene of our triumphant emancipation, was now destined to become the theatre of one of the most cowardly and brutal murders ever enacted within the precincts of the robber-haunted region that surrounded it,"[4] Canfield would later write.

After refreshing themselves, the Texans were herded into their old

---

1. Sibley, ed., *Samuel H. Walker's Account*, p. 57.
2. W.F. McMath to Mr. McMath, Esq., McMath's P. O., Tuscaloosa Co., Ala., [dated] Mexico, April 29, 1843, in *Texas Magazine* 2, pp. 453-54, says the time of arrival was 1:30 P.M.; Sibley, ed., *Samuel H. Walker's Account*, p. 57, gives the hour of arrival as 2:00 P.M.; Stapp, *Prisoners of Perote*, p. 71, says *Hacienda Salado* was reached at 3:00 P.M.
3. Quoted in Sowell, *The Life of Bigfoot Wallace*, p. 23.
4. Canfield diary, Mar. 25, 1843.

283

quarters. "On our arrival," recorded Canfield, "a violent whirlwind occurred, which with the presence of some fresh troops, and a Catholic priest was considered a bad omen."[5] An extra guard, three deep, was immediately placed on the wall surrounding the courtyard into which the prisoners were conducted.

It will be recalled that there were two courtyards in the complex of buildings at Salado. The prisoners were placed in the smaller one behind the larger courtyard through which one entered the latter from the outside. The Mexican infantry was stationed in the larger courtyard, and the "Red Caps" occupied the building which formed the wall on the west side. On entering their former quarters, the weary, handcuffed Texans were ordered to sit "upon the filthy floor of the shed that ran around the enclosure."[6]

The morning had been "clear and beautiful and the noon warm to sultriness"; but a few miles before their arrival at the *rancho,* the sky had become "suddenly overcast, and fierce gusts of wind came whistling along the plain, blinding . . . [them] with clouds of sand, and whirling the heavy leathern caps of the cavalry from their heads as lightly as though they were children's bonnets."[7] While neither action nor communication from the guard had given cause for suspicion, the somber atmosphere under which the prisoners entered the compound, the military precision of the guard, and the weather "inspired a presentiment of approaching evil in the minds of most" of the prisoners. Soon after they reached shelter, the tempest began to lull and their suspicions subsided with it.

At two o'clock a group of Mexican officers led by Colonel Huerta instead of Colonel Ortiz entered the compound and took a position on the opposite side of the low wall separating the two compounds. Colonel Ortiz so detested the task he had been ordered to carry out that he withheld "his presence from any part of the spectacle."[8] "Arrayed in the gaudy ensigns of militia authority," Huerta approached the wall, holding a piece of paper in his hand, and directed his interpreter to summon the prisoners to rise and form in double file in the rear of their own officers.

Many were the conjectures as to what the paper contained. Some even thought it contained an order for their release, as no second order had been received enforcing the one that General Mejía had refused to carry out at Saltillo.[9] "A few, therefore, of the more sanguine, pushed their way into the circle" forming "and bent their eager eyes on the" officer, "half expecting his communication to be a mandate" for their release.[10] Huerta began to read rapidly in Spanish the "Supreme Order" of March 13, 1843.

---

5. *Ibid.*
6. Stapp, *Prisoners of Perote*, p. 71; Canfield's diary, Mar. 25, 1843.
7. Stapp, *Prisoners of Perote*, p. 71.
8. *Ibid.*, p. 77.
9. Duval, *Big-Foot Wallace*, p. 221.
10. Stapp, *Prisoners of Perote*, p. 72.

When he finished, "the interpreter, in broken and tremulous tones," announced that it was a decree from the Supreme Government of Mexico of March 13, 1843,[11] directing that the reapprehended Texans should be returned to Rancho Salado, where every tenth man, "for the offense committed at that place on the 11th of February," reported Walker, in attempting to escape by using violence against their guard, was to be shot.[12] In accordance with his instructions, the interpreter, as if to show the leniency and most magnanimous spirit of the benevolent government of Mexico, informed the prisoners further "that *all* had been sentenced to the same fate, but the *humane* government had been graciously pleased to commute the just claim to the decimal exaction."[13] Lots were to be drawn at once, with the execution to follow immediately thereafter.

There were then at Hacienda Salado 176 of the 191 who had fled from Salado the month before.[14] Seventeen must die. Seventeen black beans[15] were placed in an earthen jar with 159 white ones, which were actually more of a yellow cast than white. The men were to draw in the order in which their names appeared on the Mexican's roll of the prisoners.[16]

The prisoners stood stunned by this news, and "a thrill of horror ran through the captive's souls as this sentence was pronounced by the interpreter, but expressed only in stifled murmurs."[17] "So entirely unexpected was this murderous announcement, so atrocious in its character, and so inhuman in the haste of its consummation, that a stuper seemed to pervade the whole assembly, not a word escaping from the lips of any for more than a minute."[18] As no second order had been received at Saltillo, as far as the Texans knew, except the statement made by the American wagoneers, many had become hopeful that some act of clemency might be in the offing, since Governor Mejía had refused to carry out the order to execute all of the prisoners. Soon, however, "a low clatter of the handcuffs was . . . heard, as some of the most desperate of . . . [the prisoners sought] to free themselves from their shackles."[19] The Mexican officers ordered the

---

11. *José M. Rincón a Escmo. Sr. Ministro de guerra y marina, Comandancia general del departamento de San Luis Potosí, San Luis Potosí, San Luis Potosí, Abril 1º de 1843 (Número 733)*, in *El Cosmopolita*, Apr. 19, 1843.

12. Sibley, ed., *Samuel H. Walker's Account*, p. 57.

13. Stapp, *Prisoners of Perote*, p. 72.

14. Canfield's diary, March 25, 1843; Stapp, *Prisoners of Perote*, p. 72.

15. The Alamo Museum, San Antonio, Texas, has a "white bean" 7/8" long and about 1/2" wide, reported to have been drawn by Anthony Owen. There was no Anthony Owen on the Mier Expedition, but there was a John Owen, who died in Mexico in 1843. There is little likelihood of it being an authentic bean drawn at Hacienda Salado, for the men did not keep the bean they drew, and the author has seen no claim by any prisoner of having picked up a bean after the drawing. The beans, both black and white, were laid out on the table in rows after each drawing and an accurate count kept by the Mexican officer supervising the drawing.

16. Stapp, *Prisoners of Perote*, p. 73.

17. Bell, *Narrative*, p. 51.

18. Stapp, *Prisoners of Perote*, p. 72.

19. *Ibid.*

Texans "to fall back within the shed, and the doorway or gate to the compound, and the top of the sunken wall, bristled with the muzzles of musquets." The Texans realized that in their weak and shackled condition resistance was hopeless and that "no alternative was left but to submit to the fate which Heaven in its wisdom might alter,"[20] exhibited their bravery by resignation and fortitude. "If we had known it or anticipated it," said Walker, "we would have made another attack on the guard at Saltillo, but it is now too late."[21]

While the prisoners were arranged in an extended line for the drawing, a Mexican subaltern, accompanied by a soldier, entered the yard bearing a bench and an earthen jar. The bench was placed in front of the officer who had read the order, and the earthen jar was placed on it. Several "officers stationed themselves near the earthen pot, to overlook and superintend the lottery."[22] One of the officers, bearing two bags of beans, commenced counting out the number of required white (159) and black (17) beans. He placed the white beans in the jar and then put the black ones on top. The jar was not shaken. A bandana (or handkerchief)[23] was folded and thrown over the jar. The officer in charge announced that if any man drew more than one bean and one of them happened to be a black one, he would be regarded as having drawn a black bean and would be shot.

Everything having been arranged for the lottery, a list of the names of the prisoners taken when they were recaptured was placed in the hands of the interpreter. The Texans, joined two and two by iron handcuffs,[24] were formed in a line with their officers in front.

The names of the officers were called first, beginning with the leader of the break, Ewen Cameron. Cameron is alleged to have remarked: "Well, boys, we have to draw, let's be at it."[25] As he stepped forward, William F. Wilson, who had been standing near the jar when the beans were put in and had observed that the black beans were placed on top, whispered to Cameron to "draw from the bottom"[26] or, as others phrased it, "Delve deep, Capt'n" or "Dip deep, Captain." Cameron stepped forward and without hesitation thrust his hand under the piece of cloth covering the jar, which was held high so that no one could see into it,[27] and drew out a white bean and remained silent.

Cameron was followed by the other officers. Col. William F. Wilson,

---

20. Bell, *Narrative*, p. 51.

21. Sibley, ed., *Samuel H. Walker's Account*, p. 58.

22. Duval, *Big-Foot Wallace*, p. 222.

23. Stapp says a handkerchief was placed over the jar (or "crock," as he called it). Statement made by Stapp in *Telegraph and Texas Register*, May 28, 1845.

24. Report of Orlando C. Phelps in *Daily Picayune*, May 24, 1843.

25. Green, *Mier Expedition*, p. 170.

26. Wilson, *Reminiscences of Persons, Events, Records and Documents of Texian Times*, pp. 5-7.

27. Sowell, *Early Settlers and Indian Fighters of Southwest Texas*, p. 73; "The Life of Big-foot Wallace," in *Frontier Times* 5 (Dec. 1927), p. 120.

chained to Cameron, likewise drew from the bottom, and whispered to Captain Ryon to do the same; Ryon drew with the same result, passing the word to Judge Fenton M. Gibson, Capt. William M. Eastland, and so on down the list. All of these drew the "bean of life," except Captain Eastland, who was handcuffed to Israel Canfield.[28] Eastland was the first to draw a black bean.

After the officers had drawn, the jar was given a vigorous shake and the interpreter began to call the names of the others standing in line to await their turn to draw. As a man's name was called, he stepped forward accompanied by the man handcuffed to him.[29] Thus, most of the Texans made two visits to the bench upon which the bean jug rested—once when his name was called, and again when his companion's name was called, unless in the first instance he happened to draw a black bean. According to the procedure, if the bean was black, the handcuffs that fastened the man drawing it to his companion were immediately taken off[30] and he was passed into the adjoining high-walled courtyard,[31] where a body of armed infantrymen was stationed and a Catholic priest occasionally sprinkled the earth with Holy Water to remove the pollution caused by the presence of "heretics." The condemned man was then chained to another man who had drawn a black bean.[32]

The Texans stepped forward with steady nerves to take their chance for life or death. "There was no shout of gladnes or marked change of the coutenance by those that fortune favored," reported an eye-witness. They "appeared to exhibit the same composure."[33]

The only exception was one man who was so upset by the thought of drawing a black bean that he wrung his hands and told those nearest him that he was confident he would draw a black bean. When his name was called, he refused to go until forced to do so by the bayonets of soldiers. When he arrived at the earthen jar he hesitated so long in withdrawing his hand from the vessel that a Mexican officer standing nearby "pricked him with his sword to make him withdraw it."[34] Removing his hand, he found

28. Canfield diary, June 18-July 29, 1843; Edgar Fremont Imle, "An Abstract of Biographical Data in the Texas Supreme Court Records, 1840 to 1857," M.A. thesis, University of Texas, 1937.

29. Wallace and Sensebaugh were chained together at the time of the drawing. "Life of Bigfoot Wallace," in *Frontier Times* 5 (Dec. 1927), p. 120, reprinted from "A Pamphlet Written by A. J. Sowell in 1899, and Its Publication Authorized by William A. A. Wallace, the Noted Frontier Character."

30. W. F. McMath was chained to Major J. D. Cocke, who drew a black bean. W. F. McMath, Surgeon, T. A., to Mr. McMath [of] McMath's P. O., Tuscaloosa County, Alabama, U.S.A., in *The Texas Magazine* 2, pp. 453-54; see also Bell, *Narrative*, pp. 51-52.

31. Report of Orlando C. Phelps in New Orleans *Daily Picayune*, quoted in *Northern Standard*, June 29, 1843.

32. "The Life of Bigfoot Wallace," in *Frontier Times* 5 (Dec. 1927), p. 120.

33. Letter of An Eye-Witness Participant, published in the *Planter* (Columbia), and copied by the *Northern Standard*, Feb. 10, 1844.

34. Duval, *Big-Foot Wallace*, pp. 226-27; Sowell, *Early Settlers and Pioneer Fighters of Southwest Texas* 1, p. 74.

that a fatal bean had been drawn. Turning "deadly pale," his eyes rested on it for a few minutes, but he resigned himself to his fate and never uttered another word.

The individual to whom Wallace was chained was named Sensebaugh, and was, therefore, required to draw before his companion. "Captain Wallace says," reported Sowell, "if there was ever a Christian it was this man." He prayed for himself and "Bigfoot" that they might be spared. "He drew a white bean, and afterwards, amid clanking chains in the dark dungeon of Perote, prayed and sang hymns, and thanked God that it was as well with him as it was." "It was generally believed," reported Sowell, "that Bigfoot Wallace drew two beans at Salado; that one of his comrades, a young fellow," expressed such great fear that he would draw a black bean, that Wallace gave him his white bean, "which he had just drawn," and "said he would take another chance." Sowell asked the old captain about this; he said: "No I never drew but one, and had no idea of giving it away. I could not have done so if I wished, for I heard a Mexican officer say that there would be no swapping of beans when the Beard brothers were talking about doing so, and I suppose it was from this incident that the story started in regard to me." Sowell says that Wallace told him that when he went up to draw, "he stepped up quickly, and reached for the pitcher [jar], but his hand was so large he had some difficulty, and had to squeeze his hand down to the beans."[35]

Giving further details of his drawing, Wallace said,

> I will confess frankly that when I put my hand into that pot, a spasm of fear or dread sent a momentary chill to my heart. In observing those before me I had noted that the white beans were a trifle larger than the black ones. It may have been purely imaginary, but I eventually decided by it in my choice of a bean. When I first put my hand in the pot I took up several beans at once in my fingers and endeavored to distinguish their colors by the touch, but they all felt precisely alike. I droped them and picked up two more and after fingering them for a moment, I thought one seemed larger than the other and I drew it forth. It was a white one, but not a very white one, and when I cast may eyes upon it, it appeared to me to be as black as the ace of spades. I felt certain that my fate had been sealed, but when I handed it to the Mexican officer, who received them as they were drawn out, I saw that he put it on the wall with the white beans and not in his waistcoat pocket, as he had done with the black ones. I knew I was safe.[36]

Robert Beard was too ill and exhausted from the march from Saltillo to stand in line and to walk up to draw. It is reported that he requested his brother, should the latter draw a black bean and he a white one, to ex-

---

35. Quoted in Ed. Kilman and Louis W. Kemp, *Texas Musketeers: Stories of Early Texas Battles and Their Heroes*, p. 359.

36. "The Life of Bigfoot Wallace," in *Frontier Times* 5 (Dec. 1927), p. 129; Green, *Mier Expedition*, p. 171.

change with him. Wallace, however, says they could not have made the exchange, even if they had desired to do so. When Robert Beard's name came up, the jar was carried by a soldier to where he lay on a blanket.

There is a story that Samuel McFall drew twice. Mark V. Fleming, who knew several of the Mier men, reported that McFall "first drew a white bean, which he gave to a minister in the group who was lamenting that if he drew a black bean, he would never see his family again, saying, 'Here take this; I am a gambler, I will get another white bean,' and he did," drawing a second time.[37] This story is completely false. The procedures under which the drawing took place would not have permitted a man to draw twice or to give or exchange his bean with another.

Woodland reported many years later that William Wynn, whose name was near the end of the list, drew a black bean and then attempted to deny "his name in order, if possible, to have another draw, but this did not save him."[38] When it came Van Vechten's time to draw, he kept his hand in the jar "too long to suit the officer in charge and he forced him to withdraw it. This made 'Tonkaway' so mad that he cursed loudly and pulled out a lock of his own hair,"[39] creating a hair style resembling that of a Tonkawa Indian, and giving Van Vechten the nickname that he carried through his imprisonment and later life.

After each drawing, the bean was handed to the officer supervising the drawing and the name of the individual and the color of his bean was entered on a new list.[40] The beans were laid out in rows on the bench by the officer. Often a man would plunge his hand into the jar and sift the beans between his fingers, hoping by touch to distinguish the black ones from the white.

"Boys," exclaimed one of the Texas "dare-devils," "this beats raffling all to pieces."[41] "Talking" Bill Moore announced, "Boys, I had rather draw for a Spanish horse and lose him." James A. Glasscock later reported that when he went up to draw he was "shivering."[42] Maj. James D. Cocke, to whom William F. McMath was ironed, on drawing a black bean, held it up between his thumb and forefinger and with a contemptuous smile declared, "Boys, I told you so; I never failed in my life to draw a prize."[43] Thomas L. Jones, who also drew one of the ill-fated beans, asked the interpreter to "tell the officers to look upon men who were not afraid to die for

37. D. K. Doyle, "He Knew Survivors of the Mier Expedition: Mark V. Fleming of Comanche Tells of the Men Who Drew Black," 9, 1927; and substantially repeated in *The Cattleman* (Fort Worth) 34, no. 6 (Nov. 1947), pp. 9-13, 42-43.

38. Sowell, "Benjamin Z. Boone: Story of One of the Survivors of the Famous Expedition," in *Dallas Morning News*, Aug. 4, 1901.

39. Stapp, *Prisoners of Perote*, p. 73; *The Western Chronicle* (Sutherland Springs, Texas), Nov. 2, 1877.

40. Smithwick, *Evolution of a State*, p. 275. According to Smithwick, Taney thought the white beans were the larger.

41. Quoted in Sowell, *Early Settlers and Indian Fighters of Southwest Texas*, p. 74.

42. José María Rodríguez, *Memoirs of Early Texas*, 2nd ed., p. 19.

43. Quoted in Green, *Mier Expedition*, p. 171.

their country."[44] "I am prepared," announced James M. Ogden, as he handed his black bean to the Mexican officer. Henry Whaling declared: "Well, they don't make much off me any how for I know I have killed twenty-five of the yellow-bellies."[45] He demanded his supper, saying "they shall not cheat me out of it." He was supplied with a meal of good mutton stew and beans, after which he smoked a cigar. Most of the condemned men would not eat the supper supplied them. Torrey, declaring his willingness to meet his fate, turned to one of the officers and reminded him that after the Battle of San Jacinto his family had taken one of the Mexican lads who had been captured and had "raised and educated him, and this is our requittal."[46]

Several of the Mexican officers appeared to be deeply affected by the solemnity of the gruesome scene they were witnessing. There was little doubt that they would have rejoiced if the orders for the decimation and execution could have been countermanded. It must be said that there were other Mexican officers who "leaned forward over the crock, to catch a first glimpse of the decree it uttered, as though they had heavy wagers upon the result."[47] Especially was this the case with "one little swarthy babooned-visaged chap" with a "devilish grin" who constantly sought to commiserate the individual who might hesitate in his drawing by saying: "'Take your time, my child; don't hurry yourself, my boy, be careful poor fellow'; and 'you know if you get a black bean you will be taken out and shot in ten minutes,' or, when the black bean was drawn, he would exclaim, 'Ah! that's unfortunate, but better luck next time.'"[48]

When the last black bean was drawn, three men had not yet drawn, but were never called upon to do so, as the officer turned over the jar and three white beans fell out.[49] Martin C. Wing was the last to draw a black bean. In the interval before his execution he referred often to the fact that at home he had been very religious, "but had left the beaten track of Christianity and gone sadly astray, which fact seemed to trouble him a great deal,"[50] as he now contemplated meeting his "Maker" or the "Devil."

As soon as the drawing was completed, the Mexican officers carefully counted the beans which had been drawn and checked the total number against the list of prisoners. The victims' names were read, and their persons scrutinized. The doomed men in the adjoining compound, with their

44. *Ibid.*, pp. 172-73.

45. *Ibid.*, p. 172.

46. *Ibid.*

47. Stapp, *Prisoners of Perote*, p. 73.

48. Duval, *Big-Foot Wallace*, p. 225; Sowell, *Early Settlers and Indian Fighters of Southwest Texas*, p. 74; McCaleb, *The Mier Expedition*, p. 79.

49. Sowell, *Early Settlers and Indian Fighters of Southwest Texas*, p. 75. Those who did not draw, according to Wallace, were John Brennan, Alfred S. Thurmond, and William B. Middleton. In W. A. A. Wallace to Miss Nora C. Franklin, Big Foot, Sept. 24, 1888, in "Letters of Big Foot Wallace," *Frontier Times* 8 (June 1931), pp. 417-18.

50. Sowell, *Early Settlers and Indian Fighters of Southwest Texas*, p. 75; idem, *The Life of Big-Foot Wallace*, p. 24.

interpreter (Thurmond), were placed in a small private room, and any of their fellow prisoners whom they wished to see were permitted to visit them. At the request of the doomed men, Quartermaster Gibson, Captain Ryon, Robert Smith, Trahern, Canfield, Stapp, Cameron, and possibly several others visited them.[51] The condemned were furnished with pen, ink, and paper to write to friends and relatives.

The visitors found some of the men eating their "last supper." Several were writing letters. As far as is known, only two of the letters written on this occasion have survived. Robert H. Dunham from Montgomery County scribbled this note to his mother:

<blockquote>

Mexico

Dear Mother

I write to you under the most awful feelings that a sone ever addressed a mother for in half hour my doom will be finished on earth for I am doomed to die by the hands of the Mexicans for our late attempt to escape the order issued by Santa Anna that every tenth man should be shot we drew lots I was one of the unfortunates I cannot say any thing more I die I hope with firmness may god bless you and may he in this my last hour forgive and pardon all my sins A D Headenberge will should he [live] be abl[e] to inform you farewell your affectionate sone

R H Dunham[52]

</blockquote>

Another farewell letter was written by James Masterson Ogden, cousin of Duncan Campbell Ogden, one of the Béxar prisoners. The letter was apparently written to someone named Clay in Kentucky:

<blockquote>

Clay, tell my friends that I die like a Christian thanks to Meriwether, a Methodist preacher. He has been my friend. He stripped to clothe me, he starved that I might eat. He is a relation of your neighbors.

Tell my friends I wish my old friend Crouch to preach a sermon to my friends for me and tell them I wish them all to meet me in heaven. Tell my sisters I wish them all to meet me in heaven. Tell my mother not to grieve for me, for the friend that I love is with me and my God will not forsake me. Give my love to all, to Mrs. Meriwhethr's family and old Crouch and tell them to meet me in heaven.

To Meriwether I am indebted for the favor of dying with my hands untied. Farewell, all farewell.

James Ogden[53]

</blockquote>

Cameron offered his life in place of those of the doomed men, but the

---

51. S. H. Walker to A. Sidney Johns[t]on, Prison Santiago, City of Mexico, May 4, 1843, in Army Papers (Republic), Tx-A.

52. R. H. Dunham to Mother, Mexico, [March 25, 1843], original MS, Alamo Museum, San Antonio, Texas.

53. Ogden's letter is reproduced in Wade, comp., *Notes and Fragments of the Mier Expedition* 1, pp. 146-47.

request was denied. The priest of Cedral, Luis G. Medina, was notified on March 24 that on the following day seventeen of the Texan prisoners who had fled from Salado would be *"decapitar"* ("beheaded"; "executed") in the Hacienda del Salado, and that he should be present to administer last rites to them and to receive their bodies for burial. Padre Medina was joined by Padre Don José Juan Ruemagor, who had come from Saltillo. Padre Medina reports that at 2:30 in the afternoon of March 25 he received those who were to be executed in the *capilla* (chapel) of the *hacienda*. Father Ruemagor sought to offer the "heretics" extreme absolution, but his advances were rejected.[54] Medina says that he found among the condemned some who were Catholics, others who were Protestants, and some who were not followers of any religion. He administered help "to all who did not object to dying in the bosom of our adorable religion."[55]

Major Dunham, a Protestant, and a "pious member of the Methodist Church," when asked if he would confess to the priest and receive baptism and the sacrament according to the principles of the Catholic Church, is alleged to have replied: "I confess not to man but [to] my God."[56] He knelt and prayed, after which he was requested by the rest of the men to offer up a prayer on their behalf. As he sought to comply with the request, "he was rudely stopped by the officer on duty, who sternly and profanely forbade it."[57]

Green, who was not present at the scene of the drawing and the execution, says: "Edward Este spoke of his fate with the coolest indifference, and said that he would rather be shot than dragged along in this manner." He seemed to have little desire to live since the loss of his young wife, Elizabeth Jane.[58] "Tell my friends, I die with Grace," shouted Major Cocke as his friends left the room in tears.[59] Knowing that his remains, after death, would be stripped of his clothing, he pulled off his trousers and handed them to his visiting comrades, choosing to die in this underclothes rather than that some *"pelado"* should wear his pantaloons after his death.[60]

On being separated from Israel Canfield, to whom he had been handcuffed, Captain Eastland handed what money he had to his brother-in-

---

54. *Luis G. Medina a Sr. D. S. Diego Aranda Dignisimo obispo de la Diocesis de Guadalajara, Cedral, Abril 13 de 1843,* in Documents for the Early History of Coahuila y Texas and Approaches Thereto, 1600-1843, 5. Photostat, TxU-A.

55. Bell, *Narrative,* p. 52, says only two or three of the condemned required the services of a priest; all other accounts the author has seen are either silent on the issue or say that none required such services.

56. Quoted in Bell, *Narrative,* p. 52; see also, W. P. Smith to Editor of *Texas Monument,* Pleasant Grove, Fayette Co., Oct. 25, 1850, in *Texas Monument* (LaGrange), Nov. 6, 1850. Smith reported Dunham stated: "I have been raised a Baptist, and I intend to die as I have lived—My God is my confessor."

57. Bell, *Narrative,* p. 52, says he was "interrupted and prevented by the priest himself." See also Stapp, *Prisoners of Perote,* p. 73.

58. Green, *Mier Expedition,* p. 172.

59. Quoted in *Northern Standard,* Feb. 10, 1844.

60. Green, *Mier Expedition,* p. 171.

law, Robert Smith.[61] A few minutes later, while taking leave of his comrades, Eastland remarked, "I know that some have thought me timid, but, thank God! death has no terrors for me." His parting request was, "Say to my friends that I addressed you an hour previous to my arraignment before my God. For my country I have offered all my earthly aspirations and for it I now lay down my life. I never feared death, nor do I now. For my unjustifiable execution I wish no revenge, but I die in full confidence of the Christian faith."[62]

To Henry Whaling, Trahern said: "Good bye, Henry, old boy, I am mighty sorry." To which Whaling replied: "Wash it is all right; we'll all go the same way; this is only the beginning," and he continued, "I'm going to take a good square meal and satisfy myself once; I've been hungry for a long time."[63] Cameron bid each of the doomed men a tearful farewell, especially his close friend, James Turnbull. With tears rolling down their cheeks, the friends of those about to be executed "vowed eternal hatred to the authors of this gory outrage so insulting and revolting to humanity."[64]

About six o'clock that evening, as the hour of twilight advanced, a lieutenant and a file of twenty soldiers from the "Red Cap" Company entered the courtyard, counted out nine of the unfortunate Texans, pinioned their arms behind them, and led them out of the compound with a guard on each side backed up by the whole cavalry of the escort troops.[65]

The "Red Caps" had "petitioned" for the "butcher's work," and had been selected from among those whose lives the Texans had spared in their break at Salado six weeks before. "These were the identical heroes who, with naked hands, we had disarmed and routed the morning of our break at this place," said Stapp, "and who, smarting under a sense of their disgrace, had petitioned" for the brutal work.[66]

With rhythmic tread led by a fifer and a drummer, the procession rounded the corner of the corral containing the main body of prisoners to the eastern wall. Those who had been more fortunate in the drawing were ordered to sit on the ground under guard of a strong body of sentinels with firearms cocked and with orders "to shoot the first man who should move or speak whilst the execution was progressing."[67] Quiet settled on

61. Canfield diary, June 18-July 29, 1843.

62. From an account given by Charles Keller Reese, who was not present at the drawing. *Northern Standard*, Feb. 10, 1844. Bell reports Eastland said: "Tell my wife I die in the faith in which I have lived." Bell, *Narrative*, p. 52.

63. Trahern diary, MS, Bancroft Library, University of California; see also, Buchanan, "George Washington Trahern," in *SWHQ* 58 (July 1954), pp. 65-66; Green, *Mier Expedition*, p. 172.

64. Bell, *Narrative*, p. 52.

65. Stapp, *Prisoners of Perote*, p. 73.

66. *Ibid.*, p. 75.

67. *Ibid.*, p. 73.

the compound; Texans gritted their teeth or muttered oaths as they listened to the death march. Some, with tears streaming from their eyes, sank their heads in silent prayer for their doomed comrades.[68] Deep hatred for the murderers swelled every breast.

Upon arrival at the place of execution, the condemned men were halted, "bound together with cords," and blindfolded.[69] Only a wall ten feet high, against which the condemned were made to kneel facing their executioners, separated those about to die from the main body of prisoners. Samuel H. Walker says that some of their comrades were permitted to witness the execution, but "very few had any desire to witness it."[70] Apparently, the Texans' interpreter, Alfred S. Thurmond, was among those who were eyewitnesses to the execution.[71]

Inside the compound the prisoners could hear the orders given by the Mexican officers—the halting, the order to kneel, the order to readjust the blindfolds of some of the men, the arranging of the Texans and their executioners, and the murmured prayers of the kneeling men—followed by a short interval of silence— "then the signal taps of the drum— the rattle of the muskets, as they were brought to an aim"—the command to fire—"the sharp burst of the discharge, mingled with the shrill cries of the anguish and heavy groans of the dying," as soul and suffering body parted.[72]

During the execution, one of the guards on the wall fainted and came near to falling off but was caught by a comrade. The first flurry of shots was followed by a random firing to dispatch those who had not been killed by the first volley. Some of the men were shot as many as six or seven times before death came, and Henry Whaling is reported to have received fifteen shots before his life was extinguished.[73] The inferior quality of the Mexican guns and the poor marksmanship of the "Red Caps" accounted for the mangling of some of the bodies.

The remaining eight men were marched out and the process was repeated. "They all died with more than usual firmness," recorded Samuel H. Walker, "telling us in their farewell embraces that they desired their murder to be remembered and revenged by their countrymen, and some of them also telling the Mexican officers that it was coldblooded murder and their countries should revenge their death and as small a matter as the Mexicans may think it the blood of these men may yet cost them the blood of thousands as circumstances will make it more lasting than the massacre of Fannin, which will be remembered by future generations."[74]

68. Bell, *Narrative*, p. 52.
69. Green, *Mier Expedition*, p. 174.
70. Sibley, ed., *Samuel H. Walker's Account*, p. 60.
71. Green, *Mier Expedition*, p. 174.
72. Stapp, *Prisoners of Perote*, pp. 73-74.
73. Canfield's diary, March 25, 1843; Account of Charles Keller Reese, *Northern Standard*, Feb. 10, 1844.
74. Sibley, ed., *Samuel H. Walker's Account*, pp. 60-61.

Those executed[75] at Hacienda Salado were John L. Cash of Victoria; Maj. James D. Cocke, a lawyer from Richmond, Virginia, former co-editor of the *Courier* and of the *Enquirer* of Houston; Robert Holmes Dunham of Groce's Retreat, Montgomery County; Capt. William Mosby Eastland of Fayette County; Edward E. Este, a native of New Jersey, brother-in-law of Mrs. David G. Burnet, and resident of Harris County; Robert W. Harris of Travis County, formerly of Mississippi; Thomas L. Jones, a native of Louisville, Kentucky, and a merchant in Austin; Patrick Maher of Victoria; James M. Ogden, a lawyer from Henry County, Kentucky, who lived in Austin, Texas, and was district attorney of the Third Judicial District of Texas; Christopher M. Roberts of Milam County; William H. Rowan of Fort Bend, formerly from Georgia, but came to Texas in 1840 from Apalachicola, Florida; James L. Shepherd, a lad of about seventeen years of age, formerly from Alabama and a resident of Bastrop, Texas, in 1842; Orderly Sgt. Jasper N. Mcdowell Thomson of Milam County; James N. Torrey of Harris County and a native of Colchester, Connecticut; James Turnbull of Victoria, formerly from Scotland; Henry Whaling from Victoria County; and Martin Carroll Wing, a former printer in Austin and native of Vermont, who came to Texas in the fall of 1835 with Charles DeMorse and was to have been a partner with him in the founding of the *Northern Standard* at Clarksville.

By 6:30 P.M., about four hours after the order for the decimation had been communicated to the prisoners, the bloody deed of shooting the Texans had been carried out. Referring to the reapprehended Mier prisoners and the decimation, General Woll commented: "and according to the rights of gentlemen and in conformance to the laws in similar cases they shed their blood, paying in this manner seventeen of them for their crimes."[76]

The bodies were left unburied where they had fallen so the remaining prisoners could view them the next day. A guard was placed to prevent animals from violating the corpses during the night. In spite of this precaution, it was discovered on counting the bodies the next morning that one of them, that of a Catholic, had disappeared. Speculation was rife among the guard about the seventeenth body. The priest from Saltillo had vanished during the night, so some surmised that he might be responsible for its disappearance. But why would the priest want a dead Texan? Could one of the men have survived and made his escape? Many superhuman performances had been attributed before to the terrible *"Tejanos*

---

75. James L. Trueheart to Moses Austin Bryan, Independence, Washington County, Texas [dated] San Anto Texas, Decr. 14, 1874, copy in Mier Scrapbook, TxU-A, furnishes Bryan with "a list of the Mier prisoners who were decimated at Salado Mexico taken from diary while a prisoner in Mexico." *El Diario del Gobierno*, April 8, 1843, contains a list of the decimated men.

76. *Adrián Woll a Sor. Consul Mex⁰. en Nva. Orleans, Cuerpo de ejército del Norte, General-en-jefe, Cuartel gra'l en Monterrey, Abril 19 de 1843*, in W.B. Stevens Collection, TxU-L. Am. Archives.

diablos." A check revealed that the missing body was that of James L. Shepherd.[77] A fruitless search was instituted for him.

While kneeling with his companions facing the firing squad, Shepherd, a young man of about seventeen years of age,[78] had received a ball through the side of his cheek, "cutting his face severely, but inflicting nothing more than a bad flesh-wound."[79] One of his arms was broken by another ball. He fell forward on his face, pretending to be dead. Bleeding profusely, he lay on the ground without motion or animation until the soldiers retired, when with pieces of a rag he was then able to stop the bleeding of his wounds. That night, when the guard fell asleep, he made his escape into the mountains. Shepherd worked his way northward, avoiding contact with the native population. Finally, after several days of hunger, thirst, exposure, and with his wound badly festered, he was forced to seek help near Saltillo on March 28. Taken into the city, he was recognized by one of his "executioners"[80] and was shot to death. After this second execution, Shepherd's body was carried out and left unburied on the commons, not far from the city.

Of Shepherd, Canfield reported that "our enemies" say "he was retaken a few days after [the execution] and shot together with a Mexican (who was conducting him out of the country) which was no doubt true."

The bodies of the deceased at Salado were turned over to Padre Luis G. Medina for burial at Cedral after they had been viewed by the Texans, but he was delayed in removing them for lack of carts. Even after transportation was obtained, it was not until the fourth day after the execution that he reached Cedral with the bodies. The bodies were clothed for burial, and a common grave, "truly a sepulcher," was consecrated for those who were Catholics. The Protestant, "not blessed," was buried in a separate, unconsecrated grave.[81]

"Their death," declared Charles DeMorse, editor of the *Northern Standard,*[82]

> has revealed the vindictive impulses of the Mexican villain who rules that nation; and another augmentation has been made to the hecatombs of the murdered patriots who have been perfidiously slain by his orders, after the fairest promises of honorable treatment upon capitulation. How

---

77. Canfield diary, Mar. 25, 1843.

78. Stapp, *Prisoners of Perote,* p. 74; Trahern's diary, 12; *Western Chronicle,* Dec. 14, 1877.

79. Extract of a letter from a gentleman in Monterrey, dated April 3, 1843, enclosed in I[saac] D. Marks to Daniel Webster, Secretary of State, Washington City, [dated] Consulate of the United States of America, Matamoros, April 8, 1843, no. 7, in Despatches from United States Consuls in Matamoros (Jan. 1, 1840-Dc. 29, 1848), National Archives (microfilm).

80. A later entry inserted by Canfield in his diary under date Mar. 25, 1843.

81. *Luis G. Medina a Sr. D^s. D^n. Diego Aranda dignisimo obispo de la Diocesis de Guadalajara, Abril 13 de 1843,* in Documents for the Early History of Coahuila y Texas and Approaches Thereto, 1600-1843, 5. Photostat, TxU-A.

82. *Daily Picayune,* May 24, 1843; also quoted in *Northern Standard,* June 29, 1843.

much longer shall the blood of martyred brave cry aloud from the ground for vengeance? All this could not have been, had the miscreant despot been swung by the neck, as he should have been, when captured at San Jacinto. There would have been satisfaction for previous most perfidious murder, and prevention of this new villainy, and the mal-treatment of all our citizens who have been made prisoners during the last two years.

CHAPTER 18

From Salado to Mexico City and in Santiago Prison—Arrival of Boys Wounded From Matamoros

THE MORNING AFTER THE lottery, the remaining prisoners were started on their way to the City of Mexico. First, to instill fear in the Texans of a similar fate if they should again revolt, the prisoners were marched and lined up before the stiffened forms of their murdered companions, "Laying pelmel as they had fallen."[1] Their bodies had been stripped of all clothing.[2] "How my blood did boil, when I witnessed the execution of those boys! And I made new vows to devote my life to slaying Mexicans. . . . When the Mexican war came on I hastened to the front and took my place in the ranks, and Lordy, how I spilled Mexican gore!"[3]

The drum sounded, orders were shouted, and the march began under the guard of cavalrymen commanded by Colonel Ortiz. Chained two and two, the Texians plodded along—emaciated and sore-footed—lugging their filthy sheepskins and tattered blankets and prodded by lancers on each side, monotonously crying, *"Delante! Delante!"*[4]

Their journey toward Mexico City had been delayed six weeks by the overthrow of the guard. The march now was through a desert-like plain, rarely watered by rain, and through barren mountains, spotted occasionally by a small Indian village or farm.[5] After a march of twenty-one miles the Texans were placed in a corral for the night at Las Animas, and received the first good water in four days. Late the following afternoon they reached the large *hacienda* of San Juan de Vanegas. At Vanegas the principal branch of the Sierra de Catorce ends and the two valleys of Mate-

---

1. Sibley, ed., *Samuel H. Walker's Account*, p. 61.
2. "Bigfoot" Wallace said, "We were grievously shocked when we were forced to march past our dead comrades lying naked by the roadside, their clothes having been stripped from them." Quoted in McCaleb, *The Mier Expedition*, p. 85.
3. "Greetings from Big Foot Wallace," in *Frontier Times* 12 (Oct. 1934), pp. 44-45.
4. *Adelante* (forward).
5. Bell, *Narrative*, pp. 54-55.

huala and Guadalupe el Carnicero joined to form a wide gorge that led to the Valley of Salado. It was also at Vanegas that the two roads from San Luis Potosí to Saltillo came together. The quarters and food furnished the prisoners were sumptuous in comparison with those customarily allotted to them. In general, the Texans received better quarters and food than they had between Mier and Salado.

On the second morning after leaving Salado, they were delayed three hours at San Juan while the ceremony of baptism was administered by a Catholic priest to John P. Wyatt, Richard Brown, W. Miller, and Zed Island, who voluntarily accepted the Catholic faith over the protests of their companions[6] who could not understand how any one of them could accept Catholicism. "The converts, however," reported Stapp, "seemed extremely sanctimonious and devout after the ceremony, preserving as profound a silence, touching the mysteries of their new faith, as entered apprentices of Masonry. . . . The Padre was allowed but little time to enlighten them in the doctrines of his venerable creed, and most probably their imperfect acquaintance with them, sealed their lips in decorous taciturnity."[7]

The route carried the prisoners past several large *haciendas* and across the Tropic of Cancer to Rancho Guadalupe el Carnicero, then twenty miles on March 30 to Rancho Laguna Seca and to Benado.

At Rancho Laguna Seca, where they found the water brackish, the wife of the Frenchman who operated the place added much to the comfort of the sick Texans and the gentleman himself divided his wardrobe with the prisoners. Samuel McClelland died of pleurisy at this place, in spite of the kind attention and comfort shown the prisoners by the operator's wife.[8]

During their march Colonel Ortiz showed great kindness to the prisoners and was as lenient toward them as his orders from superiors would permit. He "often extended privileges, [which] his duty as an officer forbade."[9] He tried to protect the Texans from insults from both the guards and the populace, and he always demanded comfortable quarters and suitable rations for them. He did not allow exhibitions of them in the towns and *haciendas* through which they passed, and to keep the Texans from choking on the dust raised by his cavalry he kept the cavalry at the rear of the column. The sick were permitted to ride or were placed in carts drawn by oxen.[10]

Colonel Ortiz promised that when Benado was reached, the prisoners would be permitted a day of rest since they had "borne without repin-

---

6. Canfield diary, Mar. 27, 1843; Stapp, *Prisoners of Perote*, pp. 75-76.

7. Stapp, *Prisoners of Perote*, p. 76.

8. Canfield diary, Mar. 30, 1843; see also Stapp, *Prisoners of Perote*, p. 76, and Sibley, ed., *Samuel H. Walker's Account*, p. 61-62, Walker gave the name "Le Dechonda" as "Gedediana."

9. Bell, *Narrative*, p. 55.

10. Stapp, *Prisoners of Perote*, pp. 76-77.

ing several previous long and irksome marches." On March 31 they reached Benado, where they were "received with becoming humanity, and lodged in commodious and agreeable quarters."[11] During the day of rest the prisoners were conducted by the guard to a spring-fed stream and permitted the luxury of a much-needed bath.

A leisurely march of ten miles the next day brought the prisoners to Hedionda.[12] As Las Vocas was approached on April 3 the country began to improve in appearance. Six or seven miles from San Luis Potosí, and about 130 miles from Salado, the road became wide and straight, skirted on both sides by huge clumps of prickly pears, and led directly into the city. On April 5 they reached San Luis Potosí. The prisoners were lodged in an unfinished room of the hospital, about 100 feet long and thirty feet wide, and they found four of their comrades who had been left at Salado following the revolt: Capt. John R. Baker and John A. Sansberry, wounded in the charge on the guard; Norman Woods, wounded in the Dawson fight; Thomas Colville, sick at the time of the "Battle of the Rescue." They were soon joined with the main body of prisoners and went forward with them from San Luis Potosí.[13] Places in the hospital were provided for fourteen of the new arrivals who were ill, but, in spite of the best attention and nursing, five of them died at this place. Robert Beard and E. G. Coffman died on April 8,[14] and Charles Hill, Allen S. Holderman, and Peter Rockefellow died after the main body of prisoners left the city.[15]

During the march, the iron handcuffs cut deeply into the flesh of some of the Texans and interfered with circulation. By the time he reached San Luis Potosí, one of Wallace's arms had swollen and become discolored and he feared that gangrene poisoning had developed. Wallace later declared: "I lost the use of my arm pulling my companion along who was sick and when we arrived there [at San Luis Potosí] three ladies came to see the prisoners, one of these was the Governor's wife. . . . She went back and brought the Governor and a blacksmith and cut the irons off of my arms and McMahon's arm, God bless the Governor's wife for she saved my life for I don't think I could have . . . [continued in my condition] three days longer. She brought 4 bottles of Catalan and gave them to me to rub my arm."[16] During the afternoon of the next day the Texans

---

11. Stapp, *Prisoners of Perote*, p. 76.

12. Canfield diary, Apr. 2, 1843.

13. Norman Woods to H. G. Woods, Molino del Rey, July 15, 1843, in Spellman, ed., "Letters of the 'Dawson Men,'" *SWHQ* 38 (Apr. 1935), pp. 257-60.

14. Canfield diary, Apr. 8, 1843; see also Glasscock diary, Apr. 8, 1843.

15. Stapp, *Prisoners of Perote*, p. 78; see also Glasscock diary, Apr. 10, 1843; Bell, *Narrative*, p. 56; William [Beard] to "Dear Father," Santa Ago Prison, Mexico, May 13, 1843, copy in Houston Wade Papers, Tx-A. The *Telegraph and Texas Register*, Aug. 16, 1843, reports the death of Robert Beard.

16. W. A. A. Wallace to Nora C. Franklin, Big Foot, Oct. 13, 1888, in "Letters of Big Foot Wallace," *Frontier Times* 8 (June 1931), pp. 418-19. Photostat of original may be found in TxU-A.

were relieved of their handcuffs, much to their enjoyment, and were thereafter marched singly.[17]

During the five days spent at San Luis Potosí, the Texans were supplied with weak coffee and cornbread in the morning, beef soup for dinner, and boiled beans, well flavored with *chile colorado,* and cornbread instead of *tortillas* for supper. The native element treated them kindly, but the Anglo-Americans, Germans, and French in the city treated the prisoners "with great coolness . . . inconsequence of false reports which had been circulated about us," reported Walker.[18] Especially was this true of the Americans. The year before, the Santa Fé prisoners took advantage of their generosity of permitting drafts to be drawn on the prisoners' friends in the United States, which went unpaid.[19] A German merchant was generous to some of the Mier men, giving them clothes and other items to make life a little more comfortable.

At San Luis Potosí some 300 convicts[20] were added to the ranks of the Texan prisoners. This rascally addition to the number of prisoners, plus the fact that the handcuffs had been removed from the Texans, caused the guard to be augmented by a strong body of infantry. Colonel Ortiz remained in command to conduct the prisoners to Querétaro. The Texans were kept separate from the criminals during the march.

As the march for Querétaro and Mexico City was resumed on April 10,[21] fourteen of the Mier men were left sick in the hospital at San Luis Potosí: James J. Blanton, Benjamin Z. Boone, Philip F. Bowman, Charles Hill, Allen S. Holderman, James M. Michen, John Mills, David Overton, Peter Rockefellow, John A. Sansberry, William P. Stapp, Thomas S. Tatum, Levi Williams, and William Wynn.

The route from San Luis Potosí continued south through a fertile and thickly settled country with many of the *haciendas* fenced with prickly pear or some other plant or tree.[22] The road led upward through broken country from whence the Texans got fine vistas of wide valleys delimited by blue-peaked hills. Reaching Hacienda Guadalupe el Carnicero, fifteen miles from San Luis Potosí, they spent the night.[23] On the following day, they made it to the small town of Francisco de Bayou. While there the "officers were permitted to go out into the town," but the privates were kept under guard and had to make the most of their rations of rice and tortillas. The rice had been "boiled in copper kettles that had not been in use for some time previous"; consequently, the rice "was so charged with verdigris" that only a few of the men were able to gratify their appetites.[24]

---

17. Glasscock diary, Apr. 7, 1843. Canfield gives the date of the removal of the handcuffs as Apr. 9, "preparatory to a march in the morning." Canfield diary, Apr. 9, 1843.

18. Sibley, ed., *Samuel H. Walker's Account,* p. 62.

19. Canfield diary, Apr. 5, 1843; Glasscock diary, Apr. 9, 1843.

20. Stapp, *Prisoners of Perote,* p. 78.

21. Canfield diary, Apr. 10, 1843.

22. Sibley, ed., *Samuel H. Walker's Account,* p. 63.

23. Glasscock diary, Apr. 11, 1843.

24. Stapp, *Prisoners of Perote,* p. 80.

From Francisco de Bayou they proceeded fifteen miles to Hacienda Jaral. The rich, 10,000-square-mile *hacienda* contained some 8,000 persons, numerous mills, granaries, and a store. The Marquis de Jaral,[25] one of the wealthiest men in Mexico, supplied blankets to some of those in need and distributed $25 among those destitute of means.

On leaving the *hacienda,* the prisoners were conducted through the market square and permitted to buy meat, oranges, sweet-limes, and other fruits and cake.[26] As they moved along through the market square of this and other towns, Wallace, with his height and long arms, reached out to grab *piloncillos, tamales,* fruit, and other food from the stands of vendors, much to the amusement of the soldiers and the outcries of the vendors who felt themselves robbed through the indifference of the soldiers.

Their course from Jaral lay in a southerly direction. The plain through which they passed was watered by numerous wells. A short distance brought them to the Hacienda Cubo, owned by the Count of Jaral, Don Juan Moncada. They traveled ten leagues to San Felipe, during which they crossed a spur of the Sierra Madre by a long and difficult ascent and descent. They spent the night in San Felipe.

Soon after leaving San Felipe on April 14, the Texans crossed a stony mountain pass which led them through secluded barrancas, across swift running streams, and past numerous piles of stones topped by crosses marking the graves of those murdered by robbers. They camped at Hacienda Comadré, six leagues from San Felipe.[27] Next came Dolores Hidalgo, a small town with olive trees and a grand old church made memorable by Father Hidalgo's *Grito de Dolores,* opening the Mexican Revolution on September 16, 1810. Here they camped for the night.

Finally, the Texans reached San Miguel el Grande (later known as San Miguel de Allende) on April 16, twenty-four miles from Dolores Hidalgo. San Miguel was one of the scenic towns of southwestern Guanajuanto, "the smallest, but the most densely populated."[28]

At San Miguel, previous to being locked up, Colonel Ortiz permitted about twenty of the Mier men, including Walker and John McMullen, to be taken on a tour of the town, during the course of which they were followed by a significant number of people who considered the Texans to be the "greatest curiosity" they apparently had ever seen. "Our garments," reported McMullen, "were soiled and tattered, and our condition most wretched. As we passed the doors of the houses, the women pitied us very much, and after we were locked up the Mexican girls came and threw cakes and other eatables over the walls to us, though it was strictly forbid-

---

25. Kendall, *Narrative of the Texan Santa Fé Expedition* 2, pp. 167-68.

26. A. J. Sowell, "The Life of 'Big-Foot' Wallace," reprinted from Sowell's 1899 pamphlet on Wallace, *Frontier Times* 5 (Dec. 1927), p. 121.

27. Green, *Mier Expedition*, p. 197.

28. Stapp, *Prisoners of Perote*, p. 79; see also Heriberto Frías, *Espisodios Militares Méxicanos*, Part I, pp. 278-82 (*Mapa General de la Nueva España*, 1813).

den at the time."[29] Their promenade through the city took them into a small park. "It was a yard forming a half circle with seats on the side of the circle and surrounded by beautiful shade trees with a beautiful fountain of water in the middle or center. We found a number of fashionable ladies & gentlemen sitting around though there was no conversation between them as the ladies & gentlemen did not mix as is usual with the Mexicans or English & French on such occasions. A large number of the common class followed us, but did not presume to enter amongst the lords of fashion but kept at respectful distance and looked on at us until we left, then they continued to follow us until we reached our quarters. We were quite a ragged set and I felt rather bashful at being seen by ladies of fashion & taste."[30]

Descending through a narrow valley, the prisoners reached Santa Rosa the next afternoon, and were quartered at the Hacienda de la Santa Rosa in the chapel of a deserted adobe monastery which was still in a good state of preservation. "Though long unused, it was but little dilapidated," recorded Stapp, "bearing none of those evidences of wanton violence that mark the desecration of those monastic asylums in other lands, where war or civil strife have expelled their inmates. How various or how unholy soever had been its occupants, since the removal of the saintly brotherhood, a reverential regard for its ancient usages seemed to have preserved even the most fragile portions of the building from all destruction but that which time and neglect had wrought."[31]

A march of fifteen miles the next day brought the Texans to Querétaro, the capital of the department of the same name, situated astride the Querétaro River. Querétaro was far more modern than San Luis Potosí. Its numerous public buildings, convents, and churches, with their lofty imposing domes, towers, and steeples presented to the weary Texans a grand and magnificent sight. "The houses," wrote Stapp, "are elegantly and commodiously built, and the streets, wide, with good side-walks, intersecting each other at right angles, terminating in the three largest and principal squares of that town. The magnificence of its churches and convents [especially the huge one of Santa Clara] excite universal admiration. . . . But its most imposing feature is its ten miles length aqueduct, whose massive and lofty arches [seventy-four in number], built of enormous blocks of stone, transported from a distance, must have cost millions of treasure to erect" to carry water from the mountain springs of La Cañada at San Pedro across a wide valley.[32]

The day was delightfully warm and pleasant, but the elevation of the tablelands made the nights chilly. The Texans were quartered in an old convent, adjoining the Templo de la Cruz, on the opposite side from

29. Sibley, ed., *Samuel H. Walker's Account*, p. 63.
30. Canfield diary, Apr. 17, 1843.
31. Stapp, *Prisoners of Perote*, p. 80.
32. *Ibid.*, pp. 80-81; Canfield diary, Apr. 18, 1843; Kendall, *Narrative of the Texas Santa Fé Expedition* 2, p. 191.

which they had entered the city, "a vile, dismal hole at the best." The same quarters were formerly occupied by the Santa Fé prisoners. Two of the Mier men were left sick at Querétaro.[33]

Immediately on leaving Querétaro, the road led the prisoners past the town's cemetery and down a hill to a rather flat tableland and then under one of the arches of the aqueduct. A few miles farther they commenced the ascent of a steep chain of mountains called Chapulalpa, the highest ground between the Rio Grande and Mexico City.

Passing through a gap in the mountains of Chapulalpa, the prisoners covered the remaining 170 miles to Mexico City in eight days, stopping at night along the way at Hacienda Soucé, twenty-four miles from Querétaro, where their guard was replaced and the prisoners counted and receipted. They were once more placed under lock and key until they gained the confidence of their new escort.

They marched twelve miles to San Juan del Río, in a rich and highly cultivated valley, the last town of any size before reaching Mexico City. They crossed the San Juan River. At San Juan del Río the Texans were joined by Maj. Thomas W. Murray, their second in command at Mier, who had been left sick in the hospital at San Juan.[34] As they left San Juan the next day, William Martin was left desperately ill. He died at San Juan del Río shortly after the departure of his comrades.[35]

Forty-two miles from San Juan del Río they reached the large Hacienda de Río Seco, where some of the prisoners conversed with an American on his way to the City of Mexico. From Hacienda de Río Seco, they continued to Hacienda Tordia [Jordia], distant thirty-five miles. There the Texans were placed "up stairs [of a *mesón*] in very dirty quarters."[36]

The next day they journeyed through the mountains to the small town of Tula (Tehula) on the Tula River. The Texans found Tula, one of the metropolises of the mysterious Toltecs, to be a small Indian village situated at the foot of a rocky hill in a valley about fifty miles from Mexico City. The Texans were quartered in the upper portico of an old church. Their convict comrades occupied the lower one.[37]

The guard was again changed and reduced. Eighty cavalrymen under an officer from Mexico City had been sent to take charge of the prisoners, including both the Texans and the "pressed" volunteers or convicts, bringing the number to approximately 300.[38] The new officer in charge of the escort assured the Texans that they had nothing to fear, as the English minister, Pakenham, "had requested him to treat us well," reported Walker, and he assured us "he intended to do so."[39]

---

33. Canfield diary, Apr. 18, 1843.
34. Stapp, *Prisoners of Perote*, p. 81; Glasscock diary, Apr. 20, 1843.
35. Stapp, *Prisoners of Perote*, p. 86.
36. Sibley, ed., *Samuel H. Walker's Account*, p. 64.
37. Stapp, *Prisoners of Perote*, p. 81.
38. Sibley, ed., *Samuel H. Walker's Account*, p. 64.
39. *Ibid.*

From Tula they proceeded toward Hacienda Huehuetoka (sometimes spelled Watoka or Huitoka) and Hacienda Tampantla. Poverty was visible everywhere. The almost level country near Huehuetoka formed the outer barrier to the valley of Mexico, from whence on clear days the majestic peaks of Popocatépetl and Ixtaccíhuatl could be seen rising against the northern skyline.

As the Texans approached Huehuetoka a violent whirlwind arose followed by a furious storm of wind and rain, as at Salado the afternoon of the decimation, except for the rain—an ominous foreboding. The superstitions and suspicions of the Texans were enhanced when they were locked up for the night in small rooms surrounding the courtyard.[40] The only ventilation through which air could enter the room was the keyhole, making for an "almost suffocating situation"; so, the Texans made small crude holes in the doors of their rooms and took turns breathing at them.[41]

Around eight o'clock that night, a small guard of about a dozen mounted men wearing broad-brimmed hats arrived from Mexico City, bringing an order regarding Captain Cameron. Cameron was awakened by the guard, unchained from his partner, Col. William F. Wilson, and hustled half-naked, without shoes or blanket, into another room some distance from where the prisoners were lodged. Wilson was given to understand that his time would come next. "I thought it a squally time for me," Wilson later wrote to his uncle, "but I am pretty tough, and if any one gets home, I will."[42] Also taken at the same time as Cameron was Alfred S. Thurmond, an interpreter.

Being once more ironed and a strong guard placed over him, Cameron was informed that an order had arrived from the Supreme Government for his execution to fulfill the order for shooting every tenth man—evidentially figuring to the nearest fraction in favor of the government. Actually, the government wanted to dispose of the Texan who had gained a reputation of daring and bold leadership.[43]

As William F. Wilson understood it, there was a fractional part of the tenth due, and the Supreme Government of Mexico was determined that Cameron's life should make up the deficit.[44] In his *Narrative* (p. 58), Bell

---

40. Glasscock diary, Apr. 24, 1843.

41. Canfield diary, Apr. 24, 1844. Stapp, *Prisoners of Perote*, p. 81, gives a different picture of the situation, describing Huehuetoka as "another considerable village, where comfortable quarters and an ample supply of provisions were assigned us."

42. W. F. Wilson to Wm. Wilson, Lexington, VA., [dated] Perote Castle, Aug. 12, 1844, in *Galveston Daily News*, Mar. 17, 1844, p. 2, William F. Wilson to [Uncle] ———, Rockbridge County Va., [dated] Castle of Perote, ———, 1844 (excerpts), in Wilson *Reminiscences of Persons, Events, Records, and Documents of Texian Times*, p. 8.

43. Capt. S. H. Walker to A. Sidney Johns[t]on, Galveston, Texas, [dated] Prison Santiago, City of Mexico, May 4th, 1843, in Army Papers (Texas), TxU-A; see also, alleged letter to Capt. Charles Keller Reese in *Northern Standard*, Feb. 10, 1844.

44. Wilson, *Reminiscences of Persons, Events, Records and Documents of Texian Times*, p. 9.

says no reason was given for Cameron being sentenced to die, "only that four were absent when the decimation took place at the Salado, and therefore one was wanting to make the number complete." Some writers have incorrectly said that the order for the execution originated with Santa Anna, but it seems to have come from General Tornel, the secretary of war.

On arriving in Mexico City, the Texan officers informed the foreign ministers that "the order read to the following effect—that to complete the original order read at Salado as before stated Capt. Cameron should be led out and executed." They further stated that, after the decimation had been carried out, they had been assured "that no farther atonement of blood would be required."[45]

Alexander W. Terrell years later is alleged to have said that he had the story direct from Thurmond, who had the story from Cameron, that he could have freed himself from his bonds and possibly have effected his escape, but that it would have brought hardship to the other prisoners.

Early the next morning, April 25, according to Wallace[46] the news concerning Cameron became known among the prisoners. Plans were developed as the prisoners filed out of their cells and marched to a nearby tank to wash. Each Texan now took the opportunity to fill his bosom with rocks, determined to fight for his captain and, if necessary, to die with him. The guards wanted to know why the men were collecting rocks, and were told that they were for ballast, so they would walk better; the guards made no effort to take the rocks from them. As they formed to renew the march, they demanded to know the whereabouts of their leader and what the guards intended to do with him. Threats were made, and suggestions for effecting a rescue were whispered from man to man. Apprehending the worst, the commander of the guard ordered the prisoners started at once,[47] while the officers assured the Texans that Cameron was not to be shot.[48]

As preparations for the march continued, "another old grey officer and some ten or twelve more soldiers" joined them while the Texans received their day's allowance for rations. "The old officer was very kind and obliging to the men in changing their money," reported Walker, "so much so that it attracted my attention. I saw him smile and pat several of the men on the cheek like a young lady would her lover and take their money and run off to get it changed."[49] There was a strong suspicion among the men that this new officer had been sent to perform some black deed. Walker thought it was to execute Cameron.

The march commenced and after proceeding five leagues a rest stop

45. Wm. Ryon, John R. Baker, J. G. W. Pierson, Wm. F. McMath, and F. M. Gibson to Min[ister] Plen[ipotentiary] Gr. B., U.S.A., France, and Germany, Prison Santiago 27th Apr. 1843, original MS, being the letter to the American Minister Waddy Thompson, Latin American Library, Tulane University, New Orleans, La, by permission.

46. Sowell, *Early Settlers and Indian Fighters of Southwest Texas*, p. 77.

47. Canfield diary, Apr. 26, 1843; Stapp, *Prisoners of Perote*, p. 82.

48. Stapp, *Prisoners of Perote*, p. 82.

49. Sibley, ed., *Samuel H. Walker's Account*, p. 65.

was called. At this point, the Texans and their escort were overtaken by "the old officer" and Thurmond. Although told by the Mexican officers to say nothing, Thurmond reported to his comrades that at about eight that morning, after the main body of prisoners had left Huehuetoka, he had witnessed the execution of Captain Cameron. Pen, ink, and paper were permitted Cameron, and he wrote a letter to the British minister in Mexico protesting the cruelty of the Mexican government in putting its "prisoners of war" to death,[50] especially a British subject. He protested to the Mexican officer in charge against the injustice of the order for his execution and pronounced it nothing more than cold-blooded murder. "His dying words were," reported Thurmond, *"never to be persuaded out of your own judgment."*[51]

A Mexican who witnessed the execution related the scene as follows: "They lead [led] him out, and wished to blindfold, and tie him, he refused saying that he feared not death, and he would die as a man, and a[s] soldier should *die, free* and unfettered. They then shot him, but not to kill, only to cripple. After wounding, they tied, blindfolded, and shot him as if he had been a *dog!"*[52]

Thurmond reported that the leader of the "Cow Boys" had at first determined to sell his life dearly, and for that purpose had requested the guard not to tie his hands. The request was granted and immediately after his hands were free he was shot. Eight balls struck Cameron, any one of which should have been fatal.[53] Thus perished "a brave, noble and accomplished soldier and gentleman . . . the pride and idol of his comrades and acquaintances."[54] "The murder of Cameron was an act which should have called fourth the vengance of the world on an insolent and savage race!" wrote one of the Mier men. "It was a high, a *horrid* act of barbarity! It was an awful act! enough to make *angels* weep! *Devils* laugh! and man lament! When the Mexican government saw that he did not draw the '*Black bean,*' it then had him taken out, and shot like a dog."[55]

The execution of Cameron, more than any other single act of the Mexican government, sealed the bitterness of the Mier men toward their captors.

Percy Doyle, the British acting *chargé d'affaires* to Mexico, was enraged by this act of barbarity. The Baron Alleye de Cyprey, the French minister in Mexico, "told Santa Anna that if he dared shoot another of the Texian Prisoners he would immediately demand his papers and return to his Government, for he could not stand a silent spectator of the most bar-

---

50. Alleged letter to Charles Keller Reese in the *Northern Standard*, Feb. 10, 1844; Green, *Mier Expedition*, pp. 283-86.

51. Quoted in Glasscock diary, Apr. 25, 1843.

52. Nance, ed., *McCutchan's Narrative*, p. 92; Clarence Wharton, *Texas Under Many Flags* 1, p. 384, p. 387.

53. Canfield diary, Apr. 25, 1843; Green, *Mier Expedition*, p. 285; Duval, *Big-Foot Wallace*, pp. 231-32; Stapp, *Prisoners of Perote*, p. 82.

54. Stapp, *Prisoners of Perote*, p. 82.

55. Nance, ed., *McCutchan's Narrative*, p. 92.

barous acts that ever did disgrace civilization."[56] James Trueheart recorded that Peyton A. Southall, dispatch bearer from the United States, upon
his visit to the prisoners at Perote Castle on May 13, 1843, stated that
Santa Anna was "much enraged because Cameron had been shot, blaming
Tornel, [the minister of war and marine], as the cause of it."[57]

The Mier men and some writers have blamed Santa Anna for Cameron's death because of their hatred of him. Though he was a dictator, Santa
Anna did not make all the decisions. He did not vent his hatred of Thomas
J. Green by ordering his execution or by singling him out for mistreatment.
This author does not believe that the murder of Cameron can be placed at
the doorstep of Santa Anna, who was ill during much of April, but that it
must be attributed to an order of the secretary of war and marine, who may
or may not have had the approval of Substitute President Nicolás Bravo.

After a brief rest, the march of the Mier men toward Mexico City resumed. The Texans trudged along, bitter, and angry, resolved to avenge
the murder of their leader. They camped at the small village of Tampantla, nine leagues from the City of Mexico.[58] At noon on Wednesday, April
26, four months from the day of their surrender at Mier, the Texans entered the northern outskirts of the City of Mexico.

After the formalities of changing the guard and receipting for the
prisoners, the Texans were lodged in the *Prisión Militar,* formerly a convent and ancient *Colegio de Santiago Tlaltelolco,*[59] about two miles from the
center of the city and north of the Vera Cruz road. The *Carcel* (or convent)
del Santiago had harbored the able-bodied men of the Santa Fé Expedition
and was noted for its chain gangs. "Tattered, squalid, and worn down by
fatigue, sick at heart and despondent in hope . . . [their] sufferings and
despair were alike forgotten, as . . . [the Texans] gazed with astonishment
and admiration from out the valley . . . upon the Rome of the new world
. . . and [the] palaces—the massive walls of its convents and monastic edi-
fices—draperied in the crimson hues of sunset, and mellowed by the pur-
ple shadows of the tall mountains around, gave it a look of dreamy en-
chantment that filled . . . [them] with emotions of joy and wonder," until
they found the portals of their prison closed behind them and they came
back to reality.[60]

The prison was in the better part of the city near its northern envi-
rons and some distance from San Lázaro, the lepers' prison or hospital. It
still provided housing for a few monks. "The front entrance was through
a narrow passage-way, having heavy doors on the outer and inner sides,
which were both closed at night," and before which a guard stood day and

---

56. Nance, ed., *McCutchan's Narrative,* p. 90.
57. Trueheart diary, May 19, 1843.
58. Sibley, ed., *Samuel H. Walker's Account,* p. 65; see also Glasscock diary, Apr. 25,
1843.
59. Manuel Rivera Cambas, *Mexico pintoresco, artistico, y monumental,* 2, p. 76.
60. Stapp, *Prisoners of Perote,* p. 82.

night. "In this passage-way," wrote a member of the Santa Fé Expedition the year before, "many of the soldiers forming our guard slept." The passageway led into a large yard, "having heavy stone buildings on each side, and a fountain of excellent water in the center."[61]

The prisoners occupied rooms on two sides of the inner courtyard and a sentinel stood before the door of each room. The remaining rooms on the other sides were used as a kitchen, for storage, a hospital, and a room in which mass was said on Sundays. The grounds of the prison contained a walled enclosure where thousands of cholera victims had been buried in 1833, and the effluvium was extremely offensive and sickening.[62]

The 149 Texans, now in the confines of Santiago prison, were a rough, ragged, rowdy, grim looking bunch of men. From Santiago prison, Samuel H. Walker wrote to Albert Sidney Johnston in Texas: "myself and comrades are in a tight place at last, from which we will not likely be released untill Texas strikes some decisive blow on the Riogrande and takes some of the officers and principal citizens of the government to exchange for us."[63] The first reports upon their arrival at the capital were that the Texan prisoners were to work on the road between Acapulco and Mexico City;[64] and that such of the prisoners of Perote who had fought at Salado in Texas, under Dawson, were to be brought back and placed among the Mier men to work on the road, while the other Woll prisoners in Mexico were expected to be released.

On April 27, the day after their arrival at Santiago prison, Captains Pierson, Baker, and Ryon, and Dr. McMath and Quartermaster Gibson addressed a letter to the British, American, French, and German ministers in Mexico, informing them that a number of the subjects and citizens of their respective countries had accompanied the Texans on the expedition against Mier. "If after their capture they had been treated as *prisoners of war* the undersigned could have no cause of complaint against the supreme authority of Mexico." They had "voluntarily identified themselves with one of the parties belligerent and when vanquished would necessarily have to suffer the *usual and legitimate consequences* attendant upon the condition of captives taken in authorised warfare." They then continued, "when however their treatment has not only been incompatible with but in utter and irreconcileable violation of the principles of civilized warfare we think that it is not only our right but solemn duty to appeal to the Ministers of Foreign Powers for our future protection and for the redress if possible of our past grievances." They referred to the escape, recapture,

---

61. Kendall, *Narrative of the Texan Santa Fé Expedition* 2, pp. 288-89; see also Loomis, *The Texan-Santa Fé Pioneers*, p. 237.

62. Loomis, *The Texan-Santa Fé Pioneers*, p. 274.

63. S. H. Walker to Gen. A. Sidney Johns[t]on, Galveston, Texas, [dated] Prison Santiago, City of Mexico, May 4, 1843, in Army Papers (Texas), Tx-A.

64. S. G. Norvell's report upon his arrival in New Orleans, printed in *Daily Picayune*, Feb. 16, 1843. Letter of a Dawson prisoner, dated City of Mexico, Jan. 27, 1843, reprinted from the *Western Advocate* (Austin), in *Telegraph and Texas Register*, May 3, 1843.

and decimation in violation of the terms of their second surrender as prisoners of war, and to the execution of Cameron, though "we were told," after the decimation at Salado, "that no farther atonement of blood would be required." Therefore, they declared, "Upon the Ground then of the bloody atonement at the Salado to which we were all alike subjected, upon the ground that every principle of international law has been violated in our treatment, upon the ground of common humanity, we appeal to you to demand our unconditional release it is the only redress and insufficient at that which can be offered for such illegal and outrageous conduct to prisoners of war."[65]

When the Texan wounded were transferred from Mier to Matamoros, Morgan says that he and ten others were assigned to look after them, and to carry on their work they were allowed the freedom of the town. About March 1, when word of the Texan break at Hacienda Salado reached Matamoros, Ampudia "flew into a rage" and the three boys—John C. C. Hill, William Harvey Sellers, and Gilbert R. Brush—Morgan, and the others who were out on parole, were "placed in a cell about ten feet square, with no light or anything of comfort or satisfaction."

In the evening of March 4, the door to their cell was flung open and the three boys, with seven others, were hustled out of their cell, formed in the street under a strong guard, and "secretly marched out of town . . . and sent on foot to Tampico."[66] Ampudia furnished Hill with a "beautiful little horse, saddle and bridle" and fine riding clothes. They were permitted less than "15 minutes to prepare for the journey, or an opportunity to persons charitably disposed to provide for their wants. Many of them were so disabled as to be scarcely able to walk; two were without hats, and several others had no shoes."[67]

Left at Matamoros were James Barber, who died three days later of his wounds; William Y. Scott; Francis Hughes, Edward Y. Keene; Jeffrey B. Hill; Joseph D. McCutchan; Theodore Dwight Maltby; Malcolm McCauley, who died July 14, 1843; and Ezekiel Smith.

The route through Tampico to Mexico City was a much shorter one than that through the interior of the country by way of Monterey, Saltillo, and San Luis Potosí.[68]

65. Wm. Ryon, John R. Baker, J. G. W. Pierson, Wm F. McMath, and F. M. Gibson to Min[ister] Pen[ipotentairy] Gr. B., U.S.A., France, & Germany, Prison Santiago, April 27, 1843, original MS, Latin American Library, Tulane University, New Orleans, Louisiana, by permission. The letter appears to be in the hand writing of Pierson and Ryon, and the envelope is addressed to "His Exc^y Min. Plenipo^y & & & of the U.S.A., near the Govt. of Mexico."

66. *Telegraph and Texas Register*, Apr. 5 and May 2, 1843; see also Nance, ed., *McCutchan's Narrative*, p. 74; Sibley, ed., *Samuel H. Walker's Account*, p. 65.

67. P. D. to the Editors of the *Bulletin*, Monterrey, 24th March 1843, in *New Orleans Bulletin*, Apr. 22, 1843; see also *Morning Star*, Apr. 29, 1843.

68. Nance, ed., *McCutchan's Narrative*, p. 74.

From Tampico, on April 2, Usher wrote to his sister, Mrs. Eliza Anne Barry of Wilmington, North Carolina, that "this morning very unpleasant and heartrending news" had reached them of the decimation.[69] "I am now on the eve of setting out for the City of Mexico," he said. "We leave here at four o'clock this afternoon a foot, a distance to travel one hundred and thirty leagues." Already they had traveled 600 miles since their capture.

For their journey from Tampico, the foreigners in the city took up "a small subscription" to supply them with a few of the necessities that they were greatly in need of." The foreigners and Mexicans of the city were kind "in supplying clothing and money sufficient to answer our wants on the road to Mexico," reported Usher. "We are informed that the Officer who takes charge of us to Mexico, is a very good man, God Grant it. For such a one may much alleviate our sufferings." He stated that the general belief among the prisoners was that the local citizens would also furnish the ten men with two horses when they were ready to leave on the fifteen-day journey from Tampico to Mexico City, which would be of much assistance, "as we can ride turn-about."

Their treatment in Tampico had been the best experienced as prisoners. After they left Tampico, an order arrived from Santa Anna for the release of George B. Crittenden. Through the efforts of Henry Clay and the U.S. minister in Mexico, Santa Anna had issued the order on March 12, but it did not reach Tampico until three days after the departure of the prisoners for Mexico City.[70]

At the old Convent of Santiago the main body of Mier men found eight of their ten comrades who had been sent forward from Matamoros by way of Tampico. George B. Crittenden, who had been with them, already had left for home. As soon as he had arrived at the capital he had been released and sent on his way to the coast.

En route to Vera Cruz to take passage to the United States, he stopped at Perote Castle on April 23 to visit the Texan prisoners and reported that "the prospects of the Béxar men was *[sic]* bad, and that of the Mier men worse." A letter from Gen. Waddy Thompson, the American minister, brought by Crittenden, said that the Béxar prisoners would probably all be released about June 16.[71] Crittenden reached New Orleans on May 7, by way of Havana in the steamship *Alabama*.

One of the boy prisoners who had come from Matamoros had been given considerable liberty and many privileges. This was John C. C. Hill, age fourteen, who, upon arriving in Mexico City, had been taken by the

69. Patrick Usher to [Eliza A. Barry, Wilmington, North Carolina], [dated] Tampico, April 2, 1843, in Friend, ed., "Sidelights and Supplements on the Perote Prisoners," *SWHQ* 68 (Jan. 1965), p. 371.

70. Hutchinson's diary, Apr. 9, 1843, in Winkler, ed., "The Béxar and Dawson Prisoners," *QTSHA* 13 (Apr. 1910), pp. 308-9; *Telegraph and Texas Register*, May 3, 1843; *Civilian and Galveston City Gazette*, Apr. 29, 1843.

71. Trueheart diary, Apr. 24, 1843.

escort guard directly to the National Palace to see Santa Anna. He was informed that the president was ill and unable to see him, but that he had made arrangements for him to stay with the Archbishop in his palace just across the street. There he was kindly treated until he could see the president.[72]

Hill was not closely confined. The U.S. minister in Mexico, Waddy Thompson, reported that Hill came to the legation to request that he ask Santa Anna to release him. Thompson says, "I told him to go himself, and I was sure that Santa Anna would be more apt to do it on his own account than on mine."[73] Hill took the advice, and when Santa Anna was no longer confined by illness, he went to the National Palace to see the president. Thompson related, "A few days afterwards the little fellow returned to my home very handsomely dressed, and told me he had been liberated. . . . When he requested Santa Anna to release him, the latter replied, 'Why if I do you will come back and fight me again. The Santa Fé prisoners were released on their parole of honor not to bear arms against Mexico and it was not three months before half of them had invaded the country again; and they tell me that you killed several of my Mexicans at Mier.' The little fellow replied, that he did not know how many he had killed, but that he had fired fifteen or twenty times during the battle. Very well, said Santa Anna, I will release you, and what is more, I will adopt you as my son, and educate and provide for you as such."[74] Santa Anna assured the boy's father that he would look after his son's interests. Ampudia, who had lost his son in the Battle of Mier, and Santa Anna, who had no son, wanted the boy to be sent to military school, but John declined: "I informed them that I would be of no use to Mexico as a soldier, as in case that country becoming involved in a war with the United States, I would not fight against my country."[75]

Hill was sent to the home of General Tornel, minister of war and marine, and adopted into the family "on a full footing of equality . . . and treated with the most parental kindness."[76] He was provided with a wardrobe, and was placed in the *Colegio de Minería*, there he "studied with the sons of Tornel," Manuel and Agustín. "General Santa Anna not only paid the charges of his education, but in all respects cared for him as a son."[77] He often rode in a carriage on Sundays with Santa Anna and his wife. But

---

72. Gooch-Iglehart, *The Boy Captive*, pp. 212-13; "Little John Hill the Boy Hero of Mier," in *Dallas Morning News*, Dec. 22, 1929, Feature Section, pp. 7-8.

73. Thompson, *Recollections of Mexico*, p. 76. Gooch-Iglehart gives a slightly different version, which says that Santa Anna took the initiative and sent for the boy (Gooch-Iglehart, *The Boy Captive*, pp. 227-39).

74. Thompson, *Recollections of Mexico*, p. 76.

75. John C. C. Hill interviewed, Mar. 9, 1880, by a reporter of the *Galveston News*, in *Galveston News*, Mar. 10, 1880.

76. Thompson, *Recollections of Mexico*, p. 77; see also Gooch-Iglehart, *The Boy Captive*, p. 238.

77. Thompson, *Recollections of Mexico*, p. 77; Gooch-Iglehart, *The Boy Captive*, pp. 238, 301; see also interview with Asa Hill in *Daily Picayune*, Aug. 16, 1843.

Hill "frequently visited us in our confinement," reported Stapp, "expressing the keenest solicitude for our welfare, and the most earnest hopes for our speedy deliverance."[78] He wrote regularly to relatives and friends in Texas.

Hill also asked Thompson to request the release of his father and brother. "I told him no," reported Thompson, "that he was a more successful negotiator than I was, to go and try his own hand again."[79] Hill visited the president and requested the release of his father and brother, the latter having recently reached the city from Matamoros. Santa Anna granted the request and provided clothes, money, and transportation to send Asa Hill and his son, Jeffrey Barksdale Hill, home.[80] Asa Hill's pardon, written in the president's own hand, stated that it was given in consideration of his advanced age and numerous family.[81] Asa Hill was released early in August,[82] and, carrying letters from several prisoners, reached New Orleans on Tuesday, August 15, and that evening left on the brig *Sam Houston* for Galveston and his Rutersville home in Texas. The father seemed "very well satisfied," reported the *Picayune,* "to leave his boy under the protection of the President."[83] Jeffrey Hill remained in the hospital in Mexico City.

After the arrival of the Texans at Santiago Prison from Salado, Orlando C. Phelps was brought before the president, who had seen his name on the list of Texan prisoners. His father, the jovial Dr. James A. E. Phelps, hospital surgeon of the Texan Army at San Jacinto, had three times frustrated Santa Anna's efforts to commit suicide while under house arrest in their home.[84] Santa Anna asked if he were related to Dr. Phelps of Orozimbo, and Orlando replied that he was his son. "I thought I recognized the name, Orlando, but you were a very small boy when I was in your home. You have grown much." Santa Anna instructed his secretary to order the boy's release and that he be furnished with clothing and money to get to the United States. Santa Anna "sent an aide-de-camp with him [Orlando] into the city, and purchased two to three suits of clothes for him, and gave him a room in his palace. I was informed of all this," said Waddy Thompson, "and as there was an American ship of war at Vera Cruz, about to sail to the United States, I wrote a note to Santa Anna, offering young Phelps a passage. He replied, thanking me for the offer, but declined it, saying he felt himself fortunate in having it in his power to return, in some

---

78. Stapp, *Prisoners of Perote*, p. 83.

79. Thompson, *Recollections of Mexico*, p. 77.

80. Crimmins, "John Christopher Columbus Hill; Boy Captive of the Mier Expedition," in *Frontier Times* 28 (June 1951), pp. 253-58.

81. *Daily Picayune*, Aug. 16, 1843; see also *Telegraph and Texas Register*, Sept. 6, 1843; *Northern Standard*, Sept. 30, 1843.

82. N. Woods to Dear Brothers and Sisters, Castle of Perote, September 23, 1843, in Spellman (ed.), "Letters of the 'Dawson Men,'" *SWHQ* 38 (Apr. 1935), pp. 265-66.

83. *Daily Picayune*, Aug. 16, 1843.

84. Amelia Williams, *Following General Sam Houston from 1795-1863*, p. 119.

degree, the kindness of Doctor Phelps to him, when he was a prisoner in Texas, and that he preferred sending his son home at his own expense; which he did, giving him also a draft on his factor in Vera Cruz, for whatever sum of money he might *ask for.*"[85]

The release of Phelps, commented Thomas Jefferson Green, "shows that the President of Mexico is not wholly destitute of gratitude."[86] The reaction among some of the prisoners to Orlando Phelps' release, however, was not so kind. "I have made mention of this fortunate animal [Phelps] . . . [elsewhere in this diary, wrote Canfield, and] further notice is unnecessary except that he is not worth the powder that would blow him to *any place.*"[87]

Phelps stayed at Santa Anna's palace until he left Mexico City by stage coach for Vera Cruz about May 5. He stopped at Perote Castle about lock-up time on May 8 to bid his friends goodbye and receive letters to be carried to Texas. He reached New Orleans aboard the schooner *Architect* from Vera Cruz on Monday, May 22, and was interviewed the next day by the editor of the *Picayune.*[88]

Soon after the arrival of the Mier men at Santiago prison, the English, French, and American foreign ministers received a statement about the executions of the seventeen prisoners at Salado and of Cameron at Huehuetoka. "The foreign ministers can do nothing for us," wrote Elijah Porter, "although they are trying to do something."[89] The Mier men were visited by many English, French, German, Italian, and American residents who were eager to hear their story. The visitors, especially an Italian named Gonzalvi, sent a considerable supply of clothing, hats, and shoes. Walker reported that the French, "who are always friends to the Americans," were generous in their contribution of clothing.[90]

The foreign visitors were permitted free access to the prison and prisoners, and could carry out uncensored any letter the Texans wished to send into the city or to the United States or Texas.[91] Writing the letters was not easy. Owing to poor lighting in the prison, the men often waited until they were in the open courtyard to do their writing. "You will remember," wrote McMath to his father, "that I am a prisoner and must sit down in the yard and write on my knee and [am] not allowed to be caught with a knife to mend a pen when it gets bad." He continued, "I shall look to you to succour my distressed family; however, I think they will not suffer until fall and if by chance I should get home before or by that time they will not

---

85. Thompson, *Recollections of Mexico*, pp. 75-76.

86. Green, *Mier Expedition*, p. 287.

87. Canfield diary, Apr. 26, 1843.

88. *Daily Picayune*, May 23 and 28, 1843; *Northern Standard*, June 22, 1843; *Daily National Intelligencer* (Washington, D.C.), June 3, 1843; Trueheart diary, May 8, 1843.

89. Elijah R. Porter to [John T. Porter], Prison San Tiago, Mexico, May 4, 1843, in *Cuero Star* (Cuero, Texa), March 8, 1899; clipping in Army Papers (Texas), Tx-A.

90. Sibley, ed., *Samuel H. Walker's Account*, p. 66.

91. Bell, *Narrative*, p. 68.

perish. I shall write to you as opportunity may offer and I wish you to do [so] as often as you can. Direct your letters [unsigned] to [the] care of the U.S. consul at this place." In conclusion, McMath requested his father to send him "a little money," if he could spare it, for he needed "very much to buy some clothes."[92]

One of the prisoners wrote a lengthy letter from Santiago Convent on May 4 to the editor of the *Telegraph and Texas Register,* in which he reported that James W. Robinson had opened a correspondence with Mexican authorities, "with the avowed purpose as he declared to his confidential friends of procuring his *own* personal liberty. The government here nibbled at the bait—Mr. Robinson was liberated and accepted the infamous commission under the solemn promise to use his best endeavors to bring Texas back to the fold of this degraded despotism."[93]

From San Luis Potosí on April 8 Cyrus K. Gleason wrote to his cousin, R. H. Gleason in Blenheim, New York, and handed the letter to a Mexican to be mailed. Upon arriving in Mexico City, Gleason sent letters directly to the United States "through more dependable hands." Since his capture, he said, he had "performed a journey of twelve hundred miles on foot Barefooted and almost entirely naked we arrived in this city [Mexico] on the 26th of last month [April] a period of just four months from the time of our capture." They had marched from eight to fifteen leagues per day over rough, barren country, sometimes without water all day. Gleason continued: "I have not a single shirt to my back nor scarcely anything in the shape of pantaloons. Nor have I any prospect of getting these things. Those who received money from their friends in the United States can get along very well but those that have none suffer. When I was first taken I had money sufficient to have done me eighteen months but it was all taken from me and I was left to suffer." He requested that he be sent $400 through a New York business house via Vera Cruz or the City of Mexico with a letter of credit to the American consul at Mexico City. He promised to repay the amount "with a hundred per cent." "I have sufficient property in Texas to pay it twenty times over," he assured his cousin, "but as I have not an opportunity of getting it from there I am under the necessity of calling upon you for some little assistance to alleviate my sufferings."[94]

During their incarceration at Santiago Prison, the Texans, according to Mexican standards, were well fed, although Walker claimed that in spite of all the boasted wealth and resources of the nation, they had not had a

---

92. W. F. McMath to Mr. McMath, Esq., McMath's P. O., Tuscaloosa County, Alabama, U.S.A., [dated] Mexico, April 29, 1843, in *Texas Magazine* 2, pp. 453-54.

93. Letter from a Texian Prisoner in Mexico to Messrs. Cruger & Moore, In Prison, Mexico, May 4, 1843, in *Telegraph and Texas Register*, June 14, 1843.

94. C. K. Gleason to R. H. Gleason, Blenheim, Schoharie, New York, [dated] City of Mexico, May 4, 1843 (copy June 26, 1843 by A. Daniel Favour of Lieutenant Johnson, U. States Navy, New Orleans), in Friend, ed., "Sidelights and Supplements on the Perote Prisoners," *SWHQ* 69 (July 1965), pp. 91-93.

good piece of beef since being in the country.[95] "Our rations . . . [were] pretty good," declared Glasscock, "although not suited for our tastes."[96] "We were extremely well fed and cared for in this old convent," recorded Stapp.[97] We were treated "tolerably well as respects giving," wrote Elijah R. Porter, and then as an after thought added, "[at least] some better than on the road."[98]

During their eleven-day stay in Mexico City, the prisoners improved considerably in health and flesh, as well as in spirit under the prison administration's humane discipline and a few days of rest. Their bill of fare was "a cake of corn bread and little corn flour gruel for breakfast, about 3 oz. of poor beef with soup and a cake of coarse bread for supper, beans half-cooked and a small cake of bread."[99] But it did not last.

On May 3, Benjamin Middleton died at the hospital.[100] Three days later, Saturday, May 6, the Texans were conducted to an adjoining small room decorated with rings, rivets, chains, and an anvil. They had not been chained when they arrived because there were not sufficient chains on hand. Once more they were paired by iron log chains six or eight feet long and weighing approximately twenty-five pounds.[101] Each end of the chain was attached to a ring riveted to the nearest ankle of the man as the two men stood side by side. While walking, the chain was suspended from an iron hook attached to a belt around the waist of the individual.

In the evening of May 6, Col. Francisco Barroetta, superintendent of the prison, referred to by the Texans as "Governor," visited the Texans, who were formed in single file with their heads bared to show proper respect, a testimony of submissiveness not required of them until now. The prisoners were viewed as convicts and would "be governed in every respect as the commonest criminal of the country." After being paraded, the colonel, "a morose, ill-favoured Cerberus, as ever turned bolt upon prisoner," as diplomatically as possible, informed them, "with an air and tone of the most touching philanthropy," that "the government of Mexico was too poor to support prisoners unless they labored, and that all would be expected to perform a little labor upon the public works."[102] He informed them that he was having comfortable clothes made for them, and that the clothes would be ready in a few days. The new clothes would enable them to make a respectable appearance outside of the prison walls.[103]

---

95. S. H. Walker to Gen. A. Sidney Johns[t]on, Galveston, Texas, [dated] Prison Santiago, City of Mexico, May 4th, 1843, in Army Papers (Texas), Tx-A.

96. Glasscock diary, Apr. 27-May 3, 1843.

97. Stapp, *Prisoners of Perote*, p. 83.

98. Elijah R. Porter to [John T. Porter], Prison Santiago, Mexico, May 4, 1843, in *Cuero Star*, Cuero, Tex., May 8, 1899; clipping in Army Papers (Texas), Tx-A.

99. Sibley, ed., *Samuel H. Walker's Account*, p. 66.

100. Canfield diary, Apr. 27-May 3, 1843.

101. Bell, *Narrative*, p. 60; see also Stapp, *Prisoners of Perote*, p. 5.

102. Stapp, *Prisoners of Perote*, p. 83.

103. Bell, *Narrative*, pp. 59-60.

While the colonel communicated with his superiors in the city, the Texans continued to discuss the issues among themselves, ignoring the fact that their view on the use of prisoners as laborers was contrary to those manifested by their own government toward the Mexican prisoners taken at San Jacinto in 1836, who were turned over to private parties and required to perform labor on plantaions, in sawmills, and elsewhere. A resolution was drawn declaring that they "would not work for the tyrant Santa Anna, but the Committee who drew up the resolution and signed it, strange to say," reported Walker, "are with one exception all sick."[104]

News of the plan to put the Texans to work brought many friendly visitors to the prison, among them the American minister, Waddy Thompson. He advised the prisoners to submit to the authorities as it might result in better treatment and liberation at an earlier date if the Texans voluntarily accepted whatever was required. This advice was accepted.

Soon after the foreigners left, the Texans' interpreter was taken before the colonel, who showed him the garments to be worn.[105] By early Monday morning, May 8, their prison clothes were ready and the business of robing commenced under threats that the bayonet would be used if they did not accept their new clothes willingly. In their jaunty colored, striped, coarse, woolen uniforms, the prisoners could be distinguished at a distance. Each man was supplied with a jacket, hat, and a pair of trousers "with stripes of alternate red and green," and a "coarse domestic shirt with sandals to match."[106] Leather was brought in from which the prisoners made their own sandals.

While putting on their new garb, "roars of laughter and many a merry jest on government and each other" shook the corridors of the prison; and when they had been properly groomed, "it would have puzzled Shakespeare's fantastic moralizer, the witty Lucio, to decide whether . . . [their] dress bespoke the *foppery of freedom,* or the morality of imprisonment."[107] The prisoners usually found that there was sufficient room in the shirt and pantaloons to contain another man equal in dimensions to themselves.[108] As they switched to their new prison garb, many of the men saved their civilian clothes for future use.

As soon as a few of the Texans had put on their new uniforms, five or six of them were taken out during the morning and paraded through the streets of Mexico City. Filth and wretchedness were to be found everywhere in the streets. A mob of old men, women, and children gathered to see the prisoners and to shout, *"Mueren los Gringos!" "Derriba los herejes!"* (Destroy the heretics!). "Our guard," narrated Wallace, "endeavored in vain to keep them back, and they were pressing closer and closer upon us

---

104. Sibley, ed., *Samuel H. Walker's Account,* p. 66.

105. Stapp, *Prisoners of Perote,* p. 84.

106. *Ibid.;* see also Canfield's diary, May 7, 1843.

107. Stapp, *Prisoners of Perote,* p. 84.

108. Bell, *Narrative,* p. 60.

in the most threatening manner. At last the sergeant in command of the guard told the mob if they did not give way he would turn the 'Texan cannibals' loose upon them. We heard and understood very well what he said, and to carry out the joke, and make a diversion in our favor, three or four of us grabbed as many old women and boys who had ventured in reach of us, and made out we were going to eat them at once, without salt or pepper. I clinched an old wrinkled squaw, who had been making herself very prominent in the melee, [walking backwards in front of us, grinning and making all kinds of wry faces at us] and took a good bite at her neck, but it was tougher than a ten-year-old buffalo bull's, and though I bit with a will, and can crack a hickory-nut easily with my grinders, I could make no impression on it whatever." The old woman screamed and jerked loose. "However, this unexpected demonstration on the part of the 'Gringos' took the mob completely by surprise, and they scattered like a flock of partridges, and we were molested no more that day."[109]

Returning to the prison, they found that all of the able-bodied Texans had changed into their uniforms. The prisoners were fed a breakfast of coffee and about four ounces of bread each and were told to get all of their personal gear together and to form ready for marching, "without [the] remotest hint of where they were to be taken."[110] There had earlier been reports and rumors that the Texan prisoners were to do forced labor on the road between Acapulco and Mexico City. Waddy Thompson had informed Daniel Webster that the prisoners' destination was "to the Pacific Coast to work on a public road in that quarter."[111] Could this be their destination?

---

109. Duval, *Big-Foot Wallace*, pp. 236-237; see also Sowell, *Early Settlers and Indian Fighters of Southwest Texas*, p. 78.

110. Bell, *Narrative*, p. 61.

111. Waddy Thompson to Daniel Webster, Legation of the United States of America, Mexico, March 14, 1843, in Despatches from the United States Ministers to Mexico (Mar. 12, 1842-Mar. 25, 1844), National Archives (microfilm).

CHAPTER 19

Prisoners Are Moved to the Vicinity of Tacubaya to Improve a Road

AFTER BEING PARADED ON the morning of May 8, the prisoners were supplied with crowbars, crude wooden spades or shovels, pickaxes, and mauls. A coarse "grass" or hemp sack with rawhide straps at the mouth for carrying was handed to each prisoner. In the sacks, the Texans smuggled out their old clothes for use when their freedom should be granted or an escape effected. The prisoners, chained two and two by the ankles,[1] made their first appearance in their red and green uniforms and found a contingent of cavalry ready to receive them. The prisoners were marched through several of the streets of the city, past "crowds of lazzaroni, and half-naked women and children,"[2] who followed and cheered at every step of the Texan chain gang.

The Texans were driven in a westerly direction through the suburbs of the city to Santa Anna's country place near Tacubaya. Leaving Mexico City by the Garita de Belén, the Texans were marched along the Calzada de Belén. Tacubaya was a pleasant village of scattered houses situated on the slope of the Sierra de las Cruces. It contained a number of pretty country homes of the capital's opulent who resided there for short periods during the summer months. Santa Anna lived in a large, two-story house with windows opening on all four sides, known as the Archbishop's Palace, formerly a convent.

Some of the Santa Fé prisoners had been sent to work upon the road at Tacubaya, and had reported that they had been treated well by the local inhabitants. The Mier prisoners arrived at Tacubaya at about one in the afternoon and were marched through the streets, passing near the president's palace. They were lodged in a small room with no space to lie down. An hour later they were ordered outside, where they were met by Col.

---

1. Stapp, *Prisoners of Perote*, p. 85.
2. *Ibid.*

319

Joaquín Rangel, who informed them in a mixed jargon of Spanish and French that he was to superintend their work of improving the road from the Obispado to Tacubaya. In an effort to be as friendly as possible, he informed the prisoners that they would be treated with great humanity and as "gentlemen" and that they would be expected to perform a moderate degree of work.

As soon as the colonel retired, the Texans were marched to El Santuario de la Piedad, an old Dominican convent about a mile and a half east of Tacubaya, to be lodged until other quarters could be arranged.[3] They were required to wear their chains day and night, but "no one ever thought of sleeping in them, kicking them off like old shoes the moment the key was turned" on them; but with "the first hail of the sentinel next morning, . . . all were refettered as securely as before."[4]

The next day the Texans were ordered to put on their new uniforms and were marched to see Santa Anna, taking their tools with them.[5] "Everything wore the appearance of work," and Canfield suddenly found himself quite unwell and was taken from the group and sent to the hospital in Mexico City.[6] The prisoners arrived before the palace about ten o'clock. From a window the president reviewed them, after which they were permitted to sit in the shade of trees until noon, when they were marched down to the foot of the street. Here ladies presented them with cigars, and the prisoners spent the afternoon lounging in the shade until they were returned to their quarters.

May 10 was spent in their uncomfortable quarters. These were so poor and small that their guard obtained permission to transfer the prisoners on May 11, with all their road-building equipment and bedding, to a deserted old Powder Mill (*Molino del Rey,* or King's Mill), a range of low, massive stone buildings,[7] situated in Chapúltepec Forest. From Tacubaya, a narrow, winding road, descending gradually through smooth open land, led to the southern end of the building of the *Molino.* En route to their new quarters, Henry Journeay, being sick, was unable to carry the load given to him by the guard, for which he was whipped.

In spite of the rundown condition of *Molino de Rey,* the Texans found their new quarters "quite comfortable"[8] and less secure, although the rooms were still somewhat small and crowded. Each prisoner was furnished with a mat made from rushes which served as a bed, without blanket, unless he were fortunate enough to possess one. An area of about an acre was available for recreation and exercise in the daytime when the men were not working. A nearby chapel, in which mass was said each Sunday, was available to the Texans. Early in the evening the guard was always

---

3. Canfield diary, May 8, 1843.
4. Stapp, *Prisoners of Perote,* p. 103.
5. Sibley, ed., *Samuel H. Walker's Account,* p. 67.
6. Canfield diary, May 9, 1843.
7. Glasscock diary, May 11, 1843.
8. *Ibid.*

doubled for the night, and the men were required to remain in their cells. Mexican convicts prepared their food. "Our fare here was as villanous as a parsimonious commissary and filthy cook could make it," declared Stapp.[9] The prisoners were breakfasted at six in the morning, returned to dinner at noon, and to supper at five in the afternoon.

Each morning a large kettle filled with *atole* sweetened with a little sugar was brought and each man received nearly a pint and one small cake of coarse brown bread.[10] This was regarded as sufficient until the noon meal. At noon each man was served four to six ounces of boiled lean beef, often spoiled, with a pint of "miserable soup" made of the water in which the meat had been cooked, and a five or six ounce loaf of coarse brown bread.[11] Sometimes beans were served at noon. At night the menu consisted of a half pint of boiled beans, and another portion of brown bread. If beans had been served at noon, the breakfast menu was repeated, "this being insufficient to satisfy the cravings of hunger, and the quality of the food [was] such, that none but strong men could be induced to eat it." Waters described the rations as worse than he was accustomed to feed to his dogs.[12]

The quality and quantity of the regular fare furnished the Texans laboring on the road were unsatisfactory for the maintenance of good health in large, vigorous men. But, with the small monetary allowances occasionally permitted by the government, plus small contributions the prisoners received from time to time from friends within and without Mexico, they purchased oranges, melons, sweet limes, bananas, zapotes, and other fruits and vegetables.

On several occasions the prisoners were surprised by the ladies of the village, as was the case on Wednesday, May 24, with a well-prepared and tasty dinner. On other occasions, some of the ladies residing where small parties of Texans might be working near their homes "supplied the captives with many comforts that tended to alleviate a helpless condition."[13]

On May 12 the Texans were marched to the public road connecting the Archbishop's Palace with Tacubaya to commence their labors upon the road, which was only approximately 600 yards in length.[14] The overseer, Colonel Rangel, selected the Texan officers as his deputies and explained that the roadbed was "to be covered with a layer of large pebbles," on which was put a layer of smaller pebbles, with dirt, "and the whole pounded hard with heavy mauls."[15] The center line of stones was to be higher than the others, thus giving a curvature to the road to facilitate drainage.

9. Stapp, *Prisoners of Perote*, p. 87.

10. Canfield diary, May 21, 1843.

11. Stapp, *Prisoners of Perote*, p. 87; see also Canfield diary, May 21, 1843.

12. *Telegraph and Texas Register*, Aug. 16, 1843.

13. Bell, *Narrative*, p. 67.

14. Glasscock reported the distance to be a quarter of a mile (Glasscock diary, Sept. 4, 1843).

15. Stapp, *Prisoners of Perote*, p. 88.

After issuing his instructions concerning the grade, width, type of construction desired, and the manner of performing the work, the young colonel left the Texans to the task assigned them under the supervision of a small guard.

The prisoners were divided into squads. One group of approximately sixty men performed the work of "Jacks and Jennys," or, as Glasscock said, "the work of Asses."[16] They moved in double file, carrying rocks, gravel, sand, or dirt in their grass sacks. Other squads with mauls, picks, and heavy iron crowbars dug up the ground, leveled it, broke up the stones, and worked the roadbed into shape.

The work done by the Texans during their five months near Tacubaya was of little real advantage to the Mexican government, and to the Texans it was loathsome and burdensome. In all, they improved only 600 yards of road with a topping of sand and stones a foot deep. Their policy was to do as little as possible without endangering their lives. Their working hours were from seven to five daily, except Sundays and feast days, with an intermission of two hours at noon.[17] Each morning the guard marched them out to work, left a sentry or two to see that they did not escape, then retired to their parade ground to pass the day, returning at noon and at sunset for them.[18] The guard had no interest in the work and felt no responsibility for it. Its duty was to see that the prisoners did not run off.[19]

As soon as Colonel Rangel had given his orders, twelve to fifteen of the Texans set to work in earnest, digging, pounding, and shoveling sand and gravel as though they expected to receive some sort of reward for their exertions. The others retired to the shade of a clump of ash, where they spent the remainder of the day in spite of remonstrances from their officers who entreated and sought to reason with them to do at least some work. For weeks, many of the prisoners did nothing but loll under the trees, "sleeping and gossiping of homes and friends," or engaging "in elaborate and curious calculations of the enormous lapse of time required to finish the stupendous work" assigned them. "If the Mexican Government called this work, they were willing to perform it on these easy terms, but this like all other terrestrial enjoyments had to come to an end."[20]

After several weeks of a virtual vacation from work, during which time only a few rods of road were completed, Colonel Rangel concluded that more stringent discipline would have to be imposed. The Texan officers who had served as his assistants in building the roadbed had failed to produce results, so they were replaced with "a set of ferocious brute convicts" brought from Santiago prison, who were instructed to get the maximum

16. Glasscock diary, May 14-20, 1843.
17. Canfield diary, May 21, 1843; see also, Glasscock diary, May 21, 1843.
18. Stapp, *Prisoners of Perote*, p. 87.
19. *Ibid.*
20. Bell, *Narrative*, p. 62.

labor possible out of *los flojos* (the lazy ones). They had instructions to whip the prisoners if they did not work.

The new overseers carried rods five feet in length, resembling ox-goads, which they did not hesitate to use to prod a prisoner. Thus, "Armed with cudgels, and supported by a score of soldiers, they commenced business with a briskness that would have macadamized all Mexico in a twelve-month," reported Stapp, "could it have been kept up."[21]

At first, the Texans resented their use and would return blow for blow, but they learned that the guards always protected the overseers and were under instructions to shoot any Texan who resisted the authority of the overseer,[22] and that they "could no longer repudiate their tasks with impunity."[23] Picking out one or two of the weaker "loafers" among the Texans, the overseers fell on them with their cudgels, beating them mercilessly as a warning to others. Several of the Texans, witnessing the assault upon their comrades, intervened, sometimes jointly with the soldiers, to prevent the maiming or murder of an associate.

Those among the Mier men who had been Santa Fé prisoners declared that "their treatment now is a great deal worse than that of the Santa Fé prisoners ever was," reported Robert G. Waters.[24] Waters described their condition as deplorable. "The overseers (who are convicts taken from the prisons) often beat the Texians with sticks with as little ceremony as they would beat negroes. They are all chained with fetters as heavy as log chains, which many of them are scarcely able to drag."

The prisoners realized that they could no longer ignore their assignments or be pugnacious toward their overseers and guards. They made an effort to give the appearance to obey the demands of their captors, but, in reality, did little more than previously. On the other hand, the attitude toward work among some of the prisoners was not entirely negative. On occasion they volunteered for work to get outside of their cells and in hope of improving their health.[25]

On May 13, the second day at work, Samuel H. Walker was "struck by a criminal peón . . . without cause." Walker "returned him the compliment over the head with a shovel and choked him in the bargain, for which . . . [he] afterwards was severely beaten by a drunken soldier and the same overseer . . . [and] was also compelled to carry three times as much sand as usual."[26] Fortunately, the next day was Sunday and the prisoners did not have to work. On Monday and Tuesday, Walker pleaded that he was unable to work on account of injuries received on Saturday. For some time,

---

21. Stapp, *Prisoners of Perote*, p. 87.
22. Bell, *Narrative*, p. 62.
23. Stapp, *Prisoners of Perote*, p. 88.
24. J. D. Waters showed several letters he received from his relative, Robert G. Waters, to the editor of the *Telegraph and Texas Register*, the substance of which was reported in that newspaper on August 16, 1843.
25. Sibley, ed., *Samuel H. Walker's Account*, p. 71.
26. *Ibid.*, p. 657.

no more Texans were whipped. On another occasion, a Mexican convict-overseer struck William B. Middleton as he was stooping down to pick up a bag of sand. "Middleton immediately knocked him down with a stone. The guards ran up; but a Mexican officer present, seeing the whole affair, protected the prisoner,"[27] Yoakum noted.

The Texans frequently buried their crowbars, trowels, shovels, mauls, and other tools under the dirt, pebbles, and rocks thrown on the road, or "lost" or "misplaced" them; on occasion they even "sold" their tools. Wooden handles were deliberately broken so time could be lost in making repairs. It made little difference to them if the equipment were lost or broken, as the overseer was responsible for it. "When we quit the road," reported McCutchan, "we had the extreme gratification of leaving some of our overseers, to 'taste the pleasures of a prison *life*' for the loss of tools which we had destroyed or hiden. This was our sweetest consolation. I hope they had a fine time."[28]

Beyond the control of the Texans was the problem of illness, which also affected work upon the road. Because of the poor quality of their rations and the unsanitary conditions under which their meals were prepared, a number of them from time to time became ill and were excused from the work detail for the day. If the illness persisted, they were transferred to the hospital at Santiago prison in Mexico City. The climate in the Tacubaya area, although generally mild, was often warm, and the frequent rains during the summer added much to the sickness and discomfort of the men. During the months of June and July it rained nearly every day. More than one person suffered from colds, rheumatism, influenza, and other ailments.

The American minister "told them that when any of them were sick, to let him know it," and that he "would furnish them with such things as their necessities required." "It more than once occurred," Thompson reported, "that when I visited them I found some of them sick, and unable to eat the coarse food of which their rations consisted. When I asked them why they had not applied to me, their reply was, 'Why, sir, you have had to advance so much on our account, that we were unwilling to tax you any farther.' I had very few applications for money, and in every instance, where I regarded the advance as a loan, I have since been paid, with not more than one or two exceptions."[29]

Since sickness exempted a man from the work detail, it did not take the Texans long to exploit this avenue. It is difficult to evaluate the extent of "real" sickness among the Texan prisoners. It was not uncommon to feign illness, with all kinds of pretended aches, pains, or diseases. "Brawny fellows, who never had an hour's sickness in their lives, would drop in a fit" of the most excruciating pain and agony, "and require some ten of

27. Yoakum, *History of Texas* 2, p. 399, note.
28. Nance, ed., *McCutchan's Diary*, p. 100.
29. Thompson, *Recollections of Mexico*, pp. 94-95.

their comrades several hours to get them to quarters."[30] By May 31, two-thirds of the men were either "sick or rather very much indisposed," reported Walker.[31]

An individual had to be terribly lazy to want to go to the hospital to avoid work. There he was stripped of his clothing, had nothing more than a sheet or blanket to cover him, and was compelled to remain in bed. He was given "cornmeal gruel to eat in small quantities and after undergoing a severe operation of salts & oil and several greasings, which is resorted to in almost all cases, the patient either dies or regains his appetite in which case he had to report himself well," recorded Walker.[32]

Residence in a Mexican hospital was something to be dreaded, and for able-bodied men it soon became distasteful. Some considered imprisonment there to hold a better chance for escape, and this seems to have been the case until July 1843, when four of the Texans escaped from Mexico City. "Two days elapsed before it was found out" that they had left, which caused the authorities to be more strict thereafter. "It . . . appears from the letter [received at Perote] that they are more lenient with the Texans there than with us in this infernal Perote," recorded Trueheart. "They in Mexico, many of them, living exempt from chains, and [are] not nearly so closely watched as we are; whereas, on the other hand, we are all chained in couples with a very few exemptions, and watched with increasing care and diligence both day and night; the officers coming down to visit us at various hours of the night to be enabled if possible to find some of us separated from our companions. Our chains are also closely examined night and morning"—before lockup at night and before the prisoners are let out in the morning, "which takes place after eight" o'clock, said Trueheart.[33]

On June 3, at Tacubaya, Walker's companion in chains, Peter M. Maxwell, who had not worked a day in three weeks on account of illness, was cut loose and sent to the hospital. His only complaint was rheumatism, "which was a good complaint," the Texans learned, "to go to the hospital with as the patient is generally allowed to eat. In all other diseases starvation is resorted to."[34]

After Maxwell was released from him, Walker was chained to John McMullen; two days later McMullen was replaced with Wilson N. Vandyke, who was not feeling too well. On June 9, although Walker wanted to work, Vandyke developed a fever and the two lay in the shade all afternoon. The next day, Vandyke was separated from Walker and sent to the hospital. Walker now received as a chain-partner Patrick H. Lusk.[35]

---

30. Stapp, *Prisoners of Perote*, p. 88.
31. Sibley, ed., *Samuel H. Walker's Account*, p. 68.
32. *Ibid.*, p. 70.
33. Trueheart diary, July 27, 1843.
34. Sibley, ed., *Samuel H. Walker's Account*, p. 69.
35. *Ibid.*, p. 71.

While the Texans worked on the road near Tacubaya, the bishop's residence was Santa Anna's retreat and there was much traffic over the road between the Sanctuario de la Piedad and Tacubaya. Occasionally, Santa Anna passed along the road in a great coach drawn by six well-groomed mules and guarded by several hundred cavalry. The prisoners were informed in advance of his coming and drawn up at attention on each side of the road.

On June 10 the Texans were told to work harder than usual to have their segment of the road finished by Santa Anna's presumed birthday, June 13, and to insure success the number of officers overseeing them was increased significantly.[36]

It was mistakenly believed that the Santa Fé prisoners had been liberated on June 13, 1842,[37] in celebration of what many of the Mier men believed to be President Santa Anna's birthday; and the prisoners hoped that the president would show his appreciation for their labor by granting their freedom. Their hopes for liberation were further aroused by many of the Mexican officers, as well as by foreigners who occasionally visited the prisoners and believed that June 13 would be the day of their liberation.[38] The prisoners, with high spirits, eagerly looked forward to the coming of the day, but when it arrived, "all passed off quietly, excepting the clanking of . . . [their] chains."[39]

A presidential order of that date released political prisoners, and the Texans waited anxiously to learn if they were included in the orders; the next day they were taken out to work.[40] Their hopes for liberty quickly faded. While they were at work an old friend, the "Frenchman," visited and said he did not think that Santa Anna's order included the Texans and that their only hope for liberty was in a settlement of the differences between Mexico and Texas.[41] It was assumed that the arrival of news relative to the ill-fated Warfield and Snively expeditions against Santa Fé had caused Santa Anna to reject any thought of releasing the Mier men.[42] Instead, on June 17 Santa Anna issued a decree ordering all prisoners thereafter taken in the war against Texas be shot.[43] Robert G. Waters wrote to

---

36. June 13 was Saint Anthony's feast day, and was presumed to be Santa Anna's birthday. Santa Anna's patron saint was St. Anthony, or, as Waddy Thompson said, it was Saint Antonio. Loomis, *The Texan-Santa Fé Pioneers*, p. 133 n. 14.

37. Stapp, *Prisoners of Perote*, p. 89.

38. Sibley, ed., *Samuel H. Walker's Account*, p. 71; see also Canfield diary, June 13, 1843.

39. Canfield diary, June 13, 1843.

40. Glasscock diary, June 14, 1843.

41. Sibley, ed., *Samuel H. Walker's Account*, p. 72.

42. Stapp, *Prisoners of Perote*, p. 97.

43. Decree issued by *Antonio López de Santa Anna, Palacio nacional de México, a 17 de Junio de 1843. José María Tornel, Ministro de guerra y Marina*, in *Diario de Gobierno*, June 19, 1843; see also Waddy Thompson to Hugh S. Legaré, Secretary of State, Legation of the U. States, Mexico, June 24, 1843, in Despatches from United States Ministers to Mexico, Mar. 12, 1842-Mar. 25, 1844, National Archives (microfilm).

his uncle J. D. Waters that the Mexican guard had informed them that they were not released because "Com[modore] Moore was on the coast destroying their navy, and an army of Texians and Comanche Indians was ravaging Santa Fé."[44] The commandant explained to the prisoners that the reason they had not been released was "because the Texians had been doing a great deal of mischief about Santa Fé. I hope this may be true," recorded Walker.[45]

On June 16 the prisoners were assigned to fill the mud holes in the road from Tacubaya to Mexico City, which was expected to occupy them for a number of days. On June 17, John Owens, after an illness of some forty-eight hours, died in Powder Mill Prison.[46] On June 19, Robert Smith also died. The Texan prisoners, joined by twenty-two men returned from the hospital, began work again "at the old place near the president's palace, breaking up the work which we had done," recorded Walker, "several times over already."[47]

On June 27, Thomas Colville died suddenly "of damp cholic with the chains on him."[48] He was buried at the expense of the British consul in the burying ground for foreigners. On June 3, 1843, of the 248 men who surrendered at Mier, only 189 were still alive in Mexico. Seventeen were at Perote Castle, five in Matamoros, eight had made their escape at Mier, and 159 were at Tacubaya.[49]

Toward the end of June, Colonel Rangel was ordered by Santa Anna to investigate the construction of the road and recommend a plan for greater progress. Expressing "profound indignation" at the quality of the food being supplied the prisoners, Rangel substituted coffee twice daily for the unappetizing *atole* and ordered fresh meat furnished to the prisoners. The prisoners were told in a kind but firm manner that while he intended to see that they were treated kindly, he expected them to turn out more work. The Texan officers and interpreters were unchained, placed in charge of the different squads, and told that they would be responsible for the labor of the others,[50] and "if they did not do their duty and make the men work, they . . . [would] be put to work themselves." The criminal overseers no longer had authority to whip indolent or recalcitrant workers.[51]

---

44. Quoted in *Telegraph and Texas Register*, Aug. 16, 1843.

45. Sibley, ed., *Samuel H. Walker's Account*, p. 75.

46. Glasscock diary, June 17, 1843.

47. Sibley, ed., *Samuel H. Walker's Account*, pp. 72-73.

48. *Ibid.*, p. 75.

49. [A Mier Prisoner] to the Editor of the *New York American*, Prison of the Powder Mills, near the city of Mexico, June 3, 1832, in Niles' *National Register*, 65, p. 23 (Sept. 2, 1843). On July 4, 1843, one of the prisoners near Tacubaya wrote a letter to the editors of the New Orleans *Daily Picayune* giving a complete list of the Mier men, their nativity, and a statement of what had happened to each man. [Letter of a Texan Prisoner] to Messrs. Lumsden, Kendall & Co., Powder Mill Prison, New [near] Mexico, July 4, 1843, in *Daily Picayune*, Aug. 2, 1843.

50. Sibley, ed., *Samuel H. Walker's Account*, pp. 74-75; see also Stapp, *Prisoners of Perote*, p. 88; *Telegraph and Texas Register*, Sept. 27, 1843.

51. *Telegraph and Texas Register*, Sept. 27, 1843; *Northern Standard*, Oct. 14, 1843.

On July 10 burros were furnished to pack the sand and gravel, relieving the Texans of that burdensome task. On the 12th they were informed that Santa Anna had said he would release the Texan prisoners as soon as they had repaired certain sections of the road, amounting to about 300 yards. The prisoners placed little confidence in the report; if it could be depended on, reported Walker, "we would finish it in a very short time."[52]

As soon as they realized that Rangel's promise of improvement in their living conditions was genuine, the Texans became more co-operative. When they learned that those who worked would be relieved of their chains, within three weeks nearly the whole gang was working. Whenever a prisoner was found shirking he was rechained and "many of the emancipated were rebound, preferring mild employment in irons, to more active labour without them."[53]

By Sunday, July 23, a number of the prisoners had been unchained and the word was that all of them would be unchained by Wednesday, July 26. On July 23, William H. Beard died in Powder Mill Prison, near Tacubaya. His brother, Robert, had succumbed earlier at San Luis Potosí. On July 27, Carter Sargeant died in the hospital in Mexico City,[54] and by the time Walker, Gattis, and Wilson made their escape on July 30, nine Texans had died at Tacubaya, and Judge Usher, who had been moved to the hospital in Mexico City, was hourly expected to die "of consumption."[55] He lingered, however, until August 23, 1843. The day following Usher's death, Elijah R. Porter died in the hospital in Mexico City.

Although the prisoners received no compensation for their services on the road, some obtained money through the sale of their chains or tools. When an opportunity presented, they would "cut off their chains, smuggle them out, and sell them at a very low rate; or after having cut their chain, wear it to their work, watch a[n] opportunity to hide it in some convenient place, and sell it at some future day."[56]

Numerous holidays cluttered the Mexican calendar, and when such an occasion arrived, the Texans were put under lock and key with only a few sentries to watch them.[57] One such day it occurred to one of them that it was election day in Texas, so it was decided to hold an election for the Senate and House of Representatives. Nominations were made, speeches delivered, "offices and treats promised, and all the cajoleries and strategie of a genuine and heated contest observed. There was not fighting, tippling, or pipe-laying." Upon the votes being canvassed, amid considerable crowding and swearing at the polls, and numerous challenges, Judge Gibson was chosen to the Senate by a slim majority, and Captain Buster, who

52. Sibley, ed., *Samuel H. Walker's Account*, p. 75.

53. Stapp, *Prisoners of Perote*, p. 89.

54. Sibley, ed., *Samuel H. Walker's Account*, p. 76.

55. *Northern Standard*, Oct. 14, 1843.

56. Nance, ed., *McCutchan's Narrative*, pp. 99-100; Bell, *Narrative*, p. 65; Stapp, *Prisoners of Perote*, p. 103.

57. Stapp, *Prisoners of Perote*, p. 102.

had only recently joined the group, was elected by a complimentary vote to the House.[58]

Capt. Claudius Buster and John Toops, who had left the main body of prisoners on February 17 in search of water and had found themselves cut off by a cavalry patrol, reached and crossed the Rio Grande. While preparing something to eat at a deserted *rancho* they were surprised in the afternoon by ten Mexicans. Buster had placed his *escopeta* against a wall inside the house. A surrender was inevitable, and that night the two unfortunate Texans were tied hand and foot, placed on their backs, and then tied one to the other. Sentinels were placed over them with orders to shoot if they moved. The next day they were taken to Gen. Adrían Woll's headquarters on the west bank of the Rio Grande opposite Laredo, and then in succession to Guerrero, Monterrey, Saltillo, and San Luis Potosí, where they found Norman Woods and three others who had been left there. Woods, Buster, Toops, and several others at San Luis Potosí were sent to Mexico City with the main body of prisoners, and thence to Tacubaya and to Perote Castle.[59]

As the fourth of July approached, the Texans planned to stage a grand celebration in honor of American independence. Of course, it would be easier to celebrate if the guard should prove cooperative. On July 3 a petition was drafted and presented to President Santa Anna by a committee of Texan officers, requesting that they be excused from work on that day, "unloosened from their chains for one day," and be allowed to celebrate the anniversary of the independence of the United States, their native country, "in the spirit and after the fashion of our American sires."[60]

It was verbally reported that after some consideration the president consented "from his *unbound reverence for the signers of that heroic pronunciamento, rather than from any respect for their unworthy descendants*, who asked to observe it."[61] July 4 was declared by the commander of the guard to be a holiday, freeing the men from work, though their chains were not removed. Various committees were appointed and a speaker was selected, but no copy of the American Declaration of Independence could be procured. Every pocket was emptied of its last claco and "the proceeds of the chains and tools . . . [that] had [been] sold delivered over with scrupulous exactness."[62] The amount collected was not sufficient to procure the ham and whiskey deemed indispensable on this occasion to arouse patriotic jollity. At this stage, when it seemed as if the celebration might flop, a Yankee comrade suggested that the officers of the guard be invited to unite in

---

58. Claudius Buster to John H. Jenkins, Pesch, Washington County, Texas, June 16, 1889, original MS, Daughters of the Republic of Texas Library, The Alamo, San Antonio, Texas.

59. Stapp, *Prisoners of Perote*, pp. 97-98, 102.

60. *Ibid.*, pp. 97-98.

61. *Ibid.*

62. *Ibid.*, p. 98.

the celebration. Invitations, couched in the most courteous language, were addressed to Colonel Rangel and a number of his subordinates. Every one of the Mexican officers who received an invitation accepted, and presents from anonymous donors flooded the Texan commissary department. *Pulque,* brandy, *chayotes, chirimoyas,* pineapples, and melons of various kinds, chickens, ducks, turkeys, beef, mutton, fish, and other foods were sent. The largest room in the Powder Mill was assigned for the banquet, and portraits of Washington and Jefferson were sketched in charcoal on the walls of the festive hall. Colonel Rangel insisted on catering the table.

To aid in the celebration, a small brass cannon was sent down from the barracks "to usher in the glorious morning with the customary salutes for every state of the confederacy, but either through design or ignorance, their cartridges gave out at nine, and," reported Stapp, "we were accordingly compelled to acquiesce in this dogmatical retrenchment of the sovereignties of the Union."[63] This whole affair went off with the greatest *éclat.* They celebrated the day in true American style.

On July 5 Waddy Thompson visited the prisoners and said that President Houston had issued a proclamation calling upon all Texans to cease hostilities against Mexico.[64] Two days later the British minister sent word that he expected the prisoners to be released that month. On the same day twenty-one of the Mier men returned from the hospital in Mexico City with their spirits bolstered by a report that Santa Anna had agreed to an armistice with Texas and with further confirmation of the report of an early release. The commander of the prisoners' guard was changed, and there developed "hopes of better living in the future."[65] On July 8, 1843, it was reported that John C. C. Hill had been freed by Santa Anna. Details of his adoption by the president did not come out until later. With the adoption of the armistice[66] between Texas and Mexico the rigorous treatment of the Texan prisoners was materially mitigated.[67]

General Tornel, minister of war and marine, on July 7, 1843, sent a copy of Houston's proclamation of an armistice to General Woll, and ordered him to retire his "advanced posts, spies, parties of observation, and all forces destined to molest the enemy," and to suspend during the armistice his plans to march to the center of Texas with a strong division of cav-

---

63. *Ibid.*

64. Sibley, ed., *Samuel H. Walker's Account,* p. 74.

65. *Ibid.*

66. By the President of the Republic of Texas. A Proclamation [of an Armistice with Mexico], [dated at end]: Washington, June 15, 1843, [signed]: Sam Houston. by the President: Anson Jones, Secretary of State. [Washington: Printed at the National Vindicator Office, 1843]. [At head: Vindicator—Extra.]; see also *Writings of Sam Houston* 3, pp. 409-10.

67. *Northern Standard,* Oct. 14, 1843. Many of the prisoners were relieved of their chains, the convict overseers were removed, "and the brutal ruffians who act as their masters," reported Walker in the New Orleans *Tropic,* "are no longer allowed to cudgel and lacerate the unfortunate captives." New Orleans *Tropic,* quoted in the *Northern Standard,* Oct. 1, 1843.

alry. He was to appoint commissioners to meet with those to be appointed by "Mr. Samuel Houston."[68]

Hopes of the Texan prisoners for an early release were raised when they learned that the British warship *Scylla* had arrived at Vera Cruz with dispatches from Texas and it was further learned on Monday, July 24, 1843, that the Texan brig *Wharton* would soon arrive at Matamoros, with Commissioners Samuel May Williams and George W. Hockley to treat with Mexico. They intended "to demand as a preliminary step," reported Trueheart, "to release the Texian prisoners; unwilling to proceed in the matter unless the prisoners were first released. They may succeed in obtaining our liberty, a matter of paramount importance to us, but to bring about a reconciliation between the two governments, I hardly think probable."[69]

Working daily, the grading of the road progressed slowly. Occasionally while working a man would make good his escape, but more often those who ran off did so at night. On the night of July 29, Willis Copeland, a native of Virginia, escaped over the prison wall, using blankets torn into ropes.[70] Before his absence was discovered, three others decided to do likewise. It was clear that when Copeland's escape should become known to the Mexicans all of the prisoners would be rechained, guarded more closely, and would not be permitted "to step out of doors after sun set."[71]

Samuel H. Walker, who contemplated escape for some time, waited until he had accumulated sufficient money for his use in flight. Early in the evening on July 30, Walker and James Charles Wilson went for a walk in the park of the military academy which was connected with the prison yard. "One of the greatest curiosities we saw," reported Walker, "was the secret passage which it is said Montezuma had to the city. However, the most interesting part of our walk to me was to examine the walls for the purpose of getting out."[72] Returning to the prison, Walker, Wilson, and D. H. Gattis formulated their plan. Before the regular night shift of the guard—which was always doubled—took over, the three prisoners passed the sentinels at the door early and "scaled the walls about 8 o'clock splitting our blankets & tieing them together for the purpose of letting ourselves down with."[73]

The feat of the three "dare-devils" was no simple one, for it had to be carried out within the "view of the two sentinels, and the night was by no means so dark as we could have wished it," reported Wilson. Having

---

68. José María Tornel to Adrian Woll, Commander in Chief of the Army of the North, July 7, 1843, in *Telegraph and Texas Register*, May 8, 1844.

69. Trueheart diary, July 24, 1843.

70. Nance, ed., *McCutchan's Narrative*, p. 97; Canfield dairy, July 30, 1843.

71. Sibley, ed., *Samuel H. Walker's Account*, p. 76.

72. *Ibid.*, p. 77; see also *Telegraph and Texas Register*, Sept. 27, 1843.

73. Sibley, ed., *Samuel H. Walker's Account*, p. 76; Canfield diary, July 30, 1843; J. C. Wilson's account of his escape appeared in the *Northern Standard*, Nov. 18, 1843.

cleared the wall, the three men went to Mexico City. They had to be careful "to avoid the sentinels . . . posted in front of the numerous quartels in every part of the city."[74] When they reached the village of Guadalupe, they found a soldier on duty at the gate. "We turned to the right,"[75] said Walker, and proceeded along the ditch for a mile or less, but finding no place for crossing over the ditch, they were compelled to swim across. On the morning of July 31 they abandoned the road about six leagues from Mexico City and concealed themselves in a clump of bushes to pass the day. Taking turns, two slept and one kept watch. Soon they realized that the spot they had chosen was not so private; it turned out to be a place where shepherd boys passed the time of day while their sheep grazed in the vicinity. After near discovery several times, the Texans decided to change their hiding place. Narrated Walker, "we started across the mountain when near sunset [but] were discovered by two Mexicans who were gathering *aughmeal* [aguamiel] from the megay *[maguey]*, from which a kind of fermented liquor called pulque was made. They inquired our business etc. and then told us to go with them to the town [about a league distant] and shew our passports. This we objected to [and told them, said Wilson, that if it were necessary, 'we would kill them rather than be taken'];[76] but they insisted and we could only get clear of them by giving them one dollar which was all we had and promised them 25 more. They agreed not to say anything about us, but we thought it best to lay close until night."[77]

On the morning following the escape, when the sentinel entered the room and discovered some of his charges gone, he dashed the butt of his gun to the floor. Out of fear, he neglected to report the escape, and the loss was not discovered by the officers until the following morning.[78]

As night descended, the three Texans crossed the mountain, avoiding the road in the pass. They halted at daybreak near a small town, where they lay in hiding during the day of August 1. About sunset, notwithstanding their vigilance, they were surprised by four Mexicans with sharp wooden lances, who "surrounded the little thicket where we were concealed, and pointing their lances at our breasts, ordered us to get up and accompany them." The Mexicans herded the Texans off to see the *alcalde*. He demanded their passports, and when none could be produced, said he must hold them to be sent to Mexico City the next day to answer to the prefect. The three Texans were lodged in an old jail, which also served as a schoolhouse. "But we could not wait so long," reported Wilson.[79]

74. J. C. Wilson to ———, in *Daily Picayune*, Oct. 12, 1843, and *Northern Standard*, Nov. 18, 1843.

75. Sibley, ed., *Samuel H. Walker's Account*, p. 77.

76. J. C. Wilson to ———, in *Northern Standard*, Nov. 18, 1832.

77. Sibley, ed., *Samuel H. Walker's Account*, p. 77.

78. Sowell, *Early Settlers and Indian Fighters of Southwest Texas*, p. 29.

79. J. C. Wilson to ———, in *Northern Standard*, Nov. 18, 1843, says "about ten Leagues." I find that Wilson's account is in substantial agreement with that given by Walker, but Wilson gives some details not found in other accounts.

Much to the prisoners' surprise and delight, they soon discovered that no sentinel had been placed before the door. "We set to digging up the pavement near the door. We succeeded in getting out a kind of metal cup, in which the lower hinge of the door turned, and with a plank and a piece of oak that we found in the prison, we forced the door from its post sufficiently wide to allow a man to pass out, and in less than an hour and a half after our confinement we were again upon the road."[80]

Despite Wilson being quite unwell from pleurisy, they now moved until daybreak, then they hid on a hill until nightfall, although shepherd boys were all around them during the day. As night descended, they resumed their journey, and after going three or four leagues, discovered that they were in an elongated valley. They climbed the mountain and at daybreak, August 3, hid in the bushes until night. They discovered a trail and came to a hut, where they inquired about the road. About an hour later, they came on a small party of mounted *rancheros,* "who appeared to be much alarmed, crying out to know what nation we were but would not come near enough to receive an answer. We continued our march on the road," said Walker. He continued:

> In about 3/4 of an hour [the Mexicans returned] and demanded us to halt but would not come nearer than long rifle shot distance. They wanted us to go back to the town. This we objected to telling them we had our passports which we supposed would be good, that we worked in the mines at Mineral Del Monte, that we were already two days behind our time and as for going back we would not think of it. Wilson pulled out a sheet of paper upon which one of his fellow prisoners had written an old song ballad of 'When Shall We Three Meet Again,' and endeavoured to get them to look at it but could not get near enough to show it to them. They agreed however to go with us to the next ranch [which lay alongside the road the Texans were traveling], where they could get a light and examine it. Wilson told them it made no material difference about the light, as he could interpret it to them by moon light as it was written in English.[81]

The Mexicans insisted that they go to the *rancho.* On arrival, the three Texans stepped boldly forward and Wilson, pulling out the ballad, presented it to the local leader as a passport written in English for all three of them. The commander of the *rancheros* requested Wilson to translate it. He took the paper and made a pretty good passport out of it. *"Bueno,"* said the Mexican, who apologized for having detained the three men, who, he said, he thought were "bad men." "We told them," said Walker, "that we did not blame them atall, that their regulations were essentially necessary and that they had only done their duty. We proceeded on laughing very hearty at the hoax we had played upon them."[82]

At daybreak, Friday, August 5, the three escapees reached Real del

---

80. J. C. Wilson to ———, in *Northern Standard,* Nov. 18, 1843.
81. Sibley, ed., *Samuel H. Walker's Account,* pp. 79-80.
82. *Ibid.,* p. 79.

Monte. The three prisoners had fled Tacubaya with no other provisions than five biscuits, which they consumed the first day, and "for the remaining (five days and nights) we had no other sustenance," reported Wilson, "then a few prickly pears which we found in the mountains."[83] Wilson could not walk more than a half mile without resting. The three decided to stay on the mountain and lay by during the day. Several shepherds discovered them. The Texans explained that they were minerologists looking for small specimens of ore for the English mining company.

That night the escapees entered Real del Monte, where, through the kindness of the English residents, they were fed and furnished with clothes, money, and passports. Wilson found it necessary to remain six weeks at Real del Monte to regain his health, which he did "with the skillful treatment of an English physician."[84]

On August 5, Walker and Gattis proceeded on the road toward Tampico. Saturday, August 12, brought them to Pueblo Viejo de Tampico ("Old Town," or Ancient Tampico), from whence they proceeded to Tampico.

Walker and Gattis spent some time wandering about the town. They located U.S. Consul Franklin E. Chase and found lodging at the home of a Frenchman. On August 14 they went up the Pánuco River with a Mr. L. [Lynch], an Irishman, who had earlier befriended other Mier prisoners, to wait for the departure of a vessel to the United States. It was not until September 2 that Walker was able to obtain passage on the schooner *Richard St. John*[85] and sailed from Tampico on September 3 for New Orleans. Gattis secured passage on the schooner *Brassos* for New York, but stopped off at Key West, where he engaged in business.[86]

Shortly after Walker's return to Texas, he confronted President Houston on a street in the City of Houston and charged him with being responsible for the decimation of the Mier men because of his statements to Elliot. Houston denied making such statements and asked Walker for the source of his charge. When told that Waddy Thompson had revealed the news, Houston requested that the charges be put in writing. Walker then wrote Houston a letter:

> As your Excellency denied the truth of these statements and accused General Thompson of falsehood in our conversation the other day, this issue of falsehood is between you. . . . If they are untrue General Thompson would justly sink in the estimation of every honest man and prove to the world that high and honourable office will not prevent men from lieing. . . .
>
> As one of the prisoners who suffered from the report, whether true or false, I wish not only to be satisfied myself but to satisfy all who doubt. Will your Excellency have the kindness to introduce me to Captain Elliot

---

83. J. C. Wilson to ——, in *Northern Standard,* Nov. 18, 1843.
84. *Ibid.*
85. *Daily Missouri Republican,* Aug. 24, 1843.
86. *Telegraph and Texas Register,* Nov. 15, 1843.

that I may hear his denial in your presence of any authority from you to make statements said to be contained in his dispatch to Mr. Packenham?[87]

Houston did not reply to Walker's letter, and when the two met on a staircase in Galveston, and Houston extended his hand, Walker ignored the friendly gesture and passed on. Houston paused and called back over his shoulder, "I am very sorry you are indisposed Mr. Walker."[88]

We should take note the fate of Copeland. About three weeks after his escape he was overtaken near Matamoros. His recapture was not known to his comrades, now at Perote Castle, until he was brought there in April 1844. He reported that near the Rio Grande he had met one of the officers whom the Texans had fought at Mier, and was recognized as one of the Texian prisoners. He was arrested and taken to Monterrey, where he was "tried and found *'guilty'* of being one of the Texiano Diablos."[89] From Monterrey he was taken to Saltillo and held there before being sent to Perote Castle to join the other Texan prisoners.

Less than a month after the escape of Walker and his companions, four more—William Thompson, John Day Morgan, Robert Michael Crawford, and John Fitzgerald—escaped on August 25.[90] By climbing upon the shoulder of one of their number the escapees were able to gain the top of the wall around their compound; then they lowered themselves to the ground with a rope. They "soon came to a paper mill, where they were invited to take refreshments. . . . They were hidden for about three weeks, thus allowing time for the excitement to subside before again exposing themselves to the danger of arrest. Under cover of darkness they were taken in a carriage to the residence of the English minister [Percy Doyle], who knew all, but received them by asking, "Where were you shipwrecked?' The Texans stood in silent and puzzled confusion. Then laughing he said with an oath, 'I guess you were shipwrecked on high and dry land, were you not?' "[91]

The escaped Texans were treated well at the British legation, and "felt for a little time almost safe, as they were 'feaseted and wined' under his protection for two days. . . . Then he 'capped all' by presenting them with twenty dollars apiece, and had them driven in a carriage out of the City of Mexico after dark." They were placed on the road leading to the English silver mine at Real del Monte. En route, they occasionally met patrol-guards who stopped and questioned them, "but allowed them to pass on when they claim[ed] that they [were] miners—as instructed by the

87. S. H. Walker to His Excellency, President Sam Houston, Galveston, Oct. 28, 1843, in *Telegraph and Texas Register*, Dec. 13, 1843; copy in Thomas Jefferson Green papers, Southern Historical Collection, University of North Carolina, Chapel Hill; see also Sibley, ed., *Samuel H. Walker's Account*, pp. 10-11.

88. J. H. Kuykendall, "Sketches of Early Texas," p. 8, typed MS, TxU-A; see also Sibley, ed., *Samuel H. Walker's Account*, p. 11.

89. Nance, ed., *McCutchan's Diary,* p. 97; Stapp, *Prisoners of Perote,* p. 101.

90. *Telegraph and Texas Register,* Nov. 15, 1843; Canfield diary, Aug. 25, 1843.

91. Jenkins, ed., *Recollections of Early Texas,* pp. 136-37.

English minister [and exhibited the passports that had been furnished them]."[92] They arrived at the mining town and remained out of sight for three days while the English operators worked out a plan to help them get to the coast. Fitzgerald decided to go to Tampico, and from there attempt to get passage to New Orleans. He succeeded in reaching Texas six months later.[93]

The other three were hired by the English company to help guard a shipment of silver to Vera Cruz. They were furnished passports under fictitious names and encountered no problems until they approached Perote. Morgan, walking along with one of the Mexican guards, was startled to hear him observe in passing: "We have a good many Texans confined here!' O course, he had to ask why and wherefore, but it was somewhat akin to torture for him to quietly listen to a disinterested, cold account of the battle of Mier and its subsequent results. He says," reported Jenkins, "he waxed warm at the guard's expressions of anger and condemnation towards the Texans," but the escapees concealed their wrath, and "the guard wound up the [unpleasant] history with, Poor fellows! They fought manfully at Mier, and after all had to be brought here and put to work!' 'This is mild punishment,' Morgan remarked in reply. 'They ought to be taken out and shot!' "[94]

In Vera Cruz they applied for passports to leave the country. Despite their apprehensions, "they were kindly received, however, and their papers were fixed and they were soon in search of a conveyance. They were at supper, feeling relieved and to a certain extent, safe, when a foreigner, coming in, made a special inquiry concerning some Texans. All were mum and busily engaged in eating, as the landlord scanned the crowd about the table, and [said he] knew nothing about any Texans. As soon as possible, Morgan shoved his plate back, and retreated to the street, followed by the foreigner, who seemed never to dream that Morgan was one of the objects of his search. Morgan cooly inquired why he was seeking Texans. "I heard that there were some in there, and I wanted to hire them," he answered, but his manner was non-communicative and evasive. He was doubtless in search of the guards from the silver mine, and did not know that he talked with one of them.[95]

The three Texans concluded that they should leave Vera Cruz as soon as possible. They contracted a Yankee skipper of a schooner that was preparing to sail for New Orleans. He "'found out their little pile' and charged the very last cent for passage, twenty-one dollars apiece!" Morgan remembered that they had fair weather for the voyage and that they enjoyed a very pleasant trip to New Orleans. "At New Orleans, moneyless, friendless, and without clothes, they separated."[96]

---

92. Jenkins, ed., *Recollections of Early Texas*, pp. 136-37.
93. Wharton, *History of Fort Bend County*, p. 113.
94. Jenkins, ed., *Recollections of Early Texas*, pp. 137-38.
95. *Ibid.*, pp. 138-39.
96. *Ibid.*, p. 139.

Nine, in all, escaped at night by climbing the walls of their prison at Tacubaya.[97] Others might have escaped, but did to run the risk because friends they trusted gave assurances of release; they knew, too, that the condition of those who remained behind would thereby be rendered much worse. Another deterrent was that most of the men possessed only the prison garb furnished by the government, which would have led immediately to their detection and arrest.

On September 9 the prisoners[98] were told to prepare to return to Santiago prison. Within the hour, in irons, they were started for Mexico City and their former quarters, preliminary, according to Colonel Rangel, to being transferred to Perote Castle. Many thought they were about to be released, "but this nation," reported Maxwell, "is so much in the habit of lyeing on all occasions, that we scarcely believe the report; all we wish [is] that it may be so."[99]

On arrival at Santiago prison, the prisoners found their quarters overcrowded because a large number of Mexican convicts were confined there as well. Their quarters were so cramped that there was not enough room for all of the Texans to lie down at the same time. They believed that it was only a matter of days before they would be released and they could easily endure the inconvenience. September 11 was the anniversary of Santa Anna's victory over the Spaniards at Tampico in 1829, and September 16 was the anniversary of Mexico's declaration of independence. Surely, they thought, their freedom would be granted on one of these days. Their hopes for an early liberation were encouraged by foreign friends and even by the guard. September 11 arrived and, although they could hear in the distance a continual firing of cannon during the day, the Texans remained locked within their cells.[100]

The governor of the Castle of Perote was informed that he should prepare for additional Texan prisoners, who would be started from Mexico City on September 12.[101] No mention was made of the number to be received. Upon receipt of this information on September 14, the governor commenced preparations for receiving the new prisoners, while the Texans at Perote hoped that the news of their comrades coming hailed an early liberation of all Texan prisoners in Mexico. The arrangements, however, that were being made for the reception of their friends had "more the appearance of arranging for our winter quarters than of giving us our liberty," recorded one of the prisoners already at Perote.[102] An order went to Vera Cruz to make chains, clevises, and rivets. Those who were quar-

97. Bell, *Narrative*, p. 66.

98. P. M. Maxwell to John T. Potter, City of Mexico, September 9, 1843, in *Cuero Star*, Mar. 8, 1899, clipping in Army Papers (Texas), Tx-A.

99. *Daily Missouri Republican*, Sept. 22, 1843.

100. Trueheart diary, Sept. 14, 1843.

101. *Ibid.*, Sept. 15, 1843.

102. *Ibid.*, Sept. 19, 1843.

tered in rooms 9 and 11 were moved on September 20 to the room occupied by Colonel Fisher and his party. The walls of rooms 9, 10, and 11
were whitewashed and the floors cleaned. Room No. 10 was to be occupied
by the prisoners now confined in No. 7. The "upper stores" of the rooms
—apparently the area above the partition walls where the prisoners stored
their miscellaneous gear—were removed and the overhead areas stopped
up. The new arrangement was designed to enable the sentinels to detect
tunneling operations that might be obscured from their view by the prisoners' gear.

In the evening of September 20, the Texan prisoners in Perote Castle
were formed and marched out into the courtyard to see the new governor
of the castle, Gen. José María Jarero. "We are much pleased," reported
Trueheart, "with his manner and deportment thus far. How long it will
continue . . . [only] time will tell, the great and never failing wonder of all
things."[103]

---

103. *Ibid.*, Sept. 20, 1843.

CHAPTER 20

The Texans are Transferred
to Perote Castle

O N TUESDAY MORNING, SEPTEMBER 12, the Texans in Santiago Prison, with the exception of twenty-one who were sick in the hospital,[1] were called up to have their chains cut off by a blacksmith.[2] For the first time, the Texans revealed how mistaken their guard had been in thinking that irons made the prisoners secure from escape. "The smith, a burly soot-covered Mexican, stared and grinned with astonishment as one by one the subjects on which he was called to exercise his art, approached his block, and giving the bolt of the clevis that embraced their ankles a touch, dropped the shackles at his feet, and walked off," Stapp wrote.[3] As those left at the hospital recovered, they were transferred to Santiago Prison.[4] Left behind were David Allen, John R. Baker, David H. E. Beasley, Henry Bridger, John T. Dillon, William Dunbar, John Erwin, Jeremiah Leehan, Theodore D. Maltby, Alexander W. Mathews, James M. McMichen, William F. Millen, Maj. Thomas W. Murray, Capt. John G. W. Pierson, Henry H. Roberts, Donald Smith, Ezekiel Smith, D. H. Van Vechten, Robert G. Waters, Joseph D. Watkins, and Owen R. Willis. By early January 1844, the number in the hospital had been reduced to eighteen, some of whom possessed no clothing.[5]

It was not clear to the prisoners where they would be sent.

Before noon the 126 Texans were formed,[6] and after each was sup-

---

1. Glasscock diary, Sept. 12, 1843.
2. Bell, *Narrative,* p. 69, reports that the chains of the main body of prisoners were removed on September 11, the day before they commenced their march from Mexico City.
3. Stapp, *Prisoners of Perote*, p. 103.
4. William E. Millen to The Honorable Chargé Affaires of the Republic of Texas [Isaac Van Zandt] to the Government of the United States, In Prison at Convent Santiago, City of México, Feb. 1, 1844, in Isaac Van Zandt Letters, 1844-1847, TxU-A.
5. *Daily Picayune*, Jan. 19, 1844.
6. Canfield diary, Sept. 12, 1843.

plied with one criminal's blanket, were started on the road to the Castle of Perote to join some sixty of their countrymen. Some hoped that when all the prisoners were reunited at the castle that they would be liberated, as this was the opinion of General Thompson and other foreign friends in Mexico.[7] About noon, a guard of fifty cavalrymen herded the prisoners in a southeasterly direction through the suburbs of the City of Mexico on the road to Puebla.

Crossing the causeway, the Texans found the road flanked on each side by fields of grain and agave. Luxuriant plants grew in profusion along the ditches and overlapped the road. Adobe huts and villages dotted the countryside.

Late in the afternoon the guard and prisoners began to ascend the mountains marking the eastern edge of the valley. Near dark they were lodged for the night, eighteen miles from Mexico City, in a comfortable stone barn belonging to Rancho San Agustín. While eating their supper— two tablespoonfuls of boiled rice—the Texans were visited by three Americans from the capital who stated that they were authorized by the American minister to inform them that upon their arrival at Perote they would be freed.[8] Canfield did not place much faith in this, believing that Thompson either wished to deceive or to create among the prisoners the impression that he was concerned for their welfare, but, "I think," said Canfield, "he is 'perfectly *Mexicanized.*'" He had promised, said Canfield, and made many statements concerning his release, "and of what he has done in my behalf, but I'll wait! and make note of his future exertions"; but "I think now he is a good hand at 'wind work' only."[9]

Early the next morning the prisoners were handed eighteen and three-fourths cents each with which to procure food. The usual allowance was twenty-five cents per person per day, but the captain of the guard withheld six and one-fourth cents for the purpose, he said, to procure conveyances. It was thought that he pocketed the money, for all conveyances needed by the Texans or Mexican soldiery were usually impressed without compensation. With an early start the Texans made a long march of ten leagues, mostly through rain and hail, along a narrow road up the pine-studded Sierra Madre Occidental. The road climed to more than 10,000 feet to cross the continental divide. They descended the eastern rim of the valley by a steep road full of sharp turns. At sundown the prisoners reached a narrow ravine containing a sparkling brook, the Río Frío, upon whose banks were situated a cluster of hovels also called Río Frío.

The road, like so many others in Mexico, was marked at frequent intervals by sepulchral crosses, indicating the sites of ancient and recent murders by highwaymen and gangs of desperadoes. "Sullenly and reluctantly the inhabitants of Río Frío," reported Stapp, "pointed out to the

---

7. Bell, *Narrative*, p. 69.
8. Canfield diary, Sept. 12, 1843.
9. *Ibid.*

guard a dirty hut for our night's accommodation, nor could bribes or commands procure us beyond the most stinted supply of food to stay the fierce appetites excited by our march. They permitted us to traverse their fastness, however, without the compliment of robbing us; an indignity we resented next morning, by seizing several asses from them to mount our men, who had fallen lame on the previous day."[10]

Dripping wet from a cold rain that had fallen during the afternoon, the Texans spent a miserable night, shivering from cold and suffering from hunger, "for nothing could be bought here either for love or money."[11] After a night spent in a filthy room too small for the prisoners to lie down comfortably, the Texans were happy when the new day arrived and they could be on their way. The greater part of the day was spent descending the mountain range. During the day the Texans crossed the Puenta de Texmelucan, an aerial bridge over the icy Texmeluca stream dashing from a mountain ravine. Late in the afternoon, after a march of twenty-one miles, they descended another slope to the village of San Martín, twenty miles from Puebla, on the foot of the Río Prieto. Here they found the "huxter" women of the place waiting to sell them *sapodillas, chile con carne,* peaches, oranges, and other fruits. Ten to fifteen peaches could be procured for a single *tlaco.*[12] That night the weary band of Texans received an excellent supper and quarters that proved more comfortable than those of the previous night.

The next morning, Friday, September 15, the guard was changed, and with both captains present the roll was checked and receipted. The new captain ordered each of the prisoners to be paid *dos reales* (twenty-five cents), which was further proof to the Mier men that they had been swindled by the former captain of the guard.[13] The journey was renewed early with a northeaster whistling in their faces. At noon they halted to refresh themselves. Later in the day it rained in torrents and the road became "flooded with water as high as . . . [their] knees." Their officers were quite uneasy for fear that some of the Texans might attempt an escape during the severe storm. As La Puebla de los Angeles was approached, the country improved in appearance. The prisoners passed through a blooming and scented valley, full of large, rich plantations, each amounting to a thousand or more acres.[14]

At five in the afternoon, after a march of eight leagues, the Texans entered the gates of the picturesque city of Puebla.

Entering the city from the western side, the Texans marched along the Alameda, "from whose avenues of retired shade, poured out a lengthening throng of dames and dons, gallant cavaliers and flashing danzellas."[15] As they moved along the side of the plaza, they noted the Gover-

10. Stapp, *Prisoners of Perote,* p. 105.
11. Bell, *Narrative,* p. 70.
12. Canfield diary, Sept. 14, 1843.
13. *Ibid.,* Sept. 15, 1843.
14. *Ibid.*; Bell, *Narrative,* p. 70; Glasscock diary, Sept. 16, 1843.
15. Stapp, *Prisoners of Perote,* p. 108.

nor's Palace and directly in front of it across the square stood the beautiful cathedral of Puebla. It was perhaps equal in size to the one that they had seen in Mexico City.

Passing along the straight, wide streets, walled on each side by stately buildings, the Texans were conducted, "amidst the dying chimes of innumberable bell calling the devout to their vesper orisons,"[16] through a sea of curious eyes to the gloomy Presidio del Departamento at the edge of town. It was here that the Santa Fé prisoners were quartered. The Mier prisoners' supper consisted of two small loaves of good wheat bread, supplemented by eighteen and three-fourths cents distributed to purchase additional items of food or other necessities.

At an early hour the next morning, September 16, the Texans were aroused by the continual roar of artillery, the tolling of bells, and strains of music announcing the opening of a glorious day in the nation's history —the anniversary of Mexican independence. These manifestations of joy continued while the prisoners remained securely locked in their cells to permit the guard to participate in the patriotic festivities. Each prisoner was again supplied with two small loaves of wheat bread and money. In the middle of the afternoon a young officer who had been a prisoner in Texas took William P. Stapp and another Texan on a ramble through the city.[17]

"The streets were teeming with population, a great number having been attracted from the country and the neighboring towns by the celebration of the day. The balconies and open windows blushed with their blooming flowers and lovely women, and the lofty walls of the rooms, into which we could see," wrote Stapp, "were covered with rich-looking pictures and costly mirrors. Old monks and young friars, in their broad shovel hats and canonical habit, nuns, modistes, and fruit-girls, and the regular lords of the *pavé*, from *millionaire* to *leperos*, jostled each other on the crowded footways."[18]

As the day passed, the Mier men's hopes for liberation on this national holiday faded. About ten o'clock the next morning, the Texans, with the exception of Levi Williams, who was left behind sick, together with 110 "of the lowest and basest" Mexican criminals taken from the dungeons of the city, were again started on the road to the Castle of Perote. The criminals, including a number of deserters from the army, were destined for Vera Cruz to render service in the "volunteer forces" of the regular army.[19] En route the criminals stole from the Texans "nearly everything" they possessed, including McCutchan's only pair of extra trousers worthy the name.

The guard seemed to be in no hurry to reach the Castle of San Carlos de Perote, ninety-six miles away.[20] The road from Puebla to Perote was

---

16. *Ibid.*; Canfield diary, Sept. 15, 1843.
17. Stapp, *Prisoners of Perote,* p. 108.
18. *Ibid.*, p. 109.
19. Canfield diary, Sept. 17, 1843.
20. Glasscock diary, Sept. 17, 1843; Nance, ed., *McCutchan's Narrative*, pp. 100-01; Canfield diary, Sept. 17, 1843.

generally smooth and level, although often cut by deep gullies. They spent the first night after leaving Puebla at Amosoque (Amozoc) in a horse stable. Here many of the men were compelled to go hungry in spite of the small quantity of money they had.[21] The next morning each received his twenty-five cents allowance and all were able to procure something to eat before starting.

The road passed "a wild moorland plain, intersected by mountains, whose narrow valleys were fertile and beautifully improved," recorded Stapp.[22] After a march of three leagues they reached the small town of Acajete, where they rested briefly. Continuing for five more leagues, they arrived at Nopaluca and were crammed into a granary with the Mexican convicts, in quarters insufficient for comfort, on a small hill overlooking a fertile valley, and here they were able to obtain something to eat.[23]

On the third day they crossed a small sandy valley to camp in a large barn in a lonely plain at the Hacienda Alverez,[24] at Ojo de Agua, some thirty-five miles from Perote. In comparison to the previous night, their quarters were comfortable.

On the fourth day after leaving Puebla, September 20, they camped for the night with their "Mexican friends" at La Ventilla in a horse stable. Many were "compelled to go without any thing to eat notwithstanding each had his small portion of money."[25]

On Thursday, September 21, ten days after leaving Mexico City, the Texans commenced their march in a high wind which whipped up the sand into clouds of dust, making walking unpleasant. They passed through the village of Tepeyagualco (or Tepeyahualco), about ten miles from Perote and across a plain dotted here and there with numerous agave plants, to reach the western edge of Perote about three o'clock in the afternoon.

On arrival at Perote, the Mexican criminals were separated from the Texans, who were conducted through the streets of the straggling town to the Castle of San Carlos de Perote,[26] lying to the left of the road that ran from Mexico City to Vera Cruz and approximately a mile to the northwest of the town of Perote. It was approximately forty miles to the west of Jalapa and 160 miles southeast of Mexico City.

From a distance, the extent of ground within the castle walls and the earthen embankment around the outer *chevaux-de-frise* gave the fortifica-

---

21. Canfield diary, Sept. 17, 1843.
22. Stapp, *Prisoners of Perote*, pp. 111-12.
23. Glasscock diary, Sept. 18, 1843.
24. Canfield diary, Sept. 19, 1843.
25. *Ibid.*, Sept. 17, 1843.
26. The name "Perote" is derived from that of a Spaniard named "Pedro," owner of the plain upon which it was built, for which great gift it was called "Pedrote" or "Perote"; its true name was "San Carlos Gustavo Casasola." *Seis Siglos de Historia gráfica de México* 1, pp. 250-51, with picture on p. 251.

tion a low appearance. The fort, or castle, as it was commonly called, was situated in a narrow valley. It stood approximately 7,000 feet above sea level. Farther to the north were higher mountains, especially the Mount of Pizarro.

In spite of having been constructed in a valley, "Frost is not uncommon here," narrated Bell, "but almost as liable to come in the middle of summer as in the winter. This dreary place is frequently enveloped in clouds so dense that the view extends only a few yards, and in winter, it rains almost constantly, while during the summer an invigorating shower seldom falls."[27] By mid-August the weather was "cold enough for a fire in the room, and thick clothing."[28]

At the time of its construction, and even in 1843, the Castle of Perote was one of the strongest fortifications in Mexico, and was built to command the mountain pass leading from the coast to the City of Mexico. If so, recorded one of the Texan prisoners, it was improperly located; for, being placed "in the center of a pass, or valley, at least six miles in breadth . . . an enemy might pass on either side of the fortress, without being materially injured by the guns of the battery."[29] It had ceased to serve its intended purpose and was used "as a state prison, a refuge for troops, an arsenal," a second line of defense, if need be, for the port of Vera Cruz, "and a depot for the rich convoys that went this way."[30]

An embankment thrown up twenty feet above the level of the plain surrounded the castle at a distance of sixty-five feet from the castle walls. On this embankment was a row of upright pickets (*chevaux-de-frise*) of squared, twelve-foot cedar timbers set in cement at a distance of fifty feet from the outer edge of the moat.[31] The picket fence encompassed an area of approximately forty-four acres. The pickets measured about six inches square and were mortised in the middle by a longitudinal timber. The area between the moat and the *chevaux-de-frise*, some fifty feet, served as a parade ground. The fort was protected from an enfilading fire by four traverses across its length on each side. On each side and at the rear, flanked by the bastions, there were gates for sorties and retreats. Outside the picket fence was a ditch fourteen feet in width and eight to ten feet in depth, whose outer embankment was elevated almost to the height of the picket fence.[32]

The castle was surrounded by a moat fifteen to twenty feet deep and

27. Bell, *Narrative*, pp. 74-75.

28. Edward Manton to Hezekiah Smith, LaGrange, Fayette County, Texas, [dated] Perote, Aug. 15, 1843, in Chabot, ed., "Texas Letters," Yanaguana Society *Publication* 5, pp. 45-46.

29. Nance, ed., *McCutchan's Narrative*, p. 104.

30. Green, *Mier Expedition*, p. 240; McGrath and Hawkins, "Perote Fort—Where Texans were Imprisoned," *SWHQ* 48 (Jan. 1945), p. 344.

31. Bell, *Narrative*, p. 72, says the fence was twenty feet from the outer edge of the ditch.

32. Green, *Mier Expedition*, p. 239.

fifty feet wide. The outside wall of the moat was of stone, and the inside wall of the moat was the wall of the castle, which rose, with a slight slope or incline, to a height of approximately forty-five feet from the bottom of the moat.[33] The castle walls tapered upward from a thickness of fifteen feet at the bottom to eight at the top.

Constructed of dark, honeycombed volcanic pumice stone and cement, the main body of the fort, which covered twenty-six acres, was built in a quadrangle of 800 feet on each of the inside quadrants, with a wing or buttress projecting from each corner. The bastions at each corner of the main rampart were about 150 feet long by about 60 feet wide. At the extreme point of each bastion or rampart was a small circular lookout tower and guardhouse. At the front and rear, ramps or inclined planes were built for ascending to the ramparts.

An inclined terrace constituted the flat roof of the fortress. It reached to within six feet of the top and ran around the entire circuit of the interior walls. It was reached by broad stairways along the inner wall that ascended to the top from each angle of the fort, admission to which could be gained only through a heavy wooden gate twelve feet high.

The five-foot-thick partition walls of the rooms did not reach all the way to the fifteen-foot arched ceiling which supported the batteries above. There were fifteen entrances on each side of the fort to the casemates in which the cannon were mounted. Thus, overhead the rooms were connected with each other. The lofty arches, extending along the outer walls and facing inward toward the square, constituted forty-five rooms nineteen and a half feet wide and seventy feet in length.[34] These contained the workshops, storerooms, granaries, armories, quarters for the garrison, stables, ammunition storage areas, and the regularly numbered cells of the prisoners. The cells were at ground level, and their floors were of stone, brick, and concrete ten inches thick. The cells were entered only from the inside through a massive "folding" wooden door.[35] Each door was equipped with a huge lock. When the door of the cell was closed, the only light and fresh air came through three gratings. One was at the top of the door; another was a small window lower down in the door; and the third was a loophole at the far end of the room. The latter was some eighteen inches square on the inner side of the wall and gradually tapered through the eight-foot wall to an aperture of some four or five inches by twelve inches on the outside and had a grating at each end.[36] Usually the upper third of the shutter to the door was left open, but an iron grating covered the

---

33. Green, *Mier Expedition*, p. 239, says the height of the wall was about sixty feet; Trueheart diary, Dec. 22, 1842, says it was from forty-five to sixty feet; Nance, ed., *McCutchan's Narrative*, p. 104, says the wall was forty feet high, twelve to fifteen feet thick at the bottom, and sloped to eight feet at the top.

34. Trueheart diary, Dec. 22, 1842.

35. Bell, *Narrative*, p. 72.

36. Green, *Mier Expedition*, p. 241.

opening. The opening in the door below the shutter enabled the sentinel to keep a sharp eye on the prisoners and their movements within the cell.

At a distance of sixty feet from the arches was another block of buildings, two stories high, covered with earth on tiles for roof. The upper stories on three sides of the inner tier, fronting on the plaza, were quarters for officers attached to the garrison, while those on the western side contained the chapel and the governor's quarters.[37] The rooms of the lower basement stories were used as barracks. The powder magazine and arsenal were located in the bastions in the southeastern and northeastern wings of the fort in rooms belonging to the inside tier of rooms, and the other two wings of the fort at the time the Mier men arrived were used to store lumber. Inside the outer pickets, the fortress covered twenty-six acres, the cluster of buildings covered about ten acres.[38] The sixty-foot-wide pavement between the arches and the inner tier of buildings was described as a street or alley, which ran entirely around the inside of the castle.[39]

The open plaza in the center of the fort was about 500 feet square,[40] paved with cement and pebbles, and was "bountifully supplied with the best of water."[41] Entrance to the plaza was through arches at each corner and opposite the drawbridge. The courtyard was used for military parades, reviews, and recreation.

Two companies of infantry and one of artillery comprised the guard of the fort when the Texans were imprisoned there. "A garrison of ten thousand men would scarce suffice to man it against a vigorous investment," declared Stapp.[42]

The fort fronted toward the southeast and the town of Perote. On entering, one passed a guardhouse on the right and continued along a covered avenue over a stone bridge across the moat to a wooden drawbridge, then through a ponderous gate into a large, central courtyard. On each side of the gateway, beneath the battery, was a calaboose, near which were the quarters of the guard.[43] Directly across the courtyard was the governor's quarters. McCutchan mentions a "secret passage" behind the rear of the fort.[44] Such an exit would seem essential to a well-planned fort.

With the clanging of bells and a chorus of "*alertas*" the Texan prisoners arriving from Tacubaya and Mexico City crossed the bridge over the moat and passed through an archway into the plaza of the castle, where they were drawn up before the governor's quarters. Most of the Mier pris-

37. Stapp, *Prisoners of Perote*, p. 112; Young, *History of Mexico*, p. 319.

38. [William E. Jones to M. B. Lamar], Washington 1 Feby 1844, in Winkler, ed., "The Béxar and Dawson Prisoners," *QTSHA* 13 (Apr. 1910), p. 323; Chauncey Johnson to the Editors of the *Picayune*, Castle of Perote, June 8, 1843, in *Daily Picayune*, July 13, 1843.

39. Nance, ed., *McCutchan's Narrative*, p. 105.

40. Green, *Mier Expedition*, p. 240.

41. Chauncey Johnson to the editors of the *Picayune*, Castle of Perote, June 8, 1843, in *Daily Picayune*, July 13, 1843.

42. Stapp, *Prisoners of Perote*, p. 112.

43. *Ibid.*

44. Nance, ed., *McCutchan's Narrative*, p. 105.

oners were now in Perote Castle.[45] While the newcomers were examined, counted, and receipted, the prisoners already in the castle proceeded in chains to greet their comrades, whom they found to be in need of clothes and blankets. "We were much surprised," reported Trueheart, "to see their haggard looks and miserable appearances, most of whom were dressed as Mexican Comanches, without shoes or shirts. My feeling in thus beholding my countrymen was oppressive in the extreme. Their whole appearance indicated to me the effects of bad treatment and hard usage."[46] Yet, "I can ashure you," wrote Edward Manton to his friends in LaGrange, "it gave us no small satisfaction to meet with those we had seen in better days."[47] "Big Wal[l]ace . . . looks very thin, although in good health," reported one of the Dawson prisoners. "They have worked him thin a carrying sand on the road at Mexico."[48]

On the other hand, to one of the new arrivals, their friends who had been in Perote for six to nine months seemed to have endured great suffering and neglect. "The sad countenances and wasted appearance of these men," recorded Stapp, "but too well attested the sufferings of their long imprisonment." He further recalled, "Few and melancholy were our greetings, it being evident on both sides there was little solace to be imparted or received."[49]

By the time the main contingent of the Mier men reached Perote Castle, the Béxar-Dawson prisoners had been reduced, either by death, escape, or liberation, to forty-five with forty-four of them in Perote prison. Norman Woods arrived with the main contingent of Mier men, bringing all of the Béxar-Dawson prisoners in Mexico together. Most had been in prison at Perote Castle for nine months. Also in Perote prison were eighteen of the Mier men. On the day after the main body reached the castle, John Bradley, an uncle of Mrs. Samuel A. Maverick and one of the Dawson prisoners, received his release from prison by the influence of Andrew Jackson working through Waddy Thompson.

The process of checking in completed, the new arrivals were ordered to file off in line as their names were called, after which they were marched to their cells. The total number of Texan prisoners in Perote Castle on September 21 was 177 of the total of 202 in Mexico.[50] The Texan prisoners who had been left at Puebla reached Perote Castle on Monday, October 9, 1843. Trueheart does not specify who they were.[51]

One hundred of the new arrivals were placed under lock and key in

45. *Northern Standard*, Feb. 10, 1844.

46. Trueheart diary, Sept. 21, 1843.

47. Edward Manton to Hezekiah Smith, Castle of Perote, Sept. 22, 1843 (By the politeness of Mr. Bradley), in Edward Manton Papers (photostat), TxU-A.

48. Edward Manton to Hezekiah Smith, LaGrange, Fayette County, Texas, [dated] Castle of Perote, Sept. 22, 1843, in Edward Manton Papers (photostat), TxU-A.

49. Stapp, *Prisoners of Perote*, p. 113.

50. Trueheart diary, Sept. 22, 1843.

51. *Ibid.*, Oct. 9, 1843.

two cells on the north side of the fort, and the remaining twenty-five were assigned to two narrow archway cells, numbers 9 and 10, adjoining each other in the eastern rampart of the castle, where the San Antonio and Dawson prisoners had been held. Twenty of the latter were moved to a room on the inner plaza, "called the Capilla"—the doomed cell—the place where prisoners sentenced to death were placed three days before they were scheduled to be shot. Their new cells were much superior to previous quarters. In a third room, to the right of the Béxar-Dawson prisoners, were the sixteen Mier prisoners, including the regimental officers. All were in chains, but were reported to be in "verry good health," although those just arriving "could not boast of being so."[52]

The new arrivals found their cells overcrowded and cold. As for furniture, there was none. There was scarcely one blanket for every ten men. That night, about six o'clock, the prisoners were counted again—this time in their cells—and the door to each cell was locked and a sentinel with a loaded musket was placed before it. "By the light of a taper kept burning the whole night, he was ordered to fire upon any who might attempt to make their escape," Bell reported.[53] At intervals of fifteen minutes throughout the night the sentinel cried out in a hoarse, cracked, and scarcely human voice, "*Sentinela alierto.*"[54] Sentinels standing watch at other points in the castle joined the doleful chorus. At first, the howl of the sentinels disturbed the slumbers of the Texans, but they soon become accustomed to it.

Not until nine o'clock the next morning, when they were counted and turned over to the officer of the guard for the day, did the new arrivals receive anything to eat, and even then, their breakfast consisted only of weak coffee and a quantity of good bread.[55] Afterward all of the prisoners, including the new arrivals, were permitted the freedom of the prison yard until four o'clock in the afternoon. Between noon and one o'clock, they were supplied with small quantities of rice, bread, and four ounces of poor beef, and the water in which it had been boiled for soup mixed with a few vegetables and a pint of boiled onions. For supper, they had bread and coffee. Occasionally for variety, about once a week, the tripe or most likely the entire intestines of a beef was given to them with a small quantity of potatoes.[56]

When ordered to their cells at four o'clock, September 22, the men were redistributed so as to have only thirty or so in a single room. The Texan officers were housed separately in a room to themselves,[57] but received the same rations. The men were "allowed only to come out and take their coffee," which proved to be nothing more than hot colored water.[58]

52. Canfield diary, Sept. 21, 1843; Bell, *Narrative*, p. 71.
53. Bell, *Narrative*, p. 72.
54. Nance, ed., *McCutchan's Narrative*, p. 121.
55. Canfield diary, Sept. 22, 1843; Stapp, *Prisoners of Perote*, p. 113.
56. Bell, *Narrative*, pp. 72-73; Glasscock diary, Sept. 22, 1843.
57. Bell, *Narrative*, p. 73.
58. Trueheart diary, Sept. 22, 1843; see also Canfield diary, Sept. 22, 1843; Stapp, *Prisoners of Perote*, p. 113; Bell, *Narrative*, p. 72.

During their first four days at Perote Castle the Mier men were kept locked up most of the day and night until the guard could be strengthened. Finally, on September 24, the guard was increased by the arrival of 300 cavalry from Jalapa, and the Texans were allowed to remain out of their cells from nine in the morning until five in the evening.[59]

During the prisoners' first days in the castle the Mexican officers and soldiers seemed to allow them all the privileges they could. They were informed on September 23 that Santa Anna would visit the castle on September 30.[60] Five days after the arrival of the Mier prisoners, the new governor and commandant of the fortress, Gen. José María Jarero, inspected the Texans in their cells and inquired into their treatment and wardrobe. He assured them of humane treatment and promised to have them supplied "with shoes and clothing necessary for their comfort in this region" and with mats on which to sleep. "Therefore, according to his statement, they were to be much better and more happily situated than if they were at home, where he supposed they lived by hunting the wild deer and buffalo." In time, "these flattering promises of General Jarero, like [those of] most other Mexicans, proved measurably base and false."[61]

Possessing no orders from his government in reference to the treatment of the Texans, Jarero declared he would not compel them to work. The San Antonio, Dawson, and advance contingent of Mier prisoners had "not done any work for nearly two months" prior to the arrival of the main body of Mier men, "but expect it every day," reported Manton on September 22, 1843.[62] Believing in cleanliness, the governor suggested that the men bathe the next day in the moat. Under a strong guard, all of the Texans were conducted outside the fortifications and permitted to bathe and to walk in the moat, while the commandant looked down from the parapet upon the cleansing and frolic going on below.[63] Thereafter every three or four weeks the Texans were taken outside the prison walls, usually on Sundays, to bathe in the foul waters of the moat. The prisoners took advantage of such opportunities to search the fort from the outside to discover any outlets and lay plans for escape.

"As soon as they were turned out" of their cells on September 28, the prisoners were told that they were to be rechained. The rechaining was postponed until the afternoon, when only a part of the men could be rechained before lockup time and they with single chains. The rest of the men would be chained in the morning. On Saturday, September 30, the governor announced that the president would be at the castle "within eight days." "*Veremos*" (we shall see), recorded Trueheart.[64]

---

59. Trueheart diary, Sept. 24, 1843.

60. *Ibid.*, Sept. 23, 1843.

61. Bell, *Narrative*, p. 73.

62. Edward Manton to Hezekiah Smith, LaGrange, Fayette County, Texas, by the politeness of Mr. Bradley, [dated] Castle of Perote, Sept. 22, 1843, in Edward Manton Papers (photostats), TxU-A.

63. Stapp, *Prisoners of Perote*, pp. 113-14.

64. Trueheart diary, Sept. 27-29, 1843.

CHAPTER 21

An Epidemic Strikes and the Perote Prisoners are Forced to Work

FOUR DAYS AFTER THE arrival at the fort of the Texans from Tacu-baya, symptoms of an epidemic appeared among the closely confined prisoners. While keeping his promise not to force the men to work "until nearly the 20th of October," Governor Jarero "during that time kept all most closely confined," allowing no time for exercise, except about three hours at noon each day. The rooms had no admission for air except that which came from one end of the cell and that was limited when the door was closed, so the inmates breathed "the putrid air of a room in which thirty men were confined."[1] They also lacked warm clothing in the cold, damp cells, "and their food was so poor and so scanty that they were ema-ciated to mere skeletons."[2] And there were no amusements in the long intervals between the evening lockup time and nine the next morning, when the cell doors were opened, except "playing cards, or reading some old phamplets . . . which found their way" to their cells.[3]

Joseph D. McCutchan was among the first to suffer from the disease, and within a week's time eighty-six of the Texans were hospitalized at the same time. Only three[4] among the whole number of Texans confined at Perote escaped the epidemic, which by January 28 had claimed the lives of eighteen of the Mier men and several of the San Antonio-Dawson pris-oners. "Our number is quite reduced since we crossed the Rio Grande," wrote P. M. Maxwell from Perote Castle. "Out of 262 [actually 261], who crossed, there is 143 left, we lost 14 at Mier, 16 in the mountains . . . ; 18 shot by order of Santa Anna, 4 died on the march to Mexico; 8 died in the

---

1. Bell, *Narrative*, p. 75.
2. *Telegraph and Texas Register*, Feb. 21, 1844.
3. Glasscock diary, Oct. 11-14, 1843.
4. Nance, ed., *McCutchan's Narrative*, p. 106; Bell, *Narrative*, pp. 75-76, says sixteen of the Texans escaped the malady.

San Luis [Potosí] Hospital; 19 died in hospital (city of Mexico); and 18 here; some few run [escaped] from Mexico but there is no show [desire] to elope from here; too many walls and sentinels. We are closely guarded day and night."[5] Samuel C. Lyon wrote to Thomas Jefferson Green on February 2, 1844, "we have had a severe epidemic in the castle—70 in the hospital at one time; it has been very fatal among our men in the last month or two. Thirteen of our best men have died, among whom are Maj. Gray, Judge Sanders, Jn. Trapnall, Crews, Tremble [Trimble], Wood, and Miller of Brazoria. I have been in the hospital twice with fever and deafness; but am now well with a tremendous appetite and nothing to eat. . . . Gen. Fisher sends his respects to you and so does all hands."[6]

The castle had no hospital, but the town of Perote did and after Santa Anna visited the castle on October 7, he ordered the Texans sent there in case of illness.[7] "Here they were well cared for, the physicians and nurses being attentive," reported Stapp, "and everything appropriate of necessity or comfort being provided them."[8] The facilities at the hospital in Perote soon became "crowded with Mexicans as well as Texans," so on Saturday, October 28, the Mexicans transferred many of the sick and some of the furniture to the prison for greater convenience and to relieve the burden on the hospital in town. Within a week the number of sick had overtaxed the "military hospital's facilities at the castle and the physicians recommended that the sick be taken to the old hospital near the town of Perote."[9] John P. Wyatt died in the hospital in Perote on October 30, and was buried the next day in the graveyard for Roman Catholics, since he professed that faith after leaving Saltillo. "Poor Wyatt will find himself in strange company," recorded Canfield, "when the last Trump[et] Sounds so thought his Companions—during life."[10]

On November 6, many of the Texans engaged in moving the hospital back to Perote were themselves ill. The patients were carried on *camas* (litters) through the hot sun[11] or the chilling rain, as the occasion might be, causing some to suffer relapses. With the exception of two weeks of pleasant weather, October, November, and December were cold and disagreeable, with rain and hail falling almost daily.[12] With so many of the Texan prisoners ill, it became a problem to keep the men chained in pairs. So, the governor ordered the chains connecting the men in pairs

---

5. P. M. Maxwell to Captain J[ohn] H[emphill]. Castle of Perote, Republic of Mexico, January 23, 1844, in *Galveston Weekly News*, Feb. 24 1844; see also Glasscock diary, Sept. 21, 1843.

6. S. C. Lon to General [Thomas J. Green], Castle of Perote, February 2, 1844, in *The Planter* (Columbia), Apr. 5, 1844.

7. Bell, *Narrative*, p. 76.

8. Stapp, *Prisoners of Perote*, p. 117.

9. Canfield diary, Nov. 5 and 6, 1843; see also Trueheart diary, Nov. 6, 1843; Glasscock diary, Oct. 28, 1843.

10. Canfield diary, Oct. 3, 1843.

11. Trueheart diary, Nov. 6, 1843.

12. Canfield diary, Oct. 9-17, Nov. 2, 7-9, 12-23, Dec. 22-23, 1843.

separated midway, letting each prisoner carry his own portion of the chain.

A typical case was that of James L. Trueheart, who became ill the day after Christmas. He described his stay in the hospital:

> *Tuesday, 26th.* Today I have a chill and am obliged to go to bed. Two of my companions are also taken sick, one of whom is carried to the hospital.
>
> *Wednesday, 27th.* My disease increases, and [I] find myself worse. Another of my companions carried to the hospital.
>
> *Thursday, 28th.* Today I am carried to the hospital, feeling better than I had on the two previous days. At night my fever arose and became too intense that I soon became very delirious, so much so, that for the first three or four days, I was perfectly frantic, contending with my attendant, abusing him, and the sentinel, in getting out of my bed whenever permitted, but I soon became so weak that I laid like a dead man for nearly twenty days, neither speaking, hearing, nor seeing, and insensible to everything. The disease is usually attended with pain in the limbs, violent headache, producing in a very few days delirium, and complete prostration, reducing a person to a mere skeleton. I was blistered on the legs and on the back of my neck, but would take them off if suffered, to prevent which, I was tied. On coming to my senses the first thing I said, that my eyes might be washed, as I was unable to see for the matter that had formed about them. My life for several days was despaired of by my physician, and indeed, by everyone. But the disease at length took a favorable change, and I commenced mending immediately and continued to do so until my return to the castle. I received every care and attention while there. During the time that I was at the hospital five of my companions died. . . . As soon as I was strong enough I had permission to come out into the yard in the sun-shine, which I enjoyed very much after being so long to my bed. Four or five days I thus employed my time, which gave me a most vigorous appetite.

On February 2, 1844, after thirty-four days in the hospital, Trueheart returned to his room, leaving behind in the hospital fourteen Texans.[13]

Most of the Texans who died in Perote or at the castle were buried without a coffin on the north side of the fort in unsanctified ground. The bodies were stripped of all clothing, then wrapped in a ragged blanket. If one had accepted Roman Catholicism, he was buried in the *campo santo* (cemetery) for Catholics with greater dignity and in a wooden coffin.

In the hospital, care for the sick was provided by some of the prisoners who performed hospital duty while so many of their number were ill. After days or weeks lying in a wretched condition and sometimes tied spread eagle hands and feet to the bedposts, as in the cases of John C. Trapnall, James L. Trueheart, "Bigfoot" Wallace, and many others,[14] the

13. Trueheart diary, Feb. 2 and Mar. 18, 1844.
14. *Ibid.*, Dec. 11-12, 28, 1843.

patient either recovered or died. Trapnall did not survive the ordeal.[15] He had been robbed of all possessions, except for one blanket. A coffin was procured for his remains, and, being Roman Catholic in religion, he was buried in the *campo santo* of the castle. As late as June 1844, Freeman W. Douglass, who had been sick more or less for the last eight months, was reported to be again in the hospital.

The epidemic among the Texan prisoners in the Castle of Perote relieved many from all earthly troubles. By March 8, twenty-two had died at Perote and had been buried in the moat.[16] "The Mexican Government," commented the editors of the *Daily Picayune*, "may have the right to retain, at least a portion of them [i.e., the Mier men] prisoners of war; but it is contrary to the usages of civilized nations to incarcerate those whom the fortunes of war have thrown into their hands, in a place where the climate, combined with scantiness of raiment, must soon bring premature disease and death."[17] On arrival at New Orleans from Vera Cruz on February 2, Captain Hollingshead of the *John Barr* reported that sixteen of the Texan prisoners confined at Perote Castle had died during the past month, and that "out of the whole only eighteen are able to do any kind of labor."[18]

"Bigfoot" Wallace was among those stricken by the epidemic. He became quite unmanageable while in delirium and on several occasions tried to "'clean out' all the guard and other attendants of the hospital."[19] The guard had to "lasso" him and tie him down to the bed so "hard and fast on his back" with ropes that the "marks will show as long as he lives."[20] On the day after his fever abated and "Bigfoot" was calmer, one of the hospital attendants came to remove the blisters placed upon him while he had been delirious. Wallace later recalled:

> The rascal cooly proceeded to handle me as if I had been as devoid of feeling as a "knot on a log," tearing the blisters from my arms by main force, and causing me thereby the most horrible torture. A heavy copper stew-pan happened to be within reach of me, which I grabbed instantly, and, exerting all the strength I had, I gave him a "clew" on the side of the head with it and knocked him senseless to the floor. The guard stationed in the room immediately rushed upon me with their drawn sabres, and no doubt would have made mincemeat of me, if luckily the surgeon-general had not at that moment stepped in and interposed his authority in my behalf, and saved my life. He said that I had served the fellow I had

---

15. Canfield diary, Dec. 13, 1843; see also Glasscock diary, Dec. 13, 1843; Trueheart diary, Dec. 13, 1843.

16. S. C. Lon to General [Thomas J. Green], Castle of Perote, Feb. 2, 1844, in *The Planter* (Columbia), Apr. 5, 1844; typed transcript in the Woods Papers and Letters, TxU-A.

17. *Daily Picayune*, Feb. 8, 1844.

18. *Ibid.*

19. Duval, *Big-Foot Wallace*, p. 239; see also W[illia]m F. Wilson to "Dear Brother," Castle of Perote, April 22, 1844, in "Two Letters from a Mier Prisoner," *QTSHA* 2 (Jan. 1899), pp. 233-34.

20. W[illia]m F. Wilson to "Dear Brother" [John S. Wilson], Castle of Perote, April 22, 1844, in "Two Letters from a Mier Prisoner," *QTSHA* 2 (Jan. 1899), pp. 233-34.

knocked down exactly right; that he richly merited the chastisement, the harshness and cruelty with which he had always treated the sick and helpless.[21]

Upon Santa Anna's request in January 1844[22] for information regarding the treatment of the Texans at the hospital, the governor asked several of the Texans to sign a statement saying that they were treated well. Most of the Texans felt they had not been treated well, "having," they said, "had no more than half rations since their captivity," but Van Ness, McMath, Alsbury, and Colquhoun, who had received good treatment at the hospital from the Mexican officers "because they have had money,"[23] signed the statement "merely to curry favor with the governor," recorded Canfield.[24]

For a while the Texan physician pronounced the malady to be "jail fever," but later concluded that it was some sort of typhus, and it was so reported in New Orleans and in Texas. The prisoners thought the epidemic was caused by their confinement in badly ventilated quarters, and while this may have helped it spread it does not explain why civilians in the nearby town of Perote also contracted the disease. The illness was characterized by a "violent headache, accompanied by fever and an immediate general prostration of the system, followed up in a few hours by delirium."[25] Whatever the disease may have been, it developed suddenly and raged violently among the prisoners, the guards, and the local inhabitants of the area. Some Mexicans believed that it was brought to Perote by the Texans.

On October 6 the prisoners were told that Santa Anna would arrive the next day. Having witnessed General Canalizo installed as substitute president, but without authority to change the ministry, Santa Anna left Mexico City for his *hacienda*.[26] Hearing rumors of sickness, death, and "foul play" among the prisoners, Santa Anna stopped at the castle overnight. It was deepening twilight when the president's guard and coach came clattering over the drawbridge. Santa Anna had sent forward four cannon to participate in saluting his arrival,[27] and great preparations had been made to receive him. At dawn the following morning the chameleon of Mexican politics was on his way once more under heavy guard. As he departed, the guns of the fort again boomed forth a salute and a new flag raised in his honor fluttered in the breeze from the castle's flagpole.

The day after he left the castle, the prisoners saw Santa Anna's Manifesto to the People, which he had issued as he left Mexico City. He

---

21. Duval, *Big-Foot Wallace*, pp. 239-40; McCaleb, *The Mier Expedition*, pp. 108-9, quotes Wallace, but with some variation in wording from that given here.

22. Canfield diary, Jan. 8, 1844.

23. Glasscock diary, Jan. 8, 1844.

24. Canfield diary, Jan. 8, 1844.

25. Stapp, *Prisoners of Perote*, p. 119.

26. *Daily Picayune*, Nov. 29, 1843.

27. Trueheart diary, Oct. 6 and 7, 1843; see also Stapp, *Prisoners of Perote*, p. 114.

stated that he had proclaimed an armistice with Texas "for the purpose of learning what the Texans need and to extend to them that assistance which nations are accustomed to do their subjects when they have wandered from the path of duty, so that [as long as?] assistance or concession does not [compromise] in any way [or] manner the honor and integrity of the Mexican nation."[28]

On October 13, less than a week after Santa Anna's visit, the governor informed the Texans that they would all be released in twenty days, and "his information," reported Stapp, "was swallowed *sine grano,* not a doubt being entertained but it was derived from the president himself on his recent visit."[29] Two days later the Texans were told by their guards that they would be going to Jalapa the first of the next week.[30] The day after the death of William H. Van Horn on October 16 in the hospital at Perote, news of Jeffrey B. Hill's release was received at the castle. He was expected to leave the next day, but it was not until October 19 that he was able to start for Vera Cruz in company with twenty criminals who had been ordered to Santa Anna's *hacienda.*[31] Hill's release was requested by his younger brother, who had been adopted by Santa Anna.

Van Ness received a letter on November 12, 1843, from General Tornel apprising him that the Texans probably would be released as a result of the armistice proposed by Houston to the government of Mexico.[32] A few days later, on November 25, however, after the receipt at Perote Castle of the news of the pending armistice, all speculation in regard to an early release of the Texans was squelched by a letter received in the mail on November 26, saying that Santa Anna had stated he would not release any more of the Texan prisoners.[33]

At Santa Anna's "urgent solicitation and command," the Texan physicians were "united with the medical staff of the castle and town in post mortem examinations of such as had died, and their [report of the] inquest, accompanied by certificates of the general discipline of the prison [were ordered to be] remitted to him."[34] Commandant General Jarero instituted sanitary regulations as a result, some of which were ridiculous in the extreme. Having witnessed the Texans washing their faces at an early hour in the morning near the water barrel, it was supposed that this was one of the causes of the prevailing malady. An order was issued on November 30 saying that "if any more was ketched washing in cold water after that morning, the water barrell should be taken away."[35] The prisoners were denied the use of water before noon, both for drinking and wash-

---

28. Summation by James L. Trueheart in his diary, Oct. 9, 1843.
29. Stapp, *Prisoners of Perote*, p. 114.
30. Glasscock diary, Oct. 15-17, 1843; see also Canfield diary, Oct. 9-17, 1843.
31. Trueheart diary, Oct. 17-19, 1843.
32. Stapp, *Prisoners of Perote*, pp. 118-19.
33. Trueheart diary, Nov. 25 and 26, 1843.
34. Stapp, *Prisoners of Perote*, p. 119.
35. Glasscock diary, Nov. 30, 1843; see also Bell, *Narrative*, p. 77.

ing; and instead, for drinking purposes, were supplied with coffee and occasionally with "homeopathic doses of brandy."[36] Several of the Texans were actually thrown into solitary confinement for a time for violating the order.[37]

Another order forbade sale of fruit in the castle.[38] After his inspection of the prisoners in their cells on November 1 and at the insistence of the director of the hospital, the governor ordered the doors to the cells to be kept open during the day. So the prisoners might receive more fresh air; "otherwise," said the director, "the hospital would continue to remain full and many of the prisoners would inevitably die."[39]

On November 16, to improve living conditions in the cells, false floors were installed above the cold stone floors,[40] and Captain Valderéz promised that "tomorrow . . . he would have us all fixed comfortably." Around noon each day, weather permitting, the prisoners were allowed three hours for exercise in the plaza.[41] The castle was given a vigorous cleansing and the garrison was drilled daily. In the prisoners' quarters and about the castle different substances were burned "to dissipate the supposed disease."[42] Nourishing soups and *chile*, well fortified with peppers, became a part of the regular diet for the time being.

During these trying days there were constant rumors, sometimes founded on information received from important persons, of the release of the prisoners. On October 9 a letter from General Thompson stated that "the British Minister had told him that he thought the prisoners were to be released shortly."[43] News was received on October 29 that the British minister had been greatly displeased at the display of a British flag as a war trophy at a state reception in Mexico City and had demanded his passport. This gladdened the depressed Texan prisoners, who somehow hoped that the Mexican government would have its hands so full with a British fleet off Vera Cruz that it would be glad to let them go home.[44]

On November 6, 1843, the prisoners received word from Waddy Thompson that he had been told by General Tornel that they would be released in a few days.[45] On November 7 a rumor among the Texans was that they were going to be removed to Jalapa, and on the 10th they heard, with disbelief, that they would be released in three days. Then, three days later, Valderéz told them that in eight or ten days they would receive their freedom.[46]

36. Stapp, *Prisoners of Perote*, p. 119.
37. Bell, *Narrative*, p. 77.
38. Trueheart diary, Dec. 3 and 5, 1843.
39. *Ibid.*, Nov. 1, 1843; Canfield diary, Oct. 25 and Nov. 1-2, 1843.
40. Trueheart diary, Nov. 16, 1843.
41. Canfield diary, Nov. 1, 1843; Bell, *Narrative*, p. 25.
42. Bell, *Narrative*, p. 77.
43. Trueheart diary, Oct. 9, 1843.
44. *Ibid.*, Oct. 20, 1843.
45. Glasscock diary, Nov. 7 and 10, 1843.
46. *Ibid.*, Nov. 13, 1843.

On November 16, Van Ness went into Perote for the mail and reported that the only news he could gather was that an express had gone to Mexico City to the English minister and that the courier had informed him that it concerned the Texan prisoners, quoting Glasscock, "that we would be liberated in a few days." On the following day Captain Ryon received a letter from Mexico City saying that "Gen'l. Thompson was doing all in his power to get the chains off of us, and also keep us from work." The next day the Texans heard that they would "certainly be released on Tuesday, the 21st," but there were some doubting-Thomases among them.

When Tuesday arrived, it was rumored among the Texans that a Texas warship was lying off Vera Cruz to take them home.[47] While some believed the rumor, it is difficult to understand how anyone could think that a Texan war vessel would have been welcomed on the coast of Mexico. It shows the state of despondency of the men and their eagerness to grasp at any hope of liberation.

For a while General Jarero kept his promise and did not compel the men to work. Commencing on October 8 and continuing for several weeks, significant quantities of arms and munitions were brought into the castle, and a portion of the Texan prisoners was detailed to unload them. More muskets, bombs, swords, and ammunition arrived on October 25 "from god knows where."[48] On November 4, all of the Texan prisoners were ordered to "bring in boxes of guns and swords. I will here remark," said Glasscock in reporting the event, "for the last 2 or 3 weeks they have been receiving arms [at the castle] and they have now something like 30,000 stands on hand."[49] On the following day, normally not a work day, the prisoners were ordered "to bring in 8 wagon loads of cannon ball[s] & shells."[50]

Part of a regiment of cavalry from Queretaro on the way to Jalapa was quartered in the castle on the night of October 3, but were on their way the next day after having increased the burden upon the cleanup detail the next morning.[51] On October 19 twenty Mexican convicts who had been in the fort were removed to Jalapa as "volunteers" for Santa Anna's army,[52] and that evening the Texans were informed that they were to perform the tasks of sweeping and removing filth from the castle formerly done by the convicted criminals.[53] Up until then the main unit of the Mier men had

47. Glasscock diary, Nov. 21, 1843.
48. Canfield diary, Oct. 19-20, 1843.
49. Glasscock diary, Oct. 8 and Nov. 4, 1843.
50. *Ibid.*, Nov. 5, 1843; see also Trueheart diary, Nov. 5, 1843.
51. Trueheart diary, Oct. 3-4, 1843.
52. Stapp, *Prisoners of Perote*, p. 114; see also Canfield diary, Oct. 25, 1843; Trueheart diary, Oct. 19, 1843.
53. James A. Glasscock believed that the work was brought on by Judge Gibson, "who has been always very officious in writing to Mexican officers, . . . [and] insulted [the] Governor of this Castle." Glasscock diary, Oct. 21, 1843.

been confined to their cells except for three hours each day around noon, unless assigned to some special detail.

The officer bringing an order from the governor to put the prisoners to work was informed that the Texan gentlemen would not perform such degrading tasks as sweeping, dusting, watering, removing filth from the rooms and stables, going to the mountains to get brooms, hauling rock and sand into the fort, and a whole host of tasks. The Texans referred to the terms under which they had capitulated at Mier, but the officer pointed out that at Tacubaya they already had performed tasks assigned to them. The Texans sought "to weaken the force of the fatal precedent by an argument based on the atrocity of compelling . . . [their] obedience to an unjust and unrighteous requirement, but finding the man deaf to . . . [their] metaphysics, . . . they next insisted upon the superior respectability [of their former jobs] over the vile offices" with which they were now threatened. After listening to their side of the case, the officer declared that the Texans would be honored with the most respectable labor possible; but, in the meantime, he advised them "to offer no opposition to the inevitable necessity of obedience to the castle discipline."[54] They were guarded there "with as much if not more care than usual," in anticipation of some possible forceful action by the prisoners.[55]

The next morning no food was brought in to the cells, but instead the same officer appeared to ask if the prisoners had decided to work. The Texans repeated their protest, and without a word the officer withdrew. The doors of the cells were locked and the prisoners were denied the customary privilege of the courtyard.

Hungry and thirsty, when the key was turned in the door the next day the Texans crowded around the door, eager to receive their supplies of bread and water. While they were busily engaged in devouring the refreshments, the officer entered the cells to learn their decision about work. Seeing that they were not to be starved outright, some prisoners reaffirmed their decision not to work. The majority, however, appeared willing to bargain. They "expressed a sullen assent to the requirements, on condition of being immediately supplied with necessary provisions and chamber furniture," such as chairs, stools, tables, and beds. The officer misunderstood or ignored the bargaining attitude of the Texans. He departed, but soon returned with soldiers, a blacksmith, and a load of chains, and the work of chaining the prisoners got under way at two o'clock, Saturday, October 21, "without the slightest distinction of persons or opinions."[56]

The governor ordered that no one could leave the castle. Trueheart was awaiting the opening of the cell door to go into town to get the mail. He was much disappointed and upset when informed by one of "our members that was permitted to remain out, that an order had been sent

54. Stapp, *Prisoners of Perote*, p. 114.
55. Trueheart diary, Oct. 19, 1843.
56. Stapp, *Prisoners of Perote*, p. 116.

to chain all hands, and that the chaining was then going on. We," the San Antonio-Dawson prisoners, "express much uneasiness unless we should have the same fate," but were "soon relieved from our suspense, by the appearance of our captain [Mexican officer] in a great rage . . . applying to us approbious epithets of ungreateful[ness], and that we had repaid his kindness with ingratitude, and that he would teach us how to make representations against him; if good treatment would not suit us, he would try bad. We were then ordered to the smiths-shop to be chained with the exception of three. I had selected my partner," narrated Trueheart, "and was on the way to the forge when the captain called me, and said that I and two others might remain, and after a little persuasion he consented that all in this room might remain single. . . ."[57]

Chaining, declared Canfield, was done "because we object to do the dirty work allotted to us."[58] But the chaining was for better reasons than that: (1) because the prisoners would, at times, be working outside of the castle; (2) because it was common in Mexico to chain felons or common criminals, as the Texans were regarded by their captors; (3) because the Mexican guards were afraid of their Texan prisoners; (4) because it was one way to humiliate the Texans; and (5) because Santa Anna, no doubt, had been forced to wear chains in Texas. But there was a difference— Santa Anna had not been forced to work. All of the prisoners were ironed *dos-a-dos*, with the exception of James L. Trueheart and two others.[59] The San Antonio-Dawson prisoners were chained singly. The two individuals considered by the governor as the instigators of the opposition to working had their chains replaced with heavier ones.

Later in the afternoon, Thurmond, an interpreter and spokesman for the prisoners, obtained an interview with the governor's representative and the ruffled feelings of both parties were soothed, with, of course, the Texans relinquishing their stand on the issue of menial labor. The parley, reported Stapp, resulted in an adjustment of "our little mis-conceptions, and a steaming joint, and profusion of other delicacies, promptly placed at our disposal by the magnanimous victor, served to rob our subjection of its sting."[60]

On October 23 the officer group of the San Antonio-Dawson prisoners was told to prepare to be moved to the capilla, "very unwelcomed tidings" as they were "comparatively well fixed" where they were. At noon the men were taken to the blacksmith shop to be rechained, "but in consequence of the smith having gone to his dinner, the matter was deferred until two [o'clock] in the evening."[61] The prisoners were moved to their new quarters, and later in the afternoon their small chains were removed

---

57. Trueheart diary, Oct. 21, 1843.
58. Canfield diary, Oct. 21, 1843.
59. Trueheart diary, Oct. 21, 1843.
60. Stapp, *Prisoners of Perote*, p. 116.
61. Trueheart diary, Oct. 23, 1843.

"and larger ones substituted, eight [of us] being permitted to go single, and without a chain and the balance, six, coupled." The new quarters were more cramped and damp and cold. The next day two of the sixteen prisoners were moved to room no. 7, relieving the pressure a little.[62]

The Mexican officers did not delay in reaping the fruits of their victory, for no sooner were a few chained two and two than they were "set to work Tearing up the square & street in the fort."[63] Those who did not work in the carpenter shop or at some other skill were taken out "one room at a time" to clean the castle and to bring in sand, while the rest of the prisoners remained locked securely in their cells.[64] Details of a dozen or more captives each, led in single file by an overseer carrying a strong stick or cudgel, paraded about the castle carrying everything before them in the form of litter. "The governor's quarters came in for more than their rightful share of these interesting proofs of our diligence; windows, doors, and walls were assailed by such furious columns of powder, as to bring the old gentlemen in person to the spot to countermarch . . . [the frisky Texans] to a more distant scene of operation."[65]

Others were set to work repairing the square and the street in the fort. Bell wrote that "Small stones or peebles *[sic]* were required to pave different parts of the fortress, which were dug from the bottom of the ditch, and had to be carefully selected according to size and shape. Therefore, a party of Texans, consisting of twenty or thirty in number might often be seated on the ground, carefully selecting peebles from the sand one by one, as though they were gathering precious stones from a mine."[66] Still others, who "were extremely indignant with their occupation,"[67] were assigned the duty of collecting in baskets "the piles of filth" swept up by other details. They were under supervision "of the vilest convicts with seeming discretion to use the pole instead of the rod, the application of which keeps every one up to the mark."[68] Sometimes the refuse was loaded directly into wheelbarrows with a shovel or, more commonly, with "a plate of broken refuse tin."[69] After the wheelbarrows had been loaded, a party of Texans was paraded between a file of soldiers on each side to take the refuse outside the castle to a distance of half a mile.

Some, such as James A. Glasscock, were employed as stone masons[70] to make repairs on the fortress or the buildings on the plaza. Others cleaned the blackened walls of moss and whitewashed or painted them.

---

62. *Ibid.*, Oct. 24, 1843.

63. Glasscock diary, Oct. 21, 1843.

64. Trueheart diary, Oct. 23, 1843.

65. Stapp, *Prisoners of Perote*, p. 116; see also Bell, *Narrative*, pp. 77-78.

66. Bell, *Narrative*, p. 82.

67. Stapp, *Prisoners of Perote*, p. 116.

68. W[illia]m F. Wilson to "Dear Brother," Castle of Perote, Apr. 22, 1844. In "Two Letters from a Mier Prisoner," *QTSHA* 2 (Jan. 1899), pp. 233-34.

69. Bell, *Narrative*, pp. 77-78.

70. Glasscock diary, Jul. 10, 1844.

William Davis was assigned to the armory to clean and oil muskets. In this occupation they were closely supervised and worked under lock and key. Nevertheless, Davis was able to supply "his fellow prisoners with little saws and files of his own construction, and with these, their chains were often cut."[71] On one occasion a party of twenty-five Texans was conducted to a battery to dig weeds and grass from broken cement. At first they were furnished with a nail, but the work of digging progressed so slowly that they were finally supplied with shovels without handles. Even with these, one man, if he worked, could have done what twenty actually accomplished.[72]

The prisoners were resentful of their occupations, and disliked performing any useful work for the Mexicans. Usually a guard of fifty soldiers and two or three officers accompanied a detail of twenty prisoners, while the balance of the prisoners were kept locked in their rooms. Since they were forced to work, some prisoners seemed to get enjoyment out of performing their tasks. The sweepers in the barracks and officer quarters seemed to enjoy their assignment because of the irritation their vigorous performance caused. The "sweepers grew to relish their branch of business so well as to repine at the prospect of its speedy termination." Their supervisors were clothed with ashes and dust, and, "though frequently relieved, not an officer or subaltern could at last be found, who would venture inside the canopy of dust," under which the Texans furiously plied their task.[73]

For two days the sweepers wreaked vengeance on their masters. By the end of the second day, the authorities had had enough. The sweepers were reassigned to carrying sand and rocks in wheelbarrows into the castle to repair the fortification. Those who hauled sand and rocks had the most laborious task. The sand had to be transported from outside the fort in a cart drawn by twelve Texans, and the rock came from a quarry approximately a mile farther. For their "beast of burden," the Mexicans "rigged up rawhide harness, composed of breast and shoulder straps."[74] The men were prodded along at the points of the bayonet or long pole with a sharpened end. Large stones necessary for repairing parts of the fortress were hauled from the mountains in a cart pulled by twenty Texans yoked together.[75] Each cart hauled two loads a day. "Nor did they stop at this for in this vehicle, the Mexican officers sometimes took a pleasure excursion through the public streets of the town of Perote drawn by their captive enemies," Bell reported.[76] Wallace recalled that "the Texans let three carts accidentally get the start of them, and run off a high bluff and smash to pieces."[77]

---

71. Jenkins, ed., *Recollections of Early Texas*, p. 116.
72. Bell, *Narrative*, p. 83.
73. Stapp, *Prisoners of Perote*, p. 117; see also William F. Wilson to John S. Wilson, Castle of Perote, April 22, 1844, *QTSHA* 2 (Jan. 1899), pp. 233-34.
74. Smithwick, *Evolution of a State*, p. 275.
75. Bell, *Narrative*, p. 85.
76. *Ibid.*
77. Sowell, *Life of "Big Foot" Wallace*, p. 67.

Lieutenant Yucatanca, a native Indian, was hated by most of the prisoners. He was often appointed to "drive" the Texans at work and took delight in seeing that they did not shirk their duty; "and then [would] borrow money from them at night and pawn his coat for payment."[78]

The Texans played many tricks on the "tinselled Captains," lesser officers, and overseers who supervised their labors. The old ruses used effectively at Tacubaya were used at Perote and some new ones were added. When called out to work in the morning, several of the men "would pretend to have a very sore foot," rheumatism, or be *malo en la cabeza* (have a headache), contending that it was impossible for them to work. An interpreter would be called to examine the patient to see if the officer could understand what the particular problem was. Thus the time for beginning work by the whole party was delayed. While one small party was being examined and readied for work, "another set of wags would be sneaking off unperceived." Time was further consumed in rounding them up. Finally, when the party reached the point where the work was to be done, "little would be done unless the officer stood by all the time for the overseers were also prisoners, and even if disposed to [make the Texans] labor, they were easily bribed."[79]

Occasionally the guard sought to encourage the Texans to work by promising to free them from their chains. Threats also were made, but efforts at encouragement and intimidation never seemed to produce results.

General Jarero showed kindness toward the prisoners, and no doubt treated them as leniently as his instructions permitted. But he was determined to rehabilitate the fortress and when ordered to put the prisoners to work, he utilized their labor to that end. He often watched the prisoners at work and "if he caught any of them idling, they were immediately punished by being sent to the calaboose."[80] Jarero was particular that the Texans showed him the proper respect. When in the presence of this "capricious old soldier," every Texan captive was required to shed his "Beaver." The unceremonious or sometimes independent and stubborn fellows unthinkingly appeared occasionally in "His Excellency's" presence without uncovering their heads, and "of this they were generally soon reminded by a blow of his cane, which brought the objecting article to the ground. And thus enraged at what he supposed [was] insolence, he would visit vengeance on the whole *rebel fraternity* for having insulted the dignity of the Supreme government of Mexico in the person of one of her generals, and while his rage lasted," reported Bell, "it was stand clear little ones, and every nook and corner in the interior of the fortress that could hide a man was sure to be occupied by a Texan, skulking from work."[81]

Major Coxo, who was second in command of the fort, was responsible

---

78. Bell, *Narrative*, p. 87.
79. *Ibid.*, p. 79.
80. *Ibid.*, p. 86.
81. *Ibid.*, pp. 78-79.

for feeding the personnel of the castle and supervision of their quarters. The Texan prisoners considered the major to be "a most indefatigable persecutor." He sometimes expressed a desire to see "a few of the 'devils' shot to teach the rest good behavior." Major Coxo often went to "the cookhouse to see, as he said, whether they had plenty [of food], also whether it was good or not, and after tasting and examining it in various other ways, always pronounced it of the very best quality, and much too good for such thieves, for such rogues, as the Texans."[82]

It was customary for the cooks each morning to bring a large tin kettle of coffee made from thirteen ounces of "burnt substance" boiled in about five gallons of water, to which had been added two and a half pounds of brown sugar.[83] Each prisoner received about one-half pint. We "eat all we can get and would be glad to get more. Our breakfast," wrote Edward Manton to his uncle in Rhode Island, "consists of a piece of bread about the size of one of your biscuits; at dinner two pieces, a saucer of boiled potatoes, and the broth with onions and red pepper in it with another saucer of rice; at night a saucer of beans and then comes . . . lockup until morning. We then have liberty of the yard during the day which enables those who have money to live quite well, there being a store inside where bread and many other things can be bought, fruit is very cheap, 12 oranges for 6 cents."[84]

Upon their arrival in Texas in May 1843, Hatch and Morgan reported the prisoners were often fed tainted beef and stale, musty bread.[85] Usually the beef, bone included, was chopped into pieces and served in portions of fourteen ounces or less each for as many prisoners as were to be fed, and was boiled in water with six ounces of lard. The meat was seasoned with salt and red peppers. Another kettle contained about eleven pounds of boiled rice for sixty-two men to which had been added a pound of lard and a small quantity of onions. On the other four days out of an eight-day period, when meat was not served, Irish potatoes or highly seasoned *frijoles* were substituted.[86]

When the coffee or soup was brought, each man approached to dip his tin cup in or to have the coffee, soup, or stew ladeled out to him; then, seating themselves in small groups, the men devoured the repast and seemed to forget that they had any other home.

With funds received from relatives or drafts upon themselves or on a friend, or the erratic monetary allowance from the Mexican government, the men were able to purchase sugar, coffee, lard, fruit, onions, or red

---

82. *Ibid.*, pp. 86-87.
83. Green, *Mier Expedition*, p. 264.
84. Extract of letter of Edward Manton to [Uncle] Edward ———, Perot (Mexico), Jan. 1, 1843, in D. C. Jenckes to A. A. Gardenier, Lime Rock, R.I., Feb. 19, 1843 (cop) in Edward Manton Papers, TxU-A.
85. *Telegraph and Texas Register*, May 17, 1843.
86. Green, *Mier Expedition*, p. 264.

peppers to supplement and improve the taste of their fare.[87] Sometimes they utilized their money "to buy liquor enough to make them[selves] merry, and thus they would have a most glorious row, as they were pleased to term it, which often terminated in an Irish pitched battle and the sending of a few of the revellers to the calaboose to brood in solitary confinement over their follies."[88]

At first the condition of the Texans in respect to food was a little better at Perote than what they encountered elsewhere in Mexican prisons but we can assume that some of the letters written from Perote were intended to ease the minds of relatives. But under no circumstances can one assume that their life in prison was an easy one. The prisoners as a whole suffered great privations and often inhumane treatment.

The poor, unbalanced diet often caused dysentery. "For the last three days," recorded a prisoner on November 19, 1843, "we have received fresh potatoes instead of our usual meat ration. . . . Our captain tells us that he has no money, and there is none in the castle, for which reasons he has been unable to furnish us meat. He tried to borrow money from the prisoners, but could not secure it as on former occasions."[89] At best, the fare was meager in quantity and poor in quality. Often the meals were described as vile, greasy messes, and seasoned too highly with red peppers, garlic, or onions for Anglo-Saxon tastes. One said the fare was "little of nothing cooked in the most horrible manner imaginable; neither fit for man, or beast, yet we eat it, and do not even get enough, bad as it is."[90] When the Texans complained of the scantiness and unappetizing food, a guard "went out and collected from the back-yard a quantity of old bones and other filthy offal, and returning threw it on the ground before us," reported Wallace, "bidding us eat, as that was good enough for such abominable heretics as we were."[91]

Conditions among the prisoners grew worse as the days and weeks passed. "Our food," reported William E. Jones, "consisted of poor beef, one day in three; beans, potatoes, rice and bread—badly cooked—the rations of these articles were always small, not being sufficient for a hearty man."[92] William F. Wilson wrote, "We are in a most retched condition, badly fed, naked, [and] made to work like beasts of burthen."[93] Two pounds of coffee per day was the government's allowance for 110 men, plus ten ounces "of the worst bread" and four ounces of the "poorest beef

87. *Ibid.*, pp. 247-48; Trueheart diary, Nov. 12, 1843.

88. Bell, *Narrative*, p. 89.

89. Trueheart diary, Nov. 19, 1843.

90. Nance, ed., *McCutchan's Narrative*, p. 108.

91. Duval, *The Adventures of Bigfoot Wallace*, p. 193.

92. [William E. Jones to M. B. Lamar], Washington, 1 Feb 1844, in Winkler, ed., "The Béxar and Dawson Prisoners," *QTSHA* 13 (Apr. 1910), pp. 320-24.

93. William F. Wilson to Colonel A[masa] Turner, Republic of Mexico, Castle of Perote, Jul. 29, 1844, in *QTSHA* 2 (Jan. 1899), pp. 234-36; see also *New Orleans Bulletin*, Jan. 19, 1844.

that can be found" for each man. The meat, if thrown against the wall, would "stick like glue." Occasionally Irish potatoes or *frijoles,* mashed in water "with a little salt and a great quantity of red pepper" would be substituted every other day for the meat.

On November 16, 1843, John R. ("Dick") Johnson got drunk and picked up rats that had been killed the night before, and, recorded Glass-cock, "fetched them in and cooked them," after which he invited all the boys to partake of the meal he had prepared. "He took a piece of bread with a rat on it and a piece with beef on it, [and] gave the boys the rat to eat and he ate the beef."[94] He may not have been so drunk after all.

Colonel Carrasco and Col. John B. Hogan of Mobile, Alabama, described as an American consul and bearer of dispatches from the United States to General Thompson, visited Perote Prison on Tuesday, February 5, 1844. Hogan told the prisoners that he did not know when they would be released but assured them that "he would do all in his power" to have them liberated and that he bore important documents concerning them.[95] Carrasco carried a proposition from General Woll suggesting the release of two of the Texan prisoners to be sent as commissioners to Texas with Colonel Carrasco to seek a renewal of the armistice. One of the propositions was that Mexico be permitted to maintain a military force on the Nueces to protect the frontier. It was expected in their discussions with Santa Anna at Manga de Clavo that the two men would solicit the release of the Texan prisoners. Colonel Hogan reported that "there prevailed a tremendous excitement in the U.S." concerning the treatment of the Texan prisoners and their detention.[96] The visit of Carrasco and Hogan at the castle created much speculation among the prisoners as to which two of them "would most likely be sent to Texas as commissioners."[97]

The Texans at Perote were usually short of clothing. The clothes of a few were so rotten and threadbare that they would scarcely undergo the operation of being taken off and being put on. The clothes with which they started out were in shreds, and many had been relieved of jackets, blankets, and hats at various times, places, and occasions by the guards. Their shoes had long since played out, and some had been able to obtain replacements from time to time or to improvise. Addressing his brother John S. Wilson "from the confines of a Prison, contrary to what I ever anticipated but in character with the present condition of our Country," William F. Wilson wrote home in April 1844 that he had marched 1,500 miles, 300 of which was barefooted, through three hail storms with the

---

94. Glasscock diary, Nov. 16, 1843.
95. *Ibid.,* Feb 4-5, 1844; Trueheart diary, Feb. 5, 1844.
96. Trueheart diary, Feb. 5, 1844.
97. *Ibid.,* Feb. 6, 1844.

washes ankle deep in hail stones.[98] "It is needless for me to state," wrote Captain Buster, "that we are almost destitute of clothing."[99] A few of the men were almost naked. If their pants and shirt were washed the men found it necessary to wrap a blanket around themselves because they did not have a change of clothes. "As this is a blanket nation, we have to follow fashion, and cut quite a dash with a blanket belted on, without either coat or pants," one prisoner reported.[100] The blankets were tied around their necks, rather than the middle of the body, giving the Texans the appearance of Roman senators.[101]

Soon after the arrival of the first Mier prisoners at Perote Castle, John Black, the U.S. consul at Mexico City, sent the prisoners a trunk of clothes and a blanket each, and Captain West also sent a trunk of clothes from the capital, as well as a supply of writing materials.[102] Other friends in Mexico City sent clothing. A big problem was protecting what clothing they had from the thievery of the soldiers, overseers, and hospital attendants. Their thievery became so prevalent that the prisoners requested that no soldier be allowed to enter their quarters unless on special duty, for if they did, reported Bell, "something was sure to be stolen. They would steal the last rag of a blanket from a dying prisoner, and have been known to attempt to take the blanket from a corpse that was being interred when it was the only covering."[103] For the audacity of striking a soldier who had stolen his shirt, one of the prisoners was placed in the calaboose on December 7, 1843.[104]

Governor Jarero provided shoes and clothes to the most destitute by withholding half of the twenty-five cents per diem allowed the prisoners to buy food and other necessities. He fed them on half or less of the ration allowance, and with the money saved bought clothes and shoes. The Texans wore sandals made of goatskins for shoes. On November 3, about six weeks after the main body of the Mier men arrived at the fort, the commandant had Mexican tailors make "public clothes" for the Texans, and on the following day the new prison garb, consisting of striped woolen pantaloons and shirts, made of red, white, and green colored blanket material, was ready for their use, paid for, said Bell, out of the twenty-five cents allowed for food.[105]

For sleeping, the Texan officers had a few sheepskins which they brought from Tacubaya to place on the cold, damp, stone floor of their

---

98. W[illia]m F. Wilson to "Dear Brother" [John S. Wilson], Castle of Perote, Apr. 22, 1844, in "Two Letters from a Mier Prisoner," *QTSHA* 2 (Jan. 1899), pp. 233-34.

99. Claudius Buster to John V. Buster, Castle of Perote, Mar. 8, 1844, typed copy in Claudius Buster Papers, TxU-A.

100. [A Prisoner] to the editor of the *Galveston News*, Perote, Jan. 28, 1844, reprinted in *Telegraph and Texas Register*, Feb. 28, 1844.

101. Green, *Mier Expedition*, p. 307.

102. *Ibid.*, p. 282.

103. Bell, *Narrative*, p. 83.

104. Trueheart diary, Dec. 7, 1843.

105. Glasscock diary, Nov. 3-4, 1843; Canfield diary, Nov. 4, 1843.

cell. The privates, who were not so fortunate, found the floors quite uncomfortable, and lucky was he who had a blanket in which to curl up on the floor. During the epidemic boards were placed on the brick or stone floor. There was no way of heating the fort, which was nearly 7,000 feet above sea level, and the climate was cold and damp. It was "the most unpleasant climate I have yet visited," declared Wilson.[106] Biting winds from the surrounding snow-clad mountains blew almost incessantly. Rain fell nearly every day, except at those times in the winter months when it snowed; if it did not snow, it rained. Yet, in the summer an invigorating shower seldom fell. The only heat in the fortification was animal heat, wrote one of the prisoners.[107]

To add to the misery of the prisoners at night, bedbugs, lice, and fleas poured forth from every crevice in the walls. Even the cracks in the floors sent forth their legions. During waking hours a considerable portion of the Texans' free time each day was spent delousing body, clothes, and bedding. Fine toothed combs were a premium. In good weather the prisoners basked in the sun, "weeding" their clothes of the detestable insects. "While I write," reported Manton to his uncle, "my companion [to] whom I am chained to is sitting by me [de]lousing himself.[108]

---

106. William F. Wilson to John S. Wilson, Castle of Perote, Apr. 22, 1844, in *QTSHA* 2 (Jan. 1899), pp. 233-34.

107. William F. Wilson to Colonel A. Turner, Republic of Texas, [dated] Castle of Perote, 29th Jul 1844, in "Two Letters from a Mier Prisoner," *QTSHA* 2 (Jan. 1899), pp. 234-36.

108. Edward Manton to Uncle Edward ———, Perot (Mexico), Jan. 1, 1843, in Weyand and Wade, *An Early History of Fayette County*, pp. 22-24.

CHAPTER 22

Release—the Béxar-Dawson
Men are Freed

WHEN IT BECAME KNOWN in the United States that former President Andrew Jackson had been effective with Santa Anna in gaining the release of Bradley, Jackson was flooded by requests from relatives and friends of other Texan prisoners for assistance. Some wrote letters; others visited the Hermitage. No person in the United States exerted more influence over President Santa Anna than Jackson, and after him, "singularly as it may seem," came the influence of former President John Quincy Adams.[1]

Democratic Congressman Clement Comer Clay, B. M. Love, John Connally, Benjamin Patterson, D. M. Bradford, and D. B. Turner, all of Huntsville, Alabama, appealed to Jackson to use his influence with Santa Anna to gain the release of Thomas S. Tatum.[2] William Harbert of Denmark, Tennessee, sought assistance in the liberation of his brother, Nathaniel. He had received "several communications in relation to . . . [Nathaniel's] situation as a captive." Harbert referred to several gentlemen of influence in Tennessee known to Jackson and reminded Jackson that he had served under him in the Seminole campaign.[3] Nath Terry of Locustgrove, Limestone County, Alabama, also requested Jackson's assistance in obtaining the release of Nathaniel Harbert.

On March 22, 1843, William Gaston of Newbern, North Carolina, appealed to the U.S. Department of State requesting assistance in obtaining the release of George C. Hatch captured at San Antonio by General Woll.

---

1. *Daily Picayune*, May 8, 1844.
2. C. C. Clay to Genl. [Andrew] Jackson, Huntsville, [Ala.], Feb. 5, 1844; D. B. Turner to General Andrew Jackson, Huntsville, Ala., Feb. 7, 1844, and endorsed by B. M. Love, John Connally, Benjamin Patterson, D. H. Bradford, in Friend, ed., "Sidelights and Supplements on the Perote Prisoners," *SWHQ* 69 (Apr. 1966), pp. 516-17.
3. William Harbert to Andrew Jackson, Denmark, Tennessee, Feb. 6, 1844, in Friend, ed., "Sidelights and Supplements on the Perote Prisoners," *SWHQ* 68 (Apr. 1965), pp. 490-92.

He was informed by Secretary of State Daniel Webster that "the circumstances will not admit of our official interference at present," but that he had sent a private letter to General Thompson, the U.S. minister in Mexico, requesting him "to do any thing which he can do with propriety toward the liberation or relief of Mr. Hatch."[4]

A strong effort was made by several in the United States to effect the release of Cornelius W. Peterson, a lawyer, culminating in an effort to get the assistance of "Old Hickory" and to interest the United States Congress and the State Department in the case. From Perote Castle, Cornelius wrote to Judge Daniel Coleman, his brother-in-law. Cornelius' letter was given to George S. Houston, congressman from Athens, to be taken to Washington. Houston discovered that the Department of State, at the request of Congressman Reuben Coleman, already had written on January 4, 1843, to General Thompson in Mexico to see what could be done to secure the release of Peterson and Hutchinson.

In his appeal to Jackson, Judge Coleman stated that at the time of Cornelius' capture by General Woll, his brother-in-law "did not belong to the Texian army, . . . but was attending court as a lawyer, and he and his fellow captives only resisted the first attack of the Mexicans under the belief that they were a band of marauders." They "finally surrendered to Woll under the express stipulation," he continued, "that all the civilians (of whom he was one) should not be detained."[5] Coleman explained to Jackson that he had tried, in vain, various means to free Peterson, and "we would now appeal," he said, "to your well known humanity and love of justice to give us your powerful aid in the case." With his letter, he enclosed a copy of a letter he had received from Peterson in Perote Castle, depicting the deplorable conditions under which he lived. On the back of Coleman's letter Jackson wrote, "Judge Coleman of Alabama respecting one of the Texian prisoners. I have written to St. Anna & Thompson & hope these prisoners will be released. A. J."

From Petersburg, Virginia, on February 7, 1844, Janet Gilliam requested Jackson to use his influence with Santa Anna to free her only brother, Ludovic Colquhoun.[6] She explained that he had gone to Texas and to San Antonio "to get a proper title to some lands granted by the Government of Mexico," and while there had been captured. Mexico's minister to the United States, Juan N. Almonte, transmitted to José María Gonzáles de la Vega, minister of foreign relations and government in

4. Dan'l Webster to William Gaston, Newbern, North Carolina, Department of State, Washington, 1st Apr. 1843, in Domestic Letters, Department of State, vol. 33 (Dec. 1, 1842-Jan. 24, 1844), National Archives (microfilm).

5. Daniel Coleman to Genl. Andrew Jackson, Athens, Alabama, Sept. 17, 1843, in Friend, ed., "Sidelights and Supplements on the Perote Prisoners," *SWHQ* 68 (Apr. 1965), pp. 493-94.

6. Janet Gilliam to General [Andrew] Jackson, Petersburg, [Virginia], Feby. 7, 1844, in Friend, ed., "Sidelights and Supplements on the Perote Prisoners," *SWHQ* 69 (July 1965), pp. 88-89.

Mexico, on April 6, Jackson's letter of March 1 and a petition signed by more than ninety members of the United States House of Representatives requesting President Santa Anna to free Ludovic Colquhoun, one of the Béxar prisoners and a member of the Texas Congress at the time of his capture.[7] Almonte urged approval of the request, as to do so, "would no doubt produce a very favorable effect in the [United] States to the Supreme Magistrate of the Republic" of Mexico.

Almonte also forwarded several letters presented to him by members of the U.S. House of Representatives and Senate expressing solicitude "for the fate of three Texan prisoners who are in Perote and whose names are C. W. Peterson, William P. Stapp and Cornelius W. Peters[on]." In the best interest of Mexico's relations with the United States, he thought it wise to accede to the requests of the members of Congress, for a demonstration of such magnanimity on the part of the president would no doubt gain the admiration of the civilized world and "at the same time it would bring about an attitude in this country [the United States] in confirming the idea that I have the favor of my Government." Accordingly, Santa Anna on May 15, 1844, issued an order for the release of Ludovic Colquhoun and C. W. Peterson.[8] By the time Almonte's request arrived and was acted upon, Colquhoun and Peterson had been released to General Thompson and had left Mexico.

Secretary of State Able Upshur transmitted to Thompson a resolution from the legislature of the State of Mississippi requesting President Tyler to use his influence with President Santa Anna to bring about the release of David H. E. Beasley. Upshur instructed Thompson to "endeavor, by all proper means, to accomplish that object."[9]

George N. Downs was the concern of three congressmen from Connecticut who petitioned the State Department on December 15, 1843, to endeavor through the United States minister in Mexico to free him.[10]

After Thompson left Mexico, Secretary of State John C. Calhoun transmitted to Benjamin E. Green, acting *chargé d'affaires,* a petition to Santa Anna from a group of citizens of Tuscaloosa County, Alabama, soliciting the release of William F. McMath.[11] Upon his arrival at New Orleans,

7. *J. N. Almonte a Exmo S.ᵒʳ Ministro de Relaciónes Exteriores y Gobernación, México, [dated] Washington Abril 6, de 1844*, no. 45, LE-1070, p. 160-61, copy in Justin H. Smith Papers, Latin American Collection, TxU-A; also in San Jacinto Museum of History.

8. *José María Tornel, Ministro de Guerra y marina a E. S. Ministro de Relaciónes Exterior y Governación, México, 20 de Mayo, 1844,* copy in Justin H. Smith Papers, Latin American Collection, TxU-A.

9. A. P. Upshur to Waddy Thompson, Department of State, 17th Feb. 1844, no. 57, in Diplomatic Instructions of the Department of State. Mexico, May 29, 1833-Mar. 29, 1845, National Archives (microfilm).

10. A. P. U[pshur] to George S. Catlin, Samuel Simons and John Stewart, Department of State, Washington 23d Feby. 1844, in *ibid.*

11. J. C. Calhoun to Benjamin E. Green, Department of State, Washington, 20th Apr. 1844, no. 2, in Diplomatic Instructions of the Department of State. Mexico, May 29, 1833-Mar. 29, 1845, National Archives (microfilm).

Thompson said that as soon as the excitement in Mexico over the escape of the Mier men from Perote Castle died away, he thought Santa Anna would release the remainder of the Texan prisoners in Mexico.[12]

The requests to Jackson became so numerous that his failing health would not allow him to read all letters received, much less permit him to write them in each case; so, he said, "finding it would be endless to address him [Santa Anna] for the liberation of each, I determined, although a very delicate question, situated as Mexico and Texas are, at present, and the situation of the United States and Texas, humanity said take the responsibility, which I have done," and the day before he received his letter, he told Maunsel White he had enclosed to Col. C. Johnson in Washington City a letter addressed to Santa Anna to be transmitted by the Mexican minister in the United States to his government.[13] Jackson said that he had "couched" his letter to Santa Anna, "in such terms, rather to soothe his feelings than to irritate, bringing to his view how much the noble act of liberating the prisoners on parole will enhance his character in the estimation of the whole civilized world, when keeping them in chains will lower it, and bring upon him the frowns of the whole christian world, etc., etc., etc. Bringing to his mind, the preparation of Texas to retaliate, which the civilized nations, will unite and put down, that such a system of warfare will not, cannot, be tolerated in this enlightened age by the christian nations."

The months passed, the routine became deadly, and the men lost hope of liberation. "Our very speculations," reported one of the Texans, "grew as old and trite as our reminiscences. . . . Our only theme was ever green, racy, and exhaustless, and that was vengeance, in some form, most direful upon our oppressors."[14] Even so, there was little hope of any "vengeance" soon or for any successful assault on an ever vigilant guard. Their numbers reduced to some 150 men separated in various prisons and hospitals so distant from each other as Mexico City, Puebla, Matamoros, San Juan de Ulúa, and Perote Castle, would almost preclude any successful revolt. Even at Perote Castle, where most of the Texan prisoners were held, they were divided during the day by different assignments and at night locked in three different cells.

Escape from the hospital in town was also impossible. The patients were too weak, and as soon as a patient showed improvement he was returned to the castle and "the fact is that not a Blanket, Shoe, shirt or even a piece of bread was left to an invalid by the Mexican attendants at the hospital." Although frequent complaints were made to the physicians, "it seemed as tho' they were Concerned in this petty and rascally system of thieving."[15]

---

12. *Daily Picayune*, Apr. 13, 1844.

13. Andrew Jackson to Maunsel White, Hermitage, Mar. 4, 1844, in Bassett, ed., *Correspondence of Andrew Jackson* 6, pp. 270-71; see also *Telegraph and Texas Register*, Apr. 17, 1844; *Mobile Advertiser* quoted in *Daily Picayune*, Apr. 6, 1844.

14. Stapp, *Prisoners of Perote*, p. 120.

15. Canfield diary, Jan. 8, 1844.

By March 1844, the health of most of the Texans improved, and increased suspicion of the Texan prisoners did so as well. The Mexican officers became more vigilant. Their commands were no longer issued in mild and courteous tones, but harshly and peremptorily, reinforced by oaths and "angry expressions of look and manner. While "receiving our rations at noon" on March 1, the eve of the Texan Declaration of Independence, reported Stapp, "we were further surprised by discovering a piece of artillery drawn up at the northern terminus of the street, and so directed as to range the avenue on which our cells were situated."[16] Another cannon had been mounted in the ditch, and a third "at the hospital."[17] "Additional sentries were every where on duty, and as soon as our dinner was through with," said Stapp, "we were ordered into our rooms and locked up."[18] At dark, a line of patrols were stationed outside, "whose shrill cry of Centinela alerto resounded through the old castle at five-minute intervals throughout the night," said Bell.[19] "When morning come, we could see the whole garrison drawn up and under arms," reported Stapp.[20] The Texans remained quietly in their cells during the day and retired early to bed, not wishing to give the Mexicans any excuse for taking drastic action against them.

The vigilance and precautionary measures were explained by the governor. He called the Texan interpreter and informed him that he had received three communications that the Texan prisoners intended making a break not only at the hospital in town but also at the castle, and that one of the soldiers had reported that one of the Texans had tried to bribe him. He wanted them to know how vigilant he was, and "how futile and fatal would be any . . . attempt to rise upon our guard."[21] Bell reported that the governor told the interpreter that "he and his comrades would have but one hour to say their prayers, if another such alarm was raised."[22]

March 2 was passed quietly by the prisoners in their rooms. They celebrated Texas Independence Day by drinking eggnog, and in the evening in the midst of their low-key frolic, Duncan C. Ogden returned from the governor's office and announced that his passport had been received in the evening mail and that he would be leaving in the morning.

This was a cause for celebration, not only because it was Texas Independence Day but also because of his release. Eggnog and toasts flowed freely during the remainder of the evening. Ogden became ill during the night, probably from drinking too much eggnog.[23] He was unable to travel for several days, but finally on March 7 he felt well enough to board the stage for Vera Cruz, taking many letters with him to the United States.

16. Stapp, *Prisoners of Perote*, p. 121.
17. Trueheart diary, Mar. 1, 1844.
18. Stapp, *Prisoners of Perote*, p. 121.
19. Bell, *Narrative*, p. 89.
20. Stapp, *Prisoners of Perote*. p. 121.
21. Trueheart diary, Mar. 1, 1844.
22. Bell, *Narrative*, p. 90.
23. Trueheart diary, Mar. 2-3, 1844.

Texian charge upon the guards and victory of Salado. From Green, ...Texian Expedition Against Mier, 154.

The shooting of Captain Cameron. From Green, ...Texian Expedition Against Mier, 172.

Shooting the decimated Texians. From Green, ...Texian Expedition Against Mier, 172.

Escape from the Castle of Perote. From Green, . . . Texian Expedition Against Mier, *328.*

Narrow escape from the cavalry officer at the town of Antigua. From Green, . . . Texian Expedition Against Mier, *350.*

Separation after escape. From Green, . . . Texian Expedition Against Mier, *328.*

Texians paving the street at the Archbishop's Palace. Author's collection.

Bridge over moat leading to entrance of Perote Prison. From McGrath and Hawkins, "Perote Fort," SWHQ, 48:342.

Above: *Violin made by Henry Journeay while in Perote Castle. Courtesy Texas State Archives.*
Right: *Corridors of inner courtyard of Perote Prison, where prisoners were allowed to exercise and warm themselves in the sun. Author's collection.*

William Kinch Davis in Perote Prison. From Wharton, History of Fort Bend County, *116.*

A lookout tower of the Castle of Perote. From McGrath and Hawkins, "Perote Fort," SWHQ, *48:342.*

The making of pulque. From Mayer, Mexico, Aztec, Spanish and Republican *(1853), 2:58.*

College of Mines. From Mayer, Mexico, Aztec, Spanish and Republican *(1853), 2:248.*

Fandango. From Mayer, Mexico, Aztec, Spanish and Republican *(1853), 2:26.*

The Chamber of Deputies. From Mayer, Mexico, Aztec, Spanish and Republican *(1853), 2:247.*

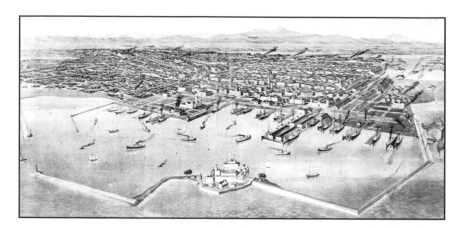

Orizaba. From Boletin Bibliografico *No. 415, May 15, 1969.*

Plaza of Vera Cruz. From author's collection.

From Boletin Bibliografico, *No. 447, Sept. 15, 1970.*

Above: *Rancheros. Author's collection.*
Left: *Popocatepetl. From Mayer,* Mexico, Aztec, Spanish and Republican *(1853), 2:223.*
Below: *Entrance to the Archbishop's Palace. From Gooch-Iglehart,* The Boy Captive of the Mier Expedition, *210.*

National Bridge — Puente Nacional, formerly called Puente del Rey. From author's collection.

Vera Cruz. From author's collection.

The Port of Vera Cruz with the Castle of San Juan de Ulua. From author's collection.

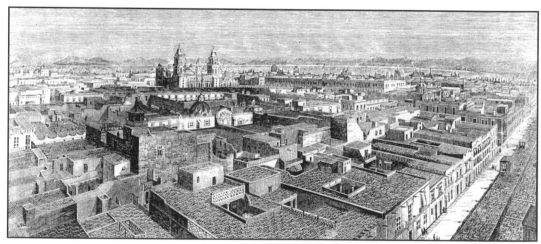

Mexico City. From Mayer, Mexico, Aztec, Spanish and Republican *(1853), 2:240.*

Chapultepec. From Mayer, Mexico, Aztec, Spanish and Republican *(1853), 1:255.*

"I've kept my promise." From author's collection.

Juan Christobal Colon Gil. From Gooch-Iglehart, The Boy Captive of the Mier Expedition.

Above: *Juan C. C. Hill, the Boy Captive, and his daughter and two grand-daughters, who were educated in the public schools of Austin, Texas. From Gooch-Iglehart,* The Boy Captive of the Mier Expedition, *309. Below: Mier prisoners. On the extreme left is Freeman W. Douglass. From Wharton,* History of Fort Bend County, *114.*

The chapel of El Encero. From Terreros, Antiguas Haciendas de México, *154.*

The church of El Jaral de la Hacienda. From Terreros, Antiguas Haciendas de México, *140.*

Map of Real del Monte. From Randall, Real del Monte, *7.*

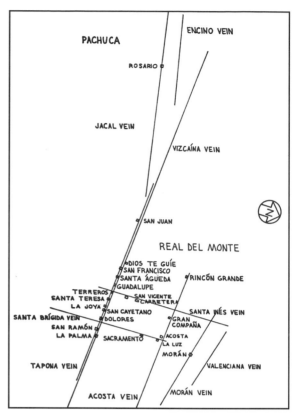

The tomb of Monument Hill. Photo courtesy of Texas Parade.

Tampico. From Mayer, Mexico, Aztec, Spanish and Republican *(1853), 2:206.*

Campeche. From Crawford (ed.), The Eagle, *179.*

Zacatecas. From Mayer, Mexico, Aztec, Spanish and Republican *(1853), 2:314.*

La "casa vieja" de El Jaral. From Terreros, Antiguas Haciendas de México, *141.*

U.S. Army Map of the Valley of Mexico. From author's collection.

Thomas Jefferson Green. Courtesy Texas State Archives.

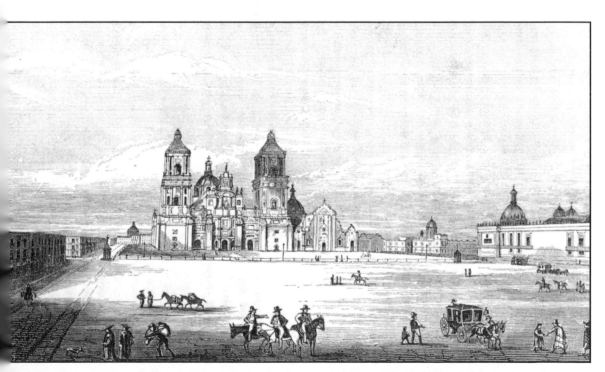

The Great Square of Mexico. From Mayer, Mexico, Aztec, Spanish and Republican *(1853), 1:420.*

Fandango. From Kendall, Gentilz: Artist of the Old Southwest, *59.*

Texians drawing the black beans at Salado. From advertising flyer for Mier Expedition Narrative *by Thomas W. Bell, 1845. Author's collection.*

Before Ogden left the prison, Israel Canfield received information on March 4 by a stage passenger that he was soon to be liberated by Santa Anna[24] through the intercession of his friends in the United States Congress, John Quincy Adams and Mahlon Dickerson. Adams, a bitter critic of slavery and a strong defender of Mexican rights in Texas, was well known and respected in Mexico. On December 14, 1843, Juan N. Almonte, the Mexican minister to the United States, recommended to his government that the request of Adams for the release of Canfield, a Mier prisoner, be granted because Adams was a good friend of Mexico.[25] Santa Anna honored the request and ordered Canfield released.

For Canfield the night of March 4 was one of excitement, anticipation, and sleeplessness. The following morning as the twelve Texan prisoners prepared to leave for San Juan de Ulúa, Captain Valderéz informed Canfield that he was to leave the castle during the morning under an escort of two dragoons to report to Santa Anna at Manga de Clavo.[26] After "taking leave of a few of my fellow prisoners who had acted the part of men," reported Canfield, he left the castle at eleven in the morning and reached Santa Anna's strongly protected residence at nine that evening, March 7. Canfield describes the scene. He "was conducted immediately to his [Santa Anna's] sitting room or parlour where I found him, his Wife, and two daughters, his interpreter being absent, he merely informed me (thro' a young lieutenant) that I was at liberty—but requested me to remain 'till his interpreter's return when he would have me conducted to Vera Cruz. [I] was soon conducted to my room and furnished with refreshments, [of] Wine, Cigaretes, &c. quite an agreeable change after an imprisonment of 15 months sleeping on stone floors with out a sufficiency to appease hunger at any one time—however I slept soundly and awoke quite refreshed on the 8th."[27]

Canfield kept to his apartment during the day of March 8. He was anxious to get out of his prison garb, but had no other clothes. The president's interpreter returned and Canfield was brought before the president. He found Santa Anna to be "rather a good looking man, rather light complexion, [of] middling size, with a countenance cool and decided."[28] Santa Anna informed him that John Quincy Adams "was *his friend* and a friend of *his* Country," and Canfield gathered that Adams had more influence with Santa Anna than any other person in the United States. Santa Anna handed Canfield a letter and requested that he deliver it to Adams. The interview concluded with an admonition from the president to young Canfield not to return to Texas again, as that territory belonged to Mexico.

24. Canfield diary, Mar. 4, 1844; see also, Trueheart diary, Mar. 5, 1844.

25. J. N. Almonte to the Minister of Foreign Relations and Government, Washington, Dec. 10 and 14, 1843, in Barker Transcripts from the *Archivo de la Secretaría de Relaciónes exteriores Reseñas politicas, 1841-1842. Estados Unidos, 1843-1845,* TxU-A.

26. Trueheart diary, Mar. 5, 1844.

27. Canfield diary, Mar. 7-8, 1844.

28. *Ibid.*, Mar. 8, 1844.

Canfield left Manga de Clavo on March 9 with two dragoons as an escort to give protection along the way. About two in the afternoon he reached Vera Cruz. He bore a letter from Santa Anna to U.S. Consul F. M. Dimond. Canfield got a shave—the first in about two years—replaced his prison garb with appropriate civilian clothes, and "took dinner at old 'Aunt Sallys,' a negress who kept a very genteel house for Vera Cruz & [which was] much frequented by the U.S. Navy officers, gamblers &c." Here he boarded until March 21, while awaiting passage to New Orleans. During his stay in Vera Cruz he collected what clothes he could and sent them in custody of the stage drivers on the Vera Cruz-Mexico City line to his "friends in prison as were most destitute."[29]

On March 3, twelve of the Texan prisoners who had been left at Convent Santiago in Mexico City arrived at the Castle of Perote on their way to the Castle of San Juan de Ulúa in Vera Cruz harbor.[30] They left behind in Mexico City three of their number and another three in Puebla.[31]

When the twelve arrived at Perote Castle, those who were headed for Vera Cruz sent a note on March 4 to the other Mier prisoners inviting them to come to see them in their cell before they left the next morning. Six of the "permanent" Texan residents of the castle were given permission to visit their friends. They were told that the twelve had been given only fifteen minutes' notice of the march from Mexico City and that they had been treated badly on the road. Their being sent to Vera Cruz, reported Trueheart, "appears very mysterious to us all.[32] Actually it was an error on the part of the officers who issued the order for the removal of the able-bodied Texan prisoners from Mexico City. The intention was to send them to join the other Mier prisoners at Perote Castle.

When new arrivals left Perote Castle, on the road near Vera Cruz they met the new British minister to Mexico, Sir Charles Bankhead, who had arrived at Vera Cruz on March 10 and was on his way to Manga de Clavo to present his credentials to President Santa Anna. He observed the Texan prisoners, in their pitiful condition, being driven toward Vera Cruz with some eighty Mexican criminals. Learning that there were several Englishmen among them, he requested that Santa Anna release them. Santa Anna readily agreed to free them.[33]

The order for the release of Major Murray and Donald Smith overtook them on their way to San Juan de Ulúa. The order also called for the release of Jeremiah Leehan, who was ill in the hospital at Puebla. News of release of these three men reached Perote Castle on March 16.[34] Murray

---

29. *Ibid.*

30. Trueheart diary, Mar. 3, 1844.

31. Capt. John. G. W. Pierson, D. H. Van Vechten, and Ezekiel Smith were left at Mexico City. Jeremiah Leehan, Alexander Mathews, and Theodore Dwight Maltby were left sick at Puebla. Nance, ed., *McCutchan's Narrative*, p. 168.

32. Trueheart diary, Mar. 4, 1844.

33. *Daily Picayune*, Mar. 31, 1844.

34. Trueheart diary, Mar. 16, 1844.

and Smith reached New Orleans on Friday evening, March 29, aboard the *John Barr*.[35] Leehan, recovering sufficiently to travel, sailed from Vera Cruz on the U.S. steamer *Poinsett* and arrived in Galveston on June 7.[36]

On March 9, 1844, Waddy Thompson visited with Bocanegra and informed him that he intended to leave Mexico City the next morning for Jalapa and from there would most probably return to the United States. He told him that Benjamin E. Green, the secretary of legation, would act as *chargé d'affaires* until the new minister arrived. Thompson left Mexico City in company with George Van Ness. On March 11 they reached the Castle of Perote, where Thompson informed the prisoners that he was leaving Mexico but that he intended to see Santa Anna before he left and to urge upon him "the case of the Mier Prisoners in the most strenuous [manner possible] and the liberation of the balance [of the San Antonio prisoners] as a personal favor to him," reported Trueheart.[37] While he could not give any assurance of what might be the outcome of his request, he assured the prisoners, "all I can, I will do."

Thompson carried letters of some of the prisoners, including one from Claudius Buster, to be mailed on his arrival in the United States. To his younger brother, Claudius Buster wrote: "I am sorry that it is not in my power to flatter you with the hope of seeing you all very soon, though for all that I know we may be liberated in a short time. The prospect, I must confess, looks very gloomy."[38] He reported that from the newspapers he saw that Congress was considering authorizing the raising of a volunteer army to invade the Rio Grande country; "the design of which is good, but I must think the effort a very lame one. I am perfectly well satisfied that an army will not be raised, but should it be the case, my advice to you is that you should stay at home at present. My absence is as much as Mother ought to lament, and there are other good weighty considerations which should prevent you from going on any campaign at your age of life. I speak from the knowledge of the evil results."

On his way to the coast from Perote, Thompson stopped for several days at Jalapa to see Santa Anna, who was "daily expected at his beautiful country seat, the Encero, five miles distant from that city."[39] Thompson called on Santa Anna in the capacity of a private individual to pay his respects upon his departure from Mexico since his functions as minister had ceased. During his stay in Mexico, Thompson had developed a good working relationship with the president, and had many kind words for him. "Santa Anna was a man of talents and many noble qualities," he informed ex-President Andrew Jackson. "You must not judge him with ref-

---

35. *Daily Picayune*, Mar. 30, 1844.
36. *Ibid.*, June 11 and 14, 1844.
37. Trueheart diary, Mar. 11, 1844.
38. Claudius Buster to Dear Brother, Castle of Perote, Mar. 8, 1844 in Wade, comp., *Notes and Fragments of the Mier Expedition* 1, pp. 88-92.
39. Thompson, *Recollections of Mexico*, p. 77.

erence to the state of things in our own happy country. He has a very different people to govern, and I think he is not only a patriot, but that he understands his countrymen and their true interests."[40]

During the course of their conversation, Santa Anna turned to the question of Texas being annexed to the United States. "It was not positively known then in Mexico that such a negotiation was on foot," recorded Thompson in his *Recollections,*

> at least I did not know it, perhaps Santa Anna did. I was not disposed to enter into any discussion with him [on the subject], but his remarks at length became so strong that I could not be silent, and I replied to him with a great deal of warmth, and at the close of a short and pretty animated discussion, I said to him—"What do you intend to do with the Texan prisoners? Do you intend to keep them here always!" "What else can I do Sir? if I release them on their parole, they will not respect it, and I gain nothing by making them prisoners, for they immediately take up arms again, as did the prisoners of the Santa Fé Expedition and I was informed that you intended to ask the release of these prisoners; but I beg that you will not do it, for great as the pleasure would be to oblige you, my duty forbids it." I told him that he knew that I was not apt to abandon my purposes, and that I would ask it, and what was more, that I knew he would release them. I added that the prisoners taken at San Antonio did not know that it was the Mexican army which was approaching, but supposed it was a band of robbers which was infesting the place; the Texans had all told me so. He replied, "I know they say so, but it is not true; Gen. Wall entered San Antonio, with cannon and music, and any one knows that robber bands have neither." "Well," [said Thompson], "if they did, they were defending their homes and their hearths, and a gallant defence they made, and a generous enemy should respect them more." "That," said he, "is putting the matter on a different footing. Are there any particular individuals of the San Antonio prisoners whom you wish released?" "Yes, there are." "Then," said he, "send me a list of their names to-morrow." "No, I will give them to you now," I replied. "Very well," said he "who are they?" I answered, "all of them. How can I distinguish between men, all strangers to me, personally, whose cases are in all respects the same, and why should you?" "Well," said he with manifest emotions, "I have been advised not to do it, and had made up my mind that I would not, but you shall take them all with you."[41]

Thompson returned to Jalapa, where he planned to continue his journey to Vera Cruz to await the arrival of the released prisoners to go home with him. At Vera Cruz the U.S. brig-of-war *Bainbridge* was standing by to take him to the United States. While awaiting the arrival of the next stage at Jalapa, Thompson wrote to Santa Anna, placing in writing his

40. Waddy Thompson to Gen. Andrew Jackson, Mexico, Sept. 24, 1843, in *Niles' National Register* 65, pp. 338-39 (Jan. 27, 1844).

41. Thompson, *Recollections*, pp. 78-79; see also *New Orleans Bulletin* quoted in *Daily National Intelligencer*, Apr. 22, 1844; *Northern Standard*, Apr. 21, 1844.

intention to leave Mexico and giving advice about Mexico's new regulations pertaining to the retail trade of foreign merchants in Mexico in order to head off criticism and quarrels with other powers. Then he made a strong plea for the release of Van Ness, the only remaining Béxar prisoner in Mexico.[42]

On March 28 Santa Anna wrote to Thompson, "It has afforded me much pleasure to grant their liberty, in the name of the Republic, to the Texans made prisoners by Gen. Woll, in the city of Béxar; and at the moment, when prompted both by my own feelings and a sincere desire to comply with your wishes, I was about to liberate all the other prisoners, I have learned that sixteen of them have escaped from the Castle of Perote, abusing the indulgence which had been extended to them. This has very much changed the aspect of things, and I cannot now offend public opinion by another act of magnanimity, of which these men have shown themselves entirely unworthy."[43]

"It has been stated on very good authority," recorded Bell, "that at the time when sixteen of the captives made their escape from Perote, by digging through the floor, Santa Anna had written an order for the release of the whole, but when he heard of the escape of these he lighted a cigar with the paper on which the order was written and observed 'that is the way I'll liberate them.' "[44]

No one could impute any unworthy motive to this act of generosity on the part of Santa Anna, for Thompson was a private citizen with no power to serve the president of Mexico in any way. Santa Anna sent-off an order immediately for the release of the men captured in the Woll campaign.[45]

On March 18, Capt. Miguel Arroyo informed the Béxar prisoners in room 7 that Van Ness had returned from Perote with the mail and with news that the Béxar prisoners were liberated.[46] Soon Van Ness appeared in the room and read a letter from Thompson saying the Béxar prisoners had been released as "a personal favor" to him, and requested that a list of the names, certified by the commandant, be sent to him. He said that he also had asked for the release of the Mier men but this had been refused. Santa Anna said the Texan commissioners for the armistice talks were expected any day and at that time "the exchange of prisoners would be immediately attended to."[47] The news of their impending release produced "great excitement and joy" among the Béxar prisoners, and the

---

42. Waddy Thompson to [Antonio López de Santa Anna], Jalapa, March 25, 1844, no. 2, in Despatches from the United States Ministers to Mexico, Mar. 12, 1842-Mar. 25, 1844, National Archives (microfilm).

43. Santa Anna to Gen. [Waddy] Thompson, Mar. 28, 1844 (extract), in *Daily Picayune*, Apr. 13, 1844; see also *Northern Standard*, Apr. 21 and May 1, 1844. The May 1 issue of the *Standard* carries an extract of Santa Anna's letter to Thompson.

44. Bell, *Narrative*, p. 94.

45. *Telegraph and Texas Register*, Apr. 17, 1844.

46. Trueheart diary, Mar. 18, 1844.

47. *Ibid.*

news of it "spread like wild fire, and seemed to be in the mouth of every person in the castle."[48]

The San Antonio prisoners were taken to the storeroom where those who were in greatest need received pantaloons, shirts, and overshirts, and two bits in *plata* (silver). Most of the men were entirely destitute of other items of clothing. The formal order for their release was awaited with eagerness. Instead, an express arrived requesting that a list of the Béxar prisoners be sent to Jalapa. The San Antonio prisoners persuaded the governor to include the names of the Salado (Dawson Fight) men on the list, which was dispatched to the president of Jalapa.

On March 23, the official order was received by stagecoach mail, along with a letter from General Thompson. All the Béxar-Dawson prisoners, except Van Ness, were instructed to report to Santa Anna at his *hacienda* at Encero, a league below Jalapa. Thompson instructed those having money to assist in bringing others to Vera Cruz where he would have all sent home.[49] The San Antonio-Salado men were locked up until mass was over the next morning. They were told to prepare to leave, and after dinner were marched off to the governor's quarters. Present were all the principal officers of the castle. The governor sought "to render the Ceremony of liberation as solemn and imposing as circumstances" would admit, wrote one of the men being released.[50] "A Bible laid open upon the table, a crucifix was by it, and a candle dimly blazed on each side of these. The commandant and officers in attendance stood around" the table while the order was read for the release, "upon certain conditions, of the prisoners taken by Woll in 1842."[51] The prisoners were required to sign an oath saying that they would never again take up arms against Mexico under penalty of being shot if apprehended. They then descended to the plaza where they found assembled the Mier prisoners who had obtained permission to congratulate and take leave of them. "I was standing in a collection of six or eight of the Mier men talking over our prospects," recorded McCutchan, "when one of the Béxar men came up saying. 'It grieves me to leave you hear; you, who, when you heard of our capture, readily took up your arms, and, though you had but a handful of men, came boldly against the enemy, that thus you may release us; but you have also been unfortunate and we must leave you behind. If ever men did deserve liberty, you are those.' His tears told that this was from his heart. This proves how a man can feel for his fellow man. But *they* are gone and

48. *Ibid.*

49. *Ibid.*, Mar. 23, 1844; see also Stapp, *Prisoners of Perote*, p. 123.

50. [Description of Release Ceremonies at Perote Castle of the Béxar-Dawson Prisoners], written by one of the men being released, was printed in the *LaGrange Intelligencer* and copied in the *Texas Democrat* (Austin), Jan. 21, 1846, and in Weyand and Wade, *An Early History of Fayette County*, pp. 354-55.

51. Weyand and Wade, *An Early History of Fayette County*, p. 355.

we are still here—likely *for life*. God only knows when we will receive our '*free* papers'—a Yankee could not even 'guess.'"[52]

The release of the San Antonio-Dawson men reduced the number of Texans remaining at Perote Castle on March 24 to 124.[53] Four of the released men remained temporarily in the castle while they sought separate passports from Santa Anna. The others, escorted by Capt. Miguel Arroyo, left for Santa Anna's *hacienda*. Three leagues brought them to Cruz Blanca, where they spent the night. Most of the Texans slept in a house where a considerable quantity of straw had been stored.

On April 25, after a march of eleven leagues through a barren and broken country, they reached Jalapa, capital of the Department of Vera Cruz. About eight the next morning they were told that a break had been made at the Castle of Perote the night after they left and that two of the escapees were reported to be in Jalapa.

---

52. Nance, ed., *McCutchan's Narrative*, p. 109.
53. *Daily Picayune*, Apr. 13, 1844; see also *Northern Standard*, May 1, 1844.

CHAPTER 23

More Escapes From Perote Castle

AFTER THE ARRIVAL AT Perote Castle of the main body of Mier men in September, a plan was conceived to bore through the floor and beneath the main wall to reach the bottom of the great moat on the outside. Beginning in February 1844, and laboring steadily for forty nights, the men in the center cell dug a tunnel two feet in diameter twenty feet from the back part of the room. The tunnel extended down eighteen feet below the floor of the cell, thence in a horizontal line thirteen feet, and then up six feet—making in all thirty-seven feet,[1] through sand and cement filled with stone. It was estimated that the foundation of the fortification reached four feet below the bottom of the moat.

The plan was to dig under the foundation and come out through the reeds in the moat adjacent to their cell. On that particular side of the castle the moat was kept free of water for purposes of health and preservation of the wall. A trap door was cut through the planks covering the floor with a piece of tin and the work of digging a shaft through the ten-inch concrete floor was begun with pieces of tin. The sand, dirt, and masonry were elevated by a hair rope tied to one of the Texan's small provision baskets and carefully hidden under boards raised six inches above the stone floor upon which the men slept, then smuggled out of the cell in the pockets of their pantaloons when the men went out to work. They scattered the debris in small driblets throughout the castle, in the moat, or when going into the mountains to work.

One of the chief engineering difficulties was that "after they had descended to a considerable depth, the carbonic acid [carbon monoxide] gas generated from the coal fires used in the castle, being heavier than the atmosphere, descended into . . . [the] pit, in which no one could labour but a few minutes before he had to ascend to prevent suffocation."[2] The

---

1. Nance, ed., *McCutchan's Narrative*, p. 119.
2. Green, *Mier Expedition*, p. 375.

380

gas became so concentrated that it nearly caused suffocation before the bottom of the pit could be reached, but fortunately the tunnel intersected a gopher hole which served as an escape for the gas.

One of the leading spirits in the tunneling operation was John Taney, who "was nicknamed 'the gopher' on account of the dexterity with which he spooned out the dirt."[3] Great secrecy cloaked the whole operation, and the plot and plans were known only to a few persons besides those participating in it. Since there was no communication between the different cells at night, the tunnel would be of value and accessible only to those in the cell in which it was dug.

So secretly did the Texans carry on their excavation that few of the other men knew about it until the morning after the break on the night of March 25. Sixteen of the twenty-seven prisoners in the room crawled through the tunnel, climbed the outer wall of the moat and the *chevaux de frise,* and disappeared into the mountains.

Those escaping included A. B. LaForge, John Johnson, Cyrus K. Gleason, Edward Keene, Richard Keene, Wiley Martin Jones, William Moore, Thomas Smith, E. D. Wright, Francis Arthur, William Wynn, John Toops, William H. H. Frensley, William T. Runyan, Stephen Goodman, and John Taney. The first nine named reached Texas safely; the others were recaptured.[4]

Once free of the castle the fugitives scattered in every direction, usually in pairs. Some, instead of taking a direct route to Texas, went in the opposite direction to elude pursuers. William Moore lay by in the mountains for the first two days, then made his way to Puebla, where he obtained assistance from several Englishmen and Americans in the city in procuring disguises and money, which enabled him to reach Tampico. Moore obtained a passport which enabled him to leave the country without a challenge. When he left Tampico, four other escapees were there awaiting transportation to New Orleans.

Richard Keene reached New Orleans on the schooner *Virginia Antoinette,* which sailed from Tampico on October 8, 1844.[5] John Taney, a relative of Roger Brooke Taney, chief justice of the United States Supreme Court, was among those who were soon recaptured.[6] Wiley Martin Jones and another escapee, making their way toward Vera Cruz, ran into an armed guard. They surprised and strangled him, stripped the Mexican's body of clothing they could use, then hurried on toward Vera Cruz. When they arrived there, Jones and his companion persuaded a Dutch ship captain to hire them as crew members even though the freighter was headed for San Francisco around Cape Horn. The captain agreed to hire them provided they could get aboard since Mexican port authorities had been

---

3. Smithwick, *Evolution of a State,* p. 276.
4. Green, *Mier Expedition,* pp. 373, 450.
5. *Telegraph and Texas Register,* Nov. 27, 1844.
6. Green, *Mier Expedition,* p. 373, 450.

alerted to be on the lookout for the escapees. They had themselves nailed in cargo boxes and were carried aboard ship before the eyes of the port inspector.

Those who remained in Perote Castle in the cell from which the escape had been made delayed as long as possible the sentinel's detection of the escape. On opening the door to the cell the next morning, the turnkey discovered the number of inmates greatly reduced. Expecting twenty-seven, he counted only eleven. In answer to his question about the others, the prisoners pointed to the huge hole in the corner of the room. "Stunned with amazement and apprehension," the poor turnkey, who the night before had securely locked the men in their cells, "could only stare down [into] the gloomy labyrinth for a time, then bounded out the door, shouting at the top of his voice as he ran toward the governor, '*Los Téjanos han salido! Los Téjanos estan bajo el castillo! Los Téjanos han escapado!*' In a minute the bells were clattering away in their turrets with a fury that threatened to bring them to the ground."[7]

Throughout the castle rang the cry, "To Arms! To Arms!" The officers rushed to their posts and the whole garrison formed ready for action. For nearly twenty minutes, in battle array, the Mexicans anxiously awaited attack from an unseen, mysterious foe lurking about the castle. "At length the commandant, having obtained some clue to the monstrous occurrence, marched boldly up at the head of about fifty men with their muskets cocked and at a charge, and forming them carefully in front of the open cells, entered brandishing his drawn sword amongst the survivors of the escapade." The eleven Texans, thinking their doom at hand, ranged against the farthest wall awaiting their fate. The governor demanded to know where and how the Texan "devils" were concealed. Three times he repeated his question to the Texans, whose attention was riveted upon the raised muskets. Nodding in the direction of the hole in the distant corner of the room, barely visible to the governor from where he stood, they let him draw his own conclusions. He advanced in the direction indicated, carefully scrutinizing the features of his informants, fearful of some new stratagem. Peering into the hole, he could scarcely comprehend that the Texans had fled. An officer was dispatched outside to search the moat for an opening. He discovered it concealed by the reeds of the moat. A soldier was ordered to descend into the hole, and when he discovered that the tunnel had an outlet, the governor "by turns stormed, raved, threatened and wept."[8]

The governor dispatched squads in all directions to search for the escapees, then returned to the center cell to vent his anger upon those who remained. He denounced them as "scoundrels and fools"—scoundrels because they had aided the toils of their comrades, and fools "because they had not acted like men of sense and fled also."[9] The eleven unhappy Tex-

---

7. Green, *Mier Expedition*, pp. 373, 450; Smithwick, *Evolution of a State*, p. 272.
8. Lelia M. Batte, *History of Milam County, Texas*, p. 49.
9. Stapp, *Prisoners of Perote*, p. 123.

ans stoutly defended themselves against the charge of being scoundrels, but admitted that they were fools for having remained.

Despite his hysteria and lamentation for his own uncertain fate, Governor Jarero vetoed the suggestion of Major Coxo that the eleven men be executed for not having informed the Mexican authorities of what was going on in their cell.[10] He ordered officers who had charge of the cells arrested, threatening them with the vengeance of Santa Anna "for neglect of duty in allowing prisoners in chains to dig such a tunnel, though the old Major . . . [had] visited the apartments every day for the express purpose of seeing that all was safe."[11] Instead of punishing the captives the governor commended their conduct as a part of their duty to escape if they could. This was a different view from that which had been taken toward those who escaped at Hacienda Salado, although in this case no Mexican soldier had been killed or injured. The chains of the prisoners were examined and all the Texans were ordered to be ironed in pairs.

Major Coxo was succeeded in his duties by Major Barilla, who was praised by the Texans as a kind and humane officer. He and several other officers, especially a young lieutenant who had been arrested for neglect of duty in letting prisoners escape, received the "silent acknowledgment" of the Texans at the time of their liberation. A court-martial was held and Captain Peneder, one of the more humane officers, was convicted and sent to the Castle of San Juan de Ulúa. Major Coxo was exonerated and restored to his previous assignment.

Ten days after the break, the governor pretended that he had received a letter from Santa Anna stating that the news of another *escapada* had "found him with a signed and sealed order" in his hands for the release of all the Texan prisoners, "which was forthwith used to light his cigarrito,"[12] saying "that is the way I'll liberate them." Bell said that the report of Santa Anna preparing to release the Texan prisoners when the news of the escape reached him was on "very good authority."[13]

On March 26 the cavalry returned empty handed without having detected a single trace of a renegade Texan, but by May 1 seven had been retaken at distances of several days' journey from the fort. Those who were apprehended were brought back to the castle, heavily ironed, interviewed, and thrown into the calaboose. They remained in solitary confinement for three weeks, and upon being released, were chained *dos-a-dos* ever after.[14] Otherwise, reported Edward Manton, they "received no worse treatment than the next."[15] Their dispositions concerning the digging of the tunnel, the conduct of their guard, and the escape were taken and distorted when

---

10. *Ibid.*, pp. 123-24.
11. *Ibid.*, p. 124
12. Bell, *Narrative*, p. 92.
13. *Ibid.*
14. Nance, ed., *McCutchan's Narrative*, p. 119.
15. William S. Fisher to ———, Castle of Perote, Aug. 4, 1843, in *Northern Standard,* Dec. 16, 1843.

entered into the minutes by the secretary. Instead of the sworn statement showing that they had spent forty nights digging the tunnel, as reported by the men, the official report said that only three nights had been so employed, putting the officers in a better light.

The San Antonio prisoners hurried as quickly as possible for fear that they might be implicated in the break and detained. They had two horses, six jacks, and $42 to get them to Vera Cruz, but they had to stop at Encero, about three miles from Jalapa, to visit with the president. Reaching Santa Anna's *hacienda* about noon, March 26, they had a cordial visit with him.[16] They thanked him for releasing them, and he provided them with a passport for the whole party. The Texans hurried on to Vera Cruz, where Thompson awaited them. Three of the prisoners took passage on the stage. The main body of Texans reached El Plan, six leagues beyond Encero, where they spent the night. Near midnight an express passed through carrying news of the escape at Perote Castle.

One of the released prisoners, anxious to get to Vera Cruz, did not tarry at El Plan but pushed on during the night and reached the *Puente Nacional,* where he was arrested under suspicion of being one of the escapees. Later in the day the remaining liberated prisoners reached *Puente Nacional* and were stopped pending the arrival of Trueheart, who carried the passport. The commandant examined the passport and pronounced it genuine.[17] They were delayed until all arrived, for some were scattered behind. When they reached El Plan there were twenty-eight in number; then the three who had taken the stage arrived, bringing the number to thirty-one as indicated in the passport, and they were told they were free to go. They rested during the heat of the day and in the late afternoon proceeded to *"el paso de Ovejas,"* two leagues farther. When they reached Santa Fé they were again stopped and counted. The officer apologized for the delay he had caused, but explained that after the break at the castle he had orders to examine the passports of all foreigners. He promised that when they started the next day he would send along a sergeant to Vera Cruz so they might not be detained on the road or on entering the city.[18]

On Friday, March 29, the Texans started at two in the morning with the hope of reaching Vera Cruz before the heat of the day. They were delayed in getting an audience with the commander, but after they found the office of the United States consul, Louis S. Hargous, they were able to deposit their bundles for safekeeping. Hargous made arrangements to feed the Texans, and General Thompson "furnished them at his own expense with many articles necessary for their comfort."[19] Yellow fever was

---

16. Bell, *Narrative*, p. 92.

17. Edward Manton to Hezekiah Smith, LaGrange, Fayette Cty, Texas [dated] Perote, August 15, 1843, in Chabot, ed., "Texas Letters," Yanaguana Society *Publications* 5, pp. 45-46.

18. Bell, *Narrative*, p. 92; see also Stapp, *Prisoners of Perote*, p. 125; Green, *Mier Expedition*, p. 327.

19. Trueheart diary, Mar. 27, 1844

raging in the city, and the Texans were anxious to get away as soon as possible. The ship's doctor "thought that there would be a great danger in receiving the Texians on board, and the commander of the . . . *[Bainbridge],* Captain Mattison, a most worthy and excellent gentleman, determined not to do so." Thompson, on the other hand, believed there would be a greater danger to the liberated Texans from yellow fever if they were left in the city for any length of time. "Capt. Mattison . . . at length agreed to receive them on board upon my taking 'all the responsibility,'" recorded Thompson, "which I did; and I was not a little rejoiced that no injury resulted from it. There was not a case of yellow fever on board."[20]

A strong north wind delayed their going aboard ship, but on Sunday, March 31, the wind began to lay and they were taken in two groups aboard the brig *Bainbridge,* where they met Waddy Thompson. On April 1, Ludovic Colquhoun came on board with General Thompson's baggage and at ten in the morning the *Bainbridge* sailed with thirty of the thirty-five released prisoners. Apparently one other, Francis McKay, arranged his own transportation and came directly from Vera Cruz to Galveston. The *Bainbridge* arrived in New Orleans about seven on the evening of Friday, April 12, after "a very fatiguing and disagreeable voyage being becalmed a part of the time and having a head wind nearly the whole way."[21] After their arrival, a plea was made by the New Orleans press for contributions of money, clothing, shoes, and other articles to relieve their destitute condition and to help them obtain passage to Texas. "They are not made of the metal of those who would solicit aid, and for this simple reason it becomes every liberal-minded man to extend to them some slight assistance," said the *Daily Picayune.*

After landing in New Orleans, reported Thompson, all the Texan prisoners called to see him and to take leave of him, "and it occurred, in more than half-a-dozen instances, that after beginning to express their gratitude to me they burst into tears, and could not finish what they had intended to say. They could have made no speech half as eloquent as those tears."[22]

In New Orleans the returning prisoners were received warmly. A subscription of nearly $500 was taken up from among the local citizens that supplied the released Texans with shirts, pantaloons, shoes, hats, and provisions. From the subscription received the San Antonio prisoners set aside enough for their own pressing needs and "unanimously agreed to send the balance, amounting to nearly $300 to their companions . . . left behind in the dungeons of Perote."[23]

When the Texan prisoners in Perote Castle learned of the generosity of the released prisoners, a meeting was held to express their appreciation. Colonel Fisher was elected chairman and a committee was appointed

20. Thompson, *Recollections of Mexico,* p. 99.
21. *Telegraph and Texas Register,* Apr. 1 and 13, 1844.
22. Thompson, *Recollections of Mexico,* p. 99.
23. Trueheart diary, Apr. 1-22, 1844.

to draft a suitable preamble and resolutions. The report embodied a spirit of praise for the thoughtfulness of their comrades and a condemnation of the Texan government.

When the Eighth Congress of the Republic of Texas met at Washington-on-the-Brazos in December 1844, Thomas Jefferson Green, representative from Brazoria County, who had escaped from Perote Castle the previous year, moved the appointment of a select committee of five members to examine documents in relation to the Texan prisoners in Mexico. Named to this committee were Green, chairman, Samuel A. Maverick and Duncan C. Ogden, two of the recently returned San Antonio prisoners, and two others.[24] The following day, the committee, through its chairman, reported a resolution expressing the gratitude of the nation to Waddy Thompson and the British diplomatic representative in Mexico, Richard Pakenham, and his successor Percy W. Doyle, "for their active interference in behalf of our fellow countrymen, while prisoners of war in Mexico." The House of Representatives unanimously adopted the proposed resolution and ordered copies of it to be sent to the three named individuals.

When the prisoners remaining at Perote read in the *Daily Picayune* reports of Thompson's praise of General Jarero as "a man of character, a gentleman, and an officer, and that he treats the prisoners not only with kindness but humanity," their rage was unbounded.[25] They told their tale of woes to a foreign visitor to the prison on June 8 who then wrote a letter to New Orleans describing the real situation. Thompson's statement in the New Orleans *Daily Picayune*, they said, was "a mockery of their miserable condition. . . . General Thompson no doubt expressed the sincere opinion which the specious manner of Jarero induced him to form"; but the prisoners, "from their long acquaintance with, and better opportunities of judging correctly of the commander of the Castle, are forced to the conclusion that he is utterly unworthy of any of the high titles conferred on him by Gen. T., and at the same time totally devoid of humanity."[26]

The editor of the *Daily Picayune* recognized the gloomy picture of the situation at Perote, and commented: "The unfortunate prisoners are now mostly, if not all, Americans, those claiming British protection having some time since been liberated; but such ever has been and ever will be the case. If a man is an American it is enough in Mexico to insure him the same severe treatment, and always has been so. We do not say that the Mier prisoners are entitled to American protection—they do not claim it—but they are entitled to such treatment as ordinarily is granted to pris-

---

24. *Journals of the House of Representatives of the Eighth Congress of the Republic of Texas*, p. 49.

25. *Daily Picayune*, July 10, 1844.

26. *Ibid.*; reported from the *Daily Picayune* in *Northern Standard*, Aug. 14, 1844, and in the *Telegraph and Texas Register*, Aug. 21, 1844.

oners of war, and it is the duty of the different foreign minister to see that they receive it."[27]

From New Orleans twenty-four of the former Béxar prisoners hastened to Texas aboard the *Neptune*.[28] From Galveston, twenty-three of them reached the City of Houston on Wednesday morning, April 24.

On their arrival in Galveston and Houston, "The San Antonio prisoners, recently released, were treated with the greatest hospitality."[29] Landing at Galveston, the citizens "greeted them with great enthusiasm, and during their stay . . . [treated them] as guests of the city."[30] In Houston on Wednesday, April 24, the press of the *Telegraph* was stopped to announce that all of the San Antonio prisoners, except Van Ness, had been released and that twenty-three of them had arrived in Houston that morning, where the mayor and members of the council "made ample provision for their comfort and convenience." "We regret to mention," said the editor of the *Telegraph*, "that no portion of the $15,000 appropriated by the last Congress, has yet been forwarded by the president for the relief of the Prisoners in Mexico."

George Van Ness, the last of the San Antonio prisoners, had been sentenced to ten years' imprisonment in the Castle of San Juan de Ulúa for having violated his parole as a Santa Fé prisoner. In January 1843, he was reported to be in chains and at labor upon the streets of Mexico City,[31] but was transferred to Perote Castle, where he enjoyed many liberties. Through the efforts of Peyton A. Southall, U.S. dispatch bearer to Mexico and the influence of General Tornel, who was well acquainted with the Van Ness family in Washington and had received from them many favors, Van Ness was released by Santa Anna on April 13, 1844.[32]

Southall and Van Ness planned to return to the United States together, but when Van Ness received his passport it only permitted him to go as far as Jalapa, with an order to visit the president at his *hacienda*. Santa Anna received him "very kindly" on April 17, and made him promise to go directly to New York rather than pass through the southern states.[33] Van Ness wrote Southall he regretted that he would not be able to return to the United States with him and to have had the pleasure of thanking him "in person for the great benefit you have rendered me—that of obtaining my liberation."

With an order from Santa Anna, Van Ness obtained from Gen. Blanco

27. *Daily Picayune*, July 10, 1844.

28. *Telegraph and Texas Register*, May 1, 1844.

29. *Daily Picayune*, May 3, 1844.

30. *Telegraph and Texas Register*, May 1, 1844.

31. *Daily Picayune*, Feb. 7, 1844.

32. Kendall, *Narrative of the Texan Santa Fé Expedition*, 2, p. 200; *Daily Picayune*, May 2, 1844; *Daily National Intelligencer*, May 10 and 15, 1844; Stapp, *Prisoners of Perote*, p. 123.

33. Geo[rge] Van Ness to Peyton A. Southall, Jalapa, Apr. 18, 1844, in *Daily Picayune*, May 2, 1844; *Telegraph and Texas Register*, May 15, 1844.

Quijano a passport that enabled him to proceed from Jalapa to Vera Cruz, where on April 29, he took passage for New York.

After the Béxar prisoners left, the Mier men, because of the escape, were confined closely twenty hours out of every twenty-four. However, the governor of the castle found that the prisoners' health was being impaired by close confinement and ordered them to work ten hours a day.[34]

Supervision of the Texans at Perote was assigned to experienced and efficient officers who maintained "a diligent and lynx-eyed scrutiny" of their persons, chains, and cells, and destroyed any hope of another successful tunneling out until the Mexicans again should become careless. The escape of prisoners from Perote Castle was regarded as a most extraordinary and daring feat. Great excitement—even fear—existed for a while. The authorities seemed to think *los tejanos diablos* could make their way through every impediment. After the escape, Colonel Fisher reported, "We are strongly guarded and closely watched, day and night."[35]

The plank flooring on which the Texans sat and slept and all other furnishings were removed, leaving nothing but the bare stone floor and the naked walls, which were carefully probed, examined, and sounded to see that no holes existed through which a Texan demon might be able to "squeeze his magic body."[36] Every mat and blanket was removed and the surface beneath it thoroughly tested. The guard commenced a daily check of all chains to see that they were neither cut nor broken. Each morning and evening a special "committee of safety," armed with "sticks, swords, and bayonets, visited our quarters," reported one of the prisoners, "and, after a Bow Street examination of our persons, proceeded to search every cranny and fissure in the wall and floor, sounding and picking the whole surface of the cells, as though they were supposed to contain as many secret passages and traps as a feudal stronghold."[37] As a matter of harassment, several of the prisoners became most cooperative in the search for tunnels. They pointed out to the guard "little crevices that they themselves scratched," and exhibited lumps of earth or pieces of mortar that they had smuggled in from the outside as proof of further plots."[38] A stricter watch was maintained at night, and the prisoners were ordered to keep perfect silence after eight o'clock, so that any sounds of scraping, pounding, digging, or sawing could be more easily detected.[39] During the day, an effort was made to work the men harder so that at night they would be too tired to labor on a tunnel.

---

34. William F. Wilson to Colonel A. Turner, Republic of Mexico, Castle of Perote, July 29, 1844, in *QTSHA* 2 (Jan. 1899), pp. 234-36.

35. William S. Fisher to ———, Castle of Perote, Aug. 4, 1843, in *Northern Standard*, Dec. 16, 1843.

36. Bell, *Narrative*, p. 92.

37. Stapp, *Prisoners of Perote*, p. 125; see also Glasscock diary, July 3, 1844; Bell, *Narrative*, p. 92.

38. Stapp, *Prisoners of Perote*, p. 125.

39. Bell, *Narrative*, p. 93.

Periodically the commandant had the prisoners moved to other rooms so he could probe for holes in the floor and walls.[40] The Texans suspected that a part of the difficulty lay with one of the Mexican officers. "There is a d—d little pup of a 2d Lieut. here by the name of [Antonio] Castro who speaks a little English, and I believe," declared Glasscock, "that he tells them [we are planning to escape] . . . when he gets a little mad at us on purpose to get the higher officers to ill treat us."[41]

In mid-June it was rumored at the castle that the current officers and soldiers were to be sent to Puebla, and a more rigid guard set over the prisoners. "I pray God sent it, for we never can fall into worse hand[s] than we are now in," wrote Glasscock.[42] Especially did the Texans want to get rid of "old Capt. Aroue [Arroyo]." "God sent the latter [that he] may leave," wrote Glasscock, "for he has been the most consumate tyrant that has ever had anything to do with us."[43]

---

40. Nance, ed., *McCutchan's Narrative*, p. 138.
41. Glasscock diary, July 3, 1844.
42. *Ibid.*, June 16, 1844.
43. *Ibid.*, July 1, 1844.

CHAPTER 24

Relief Aid to the Texan Prisoners

IN AN EFFORT TO meet the ordinary necessities of life, some of the prisoners sought the assistance of relatives and friends. By April 1844, William F. Wilson wrote, with some overstatement and to encourage someone to help him, that "the condition of most of our men have been Elevated by their friends in the United States" who had sent them money; but "as for myself sence the 25th December 42 I have been destitute of money not one cent to buy soap [to] wash my skin. Cloth is out of the question we are all Lousy as pigs."[1] He told his brother that he had drawn a draft under date of December 29, 1843, on Alexander Spiers Brown & Co. of New York for $428—money which was owed to him; but hearing nothing on February 23, 1844, he drew on Burnsides & Co. of New Orleans "as a matter of favor." By April 22, he still had received no answer.

After Green escaped, Samuel C. Lyon received letters from him written from Texas on November 8 and December 20, 1843. In the first letter, Green mentioned that Capt. Nathaniel Hoyt would send Lyon money on the next boat to Vera Cruz; but, reported Lyon on February 2, 1844, "there is none come yet; it is much needed come when it will."[2] He made clear his need for money with a postscript: "If it is convenient to you for to send me a small sum of money, I will return it when I get home. I am entirely out of clothing—no shirt on at present—jacket and pants in rags."

It was bad to be a prisoner in Mexico without money. There are many instances of men receiving money, but a majority did not. More than one wrote home begging their relatives and friends to send money or to loan

---

1. W[illia]m F. Wilson to "Dear Brother" [John S. Wilson], Botetourt County, Va [dated] Castle of Perote, Apr. 22, 1844, in "Two Letters from a Mier Prisoner," *QTSHA* 2 (Jan. 1899), pp. 233-34.

2. S. C. Lyon to General [Thomas J. Green], Castle of Perote, Feb. 2, 1844, in *The Planter*, Apr. 5, 1844; also typed transcript in Woods Papers and Letters, TxU-A.

money on their account, pledging their future discharge certificates, which "may be worth something" if Texas is annexed to the United States. "Pawn them if you can."[3]

The difficulties in obtaining money from home were many: some had no friends on whom they could depend; money was scarce in Texas and among many in the United States; for those who could and were willing to help, there were great difficulties in the transmittal of funds; and the credit standing of many of the Mier prisoners was nonexistent. Pledging future discharge certificates certainly was not appealing to a creditor because the expedition had been unauthorized, as the prisoners well knew, and they had been criticizing President Houston for saying so. Communication with the prisoners had to be devious and it was difficult to know where the prisoners would be at any given time, except for the last year of confinement, when most of them might be expected to be in Perote Castle. Finally, the war between Texas and Mexico precluded direct assistance from the Texas government, but after July 1844, monetary assistance came from the Texas government acting through Louis S. Hargous, a prominent American merchant in Vera Cruz.

If not intercepted by the Mexican authorities,[4] the money received by the prisoners from benevolent persons in Mexico was used to procure potatoes, peppers, onions, and other items to supplement their prison fare, acquire cloth or some necessary article of clothing, buy soap to wash body and clothing, obtain tobacco for chewing and smoking, buy *vino mescal,* gamble on louse races or the day of their freedom, or hire someone to wash their clothing.

The Mexican government allowed both soldiers and prisoners twenty-five cents *(dos reales)* per diem. As a common practice the prisoner's allowance was not paid to him directly, but as a matter of favoritism was allowed to some officer of the guard who supplied the rations. At Perote it was the *comisario,* Capt. José María Díaz de Guzmán ("Old Guts"), who handled the sums allowed the Texans. Captain Guzmán "was so corpulent, that, when standing still, he had often to rear back to preserve his equilibrium, on which occasions his abdominal prominence formed a huge semi-circle from his chin to his hipjoints. When moving forward, to preserve his balance, his epicurean preponderance impelled him along at a railroad speed—a kind of running pace; and, though he was the largest man, yet he was the fastest walker in the castle. When he would be coming around in the direction of our prisons," wrote Green, "the word 'Guts,' sung out by some wary sentinel [among the Texans], told us that we had no time to lose in adjusting our 'jewelry.' "[5]

---

3. Letter from a Perote Prisoner, [dated] Perote Castle, June 18, 1844, in *Telegraph and Texas Register,* July 10, 1844.

4. New Orleans *Daily Picayune,* Jan. 19, 1844. The governor ordered on November 23, 1843, that the mail man always report to him. Trueheart diary, Nov. 23, 1843.

5. Green, *Mier Expedition,* pp. 244, 262.

The avarice of the *comisario* was illustrated by the cost of the Texans' rations, estimated at eight cents per day per person, and that from the remaining portion of the money allotted them the prisoners received only forty-seven cents every two weeks, thus leaving approximately $1.91 per prisoner for the support of "Guts" and his three daughters, "whose proportions . . . but too much resembled that of their worthy sire."[6] On January 17, 1844, the prisoners at Perote Castle received twelve and one-half cents in silver from the Mexican government, bringing to 75¢ the total received to that time.[7] When Captain Guzmán died on February 22, 1844, the flags of the principal nations represented in Mexico were flown from the balconies of the castle and a cannon salute was fired in his honor. Some of the Texans regretted his death, "and others on the contrary, seem[ed] to be glad."[8]

In the castle a grocery store was maintained by Don Francisco, a retired army lieutenant, and from it almost anything needed by the garrison troops and prisoners could be obtained. The lieutenant's wife was described as being about thirty years younger than her husband, weighing approximately 250 pounds, and was by far "the most stingy *fat* woman" the thirsty Texans had ever seen. "The daughter," reported Green, "was twenty years her junior, and twenty pounds her senior; her face was marked with small-pox; she was, however, one of the best tempered women of her size. She made but slow progress in English, yet always met us with a smile. Her venerable sire still called her Nina. . . . We called her *Señorita Niña;* others of our boys, who made as slow progress in Spanish as did Niña in English, called her *Señorita, muy bonita,* with a low bow, . . . but the low bow gave it the undefinable touch. . . . With a low bow and the sight of a picayune, . . . the good creature never failed to wet their whistles."[9]

On certain days the prisoners could buy the local grades of liquor (*pulque, aguardiente,* and *vino mescal*) from the local *tienda,* or shop. Chewing tobacco was expensive and scarce, but avidly sought. If it could be obtained, it was chewed until there was no taste left in it. It was then dried and smoked.

Credit at the store was more easily obtained by the Texans than by the Mexican officers, because many of the Texans who owed small sums at the time they were liberated afterwards sent the money. The shopkeeper's own countrymen were often required to pawn articles equal in value to the credit extended.

On days when buying liquor was denied, the Texans resorted to various schemes to procure it with the connivance of the dispensers of the refreshing spirits. In the castle lived "a frisky, laughing, handsome little

---

6. Green, *Mier Expedition*, pp. 263-64; see also Canfield diary, Jan. 17, 1844; Glasscock diary, Oct. 15, 1843.
   7. Canfield diary, Jan. 17, 1844.
   8. Trueheart diary, Feb. 22, 23, 1844.
   9. Green, *Mier Expedition*, p. 276.

woman, the wife of a sergeant," who hated to see "the poor Texians suffer" the lack of brandy. Accordingly, the woman smuggled *vino mescal* into the fort in a cow's bladder. While one of their number stood guard to warn of the approach of an officer, the "good little woman" brought out the bladder, giving each Texan a suck for a picayune. After his tonsils had been properly wetted, Daniel Drake Henrie would first translate and then sing in English the "Soldier's Tear," causing the good woman to cry and pity the Texans' loved ones back home.[10]

Soldiers sent into Perote three times a week to get the mail or on some other errand also smuggled liquor. They would take a three-foot length of the intestines of a beef or a sheep, "tie up one end, fill it full [of *mescal*], tie up the other, and curl it up like a snake in the top of his cap, bring it into the castle and retail it to . . . [the Texans] at a usurious profit 'per suck.'"[11] The traveling bartender would squeeze the intestine at the lower end for the amount bought, and the customer would suck it out. Then the smuggler would pass on to the next customer and the same performance would be repeated. At least a few of the prisoners obtained enough liquor at times "to make them merry, and thus they would have a most glorious 'row'," as they termed it, which often terminated in a few of the revelers spending time in solitary confinement.[12]

After his escape and before he left Vera Cruz, Green borrowed from Louis S. Hargous, a wealthy merchant of that city, $300 and gave him a draft on John T. Green of New Orleans. He also gave another draft for $250 or $300 on the Treasury of Texas. When Charles B. Young, agent for Hargous, tried to collect the drafts in New Orleans, he found no John T. Green in that city. He also wrote to Sam Houston to collect the draft that had been given on the Texas Treasury. Houston explained on October 16, 1843, why payment of the draft had been rejected by Texas:

> Gen. Thomas J. Green had no authority to draw upon the Department for any purpose whatever. And, indeed, had he been so authorized the draft could not have been met without violation of the law on the part of the officer at the head of the Treasury Department, . . . for Congress, though aware of the capture of the said Gen. Thomas J. Green and his associates, made no appropriation or provision for their relief. The government is therefore powerless as to the payment of the draft drawn upon it. . . .
>
> It is not necessary for me to express my opinion as to the conduct of which you complain. An honest heart will always prefer the most grinding hardship to desception, dishonesty and fraud. As to Gen. Thomas Jefferson Green, I need no cautions. He may succeed in robbing defenceless women and children and in defrauding the unsuspecting; but he can

---

10. *Ibid.*, p. 278-80.
11. *Ibid.*, p. 277.
12. Bell, *Narrative*, p. 89.

never riot upon the substance of the people while I occupy my present position in the government. I know him too well for that.[13]

On the Mier Expedition and while in prison in Mexico, Green kept a journal and copies of his correspondence and other documents, probably with the expectation of writing a history of his experiences. Prior to escaping from Perote Castle on July 2, 1843, he entrusted his journal and papers to Ludovic Colquhoun, who, anticipating a search of their quarters after the men had fled, buried them.[14] When John Bradley was released on September 22, 1843, Colquhoun forwarded the papers through him to Green in Texas. Green probably received them about two months later.

One of Green's principal concerns after his return to Texas was to be elected the representative from Brazoria County to the Eighth Congress of Texas, scheduled to meet on December 4, 1843. *The Planter* of Columbia reported that "Green avows himself a candidate, not because he is opposed to either of the gentlemen [Dr. R. M. Collins and James F. Perry] now in the field, but because he made the most solemn pledges to his companions, that he would lay their condition before the next Congress, and because he believes the armistice to be designed by Santa Anna, for no other purpose than to destroy the Navy, and recall the Santa Fé Expeditions—while he (Santa Anna) makes active preparations for the invasion of Texas."[15] Two were chosen to Congress from the Brazoria District: Green and Dr. R. M. Collins.

The Texas government tried to provide assistance to the prisoners and to their families, but the aid, in the case of the prisoners, came late in their confinement. The Special Session of the Sixth Congress had adjourned on July 23, 1842, and the Seventh Congress did not meet in Special Session until two months after Woll's capture of San Antonio and continued without interruption into its Regular Session, but was near adjournment by the time the disaster at Mier was confirmed. The Eighth Congress did not meet until December 4, 1843. Houston, having little enthusiasm for those who disobeyed orders, did not see fit to call a special session of the Eighth Congress.

Great bitterness was felt by the Mier men toward the Texas government, and especially toward Houston, for the failure to afford them timely relief while in prison. But it must be said that President Houston's willingness to help relieve the needs of the Mier prisoners was no different than his willingness and the inability he had encountered in his efforts to furnish relief to the Santa Fé prisoners. On August 24, 1842, two drafts, one for $1,163.66 and another for $5,090.10 in favor of L. S. Hargous, American consul at Vera Cruz, were laid before him, but he had no power "to meet the demands." He informed Acting Secretary of the Treasury

---

13. Sam Houston to Charles B. Young, Washington, Oct. 16, 1843, in *Writings of Sam Houston* 3, pp. 436-37.
14. Green, *Mier Expedition*, p. 312.
15. *The Planter*, quoted in the *Morning Star*, Sept. 12, 1843.

M. P. Woodhouse, "I cannot describe my regret, at not having it in my power to meet the demands. The Government has not one dollar, of the funds described nor has the Executive the means to obtain them for any purpose. The situation of the Santa Fé prisoners has been known to the Honorable Congress for the two last sessions, and their attention called to their condition; but no law has been passed for their relief. There is not one dollar left at the disposition of the President, only to meet special appropriations, which have been made for the present war. The President sympathises most feelingly, for the Santa Fé Prisoners and rejoices at their return to their country and friends. If his private means would enable him to do so, he would most certainly relieve all their wants and contribute to their comforts, but he is as destitute of means as the government of Texas."[16]

Two of the participants in the Mier Expedition and two of the San Antonio prisoners returned in time to be elected to the Eighth Congress of Texas (December 4, 1843-February 5, 1844). William E. Jones represented Gonzales County, Samuel A. Maverick, Béxar County, George Bernard Erath, Milam County, and Thomas Jefferson Green, Brazoria County. Green was the most vociferous among them and loud in his condemnation of President Houston. Shortly after the arrival of John Bradley with Green's journal and papers, and on the eve of the meeting of the Eighth Congress, Green launched a bitter attack upon the president, claiming that he was responsible for the decimation of the Mier men. He published in the Galveston newspapers, and reproduced elsewhere, his correspondence with Waddy Thompson, Percy Doyle, and Ben Green regarding the Elliot letter and the decimation. Favored by "an all wise Providence and an energy befitting the fearful task," he said that he, with others, had effected their escape from prison in Mexico.

> A solemn duty I owe myself and unfortunate fellow prisoners and my country demands of me, with the evidence in my possession, to disabuse the public in what have been affirmed on one hand and unblushingly denied by President Houston and his partisans on the other—to wit that he wrote or caused to be written to Mexico by Capt. Charles Elliott, Her Britannic Majesty's *Chargé d'Affaires* at Galveston—*that the Mier Prisoners had entered Mexico contrary to law and authority, &c.* . . .
>
> But let me refer more particularly to the facts. From the date of our inglorious surrender at Mier on the 26th of December up to the middle of March, we had been treated with all the consideration which our articles of capitulation guaranteed—then came this *"merciful"* death warrant of General Houston. Santa Anna forthwith orders Gen. Méxia, Governor of Coahuila, to shoot the whole of the prisoners in his charge. . . .
>
> We lost no time in writing home for evidences of General Houston's falsehood; and they were furnished by the bushel.[17]

---

16. Sam Houston to Matthew P. Woodhouse, City of Houston 24th Aug. 1842, in *Writings of Sam Houston* 3, pp. 147-48; Conner, ed., *Texas Treasury Papers*, 3, p. 871.

17. Thomas J. Green to the People of Texas, reproduced in the *Telegraph and Texas Register*, Dec. 13, 1843, from the *Independent Chronicle* (Galveston).

On December 27, 1843, the editor of the *Telegraph* wrote that "through the kindness of Gen. Thomas J. Green" he had "been favored with a perusal of his Journal, and by permission" had copied that portion dealing with the arrival at Hacienda Salado of the Mexican cavalry unit from San Luis Potosí and the decimation, the story of which he proceeded to publish.

The editor of the *National Vindicator* in Washington accused some of the editors of opposition newspapers in the Republic of hurting "the cause, the character, the interest, and the dignity of the country" by their reckless publication of accusations of the country's leaders. The editor referred to their support and publication of Green's scathing attacks on the president and referred to Green as "a Great Bore—Gen. Thos. J. Green, of Mier expedition notoriety, is the greatest bore of the age. Not content with boring his way to the 'Halls of the Montezumas,' the object of his hopes and burthen of his ambition, he afterwards *bored* his way back once more to bore his countrymen. His frequent calls upon the Executive for information during the late session of Congress, proved that he was also soft 'about in spots.'"

For one who was so hasty to criticize other editors for hurting "the interest and dignity of the country," the editor of the *Telegraph and Texas Register* felt that his counterpart on the *Vindicator* had gone out of his way to publish a "most low, vulgar, and scrullious article against Gen. Green." "Whatever may be . . . [that individual's] faults," he said, "by his heroic achievements at Mier, his desperate enterprise in scaling the walls of the Castle of Perote, and his untiring efforts to ameliorate the condition of his imprisoned countrymen, has merited the warmest praise of his fellow citizens. . . . But when we reflect that this slander is *official* since it emanates from the *official organ of the Government,* well may we exclaim that *dignity* as well as honor has fled from our high places."[18]

Following Woll's capture of San Antonio, Congress passed a bill to exempt Béxar County citizens from the payment of direct taxes to the Republic for 1842; but through inaction by the president, the bill failed to become a law "by lapse of time."[19] A more limited bill was quickly passed and sent to the president to exempt "all persons who were captured and made prisoners during the campaign of General Woll, in September last . . . from paying taxes from the year (A. D.) one thousand eight hundred and forty-two, and as long thereafter as they shall remain prisoners of war; and that the provisions of this act shall extend to José Antonio Navarro," a Santa Fé prisoner still held in prison at San Juan de Ulúa. The law also exempted from taxation for 1842 "the estates of all those who were slain under the command of Capt. N. M. Dawson, near the Salado" on Septem-

---

18. *Telegraph and Texas Register*, Apr. 3, 1844.
19. "An Act for the Relief of Béxar County, Jan. 14, 1843," in Bills 7th Congress, Tx-A. Autograph document signed; see also *Journals of the House of Representatives of the Seventh Congress of the Republic of Texas*, pp. 233, 235-36, 238-39.

ber 18, 1842, and also the estates of "all those who were slain in the County of Béxar from the eleventh to the nineteenth of September," 1842.[20] The law made no mention of the Mier men, and it was not until a year later that a similar law gave them the same exemption. By this law, approved by the president on January 13, 1844, Congress exempted "all the real estate belonging to the successions of W[illia]m M. Eastland, and the Mier prisoners, who were decimated, by order of the Mexican Government, or fell in the Battle of Mier, or shall have died in bondage . . . from taxation, of all kinds, for and during the term of five years; . . . provided, the said real estate remain the property of the successions, or of the heirs of the deceased, during said period." The law further exempted "all persons who were made prisoners, at the battle of Mier, on the twenty-sixth December, one thousand eight hundred and forty-two" from paying taxes upon all real estate owned by them for the years 1842 and 1843, "and so long hereafter as they may continue to be prisoners." The same terms were extended to all who were taken prisoner or killed during the seizure of San Antonio by General Woll in September 1842.[21]

In the House of Representatives Thomas Jefferson Green lost no time in moving for the appointment of a special committee of five members to examine documents relative to the Texan prisoners in Mexico. The committee consisted of Green, chairman, and Selden L. B. Jasper of Houston County, Samuel A. Maverick of Béxar County, Frederick W. Ogden of Jefferson County, and John J. H. Grammont of Victoria County.[22]

The bill to exempt the citizens of Béxar County from the payment of taxes in 1842 that had failed earlier was revived in the Eighth Congress on December 15, 1843, and included not only the citizens of Béxar County but also those of Gonzales and Victoria counties "who were residing in the said [three] counties, at the date that Vásquez entered Béxar." The exemption was for the years 1842 and 1843. The bill passed the House of Representatives on December 29, and went to the Senate, where it was referred to the Committee on Finance, whose adverse report was adopted by the Senate on January 16, 1844.

Responding to a request from the House on December 22 for a copy of the correspondence of the Department of State with the British *chargé d'affaires* in Texas relative to the release of the Texan prisoners in Mexico, the president transmitted a copy of his correspondence to it on December 28, as well as a copy of his proclamation freeing all Mexican prisoners in

---

20. "An Act for the Relief of the Texian Prisoners Captured by the Mexicans during the Year one thousand eight hundred and forty-two." Approved Jan. 16, 1843, in Gammel, comp., *Laws of Texas* 2, p. 856.

21. "An Act for the Relief of the Heirs of Wm. M. Eastland and Others." Approved January 13, 1844, in Gammel, comp., *Laws of Texas* 2, p. 929; see also *Telegraph and Texas Register*, Feb. 21, 1844; *Journals of the House of Representatives of the Eighth Congress of the Republic of Texas*, p. 84; *Laws Passed by the Eighth Congress of the Republic of Texas*, p. 17.

22. *Journals of the House of Representatives of the Eighth Congress of the Republic of Texas*, p. 49.

Texas.[23] He informed the House that he hoped "soon to have it in his power, to inform the Representatives of the people, that an object so much desired, as the liberation of our captive countrymen, has been fully attained." For some, the documents proved to be disappointing, for Green and his associates had hoped to get information that Elliot had written to Mexico at Houston's request to tell Santa Anna that the Mier men had entered Mexico contrary to orders.

Late in December 1843, a group of citizens in Richmond petitioned Congress in behalf of their fellow citizens who were prisoners in Mexico for relief against creditors. These individuals, said the petitioners, "have still in the Republic effects either personal or real" which "have been or about to be sacrificed to the cupidity of their creditors by the officers of the law" who were proceeding against their property by writs of attachment for the "small debts" owed. Congress was requested to "take such action on the subject as the feelings of common humanity, and patriotism would dictate, and a sense of duty to our meritorious but suffering fellow citizens requires at our hands. So that if they should ever return to their homes, they will not find them desolated by those for whom they have suffered so long and so much."[24] The petition was referred to a select committee, headed by Joseph H. Barnard, that recommended the enactment of a law to "securely guard the rights and interests of those unfortunate men, until they shall be able to return and attend to their Affairs in person," and submitted a bill to accomplish that purpose.[25] James W. Henderson offered an amendment: "that any such prisoners against whom any such judgments shall have been rendered, during his absence, may within six months after his return, be entitled to a new trial, upon making affidavit that he had good grounds of defence, not known to his creditor."[26]

Barnard did not stop with a moratorium on the debts of the Texan prisoners in Mexico. He introduced a bill "To be entitled an Act Concerning the release of captive Texians in Mexico," saying: "That, unless certain information of the release of our fellow-citizens, now in captivity in Mexico, be received by the President of this Republic, on or before the

23. Sam Houston to the Hon. House of Representatives, Executive Department, Washington, Dec. 28, 1843, in *Journals of the House of Representatives of the Eighth Congress of the Republic of Texas*, 1st Sess., p. 93; *Writings of Sam Houston* 3, p. 498.

24. Petition of Citizens of Fort Bend County to the Senate and House of Representatives in Congress assembled, Richmond, Fort Bend County, December 27, 1843, in Memorials and Petitions—J.L. Sullivan, Tx-A. This petition was signed by thirty-four citizens of Fort Bend County.

25. Report of the Committee to whom was referred the petition from certain citizens of the County of Fort Bend to the Hon[ble] R. Scurry, Speaker of the House of Representatives, Committee Room, January 2, 1844—[signed;] Joseph H. Barnard, Chairman. The Report of the Committee is found on the reverse side of the petition of Citizens of Fort Bend County to the Senate and House of Representatives in Congress assembled, Richmond, Ford Bend County, December 27, 1843, in Memorials and Petitions—J. L. Sullivan, Tx-A.

26. *Journals of the House of Representatives of the Eighth Congress of the Republic of Texas*, pp. 104, 154, 415, 420.

first day of March now ensuing, (of which he shall make Proclamation) the Major General of Militia of this Republic is hereby required to make a public call for Volunteers, to repair to his Standard at some place designated, west of the Guadalupe river for the purpose of making an offensive campaign against the towns and settlements of our enemies, the Mexicans, situated in the valley of the Rio Grande."[27] The objectives of this expedition, he said, should be (1) to secure prisoners to be held as hostages; (2) to transfer the horrors of war from Texas to Mexican soil; and (3) to support and pay the Texan troops by the confiscation of Mexican property and the making of forced contributions upon the Mexican settlements. Barnard's proposal was referred to the Committee on Foreign Relations.[28]

The chairman of the Foreign Relations Committee of the House, William E. Jones, a former Béxar prisoner, asked the president for information on his correspondence with foreign powers, particularly in regard to the country's relations with Mexico. Houston responded two days later, January 26, referring Jones to his "message to the Honorable House of Representatives of the 1st inst. The Committee on Foreign Relations having availed themselves of the opportunity of examining all of the correspondence in the State Department on the subject referred to in your note, it is presumed they are in possession of all the information concerning it which it is in the power of the government to afford."[29]

The next day Duncan C. Ogden, representing Béxar County, offered in the House a resolution requesting the president to inform the House if "any monies had been paid out or advances . . . made by his orders, or by any persons connected with the Government, for the relief of the Mier Prisoners, within his knowledge."[30] The president responded on January 29 by transmitting "all the information which is of record in the Departments, in relation to the advances made to the Mier prisoners." Houston stated: "No appropriation having been made by Congress to meet any contingencies arising from the capture of the Mier prisoners, the Executive did not feel authorized to open an account upon the books of the Auditor. Owing to these circumstances, the demand of Mr. Hargous was not paid, and for his kindness and generosity, it was proper through his agent, to inform him that any delinquency which might exist was not attributable to the authorities of Texas."[31]

---

27. *Telegraph and Texas Register*, Jan. 17, 1844.

28. *Journals of the House of Representatives of the Eighth Congress of the Republic of Texas*, p. 155.

29. Sam Houston to William E. Jones, Chairman of the Committee on Foreign Relations, Executive Department, Washington, January 26, 1844, in *Writings of Sam Houston 3*, pp. 529-30; see also Sam Houston to the Honorable House of Representatives, Executive Department, Washington, Jan. 29, 1844, in *Journals of the House of Representatives of the Eighth Congress of the Republic of Texas*, p. 398.

30. *Journals of the House of Representatives of the Eighth Congress of the Republic of Texas*, p. 347.

31. Sam Houston to the Honorable House of Representatives, Executive Department, Washington, Jan. 29, 1844, *Journals of the House of Representatives of the Eighth Congress of the Republic of Texas*, p. 398; also in *Writings of Sam Houston 6*, pp. 542-43.

John Caldwell, a member of the coalition against Houston, moved to reject the president's communication, but failed to accomplish his objective by a vote of twelve to twenty. Chairman Jones then moved that all of the documents accompanying the president's message be rejected unanimously. The motion carried by a vote of thirty-two of the members present and voting.

The bill to secure the rights of the prisoners in Mexico went to the Senate where it was passed and sent to the president on February 2 for his approval, which he gave. The law prohibited the forced sale of "any property belonging to any citizen of Texas, who is or may be a prisoner of war, until release or death of said prisoner, or in the event of his death, administration upon his estate." It was further stated "That the act of limitations, as far as such prisoner shall be affected, either as debtor or creditor, shall remain suspended during the time of his captivity." It was also provided, "That when satisfactory proof shall be made to the Chief Justice of the county, where any such prisoner had his residence, preceding his captivity, that the property of such prisoner is liable to waste, or that his rights may be affected, it shall be the duty of said Chief Justice to appoint a suitable person, under sufficient bond and security as curator of said prisoner, which curator shall take charge of the effects of said prisoner and protect the same to the best of his power and ability."[32]

On February 5, the last day of the Eighth Congress, the president gave his approval to a "Joint Resolution for the Relief of Texian Prisoners in Mexico." By its provisions, the president was "authorized and required, forthwith, to employ any means in the reach of the Government, to feed and clothe our unfortunate countrymen, prisoners of war, who are, at present, starving in the prisons of Mexico."[33] The Congress appropriated $15,000 for carrying out the terms of the act "and all other acts upon this subject."

Although the act was passed in a secret session, it was soon publicized in the press at the risk of jeopardizing the chances of carrying out its provisions. It was discussed in the *Telegraph and Texas Register* on February 21 and again on March 20, when it was announced "that a joint resolution was passed in secret session in Congress, authorizing the President to forward a few hundred dollars to Mexico, to procure clothing and food to supply the immediate wants of the prisoners."[34] On April 3 the act appeared in print in that newspaper, and was mentioned or copied in other newspapers in Texas and in the United States, some of which, no doubt, made their way into Mexico. The Texan agent in Mexico wrote that "one of the greatest apprehensions which I had as a secret agent in the enemy country was from the editorial tribe, many of whom from the reckless

---

32. An Act to Protect the Property of Texan Prisoners of War, Approved February 24, 1844, in Gammel, comp., *Laws of Texas* 3, pp. 979-80.

33. Gammel, comp., *Laws of Texas* 3, pp. 1028-29.

34. *Telegraph and Texas Register*, Mar. 20, 1844.

manner in which they publish everything that comes to their ears are the best spies which Mexico could have in Texas."[35]

In May 1844 it was reported in the newspapers that $15,000 in specie had been deposited in the Treasury from the customs house in Galveston.[36] Thomas Jefferson Green wrote to the prisoners telling them of the appropriation and raising their hopes. In April 1844, this letter was received at the castle but according to Stapp, Fisher, and others, none of the money was received by the prisoners while confined.[37] Had the funds voted by the Texas Congress for the relief of the Mier prisoners in Mexico "ever reached their destination," reported Stapp, "they would materially have contributed to lighten our sufferings, as many suffered for the want of the most common articles of dress appropriate to the season. Though they never arrived, there was something consolatory in the assurance conveyed that we were not forgotten and abandoned by our countrymen."[38]

When, after several weeks, Houston did nothing to forward the relief aid provided by Congress, a joint resolution was passed by both houses calling upon the president for an explanation. The president sent a message to the House of Representatives, enclosing several letters from the clerk of a mercantile house in New Orleans with which he had been corresponding concerning transmittal of the money. Houston's letter was little more than a tissue of abuse of Thomas Jefferson Green. "The members of the House were so exasperated at the procedure," reported the Houston *Telegraph*, "that they immediately passed a resolution directing the Chief Clerk of the House to return the message to the President, as unworthy to be admitted on record as a part of the Journals of the House. . . . It was accordingly returned, being, we believe, the only message that was every before sent back by either house to any President."[39]

DeMorse stated in the columns of the *Northern Standard* on August 14 that he could say what he thought "of the treatment of . . . [the Mier] men; not by Mexico but by our own Government; that is, by the Executive branch of it." He referred to the appropriation of the last Congress for the relief of the Texan prisoners in Mexico, "the application of it was to be made by the Executive,—and although several thousand of hard dollars lie in the Treasurer's office unemployed, *these men got none.* A little money, would buy them many comforts; and God knows, they have shown gallantry enough, in one of the best fought fields that ever graced the annals of border warfare, to entitle them so far as we are concerned, to the ordinary comforts allowed to prisoners of war, even if Mexico will not give them the treatment which all respectable nations yield to men, who have

35. Reuben M. Potter to James B. Miller, Havana, Aug. 7, 1844, in Comptroller's Letters, Tx-A.

36. *National Vindicator* quoted in *Telegraph and Texas Register*, May 29, 1844.

37. Stapp, *Prisoners of Perote*, p. 126.

38. *Ibid.*

39. *Telegraph and Texas Register*, Mar. 20, 1844.

not by their own acts, put themselves beyond the pale of civilization; but these men have been marked for vengeance, by more than those they fought against."

A few months later, when DeMorse became better informed on the administration's efforts to furnish the relief to the prisoners, he became satisfied "that we had done him [Houston] injustice, and the prudential motives alone, prevented an explanation by the organs of Government, in answer to the charge of neglect and malfeasance."[40]

The bitter feuding between the members of the Congress and the president continued. On December 22, 1843, the House Foreign Relations Committee asked the president to supply information touching the affairs of Texas and Mexico and other countries, and also for information relating to the annexation of Texas to the United States. Houston did not reply until January 1, 1844.[41] Houston refused to furnish the desired information, but assured "the honorable House, that if they desire information on the subject of our foreign correspondence, the honorable Speaker of the House, accompanied by the Chairman and members of the Committee on Foreign Relations, will be received at the State Department at any time when the head of that Department has leisure, and they can obtain all the information that they desire upon any subject and every subject embraced in the correspondence of the Government about which they may think proper to engage.

This course is suggested by the Executive because there are papers in that Department, the publication of which might operate most prejudicially to this, as to every country, and greatly disoblige those in correspondence with us. . . ." The majority of the Foreign Relations Committee were furious, and on February 5 strongly condemned the president's refusal to furnish copies of the desired information. The committee believed that the president's insulting reply demanded "from the House of Representatives the most unqualified reprobation, and should receive the greatest rebuke which this House can offer, consistent with its own dignity and the decorum of language always proper to be observed towards a co-ordinate branch of the government."[42] They spoke of the right of the people to know what was going on between their government and other governments, and offered two resolutions of censure to support their report.[43]

The secret act providing money for the relief of the Mier men in Mexican prisons was turned over to James B. Shaw, chief clerk and acting sec-

40. *Northern Standard* quoted in *Telegraph and Texas Register*, Nov. 27, 1844.

41. Sam Houston to the Honorable House of Representatives, Executive Department, Washington, January 1, 1844, in *Journals of the House of Representatives of the Eighth Congress of the Republic of Texas*, pp. 121-24.

42. Levi Jones and Others to Hon. R. Scurry, Speaker of the House of Representatives, Committee Room, January, 1844, in *Journals of the House of Representatives of the Eighth Congress of the Republic of Texas*, pp. 457-63.

43. *Journals of the House of Representatives of the Eighth Congress of the Republic of Texas*, p. 463.

retary of the treasury, on March 30, with authorization to make the necessary arrangements for carrying out its provisions. Shaw immediately sent a letter through the Texan consular agent in New Orleans addressed to Louis S. Hargous, the U.S. consul in Vera Cruz, appointing him a special agent "to disburse money for the benefit of the Texan Citizens now prisoners in Mexico."[44]

Hargous received Shaw's communication, but he did not reply, reported Reuben M. Potter after an interview with Hargous, "because it bore outward signs of having come from Texas, and perhaps being official. All such letters are liable to be opened, though this escaped it. . . . He insists," continued Potter, "on not being compromitted by any communication which if intercepted would show him to be an agent of our Gov[ernment]." He informed Potter that he narrowly escaped losing $20,000 by the imprudence of a Texian who made public the aid which he had extended to help him escape the country; and said that if his name should appear in print as it has done in such matters he would cease all participation in the humanitarian work in which he had engaged.

In a confidential letter dated June 3, a month after he became secretary of the treasury, James B. Miller offered Reuben M. Potter, then serving as customs inspector and collector at Velasco, the appointment of secret agent of the government to go to Vera Cruz and Mexico City to carry out the duties required by an act of the Congress.[45] About two weeks later, Potter met Miller in Richmond, as Miller had instructed, and after learning the particulars of the proposed mission to Mexico, agreed to accept the mission. Potter was furnished with a draft for $2,500 to cover the first installment for the relief of the Texan prisoners in Mexico. He was to proceed immediately to New Orleans and to Vera Cruz and place the money in the hands of L. S. Hargous or, in case he declined, of some other reputable person for distribution among the Texan prisoners in Mexico. If Potter preferred, he was authorized to take the money to Perote himself and to distribute $20 to each prisoner, and while there to appoint an agent at Perote to receive and disburse money sent later. Potter was to pay José Antonio Navarro, the last of the Santa Fé prisoners remaining in Mexico, $200 and to furnish the Texan government with the number of Texan prisoners still in Mexico.

In a letter dated June 15, Miller informed Hargous that Potter had been appointed agent for the Texas government in Mexico to furnish relief to the Texan prisoners and that if he were willing to accept the agency the money would be sent by Reuben M. Potter. Two thousand dollars would be made available immediately and other installments would be deposited in any bank or commercial house in New Orleans that Hargous designated.

---

44. James B. Shaw to L. S. Hargous, Treasury Department (Texas), Washington, March 30, 1844 (Confidential), Comptroller's Letters, Tx-A.

45. James B. Miller, Secretary of the Treasury, to R. M. Potter, Treasury Department, Washington, June 3, 1844 (Confidential), in Comptroller's Letters, Tx-A.

Again, Hargous did not reply. Since Miller's letter to him bore outward signs of having come from Texas and appeared official, he did not wish to be compromised by any communication that showed him to be an agent of the Texas government.

In New Orleans, Potter found no difficulty in depositing $2,000 with the commercial house of Schmidt & Co., and in making arrangements for Hargous to draw on it and any subsequent amounts that might be deposited. From New Orleans, Potter wrote discreetly to Hargous informing him that money had been contributed for the relief of the Texan prisoners and that the contributors wished him to act as their agent for receiving and forwarding it to those unfortunate men. He requested Hargous to accept the money, and if he could not forward it himself, to employ some other reputable person to do so; or, if he could not even do that, to turn the acceptance into available funds and hold them subject to Potter's order.

Potter found it easy enough to send the money to Mexico, and had he known Hargous' attitude, it would not have been necessary for him to go there. Hargous had neglected to answer Miller's letter, so Potter went to Vera Cruz to contact him personally. In anticipation of being delayed in Mexico, he made arrangements with R. D. Blossom of New Orleans to receive letters directed by him under the fictitious name of Ebenezer Higgins to William Knot of New York, which Blossom was to readdress to the Texan secretary of state.

Potter planned to leave New Orleans at the most favorable opportunity. "I have serious objections to going on a Mexican vessel," he informed Miller on July 16, "for I would like to have the flag even of an American Merchantman over me in case I do not find it prudent to land. The cutter *Woodbury* is waiting at Vera Cruz for one of the installments of the U.S. debt; but from all that I can learn she is likely to wait long before she receives it & she is ordered not to return without it. It is probable that a U.S. vessel will soon be sent from Pensacola to carry Mr. Shannon the new American *Chargé d'Affaires* and I might perhaps obtain a passage on that vessel; but there is no certainty as to when she will sail. A steamboat goes tomorrow to Pensacola from this place & I am in a delema whether to go direct by the *Petrita,* or to Pensacola on an uncertainty."[46] In the meantime, he made arrangements for the money to be sent by the *Petrita,* but delayed as long as possible taking passage himself on the Mexican vessel. The necessity of getting the money into the hands of the prisoners, especially in view of the increased criticism in Texas because of the delay in doing so, no doubt had much to do in influencing Potter to go to Mexico on the Mexican schooner *Petrita* the morning after writing his letter to Miller on July 16.

Upon arrival in Vera Cruz, Potter hoped he would be able to stay on the *Woodbury.* Before leaving New Orleans, he urged Miller to forward

---

46. Reuben M. Potter to J. B. Miller, New Orleans, July 16, 1844, in Comptroller's Letters, Tx-A.

"within a short time" through the collector of customs in Galveston the second installment to Schmidt & Co., with the request that it be sent to Hargous and that the instructions be rewritten in New Orleans in Schmidt & Co.'s own name as to how the money was to be disposed of in order to avoid compromising Hargous.[47]

When he reached Vera Cruz on July 22, Potter sent letters ashore authorizing Hargous to draw on Schmidt & Co. for $2,000 as needed. The next day Potter went ashore to confer with Hargous in person. Hargous agreed to accept the agency and to pass the funds to the Texian prisoners through his agent at Perote. Hargous also agreed to disburse the sums due to the prisoners confined at San Juan de Ulúa.

Hargous had his own suggestions for disbursing the funds. He advised against distributing the remaining $1,800 all at once among the prisoners at Perote for fear that it might "draw the attention of the authorities to the circumstances and might lead to embarrassing the distribution of future remittances." He suggested making payments of $150 to $300 monthly "to some two or three trustworthy men among them to be divided by them among the whole." Potter suggested that the money be entrusted to Colonel Fisher, Captain Ryon, and Samuel C. Lyon but without making known to them the total amount or the source from which it had been derived. Potter also informed Hargous that all future communications between him and the Texan government should pass through R. D. Blossom or Schmidt & Co. of New Orleans. Hargous would pose as their agent in the cause of charity and humanity, and not of the Texas government.[48]

On the day Potter contacted Hargous, considered the only reliable person for the Texan mission in Vera Cruz, he learned that he had been recognized within twenty minutes after his arrival by a Mexican naval officer who had come in the customhouse boat to the *Petrita*. The officer had known Potter in Matamoros. The Mexican had been held a prisoner in Galveston after the Battle of San Jacinto, and Potter felt that he also knew that Potter had been an officer in the Texan government. Although the two had been on good terms, Potter worried that his mission might be uncovered to the Mexican authorities. Even if this former friend did not betray him, there was always the possibility that the Texan secret agent "might stumble on some other old acquaintance who would know him and love him less." Furthermore, he wrote later, "Indeed one of the greatest apprehensions which I had as a secret agent in the enemy's country was from the editorial tribe [back home], many of whom from the reckless

47. Reuben M. Potter to J. B. Miller, New Orleans, July 16, 1844 (Confidential), in Comptroller's Letters, Tx-A; Reuben M. Potter to Messrs. Schmidt & Co., New Orleans, Sept. 6, 1844.

48. L. S. Hargous to Reuben M. Potter, Vera Cruz, 19th Oct., 1844, p[e]r *Creole* to New Orleans, in Comptroller's Letters, Tx-A. Hargous' letter was sent on the vessel that carried the Texan prisoners to New Orleans.

manner in which they publish everything that comes to their ears are the best spies Mexico can have in Texas."[49]

While in Vera Cruz, Potter learned of a law passed by the Mexican Congress raising $4,000,000 by a tax on property for a new campaign against Texas. The law had not yet been promulgated, and his opinion was "that no serious attempt at resubjugation [of Texas] would be made," though some demonstration might be made for the sake of consistency.[50] There seemed to be a rising tension concerning Texas, always a favorite whipping horse for Mexican politicians. Potter considered it wise to get out of Mexico as quickly as possible, since "the renewal of hostilities and the interdiction of communications [that] had just been proclaimed" enhanced the risk of staying on. "Moreover," reported Potter, "at every visit I made on shore (and I made but three), I met with some civil or military face which I recollected better than I desired." Taking the advice of Hargous against any attempt to go into the interior, and of friends who urged him to leave Vera Cruz as soon as his business had been finished, he took the first boat "out of the Dominion of Mexico as the best for my safety." As no vessel was due to leave soon for a U.S. port, he had his U.S. passport visaed by the Spanish consul and took passage aboard the Spanish schooner *Adela* bound for Havana on July 24.

On August 28, Potter left Havana on the U.S. brigantine *Apalachicola* and reached New Orleans on the night of September 1. From New Orleans on September 5, Potter wrote Hargous that "three dollars a month to each [prisoner] is the rate had in contemplation by the contributors, and, though it is double what you propose making it, I would recommend you to observe the higher rate unless you see some particular objection. In that case be governed by your own discretion."[51] Potter took the steamer *Republic* for Galveston, arriving there on September 16, the day the prisoners for whom he had gone to Mexico to make arrangements for their relief were released.

Hargous' agent in Perote made contact with the Texan prisoners in the fortress and began to supply them with small amounts of money. This did much to alleviate their condition during the last six weeks of their confinement. Hargous reported on September 10 that in accordance with Potter's instruction to furnish the needy Texans returning home from imprisonment with transportation, that he had furnished William Ryon, William F. Wilson, William A. A. Wallace, James C. Armstrong, and Thomas S. Tatum passage to New Orleans on the bark *Anax* at the rate of $25 each. Also, he had paid an additional $25 for the passage of Joseph C. Morgan,

---

49. Reuben M. Potter to James B. Miller, Havana, Aug. 7, 1844, in Comptroller's Letters, Tx-A.

50. *Ibid.*

51. Reuben M. Potter to L. S. Hargous, New Orleans, Sept. 5, 1844 (copy), in Comptroller's Letters, Tx-A.

a Béxar man, agreeably to Potter's request, as well as Potter's own passage of $45.[52]

On September 10, Hargous reported progress toward distributing the money received from Schmidt & Co. Only the day before, he said, had he been able to get an accounting of the number and distribution of Texan prisoners in Mexico. There was a total of 118 prisoners, with 104 being in Perote Castle, three in Mexico City, one in Puebla, and ten in the Castle of San Juan de Ulúa. With this information, he said, he would be able to begin distribution in two or three days, "or as soon as I have things so arranged as neither to compromise myself nor the prisoners."[53] He thought, however, that the distribution of $150 to $200 a month among the prisoners at Perote, as agreed on by Potter and himself back in July, was too little in view of so many prisoners at that place. Since a number of prisoners had money from other sources, it appeared to him "that the distributors in the different places should be instructed to supply only the most necessitous . . . [as] the object of the doners must certainly be to give to those in want, not to those who receive funds of their own or from individual friends." He continued, "Since your departure, many of the prisoners in Perote, Mexico [City], and this place [the Castle of San Juan de Ulúa off Vera Cruz], particularly in Perote, have received remittances through me, therefore what I state I know to be correct."

Before mailing his second letter of September 10, Hargous was able to report a meeting that he had with Ryon, recently freed. Both agreed "that the best plan would be to give to each of the necessitous prisoners in Perote ten dollars a head," which would enable them to procure "some shirts and a blanket each."[54] The same would be done for the needy ones in Mexico City and at Puebla, after which no further distribution of the funds would be made until he heard from Potter.

Early in 1846, in a letter to the editors of the *Galveston News,* Fisher asserted that from the day of "their capture to the day of their release, the Mier Prisoners, never in any shape received one farthing from the government of Texas." However, on their arrival at Vera Cruz on the way home, the prisoners found $2,500, "the whole amount ever remitted to Mexico," said Fisher. "I will remark en passant that the sending of Mr. Potter, with silver to Mexico, was somewhat like sending coal to New Castle, and showed an entire ignorance of the condition of Mexico."[55] Secretary of the Treasury James B. Miller reported to President Houston on December 1, 1844, that out of the $15,000 appropriated on February 5,

---

52. L. S. Hargous to Reuben M. Potter, Vera Cruz, 10 Sept[r] 1844 (second letter of same date), in Comptroller's Letters, Tx-A.

53. *Ibid.*

54. *Ibid.*

55. William S. Fisher to the editors of the *Galveston News*, reprinted in *Northern Standard,* Jan. 21, 1846, and in *Telegraph and Texas Register,* Jan. 14, 1846.

$4,500 had been expended in behalf of the Mier prisoners, leaving an un-expended balance of $10,500.[56]

On September 16 all the Texan prisoners, except Navarro, to whom Hargous had paid $200, were released. Dr. McMath and Joseph F. Smith sailed from Vera Cruz for New Orleans on October 5 on the *Huntington,* and it was planned that the others would sail on the Mexican schooner *Rosita,* the only vessel that could be had at the time. Hargous, with the approval of Colonel Fisher and Judge Gibson, made the arrangements with the captain of the *Rosita* to furnish the men with provisions and trans-portation to New Orleans for $3,200, which was regarded as outrageous for 105 men.[57] But the maintenance of the men in Vera Cruz cost $100 a day and an additional cost of $400 to $500 was anticipated before leaving, so there was little to be gained by delay. The arrangements were only for "those in distress and without protection," and the ten or eleven prisoners who were British subjects were provided passage on the *Rosita* at the ex-pense of the British government. About $1,000 of the $2,000 which had been placed at the disposal of Hargous was spent to buy clothes for the men, "many of whom were in a perfect state of nudity."

The *Rosita* was unable to obtain permission from the Mexican govern-ment to land the men in Texas, and would have to put in at New Orleans. The transportation problem was further complicated when just as every-thing was ready for embarking the Texans, no captain could be found to go in the *Rosita* with such a disreputable, desperate, wild-eyed group of men— *"Los Tejanos Diablos!"* Arrangements were made to sell the vessel and to change it into American property under the name of *Creole.* The *Creole* accepted the same terms as contracted by the owners of the *Rosita* for transporting the Texans. On behalf of the prisoners, Hargous expend-ed $5,740.38, including the $2,000 which had been placed by the Texan government at his disposal in New Orleans. The amount spent had the approval of Fisher, Gibson, and Lyon.

The *Creole,* under the command of Captain Dessechi, sailed October 22 with all the Texan prisoners in Mexico except two, according to Fish-er's and Gibson's report, and Hargous agreed to send them on if they should appear at Vera Cruz and be in want. Hargous charged no com-mission for his services, for, he said, "having no intention of making a business of this assistance rendered, but I do most earnestly call your at-tention" to the payment of my draft for $3,740.38, which I have given agreeably to my last advises at 10% on the Collector of the port of Gal-veston to the order of Messrs. Schmidt & Co. of N. O."[58] Under date of

---

56. Report of the Secretary of the Treasury to Sam Houston, President of the Republic of Texas, Treasury Department, Washington, December 1, 1844, p. 11, in *Appendix to the Journals of the Ninth Congress of the Republic of Texas.*

57. L. S. Hargous to Reuben M. Potter, Vera Cruz, Oct. 5, 1844 p[e]r Huntington, in Comptroller's Letters, Tx-A.

58. L. S. Hargous to Reuben M. Potter, Vera Cruz, 19th Oct[r] 1844 p[e]r *Creole* to New Orleans, in Comptroller's Letters, Tx-A.

December 7, 1844, Schmidt & Co. reported to the Texas Treasury that out of the $4,434.17 which had been "placed in our hands for the benefit of the Texian prisoners," $3,740.38 had been disbursed by his company, leaving a balance of $693.79. "This according to instructions received from L. S. Hargous & Co. of Vera Cruz under date of 31 March last," reported Schmidt & Co., "we transferred to their credit and has since been disposed of by them." They informed Schmidt & Co. on August 30 *"that all explanation and detailed approved accounts* had been forwarded long ago signed by Geo. [William] S. Fisher, J. [F.] M. Gibson, & S. C. Lyon."[59]

---

59. Schmidt & Co. to James B. Shaw, Act^g Secretary of the Treasury, Washington, [dated] New Orleans, 7 December 1844, in Conner, ed., *Texas Treasury Papers* 3, p. 1060.

CHAPTER 25

The Lighter Side of
Prison Life

LIVING IN HOPE OF liberation by a "magnanimous nation," but not
sure when it would come, the prisoners maintained a sense of humor
throughout their confinement in Mexico. Always undernourished, ill-
clothed, and living among some of the worst criminals in a foreign land, *los
Tejanos* were not prone to brood over their condition. In various ways the
prisoners sought to relieve the monotony of prison life. Contact with the
outside was through visitors, correspondence with relatives and friends,
occasional visits into the neighboring village, town, or city near where they
were imprisoned, and through local and foreign newspapers.

At night, while locked up, some would sing like "a cainary bird in a
cage,"[1] while others, by the light of a two-cent candle, wrote letters, made
entries in diaries, or read a newspaper, pamphlet, or book sent by some
friend or passed to them by a Mexican officer. Letters, newspapers, periodicals, and a variety of small gifts came to the prisoners from the American minister, consuls, businessmen, Mexican officers, other Mexicans,
and foreign travelers in Mexico. Various U.S., English, Mexican, and
Texas newspapers[2] were given or lent to the prisoners. Texas newspapers
had to be smuggled into the castle. The governor of the castle frequently
gave or lent the prisoners newspapers,[3] and in the *Diario del Gobierno*, especially, they often found articles that appeared in U.S. newspapers on the
subject of Texas.[4] Through letters and newspapers the prisoners kept up
with the progress of the Texas-Mexican negotiations carried out under the

---

1. Nance, ed., *McCutchan's Narrative*, p. 110.
2. *New York American, Daily Picayune, New Orleans Bee,* various Alabama newspapers,
*Galveston Civilian, Galveston News, Northern Standard, Telegraph and Texas Register, Daily
National Intelligencer, Diario del Gobierno, El Siglo XIX, El Cosmopolita* and others; "A San
Antonio Prisoner to James P. Lowery [Lowrey], Castle of Perote, Mar. 9, 1843, in *Telegraph
and Texas Register,* June 7, 1843.
3. Trueheart diary, Mar. 11, 1844.
4. *Daily National Intelligencer*, Jan. 24, 1844.

armistice,[5] the progress of the Warfield-Snively expeditions, the activities of the Texas Navy, and events political and otherwise in Texas. Joseph D. McCutchan recorded in his diary that F. M. Dimond, the U.S. consul in Vera Cruz, "still sends us Newspapers and Periodicals, which serve to lighten our hours."[6] In Mexico City, Ben E. Green, secretary of the U.S. legation, provided copies of various U.S. newspapers to those in the hospital or in prison at Convent Santiago.

Newspapers and mail arrived in small quantities with some degree of regularity. Family news and that pertaining to public matters, especially relating to Texas and Mexico, was eagerly sought, passed around, and discussed. Letters were read and re-read many times, and though often personal in nature, were passed around for friends to read.

Still others[7] spent time writing in their journals or writing letters to friends and relatives or to the editors of newspapers, and even to Mexican, U.S., and foreign officials. Several planned to write a book on their experiences. One of the prisoners at Tacubaya, probably William P. Stapp, wrote on June 3 in anticipation of the prisoners being freed on June 13, that, "When liberated I intend taking passage for New York or Philadelphia, where I shall put in the press a full account of the whole expedition."[8]

Always longing for news from home, the prisoners frequently wrote letters begging friends and relatives to write. More than one worried about their loved ones, having heard of the sickness in Texas during the past winter. Claudius Buster was overjoyed to learn on February 21, 1844, that up to November 28 his parents, brothers, and sisters were well.[9] How many wrote from home or prison will never be known. How many letters were lost, misdirected, or intercepted by the Mexican authorities and never delivered is unknown. During the first nine months of their captivity, the Mier men were moved several times from one prison to another or left behind sick at various points, making it difficult to know where to send

---

5. Trueheart diary, Oct. 9, 14, 17, 20, 28, Nov. 9, 1843.

6. Nance, ed., *McCutchan's Narrative*, p. 123.

7. Journals or diaries kept and published by the authors after release, or in more recent times by various editors, are those of Thomas Jefferson Green (Mier), Thomas W. Bell (Mier), Anderson Hutchinson (Béxar prisoner), Israel Canfield (Mier), James A. Glasscock (Mier, largely a copy of Canfield's diary), Samuel H. Walker (Mier, used in limited areas by Green), William P. Stapp (Mier), and Joseph D. McCutchan (Mier). Diaries lost or destroyed: Duncan C. Ogden (Béxar prisoner, burned in State Capitol fire in 1881); Michael Robert Pilley (Mier, who made a record of his experiences, either in the form of a diary or reminiscences written later, of which that portion "pertaining to the Mier Expedition," reported Houston Wade, was "considered of sufficient importance that some newspaper solicited its loan" with the intention of publishing it; "however, the diary seems never to have been printed; neither was it ever returned to the owner"). Wade, comp., *Notes and Fragments of the Mier Expedition*, p. 141.

8. [A Mier Prisoner] to the Editor of the New York American, Prison of the Powder Mill, near the City of Mexico, June 3, 1843, quoted from the *New York American* in *Niles' National Register* 65, pp. 3-4 (Sept. 2, 1843).

9. Claudius Buster to John V. Buster, Castle of Perote, March 8, 1844, copy in Miscellaneous Docs., Tx-A.

them mail, but in time family and friends learned to send letters, money, and other items in care of the U.S. minister to Mexico or to one of the U.S. consuls, usually F. M. Dimond in Vera Cruz or John Black in Mexico City. Often the prisoners passed their letters to some dependable person on the stage when a prisoner went into town to meet the mail. Much of the cost of postage was borne by the U.S. legation in Mexico.[10] The prisoners sent letters and petitions to all the members of the resident diplomatic corps in Mexico and to important national and state government officials and agencies in the United States, including U.S. congressmen and senators. Letters that reached Mexico City for the Texan prisoners were forwarded by General Thompson to the individual wherever he happened to be held, and Thompson offered to send letters written by the prisoners to Texas or in the United States by way of New Orleans or some other port.[11] Letters were conveyed by some visitor returning to the States or by a released prisoner going home. The men often had no money to pay postage on their letters, and, if upon arrival in Galveston, New Orleans, Mobile, Pensacola, or elsewhere, postage was necessary to send them through the mail, it was paid by courtesy of the person carrying the letters or by the ship captain who had taken them for delivery. More often, expected letters were never written and thus never received. The low literacy rate among some of the homefolks and some of the prisoners precluded any writing.

Mail did get through to the prisoners, and in time they were permitted to have one or two of their number go to Perote to meet the stage. Through this means they gathered information about domestic and diplomatic affairs and obtained copies of U.S. and Mexican newspapers. Some of the information obtained at the stage stop was mere rumor. Outgoing letters, which were inspected by the guard, usually were spirited out of the prisons and sent without interception by the authorities. Individuals intending to visit the prison often sent word several days in advance of their willingness to convey letters to some point in the United States to be forwarded from there.

The pleas for news from home were touching and reveal the interest and concern of the prisoners in the affairs of state and for loved ones and friends. Richard A. Barkley wrote to friends and relatives in the LaGrange area on March 22, 1843, saying that he had written "some half doz[en] letters but I cant tell whether you received them or not."[12] A few weeks later Barkley wrote to Samuel A. Maverick, who had been released and returned home: "you must write to me soon and see my friends in Woods Prairie rite me all the news you can here or think of, dont fale to rite, a

---

10. Waddy Thompson to A. P. Upshur, Legation of the U. S. of America, Mexico, Oct. 29, 1843, in Despatches from United States Ministers in Mexico, Mar. 12, 1842-Mar. 25, 1844, National Archives (microfilm).

11. Green, *Mier Expedition*, pp. 258, 287, 295-96; Canfield diary, Feb. 8-11, 1844.

12. Richard A. Barkley to Robinsons and Woodses Harrell Wilsons & Others, Perote, Mar. 22, 1843, in Spellman, ed., "Letters of the 'Dawson Men' from Perote Prison, Mexico, 1842-1843," in *SWHQ* 38 (Apr. 1935), pp. 247-48.

letter from you would doo much more good than any thing I could receive while I remane in these walls . . . Tell Mrs Bradley her husband is well Col [Joseph] shaws allso, in fact we are all well to a man—be sure and rite to your unfortinate felow Prisoner give my respects to all my friends and receave my warmes[t] respect to yourslef."[13]

With few exceptions, foreigners at all times were allowed free access to the castle and to other prisons where Texans were held. They sometimes smuggled in things and could spirit out correspondence. Besides sending a package of English books, C. Consalvi, a Corsican, supplied the prisoners with gifts of bread, clothing, and medicine. The prisoners received word on Sunday, February 4, 1844, from Consalvi that he was on his way from Mexico City to New Orleans and would stop to visit with them on Monday and would convey any letters they had to the United States.[14] Several of the prisoners commenced at once to prepare their letters. Consalvi did not reach the castle until the afternoon of February 7, and was permitted by the officer of the guard to visit the prisoners in their quarters. He told them that he was on his way to the United States with his two children, "his wife—a Miss Stansfield of New York having left him at the City of Mexico to receive the embraces of a young painter of Minature[s]."[15] In the presence of an officer he was handed a number of letters to be mailed. The officer at once informed the governor that Consalvi had received letters. Governor Jarero sent for Consalvi and "expressed much dissatisfaction at his entering the castle and conversing with us," reported Trueheart, "without first notifying him, as was the custom."[16] The governor ordered Consalvi to be locked up in the calaboose until the Texan prisoners later in the evening were locked in their cells. After being detained for two hours and relieved of all letters and papers, he was released and allowed to proceed to Vera Cruz.[17] This time the Texans' uncensored letters did not get out of the castle.

In a corner of his cell, Thomas Jefferson Green improvised a desk by propping up an old door and spent many hours writing letters to individuals in Texas and the United States, to officials of both countries, and to the representatives of foreign governments in Mexico. He kept up a correspondence with Waddy Thompson, "who evinced the liveliest interest" in the prisoners' welfare.[18] Joseph Shaw, while a prisoner at Perote, spent much time studying the Bible and in writing short sermons.

James C. Wilson had plenty of time to reminiscence about his early

---

13. Richard A. Barkley to Samuel A. Maverick, Castle of Perote, April 15, 1843, in Green, ed., *Samuel Maverick: Texan*, pp. 245-47.

14. Trueheart diary, Feb. 4 and 5, 1844. Trueheart gives the name as Señor Gonzáles, but Canfield's diary, Feb. 7, 1844, speaks of "Our old friend W. C. Consalvi," whom Green, *Mier Expedition*, p. 282 and note, refers to as Señor Consalvi.

15. Canfield diary, Feb. 7, 1844.

16. Trueheart diary, Feb. 7, 1844.

17. *Ibid.*

18. Green, *Mier Expedition*, p. 258.

childhood and youth, and to long for happier days gone by. He put his thoughts in a lengthy poem for *The Planter* entitled "The Texian Captive's Dream Written in the Prison of Santiago, City of Mexico June 4th, 1843."[19] Another poem, "The Mier Prisoners's Lament," author and date unknown, appeared in the *Galveston News*.[20]

The prisoners' most frequent complaint, other than against their taskmasters, was the neglect from friends, relatives, and their adopted government. In spite of "writing time after time," complained William F. Wilson to his brother, "I never have heard from my native country but once," and that was from Governor James McDowell of Virginia to U.S. Consul John Black in Mexico City, "in favor of my friend William A Wallace," though he had written "time after time. farewell Wm. F. Wilson."[21]

In a letter to his brother, Claudius Buster showed great concern for the well-being of members of his family. On February 11, 1844, he received a letter from Mr. Hughes, a stranger, dated the previous November 28, which had been mailed from Mt. Vernon, Washington County. In scanning it, he saw his mother's name. "It is impossible to imagine the emotions of my heart on opening the letter and seeing the name of a stranger. Being mailed at Mt. Vernon, having heard of much sickness in Texas, and having upwards of twelve months labored under serious apprehensions for the health of my parents, I looked again before I dared read and saw Mother's name. Oh, thought I, it is my Father that is dead. Oh, what feelings, but when I read and saw Father's name mentioned as one living, my relief was in expressible.

"I regret most seriously," he said, "that it has been my ill fortune to render my poor Father and Mother as much unhappiness as I have, but if I am permitted to get home, I think I shall never render the same unhappiness again."[22]

Some were so impatient to hear from home that their feelings were hurt when letters did not come through promptly. In writing home to "Dear Friends," A. S. Thurmond addressed his letter to Mrs. Mary A. Willis, whom he wished to inform of the death of her husband. "I do not write to you all with the expectation of being Benefited any thing by itt," he said, "for I am satisfied that friends and relations have forsaken me or they would answer my letters for I [have] written often. . . . Tell my Mother and Brothers I am sorry that they have forsaken me, for I still have love and affection for them. I do no write to them [now] because they treat my let-

---

19. *The Planter* (Columbia), Feb. 10, 1844.

20. William Fields, comp., *The Scrap-Book: Consisting of Tales and Anecdotes, Biographical, Historical, Patriotic, Moral, Religious, and Sentimental Pieces in Prose and Poetry*, 6th rev. and enl. ed., p. 214; also in Baker, comp., *Texas Scrap-Book*, p. 417-18.

21. William F. Wilson to "Dear Brother" [John S. Wilson], Castle of Perote, April 22, 1844, in "Two Letters from a Mier Prisoner," *QTSHA* 2 (Jan. 1899), pp. 233-34.

22. Claudius Buster to John V. Buster, Castle of Perote, March 8, 1844, copy in Miscellaneous Docs., Tx-A; also reproduced in Wade, comp., *Notes and Fragments of the Mier Expedition* 1, pp. 88-95.

ters with contempt by not answering them. Give my love to all my friends and relations and to dear Mother, Brothers, Sisters and tell all that I have come very near seeing the Eliphant since I have been in hock. Nothing more but remain your friend until Death &c."[23]

"I have received no letters from you though I have written several times," wrote Thomas W. Bell to his father. "I begin to suppose you have given me up or that my letters have not reached you. It is with difficulty that I can raise a cent or two to get paper to write you on. I have received one letter from Texas. . . . I have learned many things on this unfortunate campaign; I think I have been an attentive observer of men and things since my captivity and have seen enough to disgust me with my own species; but of this again."[24] He continued, "This long captivity makes me feel more keenly the enjoyments of a happy home and friends."

"We were in hopes that the present Congress of Texas would do something for our relief," wrote P. M. Maxwell to a friend in Galveston on January 23, 1844, "but hope has fled, as we hear nothing from that quarter."[25]

Going for the mail was a highlight for the prisoners and a task eagerly sought, but there could be problems. Singly and in small groups, they went into town under guard to meet the stage to receive letters, newspapers, and gather news from the passengers. On these occasions they were allowed various and sundry privileges—to buy fruit and other items of food and of personal comfort and often an opportunity to stroll about the village. The mail arrived at Perote from Vera Cruz and Mexico City on Mondays, Thursdays, and Saturdays. The stage drivers, usually Americans, were generally kind. Some of the foreigners aboard the stage also showed sympathy, but others shunned them.[26]

Trueheart was often one of those who went into Perote for the mail. On Saturday, April 29, while in town at the stage stop, he met with several New Yorkers on their way to Mexico City, who had learned of the capture of the Texans at Béxar and Mier and expressed a desire to visit the castle. Trueheart hurriedly completed "what . . . [he] had to do [in town], so as to enable them to stay as long as possible" at the castle.[27] "When we arrived at the castle we had first to obtain permission from the governor for them to see the prisoners which accordingly [was] done, and they remain[ed] with us 30 minutes and return[ed]."

On June 10, 1843, three of the Texan prisoners went into Perote for the mail, but overstayed their time. Several officers were sent to look for

---

23. A. S. Thurmond to Mrs. Mary A. Willis, Rutherfords, Lauderdale, Tenn., [dated] Castle of Perote, Oct. 18, 1843, in Friend, ed., "Sidelights and Supplements on the Perote Prisoners," *SWHQ* 69 (Apr. 1955), p. 521.

24. Thomas W. Bell to William A. Bell Trenton, Tenn., [dated] Castle of Perote, Mar. 3, 1844, in Friend, ed., "Thomas W. Bell Letters," *SWHQ* 63 (Apr. 1964), pp. 593-95.

25. P. M. Maxwell to Captain J[ohn] H[emphill], Castle of Perote, Republic of Mexico, Jan. 23, 1844, in *Galveston Weekly News*, Feb. 22, 1844.

26. Trueheart diary, Apr. 28 [29], 1843.

27. *Ibid.*

them and returned with the three Texans that evening. "Great uneasiness [was] manifested by the Governor," who now informed the Texan prisoners that in the future none of them would be permitted to go out for the mail or to the market in town, but these restrictions were soon dispensed with. On November 20 the governor ordered that the mail man always report to him, and ten days later Trueheart commented in his diary that "The receipt of letters is decreasing every day. Our papers are also becoming more scarce."[28] It was thought that the governor was withholding some of the prisoners' mail.

In captivity, a number of the men acquired nicknames. William Moore was called "Talking Bill" because he had a "propensity to tell all that he knew of things that he had heard of, or seen or read of and the particulars of his own life from his earliest recollections up to the present time."[29] Gideon K. Lewis was called "Legs" Lewis because of his long legs; Thomas Davis was known as "Walking" Davis; and William Davis as "Tickey" Davis; and, of course, there was D. H. Van Vechten, who was known as "Tonkaway," and William Trimble as "Tecolote" ("Screech Owl") for his ability to imitate that weird night-bird.

Other forms of amusements were dancing, drawing caricatures upon the walls, playing monte or chuckluck, or gathering in small groups, half reclining upon their blankets, while one of their number recited some story, "heard a thousand times over."[30] Some became religious and sang hymns nightly.

Louse racing became a pastime for some, although no other writer or diarist except Thomas J. Green mentioned this form of entertainment. Lice, fleas, rats, and mice were problems—irritating problems—and there was little humor connected with their presence. On a bull's hide was drawn a circle about eighteen inches in diameter in charcoal with the figure of a "holy cross" in the center inside a smaller circle. The two racers were placed on the edge of the outer circle and the louse, of which there was a plentiful supply, that crossed both circles first to arrive at the *holy cross* was the winner. Bets were placed by participants and bystanders, "some crying out for the '*red*' and some for the '*white*' louse."[31] Whenever possible the men sought the sunshine during the day and exposed their blankets and clothes to its rays, flushing the lice from their hiding places. "When one of these [little] animals showed himself particularly fleet of foot, he would be captured and saved for the races."[32]

A few of the prisoners might be found repairing the only shirt or pantaloons they possessed, or making a pair of sandles from a piece of rawhide or mending those they had. In the midst of the noise following the

28. *Ibid.*, June 10-11, 1843.
29. Sowell, "Benjamin Z. Boone: Story of One of the Survivors of the Famous Expedition," in *Dallas Morning News*, Aug. 4, 1901.
30. Glasscock diary, Oct. 29, 1843.
31. Green, *Mier Expedition*, pp. 269-74.
32. *Ibid.*, p. 269.

locking of the cell door many of them slipped off their chains. If one could have looked in upon the little band busy with file, chisel, saw, and other tools, he would have witnessed "a perfect Blacksmith shop at times." Clearing their ankles of the heavy chains, they cut their "jewels" into smaller pieces and either buried them in the floor or in some crevice in the walls, or, when the opportunity afforded, cast them into the moat. "Many were the chains," wrote McCutchan, "we have destroyed for Mexico," even though it often meant punishment later.[33] Some of the chains were merely reduced by cutting off a part of them, resulting in lighter chains to wear.

While one of their party would whistle a tune several others would "pat," a practice learned from slaves, who, having no musical instruments to accompany a dance, would sing or whistle and with their hands slapping together or upon their head or breast would beat time or rhythm. Often patting was accompanied by beating time on the floor with their feet. Freeing themselves of their chains at night, the Texans skipped to the "music," of their chains and the "patting" of a fellow prisoner. "Every night for the last week (in my room)," recorded Glasscock, "we get a man to pat for us, and have a real old country reel; it is very good exercise and we do it more for our health than [for] amusement."[34] July and August were the coldest months in the year, and dancing or cutting a jig were ways of keeping warm. Often dancing went on for three hours in the evenings.

Violins and fiddles were carved with pieces of iron and glass by the carpenters and cabinetmakers from soup bones and bits of wood left in the carpenter shop.[35] One of those who carved a violin was a carpenter and cabinetmaker named Journeay. Using an old razor blade, a file, and a few pieces of broken glass, Journeay made his violin. When finished, it had tiny arrow-shaped inlaid work on the bridge and a tail piece carved and polished from soup bones. The bow was fashioned from a piece of wood left from the construction of a chair of state for Santa Anna.[36]

Another carpenter completed, after a week's labor, a fiddle on Saturday, June 22,[37] and it was expected to be put into use on Sunday when the prisoners usually did not work. Everyone looked forward to having a real *fandango*; and sure enough when Sunday arrived they had "a real country dance . . . [that] lasted pretty much all day. We have more fiddlers in our crowd," recorded Glasscock, "than one would expect in a[s] small a number as ours, there being only 7 or 8,[38] and on the 25th two more fiddles were expected to be ready by Saturday night, the 29th." And on July 2

---

33. Nance, ed., *McCutchan's Narrative*, p. 110.
34. Glasscock diary, Mar. 11, June 13 and 22, 1844.
35. N. M. Wilcox, "The Old Violin of Perote and Its Song of Liberty," in *San Antonio Express*, July 27, 1913; "The Violin of Perote," from the *San Angelo Standard-Times* in *Frontier Times* 20 (Mar. 1943), pp. 95-96.
36. Glasscock diary, June 13, 22, 1844.
37. *Ibid.*, June 22, 1844.
38. *Ibid.*, June 23, 1844.

Glasscock recorded: "This morning our boys in the carpenter shop completed two more fiddles; they are determined to have evening music, if nothing else."[39] By the end of July, they had five violins and seven or eight fiddles, and dancing had become the chief pastime on Sundays. Journeay brought home the violin he had carved. It remained in the Journeay family until 1931, when it was given by W. H. Journeay and James Journeay of Houston to the Texas State Archives.[40]

Merrily they skipped to such old tunes as "Nancy Robbins," "Resin the Bow," "Molly, Put the Kettle On," "Old Smoke," "The Buffalo Gals," "The Girl I Left Behind Me," and "Home Sweet Home," which brought forth memories and tears. The old tunes were "Sung divinely," but sometimes with so much gusto that it caused "the guard to quake with fear,"[41] and the prisoners' laughs were often so loud and long that the officer of the guard would cry out *"Silencio!"*

The Texans often went to extremes in gaiety to prevent despondency or to cover up the noise of digging out. "Many of the men," reported McCutchan, "dance at least three hours during each day and night, which bears the face of careless spirits—but these dances excite no joyful feelings—only serving to pass time away, free as practicable from painful thoughts."[42] There were a few, like Sensebaugh, to whom Wallace was chained, who placed their trust in God. Wallace considered him to be as true a Christian as any he had seen. At the midnight hour he would sing, pray, and thank God that it was as well as it was with him and his comrades.[43]

Violins and fiddles were not the only things carved by the Mier prisoners. Norman Woods, who worked briefly in the carpenter's shop before his death on December 16, 1843, carved two pipes and a spoon, which now reside in the Alamo Museum in San Antonio.[44]

On Sunday, July 21, an American by the name of Jenkins, an acquaintance of Glasscock, stopped at Perote Castle on his way to Mexico City to visit the Texan prisoners.[45] Jenkins was a portrait painter. He spent the night in Perote, but on Monday, and again on Tuesday, and apparently daily thereafter until as late as August 11,[46] he returned to the castle to continue his visitation and to paint portraits. He painted portraits of Dr. William F. McMath, Dr. William M. Shepherd, Judge Fenton M. Gibson,

---

39. *Ibid.*, July 2, 1844.

40. Chris LaPlante, Assistant Director of State Archives, to J. M. Nance, November 1, 1978, in possession of the author.

41. Nance, ed., *McCutchan's Narrative*, pp. 110, 132-33; see also Glasscock diary, June 22-23, 1844.

42. Nance, ed., *McCutchan's Narrative*, p. 132.

43. Sowell, *Early Settlers and Indian Fighters of Southwest Texas*, p. 74.

44. Trueheart diary, Dec. 16, 1843. The carvings of Norman Woods were given to the Alamo Museum by C. C. Wood of San Benito, Texas.

45. Glasscock diary, July 21-23, 1844; Nance, ed., *McCutchan's Narrative*, pp. 135-36, 139.

46. Nance, ed., *McCutchan's Narrative*, pp. 135-39.

and Col. William F. Wilson, and possibly others. (This author has been unable to locate any of these paintings.)

On the prison walls the prisoners drew crude charcoal sketches of Santa Anna, General Duran, the governor of the fort, "Old Guts," and other members of the guard, better known as "His Excellency's Satanic imps." When the annexation issue was renewed in the United States and Texas, the charcoal sketchers drew upon the walls of their cells the Lone Star of Texas surrounded by the constellation of its northern neighbor. The officer of the guard, on seeing the galaxy, charged the wall, hacking away the plaster with his sword, but no sooner had he turned his back than another and another flag sprang from "the deathblows of the last, until they [the Mexican guards] found it worse than useless to war upon the Phoenix-like spirit" of their captives.[47]

Charles McLaughlin, one of the few real artists among the Mier men, "painted the American flag in real beautiful colors upon the white prison walls," reported Woodland many years later. Just under the flag he "painted a bunch of cactus, and 'neath the cactus bush he painted a huge rattlesnake, with open jaws and tongue thrust forward in an attitude ready for the fray; 'neath this the words: 'Don't tramp on me or I will bite.'" All enjoyed the picture until the officer of the day entered the room on his tour of inspection. "No sooner did he see it than, comprehending its meaning, he flew into a rage, drew his sword," and uttering an oath with every stroke, hacked at it "until he had destroyed the entire painting."[48]

Some of the prisoners hailed with delight a trip into the mountains or into the town of Perote, for various and sundry purposes, as it permitted them to escape the frowning walls of the castle. In town they might meet some person who could assist in obtaining their release or in effecting their escape by supplying information about the roads or in carrying news of their condition to the outside world. In the mountains, there was the opportunity to spy out some trail which might be useful in eluding the guard in any attempt to escape.

The interest of James A. Glasscock and others in *belles-letters* extended to the publication of a weekly manuscript newspaper. The paper began publication on Sunday, July 14, 1844, under the title of the *Perote Meat-Axe,* and was filled with items contributed by the prisoners. Glasscock has left this description of the first issue: "It cuts some of the boys tolerably fine; the size is two sheets of foolscap pasted together. The terms are moderate, 6 locoles in advance or 8 at the end of the year; it gives the latest intelligence from China &c."[49] With the second number, dated July 21, the name of the paper was changed to *The Perote Prisoner,* with a drawing at

---

47. Green, *Mier Expedition*, pp. 377-78.

48. Woodland, "The Story of the Massacre of Mier Prisoners," in *Houston Daily Post*, Aug. 16, 1891, p. 8, col. 1.

49. Glasscock diary, July 12, 14, 1844; see also Nance, ed., *McCutchan's Narrative*, p. 134.

the head representing two men pulling a wheelbarrow.[50] The second number of the *Prisoner* was described as "a rather poor affair," and the paper was expected to "die a natural death" soon.[51] Apparently, the August 4 issue was the last.

The first of the Mier men, sixteen in number, to reach Perote Castle in March 1843, looked forward to the celebration of the anniversary of the defeat of Santa Anna's army at San Jacinto on April 21. By the arrival of that eventful day, they had accumulated seven gallons of *vino mescal*, an equal amount of ass's milk, thirty dozen eggs, several large loaves of sugar, and collected all their cooking vessels and water jugs for concocting a grand eggnog, which proved to have a powerful kick. The eggs were beaten by Colonel Fisher, Captain Reese, and Lt. Charles Clarke, while the old sailing master, Samuel C. Lyon, pounded the sugar. Egotist Green reported, "I presided over the synthetical operation of stirring in the requisite ingredients. When *I* pronounced it right, they all said, 'It is exactly the thing.'"[52] When the drink was ready, the ragged Texans, with chains riveted to their ankles, drank to the health of the Lone Star Republic. All hands pronounced the eggnog "better than the nectar of the gods, for *that* they understood to be pure, unmixed, and unadultered 'mountain dew,' while this had the 'body'; for while the juice of the agave inspired the soul, the ass's milk filled the stomach."[53]

Numerous toasts and puns were offered at the expense of Mexico and the Mexicans. Each was followed by three cheers, boisterous laughter, shouts, loud talking, and exclamations. Numerous toasts were offered to liberty and country, and to "Our wives, children, and sweethearts"; to "A fair field, and no more white flags"; and to "*Old Peg-Leg*, . . . we owe *thee* much." There were patriotic and ribald speeches, boisterous singing, and dancing to the "music" of clanking chains. As the evening wore on and the liquor circulated more freely, the hilarity and general good feeling increased. The loud noise attracted the attention of Captain Guzmán and the guard, who came to investigate. "What's this all about?" shouted Guzmán. "This is our All Saints' Day," replied one of the prisoners, and several expressed the hope that he would be kind enough not to disturb their mode of worship. Shaking his head in bewilderment, the captain conceded them the right of worship, said "*Bueno,*" and started to retire from the cell when William Trimble, one of the Dawson men, with a flashing, dare-devil expression in his eye, "squared himself, rolled his eyes entirely over the sockets, twisted his head 'clean round' on his shoulders, and gave a whoop that beat the best of owls."[54] The captain quickly turned around,

50. Glasscock diary, July 21, 1844.

51. *Ibid.*, July 27, 1844. The Mier diaries make no further mention of a newspaper after August 4, 1844.

52. Green, *Mier Expedition*, p. 259.

53. *Ibid.*, pp. 259-60.

54. *Ibid.*, p. 261; see also William Trimble's postscript to the letter of Norman Woods to [H. G. Woods and Others], Castle of Perote, September 23, 1843, in Spellman, ed., "Letters of the 'Dawson Men,' from Perote Prison, Mexico," *SWHQ* 38 (Apr. 1935), pp. 265-66.

frowned, and stood puzzled for a moment, not knowing whether to laugh or to swear; then, suddenly pointing his finger toward Trimble, he exclaimed, *"Tecolote"* ("Screech-Owl") and moved on, thus penning a name upon Trimble which he carried to his grave.

As July 4 approached, Fisher requested the commandant to exempt the Anglo-American prisoners from work on July 4 so they could celebrate the independence of the United States. The governor and commandant permitted the celebration and issued an order to exempt the men from work on that day.[55]

Up at dawn on July 4, the men began to prepare for "a big spree." "We got some eggs and liquor to have an eggnog tonight; a Dutchman by the name of [Henry] Miller, a rather . . . eccentric character, went around to the soldiers' wives and procured some 10 or 12 dresses to have a ball at night." The garrison officers voluntarily supplied them with an abundance of "cheer" for the occasion. "We were locked up at 5 o'clock into two rooms, as we had two fiddles, and we commenced, and such another time we had of it, I never seen before," recorded one of the participants: "there was scarcely a man who was drunk; we kept perfectly good order the whole time and between 9 & 10 o'clock we retired to bed, being too much corned to continued the ball any longer."[56] McCutchan, however, reported, "We dance and kick up a noise until one o'clock in the morning."[57] The next morning several of the men were "a little unwell" when the officers came for them to go to work.

On September 27, anniversary of the surrender of Mexico by the Spaniards, a twenty-one-gun salute was fired morning, noon, and late evening. The guard was unusually kind, supplying the prisoners with double rations and permitting them under heavy guard to walk outside the walls of the fortress.[58]

Daniel Drake Henrie's experience in hauling stones caused him to contrive a way to avoid such strenuous duty in the future. The night following his first day's assignment in hauling stones, he took a steel pen from Green's writing table, scratched his legs from his ankle to the knee, and wrapped them in many folds of old shirts and blankets. By the next morning, "his legs were in a high state of inflammation from their superabundance of clothing, so much so that the surgeon had the irons taken off his ankles. The consequence was, that Dan's first day of packing stones was his last. Afterward it was easy for him to increase the inflammation upon inspection days."[59]

Henry Woodland "played crazy, and so effectually did he succeed that though often caught fighting the cooks or knocking senseless a drunken

---

55. Glasscock diary, July 3, 1843.
56. *Ibid.*, July 4, 1843.
57. Nance, ed., *McCutchan's Narrative*, p. 133.
58. Canfield diary, Sept. 23, 1843.
59. Green, *Mier Expedition*, pp. 278-79.

Mexican, he would escape punishment." On one occasion, when a guard was sent to fetch him, "the guard went away in considerable disorder," crying at the top of his voice, *El Téjano es much Loco! Loco! O'Madre mía!*" and "so great was their suspicion . . . they dare not lay hands on him."[60]

Many feast days and holidays were celebrated by the Mexicans. On these days and Sundays the prisoners were generally not required to work, although occasionally a few of them might be employed at various tasks. Usually on non-work days the Texans remained locked in their cells, and always on Sundays they were kept locked in later than on weekdays, often until ten o'clock so the guard could attend mass. Normally the guard was changed at nine, at which time the prisoners were counted and turned over to the new guard. On Sundays and festival days they were locked up eighteen out of twenty-four hours in a day. Normally, after the day's chores had been performed, usually about four in the afternoon, the Texans were permitted the run of the courtyard until six, when they were again counted and locked in their cells until six the next morning, when the cell doors were opened and they were supplied coffee and other refreshments.

60. Woodland, "The Story of the Massacre of Mier Prisoners," *Houston Daily Post*, Aug. 16, 1891, p. 8, col. 1.

CHAPTER 26

Arrival of New U.S. Minister and the Release and Return of the Mier Prisoners

AN HOUR AFTER THE order for the release of Bigfoot Wallace and four others had been received at the castle, Wilson Shannon, the new United States minister to Mexico, arrived at seven o'clock on his way to Mexico City. At Vera Cruz he had been "greeted with a warmer reception by the authorities . . . then was ever tendered to a Charge d'Affaires from the United States at any former period."[1]

The stage remained overnight at the castle, thus affording Shannon an opportunity to visit with the Texan prisoners.[2] At the governor's office a number of the prisoners met Shannon, "who treated me with some kindness," reported William Wilson to his brother, "but did not give *me the $100 you sent to him*."[3] Although it was night and the prisoners were locked up in their rooms, "the governor of the fortress very kindly permitted him to visit the prisoners."[4] He "inquired particularly into the circumstances of each of the prisoners, and into the general mode of treatment which they received." He discovered that treatment varied considerably among the prisoners—that some, chained in pairs, were compelled to work as beasts of burden while others were "allowed very great indulgencies—for prisoners."[5] He reported that the Texan prisoners were confined in six rooms and that "some of them were in a wretched condition, being almost naked.

1. Correspondence to the *Picayune*, dated Pensacola, Sept. 12, 1844, in *Daily Picayune*, Sept. 15, 1844.

2. Wilson Shannon to John C. Calhoun, Legation of the U.S. of A., Mexico, Sept. 21, 1844, in Despatches from United States Ministers in Mexico, Nov. 10, 1843-Jan. 26, 1847, National Archives (microfilm).

3. W[illia]m F. Wilson to John S. Wilson, New Orleans, October 10, 1844, in Wilson, *Reminiscences of Persons, Events, Records, and Documents of Texian Times*, p. 10.

4. Wilson Shannon to John C. Calhoun, Legation of the U.S. of A., Mexico, Sept. 21, 1844, in Despatches from United States Ministers in Mexico, Nov. 10, 1843-Jan. 26, 1847, National Archives (microfilm).

5. *Daily Picayune*, Sept. 19, 1844.

They manifested a strong desire to be liberated, and solicited my interference in their behalf," reported Shannon.[6] Before leaving, he impressed
upon the prisoners that they should be patient a while longer, promising
that he would seek their release as soon as he reached the capital, "so far
as those endeavors did not conflict with his official station, as the representative of another Government."[7] He admonished those in cell no. 7 not
to leave until he had been heard from. He wanted no excuse for Santa
Anna to retain them. His parting words were, said McCutchan: "Wate with
patience, and anything that I can do for you, you may rely upon me for its
accomplishment."[8] They once more began to hope for release. Shannon's
advice and exertions in gaining their release no doubt prevented the loss
of several lives and many hardships and difficulties that the men would
have encountered in trying to escape.

While Shannon was at the castle he received an order for his protection on the road to Puebla from the governor of the castle, but his armed
escort failed him. Shannon arrived in Mexico City on the evening of
August 26. He was "robbed and plundered on the road" from Vera Cruz
to Mexico City on August 25 "by an armed banditti of all the property I
had about my person," he reported to the United States secretary of state.
"This outrage was committed in broad daylight, on the public highway
and within two miles of the City of Puebla, and while traveling not only
under the implied but express promise of the public authorities that I
should receive ample protection on my way to this city [Mexico City]," but
it seems that the driver of the stagecoach was to blame "for not having
chosen to wait for the proper escort" from their last stopping place.[9]

It was not uncommon for foreign emissaries to be robbed on the road
with the connivance of the government. Their papers, along with their
money and other valuables, were invariably taken. The papers were
turned over to the government as a part of its espionage activities and the
foreign dignitary was later compensated for his material losses, but his
papers were never returned and he was led to believe that the authorities
had been unable to find them.

Less than three months later, when Shannon took a stand with Manuel Rejón, minister of foreign relations, on a proposed invasion of Texas
by Mexico, and especially against the manner in which that invasion was
to be waged, Rejón on October 31, 1844, denied the right of the United
States, or that of any other foreign government, to interfere in what he
described as the internal affairs of Mexico. He bitterly condemned the

---

6. Wilson Shannon to John C. Calhoun, Legation of the U.S. of A., Mexico, Sept. 21,
1844, in Despatches from United States Ministers in Mexico, Nov. 10, 1843-Jan. 26, 1847,
National Archives (microfilm).

7. Bell, *Narrative*, p.96.

8. Nance, ed., *McCutchan's Narrative*, p. 144; see also *Galveston News*, Dec. 6, 1844.

9. Wilson Shannon to J. C. Calhoun, Legation of the U.S. of A., Mexico, Aug. 28, 1844,
in Despatches from United States Ministers in Mexico, Nov. 10, 1943-Jan. 26, 1847,
National Archives (microfilm); *Daily Picayune*, Oct. 1, 1844.

United States for instigating the Texas Revolution. "But it was not the so-called Texans," he said, "who were able to gain the independence of the province or who have sufficient means to maintain it; it is the people of the southern portion of the United States who have done it all, not in order to make an independent nation of Texas, but to annex it to their territory with some appearance of justice. The note to which the undersigned is replying is a proof of their insufficiency, because if their resources were adequate to sustain them against the power of the Mexican Republic it would not have been necessary for the Government of His Excellency Mr. Shannon to take their part so openly, tearing aside once for all the veil which it so long attempted to cover its strategems and its designs."[10]

Shannon found the secretary's letter "so insulting, both in its language and charges, to the government and people of the United States, and in such a flagrant breach of those rules of courtesy that should characterize international diplomatic intercourse," that he could only demand that it should be withdrawn.[11] Shannon said that to this demand he received a still "more insulting and exceptionable note so grossly offensive to the Government of the United States, that if I had consulted my own feelings, I would have demanded my passports, but in view of the consequences, which such a course would involve, and not wishing to take any step that might appear rash, I thought it best to notify the Mexican Government that the two exceptionable notes . . . should be immediately referred to my Government for instructions, and that unless they were withdrawn, all official intercourse between this Legation & the Mexican Government must cease, until those instructions were received." When the notes were not withdrawn, Shannon suspended diplomatic intercourse, without prior approval of the United States State Department.[12] For doing so, he was called home.[13]

On his way to Vera Cruz to take passage for New York, Shannon was again robbed on the road. The editor of the *Northern Standard* gave a graphic report of the incident:

> The scene of his [Shannon's] interview with them [the robbers] was some leagues east of the city of Puebla. . . . The stage was accompanied by an escort, furnished him by the Mexican government. But a few min-

10. Manuel Crescencio Rejón to Wilson Shannon, Executive Mansion, Mexico, Oct. 31, 1844, typed copy in Wilson Shannon to John C. Calhoun, Secretary of State of the U.S. of A., [dated] Legation of the U.S. of A., Mexico City, Nov. 12, 1844, in Despatches from U.S. Ministers to Mexico, Nov. 10, 1843-Jan. 26, 1847, National Archives (microfilm).

11. Wilson Shannon to John C. Calhoun, Legation of the U.S. of A., Mexico, Nov. 12, 1844, in Despatches from U.S. Ministers in Mexico, Nov. 10, 1843-Jan. 26, 1847, National Archives (microfilm).

12. Wilson Shannon to M. C. Rejón, Legation of the U.S. of A., Mexico, Nov. 8, 1844, in Despatches from U.S. Ministers in Mexico, Nov. 10, 1843-Jan. 26, 1847, National Archives (microfilm).

13. James Buchanan to Wilson Shannon, Department of State, Washington, March 29, 1845, in Diplomatic Instructions of the Department of State, Mexico, May 29, 1833-Mar. 29, 1845, National Archives (microfilm).

utes before they entered the ravine, the captain of the escort rode up, and informed him that he had passed the haunts of the robbers, and was no longer in any danger from them; and, having received the customary "gratification," retired. From what immediately after took place, there is every reason to suspect a full understanding and a collusion between the guard and the robbers. Five minutes afterwards, while the travellers were still congratulating each other upon having passed through all the dangers of the road unscathed, the stage suddenly stopped in the middle of the ravine, and seven or eight big muzzled carbines at once enlightened them as to the treachery of their escort, and reminded them of the mutability of ounces from the purses of travellers to the pockets of the road autogentry [?]. They were politely invited to conference on foot, and, making a merit of necessity, descended from the stage with as good a grace as possible. The ceremony of searching trunks and "handing over" then began. While it lasted, Gov. Shannon had an opportunity of observing the tactics of his new acquaintants. Around the stage were fourteen in number, all marked and well armed, each with a carbine, a long knife, a sword, and pistols suspended in belts around the waist. Seven remained on horseback, with carbines levelled, ready for action in case of resistance. The others dismounted, to search for and select the booty. In the distance was some fifteen or twenty others, stationed as sentinels. The search was conducted with great order and decorum, and accompanied with all the politest phrases of the Spanish language. When it was over, having duly admired Gov. Shannon's dress sword, and expressed their approbation of its workmanship, they returned it to him, together with his papers. Then, with many apologies for the detention they had caused him, they took their leave; not, however, until they had asked for him the blessing of God, and invoked in his behalf the protection of the Blessed Virgin, "Our Lade of Guadalupe."

The whole party were shortly after brought to a stand by another set of banditti intent upon the same friendly offices. The conductor, however, good naturedly assured them that the job had been done, and resumed his course. Governor Shannon is said to have lost in the two robberies to and from Mexico City, in money, clothes, and other belongings somewhere between $500 and $600.[14]

The Texan prisoners' hopes had been elevated by the first robbery of Shannon on the way to Mexico City, believing that Santa Anna would now "wish to return some great favor to him [Shannon] on account of the accident."[15] In Mexico City, Shannon had addressed a note on August 27 to Secretary of Foreign Relations Manuel C. Rejón, informing him of his arrival and his desire to present his letter of credence to the president. However, on account of the death of Santa Anna's wife and her funeral, Shannon was unable to present his credentials to the president at the

---

14. *Northern Standard*, Aug. 16, 1845; *Texas National Register*, Sept. 11, 1845.
15. Nance, ed., *McCutchan's Narrative*, p. 145.

palace in Tacubaya until September.[16] In the meantime, he wrote on August 30 to the president requesting, "as a personal favor," the release of all of the Texan prisoners, and made a strong appeal "to his liberality and generosity in their behalf." At the appointed time, he went to the palace at Tacubaya, accompanied by Ben E. Green, acting *chargé d'affaires*. Immediately after being presented to the president on September 2, he handed the letter to the president, "with the request that he would give it an early and favorable consideration." A few days later he received a reply "couched in friendly terms, but indefinite & ambiguous in relation to the discharge of the Texan prisoners."

On September 2 the guns of the Castle of Perote commenced firing at dawn, at the rate of four to the hour, and the national flag was lowered to half-mast in mourning for Santa Anna's deceased wife, Señora Ines García de Santa Anna, who had died at Puebla of a "breast complaint."[17] During the day R. W. Turner received a letter from Shannon, dated August 26, saying that on September 2 he was going to have an audience with the president and would apply for the release of the prisoners.[18]

In his audience with the president, Shannon, according to his instructions, reminded Santa Anna that the installment on the debt to the United States, due on April 30 last, had not been paid, and that "This neglect of solemn and express stipulations cannot be otherwise regarded than as a violation of national faith, injurious alike to the honor of Mexico and the interests of the United States."[19] The other difficulties in United States-Mexican relations Shannon postponed taking up "until the final action of the President in relation to the Texan prisoners had been disposed of." Shannon was beginning to understand what Ben E. Green meant back in April when he informed the American secretary of state that a remonstrance made to the Mexican government carried very little weight.

On September 5 word was received at Perote Castle by Samuel C. Lyon from Sir Charles Bankhead, the British minister, that he had applied for the release of all English subjects among the Texan prisoners and that Santa Anna had promised him that he would release them. Bankhead requested Lyon to send him immediately a list of "bona fide English subjects."[20] Also on September 5 Henry Miller received from the German consul in Mexico notice that he had obtained his release and that the order for it would be forthcoming in a few days.[21] Shannon seemed to be

---

16. Wilson Shannon to John C. Calhoun, Legation of the U.S. of A., Mexico, Sept. 21, 1844, in Despatches from United States Ministers to Mexico, Nov. 10, 1843-Jan. 26, 1847, National Archives (microfilm).

17. Crawford, *The Eagle: The Autobiography of Santa Anna*, p. 269, n. 5.

18. Glasscock diary, Sept. 2, 1844; see also Nance, ed., *McCutchan's Narrative*, p. 146; *Telegraph and Texas Register*, Nov. 23, 1844.

19. J. C. Calhoun to Wilson Shannon, Department of State, Washington, June 20, 1844, in Diplomatic Instructions of the Department of State, Mexico, May 29, 1833-Mar. 29, 1845, National Archives (microfilm).

20. Glasscock diary, Sept. 5, 1844.

21. *Ibid.*

pushing the foreign governments represented in Mexico to press for the release of their nationals among the Texan prisoners—a policy initiated by Thompson—then to press for equal consideration for the Americans. On September 8 the prisoners learned that several petitions had been presented to Santa Anna for their release, including among them one signed by 220 members of the U.S. Congress, one from John Quincy Adams, one from Waddy Thompson, and one from Juan N. Almonte, the Mexican minister to the United States.[22] "Taking every thing cooly in view, these petitions," combined with the influence of Shannon, recorded McCutchan, "we may now begin to look forward to a time when we will again breathe the free air of Heaven, untainted by the foul, infectious breath of this abandoned, degraded race."[23]

On September 9 Fisher received a letter from Shannon enclosing a copy of a letter from Santa Anna, which indicated that the reply to his request had been "No."[24]

Despondency once more descended upon the prisoners. "A bolt of death could not have struck greater consternation to our hearts," declared McCutchan.[25] "This cuts off all hope. . . . To day—and all is dark. Not *one* lighted fire of hope to which one may look. All, *all* dreary and desolate," he continued. "When oh! when will this cease? Destiny seems to answer '*with* our lives!' It would be better—*Death*—*death* alone will release us—"[26]

The Texans had been told on September 10 that they would not have to work the next day because it was a holiday in commemoration of Santa Anna's victory over the Spaniards that led to the evacuation of the port of Tampico. This was the last effort of the Spanish government to restore its control in Mexico. However, when the 11th came, there was a change in plans and the Texans were ordered out to work. When Copeland, who was playing cards, was slow to start immediately when ordered by an officer, "a dam[n] mean, low, petting fogging scoundrel, by the name of Unkatan-ka [Yucatanca][27] commenced beating on him with a large bludgeon, Copeland made a jump at him to jerk the stick out of his hands when two or three soldiers ran in cocked their guns on him and I believe," reported Glasscock, "would have shot, and was only prevented from doing [so] by us telling Copeland to let him go."[28]

Throughout the day "the old castle . . . [was] decorated with flags of all nations except poor Texas," and the cannon of the fort boomed at in-

22. Nance, ed., *McCutchan's Narrative*, p. 146.

23. *Ibid.*, p. 147.

24. *Ibid.*, pp. 148-49; Glasscock diary, Spet. 9, 1844.

25. Nance, ed., *McCutchan's Narrative*, p. 147; see also A. De Santa Anna to the E[xcellency] Wilson Shannon, Envoy &c. &c., National Palace, Sept. 5, 1844 (copy), in John Henry Brown Papers, TxU-A.

26. Nance, ed., *McCutchan's Narrative*, p. 149.

27. Bell, *Narrative*, p. 87; see also Glasscock diary, Sept. 11, 1844.

28. Glasscock diary, Sept. 10-11, 1844; see also Nance, ed., *McCutchan's Narrative*, p. 150.

tervals in celebration of the victory over the Spaniards.[29] A letter came from Benjamin E. Green, secretary of the U.S. legation, stating that he thought there was a "fair chance" of their liberation soon, and advised the boys in no. 7 to hold off for a while longer on their plans to leave without permission of the Mexican authorities. He reported that Shannon had scheduled another interview with Santa Anna on Monday, September 9, and that everything pertaining to the prisoners looked favorable. At least Shannon thought he might be able to get some of the men released.[30]

On September 12, William Atwood received a letter from Bankhead saying that he was in hopes of getting all English subjects, fourteen in number, released.[31] Pressure was mounting for the release of all the Texan prisoners.

Having received Santa Anna's negative responses to the release of the Mier prisoners, Shannon addressed a second communication requesting "a private interview." The president replied that he would be pleased to receive the U.S. minister at noon on September 12. Shannon, accompanied by Ben E. Green, called upon the president and they were "well received." As a result of their interview, Santa Anna agreed "to release all of the Texan prisoners on the 16th instant, that being the day of Mexican independence." Santa Anna wanted Shannon to inform his president "that he wished to cultivate the most amicable relations with the U. States, and that the interest of Mexico and that country was the same, and that he hoped his liberation of the Texan prisoners would be received by the President and people of the U. States as evidence of his liberality and friendly disposition."[32] Shannon thought it prudent to delay bringing up other matters of differences between the two governments "until the final action of the President in relation to the Texan prisoners" had been taken.

Orders were immediately issued, effective September 16. On September 14 Shannon received a letter from M. C. Rejón, secretary of foreign relations, saying, "His Excellency, the Constitutional President, on a day so easily remembered by the Fatherland, as that of the 16th of September, desires to give unequivocable proof to friendly nations of the magnanimity of the Mexican Republic, and of the earnest desire that it has in fomenting good relations with them, and to this end His Excellency, with heartfelt hospitality, has decreed that all Texans, who have been taken prisoners in actions of war, or invading the territory of the nation, and who are found imprisoned in whatever part of the Republic are immediately freed, solemnizing with this generous deed the day most significant for Mexicans."

---

29. Glasscock diary, Sept. 11, 1844.
30. *Ibid.*; Nance, ed., *McCutchan's Narrative*, pp. 149-50.
31. Glasscock diary, Sept. 12, 1844; Nance, ed., *McCutchan's Narrative*, p. 150.
32. Wilson Shannon to [John C. Calhoun], Legation of the U.S. of A., Mexico, Sept. 21, 1844, in Despatches from United States Ministers in Mexico, Nov. 10, 1843-Jan. 26, 1847, National Archives (microfilm).

Shortly after the death of his wife, as noted earlier, Santa Anna asked Congress for permission to go to his Manga de Clavo estate to mourn with his children. On September 12, after receiving the U.S. minister and dictating the order for the release of the Texan prisoners, Santa Anna departed for his *hacienda* without waiting for his friend and regular substitute, Gen. Valentín Canalizo. Canalizo had just reached San Luis Potosí to take command of the Army of Operations against Texas when he was notified of his elevation to provisional (substitute) president. He set out for the captial, where he arrived on September 19, and the next day he assumed the duties of provisional president from Gen. José Joaquín Herrera, president of the Council of Government.

The command of the army for the invasion of Texas was transferred to Gen. Mariano Arista, for the Mexican newspapers generally had disavowed the "disgusting barbarity" and inhuman behavior of Ampudia in his conduct of the war in Yucatán. Yet, commented the *Picayune*, with "the retirement, however temporary, of Santa Anna, and the recall of Canalizo, we are more and more convinced that the President sees the hopelessness of a contest with the Republic of 'the Lone Star.'"[33] In Mexico, more attention focused on internal problems and the rising tide of dissatisfaction against the dictatorship of Santa Anna, and the talk of invading Texas had begun to die out by September 1844.

As September 13 approached, vigorous preparations got under way at the Castle of Perote to receive Santa Anna, who was expected to visit the fortress on his way to his estate near Jalapa.[34] On the evening of September 14 the mail was received with the "*Great and glorious News*" that the Texan prisoners were "all" to be released on September 16.[35] "This almost unexpected news intoxicated many with a thrilling joy, they had never before experienced, some were so elated as to become frantic and shouts of gladness rang through the old castle, such a peal as had not been lately heard within those dismal walls."[36] While the glorious news of their release spread through the castle, Santa Anna, amid the booming of the guns of the castle, passed the fortress with his retinue on the way to his estate. It was still two days until the release would become effective, and in the meantime, the prisoners were still driven to work.[37]

Sunday, September 15, forty of the Texans, under a stronger guard than ever before, walked four miles to the old Powder Mill to carry back furniture to the castle. At three in the afternoon, on September 15, the prisoners marched into the blacksmith shop where they were relieved of their chains, and anticipation of their forthcoming release began to soar.

---

33. *Daily Picayune*, Oct. 16, 1844.
34. Glasscock diary, Sept. 13, 1844.
35. Nance, ed., *McCutchan's Narrative*, pp. 150-51.
36. Enclosure No. 4 in Wilson Shannon to John C. Calhoun, Legation of the U.S. of A., Mexico, Sept. 21, 1844, in Despatches from the United States Ministers to Mexico, Nov. 10, 1843-Jan. 26, 1847, National Archives (microfilm).
37. Bell, *Narrative*, pp. 96-97.

Greatly surprised were the "smithy" and the guard to see so many chains drop at the foot of the anvil with the least effort on the part of the wearer. McCutchan said he had worn his chain "without intermission on the same foot for better than six months," and now with its removal he could hardly walk.[38]

At four o'clock the long awaited official order for their release reached the castle. The governor sent for Fisher, and, after reading the order to him, instructed him to read it to the prisoners. The prisoners were paraded in the courtyard and Fisher read the order for their release.

When the release order for the Mier prisoners came, it was not in the way and manner it has so often been represented. Later, some of the prisoners themselves and other writers have mistakenly attributed their release to a death-bed request of Señora Santa Anna, the wife of the president who died on August 23, 1844. If that had been the case, why did Santa Anna reject on September 5, almost two weeks after the death of his wife, Shannon's first request for the release of the Texan prisoners?

That evening the prisoners put together the items they wished to take home or would need on the road. This was done quickly, since their belongings were few. A restless and sleepless night was spent as the men thought of home and began to make plans for the future. Long before daylight on September 16, the Texans were astir. They needed no prodding that morning. It was also a gala day for the Mexicans, who with considerable fanfare celebrated the anniversary of their independence. At dawn the cannon of the fortress commenced to boom, and no one, had he desired, could sleep under such noise anyway. Most of the Texans did not feel like eating anything during the day. The excitement of their release dulled appetites. "I myself," wrote McCutchan late in the afternoon, "have had [nothing] all day, and still have something of a sickly sensation at heart, and a feeling like something sweling in the throat and breast, at times almost to chokeing."[39] Most of the men folded their blankets, collected what few pieces of clothing they possessed, and tied their knapsacks and blankets in preparation for an early start for home. "Scarcely one of them had a two cent copper [coin] to buy a mouthful to eat by the way; nor even a [piece of] soap [*claco*] to pay for a dish of 'frijol[e]s' . . . or 'tortillos' to appease the cravings of a hungry appetite; but these obstacles presented nothing insurmountable in their way, since they were soon to be free, every other consideration was for the time swalloed up in that one dearest of all others, viz., Liberty," McCutchan said.[40]

Most of the men were "badly dressed," especially to appear outside the prison walls. A few had "tolerable good clothes . . . for this place," and others had "pretty good clothes and a little money but not enough to divide" with any of their comrades; "but I think we will make out—of Mexico," reported McCutchan, if only they could gain their freedom. The

---

38. Nance, ed., *McCutchan's Narrative*, p. 151.
39. *Ibid.*
40. *Ibid.*, p. 152.

prisoners were in debt to Don Francisco for an estimated $80, "for which he is well satisfied to wate," declared McCutchan, "till we reach Vera Cruz or our homes. The fact is he must *wate* this he is well aware of, and takes it easy. One of the men offered to give him an officer as security, but he refused saying 'that he had rather have the *word* of a Texian than the note of a Mexican officer.' "[41]

Great was their disappointment when they were kept waiting until three o'clock before the authorities were ready to proceed with the formalities incidental to the prisoners leaving the castle. Impatiently they waited. In the meantime, Colonel Fisher completed individual certificates testifying to the service of each prisoner being released. The following certificate was typical of those issued:

> Know all men, by these presents, that the bearer, Claudius Buster, was attached to Captain William S. Fisher's Company, As second lieutenant, on the seventeenth of October, one thousand, eight hundred and forty-two, and acted in that Capacity, up to the eighteenth day of December of the same year, at which time he was selected Captain of said Company, the latter post he has held, with honour to himself and Country, up to the present date.
>
> I do further certify &c. Given under my hand this sixteenth day of September—one Thousand eight-hundred and forty-four.
>
> William S. Fisher[42]

At three o'clock the Texans were paraded in double-file in the central courtyard of the castle. After they were kept standing for thirty minutes,[43] the men were marched to the governor's quarters, where the oath of parole was administered and signed, binding them never again to take up arms against Mexico.[44] "When called up to take the oath, some raised their right hand, some their left, and some neither raised a hand or responded to it in any way, but I believe *all*," recorded McCutchan, "or nearly so, were scinscere [sincere] in vowing *revenge* (even while the oath was being administered to them) for the fall of our companions in arms and countrymen, and for the ha[r]sh trcatmcnt which we as a body had received while in the power of the brutal foe. I made no response to the oathe, but was inwardly vowing *never* to grant mercy to a Mexican foe."[45]

After the oath had been signed, each Texan was given a *peso* by the governor to defray his travelling expenses to Vera Cruz,[46] some ninety-eight miles distant. It would in no way cover their expenses, but the prisoners thought little of it, so happy were they to be free. As each man de-

---

41. *Ibid.*

42. Certificate in the Daughters of the Republic of Texas Library, The Alamo, San Antonio, Texas.

43. Bell, *Narrative*, pp. 97-98.

44. *Ibid.*

45. Nance, ed., *McCutchan's Narrative*, p. 153.

46. Bell, *Narrative*, p. 98; Nance, ed., *McCutchan's Narrative*, p. 154.

scended the stairs from the governor's quarters to the *plaza*, he was handed an individual passport "in the presence of the troops of the garrison,
who were drawn up in front of our line," reported McCutchan,[47] which
would permit him to go wherever he chose and enjoined all Mexicans "to
treat the liberated Texans as friends and fellow citizens."[48] At five the 104
Texans stood at parade under Mexican military discipline for the last
time. As the Texans stood facing the Mexican soldiers, some thought how
happy they would be to "meet these troops face to face, and *hand* to *hand*
on a bloody field of death where *liberty* and *revenge* may be wone and life
is often lost."[49] As the ceremony of liberation progressed, Major Barilla
and several other officers who had been kind and at times even indulgent
towards the Texans "received the silent acknowledgment of the whole
party" of Mier men.[50]

Governor Jarero appeared before the troops and the former prisoners. He "delivered a short address to the soldiers and closed his remarks
to them saying—'Shout for your country' and immediately the walls of the
castle revibrated with their cry of—'Viva la República Méxicana.' Thrice
did they repeat their cry. The governor then turned to us," reported one
of the Mier men, "for an approving shout—he received something of an
half moaned yell from some, but even that was forced by them who uttered
it—and but scattering along our lines, and *Mexico* [was] not once mentioned. But the most of our little band stood motionless and silent as the
grave absorbed in our own reflections in the prospect of future *revenge*."[51]
Indelibly stamped upon their minds was the fact "that they had been the
fettered inmates of the frowning fortress" near Perote "for nearly twelve
months and captives in Mexican bondage twenty months and twenty days,
and absent from their homes, in Texas more than two years."[52]

As the ceremonies of liberation drew to a close, it commenced to rain.
Following the cheering, Jarero stood by as the Texans prepared to leave
"to embrace those [with] whom he was a little acquainted personally. He
gave me," said McCutchan, "the embrace of a friend, as he had once excused me from work when I was unable to do any thing."[53] In the rain, at
about six that evening amid a "deep and solemn roar" of a cannon salute
to them, as some of the Texans wanted to believe, followed by one to the
Mexican nation in commeration of Mexican independence, the jingle of
the chapel bells tolling vespers, and the smell of gunpowder, the Mier
men "sprang like beasts from a cage in which they had been fettered for
months" and poured through the castle gate and across the drawbridge
into the air of freedom. The weather, the hour, and the excitement re-

---

47. Nance, ed., *McCutchan's Narrative*, p. 154.
48. Bell, *Narrative*, p. 98.
49. Nance, ed., *McCutchan's Narrative*, p. 154.
50. Bell, *Narrative*, p. 87.
51. Nance, ed., *McCutchan's Narrative*, p. 154.
52. Bell, *Narrative*, p. 98.
53. Nance, ed., *McCutchan's Narrative*, p. 155.

called to memory the thrilling events "of *Mier on the 25th day of December 1842*. In less than thirty minutes . . . [they] were scattered over the valley like sheep without a shepperd, or rather wild horses, without a leader. Perfectly wild in appearance. Some three went to Mexico [City], five or six to Tampico, and the rest . . . to Vera Cruz,"[54] forty leagues distant. "Some even started, late as it was, and walked three leagues that evening," before lying down beside the road to rest until daylight. "About [forty to] fifty . . . went into the town [of Perote], one mile from the castle," where they obtained lodging for the night.[55]

As soon as daylight arrived on September 17, the men were again on the move, strung out along the road in groups of two, three, or even larger—sometimes alone. They plodded along in the rain "or rather mountain mist,"[56] which kept up all day. After going twelve miles, the road ascended "from the flat and trenched plain up the rugged mountain acclivities, winding its way through moaning forests and [by] mouldering crosses, whose omnipresent warning perpetually reminds the traveller in Mexico of the perils that surround them."[57] At noon they stopped to eat in small squads at a little town. They made a fire under a shed and cooked their meal much after the Texan camp fashion, which drew "the attention of the dark sons of pusilanimous Mexico," reported McCutchan.[58]

As the Texans made their way to the coast, they camped or took quarters at night and ate together in small groups as they had customarily done in prison. Prison life had welded all of the men into a close comradeship; but the small "mess" groups were the closest.

Louis S. Hargous, an American merchant and the United States vice consul at Vera Cruz, with the approval of Colonel Fisher and Judge Gibson, made arrangements for the Mexican schooner *Rosita*[59] to take the released prisoners to New Orleans. Just as everything seemed to be in readiness to sail, no Mexican ship captain could be found to command the *Rosita,* so the Mexican schooner was sold and converted to the *Creole* under U.S. registry. The new owners accepted the same terms as contracted by the owners of the *Rosita,* and Captain Dessechi was obtained to command it.[60] The arrangement was to transport and provide provisions for 108 men to New Orleans, reported McCutchan, "at the enormous price of *three thousand two hundred dollars,* or about *thirty dollars* each! This vessel, too, is nothing more than an old Topsail Schooner not worth (going to its real value) *fifteen hundred.*"[61]

---

54. *Ibid.,* p. 154.
55. *Ibid.,* pp. 154-55.
56. *Ibid.,* p. 155.
57. Stapp, *Prisoners of Perote,* p. 158.
58. Nance, ed., *McCutchan's Narrative,* p. 155.
59. Sometimes written "Rosetta." *Galveston News,* Nov. 8, 1844; *Telegraph and Texas Register,* Nov. 13, 1844.
60. *Telegraph and Texas Register,* Nov. 13, 1844; *Daily Picayune,* Aug. 21, 1844; L. S. Hargous to Reuben M. Porter, Vera Cruz, Oct. 5, 1844, in Comptroller's Letters (Texas), Tx-A.
61. Nance, ed., *McCutchan's Narrative,* p. 167.

The British government bore the expenses of the ten or twelve who were considered subjects of Great Britain. Hargous assumed the expense of helping the Mier men home, believing that Potter and "the people of Texas in general will do all in their power to see any disbursements paid." Already the Texan government owed him money. In all Hargous expended on his own account $3,740.38 in chartering passage for the Mier men and in furnishing them with various necessities.

When it came time to sail, only 105 went on board the *Creole.* Twelve decided to remain in Mexico for the time being, intending "by their labor to try and raise money to transport themselves from this unhospitable region, very resonably thinking," reported Bell, that their "present prospects for getting home were very dull," as there was no assurance, when they made their decision, that transportation would be available from Vera Cruz.[62] From the list of those released and those who reached New Orleans on the *Creole*, we know the twelve left behind were William Atwood, D. F. Barney, Dan Davis, John E. Dusenberry, Charles McLaughlin, Theodore D. Maltby, William H. Moore, A. Mosier, William T. Parker, William M. Shepherd, James Wilson, and William Wynn. Maltby was still convalescing at Puebla. Joseph F. Smith and William F. McMath obtained their own passage and left Vera Cruz before the main body of men. Francis Hughes and William Y. Scott returned to Texas from Matamoros. George W. Bush, who escaped while at work in the mountains on August 23, 1844, made contact with his comrades either before they reached Vera Cruz or afterward and went with the main body to New Orleans.

The Mexican government's attitude toward former Texan prisoners who wished to remain in Mexico is illustrated by the British minister's letter to Bocanegra, the minister of foreign relations, in reference to the released Santa Fé prisoners. Pakenham stated that he had received Bocanegra's note of June 18, 1842, stating that "orders had been issued to the Commandants General of Mexico and Puebla, and of the Cantonment of Jalapa to make known to the Texian prisoners, lately set at liberty by command of his Excellency the President that they may, if they think proper, remain in the Republic seeing that, as pardon has been granted to them in the name of the Mexican Nation, they are no longer considered as enemies, but that, on the contrary, they shall receive the same protection as granted by law to Foreigners in general residing in the country."[63]

By special invitation of Captain Dessechi, Colonel Fisher was invited aboard the *Creole* on Friday, October 4, to inspect the vessel and to conclude final arrangements for sailing.

Finally, on October 16, the former prisoners boarded the vessel that would take them from Mexico. McCutchan's diary provides an account of the voyage.

62. Bell, *Narrative,* p. 99.

63. Richard Pakenham to [Bocanegra], Mexico, June 20, 1842, in Chabot, ed., "Texas Letters," in Yanaguana Society *Publications* 5, pp. 157-58.

17th. *At last*! we bid adieu to land and try our fortune at sea. Some went on board at 10 o'clock A.M. Others at 12 M. Others, with myself at 2 P.M. and the last (with the exception of Fisher, Gibson, and Lyons [Lyon] at 4 P.M. At sunset this evening, with the exception of the three before mentioned, we are all on board and as merry as men could be who expect soon to see their homes, country, and friends. And I assure you that our merryment was unbounded.

I think that I have set foot on the soil of Mexico for the *last* time, untill an opportunity may offer for me to again raise an arm in defence of the rights of Texas, and for my own *deep* vengance and retribution on their heads for the unparalleled murders which they have left as monuments to their shame. . . .

18th. The vessel upon which we find ourselves is an *old* Topsail Schooner, or Brigantine, of one hundred and twenty tons burden, and every timber seems to be decayed save her masts, and they appear sound; but she has lately been coppered with new mettal, and has reasonably good riging. She has a perfect *"tub"* bottom—is said to be 17 years old, but looks to be twenty five, at least; and so all appearances will not sail more than seven "knotts an hour." Upon the whole she is a crazy, rotten old craft, not worth saving from a gale; but, perhaps, by the aid and protection of Divine providence we may reach New Orleans in her, but the case is exceedingly doubtful. However, any thing, the bottom of the gulf—or, any thing that may come in preference to this City of Perdiction and iniquity.

About 6 of clock P.M. a heavy gale arose, or came *down* from the North, and thus it is that our worst enemy, Miss Fortune, continues to bear us company, regardless of the many plain hints which we have given her to leave us. But we *should* be thankful! with no great reason to complain.

19th. During the whole of last night we experienced great inconvenience from the rolling of the vessel, but nothing serious occured. At five this morning the wind lulled, and at least [later] it again arose, but not so high as it was in the outset. At ten P.M. the wind calms down to a gentle breeze from the southward.

20th. We have fair weather and a prospect of sailing in two or three days. We are induced to hope that Fisher will come aboard to day.

21st. Oh, how this dull delay does effect the mind! The mind being wholely engroced and the feelings entirely absorbed in the one grand wish to depart, and that wish being partially satiated by a faint hope, disappointment is rendered doubly accute, and the mind double pevish and fretful. But it is, I think, a virtue in a man to accommodate his will and desire to conflicting circumstances. . . .

Tuesday, the 22nd. *All hail, most glorious morn!* The danger is past, the work is done, and we sail to day. O what an expression of joy is thare contained in that word. It is *True* this time, and no mistake. We Sail to day. Fisher, Gibson, Lyons, and the Captain of the vessel came on board half past six, and we sailed a little after seven A.M.

Up goes the fore and main sails, while the anchor is drawn from its bed to the sailors merry not[e] of Ho, he ho! and, like the light winged birds of heaven, lightly our boat gives way to the wind. Fare well! Fare Well thou base and oppressed people—if ever I press thy putrid soil again with my foot, *may it* be to reek a terrible vengance for wrongs inflicted and to free thousands of you from your galling yoke, *only* to *hurl* you into *eternity.*

We stand to the eastward to clear the breakers and shoals, running with all canvass spread and a light wind at the rate of only six miles an hour. Rather slow for we who are so gifted with impatience as this little band seem to be; but we can but awate our time; and come when it will, I will feel thankful for mercies thus bestowed.

I think that it is time that I had made some enquiry abo[u]t the commander of this craft, the crew, and the strange[r]s, of which latter I find several on our decks. I will enquiry about the matter.

To begin then with the captain of the vessel, which is my duty. He is a Native of France, speaks English verry well, has been in the gulf trade for a long time between Vera Cruz, New Orleans, and Havana, is about thirty three or four years of age, and that is all I know of him, except that he is a good looking fellow.

The crew, which is next in order, is a complete mixture of various countries. . . . Two of them are english and the other is a Scotchman. Our rightful crew are—First and second mates—cook and three seamen. The first mate is a Havana Spaniard or perhaps a Mexican; the second mate is either a creole Frenchman or a Spaniard; the cook is Frenchman; two American sailors; and one Maltese; so we have a complete assortment.

The strangers come next in order. There is a Irishman and his family (three children and a wife) who have been residing in Mexico for some time and are now going to try the United states. He is not much or he would not put his family on board with such piratical looking fellows as we are. Then thare are four others, who I do not know any thing about.

Then comes, last but not least, the Texians, who, to judge from their appearance have been raised on the Deck of a pirate ship and tutored amid scenes of *Dirt, Smoke, Fire, blood and Death!* Some (or in fact all who can raise them) have an overgrown pa[i]r of whiskers and mustachios, with long, kinked, and sunburnt hair, and for the want of hats, we generally wear a handkerchief on the head tied to a turban. *Really an interesting group.* And if this vessel does not sink before we reach our Destined port, then I will acknowledge the falacy in juding from appearances. Thare are cords of Sin and eniquity on board of us.

2 o'clock P.M. We tack and lay an northwesterly course. Breeze verry light. At nine P.M. we can still plainly distinguish the light hous[e] on the Castle of San Juan de Ulloa close in on land north west of Vera Cruz.

23d. We had a light wind all night.

The Mountain of Orazabo is in sight all day. Calm from 12 M to 2 P.M.—then a light breeze.

At sunset the wind arose, and we now have a good breeze. Seven knots per hour at sunset.

24th. We had a stiff breeze all night, and under all the canvass she could bear and all the wind she could stand our vessel only ran about 8 knots per hour. Plague on the old wash Tub bottomed thing.

We can see no land. . . .

25th. A calm from Nine A.M. to one P.M.—than a light breeze from the South East, or east south east, with which we make headway of about five knotts an hour. Owing to the peculiar roundness of the keel of our vessel and its awkward-luberly shape, we make great leeway, in consiquence of which we lay nearly north-East to make the North point; that is, if the wind be near ahead.

26th. Running as usual—slow, and not *verry* sure. The wind howls towards the north east, and we give to it—still runing on the northwest tack.

Thare is great anxiety among the men with regard to the water, as we are now drinking sour water, which was put up in wine casks, and its quite pungent in its taste.

Sunday, 27th. Still light winds, and occasionally a calm.

There are a great ma[n]y of us sea sick, though I am not yet, nor do I fear it.

We have a great row today, and I will now state the particulars. In looking around, some one found two or three ship's casks filled with water, which was to us (who have been using sour water for some time) really splendid—excellent to the taste, so we took a notion to drink a little of it, which notion we carried into effect by drawing it with a vial belonging to some of our number. But about one o'clock P.M. when the mate (1st mate, the Mexican) wanted some water on deck, he asked some of the Texians to help him, to which several assented their willingness by immediately jumping down the hatch and fastening onto a barrel, but lo! and behold! it was a barrel of the good water! When the mate discovered this he requested that it should be replaced in the hold of the vessel, and the men acted accordingly to his request, taking instead a barrel of sour water; but we determined that the sick should have good water at all hazards as long as thare would be any on board. In about an hour, or less from this, one of the sick, an Englishman by birth and George Lord by name, drew a pint of fresh water from a barrell, and was drinking it when the mate mistrusting something went below and on seeing Lord he snatched the cup from him and threw its contents in his face, for which Lord knocked him down without a word of cerimony, and would have thrashed him well, but was kept off of him by our own men. As soon as the Mate could recover his standing position, he went to the cabin and got a pare of Pistoles, which I, myself seeing communicated to Lord that he should be on his guard. Fisher told the Captain not to allow him to go below with the pistoles, but the capt. thinking [it] a useless warning, payed not attention to it; and as the Mate jumped down the hatch, several voices exclaimed at once *"Throw him overboard! kill the Mexican! if he dares attempt to draw a weapon."* But he was either too smart to attempt it, or his courage was not sufficiant. When the captain heard these hurried exclamations, mingled with the most horrid imprecations, he could no longer doubt as to the probable fate of his Mate, if he should draw a weapon and wisely judging it best to stop his mate, just at the moment when several were preparing to lay violent hands on the body of the Mexican; but he came in time to save him and his only remedy was to order the mate aft and command him not to interfear with us. The capt. was the most livid featured living man I have ever seen. He supposed that we were destitute of everything like Conscience, and feared, least in our rage, we should murder the whole crew. But he knew us not, for a man of any nation but Mexico could have had a fair fight, but the moment a Mexican or Spaniard should attempt a row, he met the whole force. Thus ended the affair with the First Mate.

Gale from the North. Oh, it is perfect scissors. We roll and pitch like a dieing whale. We were some what surprised at this storm, for about day break we were becalmed and laying to, when upon a sudden all sails were ordered in and before the time could expire, which was necessary for reafing, we were going under bare poles at a tremendous rate directly before the wind. This continued but for a moment, when up went the fore and main sail, close scafed [reafed?], then the gib with the bonnet off and we were brought up to the wind, as near as could be, then we lent away to the eastward with a vengance. The Billows rolling mountains high, the vessel reals to the blast, and on and on we spring like a thing of life.

29th. Calm, or nearly so, at 3 of clock, this morning, though the sea still runs high. The wind is South East. We run in the same tack.

The wind rised at 10 o'clock A.M.—heavy gale from the north—sea rolls mountains high—we begin to look for a long leap into Eternity.

30th. The wind subsided at 12 o'clock at night, and left a smart sea which became nearly smooth at daylight.

Calmed untill 12 o'clock M when we have a fine breeze from the north East, and we tack to the northward.

31st. The north East wind still continues and we keep the northward course.

November, 1844

Now Homewhard *[sic]* my lads. Home, Home, Sweete Home

> We are homeward bound
> Let the joyful sound
> Ease our hearts, and cheer us,
> And our foes still fear us,
> And we can sing "*Homeward bound*."

Friday 1st. We came in sight of land this morning, but the Capt. fearing a squall and wanting sea room, tacked to the southward. And thus we fare, expect such men to act in all such vessels as this. We saw lights on shore a little after dark, which gave our timid captain such a fright that he gave the order, "About Ship"—and obedient to the voice, around we swung and made way to the Southward.

Saturday, 2nd. About 8 o'clock A.M. we put about again—now stearing north east—east north East for the Balize. At 10 P.M. the animating shout of "*The Light House! the light house!*" was heard from the lookout at the Mast head, striking through our organs of hearing with the effect of electricity, and upon close investigation or examination the report was confirmed, and in the course of three hours we were laying to, under "bare Poles," awaiting the dawn of day. And oh, what comfort was that, with which we reposed within view of the coast of our Native land. Sweet and calm was the sleep which that night stole over our illfated band. And yet it was not unmingled with sensations of unfeigned fear least a gale should sweep us off, even when so near our long desired homes. Although a cessation of our troubles was desired and anxiously prayed for (that is if we prayed for any thing). Yet, looking back on the fatality which seemed to have been our attendant from the first, we could not tremble still between hope and fear; and amid all our joyous clamor and hurra, there was the sign of dread anticipation.

Sunday, 3rd. This morning the joyful sight of land met our first gaze with the dawn. And oh, happy pleasing sensation, *it is* "the land of the Free, the home of the brave."

4th. At daylight we are a long distance still below the City. I have not been on this master piece of Nature since December, 1840, and it was then night when I passed where we now are, consiquently I can amuse myslef by taking a view of the scenery of the Banks on each hand, which consists principally of large sugar plantations. But, by far the most amusing acts or objects to me are the movements of our nearest neighbors—the occupants of our vessels mate in size—a topsail schooner—who are negroes from Baltimore it seems on their way to Louisiana, and who interest themselves in viewing and commiserating our destitute condition. Some of them (among the rest a large Buck Negro) threw some tobacco over to some of the boys. I was aloft at the time and it was sufficient to excite the sympathies of an adamantive heart to see the voracious and haisty struggles which ensued to gain the small bits of tobacco thus donated by the generosity of *Slaves*. . . .

We reached the City of New Orleans at 4 o'clock P.M., and found the good citizens of that City all turned heels upwards with the election, as it was the day on which was held an election for President—we were an utter blank—having no firends, *no* home, and not much country. We could do nothing, nor did we know what we should do for something to sustain life. . . .

We hoist a signal for a pilot and tow. The pilot comes, but the Tow Boats pay no attention. However, about 8 o'clock A.M. one of the Tow Boats came down within speaking distance and then holding on steam, made the foll[ow]ing enquiries, to which the following answers were returned by the pilot. "What vessel is that, and where is she from?" "The Creole from Vera Cruz." "What are all those men doing on board?" "They are Texians released from Mexican prisons." But this even did not seem to have satisfied his curiosity, and I am under the impression that he thought us rather a suspicious looking set, which we were. He approached with caution, and at length, having become convinced of our good designs, or that we held no ill ones, he fastened on to us and off we went like an arrow. After conveying us a short distance above the separation of the three passes, he droped us, giving orders to let go our anchor and await his return with instructions, averse as they were to our desires, we could but obey, while the Tow passed down to the mouth again after another vessel. Here we felt almost over powered by the emotions which you may well suppose would animate men on again viewing the land of their people, after an incarceration of *twenty months and twenty one days* with most wretched treatment. But we had not long for reflections of this kind ere the Tow hove in sight, and Taking a Barque on one side and a Brig on the other, with two topsail scho[o]ners astern of her she started up the river with us. We were delayed, from one fault or another, on our passage up, and night closed upon us without hope of reaching the city before the following day.

5th. After sleeping all night [with others] by permission on board the vessel, I arose feeling quite hungry from having eat [or] drand [drank] nothing, nothing save water, except 1 cup of coffe, since the morning of the 4th. But I knew not where or how to satisfy my hunger. Hard and Pittiable is the wretched fate of him with whom fortune is severe, and casts upon a land distant from friends, among strangers, without food— without money—without clothes, and too ill, both in body and mind, to work. . . .

[November] 6th. We have nothing to avert the attention. I have engaged a passage on board the *New York* bound for *Texas*! Oh, the bare mention—the *thought* of that Country calles up before me recollections too painful—also too pleasin[g] for a notice of this place! *Texas* the country of my adoption—my *devotion*! The Steamer "New York," Captain Wright was to have sailed to day, but Sea Captains will not comply at *all* times with their promises. I do not aim this at *all* sea captains, but it will strike the majority.

7th. We had the pleasing knowledge this morning that we should assuredly "cut cables" this day. But about 10 of clock A.M. we received intelligence to the effect that the steam ship *Republic* had entered the river, which has induced Capt. Wright to lay untill she shall have entered port. This is far from pleasing or desirable to us, as our only wish, it seems, is to land on Texian soil. Although that country did forget us in adverse circumstances, we now, when enjoying the divine gift of sweet liberty, have a deep and lasting reverential affection for her—we feel with the poet that "thare is no place like home."

At the hour of 1 of clock P.M. the *Republic* touched the Wharf, and at 2 of P.M. the *New York* pushed off into the stream with a full head of steam, and we were soon under good headway, with hearts as light as the air.

Here, for the sake of Justice and satisfaction to all, I will mention that thare were many of the men who were anxious to come on board, promising to pay their passage as soon as they *could,* but Capt. Wright was misanthropic enough to refuse a passage to the poor fellows until John M. Brown, actuated by that same noble generosity that has characterized his career since I k[n]ew him, kindly steped fo[r]ward and offered his name to Wright as responsible for the whole amount. This was sufficient to satisfy the *Noble Captain Wright,* and all who wished it soon obtained passage on board the vessel. . . .

We lay all night at a wood yard. Some 25 miles below New Orleans. We have quite a merry time. Thare are seventy six of us on board and all (two excepted) of that number take Deck passage.

8th. By dawn of day we were under weigh and making a line towards Texas. . . .

Sunday the 10th. Ah! Great and eventful day! ever to be remembered by me as my second entrance into the land of *Texas.*

At Daylight, we found ourselves in sight of land, and bouyant were our feelings on that account. About sunrise a wind was apparent, and we feared for a moment that we should be baffled and miss our landing. However that thought was soon crushed, and we hastily neared the land. Crossing the bar, we lay for the pass between Bolliver point and that of Galveston Island. As approaching nearer, and yet nearer to the Isle, oh, what joy was thare depicted in each countenance! As they stood gazing, as if entranced, you could see happiness on every face.

With proud anticipations we reach the Wharf—not a shout—not a hurra—not a sound of wellcome, went up towards Heaven, evincing the joy of our countrymen at our return! No friendly hand was stretched out to congratulate us, save those who had, perhaps, a personal friend, or rellative among! How, then were our proud anticipations of an honorable wellcome dashed to earth! No—Oh, no—even though no glad sound wellcomed our return to home and Liberty—we yet had one proud— grand satisfaction of which the coldness of our countrymen could not deprive us! *We would soon be on the soil of that country for which we suffered, many bled, and many died!* Grand—consoling thoughts to a soldiers heart.

Now we touch and leeping on shoar soon seem mad with joy! While the concourse of people, naturally drawn togeather by the arrival of the Steamer, stand around with various remarks—some make the cold—half enquiry and half assertion, "These are the Perote prisoners," and being affirmatively answered, proced to make enquiry about Mexico—Perote— how we got off—were we released—or did we escape—and how we arrived at New Orleans? with a thousand other curiosities to satisfy—and upon being satisfied—some would retire, perhaps, to speculate in their minds upon what our situation might have been while confined in the dungeons of Mexico:—while others perhaps, a little more humane in *words,* would procede to an investigation of our situation in prison, right in our presence, and with their expressed pitty and grief at our misfortunes, would render us almost as unhappy as we were in prison. Yet it seemed that all were studiously careful to avoid an enquiry into our present condition. I, however, was provided for, for thare I had a brother, and thare I was at home! But, Great God! what was the condition of many of my companions? Without a home thare, and without a friend save among those who were as destitute as they themselves;—they were forced to stand on the wharf or wander out to seek for what they had no hope of then finding.

As for myself, upon reaching the wharf, I stood on board the steamer for the space of three or five minutes, seriously contemplating the scene around me and contrasting our brillant anticipations with our cold reception. Little had I thought that Texians would thus receive their firends. After thus standing for a short time I steped on the wharf, sullen, and despondent; not a smile to wellcome me back. On the wharf I met my Brother, who had just been informed of our arrival. Then I was *at home,* in the complete sense of the word; but, oh, how different was the situation of others! Many of them, perhaps, possessing the acquaintance of not one single individual in the city, apart from our own men, and without the means of procuring a days sustinance! What, I ask, must have been the feelings of those men thus thrown upon the *Charity* of that people for whom they had fought, bled, and suffered indignities beyond conception without a murmur, and from whom had orriginated to us the base epithets of *Coward, traitor*, and *Outlaw!*—and above all knowing as they did by experience that, that people held within their bosom but verry little of Heavens Gift—called Charity. I thank God that I am indebted to the people of Texas for naught, save the base epithet of Outlaw! Orriginating from a source still more degenerate—*Sam Houston!* He it was, who, when sorrow and trouble stood over us, at the verry time when a word from him would have procured us the protection of the Civilized World, with that natural baseness of his life, deserted us! Not content with our misfortunes, he boldly declared that the expedition was *unauthorized*, thereby bring[ing] death to many—and a protracted incarceration to others! That is one *Lie* for which Sam Houston will answer to his maker, and I doubt not but that in Eternity he will remember it. . . .

Now after a series of repeated trials and misfortunes, the majority of us are here in Galveston. We left some in Mexico, a few in New Orleans, and the remainder, seventy six in number, are about to separate, perhaps, forever. It is a sad thought, for misery has made us the family of her patronage and our feelings are those of a family; but we *must* part and many of us will Never again meet![64]

---

64. Nance, ed., *McCutchan's Narrative*, pp. 166-91.

CHAPTER 27

Back Home Through the Years

IN CONCLUDING THE STORY of the Mier Expedition, one may wonder how the survivors fared after their return home. As the years passed a number of the Mier men received recognition, honors, and responsibilities from their fellow man, but not all were successful. We can examine what the record shows and how the men were regarded, but not lengthy biographical sketches, and for some there is little reliable information—they just faded away.

Of the Mier men, Francis Menefee White served in the Convention of 1845 that gave assent to annexation and framed the first constitution of the State of Texas.[1] After statehood a number of the former Mier-San Antonio-Dawson prisoners served in the legislature of the State of Texas, while several others served at various times as officers in the state legislature.

James H. Neely of Montgomery County served as sergeant-at-arms of the Ninth Congress and of the Convention of 1845, and in the Senate of the First Legislature of the state;[2] and Francis Hughes, who had lost the use of an arm from a wound received in the Battle of Mier, served as doorkeeper in the Senate of the First Legislature, February 16 to March 13, 1846.[3]

During the war with Mexico, 1846-1848, many of the Mier men volunteered for service against their hated enemy and often were able to exact retribution for the harsh treatment they had received as prisoners. They saw in the service of a stronger nation an opportunity for greater success than they had found in 1842. At least sixty-nine Mier men, ten Béxar prisoners, and three of Dawson's command rallied to the Stars and

---

1. Gammel, comp., *Laws of Texas* 2, p. 1230; [Jennett, comp.], *Directory of the Conventions and Congresses of the Republic of Texas, 1832-1845*, pp. 41-42.
2. [Jennett, comp.], *Biographical Directory of the Conventions and Congresses of the Republic of Texas*, pp. 40, 42.
3. [Yett, comp.], *Members of the Legislature of the State of Texas*, pp. 3-5.

Stripes. Some of those who had composed the Texan Camp Guard at Mier and had not fought in the Battle of Mier, now had an opportunity for action. Eight of the apparent forty-two survivors of the Camp Guard saw service in the Mexican War. Gen. Zachary Taylor could not have asked for better fighting men than the Texans; but when the battle was over, they were most difficult to control because of their animosity and their desire to take vengeance upon the Mexicans.

When William Dunbar returned to Galveston from imprisonment in Mexico, he married Caroline Simpson on February 9, 1846. By 1850 he had moved to Bastrop, where he was elected clerk of the Bastrop County Court, and served from 1850 to 1854.[4] He died in Bastrop on December 20, 1855.[5]

After Dr. William M. Shepherd returned from Mexico, he went to New Orleans. In October 1855, he was in Columbus, Mississippi, where he edited the *Eagle*. How long he was editor of the paper is not known, but on February 13, 1858, while in Travis County, Texas, he personally signed the warrant issued to him by the State of Texas for his services on the Mier Expedition.[6]

James O. Rice of Austin, who was wounded in the Battle of Mier and had, with several other wounded Texans, escaped from the hospital in Mier on January 20, 1843, soon after his arrival home joined the Snively Expedition. With the breakup of that expedition, he returned to the Austin area, and on November 5, 1846, married Nancy D. Gilliland.[7] When Williamson County was created in 1848 Rice was one of the commissioners appointed to select the county seat. Claiming permanent disability in the service of the Republic of Texas growing out of the wound he received in the Battle of Mier, Rice was granted a league of land by the legislature on January 31, 1850. He became one of the largest landowners in Williamson County, and built his home on Brushy Creek at a site known as Blue Hill and later called Rice's Crossing. He operated a store at this location and was postmaster of the Blue Hill Post Office, 1849-1857. For a short period he operated a tanyard in Georgetown, but later returned to Travis County, where he died about 1875.[8]

Returning to Victoria after his release from Perote Castle, Daniel McDonald was elected sheriff of Victoria County on February 3, 1845. McDonald previously had been elected sheriff of Victoria County on April 19, 1839, commissioned on May 1, 1839, and re-elected on February 1, 1841.

---

4. Baker, comp., *Texas Scrap-Book*, p. 593; Dixon and Kemp, *Heroes of San Jacinto*, pp. 145, 150; Hayes, *Galveston* 1, pp. 305, 394, 406, 421; Moore, *Bastrop County*, p. 56.

5. Schoen, ed., *Monuments Erected by the State of Texas to Commemorate the Centenary of Texas Independence*, p. 177.

6. *Texas State Gazette*, Oct. 27, 1855; William M. Shepherd, Public Debt Papers, Tx-A.

7. William L. Mann, "James O. Rice: Hero of the Battle of the San Gabriel," *SWHQ* 55 (July 1951), pp. 30-42.

8. *Register of the Elected and Appointed Officials of the Republic of Texas* 1, pp. 342-43; 2, p. 121.

The people of the county had not lost faith in him because of his partici-pation in the Mier Expedition.[9]

When Leon County was created and organized in 1846, William B. Middleton, returned prisoner from Mexico, was elected its first sheriff.[10]

Upon his return from imprisonment in Mexico, John Himes Liver-good was elected justice of the peace of Precinct 3 in Lavaca County, and on December 23, 1857, he sought compensation from the state legislature for three months' service in the army.[11]

When Gideon K. Lewis returned to Texas from Mexico, he settled in Galveston. He became associated with Willard Richardson in publishing the *Galveston Weekly News* and managed the *News* when Richardson went on a tour of the country. While Richardson was away, Lewis bought out the local theatre in the city and managed both it and the *News* "with consid-erable profit to the firm."[12] As relations between Mexico and the United States became more critical, he followed Taylor's army to Corpus Christi and persuaded Samuel Bangs of the *Corpus Christi Gazette* to join him in publishing a newspaper in Matamoros to be called the *Rio Grande Herald*. The *Herald* did not materialize, although a prospectus appeared in the New Orleans *Daily Picayune* on June 14, 1846. Instead, Bangs and Lewis commenced publication of the *Matamoros Reveille* on June 14, 1846, as a semi-weekly in both English and Spanish. He joined Samuel H. Walker's Company of Texas Mounted Rangers, recruited primarily in Corpus Christi and Point Isabel, which was mustered into Federal service from April 21 to July 16, 1846. Upon being mustered out of Walker's Company, Lewis re-enlisted on January 13, 1847, in Maj. Walter P. Lane's battalion and served until June 30, 1848. In Lane's battalion he often served as an express rider, and rose to the rank of captain. Lewis settled at Corpus Christi and in 1852 formed a partnership with Richard King and Capt. Mifflin Kenedy to establish a 70,000-acre ranch on Santa Gertrudis Creek, forty miles from Corpus Christi. At the time of his death he was a candi-date for Congress from the West Texas District against Peter H. Bell, who was seeking reelection, but was shot and killed on April 14, 1855, by Dr. J. T. Yarrington for carrying on a love affair with the doctor's wife.[13]

One of the youthful members of the Mier Expedition, Robert Harper Beale, at age twenty-eight, was elected sheriff of Fort Bend County in 1850. On March 16, 1850, by action of the legislature, he was granted a league of land for having been permanently disabled in the service of his country. His disability resulted from the Battle of Mier, where he had been

9. Schoen, comp., *Monuments Erected by the State of Texas to Commemorate the Centenary of Texas Independence*, p. 164.

10. *Register of the Elected and Appointed Officials of the Republic of Texas*, 2, p. 40.

11. Spell, *Pioneer Printer: Samuel Bangs in Mexico and Texas*, p. 129.

12. *Galveston Daily News*, Apr. 8, 1851; *Texas Monument*, Apr. 16, 1851.

13. Wharton, *History of Fort Bend County*, p. 116; Sowell, *History of Fort Bend County*, p. 216; Gammel, comp., *Laws of Texas*, 3, p. 399; [Yett], *Members of the Legislature of the State of Texas*, p. 86.

shot through the lung. Yet he now took on the duties of sheriff in one of the more thickly populated counties of the state. In 1874 he was chosen sergeant-at-arms of the House of Representatives of the Fourteenth Legislature of the State of Texas.

On his return to Texas, after having escaped from prison near Tacubaya, James Charles Wilson became editor of the *Planter* at Columbia, and a candidate in March 1845, for district clerk of Colorado County. In the election there was a tie vote between Wilson and his opponent, P. J. Fish, so there had to be a runoff election. In the second vote, one more vote was cast than in the first and Wilson was elected. "The clerk elect," commented the editor of the *Texas National Register* in Washington,[14] "is said to be well qualified for the office. He is an aspiring young gentleman, with fair talents."

Wilson served in the House of Representatives of the Third Legislature and in the Senate in the Fourth Legislature. In 1851 he became a leader in the Matagorda County Southern Rights Association. In 1852 he was operating a general merchandise store in Brazoria.[15] In 1856 he became a member of the board of trustees of Soule University in Chappell Hill, Texas.

Another who served in local government after his return from Mexico was John Fitzgerald. Elected justice of the peace of the Eighth District of Harrisburg County on February 4, 1839, Fitzgerald was, after his escape from prison in Mexico, elected sheriff of Harris County on April 27, 1844, and was commissioned on May 16, 1844. He served for a year. Later he was chosen secretary *pro tempore* of the Houston City Council, and early in January 1846, was elected by the City Council to be city treasurer and secretary.[16]

When John Harvey got home, he was elected surveyor of Bastrop County on February 3, 1845, and commissioned on November 22, 1845.

Mark M. Rodgers returned to Bastrop after he was released and was elected tax assessor for the County of Bastrop in 1846. In 1848 he was elected sheriff for two years.[17]

After his return from Mexico, Fenton M. Gibson practiced law in Richmond, and between 1852 and 1854 he edited the weekly *Richmond Recorder*, successor to the *Brazos Delta*. In it he published an account of his adventures in the Mier Expedition. He later moved to Austin, where on September 1, 1856, the Texas legislature ordered the comptroller of public accounts to issue warrants to Fenton M. Gibson in the amount of $1,796.67 "for balance of pay due said Gibson for services as Quarter Master of the Mier Expedition."[18] In March 1857, Gibson became editor

14. *Texas National Register*, Aug. 7, 1845.

15. *Ibid.*, Feb. 1 and May 29, 1845; *Telegraph and Texas Register*, Jan. 28, 1846.

16. *Register of the Elected and Appointed Officials of the Republic of Texas* 2, p. 5.

17. Moore, *Bastrop County*, pp. 56–57.

18. "An Act for the Relief of Fenton M. Gibson and William Oldham," September 1, 1856, in Gammel, comp., *Laws of Texas* 4, p. 757.

of the Austin *Texas State Times,* and when the *Texas Sentinel* replaced the *Times* in the summer of 1857, he became its editor.[19]

After his return James A. Glasscock worked as a printer and served in the army during the Mexican War. He went to San Antonio in 1848 with Michael Cronican and John Henry Brown to establish the *Western Texian,* the first English-language newspaper published in San Antonio. After the death of Cronican from cholera in 1849, Glasscock became the editor of the *Western Texian* on April 27, 1849, and in November 1849, transferred his interest to Nathaniel C. Lewis and John D. Groesbeck.[20] Early in 1850 Maj. Robert S. Neighbors was sent to organize El Paso, Presidio, Worth, and Santa Fé counties. Glasscock accompanied him as far as El Paso and from there continued to the gold fields in California. In 1859 he was living in Siskuyou County, California. He died in California in 1876.

The Congress of the Republic and the state legislature passed many individual relief laws providing money and land to compensate for services performed and to provide assistance to indigent veterans or their surviving widows and children. There seems to have been no discrimination against the Mier men and their families on account of the unauthorized nature of the expedition. The discussion here will be limited to the Mier-San Antonio-Dawson men.

Congress provided on February 3, 1844, that Monia E. Goodwin, Louisiana Harris, Eliza Harris, "and other heirs at law," of Robert W. Harris, one of the decimated Mier men, should receive a Land Office certificate for 320 acres of land in place of Certificate No. 217 (2nd class) which had been issued to Robert W. Harris by the Board of Land Commissioners for Bastrop County, dated December 19, 1839.[21] Two days later, Congress appropriated $150 to pay Samuel G. Norvell, one of the San Antonio prisoners, for five months' service as a soldier under the command of Capt. John C. Hays during 1842.[22] A year later, Congress ordered the secretary of the treasury to pay William Bugg, also a returned Woll prisoner, for his service as a private in Capt. John C. Hays' Company.[23] The pay ordered by Congress for the services of Norvell and Bugg in Hays' Company did not cover the period of their imprisonment in Mexico.

On December 19, 1844, soon after their return from Mexico, four captains of the Mier Expedition petitioned the Congress of Texas on behalf of themselves and their former comrades, for "pay from the com-

---

19. Sibley, *Lone Stars and State Gazettes: Texas Newspapers before the Civil War,* pp. 357-58.

20. Day, *Black Beans & Goose Quills,* p. 102.

21. "An Act for the Relief of Monia E. Goodkin, Louisiana Harris, Eliza V. Harris, and Other Heirs at law of Robert W. Harris, Deceased," Approved, February 3, 1844, in Gammel, comp., *Laws of Texas* 2, p. 1042.

22. "Joint Resolution Making an Appropriation for the Pay of Samuel G. Novel [Norvell] for Services Rendered the Republic of Texas as a Soldier," Approved, February 5, 1844, in Gammel, comp., *Laws of Texas* 2, p. 1044.

23. "Joint Resolution for the Relief of William Bugg," Approved, January 29, 1845, in Gammel, comp., *Laws of Texas* 2, p. 1090.

mencement of the company [campaign] to the time of their release and compensation for their private expenditures in fitting themselves out and as in duty &c."[24] The petition was also presented in the House of Representatives of the Ninth Congress on December 24, 1844, by Simeon L. Jones of San Patricio, and at his request was referred to the Committee on Military Affairs of which William G. Cooke was chairman, with instructions "to enquire into the expediency of affording relief to the unfortunate persons lately returned from Mexico, and who were among the Mier prisoners, and report by bill or otherwise."[25]

The Senate Committee on Finance reported on January 6, 1845, that $4,500 had been expended upon the Mier prisoners.[26] Three weeks later, after repeated efforts in the House to pass an acceptable bill for the relief of the returned prisoners,[27] a joint resolution for the relief of the Mier prisoners and others was sent to the Senate. It reached the Senate on January 25,[28] and was read the first time on January 28. On the 29th it was referred to the Committee on Finance, and the next day the Finance Committee made its report, with a majority recommending rejection of the bill. The Senate took up the Committee's report on January 31 and voted approval of the report by a vote of six to five of the Senate. Later in the day the House was notified of the Senate's rejection of the joint resolution.[29] The next day, on a motion of Senator George A. Pattillo, the Senate reconsidered its vote on the Joint Resolution for the Relief of the Mier Prisoners and Others, and agreed to take another look at the joint resolution. When the Senate reconvened the Committee on Engrossed and Enrolled Bills reported "A joint resolution for the relief of the Mier Prisoners and others," and its report was adopted. Later in the afternoon of February 3, the "Joint Resolution for the Relief of the Mier Prisoners and Others" was read a third time, passed, and sent to the Committee on Engrossed Bills, which reported a few minutes later that "it had examined and found correctly engrossed the amendment of the Senate" to the bill. The Senate adopted the report, and rushed the bill to the House for its consideration of Senate Amendments. February 3 was the last day of the Regular Session of the Ninth Congress, so the House, upon receiving the bill at seven that evening, gave immediate attention to the Senate alter-

---

24. F. M. Gibson, Wm. Ryon, Claudius Buster, [and] J. G. W. Pierson to the Honourable the Senate and House of Representatives of the Republic of Texas in Congress assembled, Dec. 19, 1844. D. S. 2 pp. Endorsed: Mier Prisoners, Read Dec[r]. 19th 1844 & Referred to a Select Com[e] Smith, McCreary, Pillsbury, F. M. Gibson, in Memorials and Petitions, Tx-A.

25. *Journals of the House of Representatives of the Ninth Congress of the Republic Texas*, p. 106.

26. *Journals of the Senate of the Ninth Congress of the Republic of Texas*, pp. 116-22.

27. *Journals of the House of Representatives of the Ninth Congress of the Republic of Texas*, pp. 106, 120, 150, 212, 224, 269-70, 280-81, and 391-92.

28. *Journals of the Senate of the Ninth Congress of the Republic of Texas*, pp. 116-22, 219.

29. *Journals of the House of Representatives of the Ninth Congress of the Republic of Texas*, p. 367.

ations, and after a brief discussion, agreed to concur in them.[30] Shortly thereafter the Congress adjourned *sine die*. The "Joint Resolution for the Relief of the Mier Prisoners and Others" failed to become a law, owing to a "pocket veto" by Anson Jones, the new president.

Efforts by individual Béxar, Dawson, and Mier prisoners to obtain compensation or relief often were rejected by Congress. For instance, James L. Trueheart, clerk of the district court of Béxar County, asked the Ninth Congress for relief as a Béxar prisoner, but the Committee on Claims and Accounts reported on January 3, 1845, "That in the opinion of the Committee, it was inexpedient at this time, to allow holders of such claims any further relief than is now provided by law."[31]

As time passed, and before there was any general compensation or pension law, special laws were enacted to aid individual Mier-Béxar-Dawson prisoners and others who had suffered in the cause of Texas against Mexicans and Indians. Examples of some of these attempts at special relief measures for the Mier-Béxar-Dawson men and their families may be of interest.

By a joint resolution, approved February 1, 1845, and amended June 27, 1845, the Extra Session of the Ninth Congress granted one league and one labor of land out of the unappropriated public domain each to Francis Hughes, John R. Baker, Henry Wicks [Weeks], G. B. Pilant, and George W. Trahern, Mier prisoners, on account of having been permanently disabled in the service of the country.[32] While the financial condition of the Republic did not permit paying L. S. Hargous of Vera Cruz and G. B. Lamar of Savannah, Georgia, for advances they had made to the Santa Fé prisoners and their transportation home, Congress on June 24, 1845, acknowledged their claims and promised to pay them at as early a date as possible.[33]

On June 27, 1845, Congress extended the deadline established in 1840 for filing suits to clear land titles to January 1, 1847, for "all persons captured and detained by the Mexicans, as prisoners of war, in the year of our Lord one thousand eight hundred and forty-one and two, their heirs and legal representatives."[34]

When Robert H. Beale, who had escaped from the hospital in Mier and made his way to Texas, learned that those Mier prisoners who had paid their own passage and expenses home from Mexico had upon appli-

---

30. *Ibid.*, pp. 391-92.

31. *Journals of the Senate of the Ninth Congress of the Republic of Texas*, p. 101.

32. Gammel, comp., *Laws of Texas* 2, pp. 1112-14.

33. "Joint Resolution Acknowledging the Claims of L. S. Hargous and Others," Approved, June 24, 1845, in Gammel, comp., *Laws of Texas* 2, p. 1203.

34. "An Act Supplementary to An Act to Detect Fraudulent Land Certificates, and to Provide for Issuing Patents to Legal Claimants," Approved, June 27, 1845, in Gammel, comp., *Laws of Texas* 2, p. 1213; *Laws Passed by the Extra Session of the Ninth Congress of the Republic of Texas*, p. 27.

cation to the customs collector of Galveston been paid "at least some thirty one Dollars" for their passage from Vera Cruz to Galveston out of the funds appropriated by Congress for the relief of the Mier men, he sought reimbursement for his expenses home. However, when he called upon the collector for his "expenses as one of the wounded who escaped from Mier, he was advised to take the matter up with the Secretary of the Treasury Department," and he did. "Now," he told the secretary, "see if you consider me embraced in the intention of the appropriation act," and if so, "favor . . . me . . . by addressing the necessary instructions of payment to the Collector at Galveston in an envelope directed to me" at Richmond.[35]

Similarly, A. B. LaForge, who had escaped from Perote Castle with Thomas Jefferson Green and had been furnished transportation to Texas by the kindness of Louis S. Hargous, sought reimbursement from the Texas government. He wrote to the Texan secretary of the treasury, "By the advice of our mutual friend J. D. [H.] Cocke, Esqr Collector of the Customs at this port [Galveston], I herewith hand you a receipt for Twenty Five Dollars, being the amount due me by the Government of Texas, as one of the Mier prisoners—You will oblige me by forwarding an order for the amount to the Collector of this port, or transmit the same to my order in any manner you may deem proper."[36]

From Fort Bend County John A. Sansberry petitioned Congress on April 4, 1846, for a grant of land, saying that he had lost an eye while serving on the Mier Expedition.[37]

Later, Robert H. Beale, wounded in the Battle of Mier, received by a relief act of March 16, 1848, a league and a labor of land for having been permanently disabled in the service of the country.[38] On February 9, 1850, John R. Baker received recognition by the legislature of his claims against the Republic of Texas and an authorization for payment in the amount of $889.50.[39]

Samuel G. Norvell, one of the Béxar prisoners, while en route to Mexico City, had been left sick at Querétaro and had, upon his arrival in Mexico City, been released from imprisonment late in January 1843. He received through a special enactment of Congress, on February 5, 1844,

35. Robert H. Beale to W. B. Ochiltee, Secy Treasury, Washington, [dated] Richmond February 21, 1845, in Connor, ed., *Texas Treasury Papers* 3, p. 1082.

36. A. B. Laforge to Secy Treasury [John Alexander Green], Austin [dated] Galveston, Novr. 6th '45. Endorsed: Recd. Galveston Novr. 1845 from the Hon ——— Twenty Five dollars being the amount due me by the government of Texas as one of the Mier prisoners. A. B. Laforge (in Connor, ed., *Texas Treasury Papers* 3, p. 1122).

37. John A. Sansberry to the Congress of the Republic of Texas, Fort Bend County, April 4, 1846, in Memorials and Petitions (Texas), Tx-A.

38. "Joint Resolution for the Relief of Robert H. Beale, Who Was Permanently Disabled in the Service of the Country," Approved, March 16, 1848, in Gammel, comp., *Laws of Texas* 3, p. 399.

39. "An Act for the Relief of John R. Baker," Approved, February 9, 1850, in Gammel, comp., *Laws of Texas* 3, p. 761.

$150 for five months service as a soldier under the command of Capt. John C. Hays in 1842.[40]

Furthermore, Norvell was approved by the state legislature on January 19, 1850, to receive a headright of 640 acres.[41] A second relief measure was passed less than a month later to compensate Norvell and William A. A. ("Bigfoot") Wallace for service in Capt. John C. Hays' Company of Rangers. Norvell was taken prisoner at San Antonio by General Woll and Wallace was one of the Mier prisoners. Norvell was paid $650 and Wallace $487, "in accordance to provisions of an act to provide for ascertaining the debt of the Republic of Texas," dated March 20, 1848.[42]

After annexation a bill was introduced on November 19, 1849, in the House of Representatives to reimburse the Mier and Santa Fé prisoners for their services and for the loss of personal property. The bill passed the House on January 28, 1850, and the Senate on February 4, and was approved by Governor J. Pinckney Henderson on February 9. It authorized the payment of $22.50 per month to the men from the date of mustering into service until one month after the main body of prisoners were released by Mexico, plus an additional maximum of $65 for the loss of horse, arms, and equipment, for an average of $605. The law specified that the individual recipient must have been "actually taken and imprisoned." Those who were members of the Camp Guard of the Mier Expedition, or who escaped from Mier after the battle, were paid $67.50 for three months' service and given an allowance of $65 for horse and equipment, for a total of $132.50.[43]

Dr. William F. McMath, who was released from imprisonment on September 16, 1844, received $1,601 in payment of his salary, for his horse, and for equipment furnished on the Mier Expedition.[44] Thomas Jefferson Green was compensated in the amount of $3,044.[45]

The heirs of James Barber of Bastrop, on October 23, 1851, sought land from the legislature for his services on the Somervell Expedition in 1842; he continued on the Mier Expedition and was wounded in the battle at Mier and died in Matamoros on March 14, 1843.[46]

---

40. "Joint Resolution Making an Appropriation for the Pay of Samuel G. No[r]vel[l], for Services Rendered the Republic of Texas as a Soldier," Approved, February 5, 1844, in Gammel, comp., *Laws of Texas* 2, p. 1044.

41. "An Act for the Relief of Samuel G. Norvell and John H. Carter for 640 A. Land Each as their Headrights," Approved, January 19, 1850, in Gammel, comp., *Laws of Texas* 3, p. 704.

42. "Joint Resolution for the Relief of Samuel G. Norvell and William A. A. Wallace," Approved, February 8, 1850, in Gammel, comp., *Laws of Texas* 3, p. 754.

43. "A Bill to be Entitled An Act to Provide for the Pay of the Mier Prisoners," House Bill, No. 123, 3rd Legislature, State of Texas. Original MS, Tx-A; see "An Act for the Relief of Certain Persons, formerly Prisoners of War in Mexico," Approved, February 9, 1850, in Gammel, comp., *Laws of Texas* 3, pp. 594-95.

44. William F. McMath, Public Debt Papers, Tx-A.

45. Thomas Jefferson Green, Comptroller's Military Service Records, Tx-A.

46. Heirs of James Barber to the Legislature of the State of Texas, Oct. 23, 1851, in Memorials and Petitions (Texas), Tx-A.

On February 13, 1854, the Fifth Legislature provided relief in the form of land grants to several of the former Béxar-Dawson and Mier prisoners, or their widows and heirs: Rebecca Jane Fisher (widow of William S. Fisher), 640 acres; Mariana Hutchinson (widow of Anderson Hutchinson), 640 acres; Samuel G. Norvell, 836 acres; John Mills (deceased), 320 acres; Lawson Mills (deceased), 320 acres; William H. [Y?] Scott, 177 acres; William [Harvey] Sellers, 320 acres; and one third of a league of land to William Rupley, in lieu of Certificate No. 1065, issued by the Board of Land Commissioners of Harrisburg [later, Harris] County.[47]

A legislative act of September 1, 1856, authorized the comptroller of public accounts to issue a warrant to William Oldham, "for the pay which he is entitled as paymaster in Col. Cooke's Regiment in the somerville *[sic]* campaign in the year 1842, and 1843, deducting the amount already received by him as a private in said campaign."[48]

Whitfield Chalk, who had escaped from Mier after the battle, filed claim on December 23, 1857, for an additional $472.50 above what he had already collected, as if he had been a member of the Camp Guard, since he had returned home with the members of the Guard. He believed he deserved the compensation for services on the Mier Expedition from the date of mustering into service until one month after the main body of prisoners was released in Mexico. He had earlier been turned down for this amount because he had not been "actually taken and imprisoned." However, through the efforts of Senator George B. Erath, he was now paid.[49] Thus, Chalk received as much for his services on the Mier Expedition as did those who suffered a prolonged imprisonment.

It is difficult to know to what extent men of the Mier Expedition participated in the Civil War. A few of them served actively in the Confederate forces, but more, on account of age and/or infirmities and family responsibilities, probably were active on the home front protecting the Texas settlements from Indian raids by serving in the "home guards" and rendering service in a number of ways other than in active service on the battle fields of the Civil War.

One of the brigadier-generals of the Texas state troops was H. Clay Davis, who commanded Brigade No. 31.[50] Davis and McBeth deserted Colonel Fisher's command on the march to Mier.

Alfred S. Thurmond served as a captain in Gen. Tom Green's Brigade during the Civil War. In 1867, he was en route to South America on a ves-

47. "An Act for the Relief of Certain Persons therein Named," in Gammel, comp., *Laws of Texas* 4, pp. 137-41.
48. "An Act for the Relief of Fenton M. Gibson and William Oldham," Passed September 1, 1856, in Gammel, comp., *Laws of Texas* 4, p. 757.
49. Claim No. 1665, Public Debt Papers, Tx-A.
50. Marcus J. Wright, *Texas in the Civil War*, p. 59.

sel bound for Tuxpan when the vessel shipwrecked and Thurmond was drowned.[51]

With the outbreak of the Civil War, John Reagan Baker organized a home guard company and was chosen its captain. After the war, Baker moved from his home in Saluria, Matagorda County, to Hynes Bay in Refugio County, where he was elected sheriff. He later moved to Goliad County, and still later to Indianola, and entered the mercantile business. Finally, he moved in 1876 to Wilson County, where he operated a ranch and raised sheep for twelve years on Cibola Creek, five miles from Stockdale. He died in Stockdale, Wilson County, on January 19, 1904, at the age of ninety-four years.[52]

George B. Erath resigned his seat in the Texas Senate in 1861 to serve on an arbitration committee for Indian affairs. With the beginning of the Civil War, he raised an infantry company and affiliated with the 15th Texas Regiment, but was soon discharged on account of ill health. In 1864, his health improved, he was appointed major of a regiment to protect the Second Frontier District.[53]

Governor Sam Houston commissioned William Kinchen Davis on October 26, 1860, to be treasurer of Fort Bend County. During the Civil War Davis commanded a company of men for six months.[54]

Upon his return to Texas from imprisonment to Mexico, William F. Wilson was appointed quartermaster of the Second Regiment, Texas Militia, by President Houston on June 20, 1843.[55] On February 3, 1845, he was reelected sheriff of Galveston County and was commissioned on February 22.[56] On July 8, he was named Indian agent at the Omaha (Nebraska) Agency by President James Buchanan.[57] When the Civil War began, Wilson returned to Virginia, where he became a captain in the Virginia Volunteers on May 8, 1861. Less then two months later he issued a call for the formation of a company of Rangers in Winchester, Virginia, July 5, 1861, which he organized for the Confederate service.[58]

What service William M. Ryon may have performed for the Confed-

51. Baker, comp., *Texas Scrap-Book,* p. 631: Wade, "Alfred Stugis Thurmond," *Frontier Times* 16 (Aug. 1939), pp. 472-74.

52. John R. Baker, Public Debt Papers (Texas), Tx-A; Thomas P. Morris, "Sketch of Captain John Reagan Baker," *Galveston News,* Jan. 24, 1904.

53. Erath, ed., "Memoirs of Major George Barnard Erath," *SWHQ* 27 (Oct. 1923), pp. 159-60.

54. Wharton, *History of Fort Bend County,* pp. 114-16.

55. "The Wilson Scrap-Book," TxU-A; see also "The Wilson Scrap-Book," *QTSHA* 1 (Oct. 1897), p. 132.

56. *Register of the Elected and Appointed Officials of the Republic of Texas* 1, p. 377, 2, p. 34; Hayes, *Galveston* 1, pp. 279, 300, 304, 350, 394, 398, 417, 421; "The Wilson Scrap-Book," *QTSHA* 1 (Oct. 1897), pp. 132-33.

57. Commission of William F. Wilson as Indian Agent at the Omaha Agency, Dated June 5, 1858, and signed by President James Buchanan, in "The Wilson Scrap-Book," TxU-A.

58. The commission of W. F. Wilson as a Captain in the Virginia Volunteers dated May 8, 1861, and signed by Governor John Letcher, in "The Wilson Scrap-Book," TxU-A.

eracy is not clear, but it must have been important, for it was necessary for him to obtain a pardon from the president of the United States after the war. He was issued a pardon for his rebellion on July 23, 1867, by President Andrew Johnson.[59]

William Harvey Sellers, a youthful member of the Mier Expedition, fought in the Civil War. "His blade," declared the editor of the Austin *Daily Democratic Statesman*, "was one of the brightest and keenest that flashed beneath the Southern cross." Harvey Sellers was only fifteen years of age, when, without his mother's consent and without considering her need of him, he joined the Somervell Expedition to the Rio Grande. During the war with Mexico he served as first lieutenant in Capt. Tom Green's Company in Col. John C. Hays' Regiment of Texas Rangers and fought in the Battle of Monterrey. At the end of the war, he settled in Houston and engaged in the mercantile business until 1851, when he moved to New York and became a member of the commercial firm of Bowman, Sellers & Company. With the beginning of the Civil War, he "returned to Texas in 1861 and joined the Bayou City Guards & [was] elected 2nd Lt. of the company. When the company was attached to the 5th Regt. of Texas troops, he was made Adjutant; and when that command was attached to Hood's Brigade, he was continued in the office with the rank of captain, and when Hood was made division commander, he became Adjutant, with the rank of Lieut.-Colonel, and was promoted to Colonel when Hood was assigned to command the army corps. At the second battle of Manassas, Colonel Sellers commanded the left wing of Hood's army, and was afterwards recommended for promotion to the position of Brigadier by General Longstreet."[60]

When the Civil War ended, Sellers returned to New York and became a partner in the commercial house of J. H. Brower & Co. He played an important role in the establishment of the first regular steamship line between the port of Galveston and New York. Sellers remained in New York until the winter of 1867-1868, when he returned to Galveston and entered in the cotton trade, and sent the steamer *Pioneer* loaded with cotton to Liverpool. Sellers was the leading figure in founding the Merchants' Insurance Company of Galveston, in the organization of the New Wharf and Cotton Press Company, and in the formation of the Galveston Cotton Exchange on May 27, 1873. He was elected the first president of the Exchange. Sometime before his death, he took his family to Lexington, Virginia, for the education of his children. His family was still in Lexington when his sudden and unexpected death occurred in Galveston on April 10, 1874.[61]

---

59. The original pardon document is in the Fort Bend County Museum, Richmond, Texas.

60. "Galveston Sketches," pt. 2, pp. 293-95. Typed MS, Tx-A.

61. *Daily Democratic Statesman* (Austin), Apr. 14, 1874; *Galveston News*, Apr. 12, 1874; "Galveston Sketches," pt. 2, pp. 293-95.

John Rufus Alexander, at age forty-three, enrolled as a private on June 8, 1861, in a volunteer infantry company known as the "Dixie Grays," commanded by Capt. Joseph J. Cook, and on October 28, 1863, his birthday, he enlisted as a private for six months in Capt. Martin Martindale's Company of unattached infantry, Fayette County, 2nd Brigade, Gen. William Webb, commanding Texas Troops.[62]

During the State Fair of Texas in Houston in May 1873, the Texas Veterans Association was organized. Prior to the opening of the fair, Brig. Gen. Jerome Bonaparte Robertson, doctor, soldier, and civic leader of the Republic and of the State of Texas, issued a call from his home in Brenham to the old veterans of the Republic to meet in Houston at the time of the fair. Robertson had been active in promoting the cause of the veterans in Texas and his influence among them was extensive. During the closing days of the Civil War he had succeeded to the command of Hood's Texas Brigade. More recently he had been elected "secretary to the old veterans" at their meeting in Corsicana, where they had petitioned the legislature for a new pension law.

He stated that the purpose of the meeting of the veterans was to form "a permanent organization of those survivors for *mutual pleasure and benefit,* and to place correctly on the roll, the names of those who are entitled to that honor."[63] He requested those who would be unable to attend to write to him so that their names could be placed correctly on the roll. He said that a proposal would be made to divide the veterans "into two or three classes, according to date of arrival in the country, service, etc., and to include in the last class all who served a regular term of not less than three months against Mexicans or Indians up to annexation, the details to be arranged at the meeting."[64] In another letter "To the Old Veterans of Texas," which he requested be published in the *Galveston Daily News*, Robertson emphasized that those who might be unable to attend the meeting in Houston should write to him in Houston, "giving date of arrival in the country, date of service, etc., with postoffice and county of present residence, and I will see that their letters are laid before the meeting."[65]

A veteran, under the pen-name of "Prairie Cabin," wrote to the editors of the *Galveston Daily News* that he thought most of the veterans "would gladly accept the invitation to meet in Houston, or any other place, on certain public occasions, but for the plain fact that most of them

---

62. Wade, comp., *Notes and Fragments of the Mier Expedition* 1, pp. 13-14; Weyand and Wade, *An Early History of Fayette County*, pp. 273-74.

63. *Galveston Daily News*, Apr. 23, 1873.

64. J. B. Robertson to the Old Veterans of Texas, Brenham, April 21, 1873, in *Galveston Daily News*, Apr. 23, 1873; see also, *Galveston Daily News*, May 5, 1873.

65. J. B. Robertson to Eds. [*Galveston Daily*] *News*, Brenham, Apr. 21, 1873, in *Galveston Daily News*, Apr. 24, 1873.

are too poor—either to get an outfit proper for the occasion, or the means to pay their expenses."[66]

On Wednesday, May 14, 1873, one hundred and twenty-five of the old veterans met at the dance hall on the grounds of the State Fair in Houston and temporarily organized with Judge Edwin Waller as president and Moses Austin Bryan as secretary. A roll of members present was made, and a constitution adopted for a permanent organization to be known as the Veterans Association of Texas.[67] The constitution provided for annual meetings of the association, and established three classes of veterans, known as First, Second, and Third Class veterans. First Class included the surviving members of Austin's "Old Three Hundred" and soldiers, seamen, and citizens who could give proof of service in Texas between 1820 and October 15, 1836. Second Class included soldiers and seamen who could show proof of service at any time between October 15, 1836, and November 1, 1837. Third Class included those soldiers and seamen who had proof of service between November 1, 1837 and annexation in 1845. All of the Mier men were Third Class Veterans, unless they were able to establish a claim to service in one of the other two categories, and a number of them were able to do so.

Having organized and adopted a constitution, permanent officers were chosen. Frank W. Johnson was elected president; Capt. William S. Russell, who commanded a company in the Battle of Velasco in 1832, vice-president; Walter P. Lane, second vice-president; and George Bringhurst, recording secretary.[68] Following the election of officers, Col. Guy M. Bryan made a patriotic and stirring address.

The state conventions of 1874 and 1875 of the Texas Veterans Association were held in Houston, but thereafter the annual meeting was held in some thirteen different cities in the state and took place during the week of April 21, San Jacinto Day.[69] In May 1874, in the fifth annual State Fair in Houston, seventeen of the former Mier prisoners attended the second annual convention of the Texas Veterans Association.[70]

The editor of the *Galveston Daily News* met Edward Manton of Fayette County, a Dawson prisoner; Andrew Meill of Galveston; and James L. Trueheart of San Antonio, both Béxar prisoners captured by Gen. Adrián Woll. Out of the fifty-two prisoners taken at Béxar (San Antonio) by General Woll, only ten were known to be living in 1874, and only Neill and Trueheart of the ten attended the veterans meeting that year. Of the fif-

66. *Galveston Daily News,* Apr. 19, 1873.
67. *Ibid.,* May 15, 1873.
68. *Ibid.,* May 15, 18 (Supplement), and 20, 1873.
69. *Ibid.,* May 19, 1874.
70. Attending were John Rufus Alexander, John Bate Berry, Benjamin Boone, Henry Bridger, Claudius Buster, John [James H.] Calvert, William [A.] Clopton, William Davis, Freeman W. Douglass, Jeffrey B. Hill, G. [John] H. Livergood, George Lord, William B. Middleton, Orlando C. Phelps, William Ryon, D. H. [Van] Vechten, and Henry Woodland. *Galveston Daily News,* May 24, 1874.

teen Dawson men captured near Salado on September 18, 1842, only Edward Manton of Fayette County and Milvern Harrell of Gonzales County were alive in 1874.[71]

During the Fair, the veterans, 425 strong, were led in parade through the streets of the city by a band. Col. Charles DeMorse made the principal speech, giving a review of the history of Texas, and the Rev. Z. N. Morrell, pioneer Baptist minister, offered a prayer. Governor Richard Coke attended the meeting but declared that he was not there to make a speech, but to observe, and in behalf of the people of Texas to honor and greet the veterans. He told them that in April he had signed a pension bill in their behalf. This was the new pension law, which was approved on April 21, 1874 (San Jacinto Day).

The pension law was more comprehensive than one enacted in 1870 by the "scalawag" government of Governor Edmund J. Davis. It granted "pensions to the Surviving Veterans of the Revolution which separated Texas from Mexico, including the Santa Fé and Mier Prisoners, the Survivors of the Company of Captain Dawson, who was massacred near San Antonio in the year 1842; the Survivors of those who were captured in the City of San Antonio in the fall of the year 1842, and taken to the Castle of Perote and confined therein; and the Survivors of Deaf Smith's Spy Company; and to provide for the liquidation and settlement of all arrearages due said Veterans under an Act of the thirteenth of August, 1870, previous to the first of July, 1874."[72] The law provided an annual pension of $150, commencing July 1, 1874, payable semi-annually on January 1 and July 1 of each year, "for and during their natural lives." In any case where the individual may have been permanently disabled by means of wounds received in actual service, or who may now be disabled by loss of sight, or limb, from any cause," he was to receive "an additional pension of one hundred and fifty dollars for the same time and upon the same terms."

Also, "in recognition of the gallant deeds and services rendered by the Patriots that fought for the independence of Texas," the law provided for a silver medal to be given to every soldier who had participated in the battles for independence. "The medal on one side to have the name of the veteran, company and regiment, and on the other side a Lone Star of Texas."[73]

In 1879 the Legislature extended the privilege of wearing a medal to all veteran soldiers and seamen of the Provisional Government and of the Republic of Texas "who [had] served a tour of duty prior to annexation," and specified that the medal was to be of "the same size and in all respects similar to the medal prepared by Colonel John Forbes, commissary general of the army of independence of the Texas republic, and one of the veterans under the provisions of said act of 1874, and in accordance with instructions from his excellency Governor Richard Coke."[74]

---

71. *Galveston Daily News*, May 24, 1874.

72. Gammel, *Laws of Texas* 8, pp. 116-20.

73. *Ibid.*

74. "Joint Resolution Relating to Medals for Texas Veterans," Approved, April 17, 1879, in Gammel, *Laws of Texas* 8, pp. 1492-93.

The medal was not awarded by the state for meritorious service, but was *"permitted"* to be procured, engraved, and embossed by the veteran "at his own expense," after first obtaining from the governor "a letter of authority, authorizing" him to have such a medal cast.

Occasionally special relief laws were passed to meet neglected promises or to provide added relief. Mrs. M. A. C. Wilson, widow of Col. William F. Wilson of the Mier Expedition and sheriff of Galveston County, petitioned the legislature for the headright claim of 640 acres that her husband, now deceased, had been granted on December 6, 1838, but which had never been transmitted to him, and also for bounty warrant No. 5,031, for 640 acres issued September 6, 1838, and not received. Both claims were approved as "valid and subsisting claims against the state."[75]

In the late years of his life, the colorful old frontiersman and Indian fighter, William A. A. ("Bigfoot") Wallace, fell in need of assistance. A relief law was passed by the legislature, approved on March 30, 1889, giving him a certificate to locate and receive 1,280 acres from the public domain, for, said the legislature, he "has rendered the state great service and is now in necessitous circumstances."[76]

Attending this last meeting of the Texas Veterans Association were J. W. Darlington of Taylor; A. J. Kirchville [Kercheville] of Kyle; William P. Zuber of Austin; Milvern Harrell of Waelder; Alphonso Steele of Mexia; and Col. Asa Collingsworth Hill of Oakville. A memorial service for the veterans was held at the First Presbyterian Church in Austin on Saturday morning, April 20, in which the Daughters of the Republic of Texas took a leading part and several of their members addressed the group.

Some twenty years later, and a few days after an interview with Mart V. Fleming of Comanche, Texas, whose sister, Mary Elizabeth Fleming, had married Whitfield Chalk in 1847, D. K. Doyle reported in the *Dallas Morning News* of January 9, 1927,[77] that some twenty years ago the last meeting of the Mier prisoners was held in Austin, at which time there were six survivors. Fleming reported that when he was six or seven years old Shapley P. Ross often camped near the Fleming home in what is now Williamson County, and he reported that he had often listened to the tales told by some of the men who had been on the Mier Expedition.

Thus comes to an end the story of a small adventurous band of Texans of varying backgrounds and abilities, who loved, served, and died for their adopted country.

---

75. "An Act for the Relief of Mrs. M. A. C. Wilson, Widow of William F. Wilson," Approved, March 22, 1879, in Gammel, comp., *Laws of Texas* 9, p. 7.

76. "An Act for the Relief of William A. A. Wallace and to Grant Him a Certificate for 1,280 acres of Land," Approved, March 30, 1889, in Gammel, *Laws of Texas* 9, p. 1396.

77. D. K. Doyle listed the survivors in 1907 as Whitfield Chalk, William A. A. Wallace, Bate Berry, Mr. ———— Gore, Claudius Buster, and Caleb St. Clair. The truth is Claudius Buster died December 27, 1889; John Bate Berry died December 20, 1891; "Big Foot" Wallace died January 7, 1899; Whitfield Chalk died May 18, 1902, age ninety-two, in Lampasas County; Caleb St. Clair had died before 1907; and there was no one by the name of ———— Gore on the Mier Expedition.

Epilogue

IN ITS FRONTIER RELATIONS with Mexico after its victory at San Jacinto, Texas suffered numerous raids along its southern and southwestern frontier and four significant humiliating confrontations with major Mexican armed forces. The first, the Santa Fé Expedition of 1841, was a disgraceful surrender of an officially authorized expedition, hopefully bent on a peaceful mission to New Mexico, a Mexican department, to extend the exaggerated claim of jurisdiction of the Republic of Texas over that territory. The claim of jurisdiction was made by the Texas Congress in 1836, which set the southern and western boundaries of the new republic at the Rio Grande from its mouth to its source. The Santa Fé Expedition was not authorized by the Congress, nor was it the responsibility of that body. It was launched by President Mirabeau B. Lamar, who had become frustrated in his efforts to negotiate a treaty of peace and boundaries with Mexico.

Thus provoked, Mexico twice, once in March and again in September 1842, sent units of its regular army into Texas to seize San Antonio, but only in the latter instance was there a bloody encounter, followed by a hasty withdrawal of General Adrián Woll's troops.

In the fourth and last major confrontation, the initiative was with Texans, who sought retaliation against an enemy whose hit-and-run tactics on the frontier fomented a strong desire to carry the war into the enemy's territory. Mexico refused to recognize the *de facto* independence of Texas. For the purpose of bringing war home to Mexico, the Somervell Expedition was launched by President Sam Houston in the fall and winter of 1842. Brig. Gen. Alexander Somervell marched to the Rio Grande with authority to cross the river if he thought conditions were suitable for success and carry the war into Mexico.

Somervell captured Laredo without a fight and then advanced down the east bank of the river to Guerrero, where he crossed and seized that undefended town. He spent one night near the west bank of the river and recrossed to the Texan side, where he concluded it to be unwise to remain longer because of conditions within his forces and the belief that strong enemy forces were assembling to block his advance. He ordered his men to return to the settled area of Texas. The order touched off another revolt in his ranks. Already 187 of the drafted militiamen had abandoned the expedition in Laredo and returned home. Now some 309 men determined to continue down the river with the intent of attacking and, as they said, "ranking down," the Mexican towns below. Thus was born what came to be known as the Mier Expedition, an episode in the frontier relations between Texas and Mexico during the days of the Republic of Texas. The expedition marched under neither the authority nor the flag of the Republic of Texas. Its personnel assumed that they had a right under the laws of Texas to do what they did. When their rash conduct culminated in disaster at Mier, President Houston, without success, insisted that the Mexican government should honor and respect the terms under which the men had surrendered at Mier on December 26, 1842. The men of the expedition blamed Houston for their predicament.

While the Texans generally sympathized with the Mier men and had compassion for their families, the majority believed that they had acted irrationally and had used poor judgment.

To say that the results of the Mier Expedition were all negative would be a misstatement. The Santa Fé, Mier, Warfield, and Snively expeditions, of the period 1841-1843, all failed to accomplish their objectives, but they all showed the Mexicans that Texas was not to be trampled upon; that she was determined to maintain her independence; and that she stood ready to repel any Mexican raids upon her frontiers. On the other hand the Texans learned that Mexico was no push-over, and that she, too, would defend her frontiers, although she knew, but would not acknowledge, that the Province of Texas was forever lost to her. Thereafter, neither Texas nor Mexico made any major effort to attack the frontier of the other, but there still lingered the question of what was the boundary between the two nations. The question of boundary was not to be resolved until the conclusion of the war between the United States and Mexico in 1848.

Appendix

MIER EXPEDITION PERSONNEL
December 19, 1842–September 16, 1844

STAFF AND COMMAND

Name	Rank	Residence	Native State or County	Remarks
Fisher, William S.	Colonel Command'g	Washington	Virginia	Wounded in hand, Battle of Mier; released Sept. 16, 1844
Green, Thomas Jefferson	Aide	Brazoria	North Carolina	Commander of Flotilla & right wing; later received pay as Lt. Col.; escaped Perote Castle, July 2, 1843
Murray, Thomas W.	Adjutant-General	Victoria	Ireland	Left in Santiago Prison, Feb. 12, 1843; remained in Hospital Santiago, Sept. 12, 1843; Released to British minister, March 14, 1844; reached New Orleans, March 29, 1844
Gibson, Fenton M.	2nd Quarter-Master	Fort Bend	Georgia	From Wm. Ryon's Co.; released Sept. 16, 1844
Shepherd, William M.	Surgeon	Liberty	Virginia	From Wm. Ryon's Co.; released Sept. 16, 1844; did not return home immediately
McMath, William F.	Assistant Surgeon	Washington	Georgia	Released Sept. 16, 1844; left Vera Cruz Oct. 11, 1844, on *W. J. Huntington* for New Orleans
Sinnickson, John J.	Assistant Surgeon	Brazoria	New Jersey	From Charles K. Reese's Co., bearer of white flag at Mier; retained at Mier temporarily to take care of Texan wounded; released at Molino del Rey, near Tacubaya, July 21, 1843

COMPANY A — CAPTAIN EWEN CAMERON'S COMPANY

Name	Rank	Residence	Native State or County	Remarks
Cameron, Ewen	Captain	Victoria	Scotland	Shot by order of Mexican government at Huehue-toka, April 25, 1843
Ackerman, Peter A.	Private	Bastrop	New York	Released Sept. 16, 1844
Anderson, George W.	2nd Sgt.	Victoria	Scotland	Left in mountains, Feb. 18, 1843; reached Texas
Arthur, Francis	Private	Fayette	Massachusetts	Escaped from Perote Castle, March 25, 1844; re-captured; released Sept. 16, 1844
Baker, John Reagan	1st Lt. & Capt. Spy Co.	Refugio	Tennessee	Wounded at Salado, Feb. 11, 1843; left at Santago Hospital, Sept. 12, 1843; released Sept. 16, 1844
Bobo, Lynn	Private	Victoria	South Carolina	Wounded at Mier (broken thigh); died of wound at Matamoros, late Feb. or early March, 1843
Bray, Fernando	Private	Victoria	Germany	Musician; left in mountains, Feb. 18, 1843; not heard from; presumed dead
Brennan, John	Private	Victoria	New York	Interpreter; released Sept. 16, 1844
Canfield, Israel	Orderly Sgt.	Refugio	New Jersey	Released March 5, 1844
Cash, John L.	Orderly Sgt.	Victoria	Pennsylvania	Shot at Salado, March 25, 1843
Cocke, James Decatur	Major, in ranks as Brigade Sgt.	Harris	Virginia	Shot at Salado, March 25, 1843
Colville, Thomas	Private	Refugio	Scotland	Died at Powder Mill Prison, June 20, 1843
Dillon, John Thomas	Private	Victoria	Tennessee	Left at Santiago Hospital, Sept. 12, 1843; at San Juan de Ulúa Castle when released Sept. 16, 1844
Downs, George N.	Private	Victoria	Connecticut	Released Sept. 16, 1844
Glasscock, James Abner	Private	Victoria	Kentucky	Released Sept. 16, 1844
Gleason, Cyrus King	Private	Victoria	New York	Escaped Perote Castle, March 25, 1844; arrived in New York
Hoffer, John	Private		Pennsylvania	Released Sept. 16, 1844
LaForge, Alfred B.	Private	Liberty	New York	Escaped Perote Castle, March 25, 1844; arrived in New York

Lee, Alfred Alonzo	2nd Lt.	Victoria	Pennsylvania	Released Sept. 16, 1844
Leehan, Jeremiah	Private	Victoria	Ireland	Left sick at Santiago Hospital, Sept. 12, 1843; later moved to Puebla, where he was sick when liberated to the British minister, March 14, 1844; reached Galveston, June 7, 1844
Lewis, Gideon K.	Private	Victoria	Ohio	Captured Dec. 24, 1842, before the Battle of Mier; released Sept. 16, 1844
Lord, George	Private	Victoria.	England	Released Sept. 16, 1844
Lusk, Patrick Henry	Private	Washington	Tennessee	Captured Dec. 25, 1842, before the Battle of Mier; released April 23, 1844
McClelland, Samuel	Private	Liberty	Ireland	Died at Laguna Seca Rancho, March 30, 1843
McDonald, Daniel	Private	Victoria	New York	Released from Perote Castle, August 19, 1844
McKindel, John Alexander	Private	Harris	Scotland	Mortally wounded; died in hospital at Mier, Jan. 1843
McMichen, James M.	Private	Victoria	Virginia	Died, Santiago Hospital, Mexico City, Nov. 20, 1843
McMullen, John	Private	Galveston	Maryland	Released Sept. 16, 1844
Maher, Patrick	Private	Victoria	Ireland	Shot at Salado, March 25, 1843
Mallon, Nathaniel R.	Private	Béxar	Massachusetts	Wounded in Battle of Mier; escaped from hospital at Mier, Jan. 20, 1843
Martin, William J.	Private	Jackson	Kentucky	Died at San Juan del Río, late April 1843
Mathews, Alexander	Private	Gonzales	Tennessee	Released Sept. 16, 1844
Mills, John	Private	Victoria	Tennessee	Released Sept. 16, 1844
Mills, Lawson F.	Private	Victoria	Tennessee	Released Sept. 16, 1844
Morehead, William T.	Private	Victoria	Germany	Left in the mountains, Feb. 18, 1843; escaped to Texas
Mosier, Adam	Private	Matagorda	Louisiana	Released Sept. 16, 1844; did not return home immediately
Muller, Henry	Private		Germany	Released Sept. 16, 1844
Neely, James H.	Private	Montgomery	Alabama	Released Sept. 16, 1844
Parker, William T.	Private		Kentucky	Released Sept. 16, 1844; did not return home immediately
Peacock, James T.	Private	Victoria	Tennessee	Released Sept. 16, 1844

Rockefellow, Peter	Private	Jackson	New York	Died at San Luis Potosí sometime between April 10-30, 1843
Rupley, William	Private	Victoria	Pennsylvania	Wounded in Battle of Mier escaped from hospital at Mier, Jan. 20, 1843
Simons, Joseph M.	Private	Jackson	England	Died at Perote Castle, Dec. 3, 1843
Sweezy, John (boy)	Private	Victoria	Pennsylvania	Released Sept. 16, 1844
Tatum, Thomas S.	Private	Matagorda	Tennessee	Released at Perote Castle, Aug. 24, 1844
Thompson, William	Private	San Patricio	England	Escaped from Powder Mill Prison, Aug. 25, 1843
Thurmond, Alfred Sturgis	Private	Victoria	Tennessee	Interpreter; witnessed execution of Cameron; released Sept. 16, 1844
Tower, Isaac S.	Doctor	Victoria	New York	Killed in Battle of Mier, Dec. 26, 1842
Trahern, George Washington (boy)	Private	Victoria	Mississippi	Slightly wounded at Salado, Feb. 11, 1843; released Sept 16, 1844
Turnbull, James	Private	Victoria	Scotland	Shot at Salado, March 25, 1843
Turner, Robert W.	Private	Victoria	Ohio	Released Sept. 16, 1844
Usher, Patrick	Private	Jackson	Ireland	Sick in Matamoros; marched via Tampico to Mexico City; died in Santiago Hospital, Mexico City, Aug. 23, 1843
Van Horn, William H.	Private	Victoria	New York	Died in hospital, Perote, Oct. 6, 1843
Walker, Samuel Hamilton	Private	Galveston	Maryland	Captured before Battle of Mier; escaped from Tacubaya, July 30, 1843
Weeks, Henry D.	Private	Victoria	New York	Wounded in Battle of Mier; escaped from hospital at Mier, January 20, 1843
Whaling, Henry N.	Private	Victoria	Indiana	Shot at Salado, March 25, 1843
White, Alvin E.	Private	Refugio	Vermont	Killed in Battle of Mier, Dec. 26, 1842
White, Francis M.	Private	Galveston	Maryland	Released Sept. 16, 1844
Willoughby, Robert	Private	Victoria	England	Released Sept. 16, 1844
Wright, E. D.	Private	Washington	North Carolina	Escaped from Perote Castle, March 25, 1844
Wynn, William	Private	Montgomery	Kentucky	Released Sept. 16, 1844; did not return home immediately

TOTAL IN BATTLE OF MIER   61

CAMP GUARD

Name	Rank	Residence	Native State or County	Remarks
Canty, John	Private			
Earnest [Ernst?], H.	Private	Jackson		A Dutchman [German?]
O'Donnell [Donnally or Donally], Michael	Private	Refugio		Remained behind with Camp Guard without orders
Ward, William	Private			
Yates, Andrew Janeway	Private	Galveston	Connecticut	Remained behind with Camp Guard without orders

TOTAL IN CAMP GUARD   5

TOTAL RANK AND FILE IN COMPANY   66

COMPANY B — CAPTAIN WILLIAM M. EASTLAND'S COMPANY

Name	Rank	Residence	Native State or County	Remarks
Eastland, William Mosby	Captain	Fayette	Tennessee	Shot at Salado, March 25, 1843
Alexander, Mathew W.	Private	Jackson	Tennessee	Left in Hospital Santiago, Sept. 12, 1843; released Sept. 16, 1844
Barber, James	Private	Bastrop	Massachusetts	Wounded in Battle of Mier; died of wounds, Matamoros, March 14, 1843
Bell, Thomas W.	Private	Fayette	North Carolina	Released Sept. 16, 1844
Blackburn, John L. D.	Private	Fayette	Tennessee	Escaped from mountains to Texas
Blanton, James J.	2nd Sgt.	Fayette	Georgia	Ensign and flag bearer of Company; died in Santiago Prison, Mexico City, May 13, 1843
Bowman, Philip F.	Private	Bastrop	New York	Released Sept. 16, 1844
Brown, Richard	Private	Liberty	Pennsylvania	Released Sept. 16, 1844
Clopton, William Anthony	2nd Lt.	Bastrop	Tennessee	Released Sept. 16, 1844
Coffman, Elkin G.	Private	Bastrop	Tennessee	Died at San Luis Potosí, April 8, 1843
Cox, Thomas Washington	1st Lt.	Fayette	Illinois	Escaped from mountains to Texas
Davis, William	Private	Bastrop	Maryland	Released Sept. 16, 1844
Dunbar, William	Private	Bastrop	Tennessee	Left in Hospital Santiago, Sept. 12, 1843; released Sept. 16, 1844

Dunham, Robert Holmes	Private	Montgomery	Tennessee	Shot at Salado, March 25, 1843
Gibson, William	Private	Travis	Ohio	Released Sept. 16, 1843
Grubbs, Friendly	Private	Montgomery	Alabama	Released Sept. 16, 1844
Hanna, Andrew Barry	Private	Montgomery	South Carolina	Left with the Mexican troops at Salado, Feb. 11, 1843; released Sept. 16, 1844
Harrison, F. W. T.	Private	Washington	Alabama	Released Sept. 16, 1844
Hays, Lewis	Private		South Carolina	Wounded in Battle of Mier; escaped from hospital at Mier, Jan. 20, 1843
Hedenburg, Abraham D.	Private	Montgomery	New York	Released Sept. 16, 1844
Hill, Asa	Private	Fayette	North Carolina	Released in Mexico City about Aug. 1, 1843; reached New Orleans, Aug. 15, and Galveston, Aug. 20, 1843
Hill, Charles	Private	Bastrop	England	Died at San Luis Potosí, late April, 1843
Hill, Jeffrey Barksdale	Private	Fayette	Georgia	Wounded in right thigh at Mier; liberated at Perote Castle, Oct. 18, 1843; and left for home, Oct. 19, 1843
Hill, John Christopher	Private	Fayette	Georgia	Youngest boy in Battle of Columbus (boy) Mier; adopted by Ampudia; retained at Matamoros, but later marched to Mexico City via Tampico; adopted by Santa Anna; lived permanently in Mexico
Holderman, Allen S.	Private	Bastrop	Kentucky	Captured on Dec. 24, 1842, before the Battle of Mier; died at San Luis Potosí, late April 1843
Jackson, Edward B.	Private	Liberty	Pennsylvania	Released Sept. 16, 1844
King, Richard Baxter	Private	Montgomery	Tennessee	Released Sept. 16, 1844
McGinley, John	Private	Montgomery	Pennsylvania	Released Sept. 16, 1844
McLeyea, William J.	Private	Bastrop	Pennsylvania	Wounded in Battle of Mier; died of wounds at Mier, Jan. 1843
Middleton, Benoni	Private	Liberty	Illinois	Died in hospital, Mexico City, May 3, 1843
Middleton, William Benjamin	Private	Montgomery	Illinois	Released Sept. 16, 1844

Morgan, John Day	Private	Bastrop	England	Attended sick and wounded at Mier and Mata-moros; left sick at Matamoros; marched from Matamoros to Mexico City via Tampico; escaped from Tacubaya, Aug. 25, 1843
Nealy, John H.	Private	Austin	South Carolina	Left in mountains, Feb. 18, 1843; not heard from
Nelson, Thomas King	3rd Sgt.	Fayette	Tennessee	Released Sept. 16, 1844
Oats, Harbert H.	Private	Fayette	Kentucky	Slightly wounded in Battle of Mier; transferred from hospital in Mier to Matamoros marched via Tampico to Mexico City; released Sept. 16, 1844
Randolph, Perry D.	Private	Montgomery	Alabama	Recaptured after break; died at Benado, Feb. 25, 1843, from drinking too freely of water
Rogers, Marcus M.	Private	Bastrop	Tennessee	Released Sept. 16, 1844
Sanders, Leonidas	Private	Montgomery	Tennessee	Died in Hospital Perote, Jan.12, 1844
Sellers, William Harvey (boy)	Private	Fayette	Tennessee	Retained at Matamoros; later marched via Tampico to Mexico City; released Sept. 16, 1844
Sergeant, Carter	Private	Bastrop	Kentucky	Departed his comrades, Feb. 12, 1843, with horse, gun, and ammunition; recaptured by Mexicans; died in hospital, Mexico City, Aug. 3, 1843
Sergeant, William	Private	Bastrop	Kentucky	Departed his comrades, Feb. 12, 1843, with horse, gun, and ammunition; recaptured by Mexicans; released Sept. 16, 1844
Shepherd, James L.	Private	Bastrop	Alabama	Shot at Salado, March 25, 1843; crawled off during night; later executed at Saltillo
Smith, Donald	Private	Bastrop	Scotland	Left in Hospital Santiago, Sept. 12, 1843; released to British minister, March 14, 1844; reached New Orleans, March 29, 1844
Smith, Robert H. M. C.	Private	Fayette	Tennessee	Died in Hospital Santiago, June 18, 1843
Taney, John	Private	Bastrop	Maryland	Escaped from mountains, but recaptured near the Rio Grande; released Sept. 16, 1844

Ury, James	Private	Bastrop	South Carolina	Wounded in Battle of Mier; died of wounds at Mier in Jan. 1843
Van Vechten, D. H.	Private	Fayette	Kentucky	Left in Hospital Santiago, Sept. 12, 1843; released Sept. 16, 1844
Williams, Levi	Private	Bastrop	Missouri	Released Sept. 16, 1844
Wilson, James	Private		New York	Released Sept. 16, 1844; did not return home immediately
Wilson, Zaccheus	Private	Montgomery	Tennessee	Died at Perote, Dec. 6, 1843
Wing, Martin Carroll	Private	Travis	New York	Shot at Salado, March 25, 1843
Wyatt, John P.	1st Sgt.	Fayette	Georgia	Died at Perote, Oct. 21, 1843

TOTAL IN BATTLE OF MIER   52

CAMP GUARD

Name	Rank	Residence	Native State or County	Remarks
Allen, George W.	Private	Travis		
Ambrose, M.	Private			
Bissell, Theodore	Private	Travis	Connecticut	
Buckman, Oliver	4th Sgt.	Bastrop		
Clark, Henry	Private	Refugio		
Holton, William S.	Private	Bastrop	Pennsylvania	
Hudson, David	Private			
Martin, Edward	Private			
Vincent, E. H.	Private			

TOTAL IN CAMP GUARD   9
TOTAL RANK AND FILE IN COMPANY   61

COMPANY C — CAPTAIN JOHN G. W. PIERSON'S COMPANY

Name	Rank	Residence	Native State or County	Remarks
Pierson, John Goodloe Warren	Captain	Montgomery	North Carolina	Left in Hospital Santiago, Sept. 12, 1843; released Sept. 16, 1844
Alexander, Anthony W.	Private	Milam	Ohio	Released Sept. 16, 1844
Bideler, John	Private	Milam	Pennsylvania	Wounded at Mier; escaped from hospital in Mier, Jan. 20, 1843
Boswell, Ransom P.	Private	Milam	Georgia	Released Sept. 16, 1844

Chalk, Whitfield	Private	Milam	North Carolina	Escaped from Mier after the battle, Dec. 26, 1842
Harris, Robert W.	Private	Travis	Mississippi	Shot at Salado, March 25, 1843
Hughes, Francis (Frank)	Private	Milam	Pennsylvania	Wounded in Battle of Mier; left at Matamoros, Jan. 14, 1843; still there when released Sept. 16, 1844, and returned home from there
Humphries, Jacob J.	Private	Milam	Tennessee	Released Sept. 16, 1844
Jones, Wiley Martin	Private	Milam	Alabama	Escaped from Perote Castle, March 25, 1844; reached Texas
Lyons, John	Private	Milam	Ireland	Killed in break at Salado, Feb. 11, 1843
McFall, Samuel C.	Private	Milam	Missouri	Released Sept. 16, 1844
Maxwell, Peter Menard	1st Sgt.	Liberty	Illinois	Released Sept. 16, 1844
Moore, William H. ("Talking Bill")	Private	Milam	Canada	Released Sept. 16, 1844; did not return home immediately
Oldham, William	Private	Milam	Virginia	Escaped from the mountains; reached Texas
Porter, Elijah R.	Private	Milam	Tennessee	Died in hospital, Mexico City, Aug. 24, 1843
Rice, James O.	Private	Travis	South Carolina	Wounded in Battle of Mier; escaped from hospital at Mier, Jan. 20, 1843
Roberts, Christopher M.	Private	Milam	Tennessee	Shot at Salado, March 25, 1843
Runyan, William J.	Private	Sabine	Georgia	Escaped from Perote Castle, March 25, 1844; recaptured; released Sept. 16, 1844
St. Clair, Caleb	Private	Gonzales	New York	Escaped from Mier after the battle, Dec. 26. 1842
Scott, William Y.	Private	Milam	Georgia	Wounded in Battle of Mier; left at Matamoros, Jan. 14, 1843; released there on Sept. 16, 1844, and returned home from there
Sullivan, Daniel C.	Private	Milam	Missouri	Released Sept. 16, 1844
Thompson, Jasper Newton McDonald	Orderly Sgt.	Milam	Tennessee	Shot at Salado, March 25, 1843
Thompson, Thomas A.	Private	Milam	Kentucky	Released Sept. 16, 1844
Yocum, Jesse	Private			Killed accidentally, Dec. 23, 1842

TOTAL IN BATTLE OF MIER   23

CAMP GUARD

Name	Rank	Residence	Native State or County	Remarks
Erath, George Bernard	Private	Milam	Austria	
Oldham, Thomas	Private	Milam		
Owens, John	Private		Pennsylvania	

TOTAL IN CAMP GUARD 3

TOTAL RANK AND FILE IN COMPANY 27

COMPANY D — CAPTAIN CLAUDIUS BUSTER'S COMPANY

Name	Rank	Residence	Native State or County	Remarks
Buster, Claudius	Captain	Washington	Kentucky	After escape at Salado, re-captured on the Rio Grande, some 30-40 miles above Laredo, in late February or early March, 1843; released Sept. 16, 1844
Armstrong, James	Private	Washington	Tennessee	Released at Perote Castle, Aug. 24, 1844
Barney, Daniel F.	Private	Washington	Kentucky	Remained with the Mexicans at Salado, Feb. 11, 1843; released Sept. 16, 1844; did not return home immediately
Bassett, R. P.	Private	Washington	Kentucky	Killed in Battle of Mier, Dec. 26, 1842
Brenham, Richard Fox	Doctor	Travis	Kentucky	Killed in break at Salado, Feb. 11, 1843
Bush, George W.	Private	Washington	Canada	Remained with the Mexicans after the break at Salado, Feb. 11, 1843; escaped from near Perote, Aug. 23, 1844, while out hauling rocks
Calvert, James H.	Private		Tennessee	Left in the mountains Feb. 18, 1843; recaptured near the Rio Grande and taken to San Fernando and then to Monterrey and Saltillo; released from Perote Castle, Sept. 16, 1844
Crawford, Robert M.	Private	Victoria	South Carolina	Escaped from Tacubaya, Aug. 25, 1843; reached New Orleans
Davis, Campbell	Private	Washington	Tennessee	Died from overdose of laudnum, Castle of Perote, Feb. 16, 1844

Dixon, John	Private	Harrison	Indiana	Killed in Battle of Mier, Dec. 26, 1842
Edwards, Leonidas D. F. (boy)	Private	Washington	Tennessee	Released Sept. 16, 1844
Hallowell, Daniel R.	Private		Tennessee	Remained with the Mexicans after the break at Salado; died at Perote, Dec. 11, 1843
Hannon, William H.	Private	Washington	Georgia	Killed in Battle of Mier, Dec. 26, 1842
Hensley, Charles	Private	Washington	Tennessee	Released Sept. 16, 1844
Hobson, William J.	Private	Gonzales	Kentucky	Killed in Battle of Mier, Dec. 26, 1842
Jackson, William A.	Private	Harris	Ireland	Killed in Battle of Mier, Dec.26, 1842
Jones, John E.	Private	Harris	England	Killed in Battle of Mier, Dec. 26, 1842
Kaigler, William	Private	Béxar	Georgia	Released Sept. 16, 1844
Keene, Edward Y.	1st Sgt.	Washington	Kentucky	Wounded at Mier; marched from Matamoros via Tampico to Mexico City; escaped from Perote Castle, March 25, 1844
Keene, Richard	Private	Washington	Kentucky	Remained with the Mexicans at Salado, Feb. 11, 1843; escaped from Perote Castle, March 25, 1844
Lockerman, Stanley	Private	Colorado		Mortally wounded in Battle of Mier; died at Mier
McCutchan, Joseph D.	Private	Washington	Tennessee	Sick at Matamoros; marched from Matamoros via Tampico to Mexico City; released Sept. 16, 1844
Millen, William E.	Private	Harris	Virginia	Left in Hospital Santiago, Sept. 12, 1843; released Sept. 16, 1844
Mitchell, William	Private	Washington	Missouri	After escape at Salado and recapture, died at Benado, Feb. 25, 1843, from drinking too freely of water
Ogden, James Masterson	Private	Travis	Virginia	Shot at Salado, March 25, 1843
Overton, David	Private	Brazos	Mississippi	Released Sept. 16, 1844
Rice, Lorenzo D.	Private	Béxar	Maryland	Killed in the break at Salado, Feb. 11, 1843
Smith, Thomas S.	2nd Sgt.	Washington	Maryland	Escaped from Perote Castle, March 25, 1844; reached Texas

Toops, John	Private	Washington	Ohio	After escape at Salado recaptured on the Rio Grande, some 30-40 miles above Laredo, in late Feb. or early March 1843; released Sept. 16, 1844
Watkins [alias Watts?] John D.	Private	Washington	Louisiana	Left in Hospital Santiago, Sept. 12, 1843; released Sept. 16, 1844
Young, James	Private	Brazoria	New York	Released Sept. 16, 1844

TOTAL IN BATTLE OF MIER   31

CAMP GUARD

Name	Rank	Residence	Native State or County	Remarks
Bonnell, George William	Private	Travis	New York	On special assignment afternoon of Dec. 25, 1843; joined Camp Guard; killed on the Rio Grande by Mexican troops, Dec. 27, 1842
Furman, A.	Private			Sick at time of Battle of Mier
Hackstaff, S. L.	Private			On special assignment afternoon of Dec. 25, 1842; joined Camp Guard
Hensley, William R.	Private	Washington	Tennessee	Sick at time of Battle of Mier
Hicks, Milton				Sick at time of Battle of Mier
Hyde, Archibald C.	Private	Travis	Connecticut	
McQueen, William	Major			Sick at time of Battle of Mier
Ransom, Thomas J.	Private			Sick at time of Battle of Micr
Smith, Gabriel	Private			Sick at time of Battle of Mier
Vaughan, Joseph E.	Major			Sick at time of Battle of Mier
Watson, Robert H.	Doctor	Houston		On special assignment afternoon of Dec. 25, 1842; joined Camp Guard
Wilkinson, Warren G.	1st Lt.	Washington		

TOTAL IN CAMP GUARD   12

TOTAL RANK AND FILE IN COMPANY   43

COMPANY E — CAPTAIN WILLIAM M. RYON'S COMPANY

Name	Rank	Residence	Native State or County	Remarks
Ryon, William M.	Captain	Fort Bend	Kentucky	Received slight head wound in Battle of Mier; released at Perote Castle, Aug. 24, 1844
Allen, David	Private	Harris	Connecticut	Wounded at Mier; later removed to Matamoros; marched from Matamoros via Tampico to Mexico City; left in Hospital Santiago, Sept. 12, 1843; released Sept. 16, 1844
Armstrong, Alexander	Private	Fort Bend	Louisiana	Released Sept. 16, 1844
Barney, Jr., Stephen A.	4th Sgt.	Fort Bend	Vermont	Released Sept. 16, 1844
Beale, Robert Harper	Private	Fort Bend	District of Columbia	Wounded in Battle of Mier; escaped from hospital in Mier, Jan. 20, 1843
Beard, Robert S.	Private	Fort Bend	Missouri	Died at San Luis Potosí, April 8, 1843
Beard, William H.	Private	Fort Bend	Missouri	Died at Hospital Santiago, July 23, 1843
Bennett, Samuel P.	Private	Austin	Tennessee	Died in hospital in Perote, Dec. 7. 1843
Brush, Gilbert Russell (boy)	Private	Fort Bend	New York	Left at Matamoros when prisoners marched inland; later marched from Matamoros via Tampico to Mexico City; released Sept. 16, 1844
Bryant, W. Barney C.	Private	Fort Bend		Died of pneumonia at Saltillo, March 9, 1843
Burke, James	Private	Fort Bend	Ohio	Died in hospital in Perote, Feb. 20, 1844
Burras, A. F.	Private	Austin	Kentucky	Died in hospital in Perote, Dec. 6, 1843
Cody, William D.	Private	Austin	Georgia	After escape at Salado, left in mountains; not heard from
Copeland, Willis	Private	Nacogdoches	Virginia	Escaped from Tacubaya, July 29, 1843; recaptured near the Rio Grande; released Sept. 16, 1844
Crittenden, George B.	2nd Lt.	Fort Bend	Kentucky	Graduated West Point Military Academy, 1832; left sick at Matamoros; marched from Matamoros via Tampico to Mexico City; Santa Anna agreed on March 15, 1843, to liberate him, but it was not until about April 21-22 that the order could be carried out

Daugherty, Patrick H.	Private		Ireland	Escaped from Tacubaya while at work; reached New Orleans
Davis, William Kinchen	Private	Fort Bend	Alabama	Wounded in left hand in Battle of Mier; released Sept. 16, 1844
Dusenberry, John E.	Private	Harris	New York	Released Sept. 16, 1844; did not return home immediately
Este, Edward E.	Private	Harris	New Jersey	Shot at Salado, March 25, 1843
Fitzgerald, John	Private	Fort Bend	Ireland	Escaped from Powder Mill Prison, Aug. 25, 1843
Frensley, William H. H.	3rd Sgt.	Fort Bend	Tennessee	Escaped from Perote Castle, March 25, 1844; recaptured; released Sept. 16, 1844
Gattis, B. H.	Private	Travis	Alabama	Wounded at Mier; moved to Matamoros; marched from Matamoros via Tampico to Mexico City; escaped from Powder Mill Prison, July 30, 1843; arrived New Orleans
Gibson, Fenton M.	2nd Quarter Master	Fort Bend	Georgia	See Staff and Command
Goodman, Stephen	Private	Fort Bend	Alabama	Escaped from Perote Castle, March 25, 1844; recaptured; released Sept. 16, 1844
Grosjean, John C.	Private		France	Died in Hospital Perote, Dec. 21, 1843
Island, Zed	Private	Béxar	Germany	Died in Hospital Perote, Dec. 20, 1843
Jones, Thomas L.	Private	Travis	Kentucky	Shot at Salado, March 25, 1843
Kelley, Charles S.	Private	Fort Bend	Connecticut	Released Sept. 16, 1844
Kuykendall, Wyatt Hanks	Private	Fort Bend	Tennessee	Wounded in Battle of Mier; died a few hours afterwards
Lacy, John	Private	Galveston	Ireland	Released Sept. 16, 1844
McCauley, Malcolm	Private	Harris	Scotland	Wounded in Battle of Mier; died of wounds at Matamoros, July 14, 1843
McDade, Samuel	Private	Fort Bend		Died at Nueva Reynosa of illness sometime after Jan. 6, 1843
Maltby, Theodore Dwight	Private	Fort Bend	Connecticut	Received severe head wound in Battle of Mier; left in Hospital Santiago, Sept. 12, 1843; later moved to Puebla, and was sick there when released on Sept. 16, 1844; but was left behind at hospital in Puebla; later went to New Orleans
Morrell, Homer Virgil	Private	Fort Bend	Georgia	Released Sept. 16, 1844

Morris, William	Private	Fort Bend	Louisiana	Died in hospital, Mexico City, Aug. 6, 1843
Pilant, George B.	Private	Fort Bend	Tennessee	Wounded in Battle of Mier; escaped from hospital at Mier, Jan. 20, 1843
Pilley, Michael Robert	Private	Harris	England	Released Sept. 16, 1844
Pitts, E. H.	Private	Fort Bend	Georgia	Released Sept. 16, 1844
Rice, Sanford	Private	Harris	New York	After escape at Salado, left in mountains; not heard from
Riley, Francis	Private	Fort Bend	Ireland	Released Sept. 16, 1844
Roark, Andrew Jackson	2nd Sgt.	Fort Bend	Tennessee	Released Sept. 16, 1844
Roberts, Henry H.	Private	Harris	North Carolina	Left in Hospital Santiago, Sept. 12, 1843; released Sept.16, 1844
Rowan, William H.	Private	Fort Bend	Georgia	Shot at Salado, March 25, 1843
Sansberry, John A.	Private	Fort Bend	Kentucky	Lost an eye and a leg in the break at Salado; left in hospital at San Luis Potosí, April 10, 1843; released Sept. 16, 1844
Shepherd, William M.	Doctor	Liberty	Virginia	See Staff and Command; Detailed Dec. 26, 1842 as Surgeon
Shipman, John M.	1st Lt.	Fort Bend	Missouri	Died in hospital, Mexico City, May 21, 1843
Smith, Ezekiel	Private	Gonzales	Virginia	Sick at Matamoros; marched from Matamoros via Tampico to Mexico City; left in Hospital Santiago, Sept. 12, 1843; released Sept. 16, 1844
Torrey, James N.	Private	Harris	Connecticut	Shot at Salado, March 25, 1843
Waters, Robert G.	1st Sgt.	Fort Bend	South Carolina	Left in Hospital Santiago, Sept. 12, 1843; released at Mexico City, Feb., 1844
White, James S.	Private		Pennsylvania	Died in Perote Hospital, Nov. 28, 1843
Whitehurst, Frederick W.	Private	Fort Bend		Released Sept. 16, 1844
Willis, Owen N. Reuben	Private		Tennessee	Left in Hospital Santiago, Sept. 12, 1843; died there Sept. 16, 1843
Wilson, William F.	Private	Liberty	Virginia	Released at Perote Castle, Aug. 24, 1844
Woodland, Henry	Private	Harris	Indiana	Released Sept. 16, 1844

TOTAL IN BATTLE OF MIER   54

CAMP GUARD

Name	Rank	Residence	Native State or County	Remarks
Brown, Edward	Private	Fort Bend	Florida	
Buckhannan, James	Private	Montgomery	Georgia	
Dressler, William E.	Private			
Gilpin, Ralph	Private			
Kuykendall, Moses	Private			
Lucas, Z.	Private			
Schneider, ———	Private			

TOTAL IN CAMP GUARD   7

TOTAL RANK AND FILE IN COMPANY   61

COMPANY F — CAPTAIN CHARLES K. REESE'S COMPANY

Name	Rank	Residence	Native State or County	Remarks
Reese, Charles Keller	Captain	Brazoria	Kentucky	Joined the Mexican troops at Salado, taking horse, gun, and ammunition; escaped from Perote Castle, July 2, 1843; arrived in New Orleans
Alexander, John Rufus	Private	Brazoria	Missouri	After escape at Salado, reached Texas
Atwood, William W.	Private	Brazoria	England	Released Sept. 16, 1844; did not immediately return home
Austin, James	Private	Brazoria	Missouri	Killed in Battle of Mier, Dec. 26, 1842
Beasley, David H. E.	Private	Brazoria	North Carolina	Left in Hospital Santiago, Sept. 12, 1843; released Sept. 16, 1844
Berry, John Bate	Private	Bastrop	Indiana	Released Sept. 16, 1844
Berry, Joseph	Private	Bastrop	Indiana	Killed in Battle of Mier, Dec. 26, 1842
Boone, Benjamin Zachariah	Private	Matagorda	Missouri	Released Sept. 16, 1844
Bridger, Henry	Private	Gonzales	Pennsylvania	Left in Hospital Santiago, Sept. 12, 1843; released Sept.16, 1844
Clarke, Charles A.	1st Lt.	Brazoria	Louisiana	Joined the Mexican troops at Salado, Feb. 11, 1843; released from Perote Castle, Aug. 22, 1843
Clark, George Wilson	Private	Jackson	Missouri	Released Sept. 16, 1844

Davis, Daniel	Private	Victoria	Kentucky	Joined Mexican troops at Salado, Feb. 11, 1843; released Sept. 16, 1844; did not return home immediately
Davis, Thomas	Private	Washington	New York	Released Sept. 16, 1844
Douglass, Freeman W.	2nd Lt.	Brazoria	Georgia	Released Sept. 16, 1844
Erwin, John	Private		Pennsylvania	Left in Hospital Santiago, Sept. 12, 1843; died in hospital, Mexico City, Oct.14, 1843
Harvey, John	Private	Brazoria	Kentucky	Released Sept. 16, 1844
Henrie, Daniel Drake	Private	Brazoria	Ohio	Former midshipman in U.S. Navy; escaped from Perote Castle, July 2, 1843; reached New Orleans
Johnson, John R.	1st Sgt.	Béxar	Virginia	Escaped from Perote Castle, March 25, 1844; reached Texas
Journeay, Henry	Private	Matagorda	New York	Released Sept. 16, 1844
Lewis, Alexander John	Private	Brazoria	Alabama	After break at Salado, left in mountains; never heard from
Livergood, John Himes	Private	Jackson	Pennsylvania	Released Sept. 16, 1844
Lyon, Samuel C.	Private	Brazoria	England	Sailing Master; released Sept.16, 1844
McLaughlin, Charles	Private	Harris	England	Draftsman; released Sept. 16, 1844; did not return home immediately
Miller, William H.	Private	Brazoria	Tennessee	Died at Perote, Dec. 17, 1843
Moore, William	Private	Fort Bend	Missouri	Escaped from Perote Castle, March 25, 1844; reached Texas
Owen, John	Private	Brazoria	Pennsylvania	Died at Powder Mill Prison, June 17, 1843
Phelps, Orlando C. (boy)	Private	Brazoria	Mississippi	Released at Mexico City, April 26, 1843
Reese, William Erwin (boy)	Private	Brazoria	Kentucky	Joined the Mexican troops at Salado; released at Tacubaya, March 15, 1843; or shortly thereafter, at the request of General Ampudia
Sensebaugh, T. J.	Private	Washington	Tennessee	Released Sept. 16, 1844
Sinnickson, John J.	Doctor	Brazoria	New Jersey	See Staff and Command
Smith, Joseph F.	Private	Refugio	Kentucky	Released Sept. 16, 1844; left Vera Cruz Oct. 11, 1844, on the *W. J. Huntington* for New Orleans

Name	Rank	Residence	Native State or County	Remarks
Stapp, William Preston	Private	Jackson	Kentucky	Released from Perote Castle, May 10, 1844
Vandyke, William N.	Private	Jackson	Georgia	Released Sept. 16, 1844
Wallace, William Alexander Anderson ("Bigfoot")	Private	Béxar	Virginia	Received slight wound in left arm from bayonett in Battle of Mier; released at Perote Castle, Aug. 24, 1844
Wilson, James Charles	Private	Brazoria	England	Left sick at Matamoros; marched from Matamoros via Tampico to Mexico City; escaped from Powder Mill Prison, July 30, 1843
Zumwalt, Isaac K.	Private	Jackson	Missouri	Released Sept. 16, 1844

TOTAL IN BATTLE OF MIER   36

CAMP GUARD

Name	Rank	Residence	Native State or County	Remarks
Callender, Sidney S.	Private	Fort Bend		
Cronican, Michael	Private	Fort Bend	Massachusetts	
Hancock, F.	Private		Missouri	
Phelps, Virgil H.	Private	Brazoria	Mississippi	
Walton, George W.	Private		Missouri	
Warren, Thomas	Private			
West, Guilford	Private			

TOTAL IN CAMP GUARD   7

TOTAL RANK AND FILE IN COMPANY   43

RECAPITULATION

	In Battle of Mier	Camp Guard	Other	Total
Staff and Command 3 Staff Members listed on Company Rolls	4			4
Company A — Capt. Ewen Cameron's Company Captured Dec. 24, 1842— Gideon K. Lewis Company Total	60	5	1	66
Company B — Capt. William M. Eastland's Company Captured Dec. 24, 1842— Allen S. Holderman Company Total	51	9	1	61

Company C — Capt. John G. W. Pierson's Company Killed accidentally Dec. 23, 1842—Jesse Yocum				
Company Total	23	3	1	27
Company D — Capt. Claudius Buster's Company				
Company Total	31	12		43
Company E — Capt. William M. Ryon's Company Two listed on Company Roll, who were assigned to staff and Command				
Company Total	54	7		61
Company F — Capt. Charles K. Reese's Company One turned back after crossing the river to do battle—Michael Cronican—joined Camp Guard	36			
One listed on Company Roll, who was assigned to Staff and Command				
Company Total		1		43
Desertions prior to arrival before Mier (Henry Clay Davis and John MacBeth)			2	2
	259	43	5	307

Bibliography

Tx-A = Texas State Archives
TxU-A = University of Texas at Austin Archives

A. Primary Sources

1. Public Documents.

a. Manuscripts.

Barker, [Eugene C.]. Transcripts from the *Archivo de la Secretaría de Relaciónes Exteriores Internacional. Estados Unidos, 1842-1847.* TxU-A.

Bastrop County, [Texas]. Tax rolls, 1837-1910. Austin, Texas: Texas State Library Records Division (1979). Microfilm. 4 reels.

Béxar County, [Texas]. Minutes of the District Court of Béxar County. Vol. 8.

County (Texas) Tax Rolls, 1837-1845. 24 vols. State Comptroller's Office, Austin, Texas.

Documents for the Early History of Texas, Coahuila, and Approaches Thereto, 1600-1843. 30 vols. Photostats, TxU-A.

Fayette County, Texas. Deed Records, County Courthouse, LaGrange, Texas.

———. District Court Minutes. County Courthouse, LaGrange, Texas.

Fort Bend County, Texas. Probate Papers, County Courthouse, Richmond, Texas.

Great Britain. Public Records Office (London). Foreign Office Papers. FO. 50 (Texas), 50 (Mexico), 5 (United States), 72 (Spain), and 27 (France).

Goliad, Texas. Minutes of Common Council, 1841-1846, County Courthouse, Goliad, Texas.

Gonzales, Texas. Early Gonzales Records, Tx-A.

Laredo Archives. Records of the City of Laredo, Texas. Library of St. Mary's University, San Antonio, Texas, Boxes 6-12. Xerox copy in Texas State Archives, Austin, Texas, Boxes 1-3; also a copy in the Béxar County Archives, made from microfilm copies of the original manuscripts.

Matamoros, Mexico. City Records, vols. 1-57 (1811-1859). Photostats in TxU-A.

Memorials and Petitions (Texas), (Restored Documents), Tx-A.

Mexican Archives. *Archivos de la Nación, MS, Provincias Internas,* vol. 12.

Military State Register (Alabama). Military Division, Alabama State Department of Archives and History.

Pension Applications. Republic of Texas. Tx-A.

Pension Papers (Texas). Tx-A.

"Record Book of the General & Special Orders and Letters of the South Western Army, November 1842 - [January 1843], A." MS. Manuscript Division, New York Public Library.

"Relaciónes Exteriores Asuntos Varios Comercio Estados Unidos, 1825-1849," Barker Transcripts from the *Archivo de la Secretaría.* TxU-A.

"Relaciónes Exteriores Reseñas Politicas, 1841-1842." Estados Unidos, 1842. Barker Transcripts from the *Archivo de la Secretaría.* TxU-A.

San Antonio, Texas. Calendar of the Records of the Probate Court of San Antonio, Texas, May 29, 1837 to December 6, 1878. Transcript. Translated by María A.C. Saldana. (Included in the calendar are Final Records, Vol. A. Red, 1838-1841; Final Records, Vol. E, Red, 1850-1859; Final Records, Vol. D; Red, 1851-1857; Probate Court Minutes, Vol. D, Black, 1857-1859; Probate Court, Bond Record, Vol. A-B, 1855-1882). TxU-A.

————. A List of City Officials and a Calendar of the City Hall Records, 1837-1890. Typescript. TxU-A.

————. Minutes of the City Council, 1837-1849. Journal A. Transcribed, translated, and typed by the Texas Works Progress Administration. TxU-A.

Smith, Justin H. "Transcripts," Vol. V, Latin American Collection, University of Texas at Austin Library.

Somervell Campaign. Compiled Military Service "Muster Rolls" for General Land Office of Texas, Austin, Texas.

Spanish Archives of Texas. Vol. IX. General Land Office of Texas, Austin, Texas.

Texas Adjutant General's Papers, 1836-1869. Transcripts, Tx-A.

————. Army Papers, 1841-1846. Tx-A.

————. Audited Military Claims. Tx-A.

————. Comptroller's Military Service Records. Tx-A.

————. Comptroller's Papers. Tx-A.

————. Congress. Bills and Unapproved Acts, 7th and 8th Congresses. Tx-A.

————. ————. Memorials and Petitions, 1st - 9th Congresses, Tx-A.

————. Bills, 7th-9th Congresses. MS, Tx-A.

————. Claim Papers. See Miscellaneous Claim Papers. Tx-A.

————. Committee Reports. Tx-A.

————. Congressional Papers. Tx-A.

————. Custom House Records (Galveston), 1836-1846. Rosenberg Library, Galveston, Texas.

————. Department of State. Consular Correspondence, 1838-1875. Tx-A.

————. ————. Consular Letters, 1835-1844. Microfilm. TxU-A.

————. ————. Consular Papers, 1835-1846. Tx-A.

————. ————. Domestic Correspondence, 1835-1846. Tx-A.

————. ————. Domestic Correspondence, undated. Tx-A.

————. ————. Foreign Letters, 1842-1846. Tx-A.

————. ————. Legation Records, May 1839-Aug. 1844. Tx-A.

————. ————. Letterbook: Home Letters, II (1842-1846). Tx-A.

————. Executive Records. Tx-A.

————. Executive Records, of the Second Term of General Sam Houston's Administration of the Government of Texas, December, 1841-December, 1844. Tx-A.

————. General Land Office. Compiled Military Service Rolls, Mier Expedition.

————. ————. Compiled Military Service Rolls, Vásquez Expedition.

————. ————. Compiled Military Service Rolls, Somervell Campaign, 1842.

————. ————. Compiled Military Service Rolls, Woll Campaign, 1842.

————. ————. Land Bounty Files.

————. ————. Land Surveys. Original Field Notes, Book 7.

————. Memorials and Petitions, 1846-1920. Tx-A.

————. Mier Muster Rolls. Tx-A.

————. Military Affairs Papers. Tx-A.

————. Military Claims Papers. Tx-A.

————. Militia Rolls. Tx-A.

————. Miscellaneous Documents. Tx-A.

————. Miscellaneous Claims Papers. Tx-A.

————. Muster Rolls, Minute Men. Tx-A.

————. Muster Rolls of the Soldiers of the Republic. Tx-A.

————. Public Debt Papers, 1848-1854. Tx-A.

————. Rangers. Muster Rolls, 1830-1860. Tx-A.

————. ————. Muster Rolls, undated. Tx-A.

————. ————. Receipt Rolls, 1830-1860. Tx-A.

————. Record of Executive Documents from the 18th Dec. 1838, to the 14th Dec. 1841. Tx-A.

————. [Register of the] Elected and Appointed Officials of the Republic of Texas, 1835-1846. 2 vols. MS, Tx-A.

————. Republic Papers, 1835-1846. Tx-A.

————. Texas Republic Papers, 1831-1846. Executive Letter Book, No. 35. Tx-A.

————. Republic Pension Papers, 1835-1846. Executive Letter Book, No. 35. Tx-A.

————. Republic Pension Papers, 1870-ca. 1900, Tx-A.

————. Treasury Department. [Galveston Custom House records under the Republic of Texas, Gail Borden, Jr., Collector, 1835-1846]. Microfilm copy, Southern Methodist University Library, Dallas, Texas.

————. State. Comptroller. Circular. Austin, November 28, 1870. [In regard to payment of pensions to "surviving veterans of the Revolution which separated Texas from Mexico, including the Mier prisoners."] A. Bledsoe, Comptroller. Broadside. Tx-A; TxU-A.

United States. Consular Despatches. Campeche, 1820-1880. National Archives, Washington, D.C.

————. ————. Chihuahua, 1830-1906. National Archives, Washington, D.C.

————. ————. Matamoros, 1837-1848. National Archives, Washington, D.C.

————. ————. Mazatlán, 1826-1906. National Archives, Washington, D.C.

————. ————. Mexico City, March 26, 1832-Dec. 30, 1845. National Archives, Washington, D.C.

————. ————. Tabasco, 1832-1874. National Archives, Washington, D.C.

————. ————. Tampico, May 29, 1824-Nov. 27, 1857. National Archives, Washington, D.C.

————. ————. Vera Cruz, 1822-1846. National Archives, Washington, D.C.

————. Correspondence and Reports of American Agents and Others in Texas, 1836-1845. Justin H. Smith Transcripts, University of Texas at Austin Library.

————. Department of State. Diplomatic Instructions, May 29, 1833-March 29, 1845. National Archives, Washington, D.C.

————. ————. Domestic Letters, Jan. 30, 1837-April 30, 1846 National Archives, Washington, D.C.

————. ————. Instructions of the Department of State, Mexico (May 29, 1833-March 29, 1843). National Archives, Washington, D.C.

————. ————. Despatches from United States Ministers in Mexico, 1823-1848. National Archives, Washington, D.C.

————. ————. Resignation and Disinclination File, 1839-1846. National Archives, Washington, D.C.

b. Printed Material.

Abstract of All Original Texas Land Titles Comprising Grants and Locations to August 31, 1941. 8 vols. [Austin: General Land Office, 1941-1942].

Abstract of Original Land Titles in the General Land Office. See Mary Lewis Ulmer (comp.), *An Abstract of Original Titles in the General Land Office.*

Adams, Ephraim D. (ed.). *British Diplomatic Correspondence Concerning the Republic of Texas, 1836-1846.* Austin, Texas: Texas State Historical Association, 1917.

————. "Correspondence from the British Archives Concerning Texas, 1837-1848." *Quarterly of the Texas State Historical Association* XV-XXI (1911-1918).

Almanáque Imperial para el año de 1866. México: Imp. de J.M. Lara, 1866.

Beerstecher, Jr., Ernest. "Historical Probate Extracts, Harris[burg] County, The Republic of Texas," *Texana* VII (1969), pp. 247-294; VIII (Winter 1970), pp. 47-90.

Benetz, Margaret Diamond (ed.). *The [Caleb] Cushing Reports: Ambassador Caleb Cushing's Confidential Diplomatic Reports to the United States Secretary of State, 1843-1844: Mexico, Egypt, the Barbary States, India, Ceylon.* Salisbury, N.C.: Documentary Publications, 1975.

Binkley, William C. (ed.). *Official Correspondence of the Texas Revolution, 1835-1836.* 2 vols. New York: D. Appleton & Company, Inc., 1936.

Brito, José. *Legislación Méxicana. Indice alfabetico razónado de las leyes, decretos, reglamentos, ordenes y circulares, que se han expedido desde el año de 1821 hasta el de 1869.* 3 vols. México, 1872-73.

Burlage, John, and J.B. Hollingsworth (comps.). *Abstract of Valid Land Claims, Compiled from the Records of the General Land Office and Court of Claims of the State of Texas.* Austin, Texas: Printed by John Marshall & Co., 1859.

Carter, Clarence Edwin (comp. and ed.). *The Territorial Papers of the United States.* Vol. XIX (The Territory of Arkansas, 1819-1825) Washington: Government Printing Office, 1953.

Coast Depot and Shipping Port of the Valley of the Río Grande, and the Provinces of Mexico Tributary Thereto, with the Government Map of that Region of Country, published in 1850, together with the Report of the Explorations of the Río Grande. New York: Pridney & Russell, printers, 1850.

Colección de Documentos historicos Méxicanos formada por orden del c. subsecretario de Guerra y Marina con acuerdo del c. Presidente constitucional de la república. 4 vols. México: *Liberia de la Vda. de Ch. Bouret,* 1920-1926.

Colección de las Leyes, Decretos y Providencias Importantes espedidas Por Las Supremas Authoridades de la República Méxicana. Formada y publicada en obsequio de los suscritores del Repúblicano. Año de 1838. México: *Ignácio Cumplido,* 1846.

Compilation of the Messages and Papers of the Presidents, A. 20 vols. New York: Bureau of National Literature, Inc., 1917.

Compiled Index to Elected and Appointed Officials of the Republic of Texas, 1835-1846. Austin: State Archives Division, Texas State Library, 1981.

Compiled Service Records of Volunteer Soldiers during the Mexican War in Organizations of the State of Texas. Microfilm. Washington: The National Archives and Records Service, General Services Administration, 1959.

Connor, Seymour V. (ed.). *Texas Treasury Papers: Letters Received in the Treasury Department of the Republic of Texas, 1836-1848.* 3 vols. Austin, Texas: Texas State Library, 1955.

Correspondencia entre los Señores J.N. Almonte, Arrongoiz Consul de N. Orleans a los Sres. Pedro Fernández del Castillo y Joaquín Velázquez de León, sobre Texas y los E.E.U.U. 1841-1843, México: *Biblioteca Aportacion Historica, Segunda Serie,* Editor Vargas Rea, 1949 (the original letters are in the *Biblioteca Nacional*).

Correspondence Relating to a Treaty of Peace between Mexico and Texas, upon the Basis of an Acknowledgment of the Independence of the Latter. Washington: National Register Print, [1845].

Dallam, James. *A Digest of the Laws of Texas Containing a Full and Complete Compilation of Land Laws, together with Opinions of the Supreme Court.* Baltimore, 1845.

————. (comp.). *Opinions of the Supreme Court of Texas from 1840 to 1844 Inclusive.* Originally published in 1845. Reprint, St. Paul, 1883.

Day, James M. (comp. and ed.). *Post Office Papers of the Republic of Texas, 1836-1839.* 2 vols. Austin, Texas: Texas State Library, 1966-1967.

Documents of Major Gen. Sam Houston, Commander-in-Chief of the Texian Army, to His Excellency David G. Burnet, President of the Republic of Texas; Containing a Detailed Account of the Battle of San Jacinto. Austin, Texas: Pemberton Press, 1964.

Dublán, Manuel, and José María Lozano (comps.). *Legislación mexicana ó Colección Completa de las Disposiciónes expedidas Desde la Independencia de la Republica. Ordenada por . . . Manuel Dublan y José María Lozano. Edición Oficial.* Tom I [-V]. México: *Imprenta del Comercio á cargo de Dublán, Luzano, hijos, 1876.*

Emory, William H. *Report of the United States and Mexican Boundary Survey, Made Under the Direction of the Secretary of the Interior* (34th Cong., 1st Sess., *Exec. Doc.* 135). 3 vols. Washington, D.C.: Cornelius Wendell, printer, 1857.

Freemasons. Texas. Grand Lodge. *Transactions,* Texas Lodge of Research, A.F. & A.M., 1959-1961. Waco, Texas: 1961.

Gammel, H. P. N. (comp.). *Laws of Texas, 1822-1897.* 10 vols. Austin, Texas: The Gammel Book Co., 1898.

Garrison, George P. (ed.). *Diplomatic Correspondece of the Republic of Texas* in *Annual Report of the American Historical Association,* 1907. vol. II; 1908, vol. II, pts. 1-2. Washington: Government Printing Office, 1908-1911.

de la Garza, Juan Nepomuceno. *Que informado este gobierno . . .* Monterrey, 1845. Broadside. Signed by both Governor de la Garza and Francisco Margain with their rubrics. Dated Monterrey, April 27, 1845.

Gracy, Alice Duggan, Jane Sumner, and Emma Gene Seale Gentry (comps.). *Early Texas Birth Records, 1833-1878.* 2 vols. in 1. Easley, S.C.: Southern Historical Press, c1978.

Herrera, D. José J[oaquín] de. *Discurso pronunciado ante el Congreso general . . . al prestar el juramento para entrar al ejércicio de la presidencia constitucional de la república y contestación del exmo sr. presidente de la Camara dediputados D. Demetrio Montes de Oca.* Mexico, 1845.

Houston, Sam. *Houston's Archives Messages, Jan. 24 and Feb. 2, et seq. and Report of Archive Committee. Morning Star* (Houston), Feb. 9, 1843.

Hunt, Memucan. *Boundary—United States and Texas. House Exec. Doc.,* No. 51, 27th Cong., 2d Sess. Washington, D.C.: 1842.

Hyde, A[rchibald] C., et al. *Address Delivered in the Senate and House of Representatives, of the Legislature of Texas, on the Death of Gen. Forbes Britton and Maj. Sam Bogart, by Hons. A.C. Hyde, B.F. Neal, J.W. Throckmorton, Thos. Lewelly, A.M. Hobby and A.B. Norton.* Austin City: Printed at the Southern Intelligencer Book Printing Establishment, 1861.

Ingmire, Frances Terry (comp.). *Texas Frontiersmen, 1839-1860: Minute Men, Militia, Home Guard, Indian Fighter.* St. Louis, Mo.: Ingmire Publications, 1982.

———. (comp.). *Texas Ranger Service Records, 1830-1846.* St. Louis, Mo.: F. T. Ingmire, c1982.

Jenkins, John H. (ed.). *Memoirs of John Forester: Soldier, Indian Fighter, and Texas Ranger in the Republic of Texas.* Austin, Texas: The Pemberton Press, 1969.

———. (ed.). *The Papers of the Texas Revolution, 1835-1836.* 10 vols. Austin, Texas: Presidial Press, 1973.

Jones, Anson. *Memoranda and Official Correspondence Relating to the Republic of Texas, Its History and Annexation—Including a Brief Autobiography of the Author.* New York: D. Appleton & Co., 1859.

Kinnaird, Lawrence (ed. and trans.). *The Frontiers of New Spain: Nicolás de Lafora's Description, 1766-1768.* Berkeley: University of California Press, 1958.

Manning, William R. (ed.). *Diplomatic Correspondence of the United States: Inter-American Affairs, 1831-1860.* Vol. VIII (Mexico, 1831-1848); and Vol. XII (Texas and Venezuela). Washington: Carnegie Endowment for International Peace, 1937 and 1939.

Mateos, Juan Antonio (comp.). *Historia parlamentaria de los congresos méxicanos de 1821 a 1857.* 2 vols. Mexico: 1877.

Miller, Thomas L. (comp.). *Bounty and Donation Land Grants of Texas, 1835-1888.* Austin, Texas: University of Texas Press, 1968.

Nance, Joseph Milton (trans. and ed.). "Brigadier General Adrián Woll's Report of His Expedition into Texas in 1842,"*Southwestern Historical Quarterly* LVIII (April 1955), pp. 523-52.

Osburn, Mary McMillan (ed.). "The Atascosita Census of 1826," *Texana* I (Fall 1963), pp. 299-321.

Personas Que Han Tenido a Su Cargo La Secretaría de Relaciónes Exteriores, desde Abril de 1823 hasta la Caida del Segundo Imperio (Archivo Historico Diplomatico Méxicano, Num. 6). México, D.F.: 1924.

Program of the Forty-Fourth Annual Meeting of the Texas State Historical Association, Austin, April 26-27, 1940. Austin: Texas State Historical Association, 1940.

Relaciónes diplomaticas hispano-méxicanas, 1839-1898; Documentos procedentes del Archivo de la Embajada de España en Mexico. Serie I-Despachos generales, III (1844-1846). México [City]: El Colegio de México, 1949.

Richardson, James D. (ed.). *A Compilation of the Messages and Papers of the Presidents, 1789-1897.* 10 vols. Washington, D.C.: Government Printing Office, 1896-99.

Schoen, Harold (comp.). *Monuments Erected by the State of Texas to Commemorate the Centenary of Texas Independence.* Austin, Texas: Commission of Control for Texas Centennial Celebrations, 1938.

Smith, W. Broadus (comp.). *Naturalization Records, 1837-1870: Washington County, Texas.* n.p., 1968.

Smither, Harriet (ed.). *Journals of the Fourth Congress of the Republic of Texas, 1839-1840.* 3 vols. in 1. Austin, Texas: Von Boeckmann-Jones Co., [1931?].

———. *Journals of the Sixth Congress of the Republic of Texas.* 3 vols. Austin, Texas: Von Boeckmann-Jones Co., 1940-1945.

Taylor, Virginia H. *The Spanish Archives of the General Land Office of Texas.* Austin, Texas: The Lone Star Press, 1955.

Taylor, Virginia H., and Mrs. B. Brandt (eds.). *Texas Treasury Papers: Letters Received in the Treasury Department of the Republic of Texas, 1836-1846.* Vol. 4, *Supplement and Letters Received from the Military Department.* Austin, Texas: Texas State Library, 1956.

Tena Ramírez, Felipe (comp.). *Leyes fundamentales de México, 1808-1875.* 6th ed. rev., *aumentada y puesta al día.* México: Editorial Porrúa, 1975.

Texas. Republic. Congress. *Republic of Texas. Fifth Congress. First Session, 1840-1841.* Austin: Cruger and Wing, Public Printers, 1841.

———. ———. ———. *Appendix to the Journals of the House of Representatives. Fifth Congress.* Printed at the Gazette Office. [Austin: 1841].

———. ———. ———. *Journals of the Senate of the Republic of Texas. Fifth Congress. First Session.* By order of the Secretary of State. Houston: Printed at the Telegraph Office, 1841.

———. ———. *Journals of the Senate of the Republic of Texas. Sixth Congress, 1841-1842.* Austin, Texas: S. Whiting, Public Printer, 1842.

———. ———. *Journals of the House of Representatives of the Seventh Congress [Called and Regular Sessions] of the Republic of Texas. Convened at Washington on the 14th Nov., 1842.* Washington: Thomas Johnson, 1843.

———. ———. *Appendix to the Journals of the House of Representatives. Seventh Congress.* Printed at the Vindicator Office. [Washington, 1843].

———. ———. *Journals of the Senate of the Seventh Congress of the Republic of Texas. Convened at Washington on the 14th Nov., 1842.* Washington: Thomas Johnson, Public Printer, 1843.

———. ———. *Journals of the House of Representatives of the Eighth Congress of the Republic of Texas.* Houston: Cruger & Moore, 1844.

———. ———. *Journals of the Senate. Eighth Congress of the Republic of Texas.* Houston: Cruger & Moore, 1844.

———. ———. *Journals of the House of Representatives of the Ninth Congress of the Republic of Texas.* Washington, Texas: Miller and Cushney, 1845.

———. ———. *Journals of the Senate of the Ninth Congress of the Republic of Texas.* Washington: Miller & Cushney, 1845.

———. ———. *Appendix to the Journals of the Ninth Congress of the Republic of Texas.* Washington: Miller & Cushney, 1845.

———. ———. *Journals of the House of Representatives of the Extra Session, Ninth Congress, of the Republic of Texas.* Washington: Miller & Cushney, 1845.

———. ———. *Journals of the Senate of the Extra Session, Ninth Congress, of the Republic of Texas.* Washington: Miller & Cushney, 1845.

———. ———. *Journals of the Secret Session of the Extra Session of the Senate, Ninth Congress of the Republic of Texas* [Appendix to] *Journals of the Senate of the Extra Session, Ninth Congress of the Republic of Texas.* Washington: Miller & Cushney, 1845.

———. ———. Senate. *Secret Journals.* See Winkler, E.W. (ed.). *Secret Journals of the Senate.*
    . . .

———. Republic. Conventions. *Journals of the Convention, Assembled at the City of Austin on the Fourth of July, 1845, for the Purpose of Framing a Constitution for the State of Texas.* Austin, Texas: Miner & Cruger, 1845. Facsimile edition by Hart Graphics & Office Center, Inc., Austin, Texas, 1974.

———. ———. ———. Department of War and Marine, *Report of the Secretary of War and Marine,* [dated] 30th Nov. 1843, and signed by G.W. Hill, [Secretary of War and Marine]. Washington: Printed by Thomas Johnson, 1844.

———. ———. *Report of the Acting Secretary of War and Marine,* [dated:] Department of War and Marine, Washington, 30th Nov. 1844, [and signed by] M.C. Hamilton, Acting Secretary of War and Marine, [Washington:] Vindicator Office, 1844.

————. ————. *Laws Passed by the Sixth Congress of the Republic of Texas*. Austin: S. Whiting, 1842.

————. ————. *Laws Passed by the Seventh Congress of the Republic of Texas*. Washington: Thomas Johnson, 1843.

————. ————. *Laws Passed by the Eighth Congress of the Republic of Texas*. Houston: Cruger & Moore, 1844.

————. ————. *Laws Passed by the Ninth Congress of the Republic of Texas*. Washington: Miller & Cushney, 1845.

————. ————. *Laws Passed at the Extra Session of the Ninth Congress of the Republic of Texas*. Washington, 1845.

————. ————. Militia. *Attention Headquarters, 4th Regiment, 2d Brigade, Texas Militia, Galveston, Oct. 23, 1842, Order-No. 30*. By order of Alden A.M. Jackson, Col. Commanding, C. G. Bryant, Act. Adj. Galveston, 1842. Broadside. Copy, Tx-A.

————. ————. President. *Message to the Seventh Congress*. [Washington, Dec. 1, 1842]. Washington: Printed at Texian and Brazos Farmer Office, 1842.

————. ————. *By the President of the Republic of Texas. A Proclamation. Calling the regular session of the Seventh Congress to meet at Washington, Texas, instead of at Austin, on December 5, 1842*. Dated at end: November 21, 1842, and signed:] By the President, Sam Houston. Anson Jones, Secretary of State. Washington: Printed at the Texian and Brazos Farmer Office, 1842.

————. ————. *By the President of the Republic of Texas. A Proclamation of an Armistice with Mexico*. Washington, June 15, 1843, and signed Sam Houston. By the President: Anson Jones, Secretary of State. Washington: Printed at the National Vindicator Office, 1843.

————. ————. *By the President of the Republic of Texas. A Proclamation Ordering Congress to assemble in annual session on December fourth, next, at Washington, instead of Austin, peace with Mexico not yet having been established, and the latter city being situated upon "the extreme frontier."* Dated at end: Washington, Nov. 4, 1843, and signed Sam Houston. By the President, Anson Jones, Secretary of State. Washington: Printed at the National Vindicator Office, 1843.

————. ————. *Message of the President of the Republic of Texas to the Eighth Congress, December 13, 1843*. Washington: Thomas Johnson, 1843.

————. ————. *President Houston's Annual Message, to the Congress of the Republic of Texas*, December 4, 1844. Washington: National Register Office, 1844.

————. State. *General and Special Laws of the State of Texas, Passed by Forty-fourth Legislature at the Regular Session Convened at the City of Austin, January 8, 1935 and Adjourned May 11, 1935*. 2 vols. Austin, Texas: Published under Authority of the State of Texas, [1935].

————. Legislature. *Journals of the House of Representatives of the State of Texas. Fourth Legislature*. Published by Authority. Austin: Printed by William H. Cushney & Hampton, "State Gazette Office," 1852.

————. ————. *Journal of the House of Representatives of the Second Called Session of the Thirty-Eighth Legislature Begun and Held at the City of Austin, April 16, 1923*. Austin, Texas: Von Boeckmann-Jones Co., 1923.

————. ————. *Journal of the Senate of Texas being the Regular Session, Nineteenth Legislature, Begun and Held at the City of Austin, January 13, 1885*. Austin: E.W. Swindells, 1885.

————. ————. Laws. *General Laws of the State of Texas Passed at the Regular Session of the Twenty-First Legislature Convened at the City of Austin, January 8, 1889, and Adjourned April 6, 1889*. Austin, 1889.

————. ————. ————. *General Laws of the State of Texas Passed at the Regular Session of the Twenty-Seventh Legislature Convened at the City of Austin, January 8, 1901, and Adjourned, April 9, 1901*. Austin, Texas: Von Boeckmann, Schutte & Co., 1901.

Tyler, John. *Correspondence with the Government of Mexico*. Sen. Doc. 325, 1842. Washington, 1842.

Ulmer, Mary Lewis (comp.). *An Abstract of Original Titles of Record in the General Land Office*. Reprint of 1838 ed. Austin, Texas: The Pemberton Press, 1964.

United States. Census, 1850. Microcopy No. 432. *Population Schedules of the Seventh Census of the United States, 1850.* Roll 908 (Texas). National Archives, Washington, D.C.

————. Congress. *Senate Executive Documents*, 31st Cong., 1st Sess., Vol. III, No. 32 (Serial No. 558). Washington, D.C.: Union Office, [1850].

————. ————. *Senate Executive Documents*, 32nd Cong., 2nd Sess., Vol. III, No. 14 (Serial No. 660). [No imprint].

————. *Congressional Record*, 75th Cong., 3rd Sess., Appendix, Vol. 83, Pt. 10 (March 28, 1938-June 1, 1938). Washington: Government Printing Office, 1938.

Weeks, William F. (comp.). *Debates of the Texas Convention.* Houston: Telegraph and Texas Register Press, 1846.

White, Gifford E. (ed.). *The 1840 Census of the Republic of Texas.* Austin, Texas: Pemberton Press, 1966.

Wilson, James C. *Circular of the Commissioner of Claims, of the State of Texas, September, 1856.* Austin, Texas: Printed at the Southern Intelligencer Book Office, 1856.

Winkler, E.W. (ed.). *Secret Journals of the Senate, Republic of Texas, 1836-1845.* Edited from the original records in the State Library and the Dept. of State by Ernest William Winkler. Austin, Texas: Austin Printing Co., 1911.

[Woll, Adrián]. *Expedición hecha en Tejas, por una parte de la División del Cuerpo de Egército del Norte.* Monterrey: *Impreso por Francisco Molina,* 1842.

Vermont, State of. *Roster of Soldiers in the War of 1812-14.* Prepared and published under the direction of Herbert T. Johnson, Adjutant General, 1933. [St. Albans: The Messenger Press, 1933].

2. Private Papers, Letters, and Memoirs.

a. Manuscripts and Typescripts.

Adams, Harvey Alexander. "[Journal of An] Expedition Against the Southwest in 1842 and 1843." Typed MS, TxU-A.

Alexander, John R. "Narrative Account of the Mier Expedition." Typed MS., TxU-A.

Allen, A.C. and O.F. Papers. Tx-A.

Bell Family Papers, 1827-1860. TxU-A.

Billingsley, Jesse. Papers, 1835-1889. TxU-A.

Brown, John Henry. Papers, 1835-1872. TxU-A.

————. "Autobiography." MS, TxU-A.

Bryan, Guy Morrison. Letters to. TxU-A.

————. Papers, 1843-1855. TxU-A.

Bryan, John A. Papers, 1841-1872. TxU-A.

Bryan, Moses A. Papers, 1821-1888. TxU-A.

Burleson, Edward. Papers, 1821-1876. TxU-A.

Burleson, Jonathan. Papers, 1839-1867. TxU-A.

Burnet, David G. Papers, 1821-1869. Rosenberg Library, Galveston, Texas.

————. Papers, 1830-1890. TxU-A.

Burnet, Isabella Neff. Papers. University of Virginia Library.

Buster, Claudius. Papers. Daughters of the Republic of Texas Library, The Alamo, San Antonio, Texas.

Canfield, Israel. "Narrative of the Texan Expedition under the command of Col. Wm. S. Fisher, from their entry into Mier, December 23d 1842 until the narrator's liberation, March 7th, 1844." MS, Tx-A.

————. Papers. Tx-A.

Cartwright, Mathew. Papers, 1830-1871. TxU-A.

Chalk, Whitfield. "Reminiscences of Whitfield Chalk," Round Rock, Texas: March 4, [c1900]. Rosenberg Library, Galveston, Texas.

Clark, James. Papers, 1827-1845. TxU-A.

Crittenden, George B. Papers. Tx-A.

Dancy, John W. Diary. TxU-A.

Davenport, Harbert. Manuscripts. TxU-A.

Donelson, Andrew Jackson. Papers. Library of Congress, Washington, D.C.

Duerr, Christian Friederich. Diary, March 21, 1839-Dec. 31, 1844. Typed copy in TxU-A, from original in the Library of Baylor University, Waco, Texas.

Dyer, J.O. "Historical Notes of Galveston," MS, Rosenberg Library, Galveston.

Fontaine, W.W. Papers, 1785-1846. TxU-A.

Ford, John Salman. Memoirs of John S. Ford, and Reminiscences of Texas History from 1836 to 1888. 8 vols. Typed transcript, Tx-A.

————. Papers, 1815-1860. TxU-A.

Fowler, Littleton A. Papers, 1826-1883. Typed transcript, TxU-A.

Franklin, Ben C. Papers, 1805-1889. TxU-A.

Fulmore, Z.T. Papers. TxU-A.

Fulton, J.C. and G.W. Papers, 1836-1846. TxU-A.

Glasscock, James A. "Diary of the Texan Mier Expedition, 1842-1844." MS., Tx-A; photo-copy, TxU-A.

Goodman, H. H. Papers, 1838-1844. TxU-A.

Green, Thomas Jefferson. Papers, 1834-1845. Archives, University of North Carolina Library, Chapel Hill, N.C. Some Thomas J. Green Papers are in Tx-A. and TxU-A.

Grover, George W. Papers. Rosenberg Library, Galveston, Texas.

————. "Scrap Book." Rosenberg Library, Galveston, Texas.

Grover, Walter E. "A Historical Sketch of Galveston Island West of the City Limits." Rosenberg Library, Galveston, Texas.

Hill, John C. C. Papers. Mrs. R.B. Thrasher, Austin, Texas; also, Joseph E. Blanton, Albany, Texas.

Holley, Mary Austin. Papers, 1829-1846. TxU-A.

Houston, Sam. Unpublished Correspondence (copies of scattered original letters). 12 vols. of transcripts. TxU-A.

Hunt, Memucan. Papers. Tx-A.

Hunt, Mrs. Memucan. Diary. Tx-A.

Irion, Robert A. Collection. TxU-A.

Jackson, Andrew. Unpublished Correspondence. Library of Congress, Washington, D.C.

Jenkins, Sr., John H. "Personal Reminiscences of Texas History Relating to Bastrop County, 1828-1847, as dictated to his daughter-in-law, Mrs. Emma Holmes Jenkins of Bastrop, Texas." Typed transcript. TxU-A.

Johnston, Albert Sidney. Papers. Howard Tilton Memorial Library, Tulane University, New Orleans, Louisiana.

Jones, Anson. Memorandum Books, nos. 1-3. TxU-A.

Karnes, Henry W. Papers. Tx-A.

Kemp, Louis Wiltz. Papers. Tx-A.

————. Texas Collection (I - General alphabet of settlers and events. 68 vols.; II - Books of dates — Chronology of Texas History. 4 vols; III - Mier Expedition, 4 vols.). Tx-A.

Kuykendall, James Hampton and William. Papers, 1822-1897. TxU-A.

————. Letters of, 1841-1845. TxU-A.

————. "Sketches of Early Texas." Typed MS, TxU-A.

Lewis, Ira A. Papers, 1813-1873. TxU-A.

Littlejohn, E.G. (comp.). "Texas Scrapbook," 2 vols. Texas Historical Collection, Rosenberg Library, Galveston, Texas.

Lord, George. "Reminiscences of the Texan Mier Expedition." Typed MS, Tx-A.

McCutchan, Joseph D. "Narrative of the Mier Expedition." MS, Rosenberg Library, Galveston, Texas; photostat copy, TxU-A.

McLean, Ephraim. "My Connections with the Mexican War," Paper read to the Texas Historical Society, October 12, 1896, MS, Rosenberg Library, Galveston, Texas.

McLeod, Hugh D. Papers. Tx-A.

Manton, Edward. Papers, 1818-1891. Photostats of originals, TxU-A.

Maverick, Samuel Augustus. Diaries, Miscellaneous, 1829-1843. See Samuel Augustus Maverick Papers, TxU-A.

————. Papers, 1825-1888. TxU-A.

Menefee, John S. Papers, 1831-1859. Photostats, TxU-A.

Menefee, William C. Papers, 1831-1845. TxU-A.

Miller, Dr. James Weston. Diary, 1844-1849. TxU-A.

Miller, Washington D. Papers, 1833-1860. Tx-A; some W.D. Miller Papers in Hardin-Simmons University Library, Abilene, Texas.

Miscellaneous Collection. MS. Texas History Society Collection, Rosenberg Library, Galveston, Texas.

Morgan, James. Papers, 1809-1881. Rosenberg Library, Galveston, Texas.

Navarro, José Antonio. Memoirs. Béxar Archives, TxU-A.

———. Papers. Photocopy, TxU-A.

Nicholson, James. Papers, 1826-1846. TxU-A.

Pease, Elisha M. Papers. Austin Public Library, Austin, Texas.

Perry, James F. Papers. Tx-A.; Transcripts, TxU-A.

Pierson, Edmund. "Goodloe Warren Pierson." MS, in possession of Miss Irene Wendel, Bryan, Texas.

Pierson, John Goodloe Warren. Papers. Robertson Colony Collection, University of Texas at Arlington, Arlington, Texas.

Reding, William R. Papers, 1837-1874. TxU-A.

Ross, Reuben. Papers, 1821-1865. TxU-A.

Rusk, Thomas J. Papers, 1823-1854. TxU-A; Papers, 1837-1854, Duke University Library, Durham, N.C.

Seguín, Juan N. Papers. TxU-A.

Sherman, Sidney. Papers. Rosenberg Library, Galveston, Texas.

Smith, Ashbel. Papers, 1830-1850. TxU-A.

Smith, Henry. Papers, 1822-1846. TxU-A.

Smith, Justin H. Correspondence and Reports of American Agents and Others in Texas, 1836-1845; Notes and Letters Collected. MS, Latin American Collection, TxU-A.

Smith, Sam S. Mier Expedition Muster Rolls, 1842. Sam S. Smith Collection, TxU-A.

Starr, James Harper. Papers, 1830-1850. TxU-A.

Steele, William H. Memorandum. Mrs. T.S. Sutherland Collection, Robertson Colony Collection, University of Texas at Arlington, Arlington, Texas.

Sterne, Adolphus. Papers. Tx-A.

Streeter, Thomas W. Collection. Yale University Library.

Stuart, Ben C. Papers and Scrapbooks, 1872-1926. Rosenberg Library, Galveston, Texas.

Swartwout, Samuel. Papers, 1834-1902. TxU-A; also some papers in Rosenberg Library, Galveston, Texas.

Texas. Republic. Election Register, 1836-1842, Book No. 255. Tx-A.

———. ———. Bonds, Oaths and Resignations. Tx-A.

Thompson, Waddy. Papers, 1824-1848. TxU-A.

Trahern, George Washington. Reminiscences. MS, Bancroft Library, University of California, Berkeley, California.

———. "George W. Trahern. By Himself. A Member of Captain Ewen Cameron's Company A at the Battle of Mier and A Prisoner of Perote. Service through the Entire Mexican War with General Zachary Taylor." Copied from the original Trahern Manuscripts in Bancroft Library, University of California [and given to Dr. Wm. E. Howard, compliments of Louis Lenz. 11/27/46]. Tx-A.

Van Zandt, Isaac. Letters, 1839-1847. Transcripts, TxU-A.

Wade, Houston. Papers. Tx-A.

———. "History of the Mier Expedition Notebook," L. W. Kemp Collection, TxU-A.

———. "Whitfield Chalk." MS, Biographical Notes, Tx-A.

Wagner, H.R. Manuscript Collection. Yale University Library, New Haven, Connecticut.

Wallace, William A.A. Papers. Daughters of the Republic of Texas Library, The Alamo, San Antonio, Texas; also, some Wallace papers in TxU-A.

Webb, William G. "History of John C.C. Hill," Tx-A.

Wilson, Mrs. M.A.C. Scrap Book. Texas State Historical Association, Austin, Texas.

———. Scrap Book. Texas State Historical Association, Austin, Texas.

Wolters, Jacob F. "Dawson Men and the Mier Expedition." Unpublished MS., Rosenberg Library, Galveston, Texas.

Woodhouse, Matthew P. Papers. Tx-A.

Woodland, Henry. "Life and Adventure of Henry Woodland: A Texas Veteran and Mier

Prisoner." Original in possession of L.W. Kemp, Houston, Texas; transcript in Center for American History, University of Texas at Austin, 1957.

Woods, Norman B. Papers and Letters: Perote Letters, Deeds, etc., 1829-1899. Typed MS. from originals loaned by Mrs. D. C. Glimp, Lometa, Texas, 1934. TxU-A.

b. Printed.

"A Leaf from Memory. Scene On the Battle-Field of Salado. By An Old Texian," *Texas Almanac*, 1860, pp. 72-74.

———. "Adventures of a Mier Prisoner; Thrilling Story of John Rufus Alexander, a Member of the Ill-Fated Expedition to Mexico," *Frontier Times* II (Apr. 1925), pp. 17-30.

Allen, L[ewis] L[eonidas]. *Pencillings of Scenes upon the Rio Grande; originally published bu* [?] *the Saint Louis American*. By the Rev. L. L. Allen, Late Chaplain in the Louisiana Volunteers, in the United States Service, Upon the Rio Grande. 2nd ed. enl. and improved. New York, 1848.

Audubon, John Woodhouse. *Audubon's Western Journal, 1849-50* (in Northern Mexico, Texas, and California), in *Magazine of History*, extra no. 14, originally published in 1852; original and complete journal published at Cleveland in 1906 under title: *Audubon's Western Journal*.

Baker, Gen. Moseley. *To the Hon. John Quincey Adams, and the Other Twenty Members of Congress Who Addressed "the People of the Free States of the Union," Remonstrating Against the Annexation of Texas to the American Union*. Washington, 1843; originally published in Houston, Texas, in October 1843.

Barbour, Brevet Major Philip Narbonne. *Journals of the Late Brevet Major in the 3rd Regiment, United States Infantry, Written during the War with Mexico—1846*. Edited by Rhoda van Bibber Tanner. New York: Doubleday, 1936.

Barker, Eugene C. (ed.). *The Austin Papers, in Annual Report of the American Historical Association for the year 1919*, Vol. II, pts. 1-2, and 1922, Vol. II. 2 Vols. Washington, D.C.: Government Printing Office, 1924-1928.

———. (ed.). *The Austin Papers*, Vol. III. Austin: University of Texas Press, 1927.

———. *The French Experience in Mexico, 1821-1861: A History of Constant Misunderstanding*. Chapel Hill: University of North Carolina, c1979.

Barker, Nancy Nichols (trans. and ed.). *The French Legation in Texas*. 2 vols. Austin: Texas State Historical Association, 1971-1973.

Barnes, Charles M. (comp.). *Antonio Menchaca Memoirs*. Yanaguana Society *Publications*, II. San Antonio, Texas: Artes Gráficas, 1937.

Bartlett, John Russell. *Personal Narrative of Explorations and Incidents in Texas, New Mexico, California, Sonora, and Chihuahua, Connected with the United States and Mexican Boundary Commission during the Years 1850, '51, '52, and '53*. New York: D. Appleton & Co., 1854.

Bassett, John Spencer (ed.). *The Correspondence of Andrew Jackson*. 7 vols. Washington, D.C.: Carnegie Institute of Washington, 1926-1935.

Becerra, Francisco. *A Mexican Sergeant's Recollections of the Alamo and San Jacinto as Told to John S. Ford in 1875*. Austin, Texas: Jenkins Publishing Co., 1980.

Bell, Thomas W. *A Narrative of the Capture and Subsequent Sufferings of the Mier Prisoners in Mexico, Captured in the cause of Texas, December 26th 1842 and Liberated Sept. 16, 1844. By Thos. W. Bell One of the Captives*. Printed for the author at the Press of R. Morris & Co., De Soto County, Mississippi, 1845. Reprinted by the Texian Press, Waco, Texas, 1964.

Berlandier, Jean Louis. *Journey to Mexico During the Years 1826 to 1834*. Translated by Shelia M. Ohlendorf, Josette M. Bigelow, and Mary M. Standifer. 2 vols. Austin, Texas: Texas State Historical Association, 1980.

Bryan, Guy M. "Speech of . . . before the Texas Veterans, delivered in the City of Houston, May 14, 1873," in *Texana* VIII (1970), pp. 92-107.

Carefoot, Jean (ed.). *A Guide to Genealogical Resources in the Texas State Archives*. Austin: Archives Division, Texas State Library, 1984.

Carl, Prince of Solms-Braunfels. *Texas, 1844-1845*. Houston, Texas: Anson Jones Press, 1936.

Carleton, James Henry. *The Battle of Buena Vista, with the "Army of Occupation" for One Month*. New York: Harper and Brothers, 1848.

Carpenter, Mrs. V. K. (transcriber). *The State of Texas Federal Population Schedules, Seventh Census of the United States, 1850.* Huntsville, Arkansas: Century Enterprises, Genealogical Services, 1969.

Carpenter, William W. *Travels and Adventures in Mexico: In the Course of Journeys of Upwards of 2500 Miles, Performed on Foot. Giving an Account of the Manners and Customs of the People, and the Agricultural and Mineral Resources of that Country.* New York: Harper, 1851.

Castañeda, Carlos E. *The Mexican Side of the Texan Revolution* [1836]. Dallas, Texas: P.L. Turner Company, 1928. 2nd ed., 1970.

Chabot, Frederick C. (ed.). *The Perote Prisoners: Being the Diary of James L. Trueheart Printed for the First Time Together with an Historical Introduction.* San Antonio, Texas: The Naylor Company, 1934.

———, (ed.). *Texas Letters*, Vol. V of *Yanaguana Society Publications.* San Antonio: Yanaguana Society, 1940.

Chamberlain, Samuel E. *The Recollections of a Rogue: My Confession.* Written and Illustrated by Samuel E. Chamberlain. Introduction and Postscript by Roger Butterfield. New York: Harper & Brothers, c1956.

Chance, Joseph E. (ed.). *The Mexican War Journal of Captain Franklin Smith.* Jackson and London: University Press of Mississippi, 1991.

Cocke, Maj. James D., *et al.* "The Texas Expedition Under Col. W. S. Fisher, and Battle of Mier," in *Morning Star* (Houston), Mar. 4-7, 1843.

[Coleman, Robert M.]. *Houston Displayed; or Who Won the Battle of San Jacinto? By a Farmer in the Army.* Reprinted from the Velasco edition of 1837. Houston: Printed at the Telegraph Office, 1841.

Colt, Samuel. *Saml. Colt's Own Record of Transactions with Captain [Samuel H.] Walker and Eli Whitney, Jr. in 1847.* Foreword and notes by John E. Parsons. Hartford, Conn.: Connecticut Historical Society, 1949.

Crawford, Ann Fears (ed.). *The Eagle: The Autobiography of Santa Anna.* Austin, Texas: Pemberton Press, 1967.

Crofford-Gould, Sherry. *Texas Cemetery Inscriptions: A Source Index.* San Antonio, Texas: Limited Editions, 1977.

Croffut, W. A. (ed.). *Fifty Years in Camp and Field: Diary of Major General Ethan Allen Hitchcock.* New York: G. P. Putnam's Sons, 1909.

Cushing, Caleb. See Benetz, Margaret Diamond (ed.). *The [Caleb] Cushing Reports.*

Davis, Robert E. (ed.). *Diary of William Barret Travis: Hero of the Alamo.* Waco, Texas: Texian Press, 1966.

Day, James M. (ed.). "Diary of James A. Glasscock, Mier Man," in *Texana* I (Spring 1963), pp. 85-119; (Summer 1963), pp. 225-38.

——— (ed.). "Israel Canfield on the Mier Expedition," in *Texas Military History* III (Fall 1963), pp. 165-99.

Delgado, Col. [Pedro Francisco]. *Mexican Account of the Battle of San Jacinto.* Translated from the Spanish. Written by Col. Delgado, Aide to General Santa Anna. Deer Park, Texas: W. C. Day, Superintendent San Jacinto State Park, 1919.

Doubleday, Rhoda Van Bibber Tanner (ed.). *Journals of the Late Brevet Major Philip Norbourne Barbour . . . and His Wife, Martha Isabella Hopkins Barbour, Written During the War with Mexico—1846.* New York: G.P. Putnam's Sons, 1936.

Erath, Lucy A. (ed.). "Memoirs of Major George Bernard Erath," in *Southwestern Historical Quarterly* XXVII (Jan. 1923), pp. 207-55; (Apr. 1923), pp. 255-79; (July 1923), pp 27-51; (Oct. 1923), pp. 140-63.

———. (ed.). *The Memoirs of George B. Erath, 1813-1891.* Dictated to and arranged by Lucy A. Erath. The Heritage Society of Waco *Bulletin* Number Three. Waco, Texas: Heritage Society of Waco, 1956.

Falconer, Thomas. *Expedition to Santa Fé: An Account of Its Journey from Texas through Mexico with Particulars of Its Capture.* New Orleans, 1842.

———. *Letters and Notes on the Texan Santa Fé Expedition, 1841-1842.* New York: Dauber & Pine, 1930.

Fisher, Howard T., and Marion Hall Fisher (eds.). *Life in Mexico; the Letters of Fanny Calderon de la Barca, With New Material from the Author's Private Journals.* [1st ed.] Garden City, N.Y.: Doubleday, 1966.

Fisher, Orceneth. *Sketches of Texas in 1840*. Waco, Texas: Texian Press, 1964. First published in 1841: Springfield, Illinois: Wolters & Weber.

Fisher, William S. (comp.). "A List of Officers Actually in Service of the Army of the Republic of Texas," on May 10, 1836. *Texana* V (Spring 1967), pp. 79-81.

Forester, John. *Memoirs of John Forester, Soldier, Indian Fighter, and Texas Ranger in the Republic of Texas*. Foreword by John H. Jenkins. Austin, Texas: Pemberton Press, 1969.

Freund, Max (trans. and ed.). *Gustav Dresel's Houston Journal: Adventures in North America and Texas, 1837-1841*. Austin: University of Texas Press, 1954.

Friend, Llerena B. (ed.). "Sidelights and Supplements on the Perote Prisoners," *Southwestern Historical Quarterly* LVIII, (Jan. 1965), pp. 366-74; (Apr. 1965), pp. 489-96; LIX (July 1965), pp. 88-95; (Oct. 1965), pp. 224-30; (Jan. 1966), pp. 377-85; (April 1966), pp. 516-24.

———— (ed.). "Thomas W. Bell Letters," *Southwestern Historical Quarterly* LXIII (July 1959), pp. 99-109; (Oct. 1959), pp. 299-310; (Jan. 1960), pp. 457-68); (April 1960), pp. 589-99.

Furber, George C. *The Twelve Months Volunteer; or, Journal of a Private in the Tennessee Regiment of Cavalry in the Campaign in Mexico, 1846-7 . . . with a Description of Texas and Mexico, As Seen on the March*. Cincinnati: J.A. & V.P. Jones, 1849.

Gardiner, C. Harvey. *Mexico, 1825-1828: The Journal and Correspondence of Edward Thornton Tayloe*. Chapel Hill, N.C.: University of North Carolina Press, 1959.

Gilliam, Albert M. *Travels in Mexico during the Years 1843 and 44, including a Description of California, the Principal Cities & Mining Districts of that Republic; the Oregon Territory, etc.* New and complete ed. Aberdeen, 1847.

Gray, William Fairfax. *From Virginia to Texas, 1835; Diary of Col. Wm. F. Gray, Giving Details of His Journey to Texas and Return in 1835 1836 and Second Journey to Texas in 1837*. Houston, Texas: Gray, Dillaye & Co., Printers, 1909. Reprinted: Houston, Texas: Fletcher Young Publishing Co., 1965.

Green, Rena M. (ed.). *Memoirs of Mary A. Maverick: Arranged by Mary A. Maverick and Her Son Geo[rge] Madison Maverick*. San Antonio, Texas: Alamo Printing Company, 1921.

Green, Mary Rowena (ed.). *Samuel Maverick, Texan, 1803-1870. A Collection of Letters, Journals and Memoirs*. San Antonio, Texas: Privately printed, H. Wolff, printer, N.Y., 1953.

Green, Thomas Jefferson. *Address of General Thomas J. Green, Upon the Breaking of Ground On the Atlantic and Pacific Railroad, the Fourth of July, 1854, At the City of Marshall, Texas*. Marshall, Texas: Printed at the "Meridian" Office, 1854.

————. *Journal of the Texian Expedition Against Mier, Subsequent Imprisonment of the Author, His Sufferings and Final Escape from the Castle of Perote with Reflections upon the Present Political and Probable Future Relations of Texas, Mexico, and the United States*. New York: Harper & Brothers, 1845. Facsimile reprint: Austin: Steck & Co., 1935.

————. *Letter of General Thomas J. Green, of California, to the Hon. Robert J. Walker, upon the Subject of Pacific Railroad, September 19, 1853*. New York: Siebells & Maigne, 1853.

————. *Reply of Gen. Thomas J. Green to the Speech of General Sam Houston in the Senate of the United States, August 1, 1854*. [Washington? 1855]. [Dated] Washington City, February 15, 1855. To the Honorable Senate of the United States.

————. "The Texan Expedition Against Mier, 1842: Petition of Gen. Thos. J. Green," in *Publications* of the Southern Historical Association III (April 1899), pp. 115-121.

————. *To the Electors of the Western Congressional District of the State of Texas*. New York: Published at the Office of the Daily & Weekly Globe, by Levi D. Slamm & C. C. Childs, 1845. Signed by Thomas J. Green, City of New York, Oct. 25, 1845.

Green, Wharton J. *Recollections and Reflections: An Autobiography of Half a Century and More*. Raleigh, N.C.: Edwards and Broughton Printing Company, 1906.

Greer, James K. (ed.). "Journal of Ammon Underwood, 1834-1838," *Southwestern Historical Quarterly* XXXII (Oct. 1928), pp. 124-151.

Gulick, Charles A., *et al.* (eds.). *The Papers of Mirabeau Buonaparte Lamar*. 6 vols. Austin, Texas: A. C. Baldwin & Sons, 1921-1927.

Hamilton, James A. *Reminiscences of James A. Hamilton; or, Men and Events, at Home and Abroad, during Three Quarters of a Century*. New York: Charles Scribner and Company, 1869.

Hammond, John Hays. *The Autobiography of John Hays Hammond*. New York: Farrar & Rinehart, Inc., [1935].

Hardy, Robert William Hale. *Travels in the Interior of Mexico, in 1825, 1826, 1827, & 1828*. Glorieta, N.M.: Río Grande Press, 1977.

Harkort, Edward. *In Mexican Prisons: The Journal of Edward Harkort, 1832-1834*. Edited by Louis E. Buster. College Station: Texas A&M University Press, 1986.

Harrell, Milvern. "Reminiscences of Milvern Harrell, The Only Living Survivor of the Dawson Massacre," *Dallas Morning News*, June 16, 1907.

Harris, Mrs. Dilue. "The Reminiscences of Mrs. Dilue Harris," *Quarterly of the Texas State Historical Association* II (Oct. 1900), pp. 86-127; (Jan. 1901), pp. 155-189.

Hill, Lucy A[manda] (comp.). "Genealogy of the Hills." Copy in possession of Joseph E. Blanton, Albany, Texas.

Holland, J. K. "Reminiscences of Austin and Old Washington," *Quarterly of the Texas State Historical Association* I (Oct. 1897), pp. 92-95.

Hollon, W. Eugene, and Ruth L. Butler (eds.). *William Bollaert's Texas*. Norman: University of Oklahoma Press, 1956.

Holmes, John. *Texas: A Self-Portrait*. New York: Harry N. Abrams, Inc., 1983.

Hooton, Charles. *St. Louis' Isle, or Texiana; With Additional Observations Made In the United States and In Canada, With A Portrait and Other Illustrations*. London: Simmonds & Ward, 1847.

Houston, Sam. *Life of General Sam Houston*. 1st ed. Washington: Printed by J. T. Towers, [1855]. Partly prepared by Houston himself and written in the third person.

———. Answering Commodore E. W. Moore, July 15, 1854. *Congressional Globe, Appendix, 1853-1954*, 1st Sess., 33d Cong. pp. 1080-86; also in *Writings of Sam Houston* VI, 30-64.

———. Remarks Concerning E. W. Moore, July 12, 1854. *Congressional Globe, Part III, 1853-1854*, p. 1700; also in *Writings of Sam Houston*. Speech in U.S. Senate on Santa Fé Question and the Conduct of Texan Soldiers in the Mexican War, June 29, & July 3, 1850. *Congressional Globe* XXII, Part 2, 1st Sess., 31st Cong., 1849-1850, pp. 1320-21, 1711-16; also in *Writings of Sam Houston* V, 167-193; William Carey Crane, *Life and Literary Remains of Sam Houston of Texas*, reprint ed. 1972, pp. 375-93.

———. *Speech of Hon. Sam Houston of Texas, in the Senate of the United States, August 1, 1854, on Texan Affairs—Thomas Jefferson Green*. Washington: Congressional Globe Office, 1854; also in *Writings of Sam Houston*, VI, 74-95.

———. *The Texas Navy*. Washington, c. 1849.

———. *Letter to Santa Anna*. Washington, 1852.

———. *The Life of Sam Houston. The Hunter, Patriot, & Statesman of Texas*. (The only Authentic memoir of him ever published.) Philadelphia: Published by G. G. Evans, 1860.

Hughes, Benjamin F. *Diary of Benjamin F. Hughes, 1835-1875*. [n.p., n.d.]. Copied from the original loaned to the Texas Centennial Exposition by Irving Morris, 1936. Copy is in the Southern Methodist University Library, Dallas, Texas.

Hunter, John Warren. *Adventures of a Mier Prisoner, Being the Thrilling Experiences of John Rufus Alexander who was with the Ill-Fated Expedition which Invaded Mexico*. Bandera, Texas: Frontier Times, [1912].

——— (ed.). *Texan Tells the Story of the Mier Expedition with Mexico: John Rufus Alexander's Reminiscences*. [n.p., n.d.].

Hunter, Marvin. *Texan Tells A True Story of the Famous Mier Expedition into Mexico; John Rufus Alexander's Reminiscences Tell One of the Most Daring Adventures in American History*. Rev. and arranged for publication by John Warren Hunter. [San Antonio? 1915?].

Hutchinson, Anderson. "Hutchinson's Diary," in E. W. Winkler (ed.), "The Béxar and Dawson Prisoners," *Quarterly of the Texas State Historical Association* XIII (April 1910), pp. 294-13.

Jenkins, John Holmes, III (ed.). *Recollections of Early Texas: The Memoirs of John Holland Jenkins*. Austin, Texas: University of Texas Press, 1958.

Kelsey, Anna Marietta. *Through the Years: Reminiscences of Pioneer Days on the Texas Border*. San Antonio: Naylor Co., (1952).

Kemp, Louis Wiltz (ed.). "The Joseph H.D. Rogers Letters," *Southwestern Historical Quarterly* LV (July 1951), pp. 102-10; (Oct. 1951), pp. 254-61.

Kendall, George Wilkins. *Narrative of the Texan Santa Fé Expedition, Comprising a Description of a Tour through Texas and Across the Great Southwestern Prairies, the Comanche and Caygua Hunting-Grounds, with an Account of the Suffering from Want of Food, Losses from Hostile Indians, and Final Capture of the Texans and Their March as Prisoners, to the City of Mexico. With Illustrations and a Map.* 2 Vols. Reprint: Austin, Texas: The Steck Company, 1935.

King, C. Richard (ed.). "Andrew Neill's Galveston Letters," *Texana* III (Fall 1965), pp. 203-17.

Kuykendall, J. H. "Reminiscences of Early Texas: A Collection from the Austin Papers," *Quarterly of the Texas State Historical Association* VI (Jan. 1903), pp. 236-53.

La Fora, Nicolás de. *Relación del viaje Que hizo a Los Presidios internos situados en la frontera de la America septentrional perteneciente al Rey de España con un liminar bibliográfico y acotaciónes por Vito Alessio Robles.* Mexico, D.F.: Editorial Pedro Robredo, 1939.

Lane, Walter P. *The Adventures and Recollections of General Walter P. Lane: A San Jacinto Veteran, Containing Sketches of the Texan, Mexican and Late Wars with Several Indian Fights Thrown In.* Ed. by J.W. Pope. Marshall, Texas: Tri-Weekly Herald Print, 1887. Reprints: Marshall, Texas: News Messenger Publishing Co. [c1928]; facsimile ed., Austin, Texas; Pemberton Press, 1970.

Latham, Francis S. *Travels in the Republic of Texas.* Austin: Encino Press, 1971.

"Leaf from Memory: Scene on the Battle-Field of Salado," by an Old Texian, in *Texas Almanac*, 1860, pp. 72-74.

Lee, Nelson. *Three Years Among the Comanches: The Narrative of Nelson Lee, The Texas Ranger. Containing a Detailed Account of His Captivity Among the Indians, His Singular Escape through the Instrumentality of His Watch, and Fully Illustrating Indian Life As It Is On the War Path and In the Camp.* Albany: Baker Taylor, 1859. New ed. Norman: University of Oklahoma Press, 1957.

Linn, John J[oseph]. *Reminiscences of Fifty Years in Texas.* Published for the author. New York: D. & J. Sadler & Co., 1883. Reprinted: Austin, Texas: Steck Company, 1935.

Looscan, Adele B. (ed.). "Journal of Lewis Birdsall Harris, 1836-1842: Personal History of My Son," *Southwestern Historical Quarterly* XXV (July 1921), pp. 3-71; (Oct. 1921), pp. 131-46; (Jan. 1922), pp. 185-97.

——. "Letter from a 'Mier' Prisoner to His Mother," *Quarterly of the Texas State Historical Association* V (July 1901), pp. 66-68.

Lord, George. [Memoirs]. Partial printing of in *Memorial and Genealogical Record of Southwest Texas.* Chicago: Goodspeed Brothers, 1894, pp. 59-63.

McClintock, William A. "Journal of a Trip through Texas and Northern Mexico in 1846-1847," *Southwestern Historical Quarterly* XXXIV (July 1930), pp. 20-37; (Oct. 1930), pp. 141-58; (Jan. 1931), pp. 231-56.

McLean, Malcolm D. (comp. and ed.). *Papers Concerning Robertson's Colony in Texas: Introductory Volume: Robert Leftwich's Mexican and Letterbook, 1822-1824.* Arlington, Texas: The University of Texas at Arlington Press, 1986.

Marcy, R[andolph] B[arnes]. *Thirty Years of Army Life on the Border.* New York: Harper and Brothers, Publishers 1866.

Mares, José Fuentes. *Poinsett: Historia de un gran Intrigo.* México, 1964.

Mayer, Brantz. *Mexico, Aztec, Spanish and Republican: A Historical, Geographical, Political, Statistical and Social Account of that Country from the Period of the Invasion by the Spaniards to the Present Time; with a View of the Ancient Aztec Empire and Civilization; A Historical Sketch of the Late War; and Notices of New Mexico and California.* 2 vols. Hartford: S. Drake and Company, 1853.

——. *Mexico As It Was and As It Is . . . with Numerous Illustrations on Wood, engraved by Butler from Drawings by the Author.* New York: J. Winchester, 1844; ed. 1847; Philadelphia: G. B. Zieber & Company, 1847; ed. New York, 1864.

Medearis, Mary (ed.). *Sam Williams: Printer's Devil; Memorabilia, Some Ante-Bellum Reminiscences of Hempstead County, Arkansas.* Hope, Arkansas: Etter Printing Company, 1979.

"Meeting of Texas Veterans in the City of Houston, On the 13th May, 1873," *Texana* VII (Spring 1969), pp. 82-91.

Menchaca, Antonio. *Memoirs*, ed. by Frederick C. Cabot and published in Yanaguana Society *Publications*, II. San Antonio, Texas: Yanaguana Society, 1937.

Mier Prisoners. Unpublished letter of, *San Antonio Express*, Feb. 9, 1908, p. 27.

Morrell, Z[enos] N. *Flowers and Fruits in the Wilderness or Forty-Six Years in Texas and Two Winters in Honduras*. 4th ed. rev. Dallas, Texas: W.G. Scarff & Co., Publishers, 1886.

Moore, E.W. *To the People of Texas: An Appeal in Vindication of His Conduct of the Navy*. Galveston, Texas: Civilian and Galveston Gazette Office, 1843.

Mullins, Mary Day (comp.). *Republic of Texas: Poll Lists for 1846*. Baltimore: Genealogical Publishing Co., Inc., 1974.

Nance, Joseph Milton (ed.). *Mier Expedition Diary: A Texan Prisoner's Account. By Joseph D. McCutchan*. Austin: University of Texas Press, 1979.

"Narrative of Mier and Perote, By One of the Expedition," *The Planter* [or *Planter's Gazette*] Columbia, Sept. 23, 1843.

Oates, Stephen B. (ed.). *Rip Ford's Texas, by John Salmon Ford*. Austin: University of Texas Press, 1963.

Pace, Eleanor Damon (ed.). "The Diary and Letters of William P. Rogers, 1846-1862," *Southwestern Historical Quarterly* XXXII (April 1929), pp. 259-99.

[Page, Frederic Benjamin]. *Prairiedom: Rambles and Scrambles in Texas or New Estremadura by a Suthron*. New York: Paine & Durgess, 1845.

Pirtle, Lela Neal (ed.). *Life on the Range and On The Trail As Told by R.J. (Bob) Lauderdale and John M. Doak*. San Antonio, Texas: The Naylor Company, c1936.

Pope, J. W. (ed.). *The Adventures and Recollections of General Walter P. Lane: A San Jacinto Veteran, Containing Sketches of the Texan, Mexican and Late Wars with Several Indian Fights Thrown In*. Marshall, Texas: News Messenger Publishing Co., 1928.

Raines, C. W. (ed.). *Six Decades in Texas or Memoirs of Francis Richard Lubbock*. Austin, Texas: Ben C. Jones & Co., 1900.

Red, W. S. "Allen's Reminiscences of Texas, 1838-1842," *Southwestern Historical Quarterly* XVII (Jan. 1914), pp. 283-305; XVIII (Jan. 1915), pp. 287-304.

Reese, Charles K. "Captain Reese's Account of the Drawing of the Beans," *Northern Standard* (Clarksville), Feb. 10, 1844. This account is erroneously attributed to Capt. Charles K. Reese.

Reid, John C. *Reid's Tramp, or A Journal of . . . Travel Through Texas, New Mexico, Arizona, Sonora, and California*. Selma, Alabama: J. Hardy & Co., 1858.

Rodríguez, José María. *Rodríguez Memoirs of Early Texas*. 2nd ed. San Antonio, Texas: Passing Show Printing Company, 1913. Reprint: San Antonio, Texas: Standard Printing Co., 1961.

Roemer, Ferdinand. *Texas with Particular Reference to German Immigration and the Physical Appearance of the Country Described through Personal Observation* [1845-1847]. Translated from the German by Oswald Mueller. San Antonio: Standard Printing Co., 1935.

Ruxton, George Frederick. *Adventures in Mexico and the Rocky Mountains*. New York: Harper & Brothers, 1848.

Samson, William Holland (ed.). *Letters of Zachary Taylor, from the Battlefields of the Mexican War; Reprinted from the Originals in the Collection of Mr. William K. Bixby, of St. Louis, Mo.; with an Introduction, Biographical Notes, an Appendix, and Illustrations from private plates*. Rochester, N.Y.: The Genesee Press, 1908.

Santa Anna, Antonio López de. *Mi Historia, Militar y Politica, 1810-1874: Memorias Ineditas*. García ed. Mexico, 1905.

Shanks, Henry Thomas (ed.). *The Papers of Willie P. Mangum*. 5 vols. Raleigh, N.C.: State Department of Archives and History, 1953.

Sibley, Marilyn McAdams (ed.). *Samuel H. Walker's Account of the Mier Expedition*. Austin, Texas: Texas State Historical Association, 1978.

Smith, Ashbel. *Reminiscences of the Texas Republic: Annual Address Delivered before the Historical Society of Galveston, December 15, 1875*. Galveston: Published by the Society, 1876.

Smither, Harriet (ed.). "Diary of Adolphus Sterne," *Southwestern Historical Quarterly* XXX-XXXVIII (1926-1935).

Sowell, A. J. "Benjamin Z. Boone: Story of One of the Survivors of the Famous Expedition," *Dallas Morning News*, Aug. 4, 1901.

Spellman, L. U. (ed.). "Letters of the 'Dawson Men' from Perote Prison, Mexico, 1842-1843," *Southwestern Historical Quarterly* XXXVIII (April 1935), pp. 246-69.

Stapp, William Preston. *The Prisoners of Perote: Containing A Journal Kept by the Author, Who Was Captured by the Mexicans, at Mier, December 25, 1842, and Released from Perote, May 16, 1844.* Philadelphia: G. B. Zieber, 1845. Reprint: Austin, Texas: University of Texas Press, 1977.

"The Texas Expedition Against Mier, 1842: Petition of Gen. Thos. J. Green," in *Publications* of the Southern Historical Association III, no. 2 (Apr. 1899), p. 114.

Thompson, Waddy. *Recollections of Mexico.* New York: Wiley and Putnam, 1846.

Thwaites, R. G. (ed.). *Early Western Travels, 1748-1846.* 32 vols. Cleveland, Ohio: A. H. Clark Co., 1904-1907.

"Two Letters from a Mier Prisoner," *Quarterly of the Texas State Historical Association* II (Jan. 1899), pp. 233-34.

Tyler, Lyon Gardiner. *The Letters and Times of the Tylers.* 3 vols. Richmond, Va.: Whittet & Sheppearson, etc., 1884-1896.

Wallace, William A.A. ("Big Foot"). "Letters of 'Big Foot' Wallace," *Frontier Times* VIII (June 1930), pp. 417-19.

Williams, Amelia, and Eugene C. Barker (eds.). *The Writings of Sam Houston, 1813-1863.* 8 vols. Austin: University of Texas Press, 1938-1943.

Wilson, Clyde N. *et al.* (eds.). *The Papers of John C. Calhoun.* 20 vols. Columbia: University of South Carolina Press, 1959-61.

Wilson, James C. *Address on the Occasion of Removing the Remains of Captains Walker and Gillespie, on the Twenty-First of April, A.D. 1856.* Published by a Committee of Citizens. San Antonio, Texas: Printed at the Office of the San Antonio Ledger, [1856].

Winkler, Ernest W. (ed.). "The Béxar and Dawson Prisoners," *Quarterly of the Texas State Historical Association* XIII (Apr. 1910), pp. 292-32.

——— (ed.). "The Bryan-Hayes Correspondence," *Southwestern Historical Quarterly* XXX (June 1926), pp. 68-74.

——— (ed.). *Manuscript Letters and Documents of Early Texans, 1821-1845.* Austin, Texas: The Steck Company, 1937.

Wislizenus, A. *Memoir of A Tour to Northern Mexico, Connected with Col. Doniphan's Expedition in 1846-47.* Washington, 1848. (U.S. Senate Misc. Docs., I, no. 26, 30th Cong., 1st Sess.)

[Woodland, Henry]. "The Story of the Massacre of Mier Prisoners: Mr. Henry Woodland, Who Once Lived Near Houston, and Was One of the Captured, Tells of Their Trials and Hardships," *Houston Daily Post*, Aug. 16, 1891, p. 8, col. 1. Article signed by "A. W. P."

3. Maps.

Aranzas Bay, As Surveyed by Capt. Monroe of the "Amos Wright." Southampton, 1841.

Arbingast, Stanley A., Calvin P. Blair, *et al. Atlas of Mexico.* Austin: Bureau of Business Research, University of Texas at Austin, 1975.

Arbingast, Stanley Alan, and Others. *Atlas of Texas.* 5th rev. ed. Austin: University of Texas at Austin, Bureau of Businesss Research, 1976.

Arrowsmith, John. *Map of Texas: Compiled from Surveys in the Land Office of Texas and Other Official Surveys.* London: Published by John Arrowsmith, 1841.

Blake, J. Edmund. "The Map of the Country in the Vicinity of San Antonio de Béxar," 1845. Original in the National Archives, Washington, D.C.

Brackettville [Texas]. Quadrangle, May 1897 ed. Reprinted in U.S. Department of the Interior, *Geological Survey.* Washington, D.C.: Government Printing Office, 1932.

Bradford, Thomas G. *Texas* [Republic of Texas]. n.p., n.d. [Boston, 1838].

Canalizo, Valentín. *"Plano topografico que comprehende por el N. hasta Vejar, por el E. hasta San Patricio, por S.E. hasta Camargo, por el S. O. hasta Saltillo, por el O. hasta Monclova."* 1838. In Center for American History, University of Texas at Austin.

Castañeda, Carlos E., and Early Martin, Jr. *Three Manuscript Maps of Texas by Stephen F. Austin, with Biographical and Bibliographical Notes.* Austin, Texas: Privately printed, 1930.

Central America Including Texas, California, and the Northern States of Mexico [1842]. [London:] Published by the Society for diffusion of Useful Knowledge by Chapman & Hall, 186 Strand, 1842.

Cline [Texas] Quadrangle. Reprinted in U.S. Department of the Interior, Geological Survey. Washington, D.C.: Government Printing Office, 1949.

The Coast of Texas: From Documents Furnished by W. Kennedy, Esq., H. M. Consul at Galveston. London: Published according to Act of Parliament at the Hydrographic Office of the Admiralty, August 26, 1844.

Dimmit County, Texas. U.S. Department of Agriculture Soil Survey, 1938, no. 4, issued April 1943.

Disturnell, John. *Mapa de los Estados Unidos de México, Segun le organizado y definido de los varias actas del Congreso de diche República y construido por las mejores authoridades*. Rev. ed. Nueva York: Lo Publican J. Disturnell, 1846. Photocopy, Tx-A.

Early Spanish and Mexican Land Grants, Map of. Corpus Christi-Brownsville area. See Tom Lea, *The King Ranch* I, 378-79.

Emory, William H. *Map of Texas and the Countries Adjacent: Compiled in the Bureau of the Corps of Topographical Engineers from the Best Authorities for the State Department . . .* [Washington, D.C.:] Published by order of the United States Senate, 1844.

[Galveston]. *A Large, Detailed Coast Survey Chart of Galveston Bay, Noting the Shoreline in Detail, Bolivar Peninsula, Turtle Bay, etc., with Many Soundings. Detailed insets of Clopper's Bar ("indicating proposed Site for a Light House") and Red Fish Bar*. Washington, 1851.

García y Cubas, Antonio. *Atlas geográfico estadistico é historico de la república méxicana*. México City: J. M. Fernañdez de Lara, 1858.

Hooker, W. "Map of the State of Coahuila and Texas." Published as frontispiece in Mary Austin Holley, *Texas*. Austin, Texas: The Steck Company, 1935.

Ikin, Arthur. "Map of Texas." J. & C. Walker, Lithographers. Published as frontispiece in Arthur Akin, *Texas: Its History, Topography, Agriculture, Commerce, and General Statistics*. London: Sherwood, Gilbert, and Piper, 1848.

Map of San Marcos Road Expedition, 1840-41, in *Texas Military History* VI (Summer 1967), p. 130.

Map of Texas and Part of New Mexico Compiled in the Bureau of Topograph^c Eng^r Chiefly for Military Purposes. New York: H.F. Walling Map Establishment, 1857.

Map of Texas from the Most Recent Authorities. Philadelphia: Thomas Cowperthwait & Co., 1845.

Mapa de los Estados Unidos Méxicanos arreghada a las distribución que en diversos de. . .ha hecho del territorio el Congreso general Méjicano. Paris: Publicado por Rosa, 1837.

Mexico & Guatimala [sic] with the Republic of Texas. Edinburgh: W. Lizars, [1836?].

Morse, Sidney E., and Samuel Bangs. *Texas [1844]*. New York: 1844.

New Map of Texas, 1841. n. p.: Day & Haghe Lithographers to the Queen, [1844].

New Map of Texas, Oregon, and California with the Regions Adjoining, A. Philadelphia: Published by S. Augustus Mitchell, 1846.

Preliminary Chart of the Entrance to Matagorda Bay, Texas. Washington, 1857.

Preliminary Chart of the Sea Coast of Texas in the Vicinity of Galveston. Washington: 1856.

"Southwest Texas." U.S. Department of Agriculture, *Field Operations of the Bureau of Soils*, 1911, no. 28.

State of Texas, by Prof. H. D. Rogers and A. Keith Johnston, F. R. S. E. London & Massachusetts, [1857?].

[Texas]. *An Early Map of the State, Now Showing Many Counties, including a Huge Presidio, but the Panhandle Still Undivided. Notes on Topography (Salt Plains, Rolling Table Lands), Many Indian Tribes located, including the Comanches and Lipans. Inset of the "Vicinity of Galveston City."* Philadelphia, 1852.

[Texas]. *From Map of the State of Texas Prepared under the Direction of* Brvt. Ma^j. G. L. Gellespie, Capt. Eng^r U.S.A., 1865.

Texas. Part of New Mexico. Drawn and engraved by J. Bartholomew. Edinburgh, 1865.

Topographical Map of the Republic of Texas, and North Mexico with the Contiguous American States, and Territories, A. Unsigned and undated [ca. 1844]. MS, TxU-A.

Uvalde [Texas] Quadrangle, Feb. 1898 ed. Reprinted in U.S. Department of the Interior *Geological Survey*. Washington, D.C.: Government Printing Office, 1931.

Williams, C. S. *Map of Texas from the Most Recent Authorities*, [1845]. Philadelphia: C. S. Williams, 1845.

Wilson, James T. D. *A New & Correct Map of Texas. Compiled from the Most Recent Surveys & Authorities to the Year 1845*. New Orleans: Published by R. W. Fishbourne, [1845].

Wyld, James. *Wyld's Map of Texas, 1840*. London, Published by James Wyld, Geographer to the Queen . . . 1840.

Yeager, B. E. *A New Map of Texas with the Contiguous American & Mexican States: Compiled from the Latest Authorities*. Galveston, Texas: E. Yeager, 1840.

"Zavalla County, Texas." U.S. Department of Agriculture, *Soil Survey*, 1934, no. 21 (issued June 1940).

4. Newspapers.

Abingdon Virginian (Abingdon, Va.), 1839-1917.

Advocate and the People's Rights (Brazoria), Nov. 23, 1833-Mar., 1834.

Aguila Mexicana (Mexico, D.F.), Jan. 1-30, 1843.

Arkansas State Gazette (Little Rock), Aug. 26, 1828; Mar. 23, 1830; Sept. 1, 1835-Apr. 1, 1846.

Austin City Gazette, Oct. 17, 1839; Mar. 4 and Dec. 30, 1840; Feb. 19, 1942.

Austin Daily Statesman, Apr. 19, 20, and 22, 1907.

Austin Statesman, Feb. 19, 1904.

Bastrop Advertiser, Apr. 18, 1885.

Boletín de San Luis Potosí, El, Núm. Extraordinario, Mar. 15, 1843.

Brazoria People (Brazoria), June 29, 1838.

Brazos Courier (Brazoria), Dec. 3, 1839-Dec. 22, 1840.

Brazos Farmer (Washington, Texas).

Charleston Courier (Charleston, S.C.), Feb. 14, 1843.

Civilian and Galveston City Gazette, Oct. 12, 1842-Sept. 7, 1844; Sept. 25, 1848. Also as *Galveston Civilian*.

Colorado Gazette (Matagorda), 1839-1842.

Colorado Gazette and Advertiser (Matagorda), Nov. 9, 1839-Nov. 16, 1839; Jan. 11, 1840-June 4, 1842.

Colorado Tribune (Matagorda), 1849-1852.

Columbia Democrat (Columbia, Texas), Oct. 19, 1853-July 24, 1855.

Commercial Bulletin (New Orleans), Mar. 15, 1838.

Le Courrier Français (México City), [1844-1846].

Congressional Globe (Washington, D.C.), 1841-1855.

Constitutional Advocate and Texas Public Advertiser (Brazoria), Sept. 5, 1832-June 15, 1833.

Constitutionalist (Augusta, Ga.), Apr. 8, May 18, 1843.

Corpus Christi Caller-Times, Nov. 13, 1960.

Corpus Christi Gazette, Jan. 1-Apr. 2, 1846.

Cosmopolita, El (Mexico City), Sept. 2, 1842-July 23, 1843.

Crescent City (New Orleans), [Oct. 6, 1840-July 11, 1842].

Crystal Reflector (Corpus Christi), June, 1939.

Cuero Star (Cuero, Texas), Mar. 8, 1899.

Daily Courier (Charleston, S.C.), Oct. 30, 1854.

Daily Globe and Galveston Commercial Chronicle, Nov., 1845-Dec., 1845.

Daily Missouri Republican (St. Louis), Jan. 2, 1843-Apr., 1844.

Daily National Intelligencer (Washington, D.C.), 1841-Dec. 31, 1844.

Daily National Register (Washington, D.C.), Jan. 2, 1843-Feb. 27, 1846.

Daily Picayune (New Orleans), July 7, 1841-Oct. 27, 1848.

Daily Tropic (New Orleans), Apr. 19, 1843.

Dallas Daily Herald, Mar. 25, 1880-1883.

Dallas Herald, Dec. 3, 1855-1856.

Dallas (Evening) Journal, Apr. 14, 1914-June, 1938.

Dallas Morning News, Apr. 23, 1893; Dec. 20, 1896; Aug. 4, 1901; Oct. 22, 1905; June 16, 1907; Sept. 12, 1912; Dec. 22, 1919; June 9, 1927; June 23 and Dec. 22, 1929; Oct. 19, 1930; Feb. 21, 1932; Sept. 24, 1933; Nov. 3, 1954; Sept. 24, 1957; Apr. 10, 1959; Feb. 17, 1965.

————. Index for 1918.

Democrat and Planter (Columbia), Oct. 9, 1855-Oct. 22, 1861; Dec. 3, 1861.

Democratic Telegraph and Texas Register (Houston), July 29 and Dec. 7, 1846; June 29 and July 13, 1848.

Diablo Conjuelo, El (México City), Jan. 12-June 10, 1843.

Diana de Matamoros, La, June 24, 1846.

Diario del Gobierno de los Estados Unidos Méxicanos (México City), Feb. 10, 1835-Sept. 12, 1847.

El Paso Herald Post, Sept. 28, 1983.

Fayette County Record (LaGrange, Texas), June 11, 1931.

Federal Union (Milledgeville, Ga.), May 4 and 25, July 13, Nov. 22, 1847.

Fort Worth Star-Telegram, May 26, 1922.

Fredericksburg Standard (Fredericksburg, Texas), May 1, 1931.

Gaceta del Gobierno del Estado do los Tamaulipas (Tampico), Mar. 18, 1843.

Gaceta de Victoria, La., [Feb. 1843].

Galveston Commercial Adveriser, July, 1842-Aug., 1844.

Galveston Daily News, March 17, Nov. 5, Dec. 6, 1844; June 24, 1848; Mar. 17, 1874; Dec. 8, 1878; Mar. 9 and 10, 1880; Feb. 17, 1881; Apr. 23, 1888; Jan. 24 and Feb. 19, 1904; Mar. 31, 1907.

Galveston Times, Mar. 27-May 16, 1843.

Galveston Weekly News, [Feb. 1844-Sept. 1845].

Gonzales Inquirer, Apr. 14-21, 1855.

Houston Chronicle Magazine, June 8, 1947.

Houston Daily Post, Apr. 14-21, 1855; Sept. 16, 1891; Feb. 9, 1930; Apr. 19, 1936; Sept. 11, 1967; Mar. 24, 1968.

Houston Post-Dispatch, May 26, 1919; Sept. 30, 1928.

Houstonian Weekly, [Apr. 1841-June 1843].

Independent Chronicle (Galveston), Aug. 1, 1843-Apr., 1844.

Indianola Bulletin, Mar. 11, 1852-Feb. 17, 1853; [Mar. 3, 1853-May 24, 1864].

LaGrange Intelligencer, Jan. 25-Sept. 5, 1844.

LaGrange Journal, June 12, 1929; June 16-Sept. 28, 1931; Aug. 3, 1933; Sept. 20, 1934; Feb. 22-May 16, 1940; June 5, 1941.

LaGrange Paper, The, Feb. 22-Aug. 4, 1856.

Latigo de Texas, El (Matamoros), [Jan. 23, 1843-Dec. 20, 1844].

Lexington Observer (Lexington, Ky.), Oct. 16, 1844.

London Times, Oct. 19, 1843; Apr. 3 and Sept. 6, 1844.

Lucero de Tacubaya, El (Tacubaya, Mex.), [1844].

Marshall Review, Apr. 8, 1843.

Matamoros Reveille, June 24, 1846.

Mississippi Free Trader (Natchez), Aug. 4, 1835-Apr. 1, 1846.

Mississippian (Jackson), May 25, 1838-Apr. 1, 1846.

Mobile Register and Journal, Dec. 31, 1844.

Morning Star (Houston), Apr. 8, 1839-Feb. 3, 1846.

Nacional, El (Jalapa), Dec. 15, 1842.

Nashville Republican Banner, Apr. 22, 1837-Apr. 1, 1846.

National Intelligencer (Houston), Mar. 1, 28, Apr. 18, May 9, June 20, July 4, 1839.

National Vindicator (Washington), July 1, Nov. 25, Dec. 16, 20, 1843; Jan. 13, Feb. 5, 10, Apr. 13, 20, 1844.

The New Era (LaGrange), May 17, 1872.

New Orleans Bee, Jan. 13-Sept. 25, 1843.

New Orleans Commercial Bulletin, Mar. 15, 1838.

New Orleans Daily Bulletin (also as *New Orleans Bulletin*), Jan. 21-Sept. 20, 1843.

Niles' National Register (Baltimore), 1839-1848.

Northern Standard (Clarksville), Aug. 20, 1842-Oct. 11, 1856.

Old Capitol, The (Columbia, Texas), Feb. 4, 1888.

Planter, The (Columbia, Texas), Sept. 23, 1843; Feb. 10, Apr. 5, 1844. Title varies: *Planter's Gazette.*

Provisional, El (Matamoros), Oct. 7, 14, 1842.

Red-Lander (San Augustine), [May 27, 1841-Apr. 1843].

Republican Banner (Nashville), Aug. 22, 1837-Apr. 1, 1846.

St. Louis Globe-Democrat, July 30, 1905.

San Antonio Daily Express, Nov. 19, 1905; Feb. 9, 1908; Sept. 15, 1912; July 27, 1913; June 21, 1929; Feb. 25, June 24, 1934. Title varies: *San Antonio Express.*

San Antonio Express-News, Aug. 10, 1963; Apr. 19, 1964; Jan. 23, 1972; May 15, 17, 1975.

San Antonio Herald, Apr. 26, 1855; Aug. 24, 1872. Title varies: *San Antonio Daily Herald.*

San Antonio Light, Feb. 13, 1938; July 19, 1968.

San Antonio Tri-Weekly Herald, Sept. 2, 1865.

San Antonio Weekly Herald, June 12, 1855-Nov. 28, 1874.

Saturday Courier (Philadelphia), Apr. 26, 1845.

Seguin Enterprise, Dec. 28, 1906; July 22, 1938.

Semañario de Monterrey, Feb. 2 and 9 (Supplement), 1843.

Semañario Politico del Gobierno del Nuevo León, El (Monterrey), Dec. 29, 1842; Feb. 2, 23, Mar. 9, 1843.

Siglo Diez y Nuve [XIX], El (México City), Oct. 8, 1841-1845. Suspended publication: Jan. 16-Mar. 1, 1843.

Southern Intelligencer (Austin), Nov. 19, 1856-Dec. 16, 1857.

State Gazette (Austin), May 18, 1850.

Telegraph and Texas Register (Houston), Dec. 11, 1839-1845.

Texas Democrat (Austin), Jan. 21, Dec. 16, 1846; Jan. 6, 1847.

Texas Monument (LaGrange), [July 10, 1850-1853].

Texas Mute Ranger (Austin), May 1878 (vol. 1, no. 3); Nov. 1881; Feb. 1882; Feb. 1883, pp. 101-07; Mar. and May 1883.

Texas National Register (Washington-on the Brazos; moved to Austin, Nov. 15, 1845), Dec. 7, 1844-Jan. 10, 1846.

Texas Sentinel (Austin), Jan. 15, 1840-Nov. 11, 1841.

Texas State Gazette (Austin), 1845-Sept. 13, 1851; June 12, 1852; Mar. 19, Apr. 2, 9, May 21, Oct. 1, 1853; 1856-1858.

Texas Times (Galveston), Oct. 18, Nov. 2-23, Dec. 731, 1842; Jan. 7, Feb. 4, 11-Apr. 22, 1843.

Texian and Brazos Farmer (Washington, Texas), Jan. 28, Apr. 8, 1843.

True Issue (LaGrange), [Oct.-Dec. 22, 1855-June 17, 1865].

Views Tribune (Houston Post), Aug. 25, 1928 (Magazine Section of the *Houston Post*).

Voto de Coahuila, El (Saltillo), Aug. 20, Dec. 31, 1842.

Weekly Bulletin (New Orleans), Feb. 25, 1843.

Weekly Citizen, The (Houston), Dec. 9, 1843-Jan. 1844.

Weekly Crescent City (New Orleans), Mar. 14-May 30, 1841.

Weekly Herald, The (New York), Jan. 1, 1853.

Weekly Messenger (Russellville, Ky.), Nov. 21, 1828.

Western Advocate (Austin). Prospectus of the *Western Advocate* [signed and dated at end:] George K. Tuelon. Austin, February 4, 1843. Austin: Printed at the *Western Advocate* Office, 1843. Broadside.

Western Chronicle (Sutherland Springs), Nov. 2, Dec. 14, 1877.

Western Texian (San Antonio), [1848-1856].

Williamson County Sun (Georgetown), June 16, 1950.

B. Secondary Sources

1. Manuscripts and Typescripts.

Adams, Allen F. "The Leader of the Volunteer Grays: The Life of William G. Cooke, 1808-1847." Master's thesis, Southwest Texas State Teachers College, 1940.

Affleck, J. D. "History of John C. Hays," Pts. I-II. Typed MS, TxU-A.

Barker, Bernice. "The Texan Expedition to the Río Grande in 1842." Master's thesis, University of Texas, 1929.

Benavides, Ilma M. "General Adrián Woll's Invasion of San Antonio in 1842." Master's thesis, University of Texas, 1952.

Berge, Dennis. "The Mexican Response to United States Expansionism, 1845-48." Ph.D. dissertation, University of California at Berkeley, 1965.

Boener, Gerald. "Austin, 1836-1877." Typed MS, Tx-A.

Boozer, Jesse Beryl. "The History of Indianola, Texas." Master's thesis, University of Texas, 1942.

Brack, Gene Martin. "Imperious Neighbor: The Mexican View of the United States, 1821-1846." Ph.D. dissertation, University of Texas, 1967.

Breeding, Sr., S. D. (comp.). "George Washington Glasscock of Kentucky and Texas and His Family." MS, Tx-A.

Brennan, Mary Estes. "American and British Travellers in Mexico." Ph.D. dissertation, University of Texas at Ausin, 1973.

Bridges, Jim L. "History of Fort Bend County, 1822-1861." Master's thesis, University of Texas, 1939.

Brown, Alma Howell. "The Consular Service of the Republic of Texas." Master's thesis, University of Texas, 1929.

Brown, Frank. "Annals of Travis County and the City of Austin from the Earliest Times to the Close of 1875." 13 vols. Typescript, Tx-A and TxU-A.

Cale, Ada Warren. "Texas Frontier Problems, 1836-1860." Master's thesis, St. Mary's University, San Antonio, Texas 1944.

Catterton, Conn Dewitt. "The Political Campaigns of the Republic of Texas of 1841 and 1842." Master's thesis, University of Texas, 1935.

"Corrections and Narratives to be Erected Around the Tomb and Placed on the Monument at Monument Hill State Historic Site," Typed MS, Museum, Monument Hill State Park, LaGrange, Texas.

Cotner, Thomas Ewing. "The Military and Political Career of José Joaquín Herrera, 1792-1854." Ph.D. dissertation, University of Texas, 1947.

Cottrell, Dorothy. "Texas Reprisals Against Mexico in 1843." Master's thesis, University of New Mexico, 1934.

Crane, Robert Edmund Lee. "The Administration of the Customs Service of the Republic of Texas." Master's thesis, University of Texas, 1939.

———. "The History of the Revenue Service and the Commerce of the Republic of Texas." Ph.D. dissertation, University of Texas, 1950.

Cravens, Lucy Elizabeth. "The Congressional History of the Annexation of Texas." Master's thesis, University of Texas, 1927.

Crawford, Polly Pearl. "The Beginnings of Spanish Settlement in the Lower Río Grande Valley." Master's thesis, University of Texas, 1925.

Crisp, James Ernest. "Anglo Texan Attitudes toward the Mexicans, 1821-1845." Ph.D. dissertation, Yale University, 1976.

Crimmins, Martin L. "Captain Ewen Cameron: A Hero of the Battle of Mier." Typed MS, Jenkins Garrett Library, Special Collections, The University of Texas at Arlington.

Crook, Garland Elaine. "San Antonio, Texas, 1846-1861." Master's thesis, Rice University, 1964.

Davenport, Herbert. "Notes from An Unfinished Story of Fannin and His Men." Typed MS, Texas A&M University Library.

Day, Donald E. "A Life of William Shannon, Governor of Ohio, Diplomat, Territorial Governor of Kansas." Ph.D. dissertation, Ohio State University, 1978.

Deviney, Marvin Lee. "The History of Nueces County in 1850." Master's thesis, University of Texas, 1933.

Dixon, Sam H. "The Heir of Encero. A Tale of Mexico, and Relating to the Mier Expedition of 1842." MS, Tx-A.

Downs, Fane. "The History of Mexicans in Texas, 1720-1845." Ph.D. dissertation, Texas Tech University, 1970.

Duerr, Christian Friedrich. Diary, March 21, 1839-Dec. 31, 1844. MS, Baylor University Library; transcript in TxU-A.

Dyer, J.O. "Historical Notes of Galveston." Rosenberg Library, Galveston, Texas.

Eliot, Lynn. "Ewen Cameron, Adventurer." MS, Jenkins Garrett Library, Special Collections, The University of Texas at Arlington.

Flaccus, Elmer William. "Guadalupe Victoria: Mexican Revolutionary Patriot and First President, 1786-1843." Ph.D. dissertation, University of Texas, 1951.

Fluth, Alice Freeman. "Indianola Early Gateway to Texas." Master's thesis, St. Mary's University, San Antonio, Texas, 1939.

Fox, Neal B. "A Correlated Study-Unit of a Diary of the Expedition Against the Southwest, 1842-1843." Master's thesis, Southwest Texas State Teachers College, 1947.

Fritz, Naomi. "José Antonio Navarro." Master's thesis, St. Mary's University, San Antonio, Texas, 1941.

"Galveston Sketches." Typescript, Tx-A.

Gambrell, Thomas DeWitt. "The Army of the Republic of Texas, 1836-1846." Master's thesis, University of Texas, 1917.

Goerner, Walter John. "Indianola: A Historic Landmark of Early European Pioneers in Texas." Master's thesis, Southwestern University, 1930.

Gore, Walter Reece. "The Life of Henry Lawrence Kinney." Master's thesis, University of Texas, 1948.

Graf, LeRoy P. "The Economic History of the Lower Río Grande Valley, 1820-1875." 2 vols. Ph.D. dissertation, Harvard University, 1942.

Graham, Stanley Sitton. "Garrison Life of the Mounted Soldier on the Great Plains, Texas, and New Mexico Frontiers, 1833-1865." Master's thesis, North Texas State University, 1969.

———. "Life of the Enlisted Soldier on the Western Frontier, 1815-1845." Ph.D. dissertation, North Texas State University, 1972.

Grant, Mary Catherine. "The Texan Expedition to Santa Fé." Master's thesis, Washington University, 1930.

Griffin, Roger Allen. "Connecticut Yankee in Texas: A Biography of Elisha Marshall Pease." Ph.D. dissertation, University of Texas, 1973.

Grover, Walter E. "A Historical Sketch of Galveston Island West of the City Limits." Typed MS, Rosenberg Library, Galveston, Texas.

Halfin, Mrs. Hardie Nancy. "Statement on William P. Stapp." Typed MS., Tx-A.

Hall, Jacqueline Rankin (comp.). "A Calendar of the Memorials and Petitions to the Legislature from 1877 to 1937." Master's thesis, University of Texas, 1938.

Hambric, Jacqueline Barnett. "The Frontier Times Magazine, 1923-1954: An Index and Brief History." 2 vols. Master's thesis, Texas A&M University, 1979.

Hancock, Walter Edgar. "The Career of General Antonio López de Santa Anna (1794-1833)." Ph.D. dissertation, University of Texas, 1933.

Huckeba, Lula B. (comp.). "A Calendar of the Memorials and Petitions to the Legislature of Texas from 1846 to 1860." Master's thesis, University of Texas, 1935.

Harding, Jocobina B. "A History of the Early Newspapers of San Antonio, 1823-1874." Master's thesis, University of Texas, 1951.

Harris, Helen Willits. "The Public Life of Juan Nepomuceno Almonte." Ph.D. dissertation, University of Texas, 1935.

Hill, James Lyle. "The Life of Judge William Pitt Ballinger." Master's thesis, University of Texas, 1937.

Huckeba, Lula B. "A Calendar of the Memorials and Petitions to the Legislature of Texas from 1846 to 1860." Master's thesis, University of Texas, 1935.

Huson, Hobart. "Iron Men: A History of the Republic of the Río Grande and the Federalist War in Northern Mexico." [1940] One of sixtuplicate typed copies of the original MS, TxU-A.

Imle, Edgar Fremont. "An Abstract of Biographical Data in the Texas Supreme Court Reports, 1840-1857." Master's thesis, University of Texas, 1937.

Jones, Clyde V. "Fayette County, Texas." Master's thesis, St. Mary's University, San Antonio, Texas, 1948.

Kemp, L. W. "Men of Mier." L. W. Kemp Collection, TxU-A.

King, John Morrison. "English Interests in Texas, 1810-1845." Master's thesis, University of Oklahoma, 1935.

Koch, Lena Clara. "The Federal Indian Policy of Texas," *Southwestern Historical Quarterly* XXVIII (Jan. 1925), pp. 223-34; (Apr. 1925), pp. 259-86; XXIX (July 1925), pp. 19-35; (Oct. 1925), pp. 98-127.

Kuykendall, J. H. "Sketches of Early Texians." TxU-A.

Leach, J. M. "Reuben Marmaduke Potter." Master's thesis, University of Texas, 1939.

"A List of the Names of the Men Who Were Members of the Mier Expedition As They Appear on the Monument—With Corrections, Additions, References and Comments, [Including] Dawson's Men—Corrections," Typed MS, Museum, Monument Hill State Park, LaGrange, Texas.

Littlejohn, E. C. (comp.). "Texas Scrap-Book, I-II." Rosenberg Library, Galveston, Texas.

Luker, Julia Eugenia. "The Diplomatic Relations between Texas and Mexico, 1836-1842." Master's thesis, University of Texas, 1920.

McClendon, Robert Earl. "Daniel Webster and Mexican Relations, 1841-1843." Master's thesis, University of Texas, 1924.

Manheimer, Eric I. "Texan Diplomatic Relations with France, 1837-1845." Master's thesis, New York University, 1946.

Martin, Lillian Davis. "The History of the Galveston News." Master's thesis, University of Texas. 1929.

Mier Expedition Papers, 1840-1937. TxU-A.

Mier Expedition Scrapbook. TxU-A.

Moore, Robert Lee. "History of Refugio County." Master's thesis, University of Texas, 1937.

Morris, Elizabeth Yates. "James Pinckney Henderson." Master's thesis, University of Texas, 1931.

Neighbors, Alice Atkinson. "Life and Public Works of Robert S. Neighbors," Master's thesis, University of Texas, 1936.

Neighbors, Kenneth Franklin. "Robert S. Neighbors in Texas, 1836-1859: A Quarter Century of Frontier Problems." Ph.D. dissertation, University of Texas, 1955.

Nuby, Oradel. "Public Career of Memucan Hunt." Master's thesis, University of Texas, 1940.

Parish, Leonard Durvin. "The Life and Works of Nicolás Bravo, Mexican Patriot (1786-1854)." Ph.D. dissertation, University of Texas, 1951.

Pitchford, Jr., Louis Cleveland. "The Diplomatic Representatives from the United States to Mexico from 1836 to 1848." Ph.D. dissertation, University of Colorado, 1955.

Putnam, Lucile. "Washington-on-the-Brazos." Master's thesis, East Texas State Teachers College, 1952.

Ratliff, Lucile. "The Diplomatic Relations of Texas and Mexico, 1836-1846." Master's thesis, East Texas State Teachers College, 1939.

Reinhart, Kate Harmon. "The Public Career of Thomas Jefferson Green in Texas." Master's thesis, University of Texas, 1939.

Rice, Bernadine. "San Antonio, Its Early Beginnings and Its Development under the Republic." Master's thesis, University of Texas, 1941.

Robins, Jerry D. "Juan Seguin." Master's thesis, Southwest Texas State College, 1962.

Roy, Addie May. "History of Telegraph and Texas Register, 1835-1846." Master's thesis, University of Texas, 1931.

Schmitz, Joseph W. "The Diplomatic History of the Republic of Texas." Ph.D. dissertation, Loyola University, 1938.

Scholars, Fannie Baker. "Life and Services of Guy M. Bryan." Master's thesis, University of Texas, 1930.

Scott, Florence Johnson. "Spanish Land Grants in the Lower Río Grande Valley." Master's thesis, University of Texas, 1935.

Smith, Michael L. "The Role of Sam Houston in the Mier Expedition." Master's thesis, Sam Houston State University, 1969.

Smith, Margaret Harrison. "The Lower Río Grange Region in Temaulipas, Mexico." Ph.D. dissertation, University of Texas, 1961.

Spence, Mary Lee. "British Interests and Attitudes Regarding the Republic of Texas and Its Annexation to the United States." Ph.D. dissertation, University of Minnesota, 1957.

Stuart, Ben C. "Early Galveston Military Companies, 1839-1901." Rosenberg Library, Galveston, Texas.

———. "Ephraim McLean." Rosenberg Library, Galveston, Texas.

———. "Texas Fighters and Frontier Rangers." TxU-A.

Terrell, Anne Charlotte (comp.). "A Calendar of the Memorials and Petitions to the Legislature of Texas, 1861-1877." Master's thesis, University of Texas, 1936.

Tijerina, Andrew Anthony. "Tejano and Texas. The Native Mexicans of Texas, 1820-1850." Ph.D. dissertation, University of Texas, 1977.

Tymitz, John R. "British Influence in Mexico, 1840-1848." Ph.D. dissertation, Oklahoma State University, 1973.

Watkins, Mrs. Willye Ward (trans.). "Memoirs of General Antonio López de Santa Anna: Translation with Introduction and Notes." Master's thesis, University of Texas, 1922.

Weakley, Louise. "The Story of Treason in the Republic of Texas." Master's thesis, Sul Ross State Teachers College, 1942.

Wilkinson, C. A. "The Boundaries of Texas." Master's thesis, North Texas State College, 1937.

Williams, Lena S. "Calendar of the Memorials and Petitions to the Congress of Texas." Master's thesis, University of Texas, 1934.

Wooster, Ralph Ancil. "A Historical Study of the Second Presidential Administration of Sam Houston." Master's thesis, University of Houston, 1950.

2. Printed Material.

a. Books.

Abolafia-Rosenzweig, Mark. *Monument Hill State Historical Park: The Dawson and Mier Expeditions and Their Place in Texas History*. (n. p.: 2nd Printing, April 1991).

Adams, Ephraim Douglass. *British Interests and Activities in Texas, 1838-1846*. Baltimore: The John Hopkins Press, 1910.

Adler, James A. (ed.). *Comprehensive Index to the American State Papers and Serial Set Publications of the 15th to 34th Congresses (1789-1857)*. 3 vols. Washington, D.C.: Congressional Information Service, 1977.

Alamán, Lucas. *Historia de México . . . con una noticia preliminar del sistema de gobierno que regia en 1808 y del estado en que se hallan el país en el mismo año*. 5 vols. México: Impr. de V. Agueros y comp., editores, 1883-1885.

———. *Historia de Mexico desde los primeros movimientos que prepararon su independencia en el año de 1808, hasta la éxpoca presente*. 3 vols. Méjico: Impr. de J. M. Lara, 1849-52.

[Alcaraz, Ramón] (ed.). *Apuntes para ls historia de la guerra entre México y los Estados Unidos*. México: Tip. de M. Payno (hijo), 1848.

——— and Others. *Apuntes de la historia de la guerra entre México y los Estados Unidos*. 2nd ed. México City: Siglo ventiuno editores, 1974.

[Alcaraz, Ramón] (ed.). *Apuntas para la historia de la guerra entre México y los Estados Unidos*. México: Tip. de M. Payno (hijo), 1848.

[Alcaraz, Ramón], ed. *The Other Side; or Notes for the History of the War Between Mexico and the United States, Written in Mexico*. [Editors: Ramón Alcarz and Others]. Translated from the Spanish and edited with notes by Albert C. Ramsey. New York and London: J. Wiley, 1850.

Aldrich, Armistead Albert. *The History of Houston County, Texas: Together with Biographical Sketches of Many Pioneers and Later Citizens of Said County, Who Have Made Notable Contributions to Its Development and Progress*. San Antonio, Texas: The Naylor Company, 1943.

Alessio Robles, Vito. *Coahuila y Texas desde la consumación de la independencia hasta el tratado de paz de Guadalupe Hidalgo*. 2 vols. México City: *Los Talleres Gráfica de la Nación*, 1945-1946.

———. *Coahuila y Texas en la Epoca Colonial*. México, D. F.: Editorial Cultura, 1938.

———. *Monterrey en la historia y en la leyenda*. México: *Antigua liberia Robredo de J. Porrúa e hijos*, 1936.

———. *Saltillo en la historia y en la leyenda*. México City: [A del Bosque, impresor], 1934.

Allen, Irene T. *Saga of Anderson; The Proud Story of a Historic Texas Community.* 1st ed. New York: Greenwich Book Publishers, 1957 [i. e., 1958].

Almonte, Juan Nepomuceno. *Guía de Foresteros y Repertorio de conocimientos útiles.* México: Ignácio Cumplido, 1852.

The American Sketch Book: An Historical and Home Monthly. vols. 1-7. Vols. 1-3 (La Crosse, Wis.: Sketch Book Company, 1874-76), vols. 4-7 (Austin, Texas: American Sketch Book Publishing House, 1878-82).

Appleton's Cyclopaedia of American Biography, ed. by James Grant Wilson and John Fiske. 7 vols. New York: Appleton, 1888. Reprint: Detroit: Gale Research Co., 1968.

Armbruster, Henry C. *The Torreys of Texas: A Biographical Sketch.* Buda, Texas: Privately Printed, 1968.

Army and Navy Chronicle and Scientific Repository. Vols. 1-3 (Jan. 12, 1843-June 27, 1844). Washington: W. Force, 1843-1844.

Baker, D. W. C. (comp.). *A Texas Scrap-Book: Made Up of the History, Biography, and Miscellany of Texas and Its People.* New York: A. S. Barnes & Co., [1875].

Bancroft, Hubert Howe. *History of California, 1542-1890.* 7 vols. San Francisco: The History Company, 1884-1890.

———. *History of Mexico.* 6 vols. San Francisco: The History Co., 1886-1888.

———. *History of Texas and the North Mexican States.* 2 vols. San Francisco: The History Company, 1890.

Barker, Eugene C. *The Life of Stephen F. Austin.* Nashville & Dallas: Cokesbury Press, 1925. Reprint: Austin: Texas State Historical Association, 1949.

———. (ed.). *Readings in Texas History for High Schools and Colleges.* Dallas, Texas: The Southwest Press, [c1929]. Cover title: *A Comprehensive Readable History of Texas.*

Barkley, Mary Starr. *History of Travis County and Austin, 1839-1899.* Waco, Texas: Texian Press, 1963. 2nd ed.: Austin, Texas: The Steck Company, 1967.

Bartholomew, Ed. Ellsworth. *The Houston Story: A Chronicle of the City of Houston and the Texas Frontier from the Battle of San Jacinto to the War Between the States, 1836-1865.* Houston, Texas: The Frontier Press of Texas, 1951.

Bartlett, John Russell. *Personal Narrative of Explorations and Incidents in Texas, New Mexico, California, Sonora, and Chihuahua, Connected with the United States and Mexican Boundary Commission During the Year 1850, '51, '52, and '53.* 2 vols. Chicago: Río Grande Press, 1965.

Barton, Henry W. *Texas Volunteers in the Mexican War.* Waco, Texas: Texian Press, 1970.

Bate, Walter Nathaniel. *General Sidney Sherman: Texas Soldier, Statesman and Builder.* Waco: Texian Press, 1974.

Batte, Lelia M. *History of Milam County, Texas.* San Antonio, Texas: The Naylor Co., c1956.

Bauer, K[arl] Jack. *The Mexican War, 1846-1848.* New York: Macmillan Publishing Co., 1974.

Bayard, Ralph. *Lone-Star Vanguard: The Catholic Re-Occupation of Texas, 1838-1848.* Saint Louis, Mo.: The Vincentran Press, 1945.

Bayliss, Francis. *A Narrative of Major General Wool's Compaign in Mexico, in the Years 1846, 1847 & 1848.* Albany: Little & Company, 1851. Reprint: Austin: 1976 Jenkins Publishing Co.

Bebout, Lois (ed.). *Microforms in Texas Libraries: A Selective List* (1976). [Austin, Texas:] published by the General Libraries, University of Texas at Austin, 1976.

Becerra, Francisco. *A Mexican Sergeant's Recollections of the Alamo & San Jacinto as Told to John S. Ford in 1875.* Austin, Texas: Jenkins Publishing Co., 1980.

Beltrami, Giacomo Constantine. *Le Méxique.* 2 vols. Paris: Crevot, 1830.

Bernhard, Hugh J., Dorothy A. Bennett, and Hugh S. Rice, *New Handbook of the Heavens.* New York: McGraw-Hill Book Co., 1948.

Berroa, Joaquín. *México bibliograficos, 1957-1960; catalogo general de libros impresosos en México.* México, 1961.

Bill, Alfred Hoyt. *Rehearsal for Conflict: The War with Mexico, 1846-1848.* 1st ed. New York: A.A. Knopf, 1947.

Bibliography of United States-Latin American Relations since 1810: A Selected List of Eleven Thousand Published References. Comp. & ed. by David E. Trask, Michael C. Meyer, Roger R. Trask. Lincoln: University of Nebraska Press, 1968.

Binkley, William C. *The Expansionist Movement in Texas, 1836-1850.* Berkely: University of California Press, 1925.

Biographical and Historical Memoirs of Southern Arkansas. Chicago: Goodspeed, 1890. Reprint, Beasley, S.C.: Southern Historical Press, [1978].

Biographical Directory of the American Congress, 1774-1971. Washington: Government Printing Office, 1971.

Biography of Jose Antonio Navarro. By An Old Texan. Houston: Telegraph Steam Printing House, 1876. Reprint, [Austin]: Hart Graphics & Office Centers, c1976.

Bishop, Curtis, and Bascom Giles. *Lots of Land.* Austin, Texas: The Steck Company, 1949.

Blanchard, P., and A. Dauzats. *San Juan de Ulúa ou relation de L'Expédition francaise au Méxique, sous les ordres de M. Le Contre—Amiral Baudin, . . . Suivi de notes et documents, et d'un apercu general sur l'état actuel du Texas.* Paris: Chez Gide, Editeur—A. Pichan de la Forest, 1839.

Bocthel, Paul C. *The Big Guns of Fayette.* Austin, Texas: Von Boeckmann-Jones Co., 1965.

———. *Colonel Amasa Turner, The Gentleman from Lavaca and Other Captains at San Jacinto.* Austin, Texas: Von Boeckmann-Jones, 1963.

———. *The History of Lavaca County.* San Antonio, Texas: The Naylor Co., 1936. rev. ed. Austin, Texas: Von Boeckmann-Jones, 1959.

———. *On the Headwaters of the Lavaca and the Navidad.* Austin, Texas: Von Boeckmann-Jones, 1967.

———. *The Free State of Lavaca.* Austin, Texas: Weddle Publications, c1977.

———. *Sand in Your Craw; Tales of the Early History of Lavaca County.* Austin, Texas: Printed by Von Boeckmann-Jones, 1959.

Bolton, Herbert E. *Guide to Materials for the History of the United States in the Principal Archives of Mexico.* Washington, D.C.: Carnegie Institution of Washington, 1913.

———. *Texas in the Middle Eighteenth Century.* Berkeley: University of California Press, 1915.

Bonham, Dora Dieterich. *Merchant of the Republic.* San Antonio, Texas: Naylor Co., [1959].

Bonnell, George W. *Topographical Description of Texas to which is Added An Account of the Indian Tribes.* Waco, Texas: Texian Press, 1964.

Brack, Gene M. *Mexico Views Manifest Destiny, 1821-1846: An Essay on the Origins of the Mexican War.* Albuquerque, New Mexico: University of New Mexico Press, 1973.

Brackett, Albert G. *General [Joseph] Lane's Brigade in Central Mexico.* Cincinnati: H.W. Derby & Co., Publishers; New York, J.C. Derby, 1854.

Bradley, Harold Whitmen. *The American Frontier in Hawaii: The Pioneers, 1789-1843.* Stanford University, California: Stanford University Press, 1942. Reprint: Gloucester, Mass.: P. Smith, 1968.

Brooks, Nathan C. *A Complete History of the Mexican War, Its Causes, Conduct, and Consequences. Comprising An Account of the Various Military and Naval Operations, from Its Commencement to the Treaty of Peace.* Chicago: Río Grande Press, 1965. Originally published in 1849.

Broussard, Ray F. *San Antonio During the Texas Republic: A City in Transition.* Vol. V. of *Southwestern Studies.* El Paso: Texas Western Press, 1967.

Brown, John Henry. *History of Texas from 1685 to 1892.* 2 vols. Saint Louis, Missouri: L.E. Daniell, 1892-1893.

———. *Indian Wars and Pioneers of Texas.* Austin, Texas: L. E. Daniell, 189-?.

———. *The Life and Times of Henry Smith, The First American Governor of Texas.* Dallas: A. D. Aldridge and Co., 1887.

———. *Two Years in Mexico, or The Emigrant's Guide.* Galveston, Texas: Printed at the "News" Book and Job Office, 1867.

Bruce, Henry. *Life of General Houston, 1793-1863.* New York: Dodd, Mead, & Co., 1891.

Bullock, William. *Six Months Residence and Travels in Mexico; Containing Remarks on the Present State of New Spain, Its Natural Productions, State of Society, Manufactures, Trade, Agriculture, and Antiquities* London: J. Murray, 1824.

Burleson County Historical Society. *Astride the Old San Antonio Road, A History of Burleson County, Texas.* Caldwell, Texas: Burleson County Historical Society, 1980.

Burnet, David G. *Review of the Life of Gen. Sam Houston, As Recently Published In Washington City by J. T. Towers.* Galveston: News Power Press Print, 1852.

Burnet, Arthur C. *Yankees in the Republic of Texas: Some Notes On Their Origin and Impact*. Houston, Texas: For the Harris County Historical Society, Anson Jones Press, 1952.

[Bustamante, Carlos Mária de]. *Aputes para la historia del gobierno del general D. Antonio López de Santa-Anna, desde principios de octubre de 1841 hasta 6 de diciembre de 1844, en que fué depueste del mando por uniforme voluntad de la nación. Escrita por el autor de Cuadro historico de la revolución méxicana*. México: Impr. de J.M. Lara, 1845.

———. *D. Antonio López de Santa Anna*. 2 vols. in 1. Mexico: J. M. Lara, 1842.

———. *El Gabinete Méxicano durante la segunda periodo de la administración del Exmo. Señor Presidente D. Anastasio Bustamante, hasta la entresa del mando al Exmo. Señor Presidente D. Antonio López de Santa Anna*. 2 vols. in 1. México: J.M. Lara, 1842. *D. Antonio López de Santa Anna*. 2 vols. in 1. México: J. M. Lara.

———. *El Nuevo Bernal Diaz del Castillo ó sea Historia de la Invasion de los Anglo-Americanos en México*. 2 vols. Mexico: Impr. de García Torres, 1847. Reprint: México: Secretaría de Educación Publica, 1949.

Calderon de la Barca, Frances Erskine. *Life in Mexico during a Residence of Two Years in that Country*. By Madame Calderon de la Barca. Wife of the Spanish Minister to México. 1st ed. Boston and London, 1843; 2nd ed., México, 1907; 3rd ed., The Aztec, México, 1910.

———. *Life in Mexico: The Letters of Fanny Calderon de la Barca with New Material from the Author's Private Journals*. Ed. & annotated by Howard T. Fisher and Marion Hall Fisher. New York: Doubleday & Company, Inc., 1966.

Callahan, James M. *American Foreign Policy in Mexican Relations*. New York: Cooper Square Publishers, 1967.

Callcott, Wilfrid Hardy. *Santa Anna: The Story of An Enigma Who Once Was Mexico*. Norman: University of Oklahoma Press, 1936.

Campbell, T. N. *A Bibliographical Guide to the Archaeology of Texas*. Austin: University of Texas Printing Division, 1952.

Canales, Isidro Viscaya (ed.). *La Invasión de los Indios Barbaros al Noreste de México en los Años de 1840 y 1841*. Monterrey, México: Publicaciónes del Instituto Tecnologico y de Estudies Superiores de Monterrey, Serie Histórico, 1968.

Cappon, Lester J. *Virginia Newspapers, 1821-1935. A Bibliography with Historical Introduction and Notes*. New York: A. Appleton-Century Company, 1936.

Carefoot, Jean (ed.). *Guide to Genealogical Resources in the Texas State Archives*. Austin: Texas State Library, 1984.

Carreño, Alberto M. (ed.). *Jefes del ejército méxicano en 1847; biografías de generals de división, y de coronels del ejército méxicano por fines del año de 1847*. [Fly leaf says to the end of "1840"] México City: Imprenta y Folotipia de la Secretaría de Fomento, 1914.

Carroll, H. Bailey. *The Texan Santa Fé Trail*. Canyon, Texas: Panhandle Plains Historical Society, 1951.

———. *Texas County Histories: A Bibliography*. Austin, Texas: Texas State Historical Association, 1943.

———, and Milton R. Gutsch (comp. and eds.). *Texas History Theses: A Check List of the Theses and Dissertations Relating to Texas History Accepted at the University of Texas, 1893-1951*. Austin, Texas: The Texas State Historical Association, 1955.

Carroll, James M. *A History of Texas Baptists, Comprising A Detailed Account of Their Activities, Their Progress, and Their Achievements*. Edited by J.B. Carroll. Dallas, Texas: Baptist Standard Publishing Co., 1928.

Carter, James David. *Masonry in Texas: Background, History, and Influences to 1846*. Waco, Texas: Committee on Masonic Education and Service for the Grand Lodge of Texas, A.F. and A.M., 1955.

Casasola, Gustavo (comp.). *Enciciopedia historical illustrada de México, 1325-1958*. México: 1958.

———. *Seis siglos de historia gráfica de México. 1325-1900*. 2 vols. [Recapilación y fotográficas del "archivo Casasola"]. 3rd ed. México: Ediciónes G. Casasola, Ediciónes Casasola, 1966. 4th ed., México: 1969.

Castañeda, Carlos E. *Calendar to the Manuel E. Gondra manuscripts, the University of Texas Library*. Mexico: Editorial Jus, 1952.

————. *Independent Mexico in Documents: Independence, Empire, and Republic: A Calendar of the Juan E. Hernandez y Davalos Manuscript Collection: The University of Texas.* Mexico: Editorial Jus, 1954 [1955].

———— (trans.). *The Mexican Side of the Texas Revolution.* Dallas: P.L. Turner Co., [1928].

————. *Our Catholic Heritage in Texas, 1519-1936.* 7 vols. Austin, Texas: Von Boeckmann-Jones Co., 1936-58.

————, and Frederick C. Chabot. *Early Texas Album: Fifty Illustrations with Notes.* Austin, Texas: 1929.

————, and Jack Autry Dabbs (eds.). *Guide to the Latin American Manuscripts in the University of Texas Library.* Cambridge, Mass.: Harvard University Press, 1939.

Catalogue of Mexican Pamphlets in the Sutro Collection, 1623-1888. With Supplements, 1605-1887. (California State Library, Sutro Branch, San Francisco). New York: Kraus Reprint Co., 1971.

Cazneau, Jane Marie McManus (pseud., Cora [Corrine] Montgomery). *Eagle Pass or Life on the Border.* Edited with introduction by Robert C. Cotner, from original edition published in New York in 1852 by G.P. Putnam & Co. Austin, Texas: The Pemberton Press, 1966.

————. *Texas and Her Presidents; With A Glance At Her Climate and Agricultural Capabilities.* N.Y.: E. Winchester, New World Press, 1845.

Chabot, Frederick C. *With the Makers of San Antonio.* San Antonio, Texas: Artes Gráficas, 1937.

Chamberlain, Samuel E. *My Confession.* New York: Harper, [1956].

————. *Recollections of a Rogue.* London: Museum Press, [1957].

Charno, Steven M. (comp.). *Latin American Newspapers in United States Libraries.* Austin, Texas: University of Texas Press, 1968.

Chase, Mary Katherine. *Negociations de la République du Texas en Europe, 1837-1845.* Paris: Libraries Ancienne Honoré Champion, 1932.

Christian, Asa K. *Mirabeau Buonaparte Lamar.* Austin, Texas: Von Boeckmann-Jones Co., Printers, 1922.

Cisneros, José. *Riders of the Border: A Selection of Thirty Drawings. Southwestern Studies Monograph,* no. 30. El Paso, Texas: Texas Western Press, University of Texas at El Paso, c1971.

Clarke, Mary Whatley. *David G. Burnet.* Austin, Texas: Pemberton Press, 1969.

————. *Thomas J. Rusk: Soldier, Statesman, Jurist.* Austin, Texas: Jenkins Publishing Co., 1971.

Clemens, Jeremiah. *Mustang Gray; A Romance.* Philadelphia: J. B. Lippincott & Co., 1858.

[Coleman, Robert M.]. *Houston Displayed; or, Who Won the Battle of San Jacinto?* By A Farmer in the Army. Reprint from the Velasco Edition of 1837. [Houston; Printed at the Telegraph Office, 1841].

Compiled Index to Elected and Appointed Officials of the Republic of Texas, 1835-1846. Austin: State Archives Division, Texas State Library, 1981.

Conclin, George. *Texas.* Cincinnati: George Conclin, [c1840].

Connor, Seymour V. *The Peters Colony in Texas: A History and Biographical Sketch of the Early Settlers.* Austin, Texas: Texas State Historical Association. 1959.

————. *West Texas County Histories.* Austin, Texas: Archives Division, Texas State Library. 1954.

Copeland, Fayette. *Kendall of the Picayune, Being His Adventures in New Orleans, On the Texan Santa Fé Expedition, in the Mexican War, and in the Colonization of the Texas Frontier.* Norman, Okla.: University of Oklahoma Press, reprint, 1970, of the 1943 ed.

Corner, William (comp. and ed.). *San Antonio de Béxar: A Guide and History.* San Antonio, Texas: Bainbridge & Corner, 1890.

Corpus Christi: A History and Guide. Corpus Christi, Texas: Corpus Christi *Caller-Times,* 1942.

Cotner, Thomas Ewing. *The Military and Political Career of José Joaquín de Herrera, 1792-1854.* Austin, Texas: University of Texas Press, 1949.

Crane, William Carey. *Centennial Address Embracing the History of Washington County, Texas, at the Fair Grounds, Brenham, July 4, 1876.* Reprint, Brenham, Texas: Banner-Press, Inc., 1939.

————. *Life and Select Literary Remains of Sam Houston of Texas*. Philadelphia: J. B. Lippincott & Co., 1884; also, Dallas: W. G. Scarff and Co., 1884.

Cravens, John Nathan. *James Harper Starr: Financier of the Republic of Texas*. Austin, Texas: The Daughters of the Republic of Texas, 1950.

Creel, George. *Sam Houston: Colossus in Buckskin*. New York: Cosmopolitan Book Corp., 1928.

Creighton, James A. *A Narrative History of Brazoria County*. Waco, Texas: Texian Press, 1975.

Crocket, George Louis. *Two Centuries in East Texas; A History of San Augustine County and Surrounding Territory from 1685 to the Present Time*. Dallas, Texas: The Southwest Press, [1932].

Cullum, George W. (ed.). *Biographical Register of the Officers and Graduates of the U.S. Military Academy at West Point, N.Y. from Its Establishment in 1802, to 1890 with the Early History of the United States Military Academy*. 3 vols. 3rd ed. Rev. & Extended. Boston: Houghton, Mifflin and Co., 1891.

Cumberland, Charles C. *The United States-Mexican Border: A Selective Guide to Literature on the Region*. Monograph, *Rural Sociology*, Special Supplement, June 1960.

Dabbs, Jack Autry (ed.). *The Mariano Riva Palacio Archives: A Guide: University of Texas Library*. 3 vols. México: Editorial Jus., 1967-1972.

Dana, Capt. Edmund L. *Incidents in the Life of Capt. Samuel H. Walker, Texan Ranger*. Wilkes-Barre, Pa.: *Proceedings*, Wyoming Historical and Geological Society, 1882.

Daniel, L.E. *Personnel of the Texas State Government*. San Antonio, Texas: Maverick Printing House, 1892.

————. *Texas, the Country and Its Men: Historical, Biographical, Descriptive*. Austin: n.p. 1922.

————. *Types of Successful Men of Texas*. Austin: Eugene Von Boeckmann, 1890.

DeCamara, Kathleen. *Laredo on the Río Grande*. San Antonio, Texas: The Naylor Company, 1949.

Denvil y Collado, Manuel. *El reinado de Carlos III*. 6 vols. [Madrid: El Progreso editorial, 1891-96].

Davis, John L. *San Antonio: A Historical Portrait*. Austin, Texas: Encino Press, 1978.

Davis, Winfield J. *History of Political Conventions in California, 1849-1892*. Publications of the California State Library, No. 1. Sacramento: California State Library, 1893.

Dawson, Joseph Martin. *José Antonio Navarro: Co-Creator of Texas*. Waco: Baylor University Press, 1969.

Day, James M. *Black Beans & Goose Quills. Literature of the Texan Mier Expedition*. Waco: Texian Press, 1970.

———— (comp.). *Handbook, Texas Archival and Manuscript Depositories*. Texas State Library Monograph, No. 5. Austin: Texas Library and Historical Commission, 1966.

Dean, Frederick T. (comp.). *Illustrated Pocket Guide of San Antonio, Texas, Containing the Points of Interest In and About the Alamo City*. San Antonio: Alamo Advertising Bureau, c1889.

DeBow, J. D. B. *Texas: A Province, Republic, and State*. New Orleans: DeBow's Review, Sept. and Oct. 1857.

DeCordova, Jacob. *Lecture on Texas*. Philadelphia: Printed by Ernest Crozet, 1858.

————, J[acob]. *Texas: Her Resources and Her Public Men. A Companion for J. de Cordova's New and Correct Map of the State of Texas. Also including Lecture on Texas delivered by J. de Cordova, April 15, 1858*. 2 vols. 1st ed: 1858. Waco, Texas: Reprint, Texian Press, 1969. Reprint of 1st ed., 1858.

DeGarmo, Mrs. Frank. *Pathfinders of Texas, 1836-1946*. Austin, Texas: Von Boeckmann-Jones, 1951.

DeRyee, William, and R. E. Moore. *The Texas Album of the Eighth Legislature, 1860*. Austin, Texas: Miner, Lambert & Perry, 1860.

DeShields, James T. *Border Wars of Texas; Being An Authentic and Popular Account, in Chronological Order, of the Long and Bitter Conflict Raged between Savage Indian Tribes and the Pioneer Settlers of Texas*. Tioga, Texas: The Herald Company, 1912.

————. *They Sat in High Places; the Presidents and Governors of Texas, from the First American Chief Executives, 1835-36; Presidents of the Republic, 1836-46; and Governors of the State, 1846-1939*. San Antonio, Texas: The Naylor Company, 1940.

DeWees, William B. *Letters from An Early Settler of Texas*. Waco, Texas: 1968. Reprint of the original edition of 1852.

Diaz, Fernando. *Caudillos y Caciques; Antonio López de Santa Anna y Juan Alvaréz*. 1st ed. México: El Coligio de México, [1972].

Diccionario Porrúa de Historia, Biografía y Geografía de Mexico. Trecera ed. corregida y aumentada con un apendice. 2 vols. México, D. F.: Editorial Porrúa, S.A., 1971. Cuarto ed. Corregida y aumentada con un supplemento. 2 vols. México, D.F.: Editorial Porrúa, S.A., 1976.

Diekemper, Barnabas. *Guide to the Catholic Archives of Texas at San Antonio*. San Antonio, Texas: Catholic Archives, 1978.

Dietrich, Wilfred O. *The Blazing Story of Washington County*. Wichita Falls, Texas: 1950. Rev. ed., Wichita Falls, Texas: Nortex Offset Publications, 1973.

Dixon, Samuel Houston. *Romance and Tragedy of Texas History; being a Record of Many Thrilling Events in Texas History Under Spanish, Mexican and Anglo-Saxon Rule*. Houston, Texas: Texas Historical Publishing Company, [1924].

Dixon, Sam Houston, and Louis Wiltz Kemp. *The Heroes of San Jacinto*. Houston, Texas: Anson Jones Press, 1932.

Dobie, J. Frank. *Guide to Life and Literature of the Southwest*. Rev. and enl. ed. Dallas, Texas: Southern Methodist University Press, 1965.

————. *Paso del Aguila; A Chronicle of Frontier Days on the Texas Border As Recorded in the Memoirs of Jesse Sumpier*. Compiled by Harry Warren. Edited by Ben Pingenot. [Austin:] Encino Press, [1969].

————. *Tongues of the Monte*. Boston: Little, Brown, 1947. Reprinted: Austin, Texas: University of Texas Press, 1980.

Dooley, Claude, and Betty Dooley (comps.) *Why Stop? A Guide to the Texas Historical Roadside Markers*. 2nd ed. Houston, Texas: Lone Star Books, 1985.

Douglas, Claude Leroy. *Thunder on the Gulf; or, The Story of the Texas Navy*. Dallas: Turner Company, c1936. Reprinted: Fort Collins, 1973.

Duewall, L. A. *The Story of Monument Hill*. LaGrange, Texas: The LaGrange Journal, 1955.

Duffus, R[obert] L[uther]. *The Santa Fé Trail*. New York: Tudor Publishing Co., 1934.

Dunn, Frederick Sherwood. *The Diplomatic Protection of Americans in Mexico*. New York: Columbia University Press, 1933.

Duval, John C. *The Adventures of Big-Foot Wallace, The Texas Ranger and Hunter*. Macon, Georgia: J. W. Burke & Co., 1870. Numerous editions. Facsimile reprint of original; Austin, Texas: The Steck Company, 1935; a reprint ed. by Mabel Major and Rebecca W. Smith: Dallas: Tardy Publishing Company, 1936.

————. *Early Times in Texas*. Austin, Texas: H. P. N. Gammel & Co., 1892. Reprint, Austin, Texas: The Steck Company, 1935.

————. *Early Times in Texas; or, The Adventures of Jack Dobell*. Austin, Texas: H. P. N. Gammel & Co., 1892. Reprints, Austin, Texas: The Steck Company, 1935; reprint ed. by Mabel Majors and Rebecca W. Smith: Dallas: Tardy Publishing Company, Inc., 1936.

Dyer, Joseph O. *The Early History of Galveston*. Centenary edition. Part I. Galveston: Oscar Springer print, c1916.

Echanove Trujillo, Carlos. *La Vida pasiónal é inquieta de Don Crecencio Rejón. Con una carta de don Alberto María Carreño*. [México:] El Colegio de México, 1941.

Eller, E.M. *The Texas Navy*. Washington, 1968.

Elliot, Claude (ed.). *Theses on Texas History: A Check List of Theses and Dissertations in Texas History Produced in the Departments of History of Eighteen Texas Graduate Schools and Thirty-Three Graduate Schools Outside of Texas, 1907-1952*. Austin, Texas: Texas State Historical Association, 1955.

Enciclopedia de México. 10 vols. México: Instituto de la Enciclopedia de México, 1966.

Enciclopedia historica ilustrado de México, 1325-1958. México: c1958.

Ericson, Carolyn Reeves. *Nacogdoches-Gateway to Texas, A Biographical Directory 1773-1849*. Fort Worth: Arrow/Curtis Printing Company, 1974.

Ericson, Joe E. (comp.). *Judges of the Republic of Texas, 1836-1846: A Biographical Directory*. Dallas, Texas: Taylor Publishing Co., 1980.

Estado general de las fundaciónes por D. José de Escandón en la colonia del Nuevo Santander Costa del Seno Méxicano. Publicaciones del Archivo General de la Nación, XIV. México: Tallares Graficas de la Nacion, 1929.

Fay, Mary Smith. *War of 1812 Veterans in Texas*. New Orleans: Polyanthos, 1979.

Fenley, Florence. *Old Timers of Southwest Texas*. Uvalde: Hornsby Press, 1957.

Fields, William (comp.). *The Scrap-Book: Consisting of Tales and Anecdotes, Biographical, Historical, Patriotic, Moral, Religious, and Sentimental Pieces in Prose and Poetry*. 6th ed., rev. and improved. Philadelphia: Edward Meeks, 1890.

Fisher, O. C. *It Occurred in Kimble*. Houston, Texas: The Anson Jones Press, 1937.

[Folsom, George]. *Mexico in 1842: A Description of the Country: Its Natural and Political Features: with a Sketch of Its History Brought Down to the Present Year. To Which is Added an Account of Texas and Yucatan; and of the Santa Fe Expedition*. New York: Charles Folsom, 1842.

Foot, Henry S. *Bench and Bar of the South and Southwest*. St. Louis: Soule, Thomas & Wentworth, 1876.

Fortescue, J[ohn] W[illiam]. *A History of the British Army*. 13 vols. in 19. New York: AMS Press, Inc., 1976?

Fournel, Henri Jerome Marie. *Comp—Oeil historique et statistique sur le Texas*, por Henri Fournel. Paris: Delloyer, 1841.

Fowler, John. *James Pearson Newcomb: Texas Journalist and Political Leader*. Austin, Texas: Department of Journalism Development Program, University of Texas at Austin, [1976?].

Freytag, Walter P. (ed.). *Chronicals of Fayette County: The Reminiscences of Julia Lee Sinks*. n.p., 1925.

Frías, Heriberto. *Episodios militares Méxicanos; principales campañas, jornadas, batallas, combates y actos heroics que ilustran la historia del ejército nacional desde la independencia hasta el tiempo definitive de la república*. 2 vols. Paris: La Vda de C. Bouret, 1901.

Friend, Llerena. *Sam Houston: The Great Designer*. Austin: University of Texas Press, 1954.

Frost, J. *The Mexican War and Its Warriors; Comprising a Complete History of All the Operations of the American Armies in Mexico; with Biographical Sketches and Anecdotes of the Most Distinguished Officers in the Regular Army and Volunteer Force*. New Haven and Philadelphia: H. Mansfield, [1848?].

Fuller, John Douglas Pitts. *The Movement for the Acquisition of All Mexico, 1846-1848*. Baltimore: The Johns Hopkins Press, 1936.

Fulmore, Z. T. *The History and Geography of Texas As Told in County Names*. Austin, Texas: The Steck Company, 1915.

Furber, George C. *The Twelve Months Volunteer; or, Journal of a Private in the Tennessee Regiment of Cavalry, in the Campaign, in Mexico, 1846-7, etc*. Cincinnati: U. P. James, 1857.

Galván Rivera, Mariano. *Calendario Manuel y Grua de Forasteros de México por el año de 1829*. México: Impresa en su Casa, 1829.

Gambrell, Herbert P. *Anson Jones, The Last President of Texas*. Garden City, N.Y.: Doubleday & Co., 1948.

———. *Mirabeau Buonaparte Lamar, Troubador and Crusader*. Dallas: Southwest Press, [1934].

García Treviño, Ciro de la. *Historia de Tamaulipas (Anales y Efermerides)*. Segunda edición. [Ciudad Victoria? c1956].

Garrison, Curtis W. (ed.). *The United States, 1865-1900: A Study of Current Literature with Abstracts of Unpublished Dissertations*. 2 vols. Fremont, Ohio: The Rutherford B. Hayes-Lucy Webb Hayes Foundation, 1943.

Garst, [Doris] Shannon. *Big Foot Wallace of the Texas Rangers*. New York: Julian Messner, Inc., 1951.

Gilbert, Marie, Thelma Puckett, and Capt. Day Jewell. *The John Berry Family*. [N.p.: privately printed, n.d.].

[Giddings, Luther]. *Sketches of the Campaign in Northern Mexico in Eighteen Hundred Forty-Six and Seven*. New York: George P. Putnam & Co., 1853.

Gilliland, Maud T. *Wilson County, Texas, Rangers, 1837-1977*. N.p., 1977.

Gilpin, Laura. *The Río Grande: River of Destiny, An Interpretation of the River, the Land, and the People*. New York: Duell, Sloan, and Pearce, 1949.

González Obregon, Luis. *Las Calles de México . . . Leyendas y sucedidos*. 5th ed.; con prologo y elogios de don Carlos Gonzáles Peña, don Rafael López y de don Artemio de Valle-Arizpe; illustraciónes de Bardasano y Molina. [Madrid:] Ediciónes Botas, 1941.

———. *Epoca colonial. México viejo, noticias historicas, tradiciónes, leyendas y costumbres*. Nueva ed., aumentada y corr., con profusion de illustraciónes: dibujos originales, retractos, vistas, planos, sacados de litográficas, y fotográficas tomadas directamente de monumentos, monedas y medallas. México, D. F.: Editorial Patria, s.a., 1945. 9th ed. México: Editorial Patria, 1966.

———. *Las Calles de México*. [Ed. rev.]. II. *Vida y costumbres de otros tiempos*. México: Imp. M. L. Sánchez, 1927.

———. *México viejo y anecdotico*. México, etc.: V^{da} de C. Bouret, 1909.

Gooch, Fanny Chambers. *Face to Face with the Mexicans: The Domestic Life, Education, Social, and Business Ways, Statesmanship and Literature, Legendary and General History of the Mexican People, As seen and Studied by an American Woman during Seven Years of Intercourse with Them*. New York: Fords, Howard, & Hulbert, [1887].

Gooch-Iglehart, Fanny Chambers. *The Boy Captive of the Texas Mier Expedition*. Rev. ed. San Antonio, Texas: Press of J. R. Wood Printing Co., 1909.

Goodrich, S. G. *North America; or, The United States and the Adjacent Countries*. Louisville, Ky.: Norton and Griswold, 1847.

Gorman, W. A. *Boundary of Texas: On the Texas Boundary Bill and Slavery Agitation*. Washington: 1850.

Gorotiza, M.E. *Correspondencia que la mediado . . . sobre el paso del Sabina por las tropas que mandaba el Gereral Gaines*. Philadelphia: 1836.

Gouge, William M. *The Fiscal History of Texas; Embracing An Account of Its Revenues, Debts, and Currency, from the Commencement of the Revolution in 1834 to 1851-52*. Philadelphia: Lippincott, Grambo, and Co., 1852.

Grace, J. S., and R. B. Jones. *A New History of Parker County: The Garrett-Buster-Estes Family History*. Weatherford, Texas: Democratic Publishing Co., 1906.

Gray, Lois Lucille. *Old Indianola; Life in a Frontier Seaport*. San Antonio: Naylor & Co., [1950].

Green, Mary Rowena (ed.). *Samuel Maverick: Texan, 1803-1870; a Collection of Letters, Journals, and Memoirs*. San Antonio: Privately Printed, H. Wolff, N.Y., 1952 [i. e., 1953].

Green, Rena Maverick (ed.). *Memoirs of Mary A. Maverick: Arranged by Mary A. Maverick and Her Son Geo[rge] Madison Maverick*. San Antonio: Alamo Printing Co., 1921.

Green, T. J. (comp.). *A Compilation of the Names of Texians Who Engaged in the Mier Expedition, from a History of the Same*. Richmond, Texas: David Nation & Sons, Printers, 1882.

Greer, James K. *Colonel Jack Hays, Texas Frontier Leader and California Builder*. New York: E. P. Dutton & Co., Inc., 1952.

Gregory, Samuel. *Gregory's History of México. A History of México from the Earliest Times to the Present . . . Geographical View of the Country . . . State of Society . . . Anecdotes and Incidents of Mexican Life, &c*. Boston: F. Gleason, 1847.

Griffin, Charles C. (ed.). *Latin America: A Guide to Historical Literature*. Austin, Texas: University of Texas Press, c1971.

Guide to Research Materials in the North Carolina State Archives, Section B: County Records. Raleigh: Dept. of Art, Culture and History, Office of Archives and History, Division of Archives and Records Management, 1972.

Guild, Thelma S., and Harvey L. Carter. *Kit Carson: A Pattern for Heroes*. Lincoln, Nebraska: University of Nebraska Press, 1984.

Haggard, J. Villasana, and Malcolm Dallas McLean (comp.). *Handbook for Translators of Spanish Historical Documents*. Oklahoma City: Semco Color Press, 1941.

Hale, Edward Everett. *How to Conquer Texas before Texas Conquers Us*. Austin: Roger Beacham, 1978.

Hanighen, Frank Cleary. *Santa Anna, the Napoleon of the West*. New York: Coward-McCann, 1934.

Harper, Henry Howard. *Journey in Southeastern México; Narrative of Experiences, and Observations on Agriculture and Industrial Conditions.* Boston: Private print for the author by the De Vinne Prews, N. Y., 1910.

Hasse, A. R. *Index to United States Documents Relating to Foreign Affairs, 1828-1861.* In 3 parts. Part III (R-Z). Washington: Carnegie Institution, 1921.

Hasskarl, Mrs. Robert A. *A History of Brenham.* Brenham, Texas: 1933. Reprint: c1950.

————. *Brenham, Texas, 1844-1958.* Brenham, Texas: Banner-Press Publishing Co., c1958.

Hayes, Charles W. *History of the Island and the City of Galveston from the Discovery of the Island in 1526, from the Founding of the City in 1837, Down to the Year 1879.* 2 Vols. Austin: Jenkins Garrett Press, 1974.

Haynes, Sam W. *Soldiers of Misfortune: The Somervell and Mier Expeditions.* Austin: University of Texas Press, 1990.

Hefter, J. *Star Alone. The Army of the Republic of Texas.* [Bellevue, Neb.: Old Army Press, 1971].

Henderson, Harry McCorry. *Colonel Jack Hays, Texas Ranger.* San Antonio, Texas: The Naylor Company, 1954.

Henry, Robert Selph. *The Story of the Mexican War.* New York: F. Ungar, [1961, c1950].

————, William S. *Campaign Sketches of the War with Mexico.* New York: Harper & Brothers, 1847.

Herring, Hubert Clinton. *A History of Latin America from the Beginning to the Present.* 2d rev. ed. New York: Knopf, 1961.

Heusinger, Edward W. *A Chronology of Events in San Antonio: Being A Concise History of the City, Year by Year, from the Beginning of Its Establishment to the End of the First Half of the Twentieth Century.* San Antonio, Texas: Standard Printing Co., 1951.

Hill, Jr., George A. *The Hill Family of Fayetteville, Typical Texans, An Address by Geo. A. Hill, Jr., Houston, Texas, Delivered at Fayetteville, Texas, December 9, 1936, upon the Occasion of the Dedication of a Monument Erected by the State of Texas.* [Houston, 1936].

Hill, Jim Dan. *The Texas Navy, In Forgotten Battles and Shirtsleeve Diplomacy.* Chicago: University of Chicago Press, 1937.

Hill, Laurence Francis. *José de Escandón and the Founding of Nuevo Santander: A Study in Spanish Colonization.* Columbus: Ohio University Press, 1926.

History of Nueces County, The. [Prepared by] The Nueces County Historical Society. Austin, Texas: Jenkins Publishing Co., 1972.

History of Texas Together with a Biographical History of Milam, Williamson, Bastrop, Travis, Lee and Burleson Counties. Containing a Concise History of the State, With Portraits and Biographies of Prominent Citizens of the Above Named Counties, and Personal Histories of Many of the Early Settlers and Leading Families. Chicago: The Lewis Publishing Company, 1893.

Hobby, A. M. *Life and Times of David G. Burnet, First President of the Republic of Texas.* Galveston: Galveston New Office, 1871.

Hogan, William Ransom. *The Texas Republic: A Social and Economic History.* Norman: University of Oklahoma Press, 1946.

Honig, Laurence E. *John Henry Brown, Texian Journalist, 1820-1895. Southwestern Studies Mongraph,* No. 36. El Paso: Texas Western Press, 1973.

Horgan, Paul. *Great River: The Río Grande in North American History.* 2 vols. New York: Rinehart & Co., Inc., 1954.

Horr, David Ager. *American Indian Ethno-history: North Central and North Eastern Indians: [The Winnebago Indians].* New York: Garland Publihsing, Inc., 1974.

Hotchkiss, C. A. *History of Scottish Rite Masonry in Texas.* N. p.: 1916.

House, Boyce. *City of Flaming Adventure, The Chronicle of San Antonio.* [Fiesta ed.] San Antonio, Texas: Naylor Co., [1949].

————. *Cowtown Columnist: Human Interest Stories of Texas.* San Antonio: The Naylor Company, [1946].

Houston: A History and Guide. Compiled by Workers of the Writers Program of the Work Projects Administration in Texas. *American Guide Series.* Houston, Texas: The Anson Jones Press, 1942.

Hughes, W. J. *Rebellious Ranger Rip Ford and the Old Southwest.* Norman: University of Oklahoma Press, 1964.

Hunter, J. Marvin (ed.). *Jack Hays. The Intrepid Texas Ranger*. Bandera, Texas: n.d. [ca 1922].

Huson, Hobart. *El Copano: Ancient Port of Béxar and La Bahía*. Refugio, Texas: Refugio Timely Remarks, 1935.

————. *District Judges of Refugio County*. Refugio, Texas: Refugio Timely Remarks, 1941.

————. *Refugio: A Comprehensive History of Refugio County from Aboriginal Times to 1953*. 2 vols. Houston: Guardsman Publishing Company, 1953.

Houston, Cleburne. *Towering Texas: A Biography of Thomas J. Rusk*. Waco, Texas: Texian Press, 1971.

Iguiniz, Juan B. *Bibliográfia Biográfica méxicana*. México: Imprenta de la Secretaría de Rela-ciónes Exteriores, 1930.

Jackson, Jack. *Los Mesteños: Spanish Ranching in Texas, 1725-1821*. College Station, Texas: Texas A&M University Press, 1986.

Jaggers, Maida (ed.). *Rusk County History*. Henderson, Texas: Rusk County Historical Asso-ciation, 1982.

James, Marquis. *The Raven: A Biography of Sam Houston*. Indianapolis: The Bobbs-Merrill Co., Inc., 1938.

Jenkins, John H. *Basic Texas Books: An Annotated Bibliography of Selected Works for a Research Library*. Austin: Jenkins Publishing Company, 1983.

————. *Cracker Barrel Chronicles: A Bibliography of Texas Town and County Histories*. Austin: Pemberton Press, 1965.

————. *Printer in Three Republics: A Bibliography of Samuel Bangs, First Printer in Texas, and First Printer West of the Louisiana Purchase*. Austin, Texas: Jenkins Publishing Co., 1981.

[Jennett, Elizabeth LeNoir]. *Biographical Directory of the Texan Conventions and Congresses*. Austin, Texas: Book Exchange, Inc., 1941

Jewell, Day. *The John Berry Family of Berry's Creek, Texas Pioneers, Williamson County, Texas*. Rev. in 1958 by Day [n. p., 1958].

Johnson, Frank W. *A History of Texas and Texans*. Edited by E. C. Barker and E. W. Winkler. 5 vols. Chicago and New York: The American Historical Society, 1914. Rev., 1916.

Johnston, William Preston. *The Life of Gen. Albert Sidney Johnston: Embracing his Services in the Armies of the United States, the Republic of Texas, and the Confederate States*. New York: D. Appleton & Company, Inc., 1879.

Jollivet, M. *Anexion du Texas. Nouveau Documents Americas*. Paris: Bruneau, Fevrier, 1845.

Jones, Margaret Belle (comp.). *Bastrop: A Compilation of Material Relating to the History of the Town of Bastrop, with Letters Written by Terry Rangers*. Bastrop, Texas: [1936?].

Jones, William Moses. *Texas History Carved in Stone. Being Complete Copies of More Than Four-teen Hundred Inscriptions Embossed in Bronze and Carved in Stone on Buildings, Monuments, Statues, Historical Markers, and Gravestones*. Compiled in Traveling order. Houston, Texas: Monument Publishing Co., c1958.

Kaminkow, Marion J. (ed.). *Genealogies in the Library of Congress: A Bibliography*. 2 vols. Bal-timore, Md.: Magna Carta Book Co., 1972.

Kelley, Dayton (ed.). *The Handbook of Waco and McLennan County, Texas*. Waco, Texas: Texian Press, 1972.

Kemp, Louis Wiltz. *The Signers of the Texas Declaration of Independence*. Houston, Texas: The Anson Jones Press, 1944.

Kendall, Dorothy Steinbomer, and Carmen Perry. *Gentilz: Artist of the Old Southwest: Draw-ings and Paintings by Theodore Gentilz*. Austin: University of Texas Press, c1974.

Kennedy, William. *Texas: The Rise, Progress, and Prospects of the Republic of Texas*. 2 vols. Lon-don: R. Hastings, 1841. Reprint: Fort Worth, Texas: Molyneaux Craftsmen, 1925.

Ker, Annita Melville. *Mexican Government Publications: A Guide to the More Important Publica-tions of the National Government of Mexico, 1821-1936*. Washington: U.S. Government Print. Office, 1940.

Kesselus, Kenneth. *History of Bastrop County, Texas Before Statehood*. Austin: Jenkins Publish-ing Company, 1986.

Kielman, Chester V. (comp. and ed.). *The University of Texas Archives: A Guide to the Historical Manuscripts Collection in the University of Texas Library*. Austin: University of Texas Press, 1967.

King, Valentine Overton. *Valentine Overton King's Index to Books About Texas before 1889.* Facsimile ed. Austin, Texas: Texas State Archives, 1976.

Kinney, John M. (comp.). *Index to Applications for Texas Confederate Pensions.* Austin, Texas: Archives Division, Texas State Library, 1975.

Kinney County: Brackettville, Spofford, Fort Clark. Brackettville, Texas: New World Study Club, 1947?.

Kittrell, Norman G. *Governors Who Have Been, and Other Public Men of Texas.* Houston: Dealy-Adey-Elgin Co., 1921.

Konwiser, Harry M. *Texas Republic Postal System. The Postoffice and Postal Markings of the Republic of Texas.* New York: 1933.

Kubiak, Daniel James. *Ten Tall Texans.* Rev. and enl. ed. San Antonio: Naylor Co., 1970.

Lea, Tom. *The King Ranch.* 2 vols. Boston: Little, Brown, 1957.

Lester, Charles Edward. *The Life of Sam Houston: The Only Authentic Memoir of Him Ever Published.* New York: J. C. Derby, 1855.

————. *The Life of Sam Houston, The Hunter, Patriot, and Statesman of Texas: The Only Authentic Memoir of Him Ever Published.* Philadelphia: Davis, Porter & Coates, 1866.

————. *Sam Houston and His Republic.* New York: Burges, Stringer & Company, 1846.

Life of "Big Foot" Wallace, the Only Reliable History of the Famous Frontiersman . . . Facts Gathered from the Lips of the Great Ranger Captain. Austin, Texas: Steck Co., 1957.

Limmer, Jr., E. A. (ed. and comp.). *Story of Bell County, Texas.* 2 vols. Austin, Texas: Pub. by Eakin Press for Bell County Historical Commission, 1988.

Lindsey, Theresa (Kayser). *Blue Norther: Texas Poems.* New York: H. Vinal, 1925.

Lone Star State Memorial and Genealogical Record of Southwest Texas, Containing Biographical Histories and Genealogical Records of Many Leading Men and Prominent Families. Chicago: Goodspeed Bros., 1894.

Loomis, Noel M. *The Texan-Santa Fé Pioneers.* Norman, Oklahoma: University of Oklahoma Press, 1958.

————. *Short Cut to Red River.* New York: Macmillan, 1958.

————, and Abraham P. Nasatir. *Pedro Vial and the Roads to Santa Fé.* 1st ed. Norman: University of Oklahoma Press, 1967.

Lotto, F. *Fayette County: Her History and Her People.* Schulenburg, Texas: Sticker Steam Press, 1902.

Lynch, James D. *The Bench and Bar in Texas.* St. Louis: Nixon-Jones Printing Co., 1885.

MacKay, Albert G. *Encyclopedia of Freemasonry*, Rev. and enl. by Robert I. Clegg, with supplementale volume by H. L. Haywood. 3 vols. Chicago: The Masonic History Co., 1929.

McCaleb, Walter Flavius. *Big-Foot Wallace.* [2nd ed.]. San Antonio, Texas: The Naylor Co., 1960. First published c1956.

————. *The Mier Expedition.* San Antonio, Texas: Naylor Co., [1959].

McCampbell, Coleman. *Saga of a Frontier Seaport.* Dallas, Texas: Southwest Press, c1934.

————. *Texas Seaport: The Story of the Growth of Corpus Christi and the Coastal Bend Area.* New York: Exposition Press, Inc., c1952.

McClelland, Robert. *Report on the Mexican Boundary.* Senate Exec. Doc., No. 55 33d Cong., 2d Sess., March 21, 1853.

McCormick, Andrew Phelps. *Scotch-Irish in Ireland and in America as Shown in Sketches of the Pioneer Scotch-Irish Families McCormick, Stevenson, McKenzie and Bell, in North Carolina, Kentucky, Missouri and Texas.* New Orleans, 1897.

McDowell, Catherine W. (ed.). *If you Hear My Horn: The Journal of James Wilson Nichols, 1820-1887.* Austin, Texas: University of Texas Press, 1968.

McLean, William Hunter (comp.). *Everyname Index of 7,000 Entries from Indian Wars and Pioneers of Texas by John Henry Brown.* Dallas: Texas State Genealogical Society, 1977.

McNair, George L. *Texian Campaign of 1842.* [New Orleans, 1842]. Broadsheet. Copy in Archivo General de la Secretaría de Relaciónes Exteriores, México City, México.

Madray, Mrs. I. C. *A History of Bee County; With Some Brief Sketches About Men and Events in Adjoining Counties.* Beeville: Beeville Publishing Co., 1939.

Mann, William L. *Early History of Williamson County.* Georgetown, Texas: 1948.

Mansfield, Edward Deering. *The Mexican War: A History of its Origin, and a Detailed Account of the Victories Which Terminated in the Surrender of the Capital; with the Official Despatches of the General To Which is Added, the Tready of Peace, and Valuable Tables on the Strength and Losses of the United States Army.* New York: A. S. Barnes, 1848.

Marroqui, José María. *La Ciudad de México; contiene: el origen de los nombres de muchas de sus calles y plazas, del de varios establecimientos publicos y privados, y no pocas noticias curiosas y entretendias.* 3 vols. 2nd ed. [México:] Jesús Medina, 1969.

Marshall, Thomas M. *A History of the Western Boundary of the Louisiana Purchase, 1819-1841.* Berkeley: University of California Press, 1914.

Martin, Madeleine. *More Early Southeast Texas Families.* Quanah, Texas: Nortex Press, 1978.

Medearis, Mary (ed.). *Sam Williams: Printer's Devil, Memorabilia; Some Ante-Bellum Reminiscences of Hempstead County, Arkansas, Embracing Pictures of Social Life, Personal Sketches, Political Annals, and Anecdotes of Characters and Events.* Hope, Arkansas: Etter Printing Company, 1979.

México y sus alrededores: colección de monumentos, trajes y paisajes dibujados al natural y litográfiados por artistas Méxicanos. México [City]: Establecimiento Litografico de Decaen, 1855-56.

Miller, E. T. *A Financial History of Texas.* University of Texas *Bulletin* No. 37. Austin: A. C. Baldwin and Sons, 1916.

Miller, Ray. *Eyes of Texas Travel Guide—San Antonio Border Edition.* Houston: Cordovan Corp., 1979.

Miller, Mrs. Sylvanus Gerard. *Sixty Years in the Nueces Valley, 1870-1930.* San Antonio, Texas: Naylor Printing Co., 1930.

Montgomery, Robin. *The History of Montgomery County, Texas.* Austin: Jenkins Publishing Co., 1975.

Moore, Bill. *Bastrop County, 1691-1900.* Rev. ed. Wichita Falls, Texas: Nortex Press, 1977.

Moore, Francis. *Description of Texas . . .* New York: Y. R. Tanner, 1844.

Morphis, J. M. *History of Texas From its Discovery and Settlement, With a Description of Its Principal Cities and Counties, and the Agricultural, Mineral, and Material Resources of the State.* New York: United States Publishing Company, 1875.

Morris, Mrs. Harry Joseph (comp. and ed.). *Citizens of the Republic of Texas.* Dallas, Texas: Texas State Genealogical Society, 1977.

Moursund, John Stribling. *Blanco County Families for One Hundred Years.* Austin: By the Author, 1958.

Nance, Joseph Milton. *After San Jacinto: The Texas-Mexican Frontier, 1836-1841.* Austin: University of Texas Press, 1963.

————. *Attack and Counterattack: The Texas-Mexican Frontier, 1842.* Austin: University of Texas Press, 1964.

———— (comp. and ed.). *Texas Newspapers, 1813-1939. A Union List of Newspaper Files Available in Offices of Publishers, Libraries, and A Number of Private Collections.* Prepared by Historical Records Survey Program, Division of Professional and Service Preojects [of the Works Project Administration of Texas]. Houston. Texas: San Jacinto Museum of History Association, 1941.

Neighbours, Kenneth F. *Robert Simpson Neighbors and the Texas Frontier, 1836-1859.* Waco, Texas: Texian Press, c1975.

Nevins, David. *The Old West: The Texans,* by the editors of Time-Life Books, with text by David Nevins. New York: Time-Life Books, c1975.

Nixon, Pat Ireland. *A Century of Medicine in San Antonio: The Story of Medicine in Béxar County, Texas.* San Antonio, Texas: Privately Published by Author, 1936.

————. *The Medical Story of Early Texas, 1528-1853.* Lancaster, Pa.: Lancaster Press, Inc., 1946.

Oates, Stephen B. *Visions of Glory, Texans on the Southwestern Frontier.* Norman: University of Oklahoma Press, 1970.

Olivera, Ruth R., and Lilliane Crite. *Life in Mexico Under Santa Anna, 1822-1855.* Norman: University of Oklahoma Press, 1991.

Partlow, Miriam. *Liberty, Liberty County and the Atascosito District.* Austin, Texas: Pemberton Press, 1974.

Pearson, Newcomb. *The Alamo City.* San Antonio, Texas: P. Newcomb, 1926.

Pennington, Mrs. R. E. (May Amanda). *The History of Brenham and Washington County.* Houston: Standard Printing and Lithographing Co., 1915.

Peral, Miguel Angel. *Diccionario biográfico méxicano*. México City: Editorial P. A. C., 1944.

Pérez Maldonado, Carlos. *La ciudad metropolitana de nuestra señora de Monterrey, 1596-1946*. Monterrey: Impresora Monterrey, 1946.

Peterson, Harold Leslie, and Robert Elman. *The Great Guns*. New York: Grossett and Dunlap, 1971.

Pickett, Arlene. *History of Liberty County*. Dallas: Tardy Publishing Company, c1936.

Pierce, Frank C. *A Brief History of the Lower Río Grande Valley*. Menasha, Wisconsin: George Banta Publishing Co., 1917.

Pinckney, Pauline A. *Painting in Texas: The Nineteenth Century*. Austin, Texas: Published for the Amon Carter Museum of Western Art, Fort Worth, by The University of Texas Press, 1967.

Prescott, William Hickling. *History of the Conquest of Mexico*. 3 vols. ed. by John Foster Kirk. Philadelphia: J. B. Lippincott Company, c1873.

Prieto, Alejandro. *Historia, geográfia y estadista del Estado de Tamaulipas*. México City: 1873.

Puckett, Thelma, and Capt. Day Jewell. *The John Berry Family*. A brochure. Privately Printed.

Rader, Jesse L. *South of Forty; From the Mississippi to the Río Grande*. Norman: University of Oklahoma Press, 1947.

Ramírez. Kpsé Fernando. *México durante su guerra con los Estados Unidos*. México: 1905.

————. *México During the War With the United States*. Edited by Walter V. Scholes. University of Missouri Studies, vol. 23. Columbia: University of Missouri, 1950.

Randall, Robert W. *Real de Monte: A British Mining Venture in Mexico*. Austin: Published for the Institute of Latin American Studies by the University of Texas Press, 1972.

Rankin, Melinda. *Texas in 1850*. Boston: Damrell & Moore, 1850.

Rather, Ethel Zilvey. *Dewitt's Colony*. Austin, Texas: University of Texas Press, 1905.

Ray, Worth S. *Austin Colony Pioneers, Including History of Bastrop, Fayette, Grimes, Montgomery and Washington Counties, Texas and their Earliest Settlers*. Austin: 1949. Reprint: Austin: Pemberton Press, 1970.

Reeves, Frank. *Hacienda de Atotonilco*. Yerbanis, México: Atotonilco Livestock Co., 1936.

Reeves, Jesse S. *American Diplomacy of Tyler and Polk*. Baltimore: The Johns Hopkins Press, 1907.

Retratos de los personajes ilustres de la primera y segunda epoca de la independencia mexicana y notabilidades de la presente. [México: Hallase en la Estamperia de Julio Micchaud y Thomas], n. d. "Méjico: C. L. Prudhomme, 1843."

Rister, Carl C. *The Southwestern Frontier, 1865-1881*. Cleveland, Ohio: The Arthur H. Clark Co., 1928.

Rittenhouse, Jack D. *The Santa Fé Trail: A Historical Bibliography*. Albuquerque: University of New Mexico Press, c1971.

Riva Palacio, Vicente. *México a través de los siglos*. 5 vols. [México City: Publicaciones Herrericos 1939?].

Rivera, Luis Manuel del. *Mexico in 1842*. Madrid: Eusebio Aguado, 1844.

Rivera, Mariano Galvan. *Calendario Manuel y Guía de foresteros de México por la año de 1829*. México: Impresa en su Casa, 1829.

Rivera Cambas, Manuel. *Historia antigua y moderna de Jalapa y de las revoluciónes del estado de Veracruz, escrita por el ingeniero Manuel Rivera*. 5 vols. México: Impr. de I. Cumplido, 1869-1871.

————. *Los gobernantes de México*. 2 vols. México City: J. M. Aguilar Ortiz, [1872]-1873.

————. *México pintoresco, artistico y monumental: vistas, descripción, anécdotas y episodios de los lugares más notables de la capital y de los estados, aun de las poblaciónes cortas, pero de importancia geografica o historica; los descripciones contienen datos cientificos. historicas y estadisticos, arreglada escrita por Manuel Rivera Cambas*. 3 vols. México: Editora Nacior 1857. Reprint: México: Imprenta de la Reforma, 1880-83.

Rivers, Edward Nathaniel. *Adventures in Texas*. Philadelphia: 1844.

Rives, George L. *The United States and Mexico, 1821-1848; A History of the Relations Between the Two Countries from the Independence of Mexico to the Close of the War with the United States*. 2 vols. New York: C. Scribner's Sons, 1913.

Robinson, Fayette. *Mexico and Her Military Chieftains from the Revolution of Hidalgo to the Present time*. Philadelphia: E. H. Butler & Co., 1847. Reprint, Hartford, Conn.: 1848.

Romero de Terreros, Manuel. *Antiguas Haciendas de México*. México: Editorial Patria, S. A., 1956.

Rose, Victor M. *History of Victoria County, Account of its Settlement, Development, and its Progress*. Laredo: Daily Times Print, 1883.

———. *The Life and Services of Gen. Ben McCulloch*. Philadelphia Pictorial Bureau of the Press, 1888.

———. *Some Historical Facts in Regard to the Settlement of Victoria, Texas: Its Progress and Present Status*. Laredo: Daily Times Print, 1883.

Rousseau, François. *Régne de Charles III d'Espange*. 2 vols. Paris: Plon-Nourrit, 1907.

Ruxton, George Frederick. *Adventures in México, from Vera Cruz to Chihuahua in the Days of the Mexican War*. New York: Outing Publishing Co., 1915.

Saldívar, Gabriel. *História compendiada de Tamaulipas*. México City: [Editorial Beatriz de Silva], 1945.

Sánchez Lamego, Miguel A. *Apuntas Para La Historia del Armas del Ingenieros en México: Historia del Batallion de Zapadores*. Tomo IV. México, D., F.: Secretaría de la Defensa Nacional Teller Autografico, 1946.

———. *El Castillo de San Carlos de Perote*. Vera Cruz Colección Suma Veracruzanna, n. d.

———. *The Second Mexican-Texas War, 1841-1843*. Hill Junior College Monograph, No. 7. Hillsboro, Tex.: Hill Junior College Press, 1972.

Sartorius, Carl [Christian]. *Mexico About 1850*. Stuttgart: Brockhaus, 1961.

Scarborough, A. C. *The Pass of the Eagle: The Chaparral Region of Texas*. Austin: San Felipe Press, 1968.

Schmidt, Charles Frank. *History of Washington County*. San Antonio: The Naylor Company, [1949].

Schmitz, Joseph William. *Texas Culture in the Days of the Republic, 1836-1846*. San Antonio, Texas: The Naylor Company, 1960.

———. *Texan Statecraft, 1836-1845*. San Antonio, Texas: The Naylor Company, 1941.

———. *Thus They Lived; Social Life in the Republic of Texas*. San Antonio, Texas: The Naylor Company, 1935.

Schoen, Harold (comp.). *Monuments Erected by the State of Texas to Commemorate the Centenary of Texas Independence*. Austin, Texas: Commission of Control for Texas Centennial Celebration, 1938.

Schwartz, Rosalie. *Across the River to Freedom: U. S. Negroes in Mexico*. Southwestern Studies Monograph, No. 44. El Paso, Texas: Texas Western Press, 1975.

Scott, Florence Johnson. *Historical Heritage of the Lower Río Grande. A Historical Record of Spanish Exploration, Subjugation and Colonization of the Lower Río Grande Valley and the Activities of José Escandón, Count of Sierra Gorda, together with the Development of Towns and Ranches under Spanish, Mexican and Texas Sovereignties, 1747-1848*. San Antonio, Texas: The Naylor Company, 1937.

———. *Old Rough and Ready on the Río Grande*. San Antonio, Texas: The Naylor Co., 1935. Reprint, Waco, Texas: Texian Press, 1969.

Sibley, Marilyn McAdams. *Lone Stars and State Gazettes: Texas Newspapers Before the Civil War*. College Station, Texas: Texas A&M University Press, 1983.

Siegel, Stanley. *A Political History of the Texas Republic, 1836-1845*. Austin: University of Texas Press, 1956.

Simpson, Harold B. *Hood's Texas Brigade: A Compendium*. Hillsboro, Texas: Hill Junior College Press, c1977.

Smith, Justin H. *The Annexation of Texas*. New York: Barnes & Noble, Inc., 1941.

———. *The War With Mexico*. 2 vols. New York: The MacMillan Company, 1919.

Smith, S. Compton. *Chile Con Carne, or the Camp and the Field*. New York: Miller and Curtis, 1857.

Smith, W. Broaddus. *Pioneers of Brazos County, Texas, 1800-1850*. Bryan, Texas: "The Scribe Shop," 1962.

Smithwick, Noah. *The Evolution of a State; or, Recollections of Old Texas Days*. Austin: Gammel Book Co., 1900.

Sobel, Robert, and John Raimo (eds.). *Biographical Directory of the Governors of the United States, 1789-1978*. 4 vols. Westport, Conn.: Meckler Brooks, c1978.

Soldado Mexicano, 1837-1847: Organizacion, Vestuario, Equipo El. Documentos Historicos Militares, Monografia 1. Mexico: Nieto-Brown-Hefter, 1958. (In Spanish and English.)

Sosa, Francisco. *Biografía de Méxicanos Distinguides.* México: Oficina Tipográfica de la Secretaría de Fomento, 1884.

Sowell, A[ndrew] J[ackson]. *Early Settlers and Indians Fighters of Southwest Texas. . . . Facts Gathered from Survivors of Frontier Days.* Austin, Texas: B. C. Jones & Co., Printers, 1900.

————. *History of Fort Bend County, Containing Biographical Sketches of Many Noted Characters.* Houston, Texas: W. H. Coyle & Co., Printers, 1904.

————. *Life of "Big Foot" Wallace.... The Only Reliable History of the Famous Frontiersman. Many Errors of History Corrected. Facts Gathered by the Author from the Lips of the Ranger Captain, Told in a Simple, Plain Manner, without Romance, or Embellishment.* [Devine], Texas: Devine News, 1899. Reprinted, Bandera: *Frontier Times,* 1927, with the notation that in 1899 its publication had been "authorized by William A. A. Wallace." Facsimile ed.: Austin: The Steck Co. 1957.

————. *The Mier Expedition.* Extract from *History of Fort Bend County* by A. J. Sowell. Houston, Texas: The Union National Bank, 1929.

————. *Rangers and Pioneers of Texas, with a Concise Account of the Early Settlements, Hardships, Massacres, Battles, and Wars, by which Texas was Rescued from the Rule of the Savage and Consecrated to the Empire of Civilization.* 2 vols. San Antonio, Texas: Shepard Bros. & Co., 1884. Reprint, New York: Agrosy-Antiquarian, Ltd., 1904.

Speer, John W. *A History of Blanco County.* Ed. by Henry C. Armbruster. Austin, Texas: Pemberton Press, c1963.

Spell, Lota M. *Pioneer Printer; Samuel Bangs in Mexico and Texas.* Austin, Texas: University of Texas Press, 1963.

Spurlin, Charles D. (comp.). *Texas Veterans in the Mexican War: Muster Rolls of Texas Military Units.* Victoria, Texas: C. D. Spurlin, c1984.

Strode, Hudson. *Now in México.* [1st ed.] New York: Harcourt, Brace, 1947.

Swenson, Helen Smothers (comp.). *8800 Texas Marriages, 1824-1850.* 2 vols. Round Rock, Texas: H. S. Swenson, 1981.

Taylor, Paul S. *An American-Mexican Frontier; Nueces County, Texas.* Chapel Hill: University of North Carolina Press, 1934.

Texas Almanac for 1857 with Statistics, Historical and Biographical Sketches, &c. Relating to Texas, The. Galveston: Richardson & Co., 1856.

Texas Almanac for 1860.. . . Galveston: 1859.

Texas, Mexico, and the Southwest, the Republic of Texas, the Mexican War; Books, Pamphlets, Broadsides Printed in Mexico, 1813-1850. New York: 1961?.

Thompson, Henry T. *Waddy Thompson, Jr.* Columbia, S. C.: R. L. Bryan Co., 1929.

Thompson, Jerry. *Sabers on the Río Grande.* Austin, Texas: Presidial Press, 1974.

Thorpe, Thomas Bangs. *Our Army on the Río Grande, Being a Short Account of the Important Events Transpiring from the Time of the Removal of the Army of Occupation from Corpus Christi to the Surrender of Matamoros; with Descriptions of the Battles of Palo Alto and Resaca de la Palma, the Bombardment of Fort Brown, and the Ceremonies of the Surrender of Matamoros, with Descriptions of the City, etc.* Philadelphia: Carey and Hart, 1846.

Thrall, Homer S. *A Pictorial History of Texas, From the Earliest Visits of European Adventures to A. D. 1883.* St Louis, Mo.: N. D. Thompson & Co., 1883.

Tornel Y Mendivil, José María. *Tejas y los Estados-Unidos de America, en sus Relaciónes con la República Méxicana.* México: Ignácio Cumpliano, 1837. A translation was published by Carlos E. Castañeda in *The Mexican Side of the Texan Revolution.* Dallas: P. L. Turner Co., c1928.

Toro, Alfonso. *Compendio de historia de México.* 3 vols. México: Editorial Patria, 1967-1968.

Tyler, George W. *The History of Bell County.* San Antonio, 1936.

Tyler, Lyon Gardiner (ed.). *The Letters and Times of the Tylers.* 3 vols. Richmond, Va.: Whittet & Shepperson, etc., 1884-1896.

Vestal, Stanley. *Big Foot Wallace: A Biography.* Boston: Houghton Mifflin, 1942.

[Veterans Association]. *List of Pensioners Who have Received Certificates together with the Names of Persons Applying for Pension.* Austin: State Gazette book and job office, 1876.

Wade, Houston. *David Wade: A Texas Pioneer.* LaGrange, Texas: LaGrange Journal, 1943.

————, (comp.). *The Dawson Men of Fayette County*. Houston, Texas: 1932.

————, (comp.). *Notes and Fragments of the Mier Expedition*. 2 vols. LaGrange, Texas: LaGrange Journal, 1936. Reprint of articles originally published in the *LaGrange Journal* (LaGrange), 1935-1936.

Wallace, Ernest. *Charles DeMorse: A Pioneer Editor and Statesman*. Lubbock: Texas Tech Press, 1943.

Wallis, Mrs. Jonnie Lockhart, and Lawrence L. Hill. *Sixty Years on the Brazos: The Life and Letters of Doctor John Washington Lockhart, 1824-1900*. Los Angeles, Calif.: Dunn Bros.: 1930.

Ward, H. G. *Mexico in 1827*. 2 vols. London: H. Colburn, 1828.

Watson, Mrs. James (comp.). *The Lower Río Grande Valley of Texas and Its Builders*. Mission? Texas, 1931.

Webb, Walter Prescott. *The Texas Rangers: A Century of Frontier Defense*. Boston: Houghton-Mifflin Company, 1935.

Weber, David J. *The Mexican Frontier, 1825-1846: The American Southwest Under Mexico*. Albuquerque, New Mexico: University of New Mexico Press, 1982.

Weckmann, Luis. *Las Relaciónes Franco-Méxicanos*. Tomo II (1839-1867) Archivo Histórico Diplomatico Méxicano: Guías para la Historia Diplomatica de México, No. 2. México: Secretaría de Relaciónes Exteriores, 1962.

Weddle, R. S. *San Juan Bautista: Gateway to Spanish Texas*. Austin: University Press, 1968.

————, and Robert H. Thornhoff. *Drama and Conflict: The Texas Saga of 1776*. Austin, Texas: Madrona Press, c1976.

Weeks, William F. *Debates of the Texas Convention*. Houston: Telegraph and Texas Register Press, 1846.

Weems, John Edward, and Jane Weems. *Dream of Empire: A Human History of the Republic of Texas, 1836-1846*. New York: Simon and Schuster, 1971.

Weinert, Willie Mae. *Authentic History of Guadalupe County; San Antonio and Its Beginnings, 1691-1731*. Seguin, Texas: Seguin Enterprise, 1951.

Wells, Tom Henderson. *Commodore Moore and the Texas Navy*. Austin, Texas: University of Texas Press, 1960.

Weyand, Leonie Rummel, and Houston Wade. *An Early History of Fayette County*. [La Grange: LaGrange Journal Plant, 1936].

Wharton, Clarence R. *History of Fort Bend County*. San Antonio, Texas: The Naylor Company, 1939.

————. *El Presidente: A Sketch of the Life of General Santa Anna*. Austin: Gammel's Book Store, 1926.

————. *The Republic of Texas: A Brief History of Texas from the First American Colonies in 1821 to Annexation in 1846*. Houston, Texas: C. C. Young Printing Co., 1922.

————, (author and ed.). *Texas Under Many Flags*. 3 vols. Chicago and New York: The American Historical Society, Inc., 1930.

White, Gifford E. (ed.). *Character Certificates in the General Land Office of Texas*. [Austin, Texas] G. E. White, 1985.

Whitley, Glenn R. *Map and Road Guide to the Mountain Roads South of Monterrey*. Big Spring, Texas: G. R. Whiteley, 1979.

Wilbarger, J. W. *Indian Depredations in Texas*. 2nd ed. Austin, Texas: Hutching's Printing House, 1890.

Wildwood, Warren. *Thrilling Adventures Among the Early Settlers*. Philadelphia: J. Edwin Potter, 1862.

Wilkinson, J. B. *Laredo and the Río Grande Frontier*. Austin: Jenkins Publishing Co., 1975.

Williams, Alfred M. *Sam Houston and the War of Independence in Texas*. Boston and New York: Houghton, Mifflin, 1893.

Williams, Amelia. *Following General Sam Houston from 1795-1863*. Austin, Texas: The Steck Company, c1935.

Williams, Clayton. *Never Again: Texas B. C.-1861*. 3 Vols. San Antonio, Texas: The Naylor Company, 1969.

Winfield, Jr., Nath, and Judy Winfield. *Cemetery Records of Washington County, Texas, 1826-1960*. Chappell Hill, Texas?: Winfield, c1976.

Wolters, Jacob F. *Dawson's Men and the Mier Expedition. Memorial Day Address at the LaGrange*

Opera House, April 21, 1904. LaGrange, Texas: Journal Print, 1904. Reprinted, Houston: The Union National Bank, 1927.

Wooten, Dudley G. *A Comprehensive History of Texas, 1685 to 1897*. 2 vols. Dallas: W. G. Scarff, 1898.

Wortham, Louis J. *A History of Texas from Wilderness to Commonwealth*. 5 vols. Fort Worth: Wortham-Molyneaux Co., 1924.

Writers' Program of the Works Projects Administration (comp.). *Texas: A Guide to the Lone Star State*. New York: Hastings House, 1940.

Yett, Tommy (comp.). *Members of the Legislature of the State of Texas from 1846-1939*. Austin: c1939.

Yoakum, H. *History of Texas from its First Settlement in 1685 to Its Annexation to the United States in 1846*. 2 vols. New York: J. S. Redfield, 1855. Facsimile reprint, Austin, Texas: The Steck Co., 1935.

Young, Philip. *History of Mexico: Her Civil Wars, and Colonial and Revolutionary Annals; from the Period of the Spanish Conquest, 1520, to the Present Times, 1847, Including an Account of the War with the United States, Its Causes and Military Achievements continued to the Treaty of Peace, 1848*. By George C. Furber, Esq., Author of "Twelve Months Volunteer," pp. 471-573. Cincinnati: Published by J. A. & U. P. James, 1850.

Zorrilla, Luis G. *Historia de las Relaciónes Entre México y los Estados Unidos de America, 1800-1958*. 2 vols. México: Editorial Porrua, 1965-1966.

b. Articles and Periodicals.

"An Ancient Texian: The Remarkable History of John C. C. Hill, an Old Time Texan Boy," *Dallas Daily Herald*, Mar. 25, 1880.

Anonymous. "A Leaf from Memory: Scenes of the Battle-Field of Salado." By an Old Texan. *Texas Almanac for 1860*, pp. 72-74.

Armstrong, Mary K. "The Recovery of the Remains of the Mier Prisoners," *Naylor Epic Century Magazine* (Winter 1935), pp. 10-12.

Baldwin, T. B. "The Lone Star Flag of Texas," *Frontier Times* I (Nov. 1923), pp. 6-7.

Barker, Eugene C. "The Annexation of Texas," *Southwestern Historical Quarterly* I (July 1946), pp. 49-74.

———. "The Finances of the Texas Revolution," *Political Science Quarterly* XIX (Dec. 1904), pp. 612-35.

Barnes, Charles Merritt. "Houses with Histories," *San Antonio Daily Express*, Feb. 9, 1908.

Barr, Alwyn. "A Bibliography of Articles on the Military History of Texas," *Texas Military History* II (Nov. 1962), pp. 265-74; III (Spring 1963), pp. 23-32; (Summer 1963), pp. 111-13; IV (Winter 1964), pp. 285-88; VI (Spring 1967), pp. 107-10.

Barton, Henry W. "Five Texas Frontier Companies during the Mexican War," *Southwestern Historical Quarterly* LXVI (July 1962), pp. 17-30.

———. "The Problem of Command in the Army of the Republic of Texas," *Southwestern Historical Quarterly* LXII (Jan. 1959), pp. 299-311.

"The Battles of the Río Grande," *The Southern Quarterly Review*, n. s., II (1850), pp. 427-63.

Beerstecher, Jr., Ernest (ed.). "Historical Probate Extracts. Harris(burg) County, Republic of Texas," *Texana* VII (Winter 1969), pp. 247-94; VIII (Spring), pp. 47-90.

Bergen, Lynne. "Major Dunham's Black Bean," *Junior Historian*, March 4, 1965, pp. 26-28.

"Big Foot Wallace: The Texan Ranger," in *Rockbridge* (Va.) *Citizen*, reprinted in *San Antonio Daily Herald*, Aug. 24, 1872.

Billingsley, John Beldon. "A Trip to Texas, " edited by Robert L. and Pauline H. Jones, *Texana* VII (1969), pp. 201-19.

Binkley, William C. "The Last Stage of the Texan Military Operations Against Mexico, 1843," *Southwestern Historical Quarterly* XXII (Jan. 1919), pp. 260-71.

Blount, Lois Foster. "A Brief Study of Thomas J. Rusk Based on His Letters to His Brother, David, 1835-1856," *Southwestern Historical Quarterly* XXXIV (Jan. 1931), pp. 181-202; (April 1931), pp. 271-92.

Bourke, Capt. John G. "The American Congo," *Scribner's Magazine* XV (May 1894), pp. 590-610.

Bouve, P. C. "Sam Houston," *American Heroes*, pp. 270-99.

Bowden, J. J. "The Texas-New Mexico Boundary Dispute Along the Río Grande," *Southwestern Historical Quarterly* LXIII (Oct. 1959), pp. 221-37.

"Dr. Richard Fox Brenham," *Frontier Times* XVI (July 1939), pp. 439-41.

Brown, Alma Howell. "Consular Service of the Republic of Texas," *Southwestern Historical Quarterly* XXXIII (Jan. 1930), pp. 184-230; (April 1930), pp. 299-314.

Bruce, H. A. "Sam Houston and the Annexation of Texas," *Outlook* LXXXVIII (Apr. 25, 1908), pp. 954-65.

Buchanan, A. Russell (ed.). "George Washington Trahern: Texan Cowboy Soldier from Mier to Buena Vista," *Southwestern Historical Quarterly* LVIII (July 1954), pp. 60-90.

Callihan, Elmer L. "Little John Hill, the Boy Hero of Mier," *Dallas Daily Herald*, Mar. 25, 1880.

Canfield, J. H. "Bit of Secret History: Annexation of Texas," Independent (New York), LV, 914-15 (Apr. 16, 1903).

"Captain Ben McCulloch," *Frontier Times* XXIII (Dec. 1945), pp. 47-49.

"Captain Jesse Billingsley: A Texas Patriot," *Frontier Times* XVII (Nov. 1939), pp. 85-89.

"Capt. S. H. Walker," *Niles' National Register* LXX, 201-2 (May 30, 1846).

Carnack, George. "Adventure's Magnet: The Border," *San Antonio Express-News,* May 15 and 17, 1975.

Carnes, F. G. "George Lord, A Texas Pioneer," *Frontier Times* VI (July 1929), pp. 395-98.

Carroll, H. Bailey. "Steward A[lexander] Miller and the Snively Expedition of 1843," *Southwestern Historical Quarterly* LIV (Jan. 1951), pp. 261-86.

Castel, Albert, "Sam Houston's Last Fight," *American Heritage* XVII (Dec. 1965), pp. 81-87.

Chalk, Whitfield. "How Whitfield Chalk Escaped from Mier," a newspaper clipping in E. G. Littlejohn (comp.), "Texas Scrap Book," II, p. 68. Rosenberg Library, Galveston.

Christian, Asa K. "Mirabeau Buonaparte Lamar," *Southwestern Historical Quarterly* XXIII (Jan. 1920), pp. 153-70.

———. "The Tariff History of the Republic of Texas," *Southwestern Historical Quarterly* XX (Apr. 1917), pp. 335.40.

"Claudius Buster was A Mier Prisoner," *Frontier Times* XVI (June 1939) pp. 395-400.

Clay, Comer. "The Colorado River Raft," *Southwestern Historical Quarterly* LII (Apr. 1949), pp. 410-26.

Cole, Mrs. M. E. "The Old Washington I Knew," *Frontier Times* V (Jan. 1928), pp. 154-55.

"Concentration Camp Horrors Sound Familiar to Daughter of Meir *[sic]* Expedition," *Dallas Morning News*, May 18, 1941.

Coyner, C. Luther. "Peter Hansbrough Bell," *Quarterly of the Texas State Historical Association* III (July 1899), pp. 49-53.

Cox, Isaac J. "The Southwest Boundary of Texas," *Quarterly of the Texas State Historical Association* VI (Oct. 1902), pp. 81-102.

Crimmins, Martin L. "James C. Wilson, An English Hero of the Mier Expedition," *Frontier Times* XXVIII (Sept. 1951), pp. 352-53.

———. "John Christopher Columbus Hill: Boy Captive of the Mier Expedition," *Frontier Times* XXVIII (June 1951), pp. 253-58.

———. "Whitfield Chalk Escaped at Mier," *Frontier Times* XXVIII (July 1951), pp. 275-78.

Cude, Elton, "Fritzgerald—A Perote Prisoner," *Texana* VIII (1970), pp. 256-68.

Cunniff, M. G. "Texas and the Texans," *World's Book* XI, pp. 7267-88. (Mar. 1906).

Davenport, Harbert. "General José María Jesús Carabajal," *Southwestern Historical Quarterly* LV (Apr. 1952), pp. 475-83.

———. "The Men of Goliad," *Southwestern Historical Quarterly* XLIII (July 1939), pp. 1-41.

"Dawson Massacre," *Frontier Times* I (Feb. 1924), pp. 191-96.

Day, Donald, and Samuel Wood Geiser. "D. Port Smythe's Journey Across Early Texas," *The Texas Geographic Magazine* VI (Fall 1942), pp. 1-20.

Day, James M. [Guy M. Bryan, Sketch of] in "Texas Letters and Documents," *Texana* VIII (1970), pp. 91-92.

———. "Masonic Men of the Mier Expedition of 1842," *Transactions* Texas Lodge of Research, A.F. & A.M., 1959-1960-1961, pp. 347-57.

Denman, Clarence P. "The Office of Adjutant General in Texas, 1835-1881," *Southwestern Historical Quarterly* XXVIII (Apr. 1925), pp. 3302-22.

DeShields, James T. "Jack Hays: Famous Texas Ranger," *The American Home Journal: A Monthly Magazine for the Home* IV (June 1906).

Dienst, Alexander. "The Navy of the Republic of Texas," *Quarterly of the Texas State Historical Association* XII (Jan. 1909), pp. 165-203; (Apr. 1909), pp. 249-75.

Dobb, William E. "The West and the War with Mexico," *Journal of the Illinois State Historical Society* V (July 1912), pp. 159-72.

Doyle, D. K. "He Knew Survivors of Mier Expedition: Mart V. Fleming of Comanche Tells of Men Who drew Beans in Gamble for Life or Death," *Dallas Morning News*, Jan. 9, 1927.

"Drawing of the Beans by Texans," *Frontier Times* XIII (Mar. 1936), pp. 311-14.

Edwards, Herbert Rook. "Diplomatic Relations between France and the Republic of Texas, 1836-1845," *Southwestern Historical Quarterly* XX (Jan. 1917), pp. 209-41; (Apr. 1917), pp. 341-57.

Edwards, Jr., Klmer J. "An Interesting Trip to Mier, Mexico," *Frontier Times* XVIII (Mar. 1941), pp. 289-91.

Elliot, Claude. "Alabama and the Texas Revolution," *Southwestern Historical Quarterly* (Jan. 1949), pp. 315-28.

Englehart, Mrs. L. K. "Samuel Colt Lived in Texas; Patent History of the Republic of Texas," *Hobbies* LII (May 1952), p. 142.

"Erath's Famous Fight," *Frontier Times* XXVI (May 1929), pp. 179-82.

"Ewen Cameron: First 'Cowboy,'" *Texas Parade* (Apr. 1960), p. 42.

[Fisher, William S.] "A List of Officers Actually in Service in the Army of the Republic of Texas," compiled by William [S.] Fisher, Secretary of War, on May 10, 1836, in Army Papers, Tx-A, and printed in *Texana* V (Spring 1967), pp. 79-81.

Flaccus, Elmer W. "The Secret Adversary: Henry George Ward and Texas, 1825-1827," *East Texas Historical Journal* IV (Mar. 1966), pp. 5-15.

Franke, Paul. "Lottery of Death," *Houston Chronicle Magazine*, June 8, 1947.

Friend, Llerena B. "W. P. Webb's Texas Rangers," *Southwestern Historical Quarterly* LXXIV (Jan. 1971), pp. 293-323.

"General Edward Burleson," *Frontier Times* VI (June 1929), pp. 353-54.

"Gen. Walter P. Lane—His Bold Recovery of the Mier Prisoners' Bodies," *The Old Capitol* (Columbia, Texas), Feb. 4, 1888.

"George B. Erath," *Frontier Times* I (Dec. 1923), pp. 93-94.

Gilligin, Burce. "John Christopher Columbus Hill," *Junior Historian* XI (Mar. 1951), pp. 1-4.

Goolsby, William B. "Perote Prison Buried Texans' Dreams," *Frontier Times* XV (May 1938), pp. 362-65.

Graf, Leroy P. "Colonizing Projects in Texas South of the Nueces, 1820-1845," *Southwestern Historical Quarterly* L (Apr. 1947), pp. 431-48.

Green, Wharton C. "General Thomas J. Green, of Warren, North Carolina," *North Carolina University Magazine* XI, No. 5 (1892), p. 217.

Grove, Larry. "Pale Sash Lives on After Drama," *Dallas Morning News*, Feb. 27, 1965.

Gunn, Jack W. "Ben McCulloch: A Big Captain," *Southwestern Historical Quarterly* LVIII (July 1954), pp. 1-21.

Hale, Joseph W. "Masonry in the Early days of Texas," *Southwestern Historical Quarterly* LXIX (Jan. 1946), pp. 374-83.

Hardy, L. C. "Texan Types and Contrasts," *Harpers Monthly* LXXXI (July 1890), pp. 229-46.

Hart, James P. "John Hemphill—Chief Justice of Texas," *Southwestern Law Journal* III (Fall 1949), pp. 395-415.

Hatcher, John Henry. "The Navy of the Republic of Texas," *Texas Military History* V (Summer 1965), pp. 65-78.

Haugh, George F. (ed.). "History of the Texas Navy," *Southwestern Historical Quarterly* LXIII (Apr. 1960), pp. 572-79,

Henderson, Mary Virginia. "Minor Empresario Contracts for the Colonization of Texas," *Southwestern Historical Quarterly* XXXII (July 1928), pp. 1-28.

"Henry Journeay," *Frontier Times* VI (Dec. 1928), p. 95.

Henson, Margaret Swett. "Politics and the Treatment of the Mexican Prisoners after the Battle of San Jacinto, *"Southwestern Historical Quarterly* XCIV (Oct. 1990), pp. 189-230.

Hogan, William Ransom. "Rampant Individualism in the Republic of Texas," *Southwestern Historical Quarterly* XLIV (Apr. 1941), 454-80.

Hunter, [J.] Marvin. "Big Foot Wallace, The Daniel Boone of Texas," *Frontier Times* XVII (July 1940), pp. 424-27.

———. "General Benjamin McCulloch," *Frontier Times* V (June 1928), pp. 353-54.

———. "Jack Hays, Premier Texas Ranger," *Frontier Times* XXX (Jan. 1953), pp. 79-84.

———. "Jack Hays, the Intrepid Texas Ranger," *Frontier Times* IV (Feb. 1927), pp. 25-40; (Mar. 1927), pp. 17-31; (Apr. 1927), pp. 17-31; (May 1927), pp. 17-31.

———. "The Story of the Black Beans," *Frontier Times*. XXIX (May 1952), pp. 211-15.

Hunter, John Warren. "Adventures of a Mier Prisoner; Thrilling Story of John Rufus Alexander, A Member of the Ill-Fated Expedition into Mexico," *Frontier Times* II (Apr. 1925), pp. 17-30, and inside front cover.

———. "Adventures of John Rufus Alexander," *Frontier Times* XVI (Nov. 1938), pp. 61-76.

———. "The Vengeance of Bate Berry," *Frontier Times* XXX (Oct.-Dec. 1953), pp. 465-71.

———. Mary Maurine, "They Lived with a Vengeance," *Texas Parade* IV (Jan. 1940), pp. 4-5, 21-22.

"Jack Hays and His Men," *Texas Democrat*, Dec. 16, 1846.

"John C. Hays and His Men," *Niles' National Register* LXXI, 201-2 (Nov. 28, 1846).

"John McMullen Went to California in 1849," *Frontier Times* XII (Oct. 1934), pp. 5-6.

"John Reagan Baker," *Frontier Times* I (June 1924), pp. 383-90; (July 1924), pp. 405-10.

"John Twohig, A Texas Patriot," *Frontier Times* VI (Apr. 1929). p. 261.

Johnston, Marguerite. "A Boy Who Got a Black Bean Wrote A Letter," *Houston Post*, Sept. 11, 1967.

———. "The 17 Black Beans of Doom," *Temp Magazine* [of the *Houston Post*], Mar. 24. 1968. pp. 32-34.

Jones, Robert L., and Pauline H. Jones. "Memucan Hunt: His Private Life," *Texana* VI (Summer 1966), pp. 104-28; (Fall 1966), pp. 213-32.

"José Antonio Navarro Was a Patriot," *Frontier Times* I (Dec. 1923), p. 32.

Kelley, Mary E. "The Forest of Sindbad," *Frontier Times* XI (Jan. 1934), pp. 151-56.

Kemp, L. W. "History of Kenney's Fort," *Frontier Times* XXIII (June 1946), pp. 148-51.

———. "Monument Hill: The Colorful Story of a Memorial," *Texas Parade* XIII (Apr. 1953), pp. 44-47.

———. "Official Flags of the Republic of Texas," *Southwestern Historical Quarterly* LIX (Apr. 1956), pp. 487-97.

"Kenny's Fort in Williamson County," *Frontier Times* XXVIII (July 1951), pp. 278-80.

Kilman, Ed. "José Antonio Navarro: Texas Patriot," *Houston Post*, Apr. 19, 1936.

———. "Mier Expedition: Tourists Find Cold Beer Concessions in Buildings of Ancient Mexican Town Where Daring Texans Fought Nearly a Century Ago: A Modern Version," *Houston Post-Dispatch*, Sept. 30, 1928.

King, C. Richard. "James Clinton Neill," *Texana* II (Winter 1964), pp. 231-52.

———. "Newspapers that Republic of Texas Readers Didn't Read," *Texana* V (Summer 1967), pp. 117-25.

———. "Public Printing in the Republic of Texas," *Texana* VI (Winter 1968), pp. 343-72.

Koch, Mary Wilcox. "Violin Whose Music Lulled Mier Prisoners is Found," *Dallas Morning News*, Feb. 21, 1932.

Kossok, Manfred. "Prussia, Bremen and the 'Texas Question,' 1835-1845," *Texana* III (Fall 1965), pp. 227-69.

"LaGrange in 1884," in *LaGrange Journal*, June 12, 1929.

Lander, Jr., Ernest M. "General Waddy Thompson, A Friend of Mexico During the Mexican War," *South Carolina Historical Magazine* LXXVIII (Jan. 1977), pp. 32-42.

"Last Range of Big-Foot Wallace," *Frontier Times* XX (Mar. 1943), pp. 91-93.

Lastinger, W. W. "The Ill-Fated Mier Expedition," *Frontier Times* XI (Aug. 1934), pp. 499-504. First appeared in *San Antonio Express*, Sunday Morning, June 24, 1934.

"Life of Bigfoot Wallace, The." [From "A Pamphlet Written by A. J. Sowell in 1899, and Its Publication Authorized by William A. A. Wallace, the Noted Frontier Character"], *Frontier Times* V (Nov. 1927), pp. 65-80; (Dec. 1927), pp. 113-28; (Jan. 1928), pp. 161-74.

"Little John Hill, the Boy Hero of Mier," *Dallas Morning News*, Dec. 22, 1929.

Looscan, Mrs. Adele B. "Decimation of the Mier Prisoners," *Quarterly of the Texas State Historical Association* V (July 1901), pp. 66-68.

————. "Harris County, 1822-1845," *Southwestern Historical Quarterly* XVIII (Oct. 1914), pp. 195-207; (Jan. 1915), pp. 261-86; (Apr. 1915), pp. 399-409; XIX (July 1915), pp. 37-64.

Lord, Eugene. "George Lord—Pioneer," *Junior Historian* IX (May 1949), pp. 8-10.

Lott, Virgil N. "History Denies the Real Saviors of Texas to Gallant Men Who Tackled Mier Rather Than to Martyrs at Alamo We Owe Our First Lasting Peace," *Dallas Morning News*, June 23, 1929, Feature Section, p. 4.

Lubers, H. L. "William Bent's Family and Indians of the Plains," *Colorado Magazine* XIII (Jan. 1936), pp. 19-22.

McCampbell, Coleman. "Colonel Kinney's Romance with Daniel Webster's Daughter," *Crystal Reflector* (Corpus Christi), June 1939.

McCausland, Walter. "Some Early Texas Newspapers," *Southwestern Historical Quarterly* XLIX (Jan. 1946), pp. 384-89.

McClintock, William A. "Journal of a Trip through Texas and Northern México in 1846-1847," *Southwestern Historical Quarterly* XXXIV (July 1930), pp. 20-37; (Oct. 1930), pp. 141-58; (Jan. 1931), pp. 231-56.

McGrath, J. J., and Walace Hawkins. "Perote Fort—Where Texans were Imprisoned," *Southwestern Historical Quarterly* XLVIII (Jan. 1945), pp. 340-45. Also Published in *San Antonio Light*, Feb. 13, 1938.

McMurtrie, Douglas C. "Pioneer Printing in Texas," *Southwestern Historical Quarterly* XXXV (Jan. 1932), pp. 173-93.

Mann, William L. "James C. Rice, Hero of the Battle on the Gabriel," *Southwestern Historical Quarterly* LV (July 1951), pp. 30-42.

Manning, William R. "Texas and the Boundary Issue, 1822-1829," *Southwestern Historical Quarterly* XV (Apr. 1912), pp. 267-93.

————. "The Southwestern Boundary of Texas, 1821-1840," *Quarterly of the Texas State Historical Association* XIV (Apr. 1911), pp. 277-93.

Mendizabal, Miguel O. de. "Los Minerales de Pachuca y Real del Monte en la epoca, colonial," *El Trimestre Economico* VIII (1941), pp. 253-309.

Menn, Alfred E. "When Santa Anna Was Texas Captive," *Dallas Morning News*, Nov. 3, 1954.

"The Mier Expedition: Vivid Account of Texas' Invasion of Mexico—Drawing of the Black Beans," *Foster's Follies* III, pt. 1, Apr. 10, 1936; May 25, 1936, being Parts I and II, respectively. Published by Foster's Print Shop, Beaumont, Texas.

Miller, Sam. "Romance, Adventure, History and Tragedy Fill Texas Names," *Frontier Times* VII (Oct. 1929), pp. 6-8.

Miller, Thomas Lloyd. "José Antonio Navarro, 1795-1871," *Journal of Mexican American History* II (Spring 1972), pp. 71-89.

Moore, A. Gayland. "A Tale of Two Salados," *Texas Parks and Wild Life* XL (Sept. 1986), pp. 2-7.

————. "Kreische's Bluff Beer," *Texas Parks and Wild Life* XLIV (Sept. 1986), pp. 8-11.

Moore, Walter B. "Hamilton Stuart," *Texana* IV (Spring 1966), pp. 23-32.

Morgan, Ernest. "Resulted in Black Bean Drawing: A Border Town Chooses to Forget Fight of Texans, Mexicans 118 Years Ago." *Corpus Christi Caller-Times*, Sunday, Nov. 13, 1960.

Morgan, S. H. "John Day Morgan, A Texan Pioneer," *Frontier Times* IV (Feb. 1927), pp. 4-8.

Muckleroy, Anna. "The Indian Policy of the Republic of Texas," *Southwestern Historical Quarterly* XXV (Apr. 1922), pp. 229-69; XXVI (July 1922), pp, 1-29; (Oct. 1922, pp. 128-34; (Jan. 1923), pp. 184-206.

Nackman, Mark. "Anglo-Americans Migrations to the West: Men of Broken Fortunes? The Case of Texas, 1821-46," *Western Historical Quarterly* V (Oct. 1974), pp. 441-55.

————. "The Making of the Texan-Citizen Soldier, 1835-1860," *Southwestern Historical Quarterly* LXXVII (Jan. 1975), pp. 231-53.

Nance, Joseph Milton. "Adrián Woll: Frenchman in the Mexican Military Service," *New Mexico Historical Review* XXXIII (July 1958), pp. 177-86.

————. "The Flag Incident of the Texan Mier Expedition of 1842-1844," West Texas Historical Association *Yearbook* LXV (1989), pp. 5-23.

————. "Was there a Mier Expedition Flag?" *Southwestern Historical Quarterly* XCII (Apr. 1989), pp. 543-57.

Nevin, David. "A Bold Adventure that Ended in Tragedy," Time-Life Books, *The Old West: The Texans*, pp. 142-47.

Newsome, W. L. "The Postal System of the Republic of Texas," *Southwestern Historical Quarterly* XX (Oct. 1916), pp. 103-31.

Nordyke, L[ewis]. "Black Beans of Death," *Coronet* XLVI (Aug. 1959), pp. 150-56.

O'Meara, J. "The Mier Prisoners," *Californian* V, 466.

Oates, Stephen B. "Los Diablos Téjanos," in *Visions of Glory: Texans on the Southwestern Frontier*. 1st ed. Norman: University of Oklahoma Press, 1970, pp. 25-52.

"Off the Beaten Track: A Long Three Miles," *San Antonio Express-News*, Apr. 19, 1964.

Posey, Mary Johnson. "Captain William Eastland," *Frontier Times* XXI (Sept. 1944), pp. 443-45.

Presley, James. "Santa Anna in Texas: A Mexican Viewpoint," *Southwestern Historical Quarterly* LXII (Apr. 1959), pp. 489-512.

Rather, Ethel Zivley. "DeWitt's Colony," *Quarterly of the Texas State Historical Association* VIII (Oct. 1904), pp. 95-192.

Robinson, Joseph C. "Survivors of Dawson's Defeat," in *Texas Monument* (LaGrange), Aug. 27, Sept. 3 and 10, 1851.

Rogers, Marjorie. "Major George B. Erath," *Frontier Times* XVII (Dec. 1939), pp. 93-94.

————. "Old Viesca," *Frontier Times* VIII (Aug. 1931), pp. 489-92.

Roper, William L. "Ben McCulloch: Texas Hero," *Texas Parade* XIX (Oct. 1958), pp. 51-53.

R[ose], V[ictor] M. "Preserving the Relics of Mier," in *Texas Mute Ranger*, Feb. 1883.

Rumph, Catherine Elizabeth (Hixon). "Reminiscences of Perote in Bullock [County]," *Alabama Historical Quarterly* XX (Fall 1958), pp. 479-522.

Runge, J. Forrest. "The Story of the Las Moras Ranch," *Frontier Times* XXXI (Oct.-Dec. 1954), pp. 391-405.

"Samuel Augustus Maverick, Texas Patriot," *Frontier Times* V (Apr. 1928), pp. 257-60.

"Samuel Maverick in Perote Prison," *Frontier Times* XV (Sept. 1938), pp. 405-10.

"Samuel Colt Lived in Texas," *Frontier Times* XXIII (Jan. 1946), pp. 71-72.

Scott, Florence Johnson. "Historic Bean Lottery Took Place Exactly 79 Years Ago," *Fort Worth Star-Telegram*, May 26, 1922.

Shannon, H. A. "12 Miles to Mier Thunder the 300," *Dallas Morning News*, Sunday, Oct. 19, 1930.

Sibley, Marilyn McAdams. "Thomas Jefferson Green, Recruiter for the Texas Army, 1836," *Texas Military History* III (Fall 1963), pp. 129-45.

Smith, Brad H. "Mier, Which Texans Hoped to Capture, Defies the March of Time," *San Antonio Express*, Feb. 25, 1934.

Smithers, W. D., "Nature's Pharmacy and the Curanderos and the Border Trading Posts," *Sul Poss State College Bulletin* XLI, No. 3 (Sept. 1, 1961), pp. 3-57. (*Publication* of the West Texas Historical and Scientific Society, No. 18).

"Son [J. L. Brown of Houston] of Mier Expedition Survivor Visits Dallas Kin, Relates Tales of Early Texans' Heroic Lives," *Dallas Morning News*, Sept. 3, 1940, Section I p. 3.

Sowell, A. J. "The Life of Bigfoot Wallace," *Frontier Times* V (Dec. 1927). pp. 113-14.

Spell, Lota M. "Samuel Bangs: The First Printer in Texas," *Southwestern Historical Quarterly* XXXV (Apr. 1932), pp. 267-78.

Spurlin, Charles. "Ranger Walker in the Mexican War," *Military History of Texas and the Southwest* IX (1971), pp. 259-79.

Stillwell, Hart. "9 Descendants of Fatal Beans," *San Antonio Light*, July 19, 1968.

Stratton, Mrs. Ruby K. (comp.). "A History of Brazoria County," *Frontier Times* XXVII (Aug. 1951), pp. 316-21.

Stuart, Ben C. "Hamilton Stuart: Pioneer Editor," *Southwestern Historical Quarterly* XXI (Apr. 1918), pp. 381-88. Corrected version of original publication in *Galveston News*, June 3, 1917.

"A Survivor of the Mier Expedition," *Frontier Times* I (Nov. 1923), p. 23.

Syers, Ed. "Ciudad Mier Still Almost Like Attackers Saw It," *San Antonio Express-News*, Aug. 10, 1963.

————. "Off the Beaten Trail: A Long Three Miles," *San Antonio Express-News*, Apr. 19, 1964.

Terrell, Alexander W. "The City of Austin from 1839 to 1865," *Quarterly of the Texas State Historical Association* XIV (Oct. 1910), pp. 113-28.

————. "Recollections of General Houston," *Southwestern Historical Quarterly* XVI (Oct. 1912), pp. 113-36.

"A Texan of the Old Times—His Treatment As A Prisoner in Mexico," *Galveston Daily News*, Mar. 17, 1874.

"Texan Tells the True Story of the Famous Mier Expedition into Mexico: John Rufus Alexander's Reminiscences Told of one of the Most Daring Adventures in American History." Revised and Arranged for publication by John Warren Hunter, San Angelo, Texas, in *San Antonio Express*, Apr. 26, 1914.

Thompson, Jane Edward. "Overland Staging in the Fifties," *Overland Monthly*, 2nd ser., XII (July-Dec. 1888), pp. 177-90.

Thrall, H. S. (comp.). "A List of Old Texans Who Have Died and Been Killed by Mexicans and Indians from 1828-1874," in D. W. C. Baker (comp.), *A Texas Scrap-Book*, 580-85.

Tilloson, Cyrus. "Place Names of Nueces County," *Frontier Times* XXXVI (Apr. 1949), pp. 175-78.

"Tom Hancock," *Frontier Times* II (Nov. 1924), pp. 31-35.

Traylor, Maude Wallis. "Benjamin Franklin Highsmith," *Frontier Times* XV (Apr. 1938), pp. 309-17.

Traylor, Mrs. C. T. (i. e., Maude Wallis). "George Lord: A Mier Prisoner," *Frontier Times* XV (Sept. 1938), pp. 533-52.

————. [Letter of] to [J. Marvin] Hunter, Cuero, Texas, Dec. 5, 1939, *Frontier Times* XVII (Feb. 1940), pp. 187-89.

————. "Those Men of the Mier Expedition," *Frontier Times* XVI (Apr. 1939), pp. 299-309.

Townsend, Samuel. "Relates How His Uncle Saved Life of Santa Anna," *San Antonio Express*, June 21, 1929.

"The Vanished Texas of Theodore Gentilz," in *American Heritage* XXV, no. 6 (Oct. 1974), pp. 18-27.

Vásquez, Josefina Zoraida. "The Texas Question in Mexican Politics, 1836-1845," *Southwestern Historical Quarterly* LXXXIX (Jan. 1986), pp. 309-44.

"The Violin of Perote," *Frontier Times* XX (Mar. 1943), pp. 95-96.

Wade, Houston. "Alfred Alonzo Lee . . . or Alfred Allee," *Frontier Times* XVII (Aug. 1939), pp. 32-35.

"Alfred Sturgis Thurmond," *Frontier Times* XVI (Aug. 1939), pp. 472-74.

————. "Captain John Reagan Baker," *Frontier Times* XVII (June 1940), pp. 383-91; (July 1940), pp. 405-10.

————. "Collecting Data Relative to Dawson Massacre," *Frontier Times* XI (Feb. 1934), pp. 199-200.

————. "Dr. Richard Fox Brenham," *Frontier Times* XVI (July 1939), pp. 439-41.

————. "Eastland's Company," *LaGrange Journal*, Nov. 1 and 8, 1934.

————. "Edward E. Este Drew A Black Bean," *Frontier Times* XIX (Oct. 1941), pp. 31-32.

————. "The Fate of J. L. Shepherd," *Frontier Times* XIX (Nov. 1941), pp. 76-77.

————. "Michael Cronican, A Mier Fighter," *Frontier Times* XVIII (Sept. 1941), pp. 555-59.

————. "The Story of Whitfield Chalk," *Frontier Times* XVIII (Nov. 1940), pp. 77-78.

Walker, Olive Todd. "Major Whitfield Chalk, Hero of the Republic of Texas," *Southwestern Historical Quarterly* LX (Jan. 1957), pp. 358-68.

[Wallace, William A. A.]. "Greetings from Big Foot Wallace," *Frontier Times* XI (Oct. 1934), pp. 44-45.

————. "Letters of Big Foot Wallace," *Frontier Times* VIII (June 1931), pp. 417-19.

Ward, Hortense Warner. "The First State Fair of Texas," *Southwestern Historical Quarterly* LVII (Oct. 1953), pp. 163-74.

Warren, Harry. "Col. William G. Cooke," *Quarterly of the Texas State Historical Association* IX (Jan. 1906), pp. 210-19.

Weems, John Edward. "Lottery of Death," *Galveston News*, Jan. 23, 1972, Texas Star Section, pp. 6-7; also in *Texas Star* of [*San Antonio*] *Express and News*, Sunday, Jan. 23, 1972, pp. 6-7.

Weinert, Willie Mae. "Colonel Andrew Neill," *Seguin Enterprise* July 22, 1938; also in *Frontier Times* XVI (May 1939), pp. 336, 367-68.

———. "Sketch of Captain Jack Hays," *Frontier Times* XVII (Jan. 1940), pp. 175-76.

Wells, Tom H. "An Evaluation of the Texas Navy," *Southwestern Historical Quarterly* LXIII (Apr. 1961), pp. 567-71.

"When A Handful of Americans Invaded Mier," from *The Hidalgo News* (Hidalgo, Texas), in *Frontier Times* VI (Mar. 1929), pp. 246-48.

Wilbarger, J. W. "Captain Ben McCulloch," *Frontier Times* XXIII (Dec. 1945), pp. 47-49.

Willrich, Mrs. George. "Care of Tomb Extends Over Eighty Years," *Fayette County Record* (LaGrange), June 11, 1931; also in *LaGrange Journal*, June 16, 1931.

Wilcox, N. M. "The Old Violin of Perote and Its Song of Liberty," *San Antonio Express*, July 27, 1913.

Wilcox, Seb S. "Laredo during the Texas Republic," *Southwestern Historical Quarterly* XLII (Oct. 1938), pp. 83-107.

———. "The Spanish Archives of Laredo," *Southwestern Historical Quarterly* XLIV (Apr. 1941), pp. 498-500; XLIX (Jan. 1946), pp. 341-60.

Woodland, Henry. "The Story of the Massacre of Mier Prisoners," *Houston Daily Post*, Aug. 16, 1891.

Woods, J. M. "José Antonio Navarro: A Great Texan," *Frontier Times* XIX (Jan. 1942), pp. 141-42.

Wooster, Ralph A. "The Military Operations Against Mexico, 1842-1843," *Southwestern Historical Quarterly* LXVII (Apr. 1964), pp. 465-84.

Worley, J. L. "The Diplomatic Relations of England and the Republic of Texas," *Quarterly of the Texas State Historical Association* IX (July 1905), pp. 1-40.

Yates, Paul C. "Adventurer Artist of Republic Era Records Scenes from Daring and Ill-Fated Texas Expedition," *Houston Post Dispatch*, May 26, 1919.

Yoakum, Thomas P. "Henderson Yoakum, Texas Historian," *Frontier Times* XXVII (July 1950), pp. 288-92.

Young, Kevin R. "The Mier P. O. W.'s," in *Military Images* II, no. 3 (Nov.-Dec. 1980), pp. 8-9.

Zuber, William P. "The Number of 'Decimated' Mier Prisoners," *Quarterly of the Texas State Historical Association* V (Oct. 1901), pp. 165-68.

Index